Jörg Riese 6. März 1995

MOTOCOURSE
The World's Leading Grand Prix Annual

HAZLETON PUBLISHING

CONTENTS

FOREWORD by Michael Doohan	5
EDITOR'S INTRODUCTION	8
TOP TEN RIDERS OF 1994	12
CELLULAR DEVELOPMENT by Kevin Cameron	20
WATER INJECTION AND THE STEAMROLLER EFFECT Peter Clifford looks at technical developments in the 500 class	24
GRAND PRIX MOTOR CYCLE SPECIFICATIONS by Peter Clifford	30
ONLY THE LONELY Michael Scott looks at the state of racing	33
SIXTEEN YEARS, AND WHAT DO YOU GET? A history of Cagiva by Michael Scott	36
WHO WENT WHERE IN 1994 by Michael Scott	42
1994 GRANDS PRIX	49
WORLD CHAMPIONSHIP RESULTS – 1994 compiled by Kay Edge	162
SIDECAR WORLD CHAMPIONSHIP by John McKenzie	164
SUPERBIKE WORLD CHAMPIONSHIP by Johan Vandekerckhove	168
ENDURANCE WORLD CHAMPIONSHIP by Kel Edge	174
UNITED STATES ROAD RACING by Paul Carruthers	176
ISLE OF MAN TT by Mac McDiarmid	180
BRITISH NATIONAL RACING by Gary Pinchin	184
OTHER MAJOR 1994 RESULTS compiled by Kay Edge	188

Motocourse is published by Hazleton Publishing, 3 Richmond Hill, Richmond, Surrey TW10 6RE.

Colour reproduction by Barrett Berkeley Ltd, London.

Printed in England by Butler and Tanner Ltd, Frome, Somerset.

© Hazleton Securities Ltd 1994. No part of this publication may be reproduced, stored in a retrieval system or transmitted, in any form or by any means, electronic, mechanical, photocopying, recording or otherwise, without prior permission in writing from Hazleton Securities Ltd.

ISBN: 1-874557-90-X

DISTRIBUTORS

UNITED KINGDOM
Bookpoint Ltd
39 Milton Park
Abingdon
Oxfordshire OX14 4TD

NORTH AMERICA
Motorbooks International
PO Box 1
729 Prospect Ave.
Osceola
Wisconsin 54020, USA

AUSTRALIA
Technical Book and Magazine Co. Pty
289-299 Swanston Street
Melbourne
Victoria 3000

NEW ZEALAND
David Bateman Ltd
'Golden Heights'
32-34 View Road
Glenfield
Auckland 10

SOUTH AFRICA
Motorbooks
341 Jan Smuts Avenue
Craighall Park
Johannesburg

PUBLISHER
Richard Poulter

EDITOR
Michael Scott

TECHNICAL EDITOR
Peter Clifford

ART EDITOR
Steve Small

PRODUCTION MANAGER
George Greenfield

PRODUCTION EDITOR
Peter Lovering

BUSINESS DEVELOPMENT MANAGER
Simon Maurice

SALES PROMOTION
Elizabeth Le Breton

RESULTS AND STATISTICS
Kay Edge

CHIEF PHOTOGRAPHERS
Gold & Goose

ADDITIONAL DESIGN
Julian Bigg

ACKNOWLEDGEMENTS

The Editor and staff of *Motocourse* wish to thank the following for their assistance in compiling the 1994-95 edition:
Anne-Marie Gerber and Marc Pétrier (FIM), Paul Butler (IRTA), Carlo Pernat, Garry Taylor, Ian Mackay, Charlie Hennekam, Kay Edge, Dennis Noyes and Renata Nosetto (Dorna), Stefano Zaragoni and Yves Jamotte (IRRPA), Henny Ray Abrams, Gunther Wiesinger, Hans van Loozenoord, Shigehiro Kondo, Sheona Dawson-King, Diane Michiels and many others.

Photographs published in *Motocourse 1994-95* have been contributed by:
Chief Photographers: David Goldman and Patrick Gosling of Gold & Goose; Malcolm Bryan, Clive Challinor, Double Red Photographic, Kel Edge, Nigel Kinrade, John McKenzie, Don Morley, Tom Riles, Jad Sherif/Pan Images, Two Plus Two and Anton Want/Allsport.

The dust-jacket photograph shows 500 cc World Champion Michael Doohan on his HRC Honda.

The title page picture shows 250 cc World Champion Massimiliano Biaggi riding the Chesterfield Aprilia.

Pictured left: The spoils of victory for Michael Doohan.

Opposite: Carl Fogarty became Britain's first mainstream solo World Champion since Barry Sheene when he took the Superbike title on the works Ducati.

Photos: Gold & Goose

THE CRIME
CHARGED WITH PROVIDING SERIOUS LAWFUL EXCITEMENT

THE PROSECUTION

Some manufacturers can't even build a 600 that weighs so little. And none of them can build one that looks so gorgeous. Honda are the best production engineers in biking and the quality of even the tiniest brackets and lugs reveals a religious attention to functional beauty.
Performance Bikes, April 1994 - CBR900RR v Triumph Super Three

Think of a sports bike that displays a total synthesis of design from the front to the back, engine chassis, suspension all built specifically and only for the same bike and designed for each other from the start. Chances are you'll first think of a Yamaha and the Genesis philosophy, but it's Honda and their CBR900RR who've taken the design to its logical conclusion, the most single purpose road-sports bike ever built.
Fast Bikes, June 1994 - CBR900RR v Ducati 916 v Honda RVF750

On the dyno the Honda counters every punch of the 916, then deals a knockout horsepower blow. Two points to the 'Blade and victory by one point - it's faster, more powerful, sharper handling, and worth every penny of its price.
Motor Cycle News, May 18 1994 - CBR900RR v Ducati 916

Just grabbing the CBR's bars and feeling how little resistance they offer to turning gets you in the mood. The light clutch, and slight vibration that comes from a big motor bolted into such a small frame, create a seething expectation of speed and lightness that is immediately confirmed: the CBR lunges forward from 2,500rpm like a mad dog taking owner its for a walk.
Performance Bikes, April 1994 - CBR900RR v ZX-9R v Triumph Super Three

Since its launch in Australia at the end of 1991, the Honda FireBlade has set completely new standards for the opposition to aim at. Any test of pure sports bike isn't complete without some reference to how it compares to Honda's instant classic. You hear the name so much, you get fed up with it. Then you ride one on the track and the respect returns.
Motor Cycle News, May 18 1994 - CBR900RR v Ducati 916

More than ever there's a buzzing, sizzling fire about the 'Blade - even at a standstill. Stubby and chunky, tiny and flighty and a 900, impossibly. The claws of the mighty mouse Honda are now sharper than ever before.
BIKE, April 1994 CBR900RR v Triumph Super THREE v ZX-9R

THE VERDICT
GUILTY

HONDA CBR900RR FIREBLADE
STILL THE NO.1 MOTORCYCLE IN ITS CLASS
ALL MOTORCYCLES OVER 400cc CARRY A TWO YEAR UNLIMITED MILEAGE WARRANTY

THE SPIRIT • THE TECHNOLOGY • THE MOTORCYCLES

RACING WITH

Foreword
by Michael Doohan

All year long, I tried to put the World Championship out of my mind. That wasn't easy. Apart from being reminded of it all the time by other people, winning the title has to be every Grand Prix racer's ambition, or else he wouldn't be there.

I'd already faced the disappointment in 1992 of being in the lead and losing it through injury, and I didn't want to go through that again. I just tried to approach it race by race, and let the points take care of themselves.

Now it's over, and I feel at last I can enjoy it.

One of the privileges is to see my photograph on the cover of *Motocourse*. Ever since I first saw the book I wanted that. We are all in racing because we have a passion for the sport, and *Motocourse* is the one book that captures the feeling of racing with the same passion for perfection.

I have to thank Honda, of course, and also Michelin and Elf, for all their technical and other support. And especially my team. My crew chief Jeremy Burgess is more than a partner in my success. He's a vital part of it; and people just don't realise the amount of work he and the crew have put into this.

I also owe everything to the doctors who brought me back to race fitness after 1992: Dr Costa, who probably saved my leg from amputation, and Dr Louie and Dr Ting in the USA, who helped repair the damage. Without them, I might not be able to walk, let alone race.

Winning the World Championship won't change me. I'm just an ordinary guy who was lucky enough to have the opportunity and the determination, and I'm still the same person as champion as I was before I was champion.

That's not to say victory isn't sweet. I'm thrilled to have won. Now we'll start working on trying to win next year as well.

The R1100GS: a motorcycle that doesn't promise anything it can't deliver. Shown in its true light, it is, without a shadow of a doubt, an awesome proposition. Consider its wealth of mid-range torque, its impressive 80bhp at only 6,750rpm, and the security of ABS II braking.

Couple that with BMW's Telelever and Paralever suspension systems and a very imposing motorcycle becomes a pleasure to ride.

RECOMMENDED PRICE: BMW R1100GS £8295. CORRECT AT TIME OF GOING TO PRESS. INCLUDES VAT AND 12 MONTHS BMW ASSISTANCE MEMBERSHIP, BUT NOT DELIVERY, PDI AND NUMBER PLATES, ESTIMATED

APPEARANCES CAN BE DECEPTIVE.
SOMETIMES.

Suddenly, a journey to the Alps is something to savour, and the R1100GS is just the motorcycle to get you there. With its adjustable windshield and seat height, and a carrying capacity that can take the full complement of BMW luggage, two people can travel in comfort.

So, in the case of the R1100GS, the camera doesn't lie. It really is a motorcycle to overshadow everything else on the road.

THE NEW BMW R1100GS

COST £450. PERFORMANCE FIGURES: MANUFACTURER'S DATA. FOR MORE INFORMATION WRITE TO BMW INFORMATION SERVICE, PO BOX 161, CROYDON, SURREY CR9 1QB, OR FREEPHONE 0800 325600.

EDITOR'S INTRODUCTION

endangered SPECIES

One minute and 47.934 seconds said everything there is to say about Grand Prix racing. The TV cameras were locked on Michael Doohan for a full lap of the Montmelo circuit at Barcelona, following every inch of the 2.95 miles. And it was a spectacle for connoisseurs as the new World Champion exercised his art on one of the most formidable racing motor cycles ever built.

Exuding confidence and control, Doohan spun, slid and soared round the continuous sweeping turns. If front and rear wheels were ever in line with one another, it was only momentarily as he switched smoothly from one mode to another: power-on and sliding the rear or power-off and gliding the front. Black lines painted by the skimming tyres marked his progress like a vapour trail.

Here was a master craftsman at work, a sight to be treasured. Keep the videotape if you can, for it shows an endangered species.

There were many fine moments during the year: a 250 contest of such a high standard as almost to deify its protagonists; a 125 struggle that, by year's end, yielded some of the closest and best racing ever seen. But Doohan's Honda remains in the memory.

There have only ever been a handful of riders who can take a 500 to its outer limits. This is the nature of the beast. The most powerful, specialised and dedicated motor cycles in existence shouldn't be easy to ride any more than a fine violin should be easy to play. They are instruments with sufficient range to display the full talents of those with exceptional gifts.

In 1994, give or take the enigmatic John Kocinski and the erratic Luca Cadalora, there were only two riders who could be relied on to have this ability week in week out: Doohan and Schwantz. Then one of them got hurt, which meant racing was frequently a lonely business for the other.

The 500 class had to rely on the second echelon of works riders for spectacle, and they were numerous enough to make a good show of it. When Schwantz and Doohan go, probably at the end of 1995, 500 racing will be closer and more exciting than it is now. And slower.

Speed is of the essence. It's like that in racing. Or is that an over-simplification? Do you get a higher order of competition when the limits of the machinery are easier to find, the technology taken down a peg or two, and the battle for the lead closer and more numerous? Do the reserves of speed within a modern 500, attainable only by so small an elite, make it more exciting to watch one or two ridden to their limits than a gaggle of 125s all fighting over the same inch of tarmac?

My own answer is an unequivocal yes, an opinion pretty much universal among those who are regularly exposed to both circumstances. But it is not always shared by people not so intimately involved.

Why isn't racing in the 500 class closer? Has technology made the bikes too hard to ride, or has the class just temporarily run short of new talent?

We may never find out, for the current generation of 500 cc V4s are under threat on all sides. No other racing series of any importance uses these marvellous hand-wrought machines, and there is no ladder of learning available for future stars.

By the year's end, many were looking to Superbikes as the top class of the future, particularly as more and more manufacturers take a direct interest in the production-linked series. Furthermore, though the bikes are clod-hopping monsters compared with the finesse of a GP two-stroke (not for nothing does the GP paddock refer to them as 'diesels'), their lower capabilities reliably make for closer racing. As with the 250s and 125s.

Speed again. There is no place in the current Grand Prix hierarchy for Superbikes. They could hardly slot in as the top class when they are slower than the 'junior' 250s. Yet, in the current climate, there hardly seems room for both series to be sustained.

Sooner or later something will have to change and, sadly, the 500 cc class stands out as the most exposed target. The jewel in racing's crown is too lustrous for its setting.

Those beautiful, beastly, dangerous and uplifting 180 horsepower motor cycles cannot live forever. Their days are numbered and with them, perhaps, the days of GP racing as we know it.

Enjoy the 500s while you can, for we shall never see their like again.

Michael Scott
Richmond, England
November 1994

The Choice of World Champions

Make Sure It's a Michelin

Mick Doohan, World 500cc Champion 1994
Our Ultimate Research and Development Technician

THE MARK

OF A WINNER

THE TOP TEN RIDERS OF 1994

1 *Michael Doohan*
2 *Kevin Schwantz*
3 *Massimiliano Biaggi*
4 *Loris Capirossi*
5 *Kazuto Sakata*
6 *Tetsuya Harada*
7 *John Kocinski*
8 *Tadayuki Okada*
9 *Alberto Puig*
10 *Ralf Waldmann*

Michael Doohan
HONDA TEAM HRC
1994 World Championship – 1st
Race wins – 9
(MAL, SPA, OST, GER, NED, ITA, FRA, CZ, ARG)
Pole positions – 6; Lap records – 3
Born: 4 June 1965, Brisbane, Australia

Kevin Schwantz
TEAM LUCKY STRIKE SUZUKI
1994 World Championship – 4th
Race wins – 2
(JAP, GB)
Pole positions – 1; Lap records – 2
Born: 19 June 1964, Paige, Texas, USA

Wearing the long-awaited Number One plate, Schwantz went back to his buccaneering ways in 1994, a season replete with derring-do, heroism, two dazzling wins and several crashes. It was not what he would have chosen.

The die was cast three weeks before the season, when fit-and-ready Kevin fell off his mountain bike and fractured his left forearm.

The injury itself, quickly plated, was only slightly troublesome. He'd raced with worse in the past, and would soon do so again. The real cost was missing the final Suzuki pre-season tests – which in turn meant the Lucky Strike team took two races to discover a crucial dimensional error in their new bikes.

From then on, in spite of a strong win in Japan, Schwantz was trying to catch up.

After three second places, his major hope of stemming the tide came at Assen and the following more technical circuits, including Donington Park. Instead he fell again, and paid a high price.

His character forced him to keep fighting on, his title hopes dwindling race by race. He'd have been wiser to stop, since his left wrist sustained further damage at every subsequent race, to the point that it was beyond normal repair by the time yet another crash in America ended his season early.

He returned to the last races as a spectator, both wrists in plaster-casts painted in military camouflage colours 'so other people can't see them'. They were – among other things – a badge of conspicuous courage.

A lack of competition after Schwantz's injury made Doohan's first world title look easy. Racing veterans know this is seldom true. In any case, Doohan had been equally dominant against a full set of rivals in 1992, until the Assen leg injury sealed his fate.

Championship victory reliably goes to the rider who is best prepared to race hardest for longest the oftenest. Prepared in every sense: to take risks, to keep on pushing; and with the machine also prepared, so that while others are scratching to catch up, you are making only minor adjustments to match the bike to each track.

Mick's Honda was the best bike out there – but this too was to his personal credit. Doohan had to argue to get it right, after Showa and HRC foisted some unwanted suspension 'improvements' on him for the first three races.

Once he'd forced the issue, to recapture the handling balance as well as the torquey engine of his '92 machine, he embarked on a winning spree that put him in the record books. Not that he cared. After becoming the first 500 rider since Agostini to win five, and then six races in a row, he gruffly responded: 'It's 1994 now, not 1972.'

Doohan makes an art of being matter-of-fact. If people want to admire him for what he does on the bike – well, that's okay, as long as they realise that he's only there 'because I was lucky enough to get the opportunity, and determined enough to use it'. But he's more than anxious to remind them that, off the bike, he's just an ordinary bloke.

Some kind of ordinary; some bloke! The story of his fight back from near-amputation of his right leg in 1992 to domination in 1994 is an epic of hardship overcome by courage and determination.

Doohan's gift is natural. He came to road racing late, and vaulted rapidly up from Australian production bikes via Superbikes direct to the Grand Prix team.

His style includes the crucial ability to steer with the rear wheel, learned off-road at an early age; but he also uses the front wheel more than the classic ex-dirt-trackers. The hallmark of his riding in 1994 was wide sweeping cornering lines with high mid-corner speed, followed by smooth power-slides through the exits.

Doohan showed strength in a number of areas in 1994: riding creatively in Malaysia, casually in Austria and Germany, almost disdainfully at Assen, and masterfully at any number of other tracks. He was pushed hard only once, by Schwantz, at Jerez, a tight track that in theory should have favoured the latter's Suzuki. Doohan's win there was his race of the year.

He also had luck on his side, escaping unscathed from four practice accidents and two very near-misses of his own making in France. This was well deserved, after 1992...

Racing has damaged Doohan permanently – though there was hope that fresh surgery two days after the last race might restore some movement, if not strength, to his stiff right ankle.

Racing has also made him a rich man: he is now based in Monaco as a tax-haven from his Queensland home.

And racing has made him a worthy hero, to anyone with the wit to appreciate the true depth of the accomplishments which he shrugs off so lightly.

Schwantz never complained about the injury. 'It bothers me a little,' was the furthest he would go. But the pain was obvious as he waved his hand to restore circulation on the straights, and etched into his face after every race.

In these circumstances, victory in Britain was an epic feat – but no less so than the other six plaster-cast races. Weakened by injury, urgently needing race wins, Kevin fell four more times in five weekends, but kept on pushing right until the end.

Kevin Schwantz matured with his 1993 world title. He moved confidently in exalted circles when protocol (or sponsors) dictated, and was always ready with the wryest wisecrack for press and TV. He handed over the title with dignity.

But the real story of his season was one of grit, pain, determination and frustration – pressures far greater than a sportsman of his years and stature should by rights have to endure.

He bore them well. Time will tell how much they cost him in his valedictory season of 1995.

3
Massimiliano Biaggi
TEAM CHESTERFIELD APRILIA
1994 World Championship – 1st
Race wins – 5
(AUS, MAL, NED, CZ, EUR)
Pole positions – 7; Lap records – 7
Born: 26 June 1971, Rome, Italy

Dashing, flashing, dazzling and more than slightly mysterious, Max Biaggi is a perfect World Champion.

The 23-year-old Roman was a pit, paddock and grandstand favourite as much for the style in which he won, in a notably tough year, as for the fact that he did so.

Max is a go-for-it rider in the classic mould. He is also a Max of many parts.

There is Fast Max: win or bust – risk is strength. A year of intense competition yielded five wins, all displaying striking superiority; and three crashes while at or near the front. At tracks where the Honda's handling advantages were worth more than his Aprilia's extra performance, he never rode for points. Instead, his fighting instincts and riding were sharpened, his last-lap attacks a legend.

Then there's Handsome Max, with a chiselled and soulful face that often smiles, but also carries an anxious and mournful look, along with a flashing pride. Max plays the game: ringing the fashion changes with accessories ranging from scarves to his year-end Vandyke beard.

Charming Max emerged this year from the brooding introvert who'd had a bad season in 1993. 'It's easy to be cheerful when you have a chance of winning,' he explained. Max takes stardom seriously: he used the break before this season to become fluent in English.

And there's Mysterious Max, who keeps apart from racing between GPs, and whose private life is private. The inevitable rumours carried just the right whiff of scandal to be a positive asset for a 1990s hero.

Biaggi was a late-comer to motor cycle racing, shooting from local 125 production racing into the arms of Aprilia for a debut-year European title in 1991, and a first-season GP win in 1992. Then came the Honda hiatus, with turncoat Max repaid for his disloyalty by a string of crashes and only one win as he struggled with Michelin tyres.

Aprilia forgave all, and the prodigal returned in 1994, back with the bike and Dunlop tyres on which he'd achieved his prodigious early success.

Max's title was the toughest in any class. In a breathtaking year, he prevailed by riding like a demon. Risk and win. That's real racing.

4
Loris Capirossi
MARLBORO TEAM PILERI HONDA
1994 World Championship – 3rd
Race wins – 4
(OST, GER, FRA, GB)
Pole positions – 5; Lap records – 4
Born: 4 April 1973, Bologna, Italy

Loris came whisker-close to the title in 1993, and was only a little further away in 1994. That makes him a fully paid-up member of the exclusive 250 superstars club, where a generation of exceptionally talented riders have come together to send the standards vaulting.

In the end, in these circumstances, winning or losing overall is simply a matter of mathematics and chance. These went against Loris in 1994 when he hurt his hand at Brno, spoiling the last four races.

The injury was crucial, but so was the nature of the crash. It happened on the last lap, when Capirossi was trying to turn a certain third place into a knife-edge second. Had he stayed where he was, he'd have left the track still holding the title lead.

Capirossi fans – and the courteous and charming young double 125 World Champion has many – were keen to believe he'd put the old impetuous errors behind him, since his accident-rate had dropped sharply compared with last year (just one race crash, at Assen), and compared with major rival, Biaggi. Here was evidence that he had not.

Capirossi, from Bologna, is another whose progress has been sped by a combination of bravery and skill. He started racing at 14, was the youngest-ever World Champion in the 125 class at 17, then again at 18. He now moves to the 500 class, disappointed not to have added a 250 crown to his cabinet, but nevertheless ready for a new challenge.

Stand well back from the barriers.

Kazuto Sakata
TEAM SEMPRUCCI-KRONA APRILIA
1994 World Championship – 1st
Race wins – 3
(AUS, SPA, CZ)
Pole positions – 7; Lap records – 3
Born: 15 August 1966, Tokyo, Japan

The latest of the new Japanese generation to take that extra step is not as young as he looks, or as his riding over four GP years would suggest. Aggression of that order is the usual hallmark of a teenager; Kazuto Sakata is 28, and clearly a hard man.

He came late to racing, competing first at the age of 22 and rising rapidly through domestic racing to take the top 125 title in 1990. Then he came to GPs, and quickly earned a reputation for dazzling speed and an equally impressive crash record: another charger who didn't know when to stop.

His spirit and ability were recognised by Aprilia, the best talent scouts in the business, and he was recruited at the end of last year to become the first Japanese to ride for a European factory.

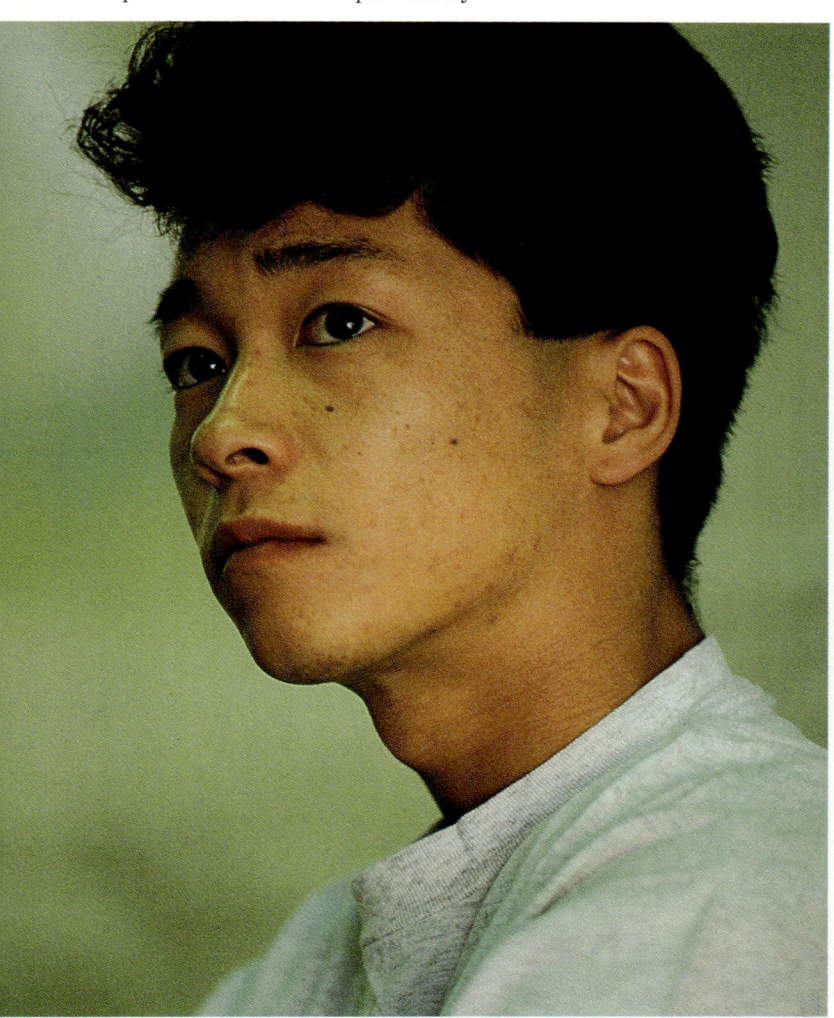

The choice was excellent, from both sides. Sakata proved able to make the best use of the Aprilia's fine chassis; it in turn brought out a much more reliable rider.

In fact, he hardly faltered all year, racking up three wins, usually in runaway style, until three races from the end, in America, when he had the chance to tie up the title. Instead, he got mixed up in a first-corner barging match, rejoining way behind the pace car; then fell heavily one lap later trying too hard to catch up.

Speaking a little English, and almost unfailingly polite in the reliable Japanese way, the little guy from Tokyo is hard for Westerners to get to grips with. His compatriots know him better – as a tough and determined character who is intensely competitive at everything he does.

The 125 class is the most intense in GP racing, with bikes evenly matched and a spread of riders from wizened veteran tacticians to wild-eyed charging teenagers. Sakata rose head and shoulders above the rabble.

Tetsuya Harada
TEAM YAMAHA MOTOR FRANCE
1994 World Championship – 7th
Race wins – 0
Pole positions – 0; Lap records – 1
Born: 14 June 1970, Chiba, Japan

The defending 250 champion had few chances to show his merit in 1994, after a crash in practice for the first race dealt him a serious hand injury. He missed only two GPs, but was not fully fit until the last part of the year.

This was also a grave blow to Yamaha – their other works rider, Kenny Roberts Junior, was out with injury too, and development to their latest bike was virtually non-existent for the first half of the year.

By the time they were both going, by year's end, it was only reasonable to suppose that the bike was way behind the standard of the race-seasoned class leaders. That makes Harada's rostrum finishes in Italy, the USA and Argentina, and his lap record in the latter race, all the more impressive.

In keeping with his enigmatic mien, his agenda at that last race remains unclear. Certainly he passed Biaggi with apparent ease on the last lap, but when repassed under power he made what may have been only a half-hearted attempt to fight back. Perhaps he had decided to help Biaggi, in the process reducing the title chances of his old Japanese rival, Okada? We shall never know.

What is certain is that Harada brings a higher plane of thinking to his tactics than others in the class. At year's end, while others played their high-risk games, Harada would be reliably close behind, saving tyres and energy for when it really mattered, at the end of the race.

Combined with his fluid, lyrically smooth riding style, he must still be regarded as a major figure in the class, in spite of his relatively poor overall finishing position in 1994.

7

John Kocinski
CAGIVA TEAM AGOSTINI
1994 World Championship – 3rd
Race wins – 1
(AUS)
Pole positions – 3; Lap records – 0
Born: 20 March 1968, Little Rock, Arkansas, USA

John Kocinski was superb in 1994. He was also pig-headed, difficult, flawed, erratic and ultimately frustrated.

His riding talent is beyond question. When things go right, he can transcend the normal limits of his machinery and come close to divinity. In this way, convincing victory in the first race in Australia was potentially devastating for his rivals. Or it would have been, had it been achieved by any other rider on any other bike.

In a strange way, the Cagiva matched John: basically brilliant, often erratic and prone to overheating. The results of both would have been better had he not damaged his hand in Germany – he was only two points off second in the final points standings. But even third was a considerable achievement.

Certainly his ability flattered the bike, while Cagiva team manager Agostini in turn flattered Kocinski, so that for most of the time – in public, anyway – he would pronounce loudly that this was the first team which had ever understood him. Indeed, had they continued their rate of improvement for one more year, they might have had a winning combination for 1995. Instead, race-winning lap record-holding one-time boy genius John was out in the cold again.

Kocinski's past is littered with failed alliances, as well as exceptional results, like his debut-season 250 title of 1990. As a result, he is regarded by several major sponsors as a Jonah.

His own confidence in his bike-setting skills is not shared by teams with whom he has worked, who mark a tendency to spiral off in all directions during practice.

These problems might yet be curable. With the right hands helping out with his professional life and his machinery, John has the talent to be a racing legend for more than just being fast and weird.

8

Tadayuki Okada
TEAM KANEMOTO HONDA
1994 World Championship – 2nd
Race wins – 2
(JAP, ARG)
Pole positions – 0; Lap records – 0
Born: 13 February 1967, Ibaragi, Japan

Tadayuki Okada is a quiet sort, often to be seen of an evening parading the paddock, taking the air with his wife and infant daughter – the very picture of stolid respectability.

His racing season was the same. The only notable rider not to fall off all year, even in practice, he put in a solid run of mainly respectable finishes, with a couple of wins straddling a mid-season slump. By the last race he was only one crash away from defeating Biaggi, who had by comparison been erratic in the extreme.

Does this make a great racer? Very nearly, in Tadayuki's case, since his crash-free record was on occasion very narrowly maintained. He may have stayed on the right side of the giddy limit, but he was still no stranger to where it lay.

More to the point, he was the only front-runner using Michelin tyres, which seem not to suit the 250s, and especially his Kanemoto Honda NSR. The combination is, as Biaggi discovered to his cost last year, very prone to severe understeer, making Okada's 1994 season all the more impressive.

Had he won the title, Okada's steadiness would inevitably have won the acclaim of all...phrases like 'mature victory' and 'Lawson-like superiority' would have tripped off the tongue.

In a year when triumph went to the dazzle factor, he perhaps looked a little dowdy by comparison.

On such illusions founder the best-planned claims to greatness.

9

Alberto Puig
TEAM DUCADOS HONDA PONS
1994 World Championship – 5th
Race wins – 0
Pole positions – 0; Lap records – 0
Born: 16 January 1967, Barcelona, Spain

10

Ralf Waldmann
TEAM HB HONDA GERMANY
1994 World Championship – 5th
Race wins – 1 (ITA)
Pole positions – 0; Lap records – 0
Born: 14 July 1966, Ennepetal, Germany

Another who achieved merit through a highly successful move up one class, wacky Ralf Waldmann managed to win a race in his debut 250 season and was a factor virtually from the start.

Certainly, the move from 125s to 250s is less of a jump than that to 500s. The riding technique remains similar, for one thing.

Indeed, Waldmann even opined that 250s were easier to race than 125s. Having a modicum of power in reserve meant that one did not have to ride so close to the limit all the time. Likewise he found the 250 easier in the wet, where the extra weight and power were usable tools of technique rather than any hindrance.

Puig's place on the roll of honour was assured almost from the first race. The gruff Spaniard, whose high regard among the cognoscenti had been somewhat tarnished by his erratic performances in the 250 class, showed himself to be an absolute natural as a 500 cc rider.

The former trials champion, who had only occasionally ridden a 500 in the past, was immediately well placed among the group of second-stringer works riders and soon out-qualified them on a regular basis, with a first visit to the front row of the grid in only the second GP.

His race results did not quite match up. There were the usual reasons – lack of experience in conserving tyres and developing race tactics, and a late-braking slow mid-corner-speed style that was better at keeping riders behind him than overtaking those ahead. More costly was a bad case of racers' wrist in his right arm, which saw him slow at the finish of almost every race, fighting stiffness and pain.

Puig left promptly after the end of the year to get his wrist seen to at the famous Mayo Clinic in the USA. All being well, he will be ready for a step up in 1995.

It is not certain that he has the talent to take that step, but there's a better than even chance that he'll visit the rostrum more often than his 1994 single shot (in Germany). He earned all his accolades this year.

This was impressive in itself – and during a year when the standard of competition would have daunted all but the brightest newcomers as well.

Ralf did best back home in Europe, going off the boil somewhat for the last three races of the year. Given the growing intensity of the battle between his more experienced rivals, this is no black mark.

Waldmann is a fun-loving sort, good-humoured in victory and defeat, and clearly enjoying his riding and racing. In the 125 class, this sometimes made him seem like a less-than-serious competitor.

His performance in 1994 proved otherwise.

winning on

3 British Supercup Champ

won on Shell 2 and

4 stroke motorcycle oils.

dave rawlins - singles
abbott + tailford - open sidecar
jason vincent - 250cc

Shell Oils

onships

 **Shell Oils**

TECHNICAL FEATURE

CELLULAR

We think we know the needs of GP bikes: they need power, tyre grip, adequate stability, quick handling. We also think we know how to supply these needs. Every year, engine power creeps up by 3-5 per cent, and is made smoother and easier to use. Tyres provide more grip and/or more controllability. Suspension becomes better able to keep tyres on the ground. Chassis qualities move along their well-established lines of development. God's in his heaven, and all's well with the world.

That may be the case in 250 racing, and especially so in 125. But somehow the improvements that have made 125s and 250s so much faster have now made 500s some ten seconds slower over the usual race distances. In a race with the ghost of technology past, 1993-94 500s would lose.

It's not so hard to see why lightweights should benefit. They have little power, so they can use more. Their lap times depend upon high corner speeds, so more tyre side grip helps. As powerbands sharpen, handling is affected as it was with 500s, so stiffer chassis translate into quicker laps.

The equation is different for 500s. Their central problem is how to steer during off-corner acceleration. Rapid acceleration shifts weight from the front to the rear, unloading the front tyre so it loses grip, making the bike run wide. Riders cannot both accelerate maximally and hold line. In dealing with this problem, the customary annual improvements somehow stopped working after 1991. Why?

First I'll offer an historical example of how the whole can be less than the sum of its excellent parts. Then I'll try to find some sense in what has happened to 500 GP bike design.

Now the example. Throughout the late 1960s, Rolls-Royce developed its new RB211 fan engine, but development failed to reach specified goals by a large margin. In a deepening crisis, Rolls recalled retired engineer, Stanley Hooker, giving him plenary powers to do whatever was necessary. Hooker found excellent performance in every section of the engine – fan, compressor stages, burner and turbines. But he also found that the responsible departments had almost no co-operative contact with one another. The result was that the output from the fan stage was quite incompatible with what the LP compressor needed as input, LP compressor output was wrong for HP input, and so on. Accordingly, Hooker went from department to department, ordering small but well-considered changes that would better integrate the performances of all the stages. Predictably, every department objected strongly, complaining that Hooker's changes would destroy their excellent stage efficiencies. When, over their objections, the changes were made, there were some local losses of efficiency – but engine thrust was increased by 6000 pounds!

The company had ignored the overall qualities on which the engine as a whole would succeed or fail, and had allowed each department to pursue its own private excellence. The problem was 'cellular development'. Hooker had the stature to see what the company's well-qualified specialists could not: the need for intelligent integration.

I argue that this same situation obtains in 500 cc Grand Prix racing. Development of major aspects of the machine occurs within essentially sealed 'cells', with only limited communication between them.

The manufacturers and the tyre makers cannot, for the best commercial reasons, reveal their long-term plans to each other, so their co-operation is at most tactical rather than strategic. Design and test functions are separated in some factories, and both are distinct from the actual race team(s), creating internal barriers.

Assumptions may be made that are valid only within a given cell, and may be downright harmful elsewhere. The chassis engineer is tempted to let the past direct the future: more chassis and form stiffness have always worked before, and the teams are still calling for more – so we'll give it to them. One embarrassing result of such 'design' has been the recent flight to the past – the adoption of chassis and forks from previous seasons.

At the separate company (cell) that makes the suspension units, slowly curling faxes pile up as the field reports come in. Are the field technicians good friends with the stay-at-home engineers? Maybe, maybe not. Riders talk to suspension technicians mainly to complain. University degrees create yet more cell walls. Engineers have them. Technicians and riders do not.

Even the most obvious assumptions, coming direct from the riders themselves, might be wrong. The violent power curves of 1988 were frightening to see in action, so we can understand the desire of riders to have them smoothed out. And so the engine department gets its marching orders: get us more power if you can, but make it smooth. They get to work.

The tyre people are ceaselessly asked for more grip, and they respond.

How can all this progress fail? It can fail if its total result steadily creeps in a direction counter to the needs of the accepted riding style of the moment. This has happened before, and it's clearly happening now. Consider some history.

Acceleration is a 500's strong suit, but accelerative weight transfer makes it hard to steer. The proven answer is to shift weight forward to put a load on the front tyre that will make it steer. Velocette had to do it in 1937 with their 500. Kel Carruthers had to do it in 1971 with his TR2-B Yamaha. It has been a recognised trend ever since. At first, this weight shift provided pure benefit, but as it grew more extreme, it brought unwanted side-effects. Rider strength and the need for quick steering limit front tyre width, but rear width has grown with power. A small front tyre, carrying an increasing share of machine weight into corners, becomes tender, increasingly liable to 'push' or go away altogether. Because of this, 500 GP bikes became progressively less stable during braking or even coasting into turns.

The Kenny Roberts 'tail-slider' style of steering was the natural response to this accumulation of change. If the motor cycle works better when accelerating, and less well during braking or coasting, then it's better to emphasise acceleration and to de-emphasise deceleration.

The classic cornering style of the 1950s had been to inscribe the arc of maximum radius into the turn and to ride it at the highest possible constant speed. This was no longer safe or possible with the new, front-heavy bikes. Roberts's dirt-track instincts were a good fit to the new conditions; he entered turns at less-than-limiting speed, got much of his turning done early with a good margin of safety, then used the remaining part of the turn as a drag-strip on which to get himself well launched down the next straight, steering the back of the machine with the throttle. The beauty of this system was that exit speed always wins over corner speed.

Against this new style, the best that front-steering classicists (Haslam and Sarron, for example) could achieve was journeyman status; and 250 riders did not successfully transfer up to the 500 class in the 1980s because the requirements were too different.

These explanations have been presented and savoured as litany for years now, but we erect dogma at our peril. Technology continues to operate but, because of the nature of Grand Prix racing, I argue that it often operates by its own rules. The pace and specialisation of GP racing discourage the appearance of big-picture generalists like Stanley Hooker. Overall planning takes a back seat to the endless round of specific, daily problems – front chatter in turn nine, a misfire at 11,000. This locks people securely within their cells.

Now consider the accumulated technology change in relation to the needs of the tail-slider riding style. To slide the back, you have to get it loose. That ought to be easy with 180 horsepower: just turn up the throttle. But it's not so easy. 'Just turning up the throttle' was what put so many riders on their heads in the 1989-90 period, when tyre grip was so extreme that grids were decimated by the infamous exit high-side accidents. What is needed is a predictable way to get the back loose, and it used to be provided for free by abrupt engine powerbands and/or poor suspension. If power output is spike-like, or if rear grip is not so good, it makes it easier to schedule a controllable rear slide.

Yet recent progress works in com-

20

DEVELOPMENT

by Kevin Cameron

A motor cycle is the sum of its parts. Do designers pay enough attention to the bottom line?

pletely the opposite direction – smoother power irons out the spikes; better suspension keeps the tyre down on the track, not bouncing in the air; better tyres strongly resist breaking loose.

Early evidence that the trends could be wrong came in weight distribution. When engines were civilised, first by electronic engine controls, then by big-bang firing order, there was no longer any need for constant forward shift of weight because the power no longer arrived with a violent jerk. Some riders began to do better with engines actually moved back in the chassis – and they found they could brake a bit harder and enter turns a bit faster because of it.

Furthermore, not all was well even with Wayne Rainey, greatest exponent of the tail-slider style. To get the bike loose despite civilised power and improved grip required him to set the suspension very hard – a well-understood technique for making a slider out of a gripper. And hard settings, combined with ever-stiffening chassis, added up to strange performance on rough tracks.

In the meantime, the changes in the nature of 500s made it possible, for the first time, for 250 and even 125 riders to move up to the 500 class without embarrassing themselves. Most significant among them is the studious and ambitious Luca Cadalora, who set several poles and has even won races this year. Traditionalists point to the easy dominance of Mick Doohan – but there is something to be learned here, too, for Doohan's style is not now the classic tail-sliding of yore. Technology change has affected him too. He says Honda's on-board computer shows him very early on the throttle, very gradually – and you can see this on the track. This is not the rushing, sliding acceleration of Wayne Rainey; this is more akin to the 250-like style of Cadalora. And the engine he chose this year is notably smooth, a complete contrast to the explosive power of 1993. This change comes not because Luca is a genius, or because Doohan is a copyist. It is change forced by accumulating new technology in the motor cycle and its tyres.

Clearly – at least for the moment – this change is for the worse. Lap times have suffered. What next? Opinion is divided. Kenny Roberts states unequivocally that better riders are the answer, trained in 'the method' – presumably his Modesto Marine Corps. The idea here is to focus on the need for rear-steering, and to make all components serve that need.

But there is another view. It holds that the current slump in 500 lap times arises from confusion over how to use unfamiliar new capabilities, and from discovery that long-running trends are not always permanent. This view trusts that riders, tuners and engineers will presently stop fixating on daily problems and will turn their intelligence to discovering how to steer motor cycles with the new capabilities. Is it best to go back to steering by intentionally destroying grip at the back? Or might the new capabilities of tyres, suspension and engines presently raise corner speeds so high that tail-sliding acceleration becomes irrelevant? The recent achievements of front-steerers like Cadalora and Kocinski support this view. And what if future motor cycles and tyres are intentionally configured to suit them? This may already be happening.

Or is there some completely different way, such as two-wheel steering in which the front is steered conventionally, but the rear is steered as some function of turn direction and throttle angle? Yamaha, for one, are known to have patents in this area.

Technology directs us if we do not direct it – and 500 racing has lost its forward momentum as a consequence. Tight focus on integrated performance must take the place of cellular development and the unexamined pursuit of trends.

ONE THAT.

Scott Russell's Kawasaki ZXR750R wore the No. 1 plate in World Superbike throughout '94. The same duo cleaned up at Daytona for the second time too.

But take away the skills of Scott, and the ZXR750 found in Kawasaki dealerships is equally tough on the opposition.

Ram Air induction, a Works-style aluminium perimeter chassis, upside-down front forks and an engine renowned for its rush of power – and you can see it's a clear winner on the streets.

Call 0800 500245 for a free range brochure giving more information on this and all the other Kawasaki street bikes.

Kawasaki
Let the good times roll.

TECHNICAL REVIEW

WATER INJECTION AND THE STEAMROLLER EFFECT

by Peter Clifford

TECHNICAL REVIEW

A mixture of finely wrought ironmongery and extensive electronics: Honda's pace-setting NSR *(below left)*. Note sealed ram-fed airbox.

Detail picture *(left)* shows Doohan's thumb brake and rear suspension adjuster on left handlebar; arrow on gilded triple clamp points to the opposition.

'What do you mean, "Can the Honda be beaten?" What do you think we did for the past four years?'

Bud Aksland had a very good point. It had been four years since Honda won the 500 cc World Championship. His team, Yamaha, won the title in 1990, '91 and '92; Suzuki won it in '93 and Yamaha finished second. By halfway through the 1994 season it didn't seem such a daft question, though. The Honda, with Mick Doohan at the helm, was steamrollering the opposition. Regularly the Hondas would have a complete lock on the speed trap figures.

Hondas have long had a reputation for being the fastest things on the track but, this year, they had apparently eradicated any weak links elsewhere. No more handling problems, nothing to spoil Doohan's almost total domination. As his race engineer Jerry Burgess said, the season was just about perfect. 'It went even better than we could have expected. To win nine races out of fourteen is not often done. I think if you look back we've had a good bike, Mick's been in super form, we're very, very happy with the way things have gone.'

Doohan was so dominant that there was hardly an instance when the team struggled, even at Donington, which had caused them problems in the past. 'We sensed that it probably wouldn't be one of our better race tracks. He was able to get out there and take pole position. Our choice of tyres for the race was a little bit soft, but I think it gave Mick a certain amount of confidence that when we come back to Donington in 1995 we'll have overcome what problems we've had there in the past and just know that we need to run a little harder rear tyre.'

But why should Donington cause a problem? 'Mick loses his time at Donington in the very slow corners. They, for one reason or another, aren't corners that Mick seems to be able to come to grips with, as he does with the faster flowing corners. Whether it's a set-up in the bike or whatever, I'm not sure. Whether Kevin's ability on the brakes makes up that time; or whether our set-up, which is not designed so much around stopping the motor cycle as keeping it flowing through the corner, handicaps us.

'At the same time, the grip overall wasn't that good and Mick's a rider who rides from feel. If he's not getting the good feel it's very difficult for him to have the confidence to go fast. Sure, he can do it, but he feels he's stepping into an area that doesn't have the safety zone that a race track with grip and feel has.'

Burgess not only feels that Doohan was riding at least as well as in 1992, when he dominated the first half of the season, but also that the bike had improved. 'It's got more power top end but at the same time we haven't sacrificed the smooth bottom power. It is a very good engine. It is very difficult to say now what we need to do without in some way changing the character of what we've got. It would be good to have more of everything we've got, but I don't think we can do that without sacrificing one area or the other. So it's going to be a very interesting winter's testing this year,' says Burgess with a chuckle. 'To see what we've got to give away, to see if what we seek is so important and where to give it away.

'Mick's happy with the geometry and that sort of thing. We'll certainly try some options. We'll jockey a few things around to get an impression but, like anything, when you start to make changes you stand a good chance of mucking it up. When you get a new golf club, someone tells you it drives ten yards further but it doesn't feel comfortable immediately, it takes time to adjust to it. With the package we've got now, any changes we make – to actually prove them better – will take a little time.'

Burgess explained just how the problems of 1993 had occurred and had eventually been ironed out. 'All through 1993 and up until the Jerez race of '94 Mick had never felt that the front was as good as the '92 bike. A lot of this was probably my fault, because in the early part of '93 Mick was obviously riding the motor cycle differently [with his injured ankle]. A lot of things didn't add up exactly as they had in '92. So you try to find reasons why it wasn't adding up, based on the premise that Showa were saying that the suspension was the same. Had Mick been fit in the early part of '93 he would have isolated this problem then. But throughout last year we just had to persevere.

'The '93 bike was pretty much supposed to be the same as the '92 bike. We got to the situation with the suspension that Mick now uses in the front – Alex and Itoh don't see any advantage in it. Mick finds it can carry his corner speed. You try and test it with Itoh, and in '93 of course we tested it with Daryl, and basically they both thought the '93 suspension was possibly a little bit better, so it got adopted. So again, if Mick had been fit to test when we did the back to back test on those two components he probably would have gone, "Oh no way, give me this one," and we wouldn't have got into the series of errors that we did.

'This year straight away again he said, "The front's not how I want it, it's not doing what I want." So we made some changes in the front forks themselves. The big, noticeable thing to me, other than Mick's absolute happiness with the set-up, was that we were then able to run much softer front tyres. So the suspension was obviously working properly rather than fighting the tyre. That was the big step forward. We knew that we'd made progress, or at least corrected a mistake that we perhaps shouldn't have made in 1993.'

So now that Burgess feels that the Honda is approaching perfection, would Schwantz find it just as perfect? 'I don't think it would be for Kevin. We don't push the avenue of the wide front tyre that seems to make the bike a lot better for braking. Mick says it's definitely better on the bumps, the casing seems to absorb a bit more. But it is not strong enough for Mick at maximum angle in the corner. There are good things for the 16.5 but it is a trade-off. Mick likes the 17, we've got the 16.5 as another tyre in the selection but we've never ever put it on the bike this year.

'As for the rear, we haven't had a lot of joy with the 16.5, because it gives us chatter. We noticed this year with the Michelin tyres that they're all sort of on the borderline for a little bit of chatter, but the gain from that is much more side grip. That's what the riders complained about in the past, lack of side grip at maximum angle. The tyre would break away very quickly, but that's not the case this year. The side grip of the tyres is absolutely fantastic.'

Schwantz has been using the 16.5-in. tyres since 1992, as his race engineer Stuart Shenton explained. 'This year we've also used the 16.5 rear in a couple of places, Donington being one, where it worked very well for us. Mugello was another, but it needs more development.

'There's perhaps more in those tyres than in the 17 now. The development is still in the early stages, but I think there is more future in the 16.5. That is one of the reasons that we are trying to use them, looking more towards the future than the present. In some respects that's

25

Gold & Goose

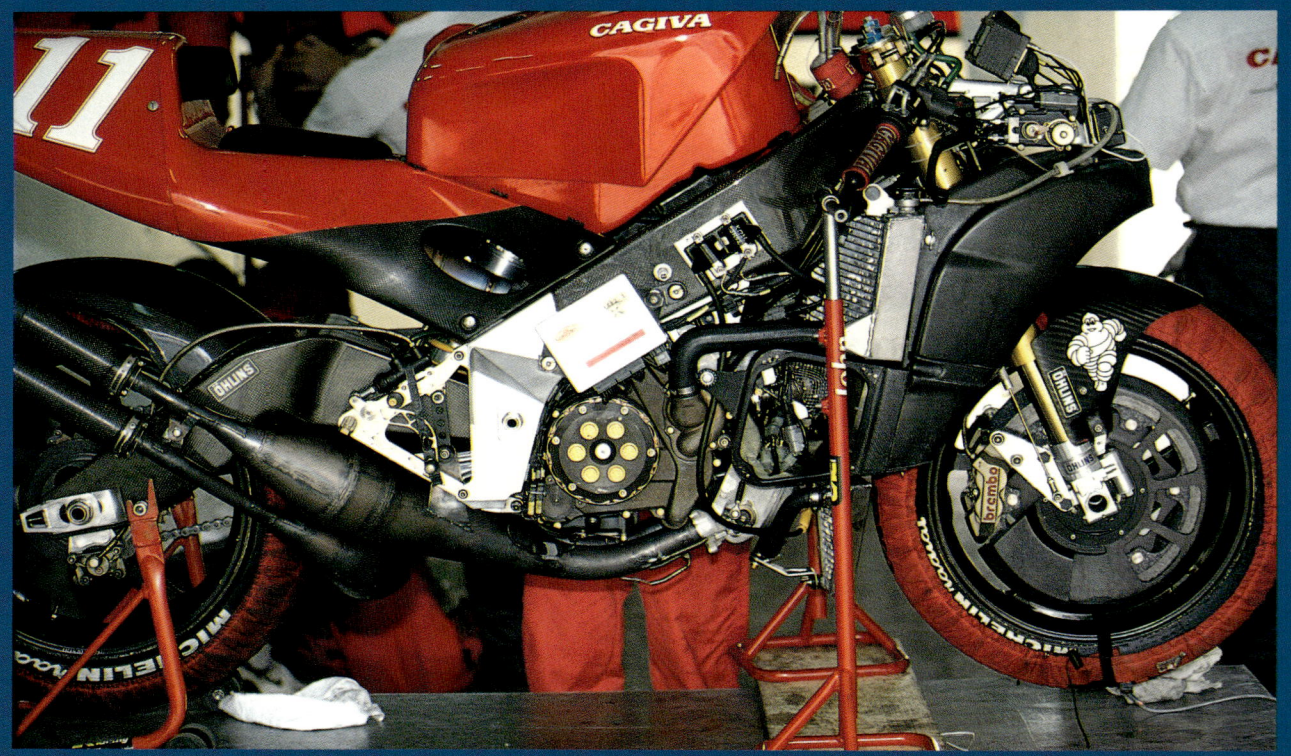

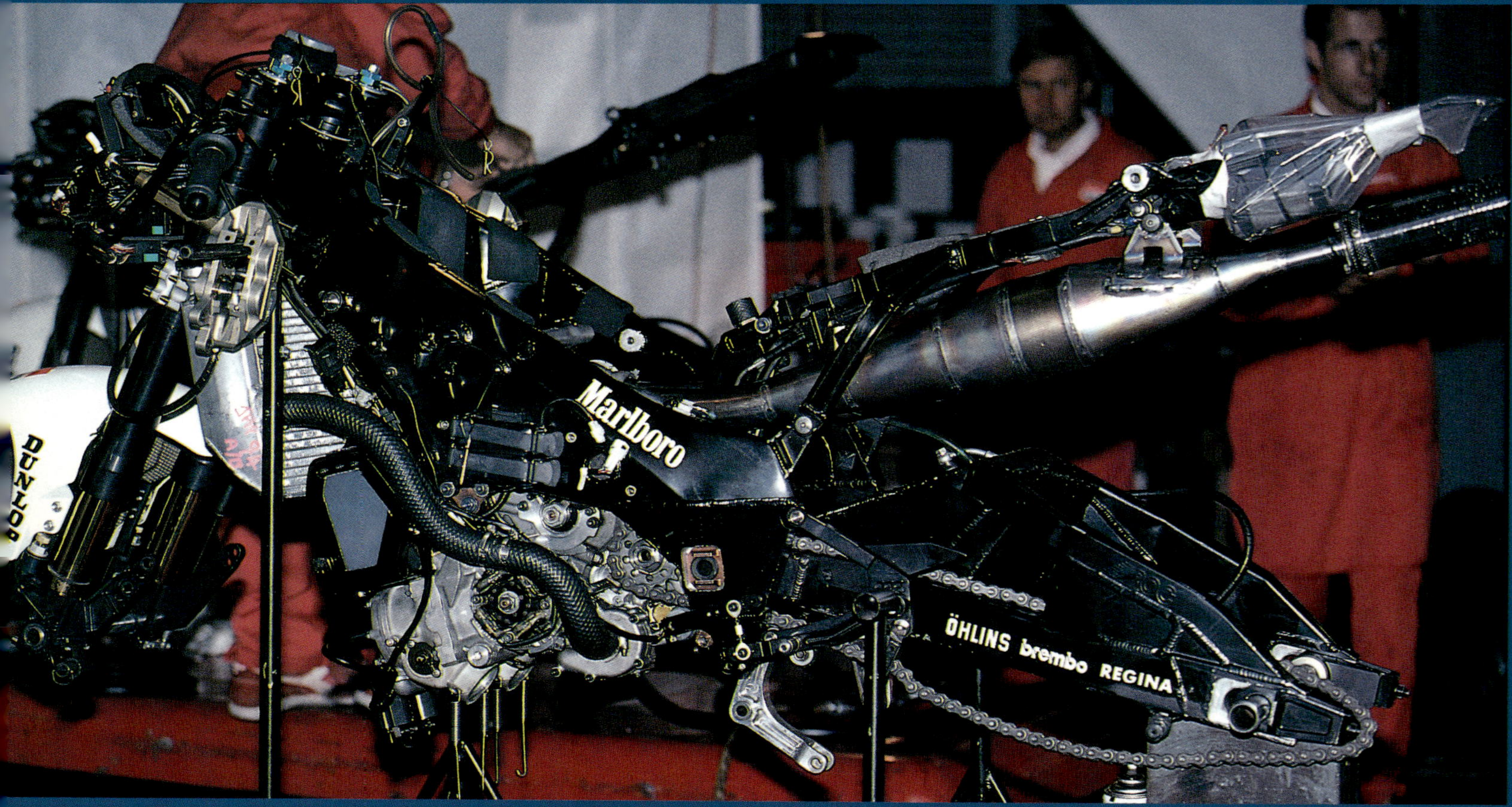

Gold & Goose

Cagiva's hybrid chassis *(top)* mated a carbon-fibre front section to an aluminium rear. Note carbon-fibre swing arm.

Above: Yamaha's Jurassic Parts policy meant they stayed with the Roc-built chassis most of the year.

Schwantz and race engineer Stuart Shenton (in glasses) contemplate the RGV, which had new brakes and experimental rear suspension. Not that you'd notice – secrecy was a policy that kept the bike well under wraps.

Anton Want/Allsport

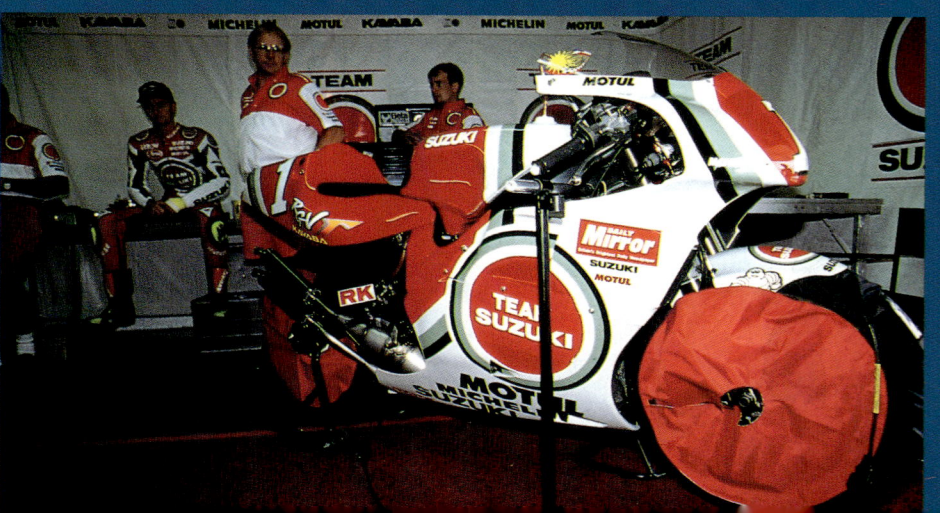

TECHNICAL REVIEW

TOP SPEEDS AT HOCKENHEIM

The Hondas still dominated the lists, but top speeds fell at Hockenheim, with NSR rider Shinichi Itoh falling short of his record 200 mph of 1993. One reason was a loss of sheer horsepower because of the switch to low-lead Avgas, another was new bumps exiting the preceding chicane. Practice times were proportionately slower, yet Doohan broke the lap record in the race. In fact, the comparison is not quite direct. The 1993 figures came from the Suzuki team's radar gun; this year's are official, from the GP timing company Delta Tre's speed trap.

	Rider	Machine	1994	1993
1	Doohan	Honda	196.7 mph	194 mph
2	Itoh	Honda	196.5	200
3	Puig	Honda	196.2	–
4	Criville	Honda	194.5	194
5	Chandler	Cagiva	192.6	190
6	Kocinski	Cagiva	191.2	–
7	Barros	Suzuki	190.7	193
8	Schwantz	Suzuki	190.4	189
9	Mackenzie	Roc	188.5	188
10	Cadalora	Yamaha	186.3	188
12	Beattie	Yamaha	184.5	198 (Honda)
25	Reggiani	Aprilia	177.1	–
	Biaggi	Aprilia	168.6 (fastest 250)	

Below: Cagiva's interesting anti-dive introduced variable-rate linkages to an old-fashioned mechanical system. The caliper is mounted on a trailing link pivoted at the wheel spindle, which operates a short adjustable link, which is in turn connected to the steering head.

wrong, if you want results, but it's a way forward for us.'

Going forward is not easy, though, as Suzuki found as they tried to improve their championship-winning 1993 bike for the '94 season. 'You have a good bike and you try to make it better,' says Shenton. 'We thought we'd made all the right moves. We did a lot of testing – the only good thing that came out of that was that when things went wrong we had a good fallback point, we didn't have to go all the way back. All this talk about using old chassis and old bikes: the only time was actually in Suzuka, where we tested an old chassis with a new engine in it. That was just at that one race meeting, and we didn't race it.

'What we have been able to do is gather data and information that will stand us in good stead for the future. Basically, without giving secrets away, it's a case of a bit more horsepower doesn't make the bike handle so good...if it's in the wrong place.

'The engine characteristics changed from last year to this year, but it wasn't recognised as a problem by either me or the riders. They felt it was better because it was stronger, and perhaps the acceleration was better. But it obviously changed the balance of the bike.'

When the Suzuki team realised that the bike was not an improvement on the 1993 machine, 'We didn't want to put the bike back to last year. We were at a stage where the riders felt that there were better qualities in this year's bike, and we needed to develop those qualities and understand them. If we didn't we'd just become stagnant.

'We've learnt from this year, and if we've got to make the same moves again then we've got to take into consideration some of the things we'd have to do to the chassis and the suspension, to work with a change in engine character.'

Though the Hondas continued to dominate the speed ratings, the Suzukis did pick up some pace – even if the power improvements could've been to blame for their handling difficulties. Internal engine improvements produced some of the speed, and more came from a new fairing featuring an airbox. 'It is something that Suzuki have been looking at for some time, with the idea that by the time we put it on the bike it would be workable,' said Shenton. 'We had it as early as testing in Jerez but Kevin didn't race on it until Hockenheim. We had to do a lot of setting up in Europe, but it had been around in Japan for a while. It is working well but we are still relatively new to it. In the future we need to be better, understand it better and get it working better.'

Honda have been working hard on their pressurised airbox designs for a number of years: different intake lengths sticking forward of the fairing leading edges have been just the most obvious signs of experimentation. Yamaha seem to have been the slowest to adopt a pressurised box as a permanent feature but not, as Team Roberts engineer Bud Aksland explains, because he does not like the idea of them. 'I am a fan of anything that will help power without stressing the engine. It's just that there probably isn't as much to be gained there as everybody would like to think there is. The mid range is kind of difficult to get right. You have to keep working on it. I think Honda's works very well, and I think Suzuki's works. We are the only ones that really don't have an effective airbox.'

Aksland freely admits that the team struggled a bit with performance this season, but that was hardly his fault. It's difficult to say if it was anyone's fault, in fact, because Yamaha tried to produce the new machine that the team had been calling for for years. Unfortunately the new bike turned out to be a disaster. They dumped it on the eve of the first Grand Prix, and it's not been seen at a GP since. So they started the season with the old engine and a rolling chassis built by Roc.

Team Roberts had problems getting the Rocs to work exactly the way that Cadalora wanted, while Beattie found them not to his liking at all. Eventually Yamaha came up with their own 1994 chassis, a very straightforward design without any of the new features, such as the co-axial final drive sprocket and swing arm pivot, that had proved such a disaster on the ditched prototype.

Beattie's season didn't go well. Cadalora, though, scored a couple of wins late on in the season, even against the ultra-fast Hondas. Kenny Roberts confirmed that they will continue to develop that bike for next season and the 'new bike' will probably never be seen again. Aksland will continue to work in parallel with the factory, looking for more power. 'I just give them ideas. We exchange information. They can only do so many things, so I try and do something a little bit different, but it doesn't always work out.'

A lot of the time it's just sheer, hard, repetitive work. 'My dynamometer is computer controlled, the acceleration path takes a minute and I've done a little over 3000 of those this year.'

At times the results are disappointing and the Hondas remain faster. 'I don't think you can say we have reached a limit,' says Aksland. 'You come up against different walls. The increases we've got over the last two years have been relatively small. It is hard to say if we'll ever see another big increase with this engine. Our biggest increase was from '90 to '91. From then on the improvements have been small.'

Kel Carruthers, race engineer to Doug Chandler for the 1994 season, says that now the improvements will always be small and that Honda will do a better job of looking for those small advances than anyone else. 'I mean, I've worked for all these companies and there is no doubt that Honda has got more resources than anyone else. In the past, if you had one really good guy to steer everybody in the right direction you could come up with something that was good enough to win the World Championship. Now it has got to the stage where all the logical stuff has been tried...how many people have got to spend how many hours to try things to see if it works or not?

'The inspired stuff's long gone. Ten years ago I'd get factory parts and change things; now you look at them and there's nothing you can do. People who think they are going to get a factory bike and make it work better are just having themselves on. Now it's a case of going back to the factory and building six more different cylinders. We'll try them and see if one of them's better. We'll try this and try that, make twenty things, and only one of them's any good – if you are lucky. Before it used to be the other way, you made five changes and each one was better. The more people and the more man hours you've got to try things, the better off you are,' concludes Carruthers.

'It's not a secret that Honda have spent a lot more money on R&D,' says Aksland. 'If they need more power it's not hard for them to get it. They've done a lot of work. It's not the number of people, it's people working with advanced technology, it's people doing research on things that we never see. Generally spending money on the future. They do things that are never successful, but they are useful purely as research projects that may pay off somewhere else.'

Aksland is not talking specifically about the electronic systems that Honda have developed to run their fuel injection or the exhaust water injection. 'I don't think that electronics are the answer. Mostly they are a

TECHNICAL REVIEW

Honda's exhaust water injection was mechanically simple, and designed to broaden the power band by slowing the responses of the expansion chamber exhausts.

band aid for a problem that you should solve another way. I don't see fuel injection as being a huge leap in horsepower, and would personally like to see fewer electronic devices on the bikes and more work done with basic engineering. I think that electronics can be a bad thing. They let you improve one area that you are working on at the time, that you want to improve, but you may have been able to improve everything if you'd done the work and been a little more careful with the design or development in the first place.

'For sure, when all the bikes are running down the straight, all the powervalves are wide open, all the jetting is going to be wide open, all the electronic controls are off. They are used for bottom end or mid range, making changes at partial throttle, refining part-throttle response, what the engine is doing in different gears, that sort of thing. As far as sheer power is concerned, the electronics are not having an effect.'

Honda have been forging ahead with electronics, although in fact, as they themselves point out, they do not see them simply as power tools but as ways of controlling engines for better exhaust emissions or fuel consumption – using the fastest motor cycles in the world to test systems that might appear eventually on anything from a commuter motor cycle to a two-stroke road car.

The exhaust water-injection system that they unveiled at the final round at Catalunya is an example. The 'Liquid Injection System' mounted on Mick Doohan's machine in Spain pumps a spray of water into the exhaust pipe just out of the cylinder to cool the gases at lower rpms. This has the effect of slowing the speed of sound in the expansion chamber, and as shock waves travel at the speed of sound, they take longer to be reflected and hence the pipe is effectively lengthened.

In this way a high rpm pipe can be made to produce more low and mid-range power. Honda also claim a reduction in hydrocarbon emissions through more efficient combustion and an improvement in fuel consumption.

The system monitors both engine speed and throttle position and then the logic chip tells the individual injectors how much water to pump into the pipes. The reservoir is a sectioned-off portion of the fuel tank, and although it has a volume of 5 litres only something over 2 litres of water is needed for a Grand Prix.

It seems that the 'Liquid Injection System' may have cost the NSR a fraction in top speed at Catalunya, but that can presumably be sorted out with further development. The advantages to low and mid-range power are claimed to be as much as 10 horsepower at 8000 rpm. The idea is not new: it has been used by both small race teams and huge corporations in the past. The Marlboro Roberts Team have tried it, but only Honda have the resources to see it through.

Honda also unveiled another electronically controlled system, the PGM suspension system, which was mounted on Alex Criville's bike at Catalunya. This programmed suspension system takes data from the engine and alters the rear suspension to better suit what the bike is doing at any point on the track, changing the compression and rebound damping automatically as the bike circulates.

An electric motor in the compression end of the unit and another in the rebound end turn cams that move damping needles to alter the valving in twelve steps. In this way it is hoped to have perfect compression and rebound damping for the different demands of braking, acceleration, mid-corner speed, etc.

The system senses engine speed, throttle position and gear position before deciding on suspension setting. There is also a manual over-ride button so that the rider can influence the system and try different settings while out on the track. It is a combined Showa/Honda project.

If Honda won the World Championship by taking the high horsepower road and eventually ironing out associated problems, then the latest 500 class newcomer, Aprilia, took the opposite track, with a twin-cylinder 400 that attempted to take full advantage of the rule allowing a twin to weigh just 145 kg compared with the four-cylinder minimum of 160 kg.

The 400 cc Aprilia missed the first three Grands Prix but was the sensation of practice at Jerez. Loris Reggiani rode the wheels off it in his classic ten-tenths style, two-wheel drifting it all the way up the kerbs. Called the RSV500, the 90° disc-

valve V-twin impressed World Champion Kevin Schwantz, who came across Reggiani in the Saturday morning session. 'Loris is doing a great job on it,' said the Texan. 'It's not slow but that's not to say I can't pull four or five bike lengths on it down the two main straights here. It's got mid-corner speed on us – through the twisty, tight sections I was having trouble staying with him.'

Aprilia engineer Jan Witteveen admitted that things were going at least as well as could be expected. 'In three tests at Mugello we basically have not had any significant problems, practically nothing. I can't speak for Loris, but talking from the technical point of view there have been no surprises. We have had the normal development problems but honestly thought we would have had more.

'The principle of the machine is that it should perform like a very powerful 250. That is the reason for going no larger than 400 cc. If the engine were bigger it would have more torque but would not rev as freely; that would alter the engine characteristics and it would no longer work like a 250.'

Reggiani said that in that respect the machine had already been a success. 'It feels exactly like a powerful 250, and that is how I ride it,' said Loris. 'It is not as fast as the works 500s at the moment – we are similar to some of the private Rocs – but we will have more power as development continues.'

Though the bike showed great early promise it suffered a variety of technical problems in its early races and was withdrawn from competition before the British Grand Prix. The company could not make engine spares fast enough, and they were still making the parts as prototype pieces rather than production items.

As a debut season the Aprilia's could not be considered stunning, but it would be a mistake to think that the company had made an error in going for a twin-cylinder design. Shenton admitted that the Suzuki's extra engine power had caused problems, and there are obvious advantages in a light, easy to handle machine. The question of how much more powerful the Aprilia has to be

before it becomes competitive, however, remains unanswered.

Honda may have the high technology lead but that does not mean they are infallible. 'I don't think that anyone's infallible,' says Carruthers. 'Honda probably make more mistakes than anybody else, in that they have a good bike one year, then they go to a bike that's not so good.

'The bike Honda have now they've basically had for about four years. I don't think they've made much progress since they first brought out the big-bang engine. They went downhill from there and have now gone back again. So I think that they are fortunate enough to have something that was good three years ago.'

Making mistakes in development direction seems to be everyone's biggest problem. Yamaha made a big mistake after the 1993 season; Suzuki's error was much slighter but that made it harder to pinpoint and correct. Despite the very high technological level involved in current 500 Grand Prix racing machines, success so often still depends on that subtle, mercurial relationship between the rider and his machine. And it is fundamentally important not only on race day but throughout testing and development.

It is so hard to quantify and control that it can be the thing that worries race engineers most. As Burgess explains, they have a great bike/rider combination but it cannot stand still. 'I think that the package is good but the thing that scares me is that a rider gets to a point where he is good enough to win the championship and he is happy with the bike. These riders, as they get older, just like other sportsmen, golfers, whatever, don't accept change as easily as younger guys.

'If we can show something that is a definite advantage in some area, we may get the situation of a rider just personally not liking that thing. This is where motor cycle development basically stops. You might be in front of the opposition for a year, but if you taper off for two years and the others are still on the climb then, suddenly, they are as good as you and still climbing. That's the worry I have.'

YOU WIN AGAIN

The 1994 YZF750R represents the pinnacle of sports motorcycle design. Featuring the latest aluminium incarnation of the Yamaha Deltabox frame, six piston brakes and advanced five valve engine technology, the YZF won both the premier UK Superbike Championships in 1993.

Despite its outstanding race success the new model features major improvements. Suspension modifications not only improve the already exquisite handling abilities of the bike, but also introduce the maximum degree of adjustment possible, to suit any individual riders preferences. Front and rear suspension both allow for compression, rebound and preload settings to be altered as required.

Such constant development is the result of feedback from racing and our commitment to research, which in turn ensures that we continue winning. It's why Yamaha have such a solid reputation for producing the sportiest sportsbikes around. And it's the reason you win again, whenever you choose Yamaha.

YAMAHA

500 cc Specifications

	Kevin Schwantz	Luca Cadalora	Michael Doohan	John Kocinski
Rider				
Machine	498 cc RGV500 Suzuki	498 cc YZR500 Yamaha	494.6 cc NSR500 Honda	498 cc C594 Cagiva
ENGINE – Type	Water-cooled four-cylinder two-stroke, twin pressed cranks, four ball bearings each.	Water-cooled four-cylinder two-stroke, twin pressed cranks, four ball bearings each.	Water-cooled four-cylinder two-stroke, single pressed cranks, five roller bearings.	Water-cooled four-cylinder two-stroke, twin pressed cranks, four roller bearings each.
Bore & Stroke	56 x 50.7 mm.	56 x 50.6 mm.	54 x 54.5 mm.	56 x 50.6 mm.
Induction	Two twin-choke 36 mm electronic power jet flat-slide Mikunis, crankcase reed-valve induction.	Two twin-choke 35 mm electronic power jet flat-slide Mikunis, crankcase reed-valve induction.	Two twin-choke 36 mm Keihins, crankcase reed-valve induction.	Two twin-choke 36 mm electronic power jet flat-slide Mikunis, crankcase reed-valve induction.
Porting	Six transfer, three exhaust.	Seven transfer, three exhaust.	Five transfer, two exhaust.	Five transfer, three exhaust.
Exhaust valve	Electronically controlled guillotine and independently controlled second chamber.	Electronically controlled cylindrical.	Electronically controlled draw bridge.	Electronically controlled cylindrical.
Ignition	Electronic with programmable advance curve linked to exhaust powervalves and carburettor power jet. NGK sparking plugs.	Electronic with programmable advance curve linked to throttle opening, exhaust powervalve and carburettor power jet. NGK sparking plugs.	Electronic with programmable advance curve linked to exhaust powervalve and throttle opening. NGK sparking plugs.	Electronic with programmable advance curve linked to throttle opening, exhaust powervalve and carburettor power jet. NGK sparking plugs.
Oil	Motul engine and gearbox.	Castrol engine and gearbox.	Elf engine and gearbox.	Agip engine and gearbox.
Other details	Single plain piston ring, needle-roller small and big end bearings.	Single plain piston ring, needle-roller small end and roller big end bearings.	Single plain piston ring, needle-roller small and big end bearings.	Single plain piston ring, needle-roller small end and roller big end bearings.
TRANSMISSION – Primary drive	Straight cut gear to clutch from right-hand end of lower crank.	Straight cut gear to clutch from right-hand end of lower crank.	Straight cut gear to clutch via cross from centre of crank.	Straight cut gear to clutch from right-hand end of lower crank.
Clutch	Dry multi-plate, nine friction and ten steel plates, six springs.	Dry multi-plate, five sintered, two organic and six steel plates, six springs.	Dry multi-plate, seven friction and seven steel plates, six springs.	Dry multi-plate, seven friction and eight steel plates, six springs.
Gearbox	Six-speed, six possible ratios for first, seven for second, fourteen for third and fourth, seven for fifth and sixth. Five different primary ratios. Drum selection. SAGS electronic cut-out gearchange.	Six-speed, nine possible ratios for first, seven for second, six for third and fourth, four for fifth and sixth. Three different primary ratios. Drum selection.	Six-speed, alternative ratios for all gears. Drum selection.	Six-speed, ten possible ratios for first and fourth, seven for second and fifth, nine for third and sixth. Drum selection. Electronic cut-out gearchange.
RUNNING GEAR – Frame	Twin-spar fabricated box-section aluminium with rear section machined from solid, bolt-on sub-frame. Ball head bearings with inserts for adjusting head angle.	Twin-spar extruded-section aluminium. Ball head bearings with inserts for adjusting head angle. (Fabricated box-section Roc manufactured frame also used.)	Twin-spar extruded-section aluminium, taper roller head bearings.	Twin-spar carbon front and aluminium rear. Taper roller head bearings with inserts for adjusting head angle.
Front suspension	Kayaba OUT telescopic forks, coil springs, oil damped, externally adjustable for both high and low speed compression and high speed rebound.	Ohlins OUT telescopic forks, coil springs, oil damped, adjustable.	Showa OUT telescopic forks, coil springs, oil damped, externally adjustable.	Ohlins OUT telescopic forks, coil springs, oil damped, adjustable.
Rear suspension	Triangulated box-section aluminium swing arm, needle-roller bearings. One Kayaba unit, coil spring, oil damped, externally adjustable for both high and low speed compression and high speed rebound with lower end linkage.	Triangulated box-section aluminium swing arm, needle-roller bearings. One Ohlins unit, coil spring, nitrogen pressure, oil damped, adjustable with lower end linkage.	Triangulated box-section aluminium swing arm, needle-roller bearings. One Showa unit, coil spring, nitrogen pressure, oil damped, adjustable with lower end linkage.	Triangulated box-section carbon swing arm, needle-roller bearings. One Ohlins unit, coil spring, nitrogen pressure, oil damped, adjustable with lower end linkage.
Wheels	Marchesini cast magnesium: 3.50 or 4.00 in. x 17 in. front and 5.25 in. x 17 in. or 6.00 in. x 16.5 in. rear.	Marchesini cast magnesium: 3.75 or 3.50 in. x 17 in. front and 6.25 in. x 17 in. rear. (5.50 in. x 18 in. or 6.25 in. x 17 in. for rain tyres.)	Honda cast magnesium: 3.50 or 3.75 in. x 17 in. front and 6.00, 6.125 and 6.25 in. x 17 in. rear.	Marchesini cast magnesium: 3.50 in. x 17 in. or 3.50 in. x 16.5 in. front and 6.00 in. x 17 in. or 6.00 in. by 16.5 in. rear.
Tyres	Michelin.	Dunlop.	Michelin.	Dunlop.
Brakes	**Front:** two AP carbon-carbon (325 mm) discs. AP six piston calipers. AP articulated pads. (Brembo brakes also tested, and used by team-mate Barros.) **Rear:** single Suzuki cast steel (210 mm) disc. Twin piston caliper.	**Front:** two Brembo carbon-carbon (Cadalora 320 mm, Beattie 290 mm) discs. Brembo four piston calipers. Brembo pads. **Rear:** single Yamaha cast steel (210 mm) disc. Brembo twin piston caliper. Brembo pads.	**Front:** two Brembo carbon-carbon (320 mm) discs. Brembo four piston calipers. Brembo pads. **Rear:** single Honda cast steel (190 mm) disc. HRC twin piston caliper. HRC pads.	**Front:** two Brembo carbon-carbon (320 mm) discs. Brembo four piston calipers. Brembo pads. **Rear:** single Brembo carbon-carbon (190 mm) disc. Brembo twin piston caliper. Brembo pads.

250 cc Specifications

	Tetsuya Harada	Tadayuki Okada	Massimiliano Biaggi	Frédéric Protat
Rider / **Machine**	249 cc TZ-M Yamaha	247.3 cc NSR250 Honda	249.6 cc AF1 93 Aprilia	247.3 cc RS250 Honda
ENGINE – Type	Water-cooled twin-cylinder two-stroke, single pressed crank, two ball and two roller bearings.	Water-cooled twin-cylinder two-stroke, single pressed crank, three ball bearings.	Water-cooled twin-cylinder two-stroke, twin pressed cranks, three ball bearings each.	Water-cooled twin-cylinder two-stroke, single pressed crank, three ball bearings
Bore & Stroke	56 x 50.7 mm.	54 x 54.5 mm.	54 x 54.5 mm.	54 x 54.5 mm.
Induction	Two 39 mm flat-slide Mikunis, crankcase reed-valve induction.	Two 38 mm flat-slide Keihins, crankcase reed-valve induction.	Two 35 x 42 mm oval bore flat-slide Dell'Ortos, disc-valve induction.	Two 38 mm flat-slide Keihins, crankcase reed-valve induction.
Porting	Seven transfer, three exhaust.	Five transfer, two exhaust.	Five transfer, three exhaust.	Five transfer, two exhaust.
Exhaust valve	Electronically controlled cylindrical.	Electronically controlled draw bridge.	Electronically controlled guillotine.	Electronically controlled draw bridge.
Ignition	Electronic with programmable advance curve linked to exhaust powervalve. NGK sparking plugs.	Electronic with programmable advance curve linked to exhaust powervalve. NGK sparking plugs.	Electronic with programmable advance curve linked to exhaust powervalve. NGK sparking plugs.	Electronic linked to exhaust powervalve. NGK sparking plugs.
Oil	Castrol engine and gearbox.	Castrol engine and gearbox.	Mobil engine and gearbox.	Motul engine and gearbox.
Other details	Single plain piston ring, needle-roller small and roller big end bearings.	Single plain piston ring, needle-roller small and big end bearings.	Single plain piston ring, needle-roller small and big end bearings.	Single plain piston ring, needle-roller small and big end bearings
TRANSMISSION – Primary drive	Straight cut gear.	Straight cut gear.	Straight cut gear.	Straight cut gear.
Clutch	Dry multi-plate, five friction and six steel plates, six springs.	Dry multi-plate, five friction and six steel plates, five springs.	Dry multi-plate, five friction and six steel plates, six springs.	Dry multi-plate, six friction and five steel plates, five springs
Gearbox	Six-speed, drum selection, alternative ratios for all gears. Electronic cut-out gearchange.	Six-speed, five possible ratios for first four gears, six for fifth and seven for sixth, drum selection. Electronic cut-out gearchange.	Six-speed, nine possible ratios for first, eight for second, four for third, three for fourth and five for fifth and sixth. Drum selection. Electronic cut-out gearchange.	Six-speed, four possible ratios for first, second and fifth gears, nine for third and fourth, six for sixth.
RUNNING GEAR – Frame	Twin-spar fabricated box-section aluminium, taper roller head bearings with inserts for adjusting head angle.	Twin-spar extruded-section aluminium with machined sections in addition, ball head bearings.	Twin-spar fabricated aluminium, taper roller head bearings with spherical seating.	Twin-spar extruded-section aluminium, with cast sections in addition, ball head bearings.
Front suspension	Ohlins OUT telescopic forks, coil springs, oil damped, adjustable.	Showa OUT telescopic forks, coil springs, oil damped, adjustable.	White Power OUT telescopic forks, coil springs, oil damped, adjustable.	Showa OUT telescopic forks, coil springs, oil damped, adjustable.
Rear suspension	Triangulated box-section aluminium swing arm, needle-roller bearings. One Ohlins unit, coil spring, oil damped, adjustable with lower end linkage.	Triangulated box-section aluminium swing arm, needle-roller bearings. One Showa unit, coil spring, oil damped, adjustable with lower end linkage.	Triangulated box-section aluminium or carbon composite swing arm, roller bearings. One White Power unit, coil spring, oil damped, electronic control of compression damping with rider handlebar choice. Lower end linkage.	Triangulated box-section aluminium swing arm, needle-roller bearings. One Ohlins or White Power unit, coil spring, oil damped, adjustable with lower end linkage.
Wheels	Marchesini cast magnesium: 3.50 in. x 17 in. front and 5.25 in. x 17 in. rear.	Honda cast magnesium: 3.50, 3.65 or 3.75 in. x 17 in. front and 5.25, 5.35 or 5.50 in. x 17 in. rear.	Marchesini cast magnesium: 3.75 in. x 17 in. front and 5.50 in. x 17 in. rear.	PVM cast magnesim: 3.50 in. x 17 in. front and 5.25 in. x 17 in. rear or HRC 5.50 in. x 17 in. rear.
Tyres	Dunlop.	Michelin.	Dunlop.	Michelin.
Brakes	**Front:** two Brembo carbon-carbon (290 mm) discs. Brembo four piston calipers. Brembo pads. **Rear:** single Yamaha cast steel (220 mm) disc. Nissin twin piston caliper. Nissin pads.	**Front:** two Brembo carbon-carbon (290 mm) discs. Brembo four piston calipers. Brembo pads. **Rear:** single Honda cast steel (180 mm) disc. Nissin twin piston caliper. Nissin pads.	**Front:** two Brembo carbon-carbon (255 mm) discs. Brembo four piston calipers. Brembo pads. **Rear:** single Brembo aluminium (184 mm) disc. Brembo twin piston caliper. Brembo pads.	**Front:** two AP carbon-carbon (273 mm) discs. AP four piston calipers. AP pads. **Rear:** single AP carbon-carbon (195 mm) disc. Nissin twin piston caliper. AP pads.

125 cc Specifications

	Dirk Raudies	Takeshi Tsujimura	Jorge Martinez	Kazuto Sakata
Rider **Machine**	*124 cc Honda*	*124 cc Honda*	*124 cc Yamaha*	*124.8 cc Aprilia*
ENGINE – Type	Water-cooled single-cylinder two-stroke, single pressed crank, two ball bearings.	Water-cooled single-cylinder two-stroke, single pressed crank, two ball bearings.	Water-cooled single-cylinder two-stroke, single pressed crank, two ball bearings.	Water-cooled single-cylinder two-stroke, single pressed crank, two ball bearings.
Bore & Stroke	55 x 54.5 mm.	55 x 54.5 mm.	56 x 50.7 mm.	54 x 54.5 mm.
Induction	One 36 mm flat-slide Keihin, crankcase reed-valve induction.	One 38 mm flat-slide Keihin, crankcase reed-valve induction.	One 38 mm flat-slide Mikuni power jet, crankcase reed-valve induction.	One 39 mm cylindrical-slide Dell'Orto, disc-valve induction.
Porting	Five transfer, two exhaust.	Five transfer, two exhaust.	Seven transfer, three exhaust.	Five transfer, three exhaust.
Exhaust valve	None.	None.	Electronically controlled guillotine.	Electronically controlled guillotine.
Ignition	Electronic. NGK sparking plugs.	Electronic. NGK sparking plugs.	Electronic. NGK sparking plugs.	Electronic. NGK sparking plugs.
Oil	Bel Ray engine and gearbox.	Elf engine and gearbox.	Cepsa engine and gearbox.	Mobil engine and gearbox.
Other details	Single plain piston ring, needle-roller small and big end bearings.	Single plain piston ring, needle-roller small and big end bearings.	Single plain piston ring, needle-roller small and big end bearings.	Single plain piston ring, needle-roller small and big end bearings.
TRANSMISSION – Primary drive	Straight cut gear.	Straight cut gear.	Straight cut gear.	Straight cut gear.
Clutch	Wet multi-plate, seven friction and six steel plates, five springs.	FCC dry multi-plate, six friction and five steel plates, four springs.	Wet multi-plate, six friction and five steel plates, five springs.	Dry multi-plate, five friction and five steel plates, six springs.
Gearbox	Six-speed, three possible ratios for first and second gears, two for third, fourth, fifth and sixth, drum selection. Electronic cut-out gearchange.	Six-speed, seven possible ratios for first and six for second, three for remaining gears, drum selection. Electronic cut-out gearchange.	Six-speed, two possible ratios for first and second, three for remaining gears, drum selection. Electronic cut-out gearchange.	Six-speed, seven possible ratios for first, second and third gears, three for fourth, fifth and sixth, drum selection. Electronic cut-out gearchange.
RUNNING GEAR – Frame	Twin-spar extruded-section aluminium, taper roller head bearings.	Twin-spar extruded-section aluminium, taper roller head bearings.	Twin-spar extruded-section aluminium, taper roller head bearings.	Twin-spar extruded-section aluminium, taper roller head bearings.
Front suspension	Kayaba OUT telescopic forks, coil springs, oil damped, adjustable.	White Power OUT telescopic forks, coil springs, oil damped, adjustable.	Kayaba OUT telescopic forks, coil springs, oil damped, adjustable.	White Power OUT telescopic forks, coil springs, oil damped, adjustable.
Rear suspension	Triangulated extruded-section aluminium swing arm, plain bearings. One Kayaba unit, coil spring, oil damped, adjustable with lower end linkage.	Triangulated extruded-section aluminium swing arm, plain bearings. One White Power unit, coil spring, oil damped, adjustable with lower end linkage.	Triangulated extruded-section aluminium swing arm, plain bearings. One Ohlins unit, coil spring, oil damped, adjustable with lower end linkage.	Triangulated extruded-section aluminium swing arm, taper roller bearings. One White Power unit, coil spring, oil damped, adjustable with lower end linkage.
Wheels	PVM cast magnesium: 2.50 in. x 17 in. front and carbon 3.50 in. x 17 in. rear.	Techno Magnesio cast magnesium: 2.25 in. x 17 in. front and carbon 3.50 in. x 17 in. rear.	Marchesini cast magnesium: 2.25 in. x 17 in. front and carbon 3.50 in. x 17 in. rear.	Marchesini cast magnesium: 2.50 in. x 17 in. front and carbon 3.50 in. x 17 in. rear.
Tyres	Dunlop.	Bridgestone.	Dunlop.	Dunlop.
Brakes	**Front:** single PVM cast steel (300 mm) discs. PVM six piston caliper. PVM pads. **Rear:** single PVM carbon-carbon (186 mm) disc. PVM twin piston caliper. PVM pads.	**Front:** single Brembo cast steel (296 mm) discs. Brembo four piston caliper. Brembo pads. **Rear:** single Honda cast steel (190 mm) disc. Nissin twin piston caliper. Nissin pads.	**Front:** single Brembo cast steel (296 mm) discs. Brembo four piston caliper. Brembo pads. **Rear:** single Yamaha cast steel (190 mm) disc. Yamaha twin piston caliper. Yamaha pads.	**Front:** single Brembo cast steel (300 mm) discs. Brembo four piston caliper. Brembo pads. **Rear:** single Brembo cast steel (180 mm) disc. Brembo twin piston caliper. Brembo pads.

THE STATE OF RACING

ONLY THE LONELY

The 1994 season proceeded smoothly and to plan. The third year of racing's new regime showed improved management, while the chill influence of Bernie Ecclestone receded with a flexible approach that allowed hard-pressed individual race promoters new freedoms to brighten up their national GPs.

The return of the French GP as well as a new South American round gave the calendar a better profile, and though there were worrying moments – especially in Argentina – the season didn't skip a beat. Overall, it seemed to have gone well. Only one thing was missing: confidence. At the end of 1994, all three main organisations involved (four if you count the manufacturers) had some sort of contingency plan to go it alone if necessary.

Twelve months ago, *Motocourse* recorded a sense of isolation, with the GPs increasingly distanced from grass-roots motor bike racing. The new year began with an unwelcome growth of this distance, and almost everything that happened thereafter only further increased the feeling of exposure. To say the classic World Championship series is on the ropes or walking the plank is to overstate the case – but only marginally.

The isolation became acute after the Japanese federation made a surprise decision to drop their All-Japan 500 class championship series at the end of 1993. Japan was the last country to run a major series for 500 cc GP two-strokes. Even more significantly, the domestic championship was an important development and proving ground for machines, and nowadays also for riders – Norifumi Abe being the latest. But though well supported by the factories, there was no second level, and grids during 1993 sometimes numbered single figures. A plan for a supply of privateer Roc Yamahas to fill the gap was well advanced, but it was too late; the premier title of the industry's home country had gone to Superbikes, like the rest of the world. The role of the industry in all this was unclear. Factory men at the GP tracks said they had been taken by surprise and all opposed the move – but nobody knew what discussions and trade-offs might have taken place higher up the factory hierarchy. So GP racing was now entirely alone.

As if the Brave New World Championship, launched in 1991, was not perfectly capable of creating enough problems of its own.

Many of these were the legacy of Bernie Ecclestone's brief involvement. He had been drawn into the IRTA hi-jack at the end of 1991, then forced at the last minute by circumstances to compromise with Dorna and the FIM. This carried with it a costly annual payment (more than $5 million) to the FIM, but it all fitted in with his vision of a new, well-heeled crowd who would gladly pay vastly increased ticket prices for the slick new racing package, and the large number of sponsors who would inevitably follow.

These turned out to be imaginary, and Ecclestone quickly understood this, promptly baling out and selling his share of the specially formed Two Wheel Promotions (TWP, part of the triumvirate who took over after the hi-jack) to Dorna. It emerged during 1994 that the price for the shares was in the region of $50 million. Even set against the steady drip of his promoter's contract for the unsuccessful German GP, this was a tidy sum – proving that while his predictions of much increased financial yields were wrong in the case of his colleagues, they were right when applied to himself.

Those left behind to struggle, after the Bernie Bubble had burst, were in some cases (like the promoters) saddled with punitive five-year contracts based on the incorrect financial projections, and in other cases under pressure from outside sources. Almost everyone in racing, from manufacturers and teams without sponsors (even HRC had failed to find a replacement for Rothmans) to hard-pressed promoters, was feeling the pinch in 1994.

This was certainly true at Dorna, now the main players in the GP business. As well as their annual burden to the FIM, the payment to Ecclestone must surely have made a serious dent in their cashflow. However, acquisition of TWP had given them complete control over all the commercial aspects of racing. They were contracted directly to the FIM on the one side for the rights, and to IRTA on the other for the teams; and they likewise had hands-on first-party contracts for sale of TV rights, track signage, event naming rights and everything else. In any case, as their officers never tired of reminding the doubters, they were not only a big company in their own right, but were furthermore 50 per cent owned by the giant Banesto Bank.

Then, late in 1993, Banesto went bankrupt. And after a government rescue their entire operation was taken over by the even bigger Banco Santander. Through no fault of their own Dorna's shares suddenly became just one of a number of unwanted items of extra baggage.

All this clearly concentrated their minds wonderfully, and there followed a major shake-up. The TV rights company divested themselves of all other business including soccer contracts, MBA basketball rights and their own branch in America. From henceforth they would concentrate on motor sport, and mainly on the bike GPs. They also replaced British managing director Richard Golding, responsible for the TWP buy-out, with a Spaniard, Carmello Espelita, who had been with them from the very start of their involvement with motor cycle racing.

Dorna did not actually increase TV sales during 1994, but they did gain coherence. Outside observers also hoped they were not being too optimistic in noting a new sense of purpose, of commitment and of long-term strategy in Dorna's new management. They may yet navigate their way out of their current predicament.

IRTA, by contrast, were largely the authors of their own misfortunes. They started off the controversial cost-cutting moves all by themselves, and by the end of the year the issue had not only opened up deep divisions within the teams' association, but had also drawn up battle lines with the factory teams, represented by their own association, the Grand Prix Manufacturers' Association (GPMA).

Clearly, in all the circumstances, this was not a good time to be alienating the factory teams, and to understand how it came about and appreciate the implications it is necessary to look at how IRTA's very structure drove it unwillingly to this impasse.

In a nutshell, IRTA, architects of the hi-jack from the FIM, stand in serious danger of being marginalised, and even pushed out of the business altogether. After all, why should Dorna, who control everything else, need an intermediary in the business of recruiting the teams?

IRTA hatched their own secret counter-plans to go it alone without Dorna, but this remained a distant contingency. Meanwhile it was important to do something – anything – to demonstrate that they were a

Above: **IRTA vice-president Serge Rosset ponders the future.**

by Michael Scott

meaningful organisation. With many teams facing financial problems, the issue of rising costs and dwindling resources needed to be addressed, although it may have been little more than a convenient issue for IRTA to take up in order to prove themselves indispensable. If so, their plan backfired.

This was inevitable, given IRTA's democratic structure – one team one vote, which means the lowliest of 125 privateers has the same voting power as Doohan's HRC squad, or the whole of Cagiva. This poses few problems when IRTA is merely arranging the paddock or taking a role in ensuring the smooth running of trackside business. But when it comes to strategy and policies, the perspectives of the participating teams are so different that it can only lead to bitter argument.

On the one hand, the works teams who make racing what it is were doubtful about the whole approach. 'Racing is like war,' said one of their number. 'When you start to count the cost, you lose.' Less arrogantly and as memorably, another explained their disquiet. 'When the recession hit, Porsche lost something like 50 per cent of their sales in the USA. They didn't respond by building Skodas.'

Rather than trying to cut costs and risk spoiling the show and reducing the status of the Grands Prix, IRTA should aim to increase the availability of funds. How about, for example, an initiative to seek out new sponsors, and to marry them up with worthwhile teams?

On the other hand, there were a number of teams who, in relative terms, were on the bread-line already. They would welcome anything that would cut costs – particularly if it could also narrow the gap between the works machines and their private bikes. It's hard to find sponsorship when the best you can guarantee is that you might get involved in a fight for tenth place.

Amid continuing argument the notion gathered momentum, rather like a runaway train at the top of a gentle but steady incline. By the German GP, a confidential IRTA memo was widely leaked (itself an indication of dissent). This document, signed by IRTA chief executive Paul Butler, set out a number of disparate cost-cutting ideas on the scatter-gun principle, and hoped to have more concrete proposals by the very next race.

This list included the following:

- to restrict all teams to one bike per rider
- to ban works specials from the 250 and 125 classes
- to introduce an age limit for 125 riders
- to require a factory entering a class to field a minimum of two riders in the first year, increasing in subsequent years
- to restrict private winter testing to Japan and Europe
- to reduce the cost of fuel and tyres
- to reduce the number of riders per class to 30/32, increasing the expense contribution fund.

Every one of these ideas could find a group of IRTA members to oppose it. Having only one bike could mean a works star and title contender might fail to qualify, should he miss out on a crucial dry practice session; an age limit for 125 riders (intended to move the veterans on to 250s) was silly; dictating the size of factory teams was none of IRTA's business; restricting testing to Europe and Japan was (as one put it) 'like holding snowmobile tests in California in summer'; and as for reducing fuel costs – the switch to low-lead Avgas this year was meant to do that, but the cost of compensatory additives had simply driven the price back up to where it was last year.

'They are only points for discussion,' said Butler disarmingly, from his unhappy position 'twixt Scylla and Charybdis; but by the end of the season angry factory men would accuse extreme elements of IRTA's privateer faction of having bulldozed the matter through without following the statutory procedure that would have given them (the factory men) a chance to apply some safeguards.

The proposal that survived, applied only to the 250 and 125 classes, was the first – to follow (vaguely) F1 practice in restricting each rider to one bike. Of course he may have a spare, and should he have the misfortune to damage his bike during practice he would be able to use it. But instead of being revved up ready in the pits, it would first have to go through its own process of scrutineering and technical inspection, which could begin only after the first bike was officially declared *hors de combat*.

To outsiders this seemed particularly half-baked, since it was hard to see any serious savings. The works teams and the luckier privateers, with two or more bikes per rider already, would still have the same number of bikes, but they would be in the back of the lorry rather than the back of the pits. The private teams with one bike per rider would still have one bike per rider. So where's the saving? And the quality of the show would suffer, with fewer bikes on the track during practice, and riders less prepared to take risks. There was also the possibility that a rider might not qualify should he suffer a crash or a breakdown that prevented him taking part in the only dry session. IRTA dealt with this by promising to remove the 'pole plus 10 per cent' qualifying cut-off rule, unleashing yet more howls of derision.

Still the train rolled on, gathering speed.

All this manoeuvring alerted others in the undergrowth – in particular the manufacturers. Formed in 1991, the GPMA had been at best a shadowy organisation, representing only the 500 class teams. It was in America, near the end of the season, that they broke cover, with an unprecedented press conference. The delegates to the top table, surrounded on all sides by lesser acolytes, themselves senior figures in the Japanese racing hierarchy, comprised a huge amount of industrial and commercial power: Claudio Castiglioni, part-owner of Cagiva, Ducati, Husqvarna et al., and GPMA chairman; Kensuke Fukatsu, Honda Motor Corporation director and chief officer of motor cycle operations; Yukio Nakamura, general manager of Suzuki's racing operations; and Kazuhiko Nomura, executive director of Yamaha. It was surely the first time in racing history that such senior industry figures, all fierce commercial rivals, had sat down together in public to

THE STATE OF RACING

The 500s come out to play. Isolated or not, they remain the greatest racing bikes in the world.

Below: The question was how to cut costs without killing the show.

ential figure, thought it offered an opportunity to cut budgets, which in turn would make it easier to find sponsors. Nonplussed factory men suspected a hidden agenda, taking money and prestige away from the smaller classes so that the 500s might benefit at their expense, creating a potential super-class along the lines of F1 car racing. But the notion had other important supporters as well – so while some decried the scheme as a blatant and possibly deceitful folly, others were hustling it through.

The final surprise came at the last race of the year, at Catalunya, where it was announced that the GPMA had accepted, at least in principle, the proposal for one bike for the 250 and 125 classes for 1995...an about-face that hinted at important concessions won for the 500 class. New members Aprilia protested violently, issuing a statement the next day condemning the decision on a number of grounds, one of which was safety. They feared that mechanics might be obliged to patch up a crashed bike hastily, to get the rider back on the track, with the obvious risk of mistakes or component failures.

Whatever the outcome of this dispute, it certainly had a purgative effect on IRTA, and left clearly drawn battle lines both within and without. It also galvanised the GPMA into unprecedented action. It is hard to predict what will happen next: another element of insecurity to undermine general confidence.

Finally, the lot of the promoters improved only marginally in 1994. Most are locked into five-year $1 million 'bubble' contracts, and all are bereft of all forms of income except for ticket sales from the vast hordes of 'bubble' spectators. In a few lucky cases, like Australia and Malaysia, government backing makes good the shortfall; other races are successful simply because they've managed by hook or by crook to hang on to their traditional big crowds. But there were lame ducks, notably in Britain, Germany and the USA, where dwindling crowds mean it's virtually impossible for promoters to make a profit.

This year, they did at least have some help from Dorna. This took the form of new freedoms to add support events and sideshows, to flesh out the somewhat sterile three-race GP format. Several promoters took advantage of this to reintroduce the flavour of a national event.

Australia had saloon car grudge races between World Champions Alan Jones and Wayne Gardner, and an ear-shattering flyover from a liberated ex-Soviet Mig fighter. Assen brought back classic bikes to regain at least a smattering of its old bike festival atmosphere. France had rocket cars, rock music and bungee jumping. Donington Park laid on a festival of wall-to-wall racing, with a full national programme going on long after the last (125) GP was over.

All were successful in improving crowd figures – not that Assen had ever had much trouble anyway; but in Britain the increase was marginal, and for a third year the promoters made a loss. Meanwhile, in Germany, promoter Ecclestone cut investment back for a bare-bones three-race (plus sidecars) GP, and the grandstands were once again pitifully empty.

Donington Park has two more years of contract to run, and to turn the expensive loss-making event into a worthwhile investment. Dorna have also tasted the disappointment of promoting a race that didn't attract the crowds, as partners with Kenny Roberts in the USA. They will now probably move the race to Elkhart Lake in Wisconsin, since they too are contracted (to themselves) to continue. And the German GP? Well, Ecclestone found a way out. From 1995 the race will take place at the new Nürburgring, and the great circuit of Hockenheim may be lost to GP racing forever.

In contrast to these special cases, there is another one in Brno. Slick professional promotion by former US racer Steve McLaughlin has not only negotiated a more favourable contract deal, with sponsors underwriting ticket prices, but has also shown how pure GP racing can still pull in the crowds – at the right prices and at the right track.

And the FIM? Well, they stayed in the background, busy no doubt with the building and commissioning of a fine new headquarters in Geneva. None of the money they received from GP racing noticeably found its way back, although other sporting disciplines felt the benefit. And one could hardly stifle a small feeling that they are now content to take the money and watch as GP racing apparently tries to destroy itself. Then, one day, no matter how bedraggled, they will take their World Championship series back again.

Some people would welcome this, and think GP racing would be improved by the wholesale withdrawal of factory teams. It would represent a return to the simpler days of GP racing, before the arrival of the money men, the professional sponsor-pleasers, the millionaire riders and the whole extra baggage of an entertainment business whose primary concern is to make money. Once again, paddocks would resound with dusty camaraderie among the race-crazy travelling circus – a band of happy-go-lucky heroes sleeping with their bikes in the backs of their vans.

It's hardly what you might call progress.

make a joint pronouncement.

In fact, taking turns at anodyne speechifying, they didn't actually say very much, beyond underlining their need for a stable GP future to justify their investment in the sport, and adding mildly that if IRTA did wish to limit the number of motor cycles, they would prefer it to be two per rider. In the traditional Japanese manner, one was left to read between the lines – where there was a clear acknowledgement that IRTA were the enemy.

There was no turning back for IRTA, however. The one-bike scheme had the support of vice-president Serge Rosset, owner of Roc, chassis-builders to the 500 privateers. Likewise 500 class Ducados Honda team owner Sito Pons, a politically influ-

35

A history of Cagiva
SIXTEEN YEARS, AND WHAT DO YOU

A HISTORY OF CAGIVA

GET?
by Michael Scott

Swan-song: Kocinski is pushed out of the Donington pits in 1994. Agostini *(left)* and Fanale *(red top)* look on. Note Japanese team technician in the background.

It was at Donington Park that Cagiva announced that they were to quit motor cycle racing. They would finish the European season, they said, and that would be that. After 12 years of trying, the game was over.

That was in 1990.

The next serious talk of retirement came at the end of 1993, in the form of a rumoured threat to Honda, who were eyeing John Kocinski for 1994. If they lost Kocinski, said Cagiva, they would quit. Or so the stories went. And, not for the first time, Japan Inc. were prepared to help their honourable (and only) European rival.

At the end of 1994, however, factory owner Claudio Castiglioni would say nothing about Cagiva's GP future, beyond insisting: 'I have never said we were going to quit.' This time, it seemed certain, he *really* didn't mean it.

Rumours of impending withdrawal had been circulating all year, ever since the company ran into well-publicised cashflow problems in March that had unpaid component suppliers refusing deliveries, temporarily halting the Ducati production line.

Furthermore, though 16 years of effort had finally forged the once tragi-comic Italian works team into a fully competitive fighting force (after any number of false starts), the cost far outweighed the returns. Cagiva had spent tens, no hundreds of millions of dollars, all to move from also-rans to almost-wins; and it wasn't getting any cheaper. Ducati's race programme, at far lower cost, had yielded a string of world and national championship titles, and continued to do so in 1994 when they took the World Superbike title. (Cagiva, of course, own Ducati.)

Cagiva were financially rescued by a consortium of banks during 1994. Leaks from Italy suggest that the rescue package carried a firm precondition – that Cagiva must stop the expensive and almost fruitless activity of GP racing.

The final factor was the imminent arrival of a new Cagiva superbike. This 750 cc four, engine designed by Ferrari, would be a head-on challenge to the Japanese in Superbike racing as well as on the road, and word from the factory was that Cagiva owners Claudio and Giancarlo Castiglioni were ready to transfer their affections to this new project, even though it was yet to be accepted for the 1995 World Superbike series.

Of all the above reasons, this was the most compelling. If there is a single common thread running through Cagiva's racing history, through all the different machines, designers, engineers and riders who have pushed the project this way and that over the years, it is the sheer enthusiasm and love of GP racing of the two brothers. Between them they built up an industrial giant on the bones of the bankrupt Aermacchi concern at Varese, and they went GP racing out of pure passion. If the new Ferrari/Cagiva superbike has stolen their hearts, then they will leave GP racing for the same reason.

At the time of going to press, there was still no official confirmation of what they intended to do in 1995. As in the past, they might easily change their minds again and come back. Perhaps this was another stratagem to manipulate the rider market – some thought they wanted to be rid of Kocinski, others that they were desperately trying to keep the American rider. The affair remained a mystery, with race team manager Giacomo Agostini professing to be as much in the dark as everybody else.

Yet the writing on the wall was clear. By the last race of the season, in Barcelona, riders and crew members were openly looking for jobs.

It really did look as though Cagiva were leaving.

Racing cannot afford to be too sentimental, yet everybody knew that they would leave a big hole in the 500 class. Cagiva were important not only because they had improved so much over the past four years, and not only because they were often technically adventurous, adding much interest to a somewhat stagnant design pool. Their greatest value was as a counterpoint to the Japanese. With them gone, it would be up to the V-twin Aprilia to fight the big three.

Looking back, nobody could speak of a glorious history. The progress of the Cagiva has been fitful in the extreme – 16 years littered with high hopes turned to disillusionment, a process repeated over and over as technical staff and riders were regularly replaced.

Time and again, the same words would be echoed. Upon joining, the rider/engineer could hardly speak highly enough of the factory's dedication to improvement, their willingness to work all hours to keep up a constant stream of new equipment and ideas, their fast response time and enormous potential. One or two years later the same people would leave, complaining about hopelessly confused development and a damaging lack of coherence. It seemed none of the big names could overcome Cagiva's tendency to try and develop too many ideas at once, when what succeeds in racing is a meticulous, even plodding sort of approach, working through one idea at a time, each to its logical conclusion. The sort of thing the Italians do so badly, and the Japanese so well.

Cagiva always went for big names. Their generosity to riders and technicians was legendary, and for every one person they did manage to imbue with enthusiasm in this way, you could be sure there would be one or two others who had been sorely tempted by the Cagiva shilling.

They always aimed for the very best of riders. They didn't always succeed in getting them, recording near-misses with Kenny Roberts, Wayne Rainey and Barry Sheene, among others. But even in the really bad early years they had good men: almost-champion Virginio Ferrari, 350 World Champion Jon Ekerold, 500 World Champion Marco Lucchinelli; then came the real big-time riders – Randy Mamola, Eddie Lawson, John Kocinski...

Many of the above were fading stars. It was the lesser-known riders who earned them their first points: Ekerold in 1982, Hervé Moineau in 1984, Juan Garriga in 1986; then Raymond Roche and Didier de Radiguès, before Mamola's first rostrum finish in 1988. But it was not until the arrival of Eddie Lawson and ex-Yamaha crew chief Fiorenzo Fanale that the policy really paid off. Their partnership coincided with the best bike yet, and together they turned it into a truly competitive 500 class racer, securing pole position twice and claiming the marque's first-ever race win in Hungary. No matter that this was a tactical win hinging on tyre choice, it was a win all the same. At last the red bikes had come of age.

Better still was to follow when they stepped in to salvage the career of erratic genius Kocinski, after he had undergone meltdown midway through his much-vaunted 250 class return on the Lucky Strike Suzuki.

John, with a big grudge against the world, was just the man to take the Cagiva one step further, claiming their first dry-weather win in the USA in 1993. Kocinski stayed with them for 1994, winning the first GP brilliantly. The story of what happened after that is an important part

37

A HISTORY OF CAGIVA

Cagiva were always willing to take technical risks. Ferrari's '83 bike *(right)* has subframes front and rear, with the square-four motor as a stressed chassis member; and a magnesium swing arm. Like many of their experiments, it was short-lived.

Below: Ferrari in 1981: Yamaha-based in-line four engine had novel belt-driven disc-valve induction.

Below right: The 1983 Cagiva was a square four. Jon Ekerold, who scored Cagiva's first point in 1982, battles to hold off privateer Gary Lingham's Suzuki at Kyalami.

Right: Marco Lucchinelli's 1984 bike: the last square four was the prettiest.

Bottom: Juan Garriga joined in 1986 after Cagiva had failed to entice Kenny Roberts. He gave them their best season yet.

A major redesign in 1987 produced a more compact engine, fitted in a special lightweight frame with an almost horizontal rear suspension unit. Wearing Bastos stripes, this was the first non-MV-coloured Cagiva, and the only time they took outside sponsorship. This is Raymond Roche's machine.

of the rest of this book – a role that Cagiva have never occupied before.

Cagiva's racing history is littered with strange tales hinting at technical piracy and secret liaisons with supposed rivals: the charge is that they caught up with the Japanese (eventually) not merely by copying them, but by actually using the same component dimensions. This suggested a more or less covert exchange of drawings or even parts, especially with Yamaha. It is common knowledge that many intimate parts of their second-generation 1987 V4 – parts such as crankshafts and pistons – were interchangeable with Yamaha components; there were also parallel chassis developments, notably the banana-curved arched swing arm of 1988, that seemed far too similar to be a coincidence.

Claudio Castiglioni, the brother with the higher public profile, was always staunch in his denials that there was any link whatsoever with Yamaha, or with anybody else. Yet tales of skulduggery had been with Cagiva right from the very start, including a persistent belief that the disappearance of a works Suzuki crankcase from the team's British headquarters in 1978 was closely linked with the appearance in 1979 of the first 'Cagiva', which appeared to have copy square-four crankcases, surmounted by a collection of freely available Suzuki RG500 production racer components. The bike was ridden by Scotsman Alex George, managing a couple of 13th-placed finishes before disappearing into history.

They were back in 1980 with the new Cagiva painted in the proud red-and-silver colours of the old MV team. There were other MV links too, including team boss Arturo Magni, who now filled the same role at Cagiva. This was a different machine, but still not entirely their own. On top of an in-line four Yamaha crankcase they'd put their own cylinders, without exhaust valves but with reed-valve induction. This was an early use of a system that took three or more years to become the class norm. But the bike was raced only once, at the Nürburgring on 24 August, in the hands of Virginio Ferrari. He qualified 25th, well off the pace.

Ferrari was a big name in Italy and was keen to help this all-Italian effort, so he resisted the temptation to join an established works team in 1981 to help further progress. This comprised another much-changed bike, and lots of troubles, culminating in characteristic fond ambitions turned to disillusionment.

The new bike was ready for the German GP at the Hockenheimring, and incorporated a number of interesting revisions compared with the original piston-port-intake Yamaha and their own reed-valve experiment of 1980. Cagiva had now grafted a gallery of rotary disc valves onto the top of the gearbox/crankcase of the straight-four engine in another piece of premature technical ambition (Yamaha adopted a somewhat similar system during 1984 for their V4). The two outer cylinders had reversed exhaust ports. But, while clever, it was slow and unreliable, and Ferrari missed several races before returning for the tenth round at Imola, complaining that the new frame built by Niko Bakker handled badly, but that the Dutchman didn't seem to care. The engine was stripped of exhaust powervalves in a bid to simplify it, but remained a long way off being competitive.

In 1982, Ferrari went to Suzuki. Cagiva were absent again for the start of the season while they developed another new bike. This was a Yamaha-like disc-valve square four, which finally arrived in July for newly signed rider Jon Ekerold, the South African iron man. Dutchman Boet van Dulmen had tested it and turned the ride down, but Ekerold, fiercely independent and the scourge of the Japanese factories, conformed to type as a Cagiva recruit, and was almost gushing about the enthusiasm of the team.

The Cagiva was now one of three Italian alternatives, the others being the Sanvenero and the Morbidelli, both of which started many more GPs. Ekerold's bike arrived in Yugoslavia; a revised model with a lower frame arrived for the ninth round, the British GP at Silverstone. Jon qualified tenth and finished 13th (points were only for the top ten at that time); he stayed away from Sweden while they looked for more horsepower. The last race of the year, at Hockenheim, was to be a milestone. As Spencer and Uncini crashed out at the final bend, leaving victory to Mamola's Suzuki, Ekerold was promoted to tenth. This was Cagiva's first World Championship point.

The year 1983 saw the classic confrontation between Freddie Spencer and Kenny Roberts. Cagiva had a different sort of stand-off, as they brought Virginio Ferrari back into the team and Ekerold found himself pushed to one side. All talk of enthusiasm was forgotten as he ranted at the third GP, the Italian at Monza: 'My mechanics treat it as a nine-to-five job,' before refusing to race the underdeveloped and ill-prepared machine. For the next three races, Cagiva had no bike for Ekerold. The third was in Austria, where Ferrari had three at his disposal. Ekerold quit in a rage.

In typical Cagiva fashion, rather than working on improving what they had they instead produced something new. One of Ferrari's Austrian bikes had a revised engine as the main frame member, with subframes front and rear to carry steering and suspension, and a magnesium swing arm. This was the work of freelance designer Valentino Ribi, and like any ground-breaking design it could hardly be expected to achieve much first time out. Nor did it. Three non-starts followed a debut 23rd; then for Britain came yet another new Ribi frame, this time a full loop all in aluminium. It never finished a race.

Enthusiasm undamped, Cagiva secured the services of ex-World Champion Marco Lucchinelli for 1984. His year on the square four didn't go well. A string of non-finishes preceded a fit of temperament in France when 'Lucky' had a fist-fight with a marshal. Cagiva had already signed up a second rider for the rest of the year, French endurance star Moineau. And as the mercurial Lucchinelli came and went, taking only one non-scoring finish in 12 races, Moineau achieved the machine's second World Championship point with a tenth in Yugoslavia.

Cagiva took another step forward in 1985, pensioning off the obsolete square four and introducing their first V4, which formed the basis of the bike that has carried them through to the present day. It was described with some wonderment as 'very like the 1983 Yamaha YZR' (it had an extra idler gear and crossshaft linking the crankshafts, which Yamaha had since dropped). But while it brought them closer to the class state of the art, it fell short in several important areas. Not only was it bulky and heavy by comparison with the Yamaha and Honda V4s, it also produced less power – the legacy of staggered inlets rather than the in-line four of the Yamaha, which in turn meant they had to use Dell'Orto carburettors rather than the Yamaha's twin-choke pair of Mikunis. The Dell'Ortos were bulkier and dictated slightly longer inlet tracts, whereas the more powerful reed-valve engines were making extra power by shortening the inlet as much as possible.

The V4's first year was not auspicious. Lucchinelli was again the team's head rider, and together they missed the first six GPs and finished only once.

Something important had happened in the meantime, however. Cagiva had persuaded the retired Kenny Roberts to test the bikes at Misano before the last race, and he had quickly been on the pace. From then on he would feel a special fondness for 'my Cagivas', and he was convinced that there wasn't much wrong with them that a little well-directed development by a top quality rider couldn't sort out. Cagiva paid him $50,000 for the test session, and offered him double that to race the bike; he wisely declined, as had Barry Sheene before him.

Instead, the best they could do for 1986 was rising young Spaniard Juan Garriga, who gave them their best season yet. Garriga qualified in the top ten four times in 11 races, and scored points twice. Eighth at the opening Spanish GP was the marque's best-ever result, and by year's end he was 17th overall, the first time Cagiva had done better than equal last in the championship.

Cagiva found it easier to recruit good riders for 1987, for they had shown they could at least attain the standards of the lower echelons of the Japanese works teams. They also had another major redesign, addressing the problems of the old CV10, which was now sufficiently changed to be redesignated the V587. The work had been done in house by engine designer Ezio Mascheroni, and not surprisingly the direction of development closely followed that of Yamaha. The angle between the vee closed right up from 90 degrees to 56, making the motor more compact; the inlets to the reed valves were arranged in line and Yamaha-type Mikuni carburettors were adopted; the total-loss Marelli ignition (requiring a bulky battery) was replaced with a Japanese Kokkuisan self-generating system.

Cagiva had signed up for the first and only time with a sponsor – Bastos, a European cigarette brand: the bikes were still red, but they had some product-identifying striping. They recruited two riders who could be regarded as good and still improving:

A HISTORY OF CAGIVA

Frenchman Raymond Roche and Belgian Didier de Radiguès.

And they signed up French engineer Alain Chevallier, until now a racing bike manufacturer in his own right. He was expected to produce a lightweight chassis, but when this was not forthcoming Cagiva's own chassis man, Gilberto Milano, built one in house, which arrived in time for the fourth race at Monza.

Roche and de Radiguès had a good year, by and large, up with the lesser works bikes more often than not, though the non-finishes were still frequent, with nine and eight respectively. But each scored points four times, with a best-ever fourth in Brazil for de Radiguès, who was 12th overall, with Roche 13th.

Now Cagiva were the strongest they had ever been. The bike still lacked performance and refinement compared with their Japanese rivals, but the gap was much, much smaller, and might be closed still further if they could sustain development.

And as a reward they managed to catch their best rider so far – Randy Mamola, on the rebound from Team Roberts, but still a leading light.

Randy and team-mate Roche rode the revised V588, which had the new arched swing arm. During the season they also switched to Ohlins suspension, adopted a new computerised programmable ignition from Marelli, and revised the bodywork to a fully enclosed design.

With its vivid red paint and Testa Rossa-like air ducts, it was the prettiest bike on the track by a big margin, but it was still not as good as its ever-improving rivals. By comparison the Cagiva was too peaky, lacking a broad powerband; and too heavy, with aluminium rather than magnesium engine cases just one reason why. They were also the only team racing with the new Pirelli tyres, an association that only just lasted the year. All the same, the results were better than ever. Mamola failed to score at nine out of 15 rounds but was three times in the top six, and in Belgium gave Cagiva their first-ever rostrum. It was now becoming necessary to take them seriously.

Randy had two more years at Cagiva, but things didn't really continue to gel.

The bike was further improved for 1989, with lightweight magnesium cases, new rotary powervalves, a new ATAC-style exhaust chamber and a new chassis. But handling problems and teething troubles dropped Mamola to 17th overall.

In 1990, Mamola's dedication to playing the fool finally got the better of the Italians. They were more serious than ever, with engine and frame further improved, and a new carbon-fibre frame waiting in the wings. Just to prove their innovative spirit, they had also tested fuel injection during 1989, though it was far from race ready. All the same, they were some years ahead of the Japanese in these trials.

Randy came close to winning in Spa, moving through like a master in the wet before finally outreaching himself and crashing; his best result was sixth. New team-mate Alex Barros did better, with a fifth place, but grandiose plans for their new three-bike team came to little in the case of Ron Haslam, who injured his hands twice in the early part of the year.

Barros was 12th, Mamola and Haslam 13th and 15th. Rather disappointing, given the amount spent on bike and riders. And, as a result, Cagiva dropped a bombshell.

They were to quit.

Or so they said.

In fact, they did nothing of the sort. Instead they were busy negotiating to recruit their greatest prize ever – four times World Champion Eddie Lawson.

It heralded their best two years so far – not only because Eddie's results were better than anything they'd dreamed of to date, but also because of the progress they made towards full maturity as a genuinely competitive racing team that need make no excuses when compared with the Japanese.

Certainly much of this was as a direct result of the influence of the quiet American and his ex-Yamaha crew chief Fanale. Steady Eddie not only brought a methodical approach but also great strength of character and steadfastness of purpose to the task, and the bike and factory responded in kind. In 1992 he had only four no-scores out of 15 races, and he was twice on the rostrum, third in Italy and in France. These were backed up by solid results elsewhere to put him sixth overall. Pole positions in both Holland and England were the icing on the cake.

The next year came Cagiva's first win, and while it may have had as much to do with tyre tactics as anything else, Lawson's first place in Hungary also required both rider and bike be good enough to take advantage of the tactics. Lawson thoroughly deserved to be the man to bring the Cagiva to victory. Ironically, he shared the honour with old adversary Giacomo Agostini, now Cagiva's new team manager.

If it hadn't been Eddie, it would have been John Kocinski, a latecomer to the Cagiva equation. In terms of development, he merely reaped the benefit from the foundations laid by Lawson and others. Yet Kocinski and the Cagiva were peculiarly suited, and his first dry-weather win, in the USA, and the second this year, in Australia, were out-and-out racing victories that owed nothing to tactics and everything to the abilities of machine and rider. As such, they gave the Cagiva a fitting swan-song – if that is what it turns out to be.

In fact Cagiva had hired Doug Chandler to replace the retired Lawson for 1993, poaching him from Suzuki. But though Doug started well, a heavy crash at Mugello left him concussed, confused and unconfident, an affliction that would take him almost a year to shake off.

The bike was now not only better than ever, but was teaching the Japanese lessons in the creative approach. Cagiva had been early on track with an effective Big Bang to follow Honda's lead in 1992; they had also been quickest to copy Honda's ram-pressurised airbox, thanks to new chief engineer, Riccardo Rosa. This year they had a hatful of new ideas ranging from a half-carbon/half-aluminium chassis to a sophisticated update of mechanical anti-dive brakes; and their engine management electronics were as good as anybody's. They also had an open attitude that was a refreshing contrast to the Japanese firms' obsessive secrecy.

Since Cagiva have yet to announce their expected withdrawal officially, it is too early for an epitaph. Yet it is appropriate to disinter the eloquent ghost-written statement made by Mamola to the press in Britain in 1990, on the occasion of their first retirement.

'It's all going to be a bit more ordinary [without Cagiva], don't you think?

'When you write your stories, say what you have to say about Cagiva and Mamola...Say I didn't try hard enough if that's what you think. But try and think of something encouraging for the brothers...

'Tell them that for all the down stuff, they were great.

'Try to tell them we want them back...we're going to miss them. I don't think we even realise how much.'

Left: Mamola in 1988, the first of three Cagiva years, *en route* to third at Spa, Cagiva's first rostrum. His 1988 machine *(below)* was closer to the Japanese rivals than ever.

Right: Eddie Lawson in action: dedication finally rewarded with the marque's first win.

Left: Lawson's stature and strength of character were crucial in helping forge Cagiva into a worthwhile team.

Bottom: Cagiva's elephant will be hugely missed from GP racing.

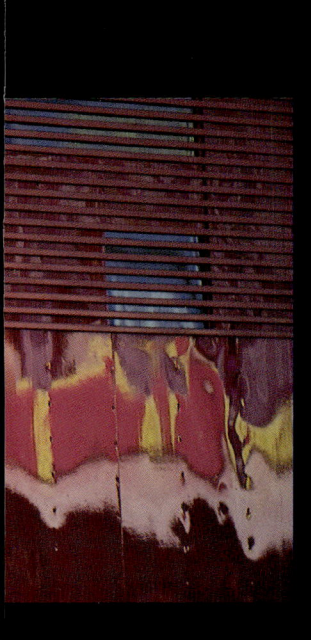

THE 1994 GRAND PRIX LINE-UP

The Leather Boys –
WHO WENT WHERE IN 1994

by Michael Scott

The year began with IRTA perilously close to scratching for entries: even the 125 class was not oversubscribed by entries of sufficient quality, as was the case last year. In the precarious financial climate there were a number of comings-and-goings at the last minute too, as sponsorship deals waxed then waned. The 500s had a fair-sized batch of regulars, but had to scrape the barrel (as it turned out) to make up numbers.

The calendar was just full too, with the European season neatly arranged round an August break for holidays, topped with the Pacific races in Australia, Malaysia and Japan, tailed with a visit to each of the Americas, and concluding as per policy in Europe, at the circuit of Catalunya. This time, Spain was the only country to host more than one race – last year they'd had *three* and Italy two. Now France was back, and Argentina had joined, achieving a far better geographical balance.

The profile of works bike was little altered in the 500 class, with an elite quartet of Roc- or Harris-equipped privateers moving halfway to paradise with Big Bang engines for their works-replica chassis. The 250 class, however, had lost Suzuki, with factory plans thwarted by various difficulties – though hope lingered for a while of a late entry. The 125s had gained, however, with the arrival of Yamaha, in semi-works guise.

500 cc: ESTABLISHMENT RULES

As ever, Honda fielded the largest force, with a combined tally of four in the official HRC and satellite lease-bike teams.

The central army was unsponsored. Having lost Rothmans backing, and after a rumoured flirtation with Pepsi had gone flat, Honda came back to go it alone, in a new variation of the factory colours, with three bikes under the Honda Team HRC banner.

Foremost was that of Michael Doohan (28 at the first GP), in his fifth straight GP year, all with the Honda factory team, and with his long-time ex-Gardner crew chief Jerry Burgess. This team had more autonomy than that of Shinichi Itoh (27), whose role is at least partly that of test pilot for factory innovations – it was he who spent much of last season riding the fuel-injected machine. This year Honda had shelved that system and were working on a Mk2 version behind the scenes, they said, though it is believed it did get to the tracks now and then, if only for practice. The third HRC bike was ridden by Alex Criville, for the 23-year-old former 125 World Champion's second season in the class. He also did some testing, notably of the latest electronically controlled rear damping.

The final Honda was a leased bike, ridden by class newcomer Alberto Puig, fresh from six straight 250 years. Now 27, the former trials champion had had only the occasional 500 ride in the past.

The other manufacturers had just two riders each.

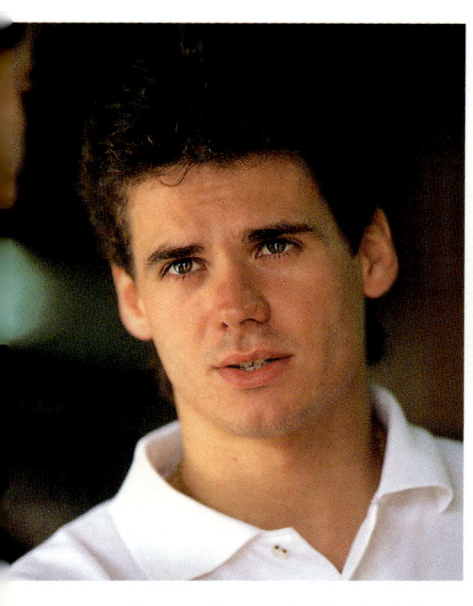

Suzuki, their Lucky Strike look updated with bold new graphics and the Number One plate, fielded Kevin Schwantz (29) and Alex Barros (24) for a second year in succession. The smallest factory team, based in Britain, had total continuity of men and machinery.

Yamaha's main effort was again with Marlboro Team Roberts, still the biggest outfit in the paddock although at first one of the least effective. One problem was the after-effects of the shock of Rainey's crash at the end of the previous season; a second was yet another false start from the factory. As in 1993, pre-season tests saw the riders ditch the all-new Yamaha – with fuel injection and a swing-arm pivot co-axial with the gearbox output drive sprocket. With time so short and the bike still so far off target, they again switched back to Old Faithful, or a parts-bin variation thereof, with a Yamaha-badged Roc based closely on the 1991 works bike, and the old carburated YZR V4 engine. A third chassis variation appeared at Assen, being a revision of 1993's reject, made by the factory from extruded complex-section tube (as is the Honda) rather than the usual box-fabrication.

The two riders labouring under these disadvantages were Luca Cadalora (29) and Daryl Beattie (23), the former in his second year with the team, the latter snapped up after being let go by Honda following a strong debut season in which he'd finished third overall, including one GP win. Both had another – not exactly cross to bear, though Beattie saw it that way – in the exclusive use of Dunlop tyres. Though clearly not quantifiably inferior to the Michelins used by the rest of the works bikes they were certainly different, leading to a number of erratic results for Cadalora (including two race wins), and to a whole season of calamity for Beattie, whose riding style simply didn't suit the rubber.

The last pair of the eight full works bikes were the two Cagivas, in the Agostini-led team. John Kocinski (26) joined halfway through last season, and had already racked up the Italian bike's first dry-weather win; Doug Chandler (28) was in his second year. They had machines that not only set new standards of good looks, as usual, but were also notably clever in several respects. As well as interesting experiments with anti-dive braking linkages and various engine electronics, they also had a gorgeous dual-medium frame, with the front part fabricated in aluminium and the rest in carbon fibre, joined beneath the tank. To this was attached the carbon-fibre swinging arm, all of which made the Cagivas the most technically adventurous machines in the class.

Lurking up with the works bikes in terms of exclusivity, but behind the slowest privateers in terms of speed, the Paton was back, to be ridden by Vittorio Scatola (35). Others riders would follow during the year, though to little effect: bravery and past four-stroke history alone are not enough to elevate a backyard effort to the level of the factories.

And at the start of the European season came the late-entered Aprilia 400 cc V-twin, ready to mount its challenge to the V4 dinosaurs. Nearly ready, anyway. It took 34-year-old veteran Loris Reggiani to a promising debut result, but ran into trouble as the season wore on.

Six privateers had Yamaha Big Bang engines in replica chassis; a seventh had a factory lease-bike with a similar power unit: Jeremy McWilliams (29) on the Team Millar bike.

The favoured few were Niall Mackenzie (32), Bernard Garcia (22), Juan Lopez Mella (28) and Laurent Naveau (27) for Roc, and Britons Sean Emmett (24) and John Reynolds (30) for Harris.

Mackenzie was again in the Bob MacLean-owned team run by *Motocourse* technical editor Peter Clifford, with new sponsors Slick 50 (oil treatment) replacing Valvoline. Garcia was in the Yamaha Motor France team, which sadly didn't last beyond three races after the French government declined to cough up the expected compensation money for the loss of Gauloises sponsorship in 1992. Roc then took over the entry on their own account.

Emmett's was the Harris entry, sponsored once more by Shell. Again he was the only rider in any class to use completely lead-free petrol, though new regulations meant that all the others had been obliged to find new formulations to comply with the latest 'low-lead' rules. Reynolds rode again in the multi-coloured livery of Padgetts, a

Top row, from left: Luca Cadalora, Alex Criville and Daryl Beattie.

The British brigade *(clockwise from below):* Sean Emmett, John Reynolds, Jeremy McWilliams and Niall Mackenzie.

All photos: Gold & Goose

43

THE LEATHER BOYS – WHO WENT WHERE IN 1994

This page, from top: Doug Chandler, Shinichi Itoh, Jean-Michel Bayle.

Opposite page: Tadayuki Okada *(top)*; Nobuatsu Aoki *(centre left)*; Doriano Romboni; and Kenny Roberts Junior *(bottom right)*.

250 cc: THE FATTED CALF SURVIVES

The biggest change was the move by Max Biaggi from Honda back to Aprilia, and to Dunlop tyres. It also turned out to be the most significant, with the rest merely shuffling around.

Wastage from last year, apart from Rainey, had robbed the class of dumped works riders Freddie Spencer and Mat Mladin, as well as such privateer stalwarts as Thierry Crine, Serge David and José Kuhn.

This made 31 names on the full-time list, short of the maximum of 36, but enough for a quorum.

There were only Michelin or Dunlop tyres available, Yokohama having withdrawn last year. All the works teams except for Roberts Yamaha were on Michelins; the privateers split almost evenly, with 11 on Dunlop and 10 (including the Paton) wearing Michelins. Notable Dunlop users included all the Britons – Mackenzie, Reynolds, Emmett and McWilliams; the top men on Michelins were Lopez Mella and Bernard Garcia.

Honda had the largest number of works bikes, with NSRs spread among no less than eight riders in separate lease-teams. None was an official factory outfit, though Erv Kanemoto's, fielding former HRC rider Tadayuki Okada, was at least notionally the closest by virtue of traditional links on many sides. Okada (27) was also the only top rider on Michelins.

The former Japanese champion was a dark horse; not so the rampant Italian stallions, two of whom were NSR-mounted for second successive years. They were former double 125 World Champion Loris Capirossi (20), and his older shadow Doriano Romboni (25). Both had won races the year before, and Capirossi had almost taken the championship.

Ralf Waldmann was fresh from the 125 class, and the 27-year-old German had an HB-backed NSR as entry-level machine, an honour not accorded to either of the Italians, who'd made the same move two years before.

Nobuatsu Aoki (22) was another to return on an NSR, with new last-minute sponsorship from Rheos for his Jha Racing machine. Likewise Wilco Zeelenberg (27), with a partly self-financed effort (one new backing deal was struck after the season had begun, but collapsed barely three races later). Spaniard Luis D'Antin (29), backed by Repsol, car radio firm MX Onda and also now by Pepsi, had acquired a works bike after his kit-bike debut last year. The last NSR was in the hands of Adrian Bosshard (31), the ex-motocrosser with the backing of Elf and the Swiss Honda Dealer team.

Lesser degrees of favour had rewarded just four riders with HRC power-up kits for their privateer RS machines. These went to Frédéric Protat (27), riding for the south of France-based Tech 3 outfit who had been displaced by the enforced withdrawal of Suzuki; to rising young Spaniard Carlos Checa (21), entered by Givi Racing; to Veitinger Honda-backed veteran Adi Stadler (29); and

long-established racing force run by a major north of England dealership.

And so the rest: Harris Yamahas for Kevin Mitchell (32), Cees Doorakkers (31) and Lothar Neukirchner (34) – a rider from the former East Germany who was allowed in after special tests at Paul Ricard (along with Scatola) convinced IRTA that he was fast enough and his team sufficiently committed. They turned out to be wrong in both respects.

Roc troops were more numerous by far: Lucio Pedercini (21), Bruno Bonhuil (34) and Marco Papa (35) were back; Andreas Leuthe (28) had returned; ex-250 men Bernard Hänggeli (33) and Jean-Pierre Jeandat (24) were back, with Jean Foray (the oldest man in racing, at 37); Cristiano Migliorati (24), son of former racer Walter, and Marc Garcia (26), older brother of Bernard, had joined; former tiddler rider Julian Miralles (28) had also moved up, though his effort was to prove ill-fated after his sponsors let him down.

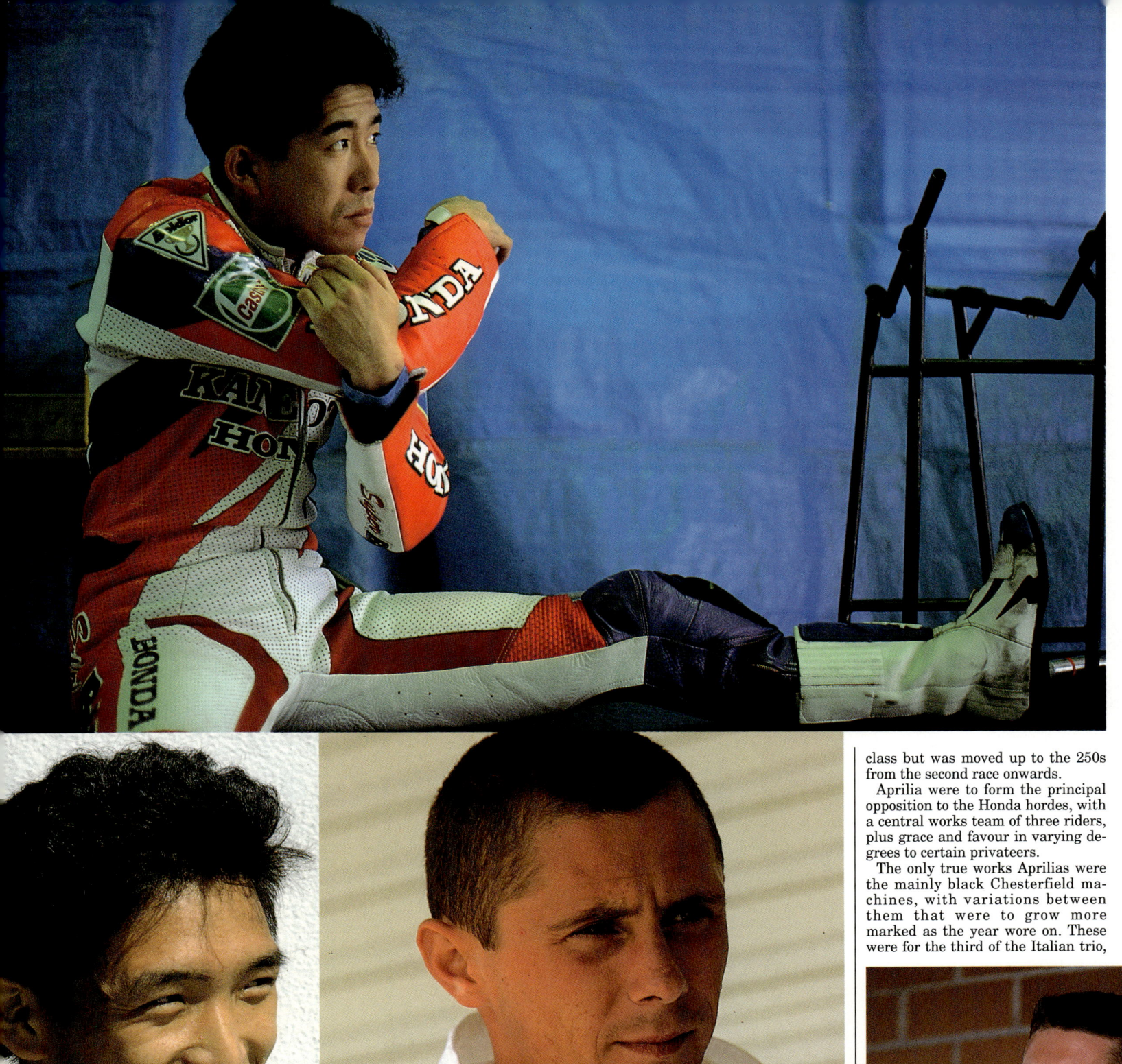

class but was moved up to the 250s from the second race onwards.

Aprilia were to form the principal opposition to the Honda hordes, with a central works team of three riders, plus grace and favour in varying degrees to certain privateers.

The only true works Aprilias were the mainly black Chesterfield machines, with variations between them that were to grow more marked as the year wore on. These were for the third of the Italian trio, to privately entered Luis Carlos Maurel (26) from Spain.

Just four stock RS Hondas closed the HRC account. One was for French newcomer Noel Ferro (19), also riding for Tech 3; the other two were in a new Anglo-Irish team, originally named Team Cotoni, but becoming Team Beckett by the end of the year amid the shifting sands of bottom-end GP racing. Originally they had entered Briton Alan Patterson and Chinese-Canadian Rodney Fee (both 24), but while the latter was still racing at year's end, there were all sorts of comings and goings during the year, including brief tenures by one-off Briton Jamie Robinson and bemused American Donnie Hough, before the other black bike ended up in the hands of another Briton, James Haydon.

The last RS was ridden by 24-year-old Marlboro Pileri junior Giuseppe Fiorillo, who started off in the 125

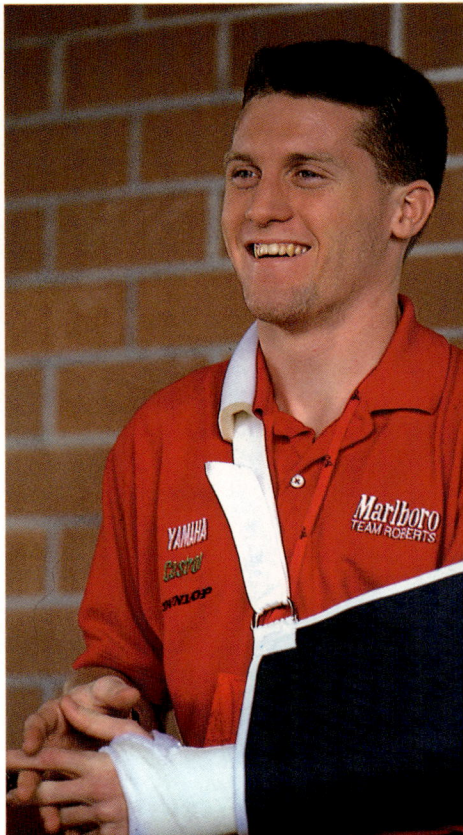

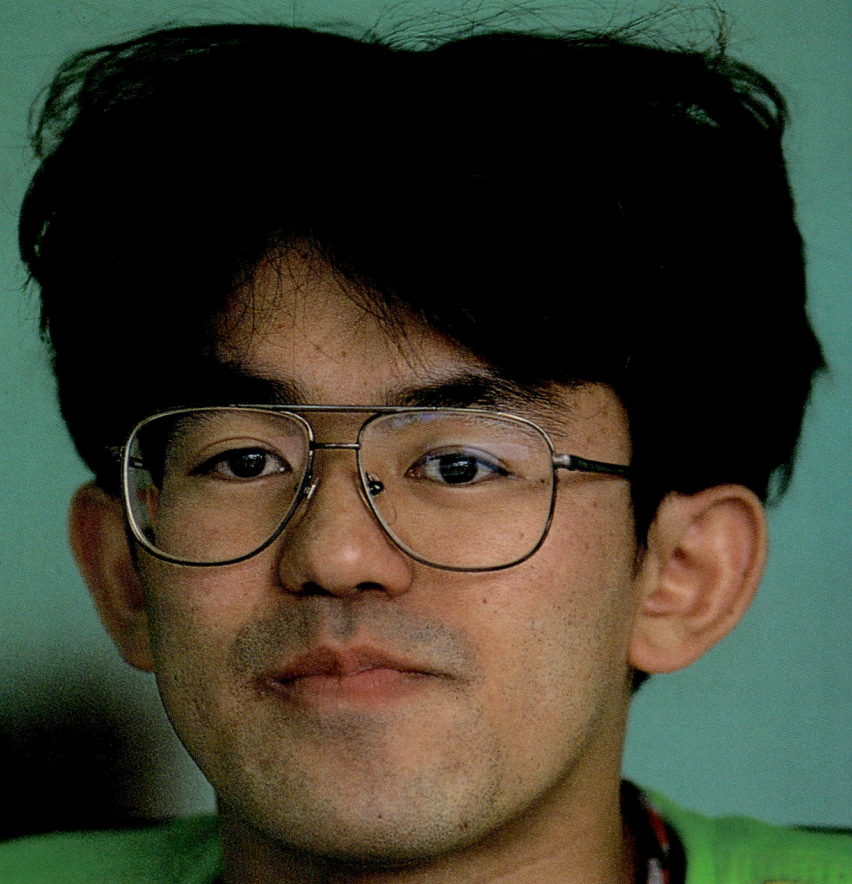

THE LEATHER BOYS – WHO WENT WHERE IN 1994

Massimiliano Biaggi, the 22-year-old returned prodigal; for last year's Aprilia star, Jean-Philippe Ruggia (28); and for probably-man Jean-Michel Bayle, elevated to top machinery in only his second GP year. The 24-year-old off-road legend had learned a lot in his first road racing season, which took place in the GP deep end; now we would see if he could put those lessons into practice.

The next echelon of Aprilia riders had at least some support from the factory, in the form of evolution parts from time to time. Chief among these was Austrian almost-man Andy Preining (33), sponsored again by porn queen Dolly Buster, whose lubricious personage was an occasional paddock adornment. Mohag Aprilia rider Eskil Suter (26) was another, the Swiss rider in his third GP season.

The Aprilia was the privateers' machine of choice. The ranks included the van den Goorbergh brothers from Holland, both Patrick (28) and Jurgen (24) among several riders on updated year-old bikes. Then there was German Bernd Kassner (29), Spanish newcomers José Luis Cardoso (18) and Enrique de Juan (23), French veteran Christian Boudinot (36) and 1992 125 World Champion Alessandro Gramigni (25), fallen on hard times after the collapse last year of Gilera. Finally there was the entry of veteran Manuel Hernandez (33), who missed the first four races injured (to be replaced by Juan Borja), and was again fitful by year's end. A late entry came from Ducados Honda Pons – a Honda (of course) for none other than Borja (24).

This left only the Yamahas, with a once-mighty force reduced to just three bikes – two works TZ-Ms and one stock TZ – and reduced still further by injury before the first race even started.

The main works entry was defending World Champion Tetsuya Harada (23), who ruined the first half of his season by incurring hand injuries in practice in Australia. The other factory bike was for Kenny Roberts Junior, the 20-year-old originally to ride in his father's Marlboro Roberts team, before Kenny Senior made the team over to Wayne Rainey at the Australian GP. But Junior was already *hors de combat* with an arm broken in a pre-season training spill which proved extraordinarily slow to mend: he missed the first ten races. His place was initially taken by US champion Jimmy Filice, and later by Japanese factory veteran Toshihiko Honma, to no great effect.

The only private Yamaha was ridden by 21-year-old Finnish newcomer Kristian Kaas, whose all-yellow outfit was frequently seen on TV as he was lapped by the leaders. Sadly the TZ proved so far off being competitive that he never did pick up the pace.

Bottom left: 250 works rider Luis D'Antin.

Top row from left: 125 gallery: Kazuto Sakata, Noboru Ueda, Peter Öttl.

Below: New 125 star Stefano Perugini.

125 cc: THE INVASION IS COMPLETED

Again it was Aprilia engineering the most significant change by their seduction, at the end of the previous season, of title runner-up Kazuto Sakata from Honda. The 27-year-old would be the first-ever Japanese racer on a European factory bike, an indication of the quality of riders now coming from the East as well as a revival in the quality of machines coming from the West.

His was one of no less than eight 'works' Aprilias, if you use the term loosely. This is the right way to use it in this class, where differences between top factory bikes and the rest are small (though crucial). In the case of Aprilia, the main mechanical differences were in the crankcases, ignition and exhausts. Plus, in Sakata's case, a hot-line to factory development.

His Semprucci-Krona team-mate was Spaniard Herri Torrontegui

THE LEATHER BOYS – WHO WENT WHERE IN 1994

Yoshiaki Katoh *(left)*, new Yamaha star.

Below: Neil 'Too-Tall' Hodgson.

Bottom: Tomoko Igata, the only girl racer to finish the season.

(26), a seasoned small-class runner heading for an up-and-down season. Peter Öttl also had a top bike for his eighth GP season, the 29-year-old German riding for Team Marlboro Aprilia Eckl; likewise Ducados-backed Carlos Giro (22), last season's erratic top works man; and Swiss Marlboro rider Oliver Petrucciani (24).

Aprilia were also grooming a pair of young Italians: Gianluigi Scalvini (22) and Stefano Perugini (19) were factory backed in the 1993 European Championships, which Perugini had won brilliantly. Now they had works bikes for their first full GP season. Of the two, Perugini was to make a real mark, claiming four rostrum finishes and two lap records in the last five races.

There were Aprilia privateers, too: Australian Garry McCoy (21), former works rider Gabriele Debbia (26), Italian girl racer Daniela Tognoli and young German Manfred Geissler (23). Only the last-named made it to the end of the season. McCoy quit controversially with three races left, Debbia was displaced by the collapse of his team after the British GP, but returned on a Honda, while 21-year-old Tognoli was sacked by IRTA for being too slow before the start of the European season.

In spite of these hordes, Hondas were the most numerous bikes, with 18 entered compared with 11 Aprilias. None were works bikes as such, but there were several with HRC kits, of varying vintages, and even distinctions of rank among these subdivisions.

The top three with access to major updates during the season were the seasoned runners: defending champion Dirk Raudies (29), back in HB colours in his own team; popular forerunner of the Japanese invasion, Noboru Ueda (26), riding for Italian team Givi Racing; and rising star Takeshi Tsujimura (19) in Sakata's old FCC Technical Sports team.

Other HRC-kitted Hondas were plentiful: veteran former champion Fausto Gresini (33), the experienced Bruno Casanova (29), too-tall Briton Neil Hodgson (20) and Marlboro Pileri riders Fiorillo (soon to depart) and Vittorio Lopez (21). Then there were the privateers, many of them from Japan: 30-year-old Akira Saito, backed by Elf Team Kepla; Haruchika Aoki – at 17 the youngest of three racing brothers and the youngest rider in any class; 21-year-old Masafumi Ono, an injury victim in 1993; the other girl in the class, Tomoko Igata (28), backed by FCC Technical Sports; the impressive newcomer Masaki Tokudome (23) on the Racing Supply machine; and Hideyuki Nakajyo (24), backed by Jha Racing.

Europe's lesser Honda men were German Oliver Koch (27); Italy's Lucio Cecchinello (24) on the second Givi Racing machine; 35-year-old Dutch veteran Hans Spaan in a valedictory year; and countryman Loek Bodelier, riding for Team Zwafink.

Which left just five on the new Yamahas, two with direct factory backing. These were the Team Aspar Cepsa bikes of Jorge Martinez (31), class veteran and multi-champion; and Yoshiaki Katoh (28), fresh from a brilliant debut title win in Japan. He was replaced after mid-season injury by Tomoko Manako, who made an immediate impact.

The other Yamahas were ridden by Stefan Prein (28) and Manfred Baumann (26), from Germany and Austria respectively; and by French newcomer Frédéric Petit (18), backed by Yamaha Motor France until their demise.

48

1994
Grands Prix

Australian Grand Prix	50
Malaysian Grand Prix	58
Japanese Grand Prix	66
Spanish Grand Prix	74
Austrian Grand Prix	82
German Grand Prix	90
Dutch Grand Prix	98
Italian Grand Prix	106
French Grand Prix	114
British Grand Prix	122
Czech Grand Prix	130
United States Grand Prix	138
Argentinian Grand Prix	146
European Grand Prix	154

Gold & Goose

WORLD CHAMPIONSHIP • ROUND 1

AUSTRALIAN GRAND PRIX

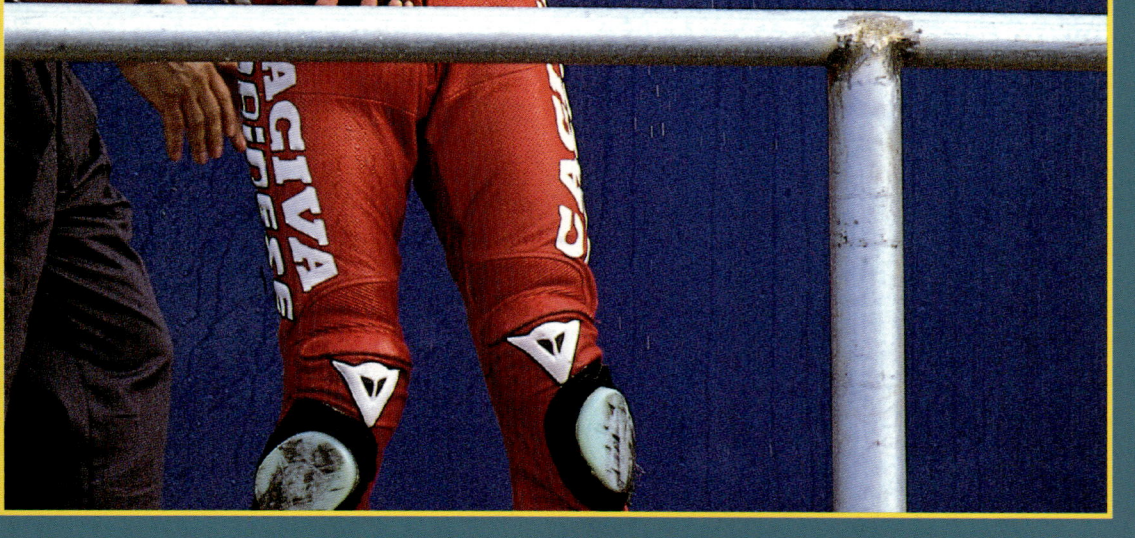

'He may kick our asses at a few tracks, but sooner or later ... he'll come all to pieces. Like a cheap watch'

Kevin Schwantz gives his assessment of John Kocinski

500 cc	KOCINSKI
250 cc	BIAGGI
125 cc	SAKATA

AUSTRALIAN GRAND PRIX

Opposite: **One squirt doesn't make a season:** Kocinski on the rostrum. Schwantz in a plaster-cast *(inset)* was to become a familiar sight.

Brave Rainey came to lay the ghosts.

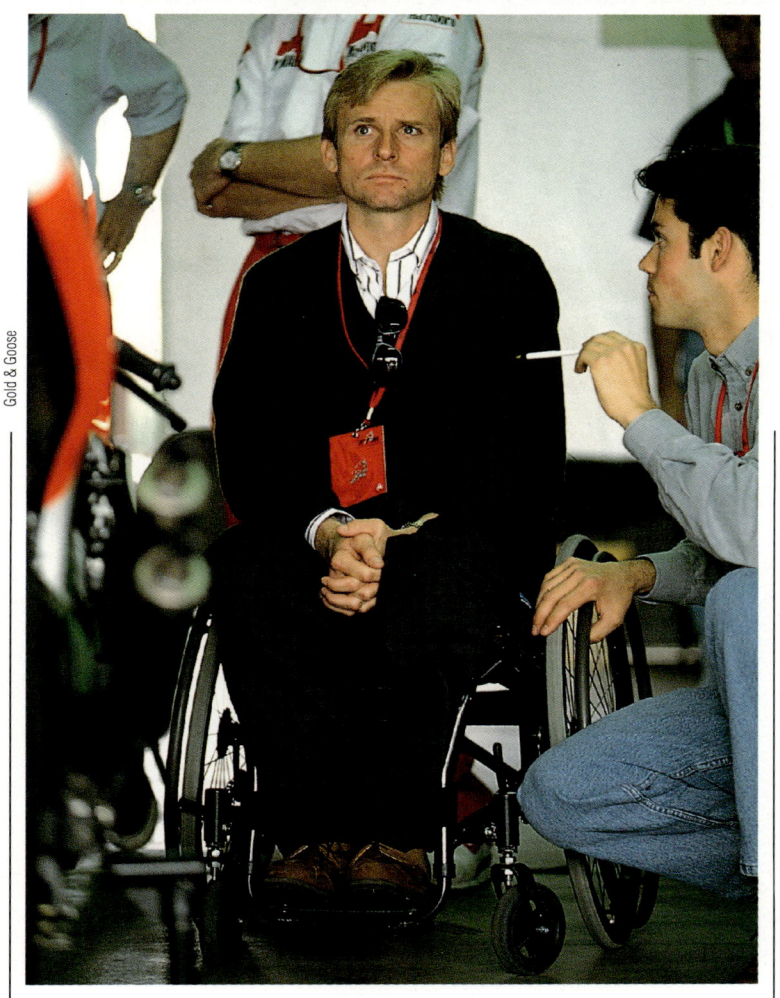

'He may kick our asses at a few tracks, but sooner or later ... he'll come all to pieces. Like a cheap watch.' Thus spoke Kevin Schwantz, with only a glance at whichever of his collection of Rolexes he was wearing at the time, of the resounding victory of John Kocinski and his oh-so-pretty red Cagiva at Eastern Creek.

Kevin's sleek silver chronometer was worn on the right hand because his left wrist was still clad in a cast, to protect the fracture that had been plated (allowing for the time difference) exactly three weeks beforehand after his ironic mountain bike crash back home in Texas. In the circumstances, the injury was something of a comfort. The World Champion at least had a tangible excuse for lagging in a lonely fourth.

Second-placed Luca Cadalora likewise had the excuse of relative 500 class inexperience. He admitted to being too cautious early on, but had redeemed himself with a magnificently daring round-the-outside move on Doohan to secure second.

But for all-time 100 per cent race favourite Doohan, there was no easy way out. He'd come to the track fit, his Honda supposedly fully tested. He'd insisted on an old-spec update, wanting nothing to do with fuel injection or any other fancy fol-de-rol – just as close a bike as he could get to the torquey original Big Bang machine on which he'd bulldozed the first half of the 1992 World Championship. The message, even when he qualified third fastest, remained quietly confident. Instead, he was humiliatingly beaten in front of his home fans, and left to mutter in disgruntled fashion about suspension problems and the need for more urgent testing.

The Australian press spared him their venom, instead complaining that the combination of an utterly dominant John Kocinski and Eastern Creek's slow corners had made for a dull and processional race. Somewhat unfair, for that's the way anyone likes to win. Perhaps it was the only reaction possible after a race that left many erstwhile heroes tending their wounds. Especially the Japanese motor cycle industry, without a single GP winner for the first time since 1976. Italian bikes had won every race, and things were very much not going as usual.

If everyone knew what was going to happen in advance, it would not be necessary to race at all; but an upset of this order sent people scurrying for reasons. Most homed in on the Creek Effect, whereby erratic changes in the Sydney track's surface made a nonsense of test data gathered here in blithe confidence in pre-season tests.

With limited choices in the Southern Hemisphere, it is almost by default that the not-so-affectionately nicknamed three-year-old Concrete Creek has become the most popular venue for now essential winter tests. As well as the open-to-all IRTA sessions a week before the GP, all three Japanese factory 500 teams and Cagiva spent time here, with Suzuki starting first, and staying the longest.

In their case, the Creek Effect was indirect. Schwantz and Barros had tested a prototototype to satisfactory conclusions here in February. Then Schwantz's arm injury meant he had to miss final shakedown tests of the production version, supposedly tidied up in line with its neat black anodised finish. Barros complained the suspension didn't feel right, but judgement was suspended until Kevin could ride the bike a week later. He too was unhappy. These were the first inklings that the production frame had inadvertent but crucial differences from the successful prototype ... but the Creek Effect served to mask this. It was only a fortnight later, after yet more unpredictable handling problems in Malaysia, that they could be sure it was the chassis playing up, not the surface.

Doohan felt more directly affected. Problems with the Honda's suspension and stability had not fully emerged in tests, but now they were chasing their tails as the physically still improving Australian upped his pace. After the race, the team realised at once that they needed more testing. Let's stay on, they suggested. 'I told them we should get the hell out of here,' said Doohan. 'We wouldn't learn anything. The way it changes, you're on a different bike every time you go out. I don't think we'll do much more testing here.'

Thus more opprobrium for the politically troubled track, to add to the steady grumble that it's too slow, tight and technical for a 500 GP bike to let rip – an aspect in which it compares very unfavourably with its beaten rival, Phillip Island. But if the Creek may lack in some areas, the organisers went all out to make up for it in others. Twice awarded IRTA's vote as the best race of the year, the organisation operated with redoubled slickness, while blanket promotion by sponsors Foster's pulled in a respectable crowd of 45,000, regaled with a variety of sideshows both aerial and terrestrial. Every effort was made to turn it into an event in its own right rather then just one of a series, a post-Ecclestone approach that was carefully noted by beleaguered European promoters. The fact remained, however, that the event is ultimately underwritten by the taxpayer, a luxury notably lacking in most other countries.

One of the extra-curricular ceremonials was emotional, indeed cathartic. On race morning, a pink convertible Cadillac ran two slow laps bearing the stricken triple World Champion Wayne Rainey, wearing dark glasses and waving to the crowd. Ignoring advice from wife and doctors, Rainey had snipped a proposed year of recuperation out of his schedule and come out of seclusion two races and six months after catastrophe at Misano had left him paraplegic. Ostensibly, the purpose was to announce the formation of Team Marlboro Rainey, taking over from Kenny Roberts to head the new 250 squad fielding Kenny Junior on a Yamaha. Another reason was to become only the third road racer (after Nieto and Agostini) to receive the FIM's Gold Medal of Motorcycling Merit from President Jos Vaessen, who spoke for many when he praised Rainey's 'lesson of courage and determination'.

The triple champion said he regretted not being able to race more than not being able to walk, and looked pale and thin as he determinedly pressed on with photocalls, as well as appearing trackside on the back of a Quad four-wheeler ridden by Kenny Roberts. Rainey also came to lay ghosts, for himself perhaps, but to the benefit of all. In this way, the bad memories could be put in the past and the new year begin clean.

For some, new problems had already arisen. Roberts Junior was spectating, nursing a broken arm that was to keep him out for ten more races. Then came Harada's misfortune. The defending 250 champion had been sixth fastest in the morning, but he ran only three laps in the afternoon. Getting up to speed he had a simple spill with serious consequences: his right hand was badly smashed, requiring delicate surgery in Australia, then again in Japan.

Many other first race stories remained shrouded in deliberate mystery. Almost as if in response to IRTA exhortations to teams to leave the front of their pit garages open, so spectators could at least glimpse the activity inside, a fresh crop of curtains proliferated, following the lead set by Team Roberts last year. The new bikes were seen only fleetingly as they whizzed in and out of the pits. If you wanted a good look, you had to go out to a trouble spot and hope someone would crash near you.

The pit lane vigil was more confusing than rewarding. Itoh's bike appeared to have the fuel-injection sensors in the exhausts, but nobody knew if they were wired up or not (they were). Cagiva gave tantalising glimpses of a two-stage rising-rate mechanical anti-dive system, though

51

you had to look hard, for it operated only on the left side, and melted into the background of the bike's gigantic new shrouded carbon Brembos. Chandler was still trying it, Kocinski didn't like it, but he didn't want to talk about it, having erected symbolic curtains of his own. 'I don't know nothin' about no anti-dive,' he insisted, the tortured triple-negative cropping up in reply to most other questions too.

Full-time Team Roberts tester Randy Mamola was watching, and remained the only regular rider of the new-for-1994 works Yamahas, which were absent from the Creek. Cadalora and Beattie exercised a variety of mix-and-match bikes with some parts dating back to 1992. They remained a cut above the new generation of sub-works Yamahas, although the Roc-framed bikes in particular were virtually identical.

These were ridden by Niall Mackenzie and Laurent Naveau, with Britons Sean Emmett and John Reynolds on Harris machines, all using Big Bang engines much like those of Team Roberts. 'It is virtually a works bike,' agreed Mackenzie, who had ridden one before. 'But though the differences are small, they're important.' Crucially, they included access to the pick of the latest tyres. Mackenzie's other problem also showed the cost of having only one bike instead of a pair. Persistent engine seizures in practice robbed him of set-up time and energy, and this ultimately denied him a race result.

Emmett particularly enjoyed the Big Bang motor, and learning how to play with the wheelspin it allows. His 'works' Harris showed an upgraded approach from the British chassis-builders, hitherto overshadowed by their high profile Roc rivals from France. It had a huge ram-airbox system similar to Cagiva's, as well as an experimental gearbox oil cooler under the fairing nose, which had a knock-on effect of also cooling the crankcases, to the benefit of incoming charge density. A more literal knock-on came on Friday, after an experiment in more radical geometry moved the front forks back. This combined with tyre fling at speed to knock the radiator off, spilling oil all over the front tyre and brakes. Emmett managed to survive without crashing. The only rider to use leadfree fuel, he had a new formulation from Shell and felt he was now closer to the rest, on their low-lead Avgas.

The 250 profile was more predictable, the biggest surprise coming from Aprilia, who had left their new bike in Europe and brought updated versions of the year-end '93 machine. This ad hoc method of avoiding early season teething troubles was crude but effective, particularly in the case of their prodigal returned. After a rogue year with Honda on Michelins, Biaggi was revelling in the bike that brought him to fame, and the Dunlop tyres he prefers.

All classes were burning the new low-lead low-octane fuel specified in the regulations, curiously without any apparent drop in horsepower. The other technical innovation came from Michelin, with a new 16.5-in. rear tyre to match their 16.5-in. front of last year. Schwantz liked it, Doohan didn't, reverting to the race-proven 17 incher. 'The main difference is it gives the tyre engineers more sidewall to play around with,' said Schwantz's man, Stuart Shenton.

Aprilia's 500 twin was absent, but its presence was felt: this is one of

AUSTRALIAN GRAND PRIX

Main picture: First lap, first 500 GP, and Kocinski is already gaining on Schwantz and Doohan, Itoh and Cadalora, Beattie, Puig and the rest.

Left: Kocinski's girlfriend Toti and team boss Agostini lead the cheers as he crosses the line.

Scott Doohan (below) found the Harris Yamaha no problem after a career on Superbikes.

the slow tracks where it might be expected to do well. Maybe next year, for news came to the Creek that Reggiani had completed successful reliability tests at Mugello the week before.

500 cc PRACTICE

The early omens were for a close race, as the top three finished a hectic final session pushing the envelope to improve on the previous quickest-ever lap (in 1992 practice), at last reversing the uncomfortable trend of bikes getting slower instead of faster.

The omens proved wrong, and the front-row men qualified in their eventual finishing order. It was Kocinski on top, for his second pole on the Cagiva (and the Italian machine's fourth), after some stiff competition from Cadalora and Doohan.

Schwantz, with his injured arm, couldn't quite match the final surge, and ended up fourth and more than a second adrift.

John had led Friday too, riding superbly, making up for the Cagiva's unexceptional acceleration with blindingly fast corner entries. He almost crashed once, running off the track at the hairpin Turn Nine after getting crossed up under brakes. In a feisty frame of mind, he refused to talk about any details. 'There's lots of other guys who could win. We've got bigger goals than just the first race.' But Chandler's top three run here last year proved the bike suited the track, while John's efforts, following on the groundwork of Lawson before him, have made it increasingly less surprising to see the Cagiva as a fully competitive motor cycle.

Cadalora secured second with a smooth and confident set of sessions on the 'old' Roc Yamaha. Typically guarded in his comments, he spoke about bettering the overall package to exploit improved front tyres for 1994. But he had a quip about the next man's top end advantage: 'Perhaps there should be a speed limit on the straight.'

Certainly, Doohan's Honda was fastest of the fast. 'I'm not going to complain about that,' he grinned. 'But it's fine on the slower bits too.' He looked good, stringing fast laps together, holding tight lines and looking confident and comfortable. Time spent testing the new smaller rear Michelins proved costly, however, and in fact he wasn't quite ready after all.

Schwantz had a question mark over his endurance. 'It's a little difficult under hard braking and hanging on under acceleration – the bike got out of shape a few times,' he said. He was aiming for a steady race and hoping to benefit from the mistakes of others. His bike was more of a problem than his arm. It was fighting back rather than responding predictably as the team ran through their setting programme.

Look who headed row two! Alberto Puig was in his first real 500 race after making his name in 250s. He showed no difficulty in switching to a 500 NSR, and was fast and aggressive from the start. Few were surprised when he fell on Friday while trying to stay with Doohan; he shrugged it off and went faster.

Row two was close: Puig was barely a tenth behind Schwantz, and merely three-thousandths ahead of Itoh; Beattie was mere tenths slower in his first Yamaha outing. Having fallen on the pit exit in the IRTA tests, he embarrassed himself further with another crash in the closing minutes of practice after being twice thwarted by traffic in an attempt to push onto the front row.

An off-form Chandler completed the row, more than one-and-a-half seconds away from Kocinski. Confidence on corner entries was the big difference, and Chandler had to be satisfied that he had at least cut almost half a second off in two days as he worked on the crucial swing in to the fast Turn One.

A displeased Barros led row three, after a Friday tumble left him with a stiff shoulder; his biggest problem, though, was with his AP carbon brakes, which simply didn't work to his satisfaction. He had grown used to Brembos when he rode the Cagiva. Criville was alongside on the final HRC bike, just trying to stay safe at a track that doesn't suit him at all. The times were beginning to stretch a little now, with the Spaniard more than two seconds down on pole.

Déjà vu – another half-second down came perennial top privateer Mackenzie. But aside from bike problems he had serious opposition from his fellow Big Bang Britons. Reynolds was three-tenths down, Emmett another tenth away, heading row four. Lopez Mella's 'screamer' was next, with wild card Scott Doohan's drone a mere two-thousandths adrift. It was Mick's elder brother's first-ever race on a racing two-stroke, but his circuit knowledge gained on Superbikes surely helped. 'People told me I'd use different lines, but though the bike turns in quicker it's not that different overall.'

Garcia's 'semi-works' Yamaha completed the row; McWilliams led the next; there were 31 starters stretching back to returned back-markers Leuthe (Roc) and Scatola (Paton), who sandwiched troubled Dutchman Doorakkers at the back. New grid-filler Lothar Neukirchner failed in this role by not qualifying after crashing on Friday.

500 cc RACE – 29 LAPS

Kocinski led into the first bend, out of the last bend, and through every bend in between. Nobody came close, nor did he ever put a wheel wrong. It was reminiscent of his 1990 domination on a 250. 'I don't know nothin' about no 250,' he snapped promptly. 'That was the past, I'm only interested in the future.'

His praise for Cagiva was of the

type that includes a barely veiled insult to someone else, in this case former mentor Roberts. 'This is the first team that has understood me,' he said. 'They did a great job with the bike, and Michelin came up with the right tyres. I just had to stay on it.' He also fingered Doohan for tipping him off with the winning tactics, after 'reading somewhere how he said it is really hard to catch up with someone at this track. After that, I tried to make a break from the start.'

Schwantz started second and held up the pursuit, unwittingly helping Kocinski gain almost a second after just one lap. Doohan whistled past him at the end of the pit straight as they started lap three, and Cadalora also went by on lap six. Then began a dour fight for second, with the Italian unable to pull the usual overtaking move into Turn One because of the Honda's straightline speed.

It took Luca until lap 13 before he found an alternative: a daring run round the outside into the hairpin Turn Two. It was definitely all or nothing, with inches to spare. Doohan said later he'd had a wobble in the first turn which slowed his exit; Cadalora's line gave him the choice of conceding the corner or crashing.

After that Luca pulled clear, but he had no hope of catching Kocinski. Indeed John was able to take the last laps relatively easily, and still win by seven seconds. 'I should have tried harder earlier on,' said Cadalora wryly.

Doohan had to be content with third, but he was not pleased. 'There's a long year ahead, but we're going to have to get our act together. I knew from the second lap I couldn't win. I could probably have ridden it a bit harder, but there were some inconsistencies in the suspension. We'll have to regroup and do some more testing.'

Schwantz was happy enough with fourth, but had a distant look in his eye. It had been the bike's twitchy handling rather than his arm injury that'd held him back, and he slackened off after a big front-wheel slide at one-third distance. 'It was always in the back of my mind that if I did push too hard and have to wrestle with it I might damage my arm,' he said.

He had been relieved of pressure from Itoh after the Japanese rider had himself dropped back, fighting such bad wheelspin that one of his crew's trackside observers thought it was clutch-slip.

Beattie had been well up until pitting after six laps, the horsepower fading fast. This left Spanish rivals Criville and Puig to fight for sixth, with Barros catching up from a slow start and yet more early brake trouble. It was resolved in the final double-apex loop when group leader Criville braked early, forcing the challenging Barros to run wide. Puig slipped through under his elbow; and they finished in that order.

Doug Chandler was a lonely ninth on the second Cagiva, never in contention and blaming an over-hard rear tyre. A long way back and equally alone came an off-colour but steadfast Reynolds, the best of the new Big Bangers after Mackenzie had retired on lap two with terminal clutch-slip. Bernard Garcia was next on his works (i.e. Roc) bike, some six seconds shy.

Then came a close privateer battle – wild card Doohan, the redoubtable Lopez Mella, and Emmett, struggling to hold on with a sticking steering damper. This ended in confusion. Kocinski was scything through them as he took the chequered flag. In fact he triggered the timing two-hundredths of a second ahead of Emmett, putting him one lap down, but half a second short of Doohan and Lopez Mella. They, almost side by side, naturally also received the flag meant for the man behind them.

In anticipation of a track invasion, the leading group were slowed at once, and ushered off the track. Lopez Mella, however, escaped, and pootled round the rest of the lap to trigger his timing beam some two minutes later. This was enough to see him classified 12th, the last rider not to be lapped. But Doohan did not complete the lap, and he was classified as a non-finisher. Of course this was crazy, and the protest that followed was dealt with in the only way possible – by taking the results from the lap before. This reinstated the one-race Australian in a well-deserved 12th, two-tenths ahead of Lopez Mella, and dropped the rest of the field by one place. Thus Emmett was 14th, and the last point went to GP first-timer Cristiano Migliorati, ahead of Big Banger Naveau.

So Cagiva led the World Championship for the first time ever; the cheap watch was bang on time. Would it last for 13 more races?

250 cc PRACTICE

The profile was a little blurred by showers that picked on the 250s, crucially in the last 15 minutes. Even so, the result was not too surprising. The front row was heart-warmingly close, just over half a second covering all four: Capirossi's Honda dominated throughout, and while Biaggi managed to squeeze his Aprilia onto the front row and Ruggia his onto the second, the Hondas looked stronger, as per pre-season tests.

Yamaha's potential remained a mystery. With KR Jnr grounded and Harada's ruinous prang, the latest TZ-M was a non-starter. Suzuki were absent too, though rumours of a late return rumbled on.

Capirossi was almost half a second down on his IRTA test time, but said he'd been foiled by the rain, which came just as he was warming up a nice soft rear tyre. Second went to Aoki's Honda. The Japanese was in similar circumstances, but astonishingly turned his quick lap with the track well spattered. 'That must have been risky,' said third-placed Biaggi, who declined to take up the challenge

AUSTRALIAN GRAND PRIX

Left: Biaggi leads Capirossi, and the duel of the season had commenced.

Below left: Dolls' Hospital – Harada and paramour after his catastrophic crash.

Right: Two Hondas, two Yamahas, one Aprilia – on the first lap Raudies is squeezed between Katoh (4) and Tsujimura, with Martinez and Giro behind.

McCoy *(below right)* was a heroic and happy third … Sakata *(bottom right)* a brilliant first.

to reclaim his second place. In fact the Italian failed to improve on his first session time, after the weather interrupted some experiments with altered chassis geometry.

Romboni completed the row, but was far more concerned by a spate of inexplicable seizures on his best bike. Neither his team nor the Honda technicians could find the cause, and in the end he decided to gamble on racing with an untested spare engine, while the offending article was sent back to Japan for examination.

Okada led row two, only two-tenths shy, and mere hundredths ahead of Ruggia who, like his Aprilia team-mate, Biaggi, had failed to improve on his Friday time. 'The changing weather spoiled the carburation,' he said, a problem that was to persist to his cost.

Then came new NSR recruits D'Antin and Waldmann, the German 125 refugee riding with familiar confidence and aggression, but narrowly escaping a fall in the run-up to his first 250 race.

Preining's semi-works Aprilia led row three from NSR new boy Bosshard, with works Honda returnee Zeelenberg next, just over two seconds down on pole. Carlos Checa's kitted RS completed the rank.

Jean-Michel Bayle's works Aprilia debut put him 14th and on row four, less than a tenth ahead of Jurgen van den Goorbergh's ageing private Aprilia. All 32 entrants qualified, the slowest being Chinese-Canadian Rodney Fee, more than seven seconds off pole.

250 cc RACE – 28 LAPS

Capirossi led away, and for most of the race, but his position was always tenuous and in the end, with a certain sense of inevitability, he cracked.

Most of the pressure came from Biaggi, climbing over the Honda's back wheel to the extent that he sometimes had to run wide to avoid a collision. At first this looked impetuous and risky, but after half-distance the roles in this game were reversed, as it became clear that Biaggi was holding tighter lines and Capirossi was beginning to get ragged.

The pair weren't quite alone. A similar Honda/Aprilia battle was being enacted close behind by Romboni and Ruggia, with the latter moving through to close on the leaders at one stage, until some scary slides prompted him to caution, and a safe fourth.

All the while the battle for the lead intensified. Biaggi nosed ahead several times, leading across the line twice; but Capirossi would always get him back, even though he was having problems with grip. 'The race was warmer than practice, and though we set the bike up well I was having trouble in the slow corners,' he said.

Loris led for most of the last lap, Biaggi poised on his back wheel. The error came near the end of it. Capirossi left his braking a fraction late for the Turn Nine hairpin, the front chattered, and he ran wide. Biaggi was ready, and dived underneath. 'I could see he was having trouble, and for the second half of the race I had the feeling I could win,' he said later.

Having lost one place through trying too hard, Capirossi wasn't finished yet. A heroic effort to catch up under brakes for the last corners carried him wide yet again. And here was Romboni, who'd closed up steadily in the closing laps, and now came onto the finish straight in Capirossi's slipstream and already travelling faster. He swerved past to lead his cursing countryman past the flag by less than four-tenths. Loris was very glum for the next few minutes, but resumed his usual grin halfway through the post-race press conference, warmly shaking the victors by the hand.

Ruggia was some four seconds behind in a safe fourth. Almost 20 seconds further back came Okada, narrowly triumphing in a race-long duel with fellow-countryman Aoki. The pair had been back and forth every lap, and were just five-hundredths apart across the line.

They had overtaken Waldmann, so taken aback by running fifth in his first-ever 250 race that he almost went off at one of the hairpins. He recovered to take an impressive solitary seventh.

Another 15 seconds back, Zeelenberg had pulled up from a poor start to join battle with D'Antin and an impressive Bayle, who lost touch only in the closing stages. D'Antin won the duel.

The next group of three comprised wild card Craig Connell, having the race of his life against veteran Preining, and NSR-equipped Bosshard. They finished in that order, just over half a second covering all three.

Another close pair disputed the last points, Checa taking 14th at the last gasp from Eskil Suter. There were 25 finishers.

125 cc RACE: 26 LAPS

The smallest class had moved up a gear, with the arrival of Yamaha as a third force. Aprilia had also become a little more serious, having lured Kazuto Sakata into a full factory team.

And this was Sakata's weekend. The first Japanese rider on a European factory bike dominated practice, and led almost from the flag to take a convincing runaway win.

Behind him, Öttl battled with Tsujimura until the Japanese rider's Honda blew up ostentatiously on the way into Turn Five at half-distance. From then on, the German was unchallenged for second.

Third on the rostrum was a genuine local hero. Now in his second GP season, Garry McCoy had qualified tenth, but was almost last away after stalling on the startline. Twentieth by the end of lap one, he kept on storming through until he was in a fierce battle for third with Gresini's Honda, which the young Aprilia rider won decisively. 'I had such an urge after messing up the start I just went for it. Usually if you don't start well in a 125 race that's the end of your chances.'

Petrucciani's Aprilia was fifth, just clear of a typical four-bike 125 pack, with Saito pipping Ueda, Torrontegui and newcomer Tokudome.

And what of Dirk Raudies? Well, he came next, but only just, after a dismal start to his title defence. Second on lap one, he found out at once that he'd made a bad tyre choice, and his handling and set-up were all to pot. Way off the pace, he dropped steadily back, only escaping relegation from the top ten by the battling Bodelier and Scalvini by a tenth of a second.

The Yamaha made a brief but glorious debut, with Katoh leaping into the lead for one splendid lap, before he slithered gracefully off. But the bikes were certainly on the pace, both Martinez and Katoh qualifying on row two. The Spanish veteran lasted five laps before copying his team-mate at Turn Nine, sliding off without injury. Perugini was another to crash, after running his Aprilia well up among the group disputing fourth early in the race.

There were 28 finishers. Briton Neil Hodgson was not among them. He made a spirited start, but crashed out early in the race and injured his hand. New Japanese girl racer Tomoko Igata finished 14th and in the points.

Photos: Gold & Goose

55

FIM WORLD CHAMPIONSHIP • ROUND 1

Foster's Australian Grand Prix

27 March 1994

500 cc
29 laps, 70.818 miles/113.970 km

Place	Rider	Nat.	Machine	Laps	Time & speed	Fastest lap	Lap
1	John Kocinski	USA	Cagiva	29	44m 37.026s 95.234 mph/ 153.264 km/h	1m 31.637s	4
2	Luca Cadalora	I	Yamaha	29	44m 43.506s	1m 31.615s	7
3	Michael Doohan	AUS	Honda	29	44m 46.272s	1m 32.004s	21
4	Kevin Schwantz	USA	Suzuki	29	45m 03.680s	1m 32.288s	7
5	Shinichi Itoh	J	Honda	29	45m 07.855s	1m 32.208s	4
6	Alex Criville	E	Honda	29	45m 10.345s	1m 32.502s	10
7	Alberto Puig	E	Honda	29	45m 10.756s	1m 32.430s	11
8	Alexandre Barros	BR	Suzuki	29	45m 10.762s	1m 32.677s	10
9	Doug Chandler	USA	Cagiva	29	45m 22.630s	1m 32.886s	8
10	John Reynolds	GB	Yamaha	29	45m 59.088s	1m 34.144s	2
11	Bernard Garcia	F	Yamaha	29	46m 04.771s	1m 34.306s	6
12	Scott Doohan	AUS	Yamaha	29	46m 09.568s	1m 34.662s	10
13	Juan Lopez Mella	E	Yamaha	29	46m 09.795s	1m 34.448s	10
14	Sean Emmett	GB	Yamaha	29	46m 10.364s	1m 34.417s	9
15	Cristiano Migliorati	I	Yamaha	28	44m 48.715s	1m 34.504s	6
16	Laurent Naveau	B	Yamaha	28	44m 54.173s	1m 35.136s	27
17	Jeremy McWilliams	GB	Yamaha	28	44m 55.808s	1m 34.808s	4
18	Jean-Pierre Jeandat	F	Yamaha	28	45m 21.668s	1m 35.626s	8
19	Bernard Hänggeli	CH	Yamaha	28	45m 30.712s	1m 36.464s	20
20	Marc Garcia	F	Yamaha	28	45m 33.512s	1m 36.508s	11
21	Julian Miralles	E	Yamaha	28	45m 47.359s	1m 36.689s	10
22	Bruno Bonhuil	F	Yamaha	28	45m 48.658s	1m 36.192s	9
23	Andreas Leuthe	D	Yamaha	28	46m 09.538s	1m 37.744s	6
24	Vittorio Scatola	I	Paton	27	44m 40.763s	1m 37.089s	24
25	Cees Doorakkers	NL	Yamaha	27	44m 57.770s	1m 38.133s	6
	Lucio Pedercini	I	Yamaha	15	DNF	1m 35.114s	11
	Jean Foray	F	Yamaha	8	DNF	1m 37.785s	6
	Daryl Beattie	AUS	Yamaha	6	DNF	1m 33.127s	3
	Marco Papa	I	Yamaha	6	DNF	1m 38.986s	3
	Kevin Mitchell	GB	Yamaha	5	DNF	1m 38.522s	3
	Niall Mackenzie	GB	Yamaha	2	DNF	1m 41.248s	2
	Lothar Neukirchner	D	Yamaha		DNQ		

Fastest lap: Cadalora, 1m 31.615s, 95.958 mph/154.429 km/h.
Lap record: Michael Doohan, AUS (Honda), 1m 31.411s, 96.171 mph/154.773 km/h (1992).

Qualifying: 1 Kocinski, 1m 30.394s; 2 Cadalora, 1m 30.523s; 3 M. Doohan, 1m 30.755s; 4 Schwantz, 1m 31.404s; 5 Puig, 1m 31.524s; 6 Itoh, 1m 31.527s; 7 Beattie, 1m 31.603s; 8 Chandler, 1m 32.151s; 9 Barros, 1m 32.278s; 10 Criville, 1m 32.455s; 11 Mackenzie, 1m 33.014s; 12 Reynolds, 1m 33.316s; 13 Emmett, 1m 33.421s; 14 Lopez Mella, 1m 33.956s; 15 S. Doohan, 1m 33.958s; 16 B. Garcia, 1m 34.288s; 17 McWilliams, 1m 34.392s; 18 Jeandat, 1m 34.948s; 19 Naveau, 1m 35.144s; 20 Pedercini, 1m 35.156s; 21 Hänggeli, 1m 35.546s; 22 Migliorati, 1m 35.670s; 23 Bonhuil, 1m 36.336s; 24 Miralles, 1m 36.442s; 25 Foray, 1m 36.818s; 26 Papa, 1m 36.910s; 27 M. Garcia, 1m 36.963s; 28 Mitchell, 1m 37.367s; 29 Leuthe, 1m 37.661s; 30 Doorakkers, 1m 37.782s; 31 Scatola, 1m 38.213s.

World Championship: 1 Kocinski, 25; 2 Cadalora, 20; 3 M. Doohan, 16; 4 Schwantz, 13; 5 Itoh, 11; 6 Criville, 10; 7 Puig, 9; 8 Barros, 8; 9 Chandler, 7; 10 Reynolds, 6; 11 B. Garcia, 5; 12 S. Doohan, 4; 13 Lopez Mella, 3; 14 Emmett, 2; 15 Migliorati, 1.

250 cc
28 laps, 68.376 miles/110.040 km

Place	Rider	Nat.	Machine	Laps	Time & speed	Fastest lap	Lap
1	Massimiliano Biaggi	I	Aprilia	28	43m 42.148s 93.874 mph/ 151.076 km/h	1m 32.658s	2
2	Doriano Romboni	I	Honda	28	43m 42.806s	1m 33.088s	3
3	Loris Capirossi	I	Honda	28	43m 42.844s	1m 32.846s	3
4	Jean-Philippe Ruggia	F	Aprilia	28	43m 46.528s	1m 32.722s	4
5	Tadayuki Okada	J	Honda	28	44m 04.738s	1m 33.338s	4
6	Nobuatsu Aoki	J	Honda	28	44m 04.784s	1m 33.548s	5
7	Ralf Waldmann	D	Honda	28	44m 14.117s	1m 34.026s	2
8	Luis D'Antin	E	Honda	28	44m 28.092s	1m 34.198s	28
9	Wilco Zeelenberg	NL	Honda	28	44m 28.124s	1m 34.328s	8
10	Jean-Michel Bayle	F	Aprilia	28	44m 29.517s	1m 34.284s	4
11	Craig Connell	AUS	Honda	28	44m 39.069s	1m 34.718s	14
12	Andy Preining	A	Aprilia	28	44m 39.468s	1m 34.818s	13
13	Adrian Bosshard	CH	Honda	28	44m 39.617s	1m 34.708s	2
14	Carlos Checa	E	Honda	28	44m 54.242s	1m 35.162s	2
15	Eskil Suter	CH	Aprilia	28	44m 54.384s	1m 35.086s	9
16	Jurgen van den Goorbergh	NL	Aprilia	28	45m 08.436s	1m 35.654s	28
17	Alessandro Gramigni	I	Aprilia	28	45m 13.542s	1m 35.780s	26
18	Frédéric Protat	F	Honda	27	44m 01.594s	1m 36.470s	5
19	José Luis Cardoso	E	Aprilia	27	44m 01.882s	1m 36.906s	7
20	Christian Boudinot	F	Aprilia	27	44m 02.518s	1m 36.696s	6
21	Luis Maurel	E	Honda	27	44m 10.256s	1m 36.622s	14
22	Juan Borja	E	Honda	27	44m 24.722s	1m 37.614s	6
23	Rene Bongers	AUS	Honda	27	44m 24.772s	1m 37.740s	3
24	Alan Patterson	GB	Honda	26	44m 03.891s	1m 40.068s	12
25	Kristian Kaas	SF	Yamaha	26	44m 11.886s	1m 40.174s	3
	Bernd Kassner	D	Aprilia	27	DNF	1m 35.835s	27
	Patrick van den Goorbergh	NL	Aprilia	17	DNF	1m 36.736s	5
	Enrique de Juan	E	Aprilia	15	DNF	1m 39.437s	13
	Rodney Fee	CAN	Honda	13	DNF	1m 39.160s	6
	Noel Ferro	F	Honda	10	DNF	1m 37.103s	7
	Adi Stadler	D	Honda	7	DNF	1m 36.171s	3
	Tetsuya Harada	J	Yamaha		DNS		

Fastest lap: Biaggi, 1m 32.658s, 94.878 mph/152.691 km/h (record).
Previous record: Tetsuya Harada, J (Yamaha), 1m 32.894s, 94.637 mph/152.303 km/h (1993).

Qualifying: 1 Capirossi, 1m 32.200s; 2 Aoki, 1m 32.584s; 3 Biaggi, 1m 32.629s; 4 Romboni, 1m 32.765s; 5 Okada, 1m 32.958s; 6 Ruggia, 1m 32.977s; 7 D'Antin, 1m 33.790s; 8 Waldmann, 1m 34.123s; 9 Preining, 1m 34.286s; 10 Bosshard, 1m 34.340s; 11 Zeelenberg, 1m 34.496s; 12 Checa, 1m 34.596s; 13 Suter, 1m 34.632s; 14 Bayle, 1m 34.888s; 15 J. van den Goorbergh, 1m 34.968s; 16 Kassner, 1m 35.214s; 17 Connell, 1m 35.246s; 18 Gramigni, 1m 35.274s; 19 Cardoso, 1m 35.616s; 20 Maurel, 1m 35.737s; 21 Stadler, 1m 36.108s; 22 Harada, 1m 36.532s; 23 Protat, 1m 36.895s; 24 Ferro, 1m 37.188s; 25 Bongers, 1m 37.317s; 26 P. van den Goorbergh, 1m 37.362s; 27 Borja, 1m 37.724s; 28 Boudinot, 1m 37.953s; 29 Patterson, 1m 38.964s; 30 de Juan, 1m 39.019s; 31 Kaas, 1m 39.053s; 32 Fee, 1m 39.464s.

World Championship: 1 Biaggi, 25; 2 Romboni, 20; 3 Capirossi, 16; 4 Ruggia, 13; 5 Okada, 11; 6 Aoki, 10; 7 Waldmann, 9; 8 D'Antin, 8; 9 Zeelenberg, 7; 10 Bayle, 6; 11 Connell, 5; 12 Preining, 4; 13 Bosshard, 3; 14 Checa, 2; 15 Suter, 1.

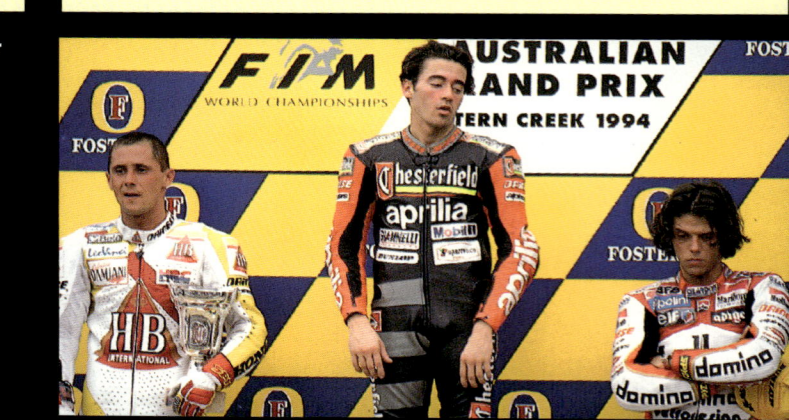

Italian stallions: Romboni was lucky for once; Biaggi looks sidelong at a glum Capirossi.

Opposite page, top to bottom: Sakata exultant, Mackenzie serious, Cadalora intent.

Eastern Creek

Turn 1, Turn 2, Turn 3, Turn 4, Turn 5, Turn 6, Turn 7, Turn 8, Turn 9, Turn 10, Turn 11, Turn 12

CIRCUIT LENGTH: 2.442 MILES/3.930 KM

125 cc

26 laps, 63.492 miles/102.180 km

Place	Rider	Nat.	Machine	Laps	Time & speed	Fastest lap	Lap
1	Kazuto Sakata	J	Aprilia	26	43m 05.474s 88.406 mph/ 142.275 km/h	1m 37.908s	3
2	Peter Öttl	D	Aprilia	26	43m 10.673s	1m 38.178s	5
3	Garry McCoy	AUS	Aprilia	26	43m 17.011s	1m 38.691s	5
4	Fausto Gresini	I	Honda	26	43m 21.014s	1m 38.648s	5
5	Oliver Petrucciani	CH	Aprilia	26	43m 30.067s	1m 39.039s	8
6	Akira Saito	J	Honda	26	43m 32.946s	1m 38.989s	3
7	Noboru Ueda	J	Honda	26	43m 33.431s	1m 39.264s	5
8	Herri Torrontegui	E	Aprilia	26	43m 33.467s	1m 39.167s	9
9	Masaki Tokudome	J	Honda	26	43m 33.937s	1m 39.370s	12
10	Dirk Raudies	D	Honda	26	43m 41.697s	1m 39.346s	5
11	Loek Bodelier	NL	Honda	26	43m 41.818s	1m 39.668s	15
12	Gianluigi Scalvini	I	Aprilia	26	43m 41.822s	1m 39.751s	8
13	Gabriele Debbia	I	Aprilia	26	43m 52.946s	1m 39.942s	6
14	Tomoko Igata	J	Honda	26	43m 53.748s	1m 39.556s	5
15	Hideyuki Nakajyo	J	Honda	26	43m 53.970s	1m 39.501s	4
16	Bruno Casanova	I	Honda	26	43m 57.450s	1m 40.015s	3
17	Haruchika Aoki	J	Honda	26	43m 57.503s	1m 40.181s	5
18	Lucio Cecchinello	I	Honda	26	44m 06.789s	1m 40.365s	3
19	Stefan Prein	D	Yamaha	26	44m 08.408s	1m 40.705s	11
20	Manfred Geissler	D	Aprilia	26	44m 08.416s	1m 40.708s	20
21	Giuseppe Fiorillo	I	Honda	26	44m 08.760s	1m 40.850s	16
22	Frédéric Petit	F	Yamaha	26	44m 29.558s	1m 40.916s	8
23	Oliver Koch	D	Honda	26	44m 30.142s	1m 41.182s	4
24	Hans Spaan	NL	Honda	26	44m 31.394s	1m 40.969s	7
25	Glen Richards	AUS	Aprilia	26	44m 40.304s	1m 41.594s	5
26	Carlos Giro	E	Aprilia	26	44m 49.754s	1m 39.650s	11
27	Masafumi Ono	J	Honda	25	43m 20.854s	1m 42.063s	24
28	Vittorio Lopez	I	Honda	25	43m 23.718s	1m 42.243s	18
	Manfred Baumann	A	Yamaha	18	DNF	1m 41.169s	8
	Stefano Perugini	I	Aprilia	14	DNF	1m 38.484s	3
	Takeshi Tsujimura	J	Honda	13	DNF	1m 38.412s	4
	Ken Fisher	AUS	Honda	7	DNF	1m 42.116s	6
	Jorge Martinez	E	Yamaha	5	DNF	1m 39.826s	4
	Neil Hodgson	GB	Honda	4	DNF	1m 39.314s	4
	Daniela Tognoli	I	Aprilia	4	DNF	1m 46.672s	3
	Yoshiaki Katoh	J	Yamaha	1	DNF	1m 45.662s	1

Fastest lap: Sakata, 1m 37.908s, 89.790 mph/144.503 km/h.
Lap record: Dirk Raudies, D (Honda), 1m 37.819s, 89.871 mph/144.634 km/h (1993).

Qualifying: **1** Sakata, 1m 37.528s; **2** Raudies, 1m 37.904s; **3** Öttl, 1m 38.016s; **4** Gresini, 1m 38.049s; **5** Martinez, 1m 38.196s; **6** Tsujimura, 1m 38.237s; **7** Torrontegui, 1m 38.252s; **8** Katoh, 1m 38.298s; **9** Ueda, 1m 38.322s; **10** McCoy, 1m 38.500s; **11** Tokudome, 1m 38.527s; **12** Petrucciani, 1m 38.676s; **13** Giro, 1m 38.858s; **14** Saito, 1m 38.899s; **15** Casanova, 1m 38.905s; **16** Scalvini, 1m 39.016s; **17** Baumann, 1m 39.087s; **18** Perugini, 1m 39.098s; **19** Aoki, 1m 39.192s; **20** Nakajyo, 1m 39.251s; **21** Debbia, 1m 39.404s; **22** Hodgson, 1m 39.465s; **23** Koch, 1m 39.531s; **24** Bodelier, 1m 39.657s; **25** Igata, 1m 39.678s; **26** Fiorillo, 1m 39.931s; **27** Cecchinello, 1m 39.960s; **28** Prein, 1m 39.988s; **29** Petit, 1m 40.089s; **30** Geissler, 1m 40.464s; **31** Fisher, 1m 41.224s; **32** Spaan, 1m 41.619s; **33** Richards, 1m 41.636s; **34** Ono, 1m 41.715s; **35** Lopez, 1m 42.418s; **36** Tognoli, 1m 42.737s.

World Championship: **1** Sakata, 25; **2** Öttl, 20; **3** McCoy, 16; **4** Gresini, 13; **5** Petrucciani, 11; **6** Saito, 10; **7** Ueda, 9; **8** Torrontegui, 8; **9** Tokudome, 7; **10** Raudies, 6; **11** Bodelier, 5; **12** Scalvini, 4; **13** Debbia, 3; **14** Igata, 2; **15** Nakajyo, 1.

Photos: Gold & Goose

WORLD CHAMPIONSHIP • ROUND 2

MALAYSIAN GRAND PRIX

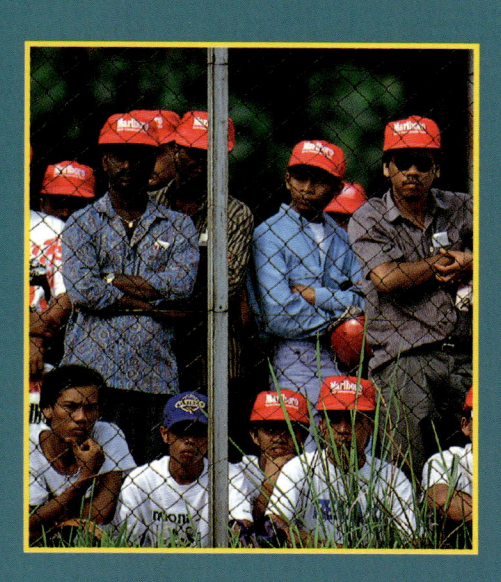

'After he came by I thought I was at the airport. His bike was so fast'

John Kocinski describing Mick Doohan's Honda

500 cc	DOOHAN
250 cc	BIAGGI
125 cc	UEDA

MALAYSIAN GRAND PRIX

Opposite: **Faceless officials, sweating pigs, leaking umbrellas and a hatless rebel added to the steamy Malaysian atmosphere; the only cold shower was of champagne, for second-placed Kocinski.**

Luckless Beattie *(left)* **proved a sitting duck for startline sniping.**

Awash with seafood, sizzling with curries, spiced with satay and lush with exotic fruits, the average buffet has to be good in Malaysia just to compete with the fresh-cooked fare of the street hawkers outside. Kuala Lumpur is a prized stop for GP gourmets living the jet-setters' high life in the glamorous world of international motor cycle racing.

Cut to a row of oddly assorted roughly painted containers behind the sheds at the back of the steaming (and sometimes reeking) pits of Shah Alam. Open the clanking door to one of these makeshift pre-fabs. It is lunchtime on the second day of practice. And there sits Michael Doohan, looking solemn as he eyes the HRC buffet, then takes yet another dry crust of white bread to chew reflectively. 'It's the only stuff you can eat here,' he insists.

The race winner was in an austere frame of mind. His Honda was wayward, and apart from the fact that it was tyre-punishingly hot, they didn't know why. 'It's unstable, breaking away out of the corners and see-sawing at high speed. It's hard to tip it in too,' explained Doohan. 'It's like the problems Suzuki had a couple of years ago, where you can't find the balance. If you get one end working the other one goes away.'

His team were going back and back, trying to replicate '93 suspension settings, so as at least to find a reference point. They were no nearer the answer after the final session, but they were closer to the truth. Whatever he did, Doohan was sliding around. So was everybody else. Perhaps it was the wakefulness of night-time hunger pangs that finally helped him see how to exploit the situation to his own advantage.

In line with mechanical fashions, the way forward was back. Instinctively rather than deliberately, Doohan harnessed a riding style that was first used at another time when everybody was sliding around. It was in the early 1980s, when engine power had vaulted beyond the capacity of chassis, suspension and especially tyres, and reigning King Kenny Roberts squared up to the classic challenge from new boy Fast Freddie Spencer.

A time of legends indeed, when the intensity of rivalry forced two major talents to create new ways of using tyres that had gone west long before they'd finished racing on them. What they did was to adapt still further their dirt-track techniques. They slowed the corner speed right down so they could pick the bikes up quickly onto the fatter part of the tyre, then open up and wheelspin away, relying on the slide to finish the turn. It was a style that served for many years, and has only recently fallen from favour as technical improvements allow a new breed of ex-250 riders to exploit higher corner speeds.

Thus on race morning came the big change. Doohan's crew dropped the ratios of the bottom three gears, which meant a lower corner speed on the track's many slow bends. It also meant even worse wheelspin, with the engine higher up the rev range, and torque multiplication greater. But more importantly it meant Mick, using tight lines with a late apex, could then pick it up and gas it while the others were still leaned over and scrabbling for grip. 'It was just something that came up in discussions with the team,' said Doohan, who dislikes mystification and shrugs off personal credit. The only surprise in the brainwave, he insisted, was that other riders hadn't done it too.

Well, maybe they couldn't, or maybe they didn't think of it in time. Kocinski later commented that his Cagiva simply hadn't been capable of that on race settings. And since he'd been on pole again, at a track where he won his first 500 GP and still held the lap record, no doubt he hadn't thought to change what he had.

Over at Suzuki, they were busy changing everything as their plight grew more confusing. Schwantz ended up on the third row of the grid, his worst position since he went full time in 1988. 'I don't even know where the third row is,' he said, while his team quipped: 'We'll take the barbecue out to the grid, because we'll meet so many new people.' Barros was having similar problems, made worse by his own difficulties with the AP brakes (he'd hoped to try Brembos, but in the circumstances there really wasn't the time). No matter which of the many possible geometric variations and combinations the technicians tried, the bike just didn't respond as expected.

By the end of the weekend they were wondering just what had changed between prototype and production bike. 'We've tried everything. The onus is now on the factory to see what's wrong,' said a baffled Stuart Shenton. And the phone lines hummed as the factory arranged emergency back-to-back comparison tests for the next weekend, not only with the prototypes but also with the pensioned-off 1993 bikes.

The conditions and the demands of the track made life hard even for those whose bikes were about right. The heat and humidity were unremitting – one victim was Briton John Reynolds, close to collapse as he finished the race in a daze. The heat also punished equipment: many bikes had supplementary radiators, while Kocinski had extra holes hacked in his fairing to cool his legs.

Then there were the handling demands of the track, which may be one of the slowest of the year (vying with Laguna Seca and possibly Buenos Aires for this dubious honour), but with one epic fast corner at the end of the straight, under ever-harder braking for the slow 'New Loop' in the opposite direction. This tests stability to the utmost; conversely the snaking slow bends require an agile bike, making the geometry compromise even harder than usual.

Front-row men Cadalora and Puig were among those to fall victim to the New Loop's difficulties, but the heaviest crash there came for a different reason, when Mackenzie's Roc Yamaha seized. Thrown high, he was lucky to be only knocked about; this was merely the latest engine problem, prompting his team to ditch their Bartol cylinders and revert to stock Yamaha equipment.

Two more victims were in the 125 class. Exciting newcomer Katoh crashed his Yamaha and mashed his hand so badly that he required skin grafts (parallel news came that countryman Harada had undergone further surgery to his hand). And Gianluigi Scalvini broke his leg badly enough for him to be helicoptered to hospital on Saturday.

Biaggi had a lucky escape. Building up speed on the straight, he was in fifth gear when a sizeable local iguana ('In fact I think it was a crocodile') ran across in front of him. He hit it and stayed on, but when he came to use the brakes they had been damaged.

Extra closed-circuit TV cameras were installed to avoid the false start problems of the 250s last year, which caused months of wrangling and tipped the balance of the title. These proved useful. In the 500 race, Kocinski on row one had clearly moved before the green, paused, then gone; Schwantz had left the third row so fast he'd collided with Beattie on the second. The film showed their innocence. The Cagiva straddled the line as the lights changed, but it is the position of the rear wheel spindle that is critical, and this was safe. Likewise Schwantz, and an embarrassing round of penalties, protests and appeals was narrowly avoided.

Racing out of packing cases is more irksome in Malaysia than elsewhere, in sapping heat and a relatively primitive paddock and pits. The tyre question made it more so. Since none worked for long, riders were hunting through the available rubberware. The problem for the works teams was the bewildering choice – far too many sizes, constructions, compounds and variations of same to be able to test every possible front/rear combination. Schwantz, Doohan and others complained; the privateers could only listen enviously.

The matter was made worse by Michelin's new 16.5-in. rear option to the regular 17 inch, matching a similar choice for the front. And there were different rim width options in all sizes. For Dunlop and Michelin it meant carrying more than 2000 tyres each to all the opening tracks; for the teams it meant extra complication beyond that of choice, since at any time they needed more wheels in the tyre warmers and ready to go. New Cagiva crew chief and long-time technical guru Kel Carruthers made a plea for sanity. 'There should be rationalisation. The regulations should specify wheel size and rim width. The tyre engineers always say they need the latitude to be able to develop better tyres. I've always said that we need to develop better engines, but we can't just add another 100 cc. We have to do it within the regulations.'

Too much latitude? Enough rope to hang themselves? A flock of proverbs came home to roost when the oldest man in the 500 class, the well-named Marco Papa (36), proved that old shoulders do not necessarily carry wise heads. Troubled by right-hand injuries from the Jerez tests, he decided to try reversing the controls: clutch on the right, throttle and brake on the left. It took three scary laps to change his mind. The right hand didn't know what the left was doing. And what was that about old dogs and new tricks?

59

MALAYSIAN GRAND PRIX

500 cc PRACTICE

Among rather unexpected results, pole was perhaps only mildly surprising. It was Kocinski's second in succession on the Cagiva. Odder was the case of ex-250 rider Puig, in his second race in the class, who qualified top Honda, on the front row ahead of Doohan.

Kocinski was short of his 1991 Yamaha record, and said his Cagiva was 'about 90 per cent. We're trying to fit the pieces of the puzzle together to make the best possible.' Riding without the anti-dive system, it was again his corner entries that made him fastest.

The only one who looked close was Cadalora, less than a tenth down, but taking a heavy tumble in the last session when the front tucked under on the infamous New Loop. He too walked away. Like Kocinski, his best time came on the cooler first day, and he was still complaining of bike balance problems after practice was over.

Puig's third was remarkable. 'I think there are a lot of 250 riders who would do well on 500s,' he said ominously – adding (of his crash): 'I'm not riding dangerously, but you have to take risks every time you get on a racing motor cycle.'

Doohan was thus the second Honda, if only by hundredths, and the experience hardly relieved his mood. Eschewing the new 16.5-in. tyres, he was battling on, with the breakthrough still to come.

Barros led row two, making some progress on Saturday to gain a second. Enjoying the heat, he was moved to say: 'At last we've found a good setting for the new bike.' This proved rather optimistic.

Beattie also improved slightly to push up alongside, although half a second slower. 'I can't seem to get the hang of it,' the ex-Honda rider said of his Yamaha – he had crashed again in the attempt – 'It's just not what I'm used to.' He was consciously trying to change his riding style, and reported some progress.

Itoh's Honda was whisper-close, the times now a second off pole. With Criville equally close to him, the three riders were covered by the span of only one-hundredth of a second.

Chandler led row three, apparently happy (or resigned) to playing second fiddle to team-mate Kocinski as he worked on regaining confidence. He found the anti-dive helped. 'It slows the initial dive a little and helps keep the back on the ground,' he said.

Schwantz was more than just surprised to find himself tenth overall, especially after having been fourth on Saturday morning. Oddly, he didn't display the expected temperament, though he did look very distant. This was different from his moodiness when knocked off pole by a few bare hundredths. 'There's nothing big wrong – just little things that compound each other,' he said, adding that his arm wasn't part of the problem. He was in and out of the pits as they tried different variations, but to no avail.

Mackenzie was alongside, largely unhurt and placed 11th, best privateer ahead of Reynolds, who completed the row.

With Emmett struggling in the heat in 19th, behind Naveau, to be the slowest of the Big Bang gang, the grid made eight rows, stretching back to Neukirchner, 30th and last, making the qualifying cut by the unimpressive margin of a tenth of a second.

500 cc RACE – 33 LAPS

By no coincidence, Doohan had been fastest in morning warm-up, and he came to the startline knowing his gamble had paid off. But it was Kocinski who jetted away, and Cadalora who seemed set to make the first challenge as two HRC Hondas dogged their heels, Doohan ahead of Itoh, for the first five laps.

Then came Criville, Puig and Chandler, with Barros soon joining the group after a mediocre start: as in Australia he'd first 'gassed up',

MALAYSIAN GRAND PRIX

Fast 500 learner Puig lays a darkie as he fends off Criville *(far left)* **and Barros.**

Bottom left: **Itoh** *en route* **to the rostrum.**

then taken a lap or two to get the brakes settled in. Schwantz was already way out of touch, ninth and unable to follow on. Instead he kept the bike calm and smooth, and awaited developments.

Up front, Cadalora couldn't quite get past the leader. Then, all of a sudden on lap six, Itoh came swooping through from fourth to second at the end of the back straight, and it began to look as though he might hold up the pursuit and let John get away for a second runaway win. But Doohan would have none of that. He dived past Itoh one lap later, and was almost instantly on Kocinski's heels.

The American was already running out of options. 'Once the tyres started going away, I was suffering in acceleration, though I could still go into the corners faster,' he explained later. This was precisely the wrong way to try and beat Doohan, as a generation of hitherto dominant European racers discovered more than a decade ago.

Doohan watched the Cagiva's spinning back wheel for less than a lap, then made his move on the esses at the start of the eighth. 'Until then,' said Kocinski, 'I thought I was in the race. After he came by I thought I was at the airport. His bike was so fast.'

It was now that Doohan's tactics paid dividends as he gave a display of the old-time religion. Much tighter on the corner exits, almost upright and on the gas, he surged ever further ahead on a tide of Honda power. The gap was better than 1.5 seconds on lap ten. At that point they started lapping slow traffic, and Kocinski was able to close up again menacingly; but by half-distance tyre wear became even more of a factor, and Doohan stretched away to win by five seconds. 'Maybe I was more used to riding out of control than the others,' was his modest comment afterwards.

In his wake, the rivals were closing up as the chequered flag drew nigh. Kocinski's hopes of a safe second melted away as he came under pressure from Itoh's fast NSR. The Japanese rider's finishing sprint put him in an attacking position – only to be foiled by a bad break in the traffic two laps from the end. So John saved second to hang on to the title lead.

Cadalora had also moved up in the last laps with a view to making his own move on Itoh, but he had been having tyre problems for too long by then. 'Too risky to try and pass,' he said, finishing one second adrift.

Puig was 11 seconds further back after a superb race. Held up behind Criville until lap eight, he'd lost touch with the leaders. But he easily outstripped his fellow-Spaniard, and though he was also sliding a lot towards the finish, he did his best lap at the end of the race, only three-tenths slower than Doohan's best, itself eight-tenths short of Kocinski's three-year-old record.

Schwantz's sixth was earned by experience, and by being there as others ran into difficulties. He passed a fading Chandler on lap 18, watched as Barros ahead of him passed Criville on lap 22, then did the same at the start of the 26th lap. Barros promptly made a mistake at the end of the straight, and Schwantz went by him as well, his waiting game rewarded. 'It's obvious we have setting problems. I did the best I could with what I had,' he explained.

Barros was a grim-faced seventh, complaining of gone-away tyres; Criville was eighth, Chandler ninth, both with similar complaints.

Some way back, Beattie finally finished an unjust but exciting race. He didn't know it was Schwantz who'd hit him on the line, saying: 'Someone must have got a bit of a roller!' Nor did he know that his front brake lever was bent. Not until the first corner. 'I grabbed, and it wouldn't move.' Standing on the rear brake, he ran straight on into the gravel trap, managing to rejoin right at the back without falling to ride doggedly through the field to tenth.

Mackenzie was 11th, down on power with a safe rich setting to avoid seizing again; Reynolds was 12th, so exhausted by the heat that he had to receive medical treatment for dehydration. Emmett was next, one lap down; and then came McWilliams, with Pedercini taking the last point.

There were 21 finishers, with Mitchell among the retirements after only one lap, with an engine that he just couldn't get to run.

250 cc PRACTICE

Aprilia had tested more than the others at Shah Alam during the winter, and it showed. Again Biaggi was the faster, although team-mate Ruggia led one session; and it was not until the end of practice that Capirossi moved up to the front row.

Crocodiles notwithstanding, Biaggi was happy with machine and set-up, as well as his three-tenths advantage over Capirossi – who in turn promised different tactics from his race-losing effort in Australia. 'I don't think it will be easy to lead all

Photos: Gold & Goose

62

MALAYSIAN GRAND PRIX

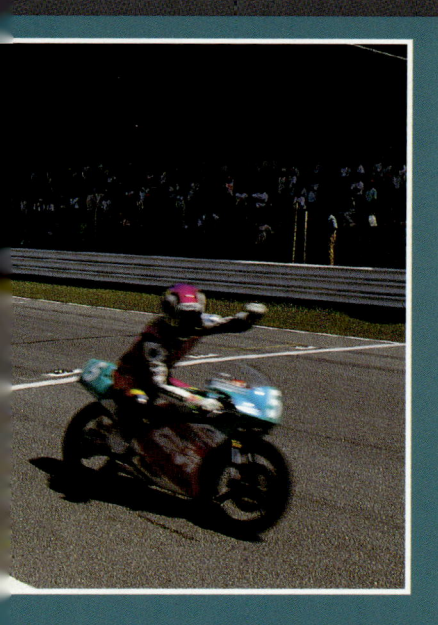

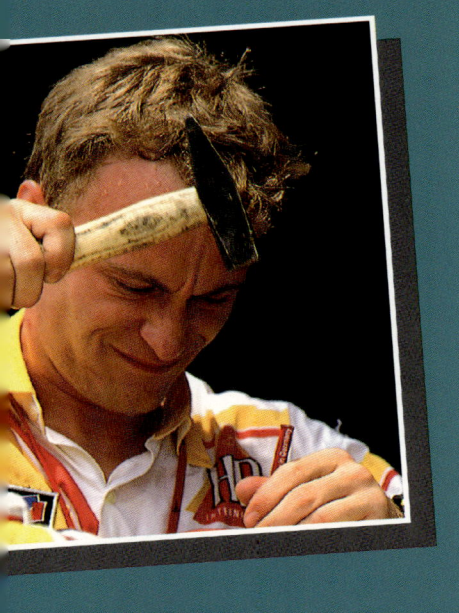

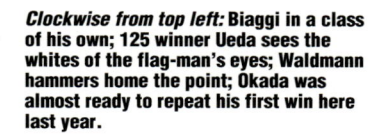

Clockwise from top left: Biaggi in a class of his own; 125 winner Ueda sees the whites of the flag-man's eyes; Waldmann hammers home the point; Okada was almost ready to repeat his first win here last year.

through this race. I expect I will have to try and come from behind.'

Ruggia ended up third, with Okada concluding the front row, more than half a second down on pole and the only fast man on Michelins. He disputed the lead here last year in the best race of his first season, and said: 'The main thing is this is an easy track to learn.'

Waldmann led row two, his class debut continuing to impress in spite of a crash on Saturday. Then came Romboni, who also had a lucky escape when his front tyre deflated at speed on the main straight. He managed to run on straight into the New Loop gravel trap and remain upright. Last year's winner Aoki was seventh, with Bayle's works Aprilia eighth, his best qualifying place yet in his second season of road racing.

The motocross star was thus adapting better to his upgraded equipment than the new NSR riders, arrayed behind him on row three: D'Antin, Zeelenberg and Bosshard, with former 125 champion Gramigni alongside, looking more assertive than he has for a long time, and earning the promise of some better tackle from Aprilia. He had another reason: there was still some hope of reviving the works Suzuki for the season, and his name was at the top of the list.

In the continued absence of Harada and KR Jnr, the top Yamaha was the TZ of local wild card Sharun Nizam, impressive in 19th, just behind Yokohama-shod Jurgen van den Goorbergh. The Dutch rider, with brother Patrick, was enjoying big improvements in this year's tyres. Another new name was Giuseppe Fiorillo, in 23rd, up from the 125 class to ride alongside Capirossi in Team Pileri. All 32 entrants qualified

250 cc RACE – 31 LAPS

It was Biaggi all the way, with not a challenger in sight from flag to flag. The Aprilia rider was in a class of his own, stretching the lead to three seconds by lap six, having broken the record one lap before. He kept on riding so hard he missed the chequered flag, racing on to close his slowing-down lap with a triumphant if belated wheelie.

'I was worried because my rear tyre went away after ten laps and I was sliding very badly,' he said. 'But I had pushed very hard at the start of the race, and I was able to control it from in front.'

Capirossi was in hot pursuit but soon found himself under attack from Okada, who got ahead on the sixth lap and was able to dominate a group comprising Capirossi, Ruggia and Aoki. Romboni was already losing ground behind, and was later to complain that insoluble set-up problems meant he was sliding badly on the fast corners.

Ruggia also soon dropped away slightly, with the return of carburation problems that meant his bike wouldn't rev out; Okada pulled ahead, meanwhile, leaving Aoki to scrap it out with Capirossi. The Japanese rider seemed to have the advantage, but he was taking a lot of risks, and Capirossi decided it was his turn to hang back and wait. 'I was sliding a lot but I could see his problems were even worse, so I thought I'd leave the attack until the last lap,' he said.

He didn't have to, for Aoki fell unhurt on the 28th, leaving a clear third to Loris.

Ruggia was a safe but glum fourth, Romboni likewise in a distant fifth. In the closing laps he had to work to stay clear of HB team-mate Waldmann, who had started brilliantly, dropped back with brake problems, then pulled up again to sixth after moving through a dice between Bayle's Aprilia and D'Antin's NSR Honda. By the finish the trio were well spaced out, but Bayle's best-ever finish showed he is coming of age as a road racer.

Zeelenberg was ninth, three seconds adrift at the finish after starting badly then moving up well, with Gramigni his last victim.

Then came Checa, Bosshard and Preining, still locked in combat, the last riders not to be lapped. Nizam showed well in 17th, after surviving a close encounter with Patrick van den Goorbergh on lap eight, which sent both of them into the dirt and lost them eight and ten places respectively. 'He outbraked me at a crazy speed then came across so he hit my brake and released it,' complained the Dutch rider. But what else should you expect of any really wild card?

There were 24 finishers, crashers among the eight retirements including Jurgen van den Goorbergh on the first lap, Borja and Suter.

When the heat-haze settled, the 250s had proved one thing for the following races on a day that got hotter and hotter. Lap records were possible in the heat, but it helped if yours was the first race.

125 cc RACE – 29 LAPS

Sakata threatened to continue his dominance with an extraordinary practice advantage over second-placed qualifier Tsujimura. The Aprilia was more than a full second faster than that Honda and all the rest, and, whatever the problems the Honda riders were having with reluctant A-kit engines, in this class it was a yawning gulf.

Raudies was third on the grid, but leapt into an immediate lead, a big contrast with Australia, for he managed to stay ahead until lap five, while Sakata had his hands full in a battle for third with Martinez's sweet-handling Yamaha.

Instead it was Ueda who forced his way into the lead, breaking the lap record on his third tour. He was seldom headed by more than a few feet, with Raudies fighting back all round the track, and leading again across the line from laps nine to 11. Now Sakata was finding his legs and he led on lap 12. The brawl was five-strong, with Tsujimura catching up and getting to third at one point.

Then Ueda really put his head down and charged.

In the closing laps his only real challenger was Sakata, who put in a strong effort and was poised to attack, only to lose ground as they lapped a back-marker.

Raudies had dropped to fifth at half-distance, while Martinez had pushed the Yamaha through to second once or twice, going back and forth with Tsujimura. Then the Japanese rider dropped back, his Bridgestone tyres sliding wildly.

Thus Martinez was third, giving Yamaha their first 125 points since 1975; Raudies was two seconds behind in fourth. Tsujimura was almost ten seconds adrift at the finish, in fifth, but safe from sixth-placed Gresini's Honda. Petrucciani's Aprilia was seventh. Then came Saito, leading a three-strong group, his Honda narrowly ahead of Torrontegui's Aprilia and Aoki's Honda.

Australian GP hero McCoy was 12th after another ride through the field. His engine had died at the first corner, and he was even passed by the pace car, but he had pulled through for a second successive race.

There were 23 finishers. Retirements included crashers Peter Öttl and impressive newcomer Alzamora.

Thus Honda avenged their defeat in Australia – but there was no room for complacency, and the pits rang with news of upgrades for Suzuka.

63

FIM WORLD CHAMPIONSHIP • ROUND 2

MARLBORO
MALAYSIAN GRAND PRIX

10 APRIL 1994

500 cc
33 laps, 71.874 miles/115.665 km

Place	Rider	Nat.	Machine	Laps	Time & speed	Fastest lap	Lap
1	Michael Doohan	AUS	Honda	33	47m 36.874s 90.566 mph/ 145.752 km/h	1m 25.925s	19
2	John Kocinski	USA	Cagiva	33	47m 42.099s	1m 25.928s	10
3	Shinichi Itoh	J	Honda	33	47m 44.852s	1m 26.092s	15
4	Luca Cadalora	I	Yamaha	33	47m 45.789s	1m 26.188s	16
5	Alberto Puig	E	Honda	33	47m 56.688s	1m 26.232s	28
6	Kevin Schwantz	USA	Suzuki	33	48m 00.219s	1m 26.272s	26
7	Alexandre Barros	BR	Suzuki	33	48m 01.928s	1m 26.676s	18
8	Alex Criville	E	Honda	33	48m 10.218s	1m 26.508s	18
9	Doug Chandler	USA	Cagiva	33	48m 17.105s	1m 26.987s	10
10	Daryl Beattie	AUS	Yamaha	33	48m 45.473s	1m 27.635s	22
11	Niall Mackenzie	GB	Yamaha	33	48m 52.029s	1m 28.092s	5
12	John Reynolds	GB	Yamaha	33	49m 00.709s	1m 27.629s	2
13	Sean Emmett	GB	Yamaha	32	47m 58.922s	1m 28.651s	4
14	Jeremy McWilliams	GB	Yamaha	32	48m 07.664s	1m 28.672s	3
15	Lucio Pedercini	I	Yamaha	32	48m 22.584s	1m 29.340s	9
16	Jean-Pierre Jeandat	F	Yamaha	32	48m 26.844s	1m 29.416s	24
17	Bruno Bonhuil	F	Yamaha	32	48m 28.488s	1m 29.486s	9
18	Marc Garcia	F	Yamaha	32	48m 28.691s	1m 29.583s	4
19	Cees Doorakkers	NL	Yamaha	32	48m 50.444s	1m 30.162s	6
20	Cristiano Migliorati	I	Yamaha	32	48m 51.800s	1m 29.447s	5
21	Andreas Leuthe	D	Yamaha	31	47m 38.856s	1m 31.066s	15
	Bernard Hänggeli	CH	Yamaha	30	DNF	1m 29.627s	13
	Julian Miralles	E	Yamaha	28	DNF	1m 29.744s	3
	Juan Lopez Mella	E	Yamaha	26	DNF	1m 28.322s	3
	Lothar Neukirchner	D	Yamaha	21	DNF	1m 32.400s	3
	Bernard Garcia	F	Yamaha	16	DNF	1m 28.071s	6
	Jean Foray	F	Yamaha	11	DNF	1m 31.072s	4
	Marco Papa	I	Yamaha	6	DNF	1m 32.415s	5
	Laurent Naveau	B	Yamaha	3	DNF	1m 28.908s	3
	Kevin Mitchell	GB	Yamaha	2	DNF	1m 41.876s	1
	Vittorio Scatola	I	Paton		DNS		

Fastest lap: Doohan, 1m 25.925s, 91.248 mph/146.849 km/h.
Lap record: John Kocinski, USA (Yamaha), 1m 25.100s, 92.133 mph/148.273 km/h (1991).

Qualifying: 1 Kocinski, 1m 25.180s; 2 Cadalora, 1m 25.264s; 3 Puig, 1m 25.672s; 4 Doohan, 1m 25.684s; 5 Barros, 1m 25.744s; 6 Beattie, 1m 26.282s; 7 Itoh, 1m 26.289s; 8 Criville, 1m 26.294s; 9 Chandler, 1m 26.408s; 10 Schwantz, 1m 26.503s; 11 Mackenzie, 1m 27.681s; 12 Reynolds, 1m 27.798s; 13 B. Garcia, 1m 27.866s; 14 Lopez Mella, 1m 28.268s; 15 McWilliams, 1m 28.286s; 16 Jeandat, 1m 28.719s; 17 Pedercini, 1m 28.930s; 18 Naveau, 1m 28.987s; 19 Emmett, 1m 29.150s; 20 Bonhuil, 1m 29.234s; 21 Migliorati, 1m 29.313s; 22 Miralles, 1m 29.465s; 23 M. Garcia, 1m 29.829s; 24 Hänggeli, 1m 29.904s; 25 Doorakkers, 1m 30.104s; 26 Foray, 1m 30.462s; 27 Leuthe, 1m 31.100s; 28 Mitchell, 1m 31.644s; 29 Papa, 1m 31.715s; 30 Scatola, 1m 32.048s; 31 Neukirchner, 1m 32.612s.

World Championship: 1 Kocinski, 45; 2 M. Doohan, 41; 3 Cadalora, 33; 4 Itoh, 27; 5 Schwantz, 23; 6 Puig, 20; 7 Criville, 18; 8 Barros, 17; 9 Chandler, 14; 10 Reynolds, 10; 11 Beattie, 6; 12 Emmett, B. Garcia and Mackenzie, 5; 15 S. Doohan, 4; 16 Lopez Mella, 3; 17 McWilliams, 2; 18 Migliorati and Pedercini, 1.

250 cc
31 laps, 67.518 miles/108.655 km

Place	Rider	Nat.	Machine	Laps	Time & speed	Fastest lap	Lap
1	Massimiliano Biaggi	I	Aprilia	31	45m 26.300s 89.152 mph/ 143.476 km/h	1m 26.847s	5
2	Tadayuki Okada	J	Honda	31	45m 32.108s	1m 27.134s	5
3	Loris Capirossi	I	Honda	31	45m 35.477s	1m 27.276s	23
4	Jean-Philippe Ruggia	F	Aprilia	31	45m 40.272s	1m 27.330s	4
5	Doriano Romboni	I	Honda	31	45m 56.083s	1m 27.807s	5
6	Ralf Waldmann	D	Honda	31	45m 57.337s	1m 28.232s	15
7	Jean-Michel Bayle	F	Aprilia	31	46m 04.252s	1m 28.436s	8
8	Luis D'Antin	E	Honda	31	46m 16.418s	1m 28.496s	4
9	Wilco Zeelenberg	NL	Honda	31	46m 19.684s	1m 28.592s	8
10	Alessandro Gramigni	I	Aprilia	31	46m 28.624s	1m 28.592s	6
11	Carlos Checa	E	Honda	31	46m 36.742s	1m 29.104s	3
12	Adrian Bosshard	CH	Honda	31	46m 37.148s	1m 28.987s	4
13	Andy Preining	A	Aprilia	31	46m 37.652s	1m 29.010s	3
14	Bernd Kassner	D	Aprilia	30	45m 30.684s	1m 29.557s	3
15	Adi Stadler	D	Honda	30	45m 40.070s	1m 30.204s	4
16	Luis Maurel	E	Honda	30	45m 40.161s	1m 30.166s	7
17	Sharun Nizam	MAL	Yamaha	30	45m 50.028s	1m 29.972s	4
18	Frédéric Protat	F	Honda	30	45m 55.672s	1m 30.552s	14
19	Noel Ferro	F	Honda	30	45m 56.437s	1m 30.772s	5
20	Giuseppe Fiorillo	I	Honda	30	46m 13.128s	1m 30.680s	2
21	Meng Heng Kuan	MAL	Yamaha	30	46m 28.166s	1m 31.475s	13
22	Alan Patterson	GB	Honda	30	46m 58.626s	1m 32.020s	4
23	Kristian Kaas	SF	Yamaha	29	45m 37.083s	1m 32.708s	3
24	Rodney Fee	CAN	Honda	29	45m 43.292s	1m 32.784s	2
	Nobuatsu Aoki	J	Honda	27	DNF	1m 27.314s	4
	Patrick van den Goorbergh	NL	Aprilia	24	DNF	1m 30.108s	2
	Eskil Suter	CH	Aprilia	18	DNF	1m 29.184s	2
	Enrique de Juan	E	Aprilia	17	DNF	1m 32.861s	2
	Christian Boudinot	F	Aprilia	7	DNF	1m 31.781s	2
	José Luis Cardoso	E	Aprilia	3	DNF	1m 30.898s	2
	Juan Borja	E	Aprilia	1	DNF	2m 37.038s	1
	Jurgen van den Goorbergh	NL	Aprilia	0	DNF		

Fastest lap: Biaggi, 1m 26.847s, 90.280 mph/145.290 km/h (record).
Previous record: Nobuatsu Aoki, J (Honda), 1m 27.415s, 89.692 mph/144.346 km/h (1993).

Qualifying: 1 Biaggi, 1m 26.618s; 2 Capirossi, 1m 26.962s; 3 Ruggia, 1m 27.124s; 4 Okada, 1m 27.359s; 5 Waldmann, 1m 27.370s; 6 Romboni, 1m 27.714s; 7 Aoki, 1m 27.752s; 8 Bayle, 1m 28.077s; 9 D'Antin, 1m 28.384s; 10 Zeelenberg, 1m 28.517s; 11 Bosshard, 1m 28.955s; 12 Gramigni, 1m 29.136s; 13 Suter, 1m 29.210s; 14 Preining, 1m 29.418s; 15 Checa, 1m 29.538s; 16 Kassner, 1m 29.593s; 17 J. van den Goorbergh, 1m 30.071s; 18 Maurel, 1m 30.240s; 19 Nizam, 1m 30.295s; 20 Stadler, 1m 30.368s; 21 Cardoso, 1m 30.387s; 22 P. van den Goorbergh, 1m 30.616s; 23 Fiorillo, 1m 30.812s; 24 Ferro, 1m 31.118s; 25 Borja, 1m 31.372s; 26 Boudinot, 1m 31.702s; 27 Protat, 1m 31.756s; 28 Kuan, 1m 32.161s; 29 Kaas, 1m 32.237s; 30 Patterson, 1m 32.264s; 31 Fee, 1m 33.267s; 32 de Juan, 1m 33.498s.

World Championship: 1 Biaggi, 50; 2 Capirossi, 32; 3 Okada and Romboni, 31; 5 Ruggia, 26; 6 Waldmann, 19; 7 D'Antin, 16; 8 Bayle, 15; 9 Zeelenberg, 14; 10 Aoki, 10; 11 Bosshard, Checa and Preining, 7; 14 Gramigni, 6; 15 Connell, 5; 16 Kassner, 2; 17 Stadler and Suter, 1.

Kocinski and Schwantz (row three) came close to a false start.

Far right: Ueda knows how to enjoy a win (top); Ruggia can only wish.

SHAH ALAM RACING CIRCUIT

- Turn 14
- Turn 13
- Turn 1
- Ford Corner
- Electrolux Corner
- MMSC Corner
- Suzuki Corner
- Lucky Strike Loop
- Shell Straight

CIRCUIT LENGTH: 2.178 MILES/3.505 KM

125 cc

29 laps, 63.162 miles/101.645 km

Place	Rider	Nat.	Machine	Laps	Time & speed	Fastest lap	Lap
1	Noboru Ueda	J	Honda	29	45m 09.031s 83.932 mph/ 135.075 km/h	1m 32.583s	3
2	Kazuto Sakata	J	Aprilia	29	45m 10.388s	1m 32.597s	26
3	Jorge Martinez	E	Yamaha	29	45m 13.806s	1m 32.790s	3
4	Dirk Raudies	D	Honda	29	45m 15.756s	1m 32.961s	9
5	Takeshi Tsujimura	J	Honda	29	45m 23.038s	1m 32.858s	11
6	Fausto Gresini	I	Honda	29	45m 33.256s	1m 32.917s	5
7	Oliver Petrucciani	CH	Aprilia	29	45m 36.836s	1m 33.800s	24
8	Akira Saito	J	Honda	29	45m 41.564s	1m 33.626s	27
9	Herri Torrontegui	E	Aprilia	29	45m 41.751s	1m 33.697s	14
10	Haruchika Aoki	J	Honda	29	45m 41.918s	1m 33.711s	14
11	Hideyuki Nakajyo	J	Honda	29	45m 42.566s	1m 33.758s	2
12	Garry McCoy	AUS	Aprilia	29	45m 58.081s	1m 34.008s	15
13	Oliver Koch	D	Honda	29	45m 58.244s	1m 33.820s	2
14	Masaki Tokudome	J	Honda	29	45m 58.409s	1m 34.049s	3
15	Bruno Casanova	I	Honda	29	46m 00.930s	1m 34.025s	2
16	Manfred Geissler	D	Aprilia	29	46m 15.438s	1m 34.356s	27
17	Neil Hodgson	GB	Honda	29	46m 16.649s	1m 33.942s	3
18	Vittorio Lopez	I	Honda	29	46m 33.095s	1m 35.102s	10
19	Masafumi Ono	J	Honda	29	46m 33.852s	1m 35.045s	10
20	Chee Kieong Soong	MAL	Yamaha	29	46m 34.995s	1m 35.019s	18
21	Lucio Cecchinello	I	Honda	29	46m 38.817s	1m 35.155s	3
22	Manfred Baumann	A	Yamaha	29	46m 45.599s	1m 35.521s	10
23	Hans Spaan	NL	Honda	28	45m 15.555s	1m 35.571s	4
	Tomoko Igata	J	Honda	19	DNF	1m 34.846s	6
	Stefan Prein	D	Yamaha	7	DNF	1m 34.908s	7
	Gabriele Debbia	I	Aprilia	6	DNF	1m 33.922s	6
	Frédéric Petit	F	Yamaha	6	DNF	1m 34.646s	4
	Emili Alzamora	E	Honda	4	DNF	1m 33.686s	3
	Peter Öttl	D	Aprilia	3	DNF	1m 38.233s	1
	Loek Bodelier	NL	Honda	2	DNF	1m 37.629s	2
	Daniela Tognoli	I	Aprilia	2	DNF	1m 41.300s	2
	Stefano Perugini	I	Aprilia	1	DNF	1m 43.790s	1
	Yoshiaki Katoh	J	Yamaha		DNS		
	Carlos Giro	E	Aprilia		DNS		

Fastest lap: Ueda, 1m 32.583s, 84.686 mph/136.289 km/h (record).
Previous record: Dirk Raudies, D (Honda), 1m 32.821s, 84.469 mph/135.939 km/h (1993).

Qualifying: **1** Sakata, 1m 31.685s; **2** Tsujimura, 1m 32.814s; **3** Raudies, 1m 32.858s; **4** Martinez, 1m 32.887s; **5** Öttl, 1m 32.896s; **6** Gresini, 1m 33.118s; **7** Ueda, 1m 33.178s; **8** Alzamora, 1m 33.184s; **9** Petrucciani, 1m 33.264s; **10** Torrontegui, 1m 33.274s; **11** McCoy, 1m 33.394s; **12** Tokudome, 1m 33.439s; **13** Nakajyo, 1m 33.496s; **14** Aoki, 1m 33.502s; **15** Prein, 1m 33.529s; **16** Katoh, 1m 33.580s; **17** Giro, 1m 33.611s; **18** Perugini, 1m 33.623s; **19** Casanova, 1m 33.627s; **20** Petit, 1m 33.693s; **21** Saito, 1m 33.742s; **22** Debbia, 1m 33.868s; **23** Bodelier, 1m 33.874s; **24** Hodgson, 1m 33.975s; **25** Cecchinello, 1m 34.102s; **26** Igata, 1m 34.116s; **27** Geissler, 1m 34.260s; **28** Koch, 1m 34.280s; **29** Ono, 1m 34.613s; **30** Lopez, 1m 35.115s; **31** Soong, 1m 35.236s; **32** Spaan, 1m 35.268s; **33** Baumann, 1m 35.563s; **34** Tognoli, 1m 36.062s.

World Championship: **1** Sakata, 45; **2** Ueda, 34; **3** Gresini, 23; **4** McCoy, Öttl and Petrucciani, 20; **7** Raudies, 19; **8** Saito, 18; **9** Martinez, 16; **10** Torrontegui, 15; **11** Tsujimura, 11; **12** Tokudome, 9; **13** Aoki and Nakajyo, 6; **15** Bodelier, 5; **16** Scalvini, 4; **17** Debbia and Koch, 3; **19** Igata, 2; **20** Casanova, 1.

Photos: Gold & Goose

WORLD CHAMPIONSHIP • ROUND 3

JAPANESE GRAND PRIX

500 cc	SCHWANTZ
250 cc	OKADA
125 cc	TSUJIMURA

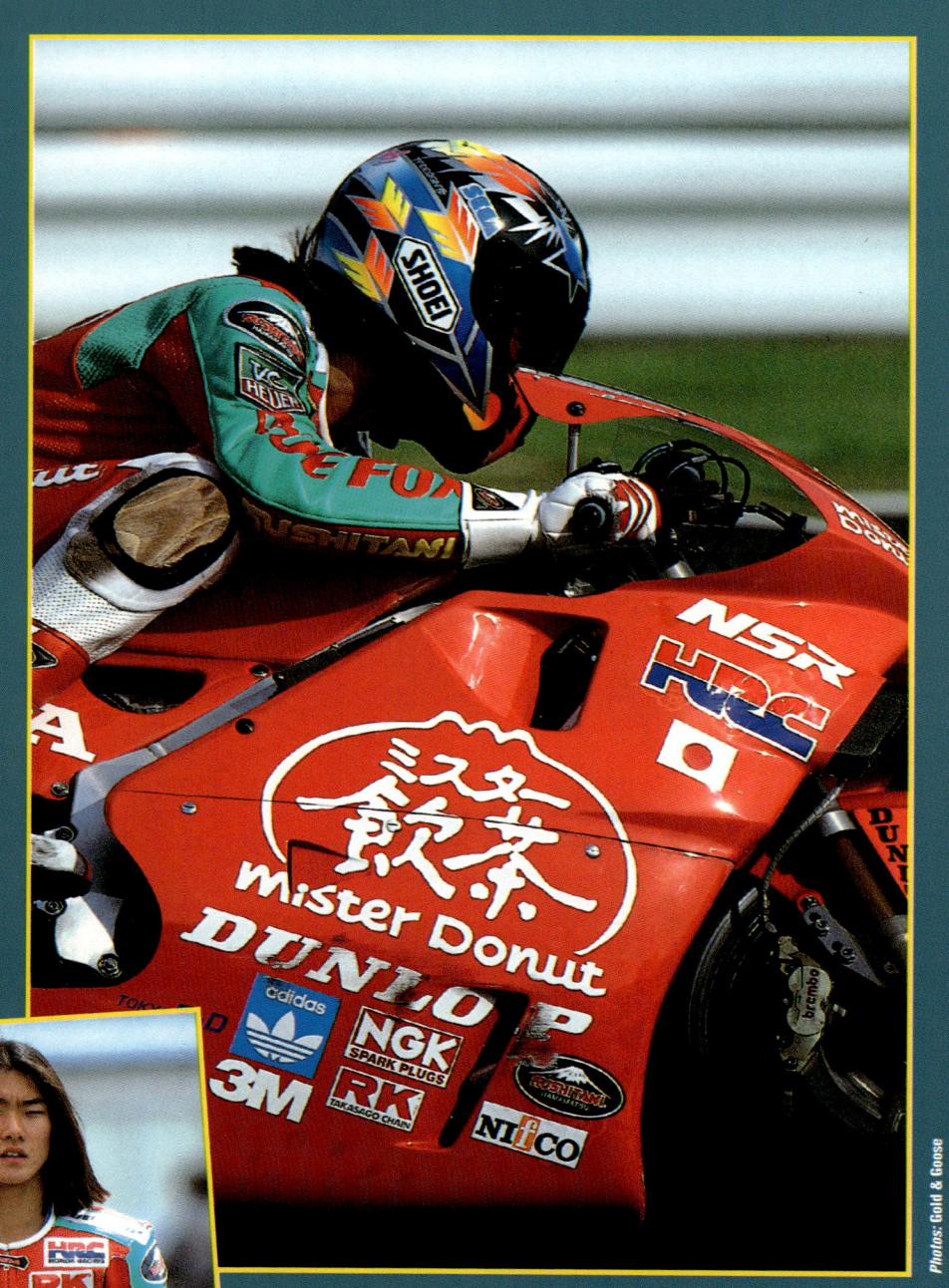

'He'd overtake in places where you just can't pass. He was brave, but it was pretty scary'
Mick Doohan on Norifume Abe

Many a dream has ended in the hay bales of Suzuka. In 1994, the trend was reversed. This time a dream began. It was that of teenager Norifume 'Norick' Abe, who had decided early in the race that he was going to try to win, or crash in the attempt. He did the latter, but only after coming far closer to the former than he had any right to expect.

Or was it the end of a nightmare? Certainly, for Doohan the sight of Abe's front wheel, fairing, and even rear wheel, was more than merely trying. Several times he shook his head as the red and green 1993 NSR Honda plunged past inside under braking for the chicane or the looping Spoon Curve, only to be repassed on the way out. 'He'd overtake in places where you just can't pass. He was brave, but it was pretty scary,' commented the Australian later. 'He'd have done better to stay behind me and Kevin and learn something rather than try and beat us all race long.'

Wild cards don't come much wilder than this. Already a teenage sensation at home after winning the All-Japan 500 title at his first attempt in 1993, and already known as a fast and crazy long-hair foreigner on the dirt tracks of California, Abe looked hairy on the track and exceedingly unlikely off it. With his slight build and youthful face topped by glossy black tresses, and a perpetual giggle on his lips, he looked more like an under-age school kid at a disco than a hard-man racer.

Abe's ride was noble and uplifting, and that he crashed with only three laps to go was neither surprising nor even disappointing, in a strange kind of way, once it was clear that he was unhurt. Having served notice of his arrival as a clear force for the future, he was fulfilling a destiny that did as much to endear him to the 72,000 fans at the track and millions more watching on TV as would the almost inevitable third place.

It was nice to see something new. The keynote elsewhere again seemed to be the revival of the old, reinforced by a move at Suzuki kept so mysterious that everybody assumed they must have more to hide than in fact they did. This led to the universal belief that Schwantz won Suzuka riding last year's bike revived. It wasn't true, but it was a long time before anybody knew that for sure.

The secrecy, which followed emergency special tests at the factory's private Ryuyo test track, was mainly on behalf of the grim-faced Suzuki men, to conceal the fact that dimen-

JAPANESE GRAND PRIX

Opposite: Wild card, or just wild? Seldom has any 500 class novice made an impact like Norifume Abe.

Abe's press-on style kept him up with Doohan and Schwantz, here early in the race.

sional differences – in other words, a manufacturing mistake – had been found between the production XR84 bikes raced in the first two rounds and their prototypes. As a result, the new bikes were undergoing hasty reconstruction, while Schwantz and team-mate Barros each had one of the XR84 prototypes, taken out of mothballs for the occasion.

There was a '93 bike (XR79) present in the pits, and Schwantz did practise on it. But really it had only come into the picture peripherally, though by whimsically dramatic means. While measuring up the prototype and production XR84s, the team wanted to have a 1993 XR79 for comparison. However, in line with factory policy, most of the bikes had already been destroyed. A show bike was eventually found in a dealership in Belgium. It was hastily stripped and the frame carried to Japan as hand luggage. But the team insist (with the benefit of hindsight) that the handbag racer was never meant to be raced.

Ah well, why buck the trend? As Cadalora quipped at a pre-race press conference when asked what version of the Yamaha he was riding: 'I don't know any more. There are some parts from 1993, some from '92, and some from the museum.' Honda were in an opposing position, now officially consigning their PGM-FI 500 cc fuel injection to their own museum, and working on a Mk2 system (actually Mk3, counting an earlier injected 250) on the bench rather than at the track. And Doohan was also playing the classic racer game: having asked for '93-spec suspension he'd been told he'd got it for this race – but his problems continued. He later said he'd been misled by Showa. This is not a first for Honda: in the Sixties Mike Hailwood became so fed up at a Suzuka test session when not given the rear dampers he'd asked for that he removed the offending units and threw them into the lake behind the pits.

Cagiva alone weren't plundering the past. Not mechanically, at least. But they'd packed their superstition in their crates, and when they were allotted pit number 13 seemed to accept that yet again Suzuka would not be kind to the interlopers in the Japanese preserve of the 500 class. Luck ran true to form, and Kocinski lost his early title lead. He had been fast in wet practice, but not in the dry, bemoaning a shortage of set-up time on a track where the Japanese bikes had many laps' advantage.

Chandler crashed his Cagiva at the hairpin on Saturday, in such a muddy spot that the stripped chassis required hosing off behind the pits – an activity done in public, revealing not only the full structural details but also the anti-dive system. This was a welcome relief from the Japanese obsession with secrecy at all costs.

The mud meant the traditional Suzuka bad weather had put in an appearance, with rain all day on Saturday, and a smattering more on race morning that left the track damp in patches for the 250 race. The wet proved risky for all on a brand new surface – the entire track had been done at a cost of $3 million to a general chorus of approval, but was inevitably a little slick in the rain. Doohan was the most illustrious victim after losing the front at speed on the way into the first turn. 'The front brake and I didn't agree,' he commented wryly. The 125 competitors in particular slithered into the mud in some numbers. Without serious injury: pole qualifier Noboru Ueda was by this stage already in a wheelchair, having wrenched his thigh on Friday, though he vowed to race – and there was much talk that the accomplished showman seemed quite able to dispense with the wheelchair when out of the paddock.

Local interest in the tiddlers was high. This is still the mainstay of the Japanese effort, in spite of impressive inroads in the larger classes. Fittingly, Honda chose their home track to respond to the increased level of factory rivalry from Aprilia and now Yamaha, bestowing a new HRC kit on a few favoured riders. This comprised the usual cylinders and exhausts, but also a new ram-fed airbox system, bringing predictable difficulties in setting up carburation in action on a system that had so far only been proved on the test bench. Tsujimura's FCC team managed this well enough for him to win the race, but there was a big element of luck involved. Dirk Raudies wasted the whole of the first day trying to make it work; then it was wet when he switched back to his older bike on Saturday. Breaking his firm rule of never testing new equipment at a GP had cost him dear – he qualified on the fifth row – but at least gave him a scapegoat when an oil seal failed in the race. It was his first machine failure in six years.

Yamaha's 125 star Katoh was still out with injury, and their 250 class problems also continued. Harada was back, but below strength, with his right hand injury making not only throttle and brake control difficult, but also hampering his ability to move his body inside the bike on left-handers. Saturday's rain bothered him, and he said he wouldn't risk riding if it stayed wet. In the end it was neither wet nor dry, and he raced bravely if unspectacularly. Meanwhile 'Junior's' arm injury was still not fixed, and Jimmy Filice was flown in to take over the young Kenny Roberts' Team Rainey Marlboro works 250. He was way off the pace on a bike that was still untested by the team and was prone to seizing; then the stubby American champion and former US GP winner, who missed out on a Grand Prix career by racing at home for too long, was knocked off in the first lap of the race.

Protective gloves and breathing apparatus were more widely seen in the pits after it became clear that the new low-lead Avgas contained compensatory additives that made it far from user-friendly. One Lucky Strike Suzuki mechanic suffered problematical 'burns' to his hands from the 'greener' new fuel. Team boss Garry Taylor, always an opponent of what he saw as too hasty a move to low-lead instead of a considered shift to no-lead, commented: 'We asked the fuel people if they can remove the dangerous chemicals, and they said yes. If they can put back the lead.'

500 cc PRACTICE

The practice that mattered was on fine, dry Friday. Saturday, when slow starters hoped to improve, was unremittingly rainy morning and afternoon, making it into a quite different game with very different results.

Cadalora beat last year's pole for the first time this year with a flier after following Schwantz, then moving past to get his head down. 'I'm a little surprised because I was so slow here last year,' he said. 'But the bike feels really good.'

Doohan was more than half a second adrift, and suggested that Luca had used extra-soft 'qualifying' tyres. Subsequent events showed he may have been more than half-right. He had rejected his new suspension parts, even though they proved more progressive, 'riding the bumps rather than hopping over them'. Only later did he discover that he'd been unknowingly subjected to an experiment by the Showa engineers, and he was not impressed. He had to wait until tests in Europe before they delivered what he'd really asked for.

Third spot went to Schwantz, his fortunes much revived after switching to the '94 prototype. He wouldn't say exactly what he was riding, and only deepened the mystery by reporting: 'We've changed the bike so it's more like what we had last year.' So too was his front-row grid position. And, as it transpired, his race.

Wild card Toshihiko Honma, a seasoned 500 class rider and old Suzuka hand, completed the front row. He was riding his 1993 All-Japan bike, which in fact dated back to 1991, and looked like it. 'I haven't raced at Suzuka for a year,' he insisted. All the same, his track knowledge was obviously valuable.

Yet agan Puig impressed, leading row two only 1.5 seconds down on pole, and almost two-tenths ahead of home hero Itoh, the Japanese rider surviving unhurt a fast Turn One

67

JAPANESE GRAND PRIX

crash on Saturday. Half a second down came Abe, in his first GP as a wild card rider, and showing no fear while staunchly refusing to have the always imminent crash.

Barros completed the row, but was not dismayed, having spent the first day refamiliarising himself with the old-style Suzuki chassis. (Only Schwantz tested at Ryuyo.)

Title leader and double poleman Kocinski was on row three and struggling to get the Cagiva right. 'The Japanese bikes have a big advantage – our bike hasn't seen the circuit before. I'm enjoying the chance of trying to fight our way out of this position.' A hatful of changes for day two would have helped a lot, he said later, but he had no chance to prove it.

He had Criville's NSR alongside, then Beattie's Yamaha, the Australian still chasing his front wheel everywhere. Next came Mackenzie, as usual the top privateer, 12th fastest on his Big Bang Roc. Chandler led row four on the second Cagiva, still lacking confidence; then came Reynolds, McWilliams and Bernard Garcia.

Wet practice was slower, of course, but was interesting and might have been crucial if race day had been rainy. One change was to the fortunes of Cagiva, with Chandler fastest in the morning, though he did crash at the ultra-slow chicane later, and Kocinski making a strong bid to lead in the afternoon, failing by one second in a widely spread array of times.

Winner of the wet contest was Barros, who just kept on getting faster and faster. 'The big thing was my front tyre. I was making the most time under brakes and into the corners,' he said. Cadalora was third, the amazing Puig fourth; then Schwantz, Chandler, Abe and Itoh. There were surprises among the privateers, too, with Laurent Naveau ninth, then McWilliams, Reynolds and Lopez Mella ahead of Beattie. Doohan had been seventh in the morning before crashing, but was 21st in the afternoon.

500 cc RACE – 21 LAPS

Cadalora left the line so fast it seemed obvious he must have jumped the start. In fact the rest had been caught napping, except for Beattie and Mackenzie. Both were most aggrieved at being docked a minute for leaving early.

Criville led the pursuit for lap one, with Schwantz behind Barros in seventh; the Texan was soon moving up, though, and was placed fourth by the end of lap two.

Cadalora was still gaining clear air. Doohan might have been closer but for a scare at the first corner. 'My brake came back to the bar. I had to grab a handful, and the bike stood on its nose.' Now, as well as his familiar suspension problems, he was very fully occupied with a heroic Abe. Every time the veteran pulled ahead Abe would fight back, visibly on the edge of his ability, but also visibly as fast as anyone on the track.

Schwantz caught the pair and passed them on lap six, breaking the lap record for the first of three times as they all closed remorselessly on Cadalora, who was feeling his tyres starting to go away. His lead shrank from three seconds on lap three to less than half a second on lap eight, with the two old rivals and the new boy now swapping around as they snapped at his heels.

Abe was the first to take the lead, at the Spoon on lap nine, only to run wide and lose the place again. He promptly attacked once more on the straight, then as they tipped to the left for the fast sweeper Cadalora had a massive slide and a fearsome wobble that threw him out of the seat. He saved it, but his time up front was over. Dunlop men later explained: 'We shouldn't have let him choose such a soft compound front tyre.'

Abe led for one more lap as Schwantz briefly tailed the troubled Cadalora, then the Suzuki was at the front for the first time at the end of the straight on lap 11.

From then on Schwantz, Abe and Doohan were at it with a vengeance. All took turns to lead, with Doohan clearly having an advantage on power, Schwantz into the turns and Abe on plain craziness. 'I don't think he was completely in control,' Doohan remarked later.

Abe survived one near-crash, and Schwantz now started to pull away, with a gap of exactly one second at the end of lap 14. He was then slowed by back-markers, and they were all together again for some classic Suzuka high-speed to-and-fro. But the Texan was riding like a true champion for the first time all year, and escaped again. 'There weren't any tactics after they caught me again,' he said. 'It was just flat out.'

Doohan might have gone with him, had Abe not kept getting in his way. Twice he shook his head as the Japanese rider came sliding past under brakes into the chicane – the

JAPANESE GRAND PRIX

'More like what we had last year.' At last, the defending champion had a race-winning bike.

test some new 16.5-in. front Dunlops to finish 28th and last, three laps behind the leaders. 'I didn't think I'd jumped the start. If it would have made any difference, I might have protested. But there's not much point,' he said.

Apart from Abe, the only other retirement was Dutchman Doorakkers.

250 cc PRACTICE

With Harada only tentative, the battle up front went on without him, the usual Japanese really wild cards – HRC Honda rider Tohru Ukawa and middle Aoki brother Takuma – mixing it with the new establishment from Europe.

In the dry, Biaggi was dominant again. 'Aprilia has never done well here before, because they have always been running untried new bikes. Our '93-and-a-half bike is good enough to win,' he said. But in the rain 1994's double-winner was less confident.

Capirossi was second in the dry, a quarter-second down, less than it might sound on such a long track, even in this close class. Loris was anxious to redress the balance, but his hothead reputation was not improved when he fell in the wet, luckily at low speed. 'I lost the front at Degner, where I crashed in the race last year. I didn't fall, but then when I looked behind to see if I could get back onto the racing line, I ran over the white line and fell off,' he explained happily.

Okada was whisper-close, managing to stamp his authority over his part-time countrymen. An old hand at Suzuka, he observed that the new, smoother surface made different demands on suspension settings, and slightly changed the character of the track.

Fourth went to Ruggia on the second Aprilia, almost 1.4 seconds slower after struggling with a repeat of his Malaysian engine problems, cured in the end by fitting new carburettors. Then he had a flat tyre. In the wet, however, he was miles the fastest morning and afternoon.

Aoki senior, the regular GP man, led the second row, another to slip off unhurt in the wet on Saturday afternoon; Ukawa was alongside him, running second fastest in the wet; then came the middle Aoki (the third brother is a 125 GP regular).

Romboni completed the row, more than two seconds down on pole, and all at sea. 'We had bad chatter problems on Friday. We've made a lot of

second time the fates got his message. Doohan ran alongside the youngster past the pits, then Abe outbraked him for the first corner. It was one risk too many. Leaving a long black stripe as his front tyre slid away, he then went somersaulting into the sand trap – more like an aircraft crash than a bike accident – lucky to escape without injury. It was a fittingly dramatic end to an electrifying GP debut. 'I was sure I could have come second,' he said later. 'But I wanted to win.'

Doohan, sliding somewhat, had lost touch with Schwantz, but did pull away from Itoh, who had joined in up front after recovering from a poor start. As usual, his peakier engine tune made his bike very fast on the straight, but by race end the effect of the sudden power on the tyres was spoiling his corner exits.

Suzuka had yielded another fine battle, proof (if any were needed) that fast tracks make for much better racing than slow ones. Behind the leaders, Cadalora soldiered on with his ruined front tyre, finishing 20 seconds adrift of Itoh, but comfortably eight seconds in front of the next battle.

This comprised Barros and Honma, banging fairings like production bike racers. On the last lap they changed places three times, with the Brazilian ahead in fifth across the line. Criville had been with them, but dropped back at the finish for seventh.

Puig was eighth, after making the mistake of a suspension experiment and also losing ground with a bad start. But he managed to fend off Kocinski, who said: 'The clutch was slipping from the start, so I just rode it home. The changes we made after first practice were good, though maybe not enough to get up with the leaders.'

Chandler was tenth, then came Bernard Garcia's Yamaha, top privateer Reynolds and McWilliams, with the Rocs of Naveau and Lopez Mella taking the last points. In fact Mackenzie had beaten Reynolds on the road, in his usual way, but the minute's penalty dropped him to 19th on the results sheet, and it was not surprising that he dropped the bike and stormed angrily out of the paddock. Emmett was 17th, sandwiched between Bonhuil and Pedercini, after catching up and scrapping with them in the closing laps.

Beattie's one-minute penalty was only one of his problems. He too had been floundering with tyres that went off, and pitted to change front and rear, using the chance to race-

Gold & Goose

69

changes, but I've had no chance to see if they work,' he said.

Row three saw the NSR of class rookie Waldmann on top. He had been sixth on Saturday, his first time on a 250 in the wet. 'Because of the smoother power it's easier than a 125 when it's slippery,' he insisted. 'Anyway, I was able to use my knee-pad whenever the front wheel started to slide.' Harada was alongside, then D'Antin's NSR; privateer Patrick van den Goorbergh completed the row.

There were 34 qualifiers, with Filice on the fifth row in the Daytona winner's first ride on a works TZ-M Yamaha, during which it seized once and wobbled always.

250 cc RACE – 19 LAPS

After 19 laps of breathtaking racing, it was an over-impulsive move by one of the Italians that decided the outcome. This time it was Biaggi, whose way-too-fast entry to the final chicane carried him from third to a short-lived first place, but also upset the until-then perfect victory plan of Capirossi. Winner Okada merely survived – but in this company that is a feat in itself.

The Japanese rider had made a brilliant start on a track still slightly damp from the overnight rain. On a modern, artificial and twisty circuit he might have been set to make a breakaway. But Suzuka is a real race track, and there was much more action to come.

The first attack came from Takuma Aoki, with fellow wild card rider Ukawa joining in at once – and from the third lap the works Honda trio were locked in thrilling combat. All the time Capirossi was closing, and he was among them on lap four.

All three Japanese riders led across the line at various stages, but nobody held any advantage for long. Then on lap 13 it was Capirossi's turn to lead past the pits for the first time, but though Aoki was to lose ground in the closing stages with his gearchange stiffening up, it was still anybody's race. It seemed highly likely that at least one of the combatants would crash, and probably more than one, since they were usually close enough to touch.

All the time, Biaggi was behind, watching and waiting. Then, at half-distance, he started closing, repeatedly setting fastest lap as he prepared for a final attack. 'I was faster through the turns, but my bike wasn't accelerating too well. I knew I'd have to wait until the last lap.'

Convinced he could win, he was almost right. A heroic piece of late braking into the chicane – the slowest corner in GP racing – took him briefly right past the group. But he was too fast and wide, and had to cut the second apex, almost falling as he then ran into the gravel trap on the exit, to rejoin a little way back for an unchastened fourth.

He could at least measure some small victory in having spoiled Capirossi's race. His tactics seemed flawless: he'd drafted past Okada on the straight and with two corners left could taste the victory. 'I was leading into the chicane, and I was sure nobody could pass me,' said Loris. 'Then this black aeroplane went by.' The surprise put him slightly off line, and gave Okada the inches he needed to take his first GP win.

'That was the hardest race of my life, and the best win of my career,' he said later. 'It was very emotional for me to hear the Japanese national anthem on the rostrum.'

Ukawa was on Capirossi's back wheel, then Biaggi, with erstwhile companion Aoki almost two seconds back in fifth.

Romboni was a lone sixth, having found himself short of grip and unable to go forward with early trackmate Biaggi. Ruggia was another five seconds adrift, stricken with minor motor problems, and also in trouble with his brakes after he was forced onto the dirt by a crashing Waldmann at the chicane on lap seven.

Aoki senior was also quite alone, almost 25 seconds behind. Then came Harada, riding cautiously, but eventually prevailing in a race-long battle with Luis D'Antin's Pepsi Honda.

Jean-Michel Bayle was 11th, also all alone; Dutchman Jurgen van den Goorbergh won the next four-strong private Aprilia tussle, with brother Patrick 13th. Andy Preining was with them, but had been penalised for jumping the start; Eskil Suter fell at the chicane on the last lap, remounting to take the last point for 15th behind Stadler.

There were 23 finishers, with neither Filice nor works man Zeelenberg among them. Both had been skittled by Adrian Bosshard's NSR Honda barely three corners from the start, after the Swiss rider had touched a white line at the second of the Esses. Other crashers included Gramigni, Borja and Rodney Fee.

JAPANESE GRAND PRIX

Left: Okada leads Capirossi, Ukawa and Biaggi in the closing stages. Soon afterwards Biaggi would try and pass the lot of them – and end up in the dirt *(inset).*

125 cc RACE – 18 LAPS

The last race of the day was another Japanese benefit, with all the fierce racing and desperate battling that that implies.

Pole qualifier Ueda climbed out of his wheelchair for the race, and took a flying start to seize a commanding early lead. It was better than five seconds after five laps; but it was not to last.

The pursuit was three-strong: Tsujimura, Sakata and Nakajyo (Honda, Aprilia, Honda), with the latter falling away behind as the other two closed up. Then came a typically furious battle, with the three countrymen swapping back and forth, and nobody able to break away.

Sakata led across the line from laps 12 to 15; then Ueda on 16 and 17. And then came the final showdown, on the last lap.

Sakata took the lead on the Esses, then Ueda had the red mist descend and, when he saw a chance to overtake, he abandoned his existing plan of settling for a safe rostrum. He forced past on the hairpin approach, led down the hill on the exit, then went flying into the Spoon Curve miles faster than the other two.

Too fast. As he tipped towards the initial apex, his Givi Honda's front wheel tucked under and he was down. He got up immediately, but the bike was too badly damaged for him to restart, and he trudged away to the barrier to slump face down, broken-hearted, as the race went on without him.

Tsujimura judged it perfectly, and had managed to pull out just over half a second at the finish, to prevent Sakata becoming the first Japanese rider to win his home GP on a foreign machine.

Nakajyo was 13 seconds down in third, with Öttl's Aprilia just two seconds behind to be the first European finisher.

Three seconds back, Akira Saito narrowly defeated wild card Tokudome (both Honda) to claim fifth; another 20 seconds away Martinez (Yamaha) did the same to countryman Herri Torrontegui's Aprilia for seventh. McCoy came through from 20th to ninth, just pipping Casanova, after yet more typical first-lap problems: this time he was knocked right back to 20th after a collision in the first bends.

Bodelier was next, ahead of Kunihiro Amano, with Koch, Geissler and Prein completing the points scorers.

The race was disastrous for World Champion Dirk Raudies, who had qualified only 17th, then had a gearbox oil seal fail on the fifth lap – the first time his bike has stopped in a race in six years. There was disappointment too for Japanese girl racer Tomoko Igata who was in ninth place when her Honda also broke down, with just four laps to go.

Top: Tsujimura needs two caps after his first win of the season.

Sakata *(above)* tried everything, but finished less than a second adrift.

Photos: Gold & Goose

FIM WORLD CHAMPIONSHIP • ROUND 3

MARLBORO GRAND PRIX OF JAPAN

24 APRIL 1994

500 cc

21 laps, 76.524 miles/123.144 km

Place	Rider	Nat.	Machine	Laps	Time & speed	Fastest lap	Lap
1	Kevin Schwantz	USA	Suzuki	21	45m 49.996s 100.170 mph/ 161.207 km/h	2m 09.439s	17
2	Michael Doohan	AUS	Honda	21	45m 53.470s	2m 09.849s	7
3	Shinichi Itoh	J	Honda	21	45m 57.985s	2m 09.858s	9
4	Luca Cadalora	I	Yamaha	21	46m 18.012s	2m 10.174s	8
5	Alexandre Barros	BR	Suzuki	21	46m 26.539s	2m 11.168s	4
6	Toshihiko Honma	J	Yamaha	21	46m 27.321s	2m 11.448s	18
7	Alex Criville	E	Honda	21	46m 31.943s	2m 11.834s	6
8	Alberto Puig	E	Honda	21	46m 44.761s	2m 12.145s	20
9	John Kocinski	USA	Cagiva	21	46m 49.376s	2m 12.014s	13
10	Doug Chandler	USA	Cagiva	21	47m 01.702s	2m 12.518s	13
11	Bernard Garcia	F	Yamaha	21	47m 19.834s	2m 13.414s	21
12	John Reynolds	GB	Yamaha	21	47m 25.406s	2m 13.197s	7
13	Jeremy McWilliams	GB	Yamaha	21	47m 44.788s	2m 14.861s	9
14	Laurent Naveau	B	Yamaha	21	47m 48.493s	2m 15.342s	3
15	Juan Lopez Mella	E	Yamaha	21	47m 57.612s	2m 15.584s	15
16	Bruno Bonhuil	F	Yamaha	21	48m 00.224s	2m 15.422s	21
17	Sean Emmett	GB	Yamaha	21	48m 02.304s	2m 16.060s	18
18	Lucio Pedercini	I	Yamaha	21	48m 02.864s	2m 16.004s	13
19	Niall Mackenzie	GB	Yamaha	21	48m 20.710s	2m 13.274s	4
20	Cristiano Migliorati	I	Yamaha	20	45m 52.740s	2m 15.816s	15
21	Jean-Pierre Jeandat	F	Yamaha	20	45m 55.008s	2m 16.096s	8
22	Marc Garcia	F	Yamaha	20	46m 02.526s	2m 16.370s	16
23	Jean Foray	F	Yamaha	20	46m 23.404s	2m 16.960s	12
24	Julian Miralles	E	Yamaha	20	46m 38.311s	2m 17.895s	6
25	Bernard Hänggeli	CH	Yamaha	20	46m 43.224s	2m 17.054s	18
26	Andreas Leuthe	D	Yamaha	20	46m 58.672s	2m 19.374s	18
27	Lothar Neukirchner	D	Yamaha	20	47m 51.305s	2m 21.747s	15
28	Daryl Beattie	AUS	Yamaha	18	48m 20.756s	2m 13.566s	16
	Norifumi Abe	J	Honda	18	DNF	2m 09.954s	8
	Cees Doorakkers	NL	Yamaha	12	DNF	2m 19.658s	4
	Kevin Mitchell	GB	Yamaha		DNQ		

Fastest lap: Schwantz, 2m 09.439s, 101.340 mph/163.091 km/h (record).
Previous record: Kevin Schwantz, USA (Suzuki), 2m 09.891s, 100.988 mph/162.524 km/h (1993).

Qualifying: 1 Cadalora, 2m 08.336s; 2 Doohan, 2m 08.995s; 3 Schwantz, 2m 09.335s; 4 Honma, 2m 09.752s; 5 Puig, 2m 09.814s; 6 Itoh, 2m 09.971s; 7 Abe, 2m 10.465s; 8 Barros, 2m 10.581s; 9 Kocinski, 2m 11.020s; 10 Criville, 2m 11.044s; 11 Beattie, 2m 11.078s; 12 Mackenzie, 2m 11.440s; 13 Chandler, 2m 12.132s; 14 Reynolds, 2m 12.706s; 15 McWilliams, 2m 12.949s; 16 B. Garcia, 2m 13.646s; 17 Emmett, 2m 13.931s; 18 Naveau, 2m 14.478s; 19 Jeandat, 2m 14.551s; 20 Lopez Mella, 2m 14.559s; 21 Pedercini, 2m 15.024s; 22 Miralles, 2m 15.658s; 23 Bonhuil, 2m 15.824s; 24 Hänggeli, 2m 16.662s; 25 Foray, 2m 17.184s; 26 M. Garcia, 2m 17.598s; 27 Migliorati, 2m 18.339s; 28 Neukirchner, 2m 19.100s; 29 Doorakkers, 2m 19.615s; 30 Leuthe, 2m 19.931s.

World Championship: 1 M. Doohan, 61; 2 Kocinski, 52; 3 Schwantz, 48; 4 Cadalora, 46; 5 Itoh, 43; 6 Barros and Puig, 28; 8 Criville, 27; 9 Chandler, 20; 10 Reynolds, 14; 11 Honma and B. Garcia, 10; 13 Beattie, 6; 14 Emmett, Mackenzie and McWilliams, 5; 17 S. Doohan and Lopez Mella, 4; 19 Naveau, 2; 20 Migliorati and Pedercini, 1.

250 cc

19 laps, 69.236 miles/111.416 km

Place	Rider	Nat.	Machine	Laps	Time & speed	Fastest lap	Lap
1	Tadayuki Okada	J	Honda	19	42m 28.242s 97.805 mph/ 157.402 km/h	2m 12.696s	18
2	Loris Capirossi	I	Honda	19	42m 28.370s	2m 12.522s	18
3	Tohru Ukawa	J	Honda	19	42m 28.556s	2m 12.872s	15
4	Massimiliano Biaggi	I	Aprilia	19	42m 30.351s	2m 12.187s	18
5	Takuma Aoki	J	Honda	19	42m 32.083s	2m 13.042s	15
6	Doriano Romboni	I	Honda	19	42m 38.538s	2m 13.456s	17
7	Jean-Philippe Ruggia	F	Aprilia	19	42m 43.901s	2m 13.180s	13
8	Nobuatsu Aoki	J	Honda	19	43m 07.349s	2m 14.851s	5
9	Tetsuya Harada	J	Yamaha	19	43m 17.999s	2m 14.377s	19
10	Luis D'Antin	E	Honda	19	43m 19.002s	2m 15.216s	19
11	Jean-Michel Bayle	F	Aprilia	19	43m 40.776s	2m 16.735s	10
12	Jurgen van den Goorbergh	NL	Aprilia	19	43m 49.825s	2m 15.710s	14
13	Patrick van den Goorbergh	NL	Aprilia	19	43m 52.574s	2m 16.443s	14
14	Adi Stadler	D	Honda	19	43m 53.160s	2m 16.592s	14
15	Eskil Suter	CH	Aprilia	19	44m 11.834s	2m 16.510s	14
16	Luis Maurel	E	Honda	19	44m 12.025s	2m 16.849s	19
17	Frédéric Protat	F	Honda	19	44m 12.745s	2m 16.879s	17
18	Giuseppe Fiorillo	I	Honda	19	44m 12.912s	2m 16.724s	17
19	Bernd Kassner	D	Aprilia	19	44m 28.893s	2m 18.210s	10
20	Noel Ferro	F	Honda	19	44m 46.873s	2m 18.498s	13
21	Andy Preining	A	Aprilia	19	44m 50.456s	2m 16.627s	18
22	Enrique de Juan	E	Aprilia	18	43m 14.491s	2m 21.824s	9
23	Kristian Kaas	SF	Yamaha	18	43m 34.252s	2m 23.090s	18
	Carlos Checa	E	Honda	14	DNF	2m 17.139s	14
	Ralf Waldmann	D	Honda	6	DNF	2m 14.212s	6
	Alessandro Gramigni	I	Aprilia	5	DNF	2m 17.443s	5
	Alan Patterson	GB	Honda	5	DNF	2m 20.645s	4
	Christian Boudinot	F	Aprilia	3	DNF	2m 20.620s	3
	José Luis Cardoso	E	Aprilia	3	DNF	2m 21.135s	3
	Rodney Fee	CAN	Honda	1	DNF	2m 36.876s	1
	Wilco Zeelenberg	NL	Honda	0	DNF		
	Adrian Bosshard	CH	Honda	0	DNF		
	Jim Filice	USA	Yamaha	0	DNF		
	Juan Borja	E	Aprilia	0	DNF		

Fastest lap: Biaggi, 2m 12.187s, 99.234 mph/159.701 km/h (record).
Previous record: Loris Capirossi, I (Honda), 2m 12.281s, 99.163 mph/159.588 km/h (1993).

Qualifying: 1 Biaggi, 2m 10.876s; 2 Capirossi, 2m 11.146s; 3 Okada, 2m 11.188s; 4 Ruggia, 2m 12.474s; 5 N. Aoki, 2m 12.638s; 6 Ukawa, 2m 12.759s; 7 T. Aoki, 2m 12.779s; 8 Romboni, 2m 13.006s; 9 Waldmann, 2m 13.296s; 10 Harada, 2m 13.702s; 11 D'Antin, 2m 14.505s; 12 P. van den Goorbergh, 2m 14.542s; 13 Bosshard, 2m 14.957s; 14 Zeelenberg, 2m 15.320s; 15 J. van den Goorbergh, 2m 15.340s; 16 Bayle, 2m 15.674s; 17 Gramigni, 2m 15.684s; 18 Checa, 2m 15.735s; 19 Filice, 2m 15.788s; 20 Suter, 2m 16.068s; 21 Preining, 2m 16.400s; 22 Maurel, 2m 16.581s; 23 Stadler, 2m 17.158s; 24 Borja, 2m 18.242s; 25 Kassner, 2m 18.609s; 26 Ferro, 2m 18.650s; 27 Boudinot, 2m 18.741s; 28 Fee, 2m 18.957s; 29 de Juan, 2m 19.177s; 30 Fiorillo, 2m 19.319s; 31 Patterson, 2m 19.438s; 32 Protat, 2m 20.115s; 33 Kaas, 2m 21.494s; 34 Cardoso, 2m 23.855s.

World Championship: 1 Biaggi, 63; 2 Okada, 56; 3 Capirossi, 52; 4 Romboni, 41; 5 Ruggia, 35; 6 D'Antin, 22; 7 Bayle, 20; 8 Waldmann, 19; 9 N. Aoki, 18; 10 Ukawa, 16; 11 Zeelenberg, 14; 12 T. Aoki, 11; 13 Bosshard, Checa, Harada and Preining, 7; 17 Gramigni, 6; 18 Connell, 5; 19 J. van den Goorbergh, 4; 20 Stadler and P. van den Goorbergh, 3; 22 Kassner and Suter, 2.

Rainey at last had a rider – but Jimmy Filice had only bad luck.

Opposite, from top: Happiness is a signed programme; Suzuka curves; Okada's home triumph almost elicited a smile.

SUZUKA CIRCUIT

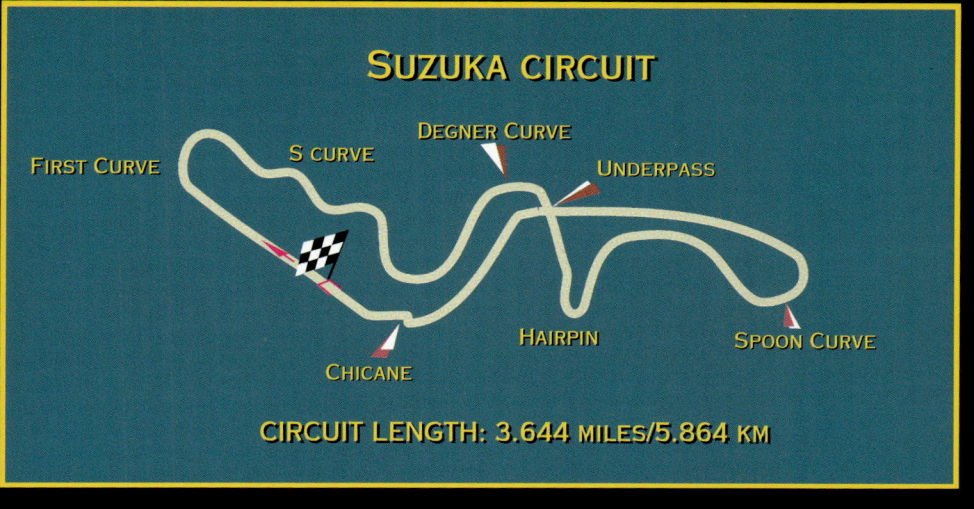

First Curve · S Curve · Degner Curve · Underpass · Hairpin · Spoon Curve · Chicane

CIRCUIT LENGTH: 3.644 MILES/5.864 KM

125 cc

18 laps, 65.592 miles/105.552 km

Place	Rider	Nat.	Machine	Laps	Time & speed	Fastest lap	Lap
1	Takeshi Tsujimura	J	Honda	18	42m 13.168s 93.209 mph/ 150.005 km/h	2m 18.912s	12
2	Kazuto Sakata	J	Aprilia	18	42m 13.838s	2m 18.756s	12
3	Hideyuki Nakajyo	J	Honda	18	42m 26.520s	2m 19.439s	12
4	Peter Öttl	D	Aprilia	18	42m 29.091s	2m 19.312s	10
5	Akira Saito	J	Honda	18	42m 31.402s	2m 19.771s	8
6	Masaki Tokudome	J	Honda	18	42m 31.484s	2m 20.235s	8
7	Jorge Martinez	E	Yamaha	18	42m 53.226s	2m 21.299s	11
8	Herri Torrontegui	E	Aprilia	18	42m 53.399s	2m 21.189s	11
9	Garry McCoy	AUS	Aprilia	18	43m 12.534s	2m 21.729s	18
10	Bruno Casanova	I	Honda	18	43m 12.892s	2m 21.767s	9
11	Loek Bodelier	NL	Honda	18	43m 23.887s	2m 22.588s	13
12	Kunihiro Amano	J	Honda	18	43m 30.818s	2m 23.119s	5
13	Oliver Koch	D	Honda	18	43m 34.470s	2m 22.946s	12
14	Manfred Geissler	D	Aprilia	18	43m 36.800s	2m 23.101s	11
15	Stefan Prein	D	Yamaha	18	43m 37.424s	2m 23.523s	13
16	Emili Alzamora	E	Honda	18	43m 40.856s	2m 23.606s	3
17	Haruchika Aoki	J	Honda	18	43m 46.958s	2m 24.195s	9
18	Fausto Gresini	I	Honda	18	43m 50.936s	2m 21.026s	3
19	Stefano Perugini	I	Aprilia	18	43m 56.600s	2m 20.979s	11
20	Carlos Giro	E	Aprilia	18	43m 57.140s	2m 24.756s	16
21	Gabriele Debbia	I	Aprilia	18	44m 09.906s	2m 25.250s	10
22	Manfred Baumann	A	Yamaha	18	44m 18.338s	2m 25.898s	3
23	Frédéric Petit	F	Yamaha	18	44m 18.458s	2m 25.625s	6
24	Masafumi Ono	J	Honda	18	44m 38.110s	2m 27.620s	11
	Noboru Ueda	J	Honda	17	DNF	2m 19.359s	15
	Tomoko Igata	J	Honda	14	DNF	2m 21.342s	11
	Hiroyuki Kikuchi	J	Honda	14	DNF	2m 23.326s	5
	Oliver Petrucciani	CH	Aprilia	11	DNF	2m 20.659s	7
	Daniela Tognoli	I	Aprilia	6	DNF	2m 39.723s	5
	Neil Hodgson	GB	Honda	5	DNF	2m 25.208s	3
	Hans Spaan	NL	Honda	5	DNF	2m 27.333s	3
	Dirk Raudies	D	Honda	4	DNF	2m 22.800s	4
	Lucio Cecchinello	I	Honda	0	DNF		
	Vittorio Lopez	I	Honda	0	DNF		

Fastest lap: Sakata, 2m 18.756s, 94.535 mph/152.140 km/h (record).
Previous record: Kazuto Sakata, J (Honda), 2m 20.231s, 93.541 mph/150.540 km/h (1993).

Qualifying: 1 Ueda, 2m 19.133s; **2** Sakata, 2m 19.933s; **3** Saito, 2m 19.995s; **4** Öttl, 2m 20.054s; **5** Nakajyo, 2m 20.122s; **6** Tokudome, 2m 20.249s; **7** Petrucciani, 2m 20.588s; **8** Gresini, 2m 20.818s; **9** McCoy, 2m 20.876s; **10** Igata, 2m 20.932s; **11** Kikuchi, 2m 21.133s; **12** Tsujimura, 2m 21.182s; **13** Perugini, 2m 21.322s; **14** Alzamora, 2m 21.385s; **15** Martinez, 2m 21.558s; **16** Koch, 2m 21.626s; **17** Raudies, 2m 22.183s; **18** Aoki, 2m 22.438s; **19** Torrontegui, 2m 22.548s; **20** Cecchinello, 2m 22.567s; **21** Bodelier, 2m 22.824s; **22** Casanova, 2m 22.869s; **23** Geissler, 2m 23.222s; **24** Prein, 2m 23.330s; **25** Hodgson, 2m 23.397s; **26** Amano, 2m 23.764s; **27** Giro, 2m 23.976s; **28** Ono, 2m 24.028s; **29** Lopez, 2m 24.508s; **30** Debbia, 2m 24.844s; **31** Petit, 2m 25.907s; **32** Spaan, 2m 26.427s; **33** Baumann, 2m 27.170s; **34** Tognoli, 2m 28.460s.

World Championship: 1 Sakata, 65; **2** Tsujimura, 36; **3** Ueda, 34; **4** Öttl, 33; **5** Saito, 29; **6** McCoy, 27; **7** Martinez, 25; **8** Gresini and Torrontegui, 23; **10** Nakajyo, 22; **11** Petrucciani, 20; **12** Raudies and Tokudome, 19; **14** Bodelier, 10; **15** Casanova, 7; **16** Aoki and Koch, 6; **18** Amano and Scalvini, 4; **20** Debbia, 3; **21** Geissler and Igata, 2; **23** Prein, 1.

Photos: Gold & Goose

WORLD CHAMPIONSHIP • ROUND 4

SPANISH GRAND PRIX

'Don't bag Honda too much – but what they gave us wasn't what they said they'd given us'
Mick Doohan

SPANISH GRAND PRIX

500 cc	DOOHAN
250 cc	RUGGIA
125 cc	SAKATA

Below left: Aprilia's new V-twin came, was seen, and was conquered – but was threatening nevertheless.

Insets. Left: Food for the multitude – Jerez is a stall-holders' paradise. *Right:* Kevin Schwantz, through a fish-eye darkly.

John Reynolds wore a distant look. 'The first time I wasn't able to pass it on the straight, I thought it must be because I'd got off the previous corner badly. So I followed him and tried again. Still couldn't get past. I had to back off and let him go, because I was afraid he'd suck me into the corners over my head.'

Reynolds's Padgetts Harris had a 1993 frame but a Big Bang works-replica motor, and with a set of solid finishes the second-year Briton headed the points for non-factory riders. A good benchmark, you might think, for a new bike making its racing debut in prototype form, with its engine in a cooking state of tune. Beat Reynolds and those of his ilk, and the next target is the full factory machines.

When that machine is the new mould-breaker from the highly successful racing department of Aprilia, the result becomes more important. By coincidence, the timing gurus Delta Tre had introduced a plethora of extra information for this race, including top speeds and section times. All eyes were on these as Loris Reggiani squirted the oh-so-pretty little 400 cc lightweight round the track, and many were the knowing glances exchanged when his name appeared in the top four during the final and fastest practice session – good enough for the front row of the grid. This didn't last, but the point was made: first, that the super-250 was close enough to being competitive out of the box to offer a real future threat to the V4 dinosaurs; and second that Jerez was well chosen as a launch pad for the pretty new pocket rocket.

Broad details of the new bike had been bandied about since last year. Chief engineer Jan Witteveen, a Dutchman based in Italy, was one of the original proponents of a differential weight limit (100 kg for twins, 130 kg for fours), but admitted that his thinking then had favoured a full-size V-twin, like Bimota's still-born effort. The idea of an overblown 250 had gelled only at Donington Park in August 1993, when there was barely one-tenth difference between the best 250 and 500 race lap times, and the race-winning average was less than 3 mph slower. Since the 250 had been Ruggia's Aprilia, a power-up version of the same thing might easily tip the balance the other way.

Now the bike was here, in factory paint, wearing the 'high-speed' 250 bodywork and using the same frame and brakes, though a slightly larger rear tyre, and looking very dainty among the chunky V4s. The bored and stroked ex-Rotax disc-valve 250 had enough new parts to be a new engine, albeit outwardly similar, and was tuned for just 110 bhp, with the eventual target being 135 or more.

In the end Loris was on the second row of the grid, although only just in the top 20 on top speed, at 251.2 km/h on Sunday morning compared with Barros's fastest Suzuki at 269.7 km/h. Even though, in the end, his practice time was slower than the best of the 250s, and despite the spate of breakdowns that were to follow, here was a real promise to enliven the class in the future.

For the present, with the packing-case races over, it was down to regular business, with a well-established mobile support army and the matter of accumulating points towards the title almost routine.

Happily, the routine at Jerez was extremely exciting, and augured well for the seven European rounds to follow. Among the rolling sherry vineyards and in front of the usual multitude of Spanish fans high drama was backed up by a number of sub-plots culminating in a ferocious record-breaking 500 race where the two remaining grand masters seized control of the high ground, and set the pace for the rest of the year.

This last made a fine sporting contest. Schwantz was on form on the 1994 prototype that had won at Suzuka; Doohan's Honda had joined the Back to the Future movement as well, to devastating effect. Basically using '92-pattern rear suspension linkage parts, which he'd finally received as requested for tests the week before at Jarama, Doohan rather anxiously revealed that he felt he'd been deceived. 'Don't bag [criticise] Honda too much, but we knew what we wanted, and they told us they gave it to us at Suzuka. But the parts were a joke. I only used them for three laps. What they gave us wasn't what they said they'd given us.'

Now he felt vindicated. The bike was working rather than fighting over the bumps, and a tendency to a punishing sort of hydraulic lock-up was gone. He could use the NSR's power out of the corners rather than shredding the tyres with it. In turn his team had been able to improve the front, and now Mick had the bike he'd been asking for.

The contrast between the two clear class leaders was finally resolved by a daring move from Doohan putting two back-markers between them five laps from the end, separating the Honda and the Suzuki for the first time all race. From then on Doohan sprinted to the flag, scything through the traffic, taking wide sweeping lines and blowing out of the bends in smooth, controlled slides, breaking the record three laps from the end. Schwantz was even faster, smashing the new record twice in the last two laps, making up time with superbly controlled late braking, rear wheel airborne as often as not, never looking risky, but ultimately not fast enough. Head and shoulders above the other 500 class riders, this was a display of brilliance to be remembered.

By contrast, the race saw the collapse of the works Yamahas. First the support act was summarily removed, with the sombre announcement from Christian Sarron that after the loss of their tobacco compensation cash, Yamaha Motor France was pulling out of everything except the factory-backed Harada 250 effort. Then there was the retirement of both Team Marlboro Roberts bikes from the race. Cadalora had a deflating rear tyre – a faulty valve; Beattie pitted saying his front tyre made the bike 'unridable'. (Dunlop's face was saved somewhat by Niall Mackenzie riding a blinder to finish eighth, close behind a much-revived Chandler on the Cagiva.) The Anglo-Japanese firm had brought a Michelin-like half-size 16.5-in. front tyre to Jerez, used by Abe and Honma in Japan, and now mainly for Beattie. But he didn't choose to race on it.

There was another fine to-do in the 250 class, very like what had happened to the 500s in Australia, when the leaders were given the chequered flag while in among a bunch of back-markers, causing confusion among some of those as yet unlapped. The stewards decreed that results should be taken from the lap before, one effect of which was to reinstate Christian Boudinot as a finisher, in 23rd place. Rather more seriously, it also reshuffled third and fourth places, giving the honour to Waldmann over Okada. The Japanese rider's team boss very properly protested, and a further FIM commission overturned the stewards' decision, reinstating Okada. Waldmann took it like a man. 'He deserved third more than me. Anyway, one of these days I'll get a rostrum finish without any help from the stewards.'

75

SPANISH GRAND PRIX

500 cc PRACTICE

The closing 15 minutes of practice were a race in themselves as times tumbled again and again, and pole changed hands three times.

Schwantz had been on top, then Doohan nosed ahead, only to be displaced by lap record-holder Barros. Then, with seconds to spare, Schwantz dashed out and set the seal on his first pole of the year with a sizzling lap, well inside the record, and half a second better than his time of the day before.

This shuffling affected the whole front row. With 15 minutes to go, Reggiani was fourth. Then Chandler knocked him down, only to be consigned to fifth himself by team-mate Kocinski, then sixth by rookie Puig. These tumbling times were helped by cooler weather on Saturday, making the surface more grippy.

Schwantz's pole confirmed his change of fortunes in ditching the flawed new 'production' chassis. Replacements were on the way; he rode the prototype, and said: 'It's not perfect, but we took a step back to get a good direction. Mainly I'm working on suspension to improve stability under braking, and generally making the bike easier to ride.'

Kocinski had switched – with Chandler – to trying Cagiva's anti-dive, though he wasn't sure he would use it for the race. Altogether he was confused, lacking the sense of direction of the first two races, in and out of the pits making changes. 'We were faster when we tested here, and the bike just isn't the same. Even the data readouts are different, though nothing major has changed. I've just been working to get it the way it was then,' he said.

He was less than two-tenths down on Schwantz, with Doohan third, less than one-tenth behind. 'The bike's better, but our speed advantage isn't worth much here – the track is all acceleration, and even the Cagiva seems as quick as us.' Significantly, his team recorded much less tyre wear with the new suspension.

Barros was still testing Brembos, as well as the team's usual AP brakes, and now finding the latter working better at a track where brakes are used hard. With them he claimed his first front-row place of the year. Some two-tenths down on Doohan, he was confident he could run with the leaders. 'Having strong tyres in the second half will decide the race.'

Puig moved through to head the second row in the closing minutes, still insisting he was only learning how to ride a 500. 'It seems that 500s suit me better than 250s, perhaps because I did a lot of motocross riding when I was younger' was his modest explanation of being able to lap just half a second slower than Schwantz.

Chandler was alongside, smiling for almost the first time all year as he finally joined the leading group. 'Things are a lot better than so far this year. I'm still having trouble getting the bike settled in the first part of the corner so I can get the power on early – it's hopping around.' He had discarded the anti-dive he used for the first three disappointing races.

Then came Reggiani's flying twin, close to a front-row start, with Loris saying he might have been faster still but for the need to do more rear-tyre testing on the slower of his pair of bikes. 'I'm happy with the second row, but I'd like to have been faster than the 250s,' he admitted. Schwantz had followed him during practice, and said: 'His mid-corner speed is higher than I could ever hope to achieve, and the bike is fast, though I was able to get four or five lengths on it on the straights.'

Criville completed the second row, after a mediocre start to practice, searching for front-end adhesion.

Even more mediocre was the performance of the works Yamahas, with both Cadalora and Beattie complaining of a lack of front-wheel grip, even with the new 16.5-in. front Dunlops that had arrived on Saturday. 'Trying tyres you've never seen before is not the way to go GP racing,' commented Cadalora, who had been in the top four on Fri-

SPANISH GRAND PRIX

Michael Doohan muscled past Kevin Schwantz on the back straight: soon Alex Barros and John Kocinski will be left behind.

Below left: Barros observes silence in memory of fellow-Brazilian Ayrton Senna, killed at Imola just one week before.

day, but dropped away to ninth, leading row three, when he failed to improve.

Itoh was alongside, complaining of continuing carburation problems and reluctant steering. Then came Beattie, who had been way off the pace on Friday, but cut 2.3 seconds off his time with the new Dunlops on Saturday. 'This is the biggest progress we've made this year,' he said.

Mackenzie completed row three, but suffered a massive crankshaft bearing failure that meant his best time remained the one he had set on Friday: a luckless season so far.

Reynolds led row four, growing disgruntled at having to work so hard for a relatively lowly position. 'There's just nothing we can do to get with the works bikes,' the Briton said. Then came Irishman McWilliams, Belgian Naveau and Roc-mounted Bernard Garcia, running with a white fairing after losing Yamaha France backing.

All 32 entrants qualified.

500 cc RACE – 27 LAPS

Barros rocketed off in the lead, pursued by Schwantz; but Kocinski in a hurry drove around the outside into second before the first downhill run. Then he tried to dive inside Barros at the final hairpin, and came close to ending his race right there as the back of the Cagiva tried to overtake the front. He was using the anti-dive, but only his skill could save him from having braked far too late.

John's unseemly haste followed an unsettling start, with his bike hesitating on the warm-up lap. He'd wanted to change to his spare, but it was too late. Now he tucked into fifth behind Criville, as Schwantz lined up to take the lead; by lap three Doohan was also ahead of Barros, while Kocinski had repassed Criville and both had joined up behind, though the Spaniard soon had a big slide and lost touch.

The remaining quartet lasted until lap 12, when Barros started to run into tyre problems and gradually dropped back. This was Kocinski's signal to move past and stay with Schwantz and Doohan, but Barros's late braking made it impossible. Once again the American tried too hard at the hairpin, and though he got ahead briefly, it was only to run wide and slip even further back. 'The only way to pass here is under brakes, and Barros is really late so he slows you up mid-corner,' said Kocinski later. 'I was real frustrated. I was gonna get by him one way or another even if both of us didn't finish.' It took him until lap 18 before he was finally past Alex – but by then he was several seconds behind the leaders, and unable to close the gap.

Not surprisingly, since the pace up front was furious.

Doohan had led for the first time on the seventh lap, moving smoothly past Schwantz at the end of the back straight, but he couldn't get away. Both riders were close to the limit, with Doohan taking sweeping lines and a faster exit speed. This meant Schwantz had trouble getting close enough to exploit his superior braking and tighter corner entries.

He managed it at the end of the pit straight at the start of lap 13, but it was a narrow lead and lasted only two more laps until he ran wide into the last slow right before the run back to the paddock area. This was partially deliberate; having failed to get away, he thought he'd shadow the Honda and wait until the end of the race to attack. All the while, the two most experienced 500 riders drew inexorably away from the Cagiva as they approached the final showdown.

The next crucial development came five laps from the end. They had already started lapping; now they came upon a group of riders – Jeandat, Marc Garcia, Foray and Miralles. The breaks came up just right for Doohan, who swooped in among them to put two between himself and Schwantz at the Dry Sack hairpin. By the time they emerged on the other side of the pack, he'd turned a gap of three-tenths into almost a full second, and now Schwantz had his work cut out.

Kevin went to it with a will, closing up a fraction every lap, even though Doohan was himself speeding up, breaking the record for the first time on lap 24. Schwantz broke the old record too, on lap 25, smashed the new one on lap 26, then again on lap 27. He was almost on the Honda's back wheel. But the race was one lap too short for him, and just right for Doohan, and the Australian won by just under half a second.

Kocinski was nine seconds back, Barros another four behind; and Criville not only hung on to fifth for his own best finish of the year, but came close to challenging the Brazilian. He had earlier managed to escape from sixth-placed Puig, who ran into tyre problems.

They were a long way clear of Chandler in seventh. The American made a bad gamble on a harder compound rear tyre, and had his hands full all race with a determined Mackenzie, who eventually finished less than two seconds behind the works Cagiva.

Reggiani's V-twin Aprilia settled straight into a lonely position between the better works riders and the second-level pack. Much as predicted, he lacked the wherewithal to attack those ahead of him, but had the speed to escape all the privateers except Mackenzie.

Reynolds was tenth and McWilliams 11th, the last riders on the same lap as the leaders; the remaining points went to Migliorati, Lopez Mella, Jeandat and Miralles.

The Yamahas went early. Cadalora had managed to pass Reggiani after a slow start, only to feel the back end go queasy as his rear tyre deflated, the wheel valve seal failed. He pitted after nine laps. Beattie lasted two more before he found his position of 11th insupportable but impossible to improve upon, with his front tyre sliding around. He retired in high dudgeon. Itoh crashed out while lying seventh with 13 laps to go.

250 cc PRACTICE

Capirossi and Biaggi had shared all the pole positions so far this year, and this time it was Loris's turn on the Honda, equalling the tally. He claimed the place most emphatically in the closing stages, fitting a softer rear Dunlop to whizz round 1.5 seconds faster than his own previous best, and a full half-second ahead of Biaggi – an advantage he didn't expect to have with the bike in racing trim.

Max was second, the Aprilia rider saying that in windy conditions on Friday 'the bike felt like a snake'. He and his team-mates, Ruggia and Bayle, were still using the 1993-and-a-half bike. Quickest on Friday, he said: 'The reed-valve Hondas have an advantage in acceleration – our disc-valve engine is more brutal out

77

SPANISH GRAND PRIX

of the slow corners, and there are many here.'

Okada's Michelins worked better here and he was only thousandths slower in third. He liked the track, comparing it to 'some Japanese circuits, especially Sugo', adding: 'Anyway, I expect to go better at a lot of European tracks where I am now racing for the second time.'

Ruggia concluded the front row. The Aprilia man had been testing a carbon-fibre swing arm, but took it off on the second day. 'It is no good to test new equipment at a race,' he said. He also complained about the difficulties in carburating the new low-lead gas. 'You get it right, then the weather changes and it's wrong again.'

The front row was covered by almost nine-tenths, thanks to Capirossi's time; Romboni missed getting on it by two-tenths, the Honda man still troubled by chatter and suspension problems that kept him short of his old rival Capirossi. New team-mate Waldmann was alongside, and had even been ahead at one point, already looking at a front-row start. Then came Aoki and D'Antin for an all-NSR row.

Zeelenberg led row three, beginning to pick up the pace as he adapted back to the Honda, with Bosshard alongside on another NSR; then Bayle's factory Aprilia with Jurgen van den Goorbergh's Yokohama-shod private Aprilia alongside in his best-ever position.

Harada was 15th fastest, on the fourth row and expecting to get slower as the race wore on, because the heavy braking here was punishing his hand; Jimmy Filice – again substituting for Roberts Junior on the other Yamaha TZ-M – was 18th, progress slowed still further by yet another engine blow-up. Team boss Rainey acknowledged: 'Jimbo would probably be faster on the stock TZ he raced in the US.'

There were 34 qualifiers, among them Jamie Robinson, the Briton taking over from Suzuka crasher Rodney Fee on the Team Cotoni Honda.

250 cc RACE – 26 LAPS

Biaggi led the first two laps from Capirossi and a gaggle, then on the third he made a slip, dropping to fourth and giving team-mate Ruggia the chance to swoop through from third to first. The other guest at the party was Romboni, third briefly, but behind Biaggi again by the end of the lap.

Okada was hanging grimly on behind while Waldmann and Aoki were catching up fast, so that by lap nine there were seven contesting the lead.

There wasn't a great deal of switching around, though Waldmann got ahead of both Japanese riders, who seemed to be fading. Then he came close to crashing at the hairpin and lost ground himself.

Biaggi and Capirossi changed places a few times, but Ruggia was in control. The picture changed on the 21st lap, though. Ruggia said later that imperfect chassis settings were punishing his tyres, and rather than risk crashing he dropped back to third.

Now Capirossi decided the time had come to run for it. At once he opened up half a second on Biaggi, and seemed set to make it even more. Biaggi couldn't bear to see it.

'I'd been having trouble with the back wheel coming up under brakes all race,' he said. Braking later into the hairpin than ever, it happened again – but he didn't have time to let it drop again before he had to turn the bike. The machine tried to swap ends, and when it landed it spat him over the high-side.

Now surely Capirossi had the race in the bag. His lead was better than 1.5 seconds and growing. Two corners later it was all over. 'What an incredible race,' he said. 'I felt I had timed it perfectly and I was sure of victory. Then my crankshaft broke.'

Ruggia had been prepared to settle for third or fourth, to avoid risks, but now saw the chance of victory, and seized it, upping his pace once more. But it was no easy ride, for all the ups and downs had given the others a chance to close up as well, and the Frenchman had Romboni pushing very hard while fighting the slides. Waldmann and Okada were there too, with only Aoki unable to join in.

At the last gasp, Ruggia held off Romboni, while Okada nipped past Waldmann. But it turned out not to be the last gasp after all. That had already happened, adjudged the stewards, the lap before, as a result of confusion with back-markers taking an early flag, in a very similar incident to that which spoiled the Australian 500 GP. The one who suffered most was Okada, who dropped from third to fourth, but of course there were others too.

One was Harada, who had surprised himself by forgetting about his painful hand and getting faster instead of slower to pull through from 16th on lap one. The World Champion battled for a while with Suter, then moved ahead of the Swiss Aprilia rider to close up on the next group. In the closing stages this was headed by D'Antin's NSR, which had itself been caught by a race-long battle between Zeelenberg and Bayle. On the final lap Harada was right behind D'Antin – but the lap before, when the results were eventually taken – he'd been behind Bayle. Thus it was Aoki fifth, then D'Antin, Bayle, Harada and Zeelenberg, with Suter three seconds back in tenth.

The next group had seen Jurgen van den Goorbergh and Carlos Checa (Honda) caught by Andy Preining's ex-works Aprilia. The Austrian seized and retired with three laps left, and Checa was some three seconds ahead of Jurgen at the finish. Next came Kassner and wild card Castilla, with Cardoso taking the final point.

There were 25 finishers, and Filice was not among them – he'd crashed out unhurt before half-distance while trying to recover from a poor start.

It was all changed back by the next race, after Team Kanemoto Honda successfully protested. Now there were 24 finishers, with Boudinot out because he took the flag too early. Among the points, Okada regained third from Waldmann, Harada seventh from Bayle, and Castilla 13th from Kassner. For those who think last-lap efforts should be rewarded, justice was done.

Either way, Okada had gained the championship lead. Japan's best rider this year still had some hard tracks to follow, but he wasn't ready to succumb to the usual Japanese problem of leaving home to go slower.

125 cc RACE – 23 LAPS

Works Aprilia rider Kazuto Sakata had claimed pole with an astonishing advantage of 1.2 seconds over second-placed Dirk Raudies's Honda, so it was not terribly surprising that after taking the lead on the third lap he galloped away into the distance, as he'd done in Australia. Ten seconds clear by half-distance, he could wave to the crowd on the last lap and still win by seven seconds.

Raudies had led the first two laps, but he was hurting all over after a heavy fall in the final practice session, and was particularly troubled by a painful throttle hand, so it was no surprise that he dropped back as the race wore on.

From laps five to seven he was pushed back to third by multi-champion Jorge Martinez on the new Yamaha. Like the Aprilia, the power deficit against the Honda was more than compensated for by the chassis's sweet handling – then a partial seizure suddenly dropped the Yamaha to ninth, in the middle of a huge pack.

Back in Europe, the European riders were still confident they could at least teach the other Japanese riders a lesson; the Aprilias of Öttl and Torrontegui both passed Raudies in one lap and took up the pursuit, to finish second and third, clear of the brawl behind.

In the closing stages, Ueda broke free from the rumble to overtake Raudies, whose resistance was tempered by caution because of his injuries. He was a close fifth, just one-tenth behind the Japanese rider.

Then came a grisly gang, which included the returned injury victim

---

Jean-Philippe Ruggia leads Loris Capirossi, Max Biaggi (yellow helmet) and Ralf Waldmann: two out of four would not finish.

Inset: Peter Öttl and Herri Torrontegui (right) lend a rare European flavour to the all-Aprilia 125 rostrum as they flank Kazuto Sakata.

Katoh, on the second Yamaha, and Honda-mounted veteran Akira Saito, until they crashed out together with eight laps left.

This left Tsujimura, Koch and Bodelier (Hondas), Martinez and Tokudome (another Honda) locked in combat, and they filled sixth to tenth places at the flag, covered by less than three seconds.

McCoy was 11th, after overtaking the slowing Perugini on the last lap. The Hondas of Haruchika Aoki and Casanova took the last points behind 13th-placed Petrucciani – the Swiss rider had crashed and remounted on lap two, to catch up with the top ten from 19th spot.

Honda riders Neil Hodgson and Fausto Gresini also crashed out, the former happily uninjured after being knocked out in a heavy high-sider.

FIM WORLD CHAMPIONSHIP • ROUND 4
GRAN PREMIO PEPSI DE ESPAÑA
8 MAY 1994

500 cc

27 laps, 74.196 miles/119.421 km

Place	Rider	Nat.	Machine	Laps	Time & speed	Fastest lap	Lap
1	Michael Doohan	AUS	Honda	27	47m 31.082s 93.696 mph/ 150.790 km/h	1m 44.258s	27
2	Kevin Schwantz	USA	Suzuki	27	47m 31.571s	1m 44.168s	27
3	John Kocinski	USA	Cagiva	27	47m 40.347s	1m 45.056s	17
4	Alexandre Barros	BR	Suzuki	27	47m 44.340s	1m 45.275s	5
5	Alex Criville	E	Honda	27	47m 45.907s	1m 45.240s	21
6	Alberto Puig	E	Honda	27	47m 52.204s	1m 45.356s	17
7	Doug Chandler	USA	Cagiva	27	48m 09.874s	1m 46.122s	18
8	Niall Mackenzie	GB	Yamaha	27	48m 11.441s	1m 46.293s	4
9	Loris Reggiani	I	Aprilia	27	48m 16.748s	1m 46.224s	10
10	John Reynolds	GB	Yamaha	27	48m 56.374s	1m 47.302s	4
11	Jeremy McWilliams	GB	Yamaha	27	49m 07.476s	1m 48.126s	6
12	Cristiano Migliorati	I	Yamaha	26	47m 47.106s	1m 48.645s	8
13	Juan Lopez Mella	E	Yamaha	26	47m 54.876s	1m 49.620s	8
14	Jean-Pierre Jeandat	F	Yamaha	26	47m 55.396s	1m 49.124s	26
15	Julian Miralles	E	Yamaha	26	47m 55.488s	1m 49.702s	20
16	Marc Garcia	F	Yamaha	26	48m 01.420s	1m 49.802s	7
17	Jean Foray	F	Yamaha	26	48m 01.822s	1m 49.550s	9
18	Andreas Leuthe	D	Yamaha	26	48m 02.137s	1m 49.366s	9
19	Cees Doorakkers	NL	Yamaha	26	48m 25.212s	1m 50.179s	26
20	Bernard Hänggeli	CH	Yamaha	26	49m 08.252s	1m 49.637s	18
21	Lothar Neukirchner	D	Yamaha	25	48m 00.862s	1m 52.870s	3
	Laurent Naveau	B	Yamaha	25	DNF	1m 47.910s	4
	Shinichi Itoh	J	Honda	14	DNF	1m 46.155s	5
	Daryl Beattie	AUS	Yamaha	11	DNF	1m 46.816s	5
	Lucio Pedercini	I	Yamaha	10	DNF	1m 49.850s	3
	Luca Cadalora	I	Yamaha	9	DNF	1m 46.544s	5
	Vittorio Scatola	I	Paton	6	DNF	1m 52.102s	6
	Marco Papa	I	Yamaha	5	DNF	1m 51.431s	4
	Bernard Garcia	F	Yamaha	2	DNF	1m 56.822s	1
	Kevin Mitchell	GB	Yamaha	1	DNF	2m 00.528s	1
	Bruno Bonhuil	F	Yamaha	1	DNF	2m 01.882s	1
	Sean Emmett	GB	Yamaha	0	DNF		

Fastest lap: Schwantz, 1m 44.168s, 94.981 mph/152.857 km/h (record).
Previous record: Alexandre Barros, BR (Suzuki), 1m 44.659s, 94.535 mph/152.140 km/h (1993).

Qualifying: 1 Schwantz, 1m 43.944s; 2 Kocinski, 1m 44.103s; 3 Doohan, 1m 44.192s; 4 Barros, 1m 44.363s; 5 Puig, 1m 44.440s; 6 Chandler, 1m 44.738s; 7 Reggiani, 1m 45.168s; 8 Criville, 1m 45.174s; 9 Cadalora, 1m 45.340s; 10 Itoh, 1m 45.461s; 11 Beattie, 1m 45.718s; 12 Mackenzie, 1m 46.562s; 13 Reynolds, 1m 46.647s; 14 McWilliams, 1m 46.825s; 15 Naveau, 1m 47.257s; 16 B. Garcia, 1m 47.402s; 17 Lopez Mella, 1m 47.794s; 18 Emmett, 1m 47.852s; 19 Migliorati, 1m 47.976s; 20 Miralles, 1m 49.112s; 21 Hänggeli, 1m 49.168s; 22 Mitchell, 1m 49.519s; 23 Foray, 1m 49.536s; 24 Bonhuil, 1m 49.679s; 25 Jeandat, 1m 49.757s; 26 M. Garcia, 1m 49.804s; 27 Leuthe, 1m 50.196s; 28 Papa, 1m 50.306s; 29 Scatola, 1m 50.448s; 30 Pedercini, 1m 50.791s; 31 Doorakkers, 1m 51.665s; 32 Neukirchner, 1m 52.608s.

World Championship: 1 M. Doohan, 86; 2 Kocinski and Schwantz, 68; 4 Cadalora, 46; 5 Itoh, 43; 6 Barros, 41; 7 Criville and Puig, 38; 9 Chandler, 29; 10 Reynolds, 20; 11 Mackenzie, 13; 12 B. Garcia, Honma and McWilliams, 10; 15 Lopez Mella and Reggiani, 7; 17 Beattie, 6; 18 Emmett and Migliorati, 5; 20 S. Doohan, 4; 21 Jeandat and Naveau, 2; 23 Miralles and Pedercini, 1.

CIRCUITO DE JEREZ

PELUQUI • EXPO 92 • ANGEL NIETO • MICHELIN • DUCADOS • DRY SACK

CIRCUIT LENGTH: 2.748 MILES/4.423 KM

250 cc

26 laps, 71.448 miles/114.998 km

Place	Rider	Nat.	Machine	Laps	Time & speed	Fastest lap	Lap
1	Jean-Philippe Ruggia	F	Aprilia	26	46m 16.824s 92.640 mph/ 149.089 km/h	1m 46.240s	3
2	Doriano Romboni	I	Honda	26	46m 17.471s	1m 46.286s	4
3	Tadayuki Okada	J	Honda	26	46m 17.579s	1m 46.233s	13
4	Ralf Waldmann	D	Honda	26	46m 17.780s	1m 46.003s	8
5	Nobuatsu Aoki	J	Honda	26	46m 25.292s	1m 46.214s	13
6	Luis D'Antin	E	Honda	26	46m 48.406s	1m 46.791s	4
7	Tetsuya Harada	J	Yamaha	26	46m 48.518s	1m 46.996s	19
8	Jean-Michel Bayle	F	Aprilia	26	46m 48.638s	1m 47.300s	21
9	Wilco Zeelenberg	NL	Honda	26	46m 49.092s	1m 47.432s	6
10	Eskil Suter	CH	Aprilia	26	46m 54.132s	1m 46.931s	18
11	Carlos Checa	E	Honda	26	47m 05.235s	1m 47.834s	9
12	Jurgen van den Goorbergh	NL	Aprilia	26	47m 08.652s	1m 47.763s	14
13	Miguel Castilla	E	Yamaha	26	47m 25.858s	1m 48.413s	13
14	Bernd Kassner	D	Aprilia	26	47m 26.000s	1m 48.554s	14
15	José Luis Cardoso	E	Aprilia	26	47m 30.905s	1m 48.656s	11
16	Oscar Sainz	E	Yamaha	26	47m 38.560s	1m 48.754s	7
17	Alessandro Gramigni	I	Aprilia	26	47m 47.737s	1m 49.243s	14
18	Frédéric Protat	F	Honda	26	47m 57.364s	1m 49.583s	24
19	Luis Maurel	E	Honda	26	47m 58.323s	1m 49.520s	6
20	Patrick van den Goorbergh	NL	Aprilia	26	48m 04.754s	1m 49.496s	24
21	Giuseppe Fiorillo	I	Honda	25	46m 28.460s	1m 49.691s	6
22	Jamie Robinson	GB	Honda	25	46m 32.790s	1m 49.977s	7
23	Enrique de Juan	E	Aprilia	25	46m 59.469s	1m 51.294s	22
24	Kristian Kaas	SF	Yamaha	25	46m 59.582s	1m 51.498s	22
	Christian Boudinot	F	Aprilia	24	DNF	1m 50.196s	5
	Loris Capirossi	I	Honda	22	DNF	1m 45.902s	9
	Andy Preining	A	Aprilia	22	DNF	1m 47.518s	11
	Massimiliano Biaggi	I	Aprilia	21	DNF	1m 45.628s	12
	Manuel Hernandez	E	Aprilia	13	DNF	1m 52.215s	4
	Jim Filice	USA	Yamaha	11	DNF	1m 47.826s	7
	Adrian Bosshard	CH	Honda	9	DNF	1m 47.686s	3
	Alan Patterson	GB	Honda	5	DNF	1m 52.582s	5
	Adi Stadler	D	Honda	2	DNF	1m 49.314s	2
	Noel Ferro	F	Honda	0	DNF		

Fastest lap: Biaggi, 1m 45.628s, 93.668 mph/150.744 km/h (record).
Previous record: Tetsuya Harada, J (Yamaha), 1m 46.303s, 93.073 mph/149.787 km/h (1993).

Qualifying: **1** Capirossi, 1m 44.928s; **2** Biaggi, 1m 45.434s; **3** Okada, 1m 45.440s; **4** Ruggia, 1m 45.817s; **5** Romboni, 1m 46.031s; **6** Waldmann, 1m 46.069s; **7** Aoki, 1m 46.071s; **8** D'Antin, 1m 46.576s; **9** Zeelenberg, 1m 46.886s; **10** Bosshard, 1m 47.000s; **11** Bayle, 1m 47.012s; **12** J. van den Goorbergh, 1m 47.036s; **13** Preining, 1m 47.614s; **14** Checa, 1m 47.633s; **15** Harada, 1m 47.802s; **16** Kassner, 1m 48.053s; **17** Gramigni, 1m 48.066s; **18** Filice, 1m 48.396s; **19** Cardoso, 1m 48.467s; **20** Suter, 1m 48.561s; **21** Sainz, 1m 48.952s; **22** Fiorillo, 1m 49.130s; **23** Castilla, 1m 49.133s; **24** Maurel, 1m 49.230s; **25** Protat, 1m 49.293s; **26** Stadler, 1m 49.528s; **27** P. van den Goorbergh, 1m 49.854s; **28** Ferro, 1m 50.311s; **29** Kaas, 1m 50.680s; **30** Robinson, 1m 51.334s; **31** Boudinot, 1m 51.380s; **32** de Juan, 1m 51.929s; **33** Hernandez, 1m 52.038s; **34** Patterson, 1m 52.501s.

World Championship: **1** Okada, 72; **2** Biaggi, 63; **3** Romboni, 61; **4** Ruggia, 60; **5** Capirossi, 52; **6** D'Antin and Waldmann, 32; **8** N. Aoki, 29; **9** Bayle, 28; **10** Zeelenberg, 21; **11** Harada and Ukawa, 16; **13** Checa, 12; **14** T. Aoki, 11; **15** Suter and J. van den Goorbergh, 8; **17** Bosshard and Preining, 7; **19** Gramigni, 6; **20** Connell, 5; **21** Kassner, 4; **22** Castilla, Stadler and P. van den Goorbergh, 3; **25** Cardoso, 1.

125 cc

23 laps, 63.204 miles/101.729 km

Place	Rider	Nat.	Machine	Laps	Time & speed	Fastest lap	Lap
1	Kazuto Sakata	J	Aprilia	23	43m 05.188s 88.025 mph/ 141.663 km/h	1m 51.470s	11
2	Peter Öttl	D	Aprilia	23	43m 11.990s	1m 51.333s	9
3	Herri Torrontegui	E	Aprilia	23	43m 15.236s	1m 51.806s	11
4	Noboru Ueda	J	Honda	23	43m 16.838s	1m 51.913s	14
5	Dirk Raudies	D	Honda	23	43m 17.371s	1m 52.022s	4
6	Takeshi Tsujimura	J	Honda	23	43m 31.546s	1m 52.556s	13
7	Oliver Koch	D	Honda	23	43m 32.169s	1m 52.494s	2
8	Loek Bodelier	NL	Honda	23	43m 32.510s	1m 52.686s	8
9	Jorge Martinez	E	Yamaha	23	43m 33.075s	1m 52.065s	4
10	Masaki Tokudome	J	Honda	23	43m 34.651s	1m 52.686s	15
11	Garry McCoy	AUS	Aprilia	23	43m 41.087s	1m 53.044s	8
12	Stefano Perugini	I	Aprilia	23	43m 41.336s	1m 52.673s	7
13	Oliver Petrucciani	CH	Aprilia	23	44m 06.721s	1m 52.368s	21
14	Haruchika Aoki	J	Honda	23	44m 11.663s	1m 54.262s	3
15	Bruno Casanova	I	Honda	23	44m 11.746s	1m 54.025s	2
16	Frédéric Petit	F	Yamaha	23	44m 11.788s	1m 54.292s	6
17	Hans Spaan	NL	Honda	23	44m 12.400s	1m 53.850s	9
18	Gabriele Debbia	I	Aprilia	23	44m 12.806s	1m 54.270s	18
19	Antonio Sanchez	E	Honda	23	44m 29.104s	1m 54.778s	9
20	Juan Maturana	E	Yamaha	23	44m 32.586s	1m 54.700s	7
21	Vittorio Lopez	I	Honda	23	44m 33.428s	1m 55.046s	21
22	Manfred Baumann	A	Yamaha	23	44m 33.718s	1m 54.856s	21
23	Masafumi Ono	J	Honda	23	44m 43.164s	1m 55.638s	11
24	Nicolas Dussauge	F	Honda	23	44m 49.782s	1m 55.606s	17
	Akira Saito	J	Honda	15	DNF	1m 52.948s	5
	Yoshiaki Katoh	J	Yamaha	15	DNF	1m 52.148s	9
	Emili Alzamora	E	Honda	10	DNF	1m 53.961s	2
	Neil Hodgson	GB	Honda	6	DNF	1m 54.163s	2
	Manfred Geissler	D	Aprilia	4	DNF	1m 53.995s	2
	Daniela Tognoli	I	Aprilia	4	DNF	2m 00.273s	4
	Tomoko Igata	J	Honda	3	DNF	1m 57.631s	3
	Stefan Prein	D	Yamaha	2	DNF	1m 55.056s	2
	Fausto Gresini	I	Honda	0	DNF		
	Lucio Cecchinello	I	Honda	0	DNF		
	Hideyuki Nakajyo	J	Honda	0	DNF		

Fastest lap: Öttl, 1m 51.333s, 88.869 mph/143.020 km/h (record).
Previous record: Ralf Waldmann, D (Aprilia), 1m 51.989s, 88.348 mph/142.182 km/h (1993).

Qualifying: **1** Sakata, 1m 50.210s; **2** Raudies, 1m 51.422s; **3** Öttl, 1m 51.474s; **4** Martinez, 1m 51.562s; **5** Ueda, 1m 51.658s; **6** Torrontegui, 1m 51.863s; **7** Tsujimura, 1m 51.930s; **8** Saito, 1m 51.969s; **9** Gresini, 1m 51.976s; **10** Petrucciani, 1m 52.106s; **11** Tokudome, 1m 52.288s; **12** Koch, 1m 52.422s; **13** McCoy, 1m 52.426s; **14** Bodelier, 1m 52.584s; **15** Prein, 1m 52.672s; **16** Alzamora, 1m 52.734s; **17** Perugini, 1m 52.966s; **18** Debbia, 1m 52.988s; **19** Hodgson, 1m 53.030s; **20** Igata, 1m 53.046s; **21** Katoh, 1m 53.050s; **22** Geissler, 1m 53.070s; **23** Aoki, 1m 53.134s; **24** Cecchinello, 1m 53.158s; **25** Spaan, 1m 53.380s; **26** Nakajyo, 1m 53.501s; **27** Casanova, 1m 53.545s; **28** Maturana, 1m 53.993s; **29** Petit, 1m 54.049s; **30** Sanchez, 1m 54.370s; **31** Baumann, 1m 55.111s; **32** Dussauge, 1m 55.554s; **33** Ono, 1m 55.820s; **34** Tognoli, 1m 55.988s; **35** Lopez, 1m 56.045s.

World Championship: **1** Sakata, 90; **2** Öttl, 53; **3** Ueda, 47; **4** Tsujimura, 46; **5** Torrontegui, 39; **6** McCoy and Martinez, 32; **8** Raudies, 30; **9** Saito, 29; **10** Tokudome, 25; **11** Gresini and Petrucciani, 23; **13** Nakajyo, 22; **14** Bodelier, 18; **15** Koch, 15; **16** Aoki and Casanova, 8; **18** Amano, Perugini and Scalvini, 4; **21** Debbia, 3; **22** Geissler and Igata, 2; **24** Prein, 1.

WORLD CHAMPIONSHIP • ROUND 5

AUSTRIAN GRAND PRIX

500 cc	DOOHAN
250 cc	CAPIROSSI
125 cc	RAUDIES

'Austria's race has scenic beauty like other tracks have gravel traps'

Photos: Gold & Goose

The Salzburgring saw Michael Doohan chalking up number two in a record string of consecutive wins. It also marked the end of the silly season. There has never been anything faintly silly about this fearsome circuit in the Alpine foothills, however. The prevailing mood is always sombre in the picturesque little valley, with its tunnel of Armco sweeping ludicrously fast across one hillside, then chicaning back along the valley floor.

Suzuka notwithstanding (and that was too far away to count), this was the first time in 1994 that the 500 riders could really measure out their power. The run up the hillside is taken wide open, running from second through to sixth gear, ending in a back-one-gear right, taken on the brink under braking. It's one of the clearest demonstrations of sheer courage all year – and also one of the most dangerous single corners – but the rest of what some whimsically call 'the back straight' tests nothing much more than pure power.

Inevitably one arrives with certain preconceptions. Usually they turn out to be correct, and were in any case already updated by IRTA tests the week before at Hockenheim, attended by all except Suzuki. They'd stayed on for private tests at Jerez. It was pretty certain that the Hondas would set the pace, the Cagivas would be found wanting, and the rest would slot in somewhere between. And that's how it turned out this year, with Yamaha's malaise deepening and the Suzukis improving, but still not quite *au point* either on power or the steadiness under braking that Schwantz can use to such good effect.

In fact, the official speed trap figures were again considered suspect because the timing loop was too late, after the very fastest bikes had already backed off; and it was late-braker Schwantz at the top of the tree at 297.8 km/h to Doohan's 296.0. Cadalora's Yamaha clocked 295.7, Criville's Honda 294.8, Chandler's Cagiva 294.7, with the 400 cc Aprilia 12th fastest at 288.0 km/h. Times for the others were probably more representative. Biaggi's Aprilia led the 250s at 263.7 km/h, followed by Aoki's Honda at 263.0, then Stadler's kitted RS Honda, tuned by Helmut Bradl's brother. 'The factory people can lease engines from us if they like,' joked Stadler. Tsujimura's airbox Honda was top 125 at 226.8 km/h, with Emilio Cuppini's factory Aprilia second at 224.3. Cuppini was

Left: **The Knockstein, a veritable miniature Matterhorn, is a Salzburgring icon, brooding over a gaggle of 125s. The name means 'cam'.**

En route to more ritual humiliation, the works Yamahas lead Lopez Mella's Roc down Austria's exclusive and unpopular driveway between pits and paddock.

riding as a substitute for the injured Gianluigi Scalvini, and qualified on the front row of the grid.

More important, however, is how quickly the bikes reach that speed, and the surging Hondas were definitely the best here, while the Yamahas and Cagivas lagged.

If this carried a sense of *déjà vu*, so be it. The phenomenon was repeated on a larger scale. This was only Doohan's second successive win, and his third of the year, but the way in which he did it was very reminiscent of the 1992 Honda steamroller. Kocinski was dropping out of the picture, nobody was coming forward to take his place, so Schwantz was left as the Australian's only title rival – and if he didn't start beating Doohan soon, he'd have to rely on breakdowns (unlikely) or injuries (sadly always possible) to keep him in touch.

Austria's race has scenic beauty and political problems like other tracks have gravel traps. These, along with a very poor crowd attendance, played a big role in there being no Austrian GP in 1992. There was still a continuing grumbling battle with local green party interests, who value the tranquillity and wildlife of this scenic valley far above the dubious privilege of hosting a GP. This year there were internal politics too, after a coup by burgeoning race promoter Steve McLaughlin, whose Moto-Motion company had ousted the long-time organisers, Arbo. McLaughlin, a former US racer, also promotes the GP at Brno, as well as the successful German Pro-Superbike series. Moto-Motion had cut ticket prices in a mainly successful attempt to bring the crowds back – they claimed a respectable 50,000; but bickering with track officials left McLaughlin so frustrated that soon afterwards he told *Motocourse*: 'There will be an Austrian GP next year, but it won't be at the Salzburgring.'

The crowd might have been even bigger but for the weather. After a week of benign sunshine, cloudbursts led to comprehensive flooding on the Thursday that had one car park knee-deep and turned the tunnel under the track into a raging torrent. This jeopardised the whole meeting, and old-timers were reminded of how the GP had been snowed off in 1980 (250 maestro Carlos Lavado was bemused by the blizzard – it was the first time the Venezuelan had ever seen snow). However, the waters subsided overnight, and while the rain returned intermittently during practice, race day was dry.

The track had gained a lot of airfence, most crucially at the right swerve that terminates the 'back straight'. Several people fell there, mostly in the wet, including Barros, Romboni and Maurel (together), Sakata and Tsujimura. This almost always involves stopping practice, and a tense wait for news of the victim: mercifully there were no serious injuries, though Sakata chipped a vertebra and Maurel broke his leg. The most serious injury of the weekend was two broken ankles, sustained elsewhere on the track by Japanese 125 racer Tomoko Igata, putting her out for several races.

The first chicane had also been revised. At the previous visit sloping kerbs had been installed, making it difficult for all but the most foolhardy to cut the second apex in the traditional way. More to the point, it made the same action more dangerous if it was done by mistake, since out-of-control riders would be launched skyward. The old almost-flush kerbing reappeared at the request of riders' rep, Franco Uncini, and cutting the corner was again obligatory for a fast lap. This spectacular and much-photographed activity was most memorably performed by Biaggi in the 250 race, filmed in slow motion as he hit the kerb with the front already tucking under, and landed on the far side in a motocrosser's flying W.

The Hondas were the target, and Suzuki had some new ammunition – an auxiliary suspension system that was literally shrouded in mystery, the mechanism kept firmly out of sight in a sort of sharks-fin cover on the rear swing arm behind the main suspension unit. Information was kept private too, on the grounds that 'some of the patents haven't been tied up yet'. This left the way clear for various fanciful theories, including one suggestion that it was an aerodynamic device which, by smoothing airflow past the rear wheel, improved the air cooling to the rear damper. Better-informed guesswork settled on a secondary or possibly even a primary damper, running directly between swing-arm and top suspension mount. This would give it a longer stroke than the usual damper operated by the spring's rising-rate linkage, offering less delicate adjustment parameters. It would also be damping wheel movement rather than spring compression, adding an interesting twist to the many ramifications of rising-rate systems. In any case, neither Schwantz nor Barros raced with it. It was seen again in Germany a fortnight later, then quietly disappeared for the next five races.

Suzuki also had a new fairing, with forward-facing engine air intakes in Honda-like vertical slots on the fairing uppers replacing the NACA ducts in the lower flanks. This meant a new ram-effect pressurised intake system like that already used by all the other factory teams, and nowadays even the top 125s. Suzuki took their time to follow the fashion, but the system worked, and stayed in place. 'It'll pull slightly taller gearing all the way up the hill,' said Schwantz.

Yamaha were still proceeding backwards, having shelved the 1994 frame for the present: even chief tester Randy Mamola was on the Roc-framed bike. Randy was at Austria, fresh from more tyre tests in Barcelona, while Dunlop had new 17-in. fronts, and a puzzled look. Both Team Roberts men were struggling, and on Sunday Cadalora pitted for a tyre change, going out again to use the rest of the race as a tyre test, as Beattie had done in Japan. But other Dunlop riders, like Puig and Mackenzie, were reporting no problems, while in the 250 class they reigned virtually supreme, if you considered Michelin-man Okada's title lead as a temporary aberration. Thus the problem must lie with the chassis or the riders, with Roberts admitting, 'We need better tyres than the others just to be in touch.'

The paddock population included Charlie Giro, the erratic 125 works Aprilia rider's 'mental problems' of a fortnight before apparently cured by sound advice from his sponsors, Ducados: 'Get back on that bike and ride it, or you're fired.' At the other end of the scale, Bernard Garcia was absent. With the collapse of Team Yamaha France he had been transferred, with his works 500 engine, to Team Roc, but his confidence had taken a knock and he was in no mood to try and rebuild it at a scary circuit like this one. His place was taken for one race by veteran endurance star Hervé Moineau.

Filice was back again, with the advent of Kenny Roberts Junior still uncertain – another round of X-rays was scheduled for the following week. Luckless so far, the US champion had been testing at Barcelona, and had at least managed to start setting up the bike. 'We made some fairly drastic changes, mainly chassis geometry. Now I feel I can ride hard. I don't know if my settings will be good for Junior, but they're better for my own self-respect.' Sadly, his luck didn't improve with his mood – he seized on the warm-up lap and missed the race; the other TZ-M Yamaha, ridden by Harada, went one lap further, seizing after the

83

AUSTRIAN GRAND PRIX

start. A similar problem afflicted Reggiani in the 500 race.

Carl Fogarty was present, with Dr Costa attending daily to the wrist the World Superbike star had broken the weekend before, while another non-participant also put in an appearance. Or at least his name did. For the first time rumours surfaced that Norifume Abe would be seen on one of Team Rainey's bikes before too much longer. This one would run and run.

Almost absent was Cagiva boss Claudio Castiglioni. His car had broken down en route, but instead of the kidnappers one might expect in Italy, this important captain of industry was recognised by some race fans, also on their way to the Salzburgring, as he stood beside the autostrada. He cadged a lift, and arrived just in time to miss a dinner held in his honour.

500 cc PRACTICE

The first day didn't count for much, with the track streaming wet and alarmingly slippery over the flat-out hill section – as Barros proved. Cadalora was fastest, then the amazing Puig in his first wet ride on a 500. They were followed by Doohan, Schwantz, Barros and Beattie. But with dry practice on Saturday and race day ditto, it meant a lot of work and risk (Doohan also fell, 'leaning it over too far' on a slower bend) for not very much reward. Riders were left with just one day to find the right gearing, chassis settings and tyres.

In the dry, Doohan's fast and now stable Honda was in complete control, simply whizzing past everything up the hill. It was fast in the turns too, which put him well ahead of most of the other Hondas. With the bike well set and the tyres chosen, the championship leader was able to wait deliberately for slower traffic and practise finding ways past it. 'The bike's the same as at Jerez. It should work well everywhere,' he said.

Schwantz had to work hard to get his Suzuki even close, with a string of desperate laps at the end that brought him to within just over sixtenths of the Honda, barely close enough for him to say: 'I think I can race with him if I can get his draft, but not beat him.' His difficulty was not so much speed as handling – 'moving around under brakes'. His best time came with the old non-ram fairing, but that was a matter of the better chassis being with the old fairing, and he swapped bodywork for the race.

Puig was third, his second time on the 500 front row. He praised the bike, but admitted, 'I don't like these really fast tracks.'

The last place on row one went to Barros, who was struggling against various minor misfortunes including an engine problem on the bike with the better chassis settings, and vice versa. He crashed for a second time in the last session at the slow chicane, luckily unhurt.

Criville led row two, his best placing this year, another beneficiary of Honda's generosity with top-end speed. He had been second at one point in the last session, but stopped for a new rear tyre and was too late to defend the position.

He was only half a second down on Schwantz, with Kocinski sixth, only half a tenth slower. The Cagiva looked strong throughout, and might have been higher, but Kocinski complained that his efforts at the end of the session had been thwarted by traffic.

Then came a relatively large gap to Cadalora, almost half a second down and complaining of continuing balance problems with the Yamaha, in spite of a batch of new tyres. 'I can only ride the bike to 75 per cent of my ability,' he complained.

Itoh was alongside to complete row two, only a tenth down, with his familiar trouble getting drive out of the bends. He had one bike fitted with the Mk2 fuel injection, which only made matters worse. He ran it in practice, but the slow-to-arrive machine was shelved before the race.

Chandler led row three, with Beattie alongside, two lame ducks showing slight if slow improvement. Importantly for both, they were on an upward curve.

At least they managed to outqualify Reggiani's V-twin Aprilia, 11th fastest, much higher than expected – especially since it was still running the Mk1 low-tune engine as at Jerez. Indeed the Italian was less than 10 km/h down on top speed, and reached his maximum very quickly. On the twists in Spain he'd been slower than the top 250; here he was a full second ahead.

Mackenzie completed row three in his usual top privateer position, but was far from happy after continuing engine problems meant that they'd again felt obliged to drop the Bartol power-up cylinders to go back to stock Yamaha parts for the Big Bang engine. 'It's nothing special. I like the track, but without speed up the hill you're lost,' he said. Ever the realist, he decided early on that he wouldn't overgear in the hope of picking up a factory bike tow up the hill.

Jeandat, in fine form, led row four from Reynolds, Naveau, McWilliams and Miralles. There were 30 qualifiers, with Neukirchner's Harris Yamaha and Scatola's Paton failing to make the cut.

Doohan (right) was untouchable now he had the suspension settled – an omen for the races to come. Schwantz (below left) was only able to fend off the attentions of Criville.

500 cc RACE – 29 LAPS

Puig leapt away in the lead, through the chicane and the first corner, but Doohan was second, and swept past on the first run up the hill to start working on a lead that rapidly became unassailable. He knew the main challenge would come from Schwantz, though he didn't know where his rival was. 'I could see his lap board and it didn't match my lap board, so I just worked on making sure nobody could get in my slipstream.' In the process he broke his own lap record on lap seven.

Schwantz had got off the line well, but then ran into a familiar intermittent Suzuki flooding problem. 'The second row and most of the third row came past me.' He ended lap one tenth, and though he carved through to second with typical assurance over the next four laps, Doohan was by then nearly four seconds gone and stretching away at almost half a second a lap. By the time he hit back-markers on lap 12 he was almost seven seconds clear.

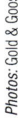

With Schwantz second, Puig dropped away gradually, but Criville went with the champion in his best race of the year, finishing less than three seconds behind the American. With 'perfect settings and tyres', plus an NSR up the hill, he was thrilled.

A little way back Puig had been joined by Kocinski and Itoh, who engaged in close combat until they ran into heavy lapped traffic with ten laps left. Puig lost touch in the mêlée, complaining later of some pain in his arm, while Kocinski moved ahead of the slithering Itoh, and seemed set to take fourth, only to run into more last-lap trouble. A hose-clip broke, and he could do nothing as his temperature gauge soared and Itoh came past again.

Well out of touch came Barros, the second Suzuki rider having started well, only to find that a tyre gamble simply hadn't paid off. The bike was sliding over the surface changes, and he got such a fright on the first lap that he didn't even try and fight, dropping back to a deeply disgruntled seventh. It might have been worse: as the race wore on, Chandler started to close up for what looked to be a last-lap challenge. Instead the American cruised into the pits with one lap to go, his Cagiva's temperature gauge also climbing as he lost coolant from a failed cylinder-base seal.

Another gap, then came Beattie. The Australian hadn't sparkled, but at least he'd kept going, saying later than his only problem was a shortage of horsepower up the hill. Teammate Cadalora had been in the top five, only to lose momentum and be passed by Beattie on lap 11, pitting soon afterwards to change both tyres before rejoining in last position to keep on testing.

This left ninth to Mackenzie, once again clearly the best privateer, and the last rider on the same lap as the leaders. Frustration was really setting in, as he saw his early hopes of getting among the works bikes recede yet again.

Reynolds was a solitary tenth, comfortably clear of a close six-bike battle that ended with Moineau taking 11th ahead of Emmett, Jeandat, Migliorati and Naveau, with McWilliams dropping off the back and out of the points after a big slide in the closing stages.

There were 22 finishers. Chandler aside, the most notable of the eight retirements was Reggiani, who toured into the pits at the end of the first lap shaking his head after a partial seizure at the end of the start straight.

250 cc PRACTICE

For the present, at least, the battle between Biaggi and Capirossi was as good natured as it was close. Honours for pole went to the former, by thousandths, with Aprilia and Honda very closely matched overall, having swapped ends over the winter. Now the Aprilia was faster, but the Honda handled better, an unthinkable equation one or two years ago.

Biaggi was anxious to draw attention to the fact that his time had come alone, whereas Capirossi's had not. 'People say I only go fast when I am following Loris, but not this time,' he said. Capirossi parried with, 'I followed Max, but I was on a part-worn tyre' – small debating advantages that mirrored their small differences on the track.

They were almost a second ahead of the two Japanese riders who completed the front row, with Okada the faster. The factory Honda rider complained of a little understeer through the chicane, but said he expected to race for the first time on the new 16.5-in. front tyre. 'I think the Michelin lasts better in the race than the Dunlops,' he said hopefully; adding, 'because I crashed here last year and spoiled my season I will be cautious tomorrow.'

AUSTRIAN GRAND PRIX

Main picture: The return of flush kerbing meant revived chicane-leaping antics, here demonstrated by Loris Capirossi and Max Biaggi.

Centre left: The race for third in the 250 class – Romboni, Waldmann, Okada.

Bottom left: Austria brings out the pensive side in most riders, especially if – like Alex Barros – they've survived a spill at one of the most dangerous spots of the season.

Bottom right: Twin Peaks – Sakata's streamlined hunchback.

Aoki was merely hundredths slower for his second front row of the year, achieved in spite of misgivings about the track, especially in the wet. 'If it rains tomorrow, I think I will stay in bed,' he said.

Harada led row two, the defending World Champion's best position of the year so far. 'My hand is a little better, but the main thing is that there is not so much braking here, so it doesn't give me so much trouble,' the Yamaha rider said. He admitted that he had used a qualifying tyre for his time, to compensate for his injury.

Waldmann was alongside, the 250 rookie showing star quality as he threatened to claim his first front row in the class. He was a tenth ahead of his HB Honda team-mate Romboni, the Italian still troubled with vexing chassis setting problems. He was also very lucky to survive virtually unscathed a crash at one of the fastest and most dangerous corners of the track on Friday; Maurel, who was also involved, suffered a suspected fractured leg.

Ruggia completed the second row, very disappointed after having won the last race. 'My engine just doesn't want to rev,' he said.

D'Antin led row three from Suter, Preining and Jurgen van den Goorbergh, the Dutchman saying: 'My bike is almost as fast as the works bikes up the hill.'

Zeelenberg led row four from Stadler, Kassner and Checa. Jimmy Filice was 18th, on row five after yet more engine trouble left him desperately short of dry laps. 'Morning warm-up is going to be real important for me,' he said. Bayle also suffered engine problems, ending up 30th out of 33 qualifiers.

250 cc RACE – 26 LAPS

This is a simple race track; this was a simple race. And thrilling.

Biaggi and Capirossi broke away from the pack early on, the former leading and the other working hard to catch up.

Then they circulated in close company until the 16th lap, when Biaggi redoubled his efforts to try and make a break. No such luck, with Capirossi breaking the lap record as he caught up again on lap 17.

The Aprilia was faster up the hill, the Honda better through the bends and chicanes. The confrontation was a classic, though it did seem to be tipped in Biaggi's favour.

The character of the track lends itself to last-lap battles, and the winner is generally whoever was second at the end of the previous lap, in a position to draft up the hill and shoot past into the final bends to control the run to the flag. Accordingly, after failing to break the draft, Max let Loris into the lead on lap 25, tucking in behind.

It almost worked. Biaggi took the lead as planned on the run up the hill. Then came the error. 'I knew his bike was better under brakes than mine, so I left my braking really late for the last corner. But the tyre slipped, and I almost crashed.'

He wobbled and ran wide, then – as he saw Capirossi come past on the inside – he opened the throttle again. Once again he slid and came desperately close to crashing, and by the time he'd recovered there was nothing left to do but follow the Honda through the chicanes and across the finish line. Capirossi was happy to accept the gift. 'It would have been very difficult to win if Max hadn't made a mistake,' he said.

The battle for third was just as tense: Romboni, Waldmann and Okada glued together, none able to escape. All led the group at various stages, but the order was settled over the last two laps, with Romboni in control, Okada next, and then the German, the trio covered by a quarter of a second across the line. Waldmann's hope of a last-lap attack had been foiled as they passed backmarker Fiorillo in the closing stages, while Romboni's forceful riding – overtaking Okada on the fast bend at the top of the hill – had settled the issue in his favour, even though the title leader had got back almost alongside at the finish.

Ruggia was sixth, the Jerez winner short of revs and power, and alone for most of the race. Likewise D'Antin, not quite able to keep his Honda with the works Aprilia.

Only 11 seconds down came an exciting battle. It included Suter, after a demon start, and the van den Goorbergh brothers, who had caught him up by means of a family slipstream sling-shot exercise, only to be slowed by Suter's late braking and slow corner speed so that Bayle and Preining closed up from behind.

At the finish, Patrick narrowly led Jurgen, followed by Suter, Bayle and Preining, the all-Aprilia group covered by less than a second.

Adi Stadler was 13th, the last rider not to be lapped, with the Aprilias of Kassner and Gramigni taking the last points.

There were 24 finishers. Harada, Filice and Checa all failed to finish the first lap because of mechanical problems; Aoki coasted to a depressed stop after three laps; and Zeelenberg pulled in after six laps with ignition trouble. He had been lying 11th.

125 cc RACE – 24 LAPS

Ueda qualified on pole, but it was close-to-home hero Raudies who sprang into the lead from his front-row start, and he was hardly headed to the finish in a race reminiscent of his string of clear wins last year.

In fact, young Garry McCoy did nose ahead once on lap 13, but that was enough to make Dirk dig even deeper and pull away again. He had switched bikes in the morning after his preferred machine gave trouble, and he was riding the A-kitted Honda with the new airbox system. 'It was faster up the hill, and though I had some trouble with the engine hesitating in the corners the power was enough to give me the win,' he said.

He was chased not only by the inspired McCoy but also by Ueda, whose enhanced airbox performance was enough for him to prevail in the last lap over McCoy's Aprilia. 'I was a bit nervous of his riding, but I knew I could beat him,' said the cheery Japanese rider.

Behind this trio the usual fierce battle saw six bikes at one stage swapping back and forth. The tussle was won in the end by Öttl's Aprilia, fractions ahead of the similar machines of Sakata and Perugini, with the Hondas of Saito and Gresini tucked right up behind. It was a heroic ride by Sakata, stiff and painful after his high-speed practice spill.

In a typical 125 brawl, ninth to 16th places were covered by less than two seconds, the pack led by front-row qualifier Emilio Cuppini, in his first race for seven months as substitute for Scalvini, injured in Malaysia. Katoh's Yamaha was in the thick of it, in 12th, but team-mate Jorge Martinez was off the back of the group in 17th, beating Bodelier by mere hundredths. Both Yamaha men had remarked on a shortage of straightline speed.

Cuppini was followed by Koch and Nakajyo with Casanova, Torrontegui and Petrucciani completing the points scorers. Tsujimura did not finish, after a fast high-sider at the top of the hill on the first lap. Igata's chicane crash came at half-distance.

Photos: Gold & Goose

OSTERREICH

22 May 1994

500 cc

29 laps, 76.328 miles/122.815 km

Place	Rider	Nat.	Machine	Laps	Time & speed	Fastest lap	Lap
1	Michael Doohan	AUS	Honda	29	37m 54.120s 120.807 mph/ 194.420 km/h	1m 17.696s	7
2	Kevin Schwantz	USA	Suzuki	29	38m 06.730s	1m 18.000s	23
3	Alex Criville	E	Honda	29	38m 09.552s	1m 18.105s	21
4	Shinichi Itoh	J	Honda	29	38m 15.350s	1m 18.116s	5
5	John Kocinski	USA	Cagiva	29	38m 18.426s	1m 18.270s	20
6	Alberto Puig	E	Honda	29	38m 23.048s	1m 18.442s	13
7	Alexandre Barros	BR	Suzuki	29	38m 29.979s	1m 18.818s	8
8	Daryl Beattie	AUS	Yamaha	29	38m 48.697s	1m 19.420s	9
9	Niall Mackenzie	GB	Yamaha	29	39m 05.026s	1m 19.988s	11
10	John Reynolds	GB	Yamaha	28	38m 06.002s	1m 20.190s	8
11	Hervé Moineau	F	Yamaha	28	38m 20.030s	1m 21.280s	20
12	Sean Emmett	GB	Yamaha	28	38m 20.286s	1m 21.158s	4
13	Jean-Pierre Jeandat	F	Yamaha	28	38m 20.685s	1m 20.908s	27
14	Cristiano Migliorati	I	Yamaha	28	38m 20.712s	1m 21.144s	20
15	Laurent Naveau	B	Yamaha	28	38m 21.276s	1m 21.188s	26
16	Jeremy McWilliams	GB	Yamaha	28	38m 24.808s	1m 21.380s	22
17	Marc Garcia	F	Yamaha	28	38m 32.880s	1m 21.345s	13
18	Julian Miralles	E	Yamaha	28	38m 36.360s	1m 21.595s	17
19	Bruno Bonhuil	F	Yamaha	28	39m 01.556s	1m 22.330s	4
20	Jean Foray	F	Yamaha	28	39m 01.638s	1m 22.404s	27
21	Kevin Mitchell	GB	Yamaha	28	39m 01.748s	1m 22.555s	14
22	Luca Cadalora	I	Yamaha	23	38m 17.634s	1m 18.647s	19
	Doug Chandler	USA	Cagiva	27	DNF	1m 19.100s	6
	Marco Papa	I	Yamaha	26	DNF	1m 24.361s	4
	Cees Doorakkers	NL	Yamaha	16	DNF	1m 23.630s	6
	Bernard Hänggeli	CH	Yamaha	15	DNF	1m 22.891s	5
	Lucio Pedercini	I	Yamaha	14	DNF	1m 22.569s	6
	Juan Lopez Mella	E	Yamaha	9	DNF	1m 22.706s	5
	Andreas Leuthe	D	Yamaha	5	DNF	1m 24.439s	4
	Loris Reggiani	I	Aprilia	1	DNF	2m 07.991s	1
	Lothar Neukirchner	D	Yamaha		DNQ		
	Vittorio Scatola	I	Paton		DNQ		

Fastest lap: Doohan, 1m 17.696s, 121.930 mph/196.226 km/h (record).
Previous record: Michael Doohan, AUS (Honda), 1m 18.021s, 121.422 mph/195.409 km/h (1993).

Qualifying: **1** Doohan, 1m 17.126s; **2** Schwantz, 1m 17.755s; **3** Puig, 1m 17.946s; **4** Barros, 1m 18.126s; **5** Criville, 1m 18.268s; **6** Kocinski, 1m 18.308s; **7** Cadalora, 1m 18.715s; **8** Itoh, 1m 18.819s; **9** Chandler, 1m 19.181s; **10** Beattie, 1m 19.590s; **11** Reggiani, 1m 20.338s; **12** Mackenzie, 1m 20.852s; **13** Jeandat, 1m 21.070s; **14** Reynolds, 1m 21.186s; **15** Naveau, 1m 21.206s; **16** McWilliams, 1m 21.230s; **17** Miralles, 1m 21.594s; **18** Emmett, 1m 21.881s; **19** Lopez Mella, 1m 21.926s; **20** Migliorati, 1m 21.994s; **21** Moineau, 1m 22.150s; **22** Pedercini, 1m 22.208s; **23** Bonhuil, 1m 22.252s; **24** M. Garcia, 1m 22.334s; **25** Mitchell, 1m 22.948s; **26** Hänggeli, 1m 22.960s; **27** Foray, 1m 23.424s; **28** Papa, 1m 24.014s; **29** Doorakkers, 1m 24.234s; **30** Leuthe, 1m 24.254s; **31** Neukirchner, 1m 25.239s; **32** Scatola, 1m 27.522s.

World Championship: 1 M. Doohan, 111; **2** Schwantz, 88; **3** Kocinski, 79; **4** Itoh, 56; **5** Criville, 54; **6** Barros, 50; **7** Puig, 48; **8** Cadalora, 46; **9** Chandler, 29; **10** Reynolds, 26; **11** Mackenzie, 20; **12** Beattie, 14; **13** B. Garcia, Honma and McWilliams, 10; **16** Emmett, 9; **17** Lopez Mella, Migliorati and Reggiani, 7; **20** Jeandat and Moineau, 5; **22** S. Doohan, 4; **23** Naveau, 3; **24** Miralles and Pedercini, 1.

250 cc

26 laps, 68.432 miles/110.110 km

Place	Rider	Nat.	Machine	Laps	Time & speed	Fastest lap	Lap
1	Loris Capirossi	I	Honda	26	35m 29.052s 115.690 mph/ 186.184 km/h	1m 20.916s	17
2	Massimiliano Biaggi	I	Aprilia	26	35m 29.552s	1m 21.014s	15
3	Doriano Romboni	I	Honda	26	35m 48.486s	1m 21.891s	11
4	Tadayuki Okada	J	Honda	26	35m 48.656s	1m 21.908s	11
5	Ralf Waldmann	D	Honda	26	35m 48.715s	1m 21.856s	6
6	Jean-Philippe Ruggia	F	Aprilia	26	36m 08.195s	1m 22.446s	5
7	Luis D'Antin	E	Honda	26	36m 23.522s	1m 22.510s	7
8	Patrick van den Goorbergh	NL	Aprilia	26	36m 34.859s	1m 23.584s	8
9	Jurgen van den Goorbergh	NL	Aprilia	26	36m 34.920s	1m 23.555s	21
10	Eskil Suter	CH	Aprilia	26	36m 35.006s	1m 23.487s	3
11	Jean-Michel Bayle	F	Aprilia	26	36m 35.036s	1m 23.059s	17
12	Andy Preining	A	Aprilia	26	36m 35.436s	1m 22.854s	17
13	Adi Stadler	D	Honda	26	36m 49.874s	1m 23.616s	10
14	Bernd Kassner	D	Aprilia	25	35m 32.940s	1m 24.108s	8
15	Alessandro Gramigni	I	Aprilia	25	35m 38.669s	1m 23.700s	9
16	Giuseppe Fiorillo	I	Honda	25	35m 57.478s	1m 24.894s	6
17	Frédéric Protat	F	Honda	25	36m 02.702s	1m 25.381s	22
18	Alexander Witting	A	Aprilia	25	36m 11.401s	1m 25.130s	21
19	Christian Boudinot	F	Aprilia	25	36m 12.384s	1m 25.837s	4
20	Alan Patterson	GB	Honda	25	36m 33.297s	1m 26.434s	12
21	Enrique de Juan	E	Aprilia	25	36m 33.382s	1m 26.320s	7
22	Hannes Maxwald	A	Yamaha	25	36m 33.568s	1m 26.466s	12
23	Rodney Fee	CAN	Honda	24	35m 44.639s	1m 27.929s	2
24	Kristian Kaas	SF	Yamaha	24	36m 12.612s	1m 28.730s	20
	José Luis Cardoso	E	Aprilia	10	DNF	1m 23.918s	6
	Wilco Zeelenberg	NL	Honda	6	DNF	1m 24.186s	5
	Manuel Hernandez	E	Aprilia	6	DNF	1m 27.755s	2
	Nobuatsu Aoki	J	Honda	3	DNF	1m 22.915s	3
	Noel Ferro	F	Honda	2	DNF	1m 31.493s	2
	Tetsuya Harada	J	Yamaha	0	DNF		
	Carlos Checa	E	Honda	0	DNF		
	Jim Filice	USA	Yamaha	0	DNF		
	Luis Maurel	E	Honda		DNS		

Fastest lap: Capirossi, 1m 20.916s, 117.078 mph/188.418 km/h ((record).
Previous record: Helmut Bradl, D (Honda), 1m 21.269s, 116.569 mph/187.599 km/h (1993).

Qualifying: **1** Biaggi, 1m 21.312s; **2** Capirossi, 1m 21.319s; **3** Okada, 1m 22.172s; **4** Aoki, 1m 22.197s; **5** Harada, 1m 22.210s; **6** Waldmann, 1m 22.253s; **7** Romboni, 1m 22.343s; **8** Ruggia, 1m 22.574s; **9** D'Antin, 1m 22.845s; **10** Suter, 1m 23.394s; **11** Preining, 1m 23.869s; **12** J. van den Goorbergh, 1m 23.884s; **13** Zeelenberg, 1m 23.943s; **14** Stadler, 1m 24.119s; **15** Kassner, 1m 24.210s; **16** Checa, 1m 24.249s; **17** Gramigni, 1m 24.597s; **18** Filice, 1m 24.792s; **19** P. van den Goorbergh, 1m 25.201s; **20** Ferro, 1m 25.224s; **21** Protat, 1m 25.287s; **22** Cardoso, 1m 25.850s; **23** Fiorillo, 1m 25.950s; **24** Boudinot, 1m 26.054s; **25** Maxwald, 1m 26.163s; **26** Witting, 1m 26.221s; **27** Patterson, 1m 26.348s; **28** de Juan, 1m 26.617s; **29** Hernandez, 1m 26.846s; **30** Bayle, 1m 26.942s; **31** Fee, 1m 27.881s; **32** Kaas, 1m 28.322s; **33** Maurel, 1m 28.726s.

World Championship: 1 Okada, 85; **2** Biaggi, 83; **3** Capirossi and Romboni, 77; **5** Ruggia, 70; **6** Waldmann, 43; **7** D'Antin, 41; **8** Bayle, 33; **9** N. Aoki, 29; **10** Zeelenberg, 21; **11** Harada and Ukawa, 16; **13** J. van den Goorbergh, 15; **14** Suter, 14; **15** Checa, 12; **16** T. Aoki, Preining and P. van den Goorbergh, 11; **19** Bosshard and Gramigni, 7; **21** Kassner and Stadler, 6; **23** Connell, 5; **24** Castilla, 3; **25** Cardoso, 1.

SALZBURGRING RACING CIRCUIT

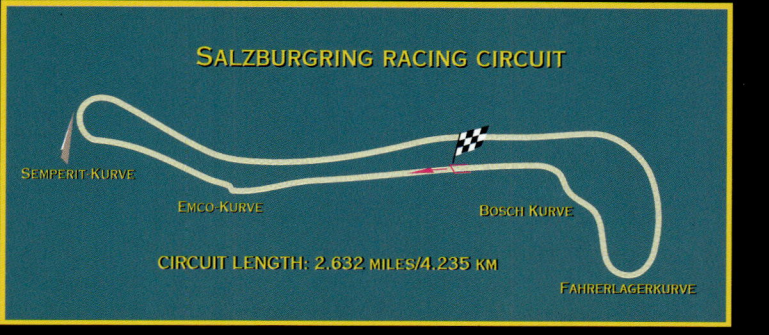

CIRCUIT LENGTH: 2.632 MILES/4.235 KM

Semperit-Kurve · Emco-Kurve · Bosch Kurve · Fahrerlagerkurve

125 cc

24 laps, 63.168 miles/101.640 km

Place	Rider	Nat.	Machine	Laps	Time & speed	Fastest lap	Lap
1	Dirk Raudies	D	Honda	24	35m 55.273s 105.491 mph/ 169.772 km/h	1m 28.950s	19
2	Noboru Ueda	J	Honda	24	35m 59.274s	1m 29.025s	10
3	Garry McCoy	AUS	Aprilia	24	35m 59.505s	1m 29.115s	10
4	Peter Öttl	D	Aprilia	24	36m 11.280s	1m 29.251s	11
5	Kazuto Sakata	J	Aprilia	24	36m 11.320s	1m 29.234s	24
6	Stefano Perugini	I	Aprilia	24	36m 11.960s	1m 29.486s	22
7	Akira Saito	J	Honda	24	36m 12.178s	1m 29.587s	22
8	Fausto Gresini	I	Honda	24	36m 12.274s	1m 29.553s	17
9	Emilio Cuppini	I	Aprilia	24	36m 17.870s	1m 29.516s	4
10	Oliver Koch	D	Honda	24	36m 18.431s	1m 29.605s	22
11	Hideyuki Nakajyo	J	Honda	24	36m 19.114s	1m 29.913s	20
12	Yoshiaki Katoh	J	Yamaha	24	36m 19.206s	1m 29.464s	17
13	Bruno Casanova	I	Honda	24	36m 19.217s	1m 29.320s	23
14	Herri Torrontegui	E	Aprilia	24	36m 19.338s	1m 29.366s	23
15	Oliver Petrucciani	CH	Aprilia	24	36m 19.576s	1m 29.497s	12
16	Stefan Prein	D	Yamaha	24	36m 19.742s	1m 29.598s	23
17	Jorge Martinez	E	Yamaha	24	36m 40.415s	1m 30.139s	6
18	Loek Bodelier	NL	Honda	24	36m 40.491s	1m 30.064s	10
19	Lucio Cecchinello	I	Honda	24	36m 59.684s	1m 31.158s	3
20	Gabriele Debbia	I	Aprilia	24	36m 59.809s	1m 31.009s	6
21	Manfred Geissler	D	Aprilia	24	37m 00.011s	1m 31.148s	9
22	Emili Alzamora	E	Honda	24	37m 00.172s	1m 31.176s	6
23	Hans Spaan	NL	Honda	24	37m 24.774s	1m 31.402s	5
24	Frédéric Petit	F	Yamaha	24	37m 24.775s	1m 31.614s	5
25	Haruchika Aoki	J	Honda	24	37m 24.831s	1m 31.899s	5
26	Vittorio Lopez	I	Honda	24	37m 25.156s	1m 32.062s	6
27	Neil Hodgson	GB	Honda	24	37m 25.268s	1m 31.802s	5
28	Carlos Giro	E	Aprilia	24	37m 25.681s	1m 32.304s	20
29	Nicolas Dussauge	F	Honda	24	37m 25.720s	1m 32.367s	5
30	Manfred Baumann	A	Yamaha	23	36m 20.216s	1m 32.882s	19
31	Gerwin Hofer	A	Honda	23	36m 53.992s	1m 34.901s	2
32	Georg Scharl	A	Honda	22	36m 03.085s	1m 36.333s	2
	Tomoko Igata	J	Honda	12	DNF	1m 31.019s	10
	Masaki Tokudome	J	Honda	5	DNF	1m 31.093s	3
	Takeshi Tsujimura	J	Honda	1	DNF	1m 37.878s	1
	Masafumi Ono	J	Honda		DNQ		

Fastest lap: Raudies, 1m 28.950s, 106.503 mph/171.400 km/h (record).
Previous record: Takeshi Tsujimura, J (Honda), 1m 29.241s, 106.156 mph/170.841 km/h (1993).

Qualifying: 1 Ueda, 1m 29.076s; 2 Sakata, 1m 29.474s; 3 Raudies, 1m 29.625s; 4 Cuppini, 1m 29.772s; 5 Petrucciani, 1m 29.882s; 6 Martinez, 1m 29.888s; 7 Öttl, 1m 30.003s; 8 Torrontegui, 1m 30.020s; 9 Gresini, 1m 30.054s; 10 McCoy, 1m 30.086s; 11 Katoh, 1m 30.119s; 12 Perugini, 1m 30.167s; 13 Prein, 1m 30.203s; 14 Tsujimura, 1m 30.338s; 15 Tokudome, 1m 30.351s; 16 Casanova, 1m 30.428s; 17 Saito, 1m 30.449s; 18 Debbia, 1m 30.731s; 19 Geissler, 1m 31.166s; 20 Nakajyo, 1m 31.223s; 21 Cecchinello, 1m 31.237s; 22 Bodelier, 1m 31.527s; 23 Dussauge, 1m 31.791s; 24 Igata, 1m 31.802s; 25 Petit, 1m 31.902s; 26 Koch, 1m 31.970s; 27 Hodgson, 1m 31.982s; 28 Spaan, 1m 32.024s; 29 Lopez, 1m 32.156s; 30 Alzamora, 1m 32.156s; 31 Aoki, 1m 32.288s; 32 Baumann, 1m 33.715s; 33 Giro, 1m 33.933s; 34 Hofer, 1m 34.786s; 35 Scharl, 1m 35.938s; 36 Ono, 1m 45.848s.

World Championship: 1 Sakata, 101; 2 Ueda, 67; 3 Öttl, 66; 4 Raudies, 55; 5 McCoy, 48; 6 Tsujimura, 46; 7 Torrontegui, 41; 8 Saito, 38; 9 Martinez, 32; 10 Gresini, 31; 11 Nakajyo, 27; 12 Tokudome, 25; 13 Petrucciani, 24; 14 Koch, 21; 15 Bodelier, 18; 16 Perugini, 14; 17 Casanova, 11; 18 Aoki, 8; 19 Cuppini, 7; 20 Amano, Katoh and Scalvini, 4; 23 Debbia, 3; 24 Geissler and Igata, 2; 26 Prein, 1.

Garry McCoy (left) scared his nearest rivals; Dirk Raudies (below) returned to winning form; likewise Loris Capirossi (bottom).

Photos: Gold & Goose

WORLD CHAMPIONSHIP • ROUND 6

GERMAN GRAND PRIX

500 cc	DOOHAN
250 cc	CAPIROSSI
125 cc	RAUDIES

Photos: Gold & Goose

GERMAN GRAND PRIX

Below left: Heading for the forests: leading 250 cc protagonists Capirossi, Romboni and Aoki.

In the 500 class John Reynolds had a '94 chassis for the first time, but crashed it *(bottom left)*. Meanwhile Luca Cadalora's left hand was trapped by the handlebar in his practice crash *(bottom right)*, and badly gashed.

'Heaving bike and rider through the air at close to 200 mph is the hardest work the engines do all season'

Reg Armstrong won the first German GP, riding a Norton at the Solitude circuit in 1952. Who will be the winner of the last one? With luck, the question may be premature; but it seemed apposite at the Hockenheimring, where it was plain (and sad) to see one of the great heartland races being run into the ground.

Victim of the financial mistakes made in the hijack of racing from the FIM by Bernie Ecclestone and IRTA, the German GP is saddled with wrong thinking and bereft of outside support. Empty grandstands for a third year in succession were an ominous reminder of the problems facing racing in general.

The poetic justice in the situation is small consolation. It was Ecclestone who based racing's economics on the view that a well-heeled new crowd could be recruited to pay inflated ticket prices. When his vision proved mistaken, it was Ecclestone who baled out within the first year. Promoters locked into five-year contracts did not have this option, and the promoter in Germany found the terms particularly punitive, making it 'impossible to make money'. The promoter's name? None other than Bernie Ecclestone.

The historic event at this historic circuit is dying on its feet. No government support has been forthcoming, while the cigarette barons aren't interested in races where their logos are covered over. Especially when they can subsidise ticket prices and attract a huge crowd to Brno from largely the same catchment area, and place their logos wherever they like. Nor is Ecclestone anxious to throw good money after bad and, beyond an ineffectual drop in ticket prices, little effort to attract or reward the spectators was apparent. And without crowds filling the vast Wagnerian grandstands, the atmosphere fell flat once again.

Only the racing remained as before. And it is always rather special at the fastest track of the year. Enjoy it while you can.

There were few surprises. The 'Ring served up its annual diet of nasty weather, perplexing engine-tuning problems, superb slipstreaming battles and raw excitement. And serious accidents too.

The weather obligingly cleared for race day, but wet practice badly cut testing time for all classes, with the 500s getting away lightest. They at least had almost two fully dry sessions; the 125s didn't have one.

This impinged on the engine-tuning difficulties. Oxygen-rich as it runs flat out through the forests – almost two miles out, and almost two miles back – the track makes unique demands on pulling power, and imposes special problems on those seeking to maximise it. Heaving a 500 cc bike and rider through the air at close to 200 mph for extended periods is the hardest work the engines do all season, in difficult and unpredictable conditions. There is always a dilemma between playing safe and setting the mixture a power-sapping over-rich, or taking the risk of seizure and going lean for speed, only to find the oxygen-overloaded air making the mixture leaner still.

Clearly a case to be tackled by self-adjusting electronic fuel injection – but not yet. Honda's Mk2 version practised in Austria, but was back on the test bench again now, and though Cagiva had tested theirs at Mugello the week before, it was also not race-ready.

One playing it close to the limits was Erv Kanemoto: his title-leading rider Okada suffered two seizures in one day, and maybe more (Honda folk never admit this if they can help it). For once Mackenzie's bike wasn't nipping up, modified stock cylinders solving the problem. But at least they'd found a reason for the bad Harald Bartol cylinders which vindicated the puzzled veteran tuner. Material problems introduced when the foundry deviated from specification had resulted in a bad batch of castings.

There were few aerodynamic adventures at this fast track. Suzuki's ram-air fairing was already one race old, while the Shell Harris team's plan to debut new fast-track bodywork for Emmett had to be shelved because they were unable to test. They stuck with their familiar bulbous cowling designed, like the new stuff, by stylist and aerodynamicist John Mockett. The Aprilia 250s donned their 'fast-track' bodywork, though, already seen on the 400 cc V-twin.

Mechanical special preparations included new cylinders and exhausts for that bike, to give Reggiani a better chance on a track where he expected to have trouble even staying with the private V4 500s, let alone the works bikes. This was the would-be giant-killer's sternest test so far, but though speed was well down, lap times were not so far off, with Loris 11th in qualifying, on the third row of the grid, his usual position. Top speed on Saturday was 26th out of 34, at 285.0 km/h, 30 km/h slower than Doohan's top-dog Honda, but 14 km/h faster than Biaggi's 250 Aprilia. Chief engineer Jan Witteveen denied rumours that he had made special larger Hockenheim cylinders for the 400 cc. 'I can't make bigger cylinders without losing rev capability, because the pistons would be too heavy, and it would overstress the bearings. They are already on the limit.' Or past it – sadly, the bike seized for a second race in succession.

Another special Hockenheim change was to the Yamaha 125s, decreed by Bartol, who is also Team Aspar's development engineer. In search of speed the cylinder dimensions were changed from Yamaha's (and Suzuki's) usual over-square 56 x 50.7 mm to square 54.4 x 54.5. This was moderately successful: although Katoh didn't finish, Martinez was up with the bunch going for second place, finally ending up seventh.

Team Roberts remained in the wilderness, the Marlboro misfortunes clocking in with perfect regularity. First Cadalora crashed in practice on one of the slower but tricky parts of the Motodrom section, the right flick after the exit from the first-gear Sachskurve. He went over the high side, and his hand was caught under the bike, gashing his left palm badly enough to put him out. Then Daryl Beattie had a double-bad race. His usual first-lap mess-up was his fault this time, when he ran into the first chicane way too fast and ended up grass tracking furiously as he dropped from near the front to close to the back. He fought his way back up to the top ten, only to run out of fuel on the last lap. 'Maybe he used more because he was alone rather than slipstreaming people,' said his shamefaced chief engineer Mike Sinclair. It was another blow to the rider who won his first GP here, on a Honda, just one year ago.

Misfortune was also waiting for John Kocinski. Fast in the wet, John was working up to try and improve his position in the dry on Saturday afternoon when he pushed too hard coming out of the first turn onto the longest and fastest straight, sliding over the white line for a spectacular one-wheel high-sider that left him with a broken finger on his left hand. He tried to ride on Sunday morning, then decided it would be safer to give it a miss.

Race day ended with a shocking crash in the sidecar class, which

91

GERMAN GRAND PRIX

caused a premature end to what three-wheeler fans said was probably the most exciting race ever. Eight outfits were locked together going for second place but then, with less than three laps left, Abbott banged into Klaffenböck at high speed and the Austrian's outfit spun into the pack, depositing hapless passenger Parzer under their wheels. All but the last two outfits got past safely; what followed looked like an air crash as disintegrating machinery somersaulted into the barriers. Parzer, the Wyssen brothers – whose machine broke into three, with part ending up in a tree – and Kumagaya miraculously escaped serious injury, but Kumagaya's passenger, Simon Prior, a 40-year-old auctioneer from Brighton, sustained head injuries that proved fatal.

Better to remember the race for the good things. Like the electrifying 250 duel where the three young Italians – what a generation of talent! – came to a showdown that saw Biaggi defy the convention that there can be no passing in the last corners. He pushed past Romboni, leaving his displaced rival livid at what he saw as dangerous tactics. 'I will set the record straight with Biaggi at the next race,' threatened hard man Romboni; to which Max replied: 'This is bike racing, not classical music.'

And the bit of German good luck that finally visited Doohan – giving him his third successive race win, and fourth this year. Twice he has lost certain victory here when a rear tyre broke up. This time he chose so hard a Michelin that it was 'like one of Fred Flintstone's tyres'. It stayed in one piece as he waited until almost half-distance for it to warm up, then he surged away on a tide of Honda power to as clear a victory as anyone could want.

500 cc PRACTICE

Despite one completely dry timed session and one mostly dry, a lack of set-up time was a common complaint even for those at the IRTA tests here earlier.

Not for pole qualifier Doohan, though, who had used those tests for extended tyre work, including running full race distance as he sought to rule out his persistent Hockenheim problem of rear tyre disintegration (the original trigger, HRC said, for development of the tyre-friendly Big Bang engine). 'It seems the tyres are a bit different this year – more slippery when you're leaned over.

Hopefully that means they'll last the race better.' His top speed was 316.6 km/h, some 5 km/h down on Itoh's 1993 barrier-breaking 200 mph. 'But it's faster than I went last year,' he grinned. 'Maybe the new fuel has knocked the edge off the speed.'

He led throughout practice, and when Schwantz closed up in the final minutes he went out and went faster still to give himself a full second's advantage. 'We didn't plan it that way,' he said. In fact they'd been trying suspension variations, then at the finish went back to the 'stock' settings used at the tests.

Schwantz also thought that some new bumps in the chicanes might have spoiled exit speed, but he too was faster than last year, and hooked onto the tail of Criville's Honda at the end of the last session to jump from seventh to second in the last ten minutes. 'I wasn't close enough to draft, but I used him as a marker. It was a flash lap, but I'll have to race at that speed if I'm gonna stay with Doohan.' The mysterious rear suspension was gone, but his chassis difficulties remained. 'The bike's twitchy. It's not comfortable or fun to ride. Missing the IRTA test here ended up costing us because of the weather.'

Third went to Puig, his third time on the 500 front row. He modestly gave his Honda the credit, but he had been fastest (ahead of Schwantz) in the morning wet session, which must have taken a certain amount of skill. And bravery. 'But I didn't enjoy it,' he said, wide-eyed. 'The 500 is so much faster than the 250 that all the braking reference points are new.'

Final front-row occupant was Barros, his time also achieved in the closing minutes following a Honda (Puig's). With his different style he had found the Suzuki less sensitive than Schwantz, but has had trouble with the AP brakes, because he brakes later and more violently, and gives them less time to reach working temperature. After unpredictable results, he was now on Brembo carbon-carbons, used previously when he rode for Cagiva.

Row two was led by last year's poleman, Itoh, who crashed on Friday in the rain, hurting his hand a little. He was short of the corner exit speed he needed to recapture his 1993 200 mph. Criville was next, half a second down, and two-and-a-half away from pole. Then came Cadalora, who had been in the top four and looked set to improve when he crashed. He was out of the race.

Chandler took his place, trying to fix a brake-dive problem, but preferring to ditch the anti-dive at faster circuits. More importantly, he was continuing his slow but steady climb back towards his earlier form. Then came Beattie, last year's winner only elevated to row two by Cadalora's crash, but likewise also reporting overdue progress after the Team Roberts Yamaha tests at Mugello. 'I honestly feel we made some major steps,' he said, vexed that the bad weather had slowed further improvements here.

Kocinski was next, angrily insisting on Saturday evening that he would be fit to race. 'My finger's not broken. I only banged it.' But it was broken, and he was out of the race too.

Thus Reggiani led row three by default, his 400 cc V-twin Aprilia rather unexpectedly 11th overall. The power-up cylinders and pipes meant he could hang in the slipstream of the private bikes instead of being outpaced, while he could gain a lot of ground through the fast and distant Ostkurve.

Mackenzie came next, in his familiar spot heading the privateers. He crashed on both Friday and Saturday. 'Brain fade,' he said, luckily unhurt. 'I missed my braking markers. There's no other track where you travel so fast for so long, and it can be quite difficult to adjust. Even if you don't brake too late the corners come at you so fast it feels as though you have.'

Bernard Garcia was back on the ex-Yamaha France Roc, now painted silver; he headed McWilliams and Reynolds, the latter also crashing. 'We have a 1994 chassis here for the first time, and it drops into the corners much more easily. But I was caught out by the cold left-hand side of the tyre at the Sachskurve.' Fellow-Briton Emmett was next, the lead-free Shell Harris Yamaha showing much less of a speed deficit than last year.

Naveau moved up to row five; Hänggeli headed row six, which also contained wild card and regular World Superbike rider Udo Mark, making an impressive GP debut. There were 32 qualifiers.

500 cc RACE – 18 LAPS

Doohan's tactics were perfect, but he wasn't sure they'd worked until the ninth lap. 'We had decided on the same hard tyre we used in testing here, but because it was cooler now we changed just before the race to the same compound but with some cuts on the left-hand side to build up tem-

Kevin Schwantz was this close to Michael Doohan until the Australian's tyres started working. Alberto Puig and Alex Barros follow on behind.

perature.' (Hockenheim is notorious for letting that side cool down, which then causes many crashes at the first-gear Sachskurve, the first left-hander for a long distance.) 'It was so hard that for the first four laps the lefts were really tricky. I thought I might have made a mistake.'

Schwantz had led into the first turn, with Puig taking over on the run out to the Ostkurve, and Doohan in fourth behind Barros.

Doohan was leading by the end of lap two, however, and seemed set to run away; Schwantz was having trouble with Puig, who could repass him on the straights. Then the American upped the pace and closed right up from a 0.4-second gap until he was challenging the Honda in the chicanes and stadium section. He could see Doohan's tyre problems, and wanted to be ready to seize any unexpected opportunities.

But by the ninth lap Doohan's rubber was up to temperature, and he simply powered ever further away, breaking his own lap record on the tenth time round, and gaining a second or more each lap to win by 13.9s. 'I was just waiting for the feeling of the tyre breaking up like it did the last two times,' he said later. 'You feel all sorts of vibrations and hear all kinds of noises.'

Schwantz could do nothing about the Honda, complaining later not so much of a shortage of top speed but of the same troublesome nervousness under braking. 'It's okay in a straight line, but I'm having problems when I try and change direction under brakes. We need to sort out a few nagging problems.'

In fact he couldn't even get away from Puig, who said later: 'For sure my bike helped me. He was faster through the chicanes, but I was much faster on the straights. It was really exciting for me to race with these guys for the first time.' Schwantz had a makeshift plan for the finish, taking control through the stadium on the penultimate trip, then doing everything to stay ahead. He secured second by almost two seconds.

This group was now miles ahead. Barros had been close at hand until lap seven, when he missed his braking point for the first chicane. He only lost one place as he threaded his way through the bales to rejoin, but a lot of distance; Criville moved through to claim a lonely fourth some 15 seconds ahead. Barros then fell into the clutches of Itoh, and the two battled to the finish, the Brazilian claiming fifth by barely a tenth.

Chandler was seventh, alone for almost the entire race; Mackenzie was eighth. He'd been ninth, with Beattie moving firmly by on the fourth lap; then the Australian sputtered obligingly to a stop on the last time round, out of petrol.

Garcia was outdistanced in a lone ninth. Then came another dice, for tenth, between Britons Reynolds and Emmett, won at the last gasp by the former. The last points went to Lopez Mella, Miralles, Naveau and Bonhuil, the last-named one lap down on the leaders.

Retirements included crashers McWilliams, who had been with Reynolds and Emmett until he fell at the Sachskurve; Migliorati, who fell on the entry to the stadium section; and wild card Mark.

Reggiani made three laps before seizing for a second race in succession.

The win marked an important milestone for Doohan. With his lead up to 28 points, he now had a one-race buffer.

250 cc PRACTICE

Biaggi's Aprilia, with an engine update to 1994 tuning specs, was fastest through the traps, 271.4 km/h to Okada's 269.9; he also led practice after the first day. But as the weather dried (the 250s got more rain than the 500s, with only one fully dry session) he ran into suspension problems, and two Hondas moved ahead.

Capirossi was best, remarkable considering he was suffering from a fever which he later said was German measles. 'My bike was a lot healthier than me.'

Romboni was second fastest, more than half a second slower, having held pole throughout most of the last session. 'I came in to change tyres for a final fast lap, but I had some chatter problems,' he said. He hoped to get back to winning, and

GERMAN GRAND PRIX

was riding hard in the chicanes to prove the point. 'You have to take risks here because of the slipstreaming on the straights.'

Biaggi had dropped to third by the finish. 'The bike's fast, but we didn't have enough dry time to get the suspension right,' he said. Okada completed the front row, insisting that any modifications Kanemoto had made to his bike for top speed were 'secret'. Also secret were his seizures.

Waldmann led row two for a second time. His move up one class had him echoing Puig's comments. 'It's like a different track on a 250,' he said. 'You come into the corners such a lot faster. But the bike stills feel safer than a 125, in spite of the speed, because it is not so lively, and the extra power makes it more stable.'

Ruggia was alongside, almost two seconds down on pole, and still dogged by engine problems that made his Aprilia much slower than Biaggi's. Already he and his sidekick/father were muttering about second-rate treatment, a grumble that was to grow. Then came the NSR Hondas of Aoki and D'Antin, the latter surviving a crash in the final session.

Harada led row three after also crashing. Luckily he didn't exacerbate his right hand injury. 'I was going quite slowly because I was waiting for a group to slipstream,' he said. He had Bayle alongside; then came the semi-works Aprilias of Preining and Kassner.

Zeelenberg continued to have trouble finding form on his works Honda, leading row four from Stadler, Patrick van den Goorbergh and Honma, the last-named riding the Team Marlboro Rainey Yamaha as the latest replacement for the still-injured Kenny Roberts Junior, who (it was now said) might be out for the whole season. And the name of Abe continued to surface as the rumours gathered intensity.

250 cc RACE – 16 LAPS

The first race of the day was a showcase for the success of the Italian system in bringing up riding talent. Biaggi leapt into an early lead, but was instantly under pressure from Romboni while Capirossi also started well and moved into third on the first lap.

Already they were back and forth, with Romboni ahead at the end of lap one and for most of the first ten laps, although there was plenty of jostling round the chicanes and long straights as Okada, Aoki and the rampant Waldmann caught the draft from behind.

On lap three it all proved too much for the young German, who ran straight at the first chicane, dropping to sixth at the front of the next group. Had there been the crowds of the old days, the stadium would have resounded with their bellows of dismay.

For the five left up front, the race was still up for grabs. As the distance wore on, Okada dropped slightly out of touch, then caught up again to take the lead for the first time on lap 11. But it was short-lived, for now Biaggi decided to up the pace and try to break the pursuit. He was almost half a second clear on lap 12, three-quarters on lap 13, then a little slip by second-placed Capirossi, leaping over one of the chicane kerbs, saw Romboni ease through and close right up again on the Aprilia.

Romboni led the penultimate lap, with Biaggi second and Capirossi third. The last lap was riveting.

Biaggi took the lead into the first chicane, Romboni and Capirossi on his tail and the Japanese riders losing touch. Biaggi held on under severe pressure all the way round the Ostkurve to the second chicane. Then came the run into the stadium.

Now Capirossi moved inside under braking to take the final corners in the lead. Max attacked straight back, trying to run underneath into the slow Sachskurve, but Capirossi wouldn't give an inch, and the Aprilia rider was forced to slow. This gave Romboni the chance to swoop round the outside to claim second.

From here on there are reckoned to be no more opportunities. Biaggi thought otherwise. As they swung into the final pair of rights he dived underneath Romboni, leaving him little choice but to run wide. This controversial but characteristic move gave him second, almost three-tenths behind Capirossi, and slightly less clear of a furious Romboni.

Capirossi was thrilled to win in spite of his illness. 'I must thank Dr Costa, because he got me ready for this race,' he said. 'Today's victory was very important because the Aprilia is faster than the Honda.' He had set a new lap record on the final lap.

Aoki claimed fourth, eight-tenths behind, with Okada a disgruntled fifth, saying that Aoki slowed him by outbraking him, then ran slower through the turns. Perfect tactics, after all.

The next battle was completely overshadowed by events up front: Waldmann fending off Harada and Ruggia, the former cautious after his practice crash, the latter still complaining about being short of power. In fact the Frenchman had been ahead of Harada and challenging Waldmann into the stadium on the last lap when the German made a slip and forced him to slow, letting the Japanese rider through as well.

Patrick van den Goorbergh had been with Harada in the opening stages, but a low battery spoiled his ignition, and he had dropped back to be embroiled in the next five-man group, battling for ninth. Victory went in the end to D'Antin's Honda, the Spaniard narrowly ahead of similarly mounted Zeelenberg, Bayle and van den Goorbergh. Preining dropped off the back to claim 13th, with Checa and Stadler taking the final points.

Honma conformed to the usual Team Rainey luck, marooned on the line with ignition problems that left his engine spluttering, and burning out his clutch trying to make up for it.

125 cc RACE – 15 LAPS

Ueda qualified on pole, with Raudies second, both running on ram-air power; Raudies had the added benefit of private tests that cured the troublesome mid-corner hesitation. Jetting for these systems involves subtle changes; less discreet was his new fairing-nose intake.

The two Honda men opened up an immediate gap as they battled to and fro for the first eight laps of the race. Raudies had most of the leading, but Ueda was always right with him.

Then the Japanese rider's gear-knob broke off, leaving just a straight lever, and though he could stamp it down all right for upshifts he had to downshift by hand, making high-speed chicane entries particularly fraught. By the time he'd managed to bend the stub of the lever so he could downshift by foot, he'd dropped back into a fierce battle for what was now second, and Raudies could win at will.

'I had problems in practice with my gearbox, jumping back to fourth gear from fifth, but we borrowed some different parts and today the bike was perfect,' the German said, after a second dominant race in his style of last year, on clearly the fastest bike out there.

The battle for second was typically fierce, with erstwhile leader Tsujimura summarily dismissed from it after a collision with Katoh that broke his seat, though he didn't fall.

By the finish the group had disintegrated somewhat, though four riders took from second to fifth within the space of a second. The victor was title leader Kazuto Sakata, who had qualified only 16th as wet weather combined with a host of small problems. 'Everything came right for the race,' he grinned, adding, 'My back hurts still from crashing at Salzburg, but I managed to forget about it.'

Third was an amazing result for GP first-timer Tomoko Manako, a novice in Japan last year and drafted in for three races to replace the injured Igata. Quite overcome, he stumbled out a few phrases about the FCC technical sports team and the bike, and could hardly stop smiling. He had beaten Öttl and Perugini in the sprint to the line.

The next big group, nine strong, was covered by little more than 1.5 seconds. It was led by the fighting Ueda from Martinez's Yamaha, the Hondas of Akira Saito and Masaki Tokudome, and front-row qualifier Oliver Petrucciani's Aprilia, followed by the Hondas of Oliver Koch, Bruno Casanova, Fausto Gresini and Lucio Cecchinello. Loek Bodelier claimed the last point.

Hans Spaan was lucky to survive unhurt a heavy crash five laps from the finish while in 22nd place. French rider Nicolas Dussauge fell on the exit from the first turn and Spaan was unable to avoid his bike. He was sent flying and landed heavily to be stretchered away, although not seriously injured.

McCoy was out even before the race, falling in morning warm-up and badly hurting his right little finger – the full extent of the injury was not discovered until the next day.

Andy Preining *(left)* struggled all year to find his previous form.

Right: The battle for third, early in the 125 cc race – Öttl leads Sakata (obscured), Katoh, Manako and Perugini, with Gresini unable to stay with the group.

Below: Already breaking away – Romboni heads Biaggi, Capirossi, Waldmann, Okada and Aoki.

A tentative Tetsuya Harada *(bottom left)* was far from fit, but came seventh.

Tomoko Manako replaced the injured girl racer, Igata, and finished on the rostrum *(bottom right)*.

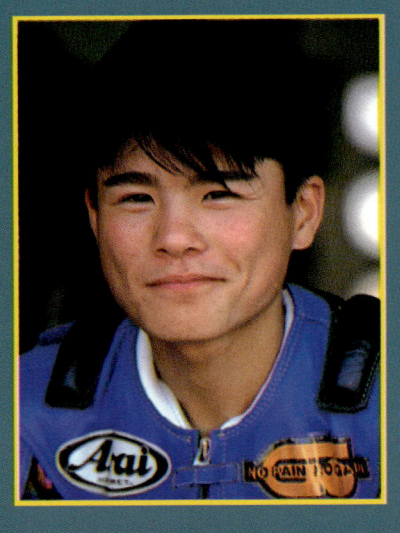

Photos: Gold & Goose

FIM WORLD CHAMPIONSHIP • ROUND 6

GROSSER PREIS VON DEUTSCHLAND

12 JUNE 1994

500 cc

18 laps, 75.960 miles/122.256 km

Place	Rider	Nat.	Machine	Laps	Time & speed	Fastest lap	Lap
1	Michael Doohan	AUS	Honda	18	35m 58.994s 126.670 mph/ 203.855 km/h	1m 58.586s	10
2	Kevin Schwantz	USA	Suzuki	18	36m 12.976s	1m 59.311s	5
3	Alberto Puig	E	Honda	18	36m 14.758s	1m 59.501s	7
4	Alex Criville	E	Honda	18	36m 18.530s	2m 00.198s	5
5	Alexandre Barros	BR	Suzuki	18	36m 32.114s	2m 00.123s	5
6	Shinichi Itoh	J	Honda	18	36m 32.287s	2m 00.728s	4
7	Doug Chandler	USA	Cagiva	18	36m 46.196s	2m 01.490s	5
8	Niall Mackenzie	GB	Yamaha	18	37m 05.284s	2m 02.342s	7
9	Bernard Garcia	F	Yamaha	18	37m 11.974s	2m 03.065s	5
10	John Reynolds	GB	Yamaha	18	37m 35.637s	2m 03.940s	3
11	Sean Emmett	GB	Yamaha	18	37m 36.056s	2m 04.044s	5
12	Juan Lopez Mella	E	Yamaha	18	37m 53.302s	2m 05.018s	5
13	Julian Miralles	E	Yamaha	18	37m 53.549s	2m 04.742s	17
14	Laurent Naveau	B	Yamaha	18	37m 53.720s	2m 04.915s	2
15	Bruno Bonhuil	F	Yamaha	17	36m 01.684s	2m 05.018s	4
16	Kevin Mitchell	GB	Yamaha	17	36m 31.822s	2m 06.788s	5
17	Andreas Leuthe	D	Yamaha	17	36m 32.180s	2m 07.498s	16
18	Cees Doorakkers	NL	Yamaha	17	36m 56.509s	2m 08.804s	5
19	Lothar Neukirchner	D	Yamaha	17	37m 17.023s	2m 10.412s	11
	Daryl Beattie	AUS	Yamaha	17	DNF	2m 01.936s	14
	Bernard Hänggeli	CH	Yamaha	16	DNF	2m 05.246s	6
	Udo Mark	D	Yamaha	14	DNF	2m 05.262s	3
	Jean-Pierre Jeandat	F	Yamaha	13	DNF	2m 05.220s	6
	Jeremy McWilliams	GB	Yamaha	12	DNF	2m 03.541s	11
	Cristiano Migliorati	I	Yamaha	10	DNF	2m 04.086s	9
	Jean Foray	F	Yamaha	8	DNF	2m 07.970s	2
	Lucio Pedercini	I	Yamaha	6	DNF	2m 04.812s	6
	Marco Papa	I	Yamaha	4	DNF	2m 11.614s	3
	Loris Reggiani	I	Aprilia	3	DNF	2m 04.471s	2
	Marc Garcia	F	Yamaha	1	DNF	2m 39.128s	1
	Luca Cadalora	I	Yamaha		DNS		
	John Kockinski	USA	Cagiva		DNS		
	Vittorio Scatola	I	Paton		DNQ		
	Manfred Erhardt	D	Yamaha		DNQ		

Fastest lap: Doohan, 1m 58.586s, 128.121 mph/206.190 km/h (record).
Previous record: Michael Doohan, AUS (Honda), 1m 58.852s, 127.833 mph/205.728 km/h (1993).

Qualifying: 1 Doohan, 1m 58.946s; **2** Schwantz, 1m 59.922s; **3** Puig, 2m 00.404s; **4** Barros, 2m 00.418s; **5** Itoh, 2m 00.538s; **6** Criville, 2m 01.081s; **7** Cadalora, 2m 01.124s; **8** Chandler, 2m 01.295s; **9** Beattie, 2m 02.038s; **10** Kocinski, 2m 02.077s; **11** Reggiani, 2m 02.702s; **12** Mackenzie, 2m 03.438s; **13** B. Garcia, 2m 03.526s; **14** McWilliams, 2m 04.104s; **15** Reynolds, 2m 04.228s; **16** Emmett, 2m 04.427s; **17** Naveau, 2m 04.433s; **18** Hänggeli, 2m 05.662s; **19** Mark, 2m 05.787s; **20** Jeandat, 2m 05.981s; **21** Lopez Mella, 2m 06.039s; **22** M. Garcia, 2m 06.142s; **23** Miralles, 2m 06.635s; **24** Leuthe, 2m 06.790s; **25** Migliorati, 2m 07.096s; **26** Pedercini, 2m 07.128s; **27** Mitchell, 2m 07.212s; **28** Bonhuil, 2m 07.521s; **29** Foray, 2m 08.314s; **30** Doorakkers, 2m 08.641s; **31** Papa, 2m 08.733s; **32** Neukirchner, 2m 10.364s; **33** Scatola, 2m 11.387s; **34** Erhardt, 2m 13.271s.

World Championship: 1 M. Doohan, 136; **2** Schwantz, 108; **3** Kocinski, 79; **4** Criville, 67; **5** Itoh, 66; **6** Puig, 64; **7** Barros, 61; **8** Cadalora, 46; **9** Chandler, 38; **10** Reynolds, 32; **11** Mackenzie, 28; **12** B. Garcia, 17; **13** Beattie and Emmett, 14; **15** Lopez Mella, 11; **16** Honma and McWilliams, 10; **18** Migliorati and Reggiani, 7; **20** Jeandat, Moineau and Naveau, 5; **23** S. Doohan and Miralles, 4; **25** Bonhuil and Pedercini, 1.

250 cc

16 laps, 67.520 miles/108.672 km

Place	Rider	Nat.	Machine	Laps	Time & speed	Fastest lap	Lap
1	Loris Capirossi	I	Honda	16	33m 43.516s 120.133 mph/ 193.336 km/h	2m 04.820s	16
2	Massimiliano Biaggi	I	Aprilia	16	33m 43.800s	2m 05.032s	12
3	Doriano Romboni	I	Honda	16	33m 43.941s	2m 05.015s	14
4	Nobuatsu Aoki	J	Honda	16	33m 44.808s	2m 05.138s	16
5	Tadayuki Okada	J	Honda	16	33m 45.141s	2m 05.106s	15
6	Ralf Waldmann	D	Honda	16	33m 57.082s	2m 05.763s	3
7	Tetsuya Harada	J	Yamaha	16	33m 57.137s	2m 06.358s	16
8	Jean-Philippe Ruggia	F	Aprilia	16	33m 57.810s	2m 06.228s	15
9	Luis D'Antin	E	Honda	16	34m 23.020s	2m 07.838s	5
10	Wilco Zeelenberg	NL	Honda	16	34m 23.074s	2m 07.640s	5
11	Jean-Michel Bayle	F	Aprilia	16	34m 23.145s	2m 07.642s	5
12	Patrick van den Goorbergh	NL	Aprilia	16	34m 23.318s	2m 07.757s	3
13	Andy Preining	A	Aprilia	16	34m 23.808s	2m 07.774s	4
14	Carlos Checa	E	Honda	16	34m 56.751s	2m 09.144s	2
15	Adi Stadler	D	Honda	16	34m 56.816s	2m 09.367s	5
16	Luis Maurel	E	Honda	16	35m 00.084s	2m 09.594s	11
17	Alessandro Gramigni	I	Aprilia	16	35m 05.942s	2m 09.413s	3
18	Jürgen Fuchs	D	Honda	16	35m 06.636s	2m 10.316s	7
19	Giuseppe Fiorillo	I	Honda	16	35m 07.652s	2m 10.680s	13
20	Noel Ferro	F	Honda	16	35m 21.614s	2m 10.789s	8
21	José Luis Cardoso	E	Aprilia	16	35m 30.596s	2m 10.894s	3
22	Kristian Kaas	SF	Yamaha	16	35m 54.860s	2m 13.446s	6
23	Manuel Hernandez	E	Aprilia	16	35m 55.038s	2m 13.008s	5
	Bernd Kassner	D	Aprilia	14	DNF	2m 09.372s	11
	Eskil Suter	CH	Aprilia	14	DNF	2m 09.498s	7
	Jurgen van den Goorbergh	NL	Aprilia	11	DNF	2m 09.730s	6
	Toshihiko Honma	J	Yamaha	11	DNF	2m 10.386s	2
	Peter Koller	D	Honda	10	DNF	2m 15.747s	3
	Frédéric Protat	F	Honda	8	DNF	2m 11.658s	2
	Alan Patterson	GB	Honda	8	DNF	2m 13.697s	3
	Rodney Fee	CAN	Honda	4	DNF	2m 15.755s	3
	Christian Boudinot	F	Aprilia	4	DNF	2m 12.668s	3
	Enrique de Juan	E	Aprilia	0	DNF		
	Adrian Bosshard	CH	Honda		DNS		

Fastest lap: Capirossi, 2m 04.820s, 121.722 mph/195.892 km/h (record).
Previous record: Loris Capirossi, I (Honda), 2m 04.889s, 121.654 mph/195.783 km/h (1993).

Qualifying: 1 Capirossi, 2m 04.853s; **2** Romboni, 2m 05.468s; **3** Biaggi, 2m 05.670s; **4** Okada, 2m 05.786s; **5** Waldmann, 2m 06.302s; **6** Ruggia, 2m 06.782s; **7** Aoki, 2m 06.896s; **8** D'Antin, 2m 07.670s; **9** Harada, 2m 07.789s; **10** Bayle, 2m 07.816s; **11** Preining, 2m 08.312s; **12** Kassner, 2m 08.723s; **13** Zeelenberg, 2m 08.992s; **14** Stadler, 2m 09.147s; **15** P. van den Goorbergh, 2m 09.250s; **16** Honma, 2m 09.398s; **17** J. van den Goorbergh, 2m 09.508s; **18** Checa, 2m 10.082s; **19** Suter, 2m 10.178s; **20** Gramigni, 2m 10.896s; **21** Boudinot, 2m 11.067s; **22** Bosshard, 2m 11.277s; **23** Ferro, 2m 11.351s; **24** Maurel, 2m 11.488s; **25** Fiorillo, 2m 11.538s; **26** Fuchs, 2m 11.935s; **27** Protat, 2m 13.504s; **28** Hernandez, 2m 14.106s; **29** Kaas, 2m 14.486s; **30** Patterson, 2m 15.609s; **31** Cardoso, 2m 15.626s; **32** Fee, 2m 15.863s; **33** Koller, 2m 16.568s; **34** de Juan, 2m 17.306s.

World Championship: 1 Biaggi, 103; **2** Capirossi, 102; **3** Okada, 96; **4** Romboni, 93; **5** Ruggia, 78; **6** Waldmann, 53; **7** D'Antin, 48; **8** N. Aoki, 42; **9** Bayle, 38; **10** Zeelenberg, 27; **11** Harada, 25; **12** Ukawa, 16; **13** J. van den Goorbergh and P. van den Goorbergh, 15; **15** Checa, Preining and Suter, 14; **18** T. Aoki, 11; **19** Bosshard, Gramigni and Stadler, 7; **22** Kassner, 6; **23** Connell, 5; **24** Castilla, 3; **25** Cardoso, 1.

125 cc

15 laps, 63.300 miles/101.880 km

Place	Rider	Nat.	Machine	Laps	Time & speed	Fastest lap	Lap
1	Dirk Raudies	D	Honda	15	34m 44.974s 109.305 mph/ 175.910 km/h	2m 17.764s	9
2	Kazuto Sakata	J	Aprilia	15	35m 01.999s	2m 18.553s	12
3	Tomoko Manako	J	Honda	15	35m 02.293s	2m 18.627s	15
4	Peter Öttl	D	Aprilia	15	35m 02.319s	2m 18.554s	6
5	Stefano Perugini	I	Aprilia	15	35m 02.920s	2m 18.735s	15
6	Noboru Ueda	J	Honda	15	35m 15.380s	2m 18.456s	4
7	Jorge Martinez	E	Yamaha	15	35m 15.478s	2m 19.027s	6
8	Akira Saito	J	Honda	15	35m 15.882s	2m 19.121s	11
9	Masaki Tokudome	J	Honda	15	35m 16.030s	2m 18.796s	6
10	Oliver Petrucciani	CH	Aprilia	15	35m 16.444s	2m 19.364s	7
11	Oliver Koch	D	Honda	15	35m 16.532s	2m 19.221s	8
12	Bruno Casanova	I	Honda	15	35m 16.852s	2m 19.235s	10
13	Fausto Gresini	I	Honda	15	35m 16.886s	2m 19.373s	7
14	Lucio Cecchinello	I	Honda	15	35m 16.970s	2m 19.250s	7
15	Loek Bodelier	NL	Honda	15	35m 39.494s	2m 20.564s	5
16	Neil Hodgson	GB	Honda	15	35m 51.756s	2m 21.824s	3
17	Frédéric Petit	F	Yamaha	15	35m 52.001s	2m 21.824s	6
18	Manfred Baumann	A	Yamaha	15	36m 26.940s	2m 24.580s	14
19	Vittorio Lopez	I	Honda	15	36m 27.046s	2m 24.163s	13
20	Carlos Giro	E	Aprilia	15	36m 27.436s	2m 24.770s	4
21	Stefan Prein	D	Yamaha	15	36m 39.645s	2m 21.004s	2
22	Emili Alzamora	E	Honda	15	36m 51.302s	2m 21.895s	2
23	Rick van Etten	NL	Honda	14	35m 05.822s	2m 29.334s	6
	Nicolas Dussauge	F	Honda	10	DNF	2m 23.302s	3
	Hans Spaan	NL	Honda	10	DNF	2m 23.402s	3
	Hideyuki Nakajyo	J	Honda	9	DNF	2m 19.115s	7
	Takeshi Tsujimura	J	Honda	8	DNF	2m 18.882s	6
	Yoshiaki Katoh	J	Yamaha	7	DNF	2m 19.273s	6
	Maik Stief	D	Honda	6	DNF	2m 21.852s	3
	Manfred Geissler	D	Aprilia	6	DNF	2m 21.544s	3
	Stefan Kurfiss	D	Honda	4	DNF	2m 20.514s	4
	Herri Torrontegui	E	Aprilia	4	DNF	2m 20.396s	3
	Gabriele Debbia	I	Aprilia	2	DNF	2m 31.762s	1
	Emilio Cuppini	I	Aprilia	1	DNF	2m 25.373s	1
	Garry McCoy	AUS	Aprilia		DNS		

Fastest lap: Raudies, 2m 17.764s, 110.285 mph/177.486 km/h.
Lap record: Kazuto Sakata, J (Honda), 2m 17.301s, 110.657 mph/178.085 km/h (1993).

Qualifying: 1 Ueda, 2m 19.260s; **2** Raudies, 2m 19.410s; **3** Gresini, 2m 19.877s; **4** Petrucciani, 2m 20.631s; **5** Cuppini, 2m 21.246s; **6** Saito, 2m 21.440s; **7** Tsujimura, 2m 21.483s; **8** Kurfiss, 2m 21.607s; **9** Öttl, 2m 21.719s; **10** Koch, 2m 21.754s; **11** Perugini, 2m 21.818s; **12** Martinez, 2m 21.832s; **13** Bodelier, 2m 22.254s; **14** Katoh, 2m 22.443s; **15** Tokudome, 2m 22.664s; **16** Sakata, 2m 22.688s; **17** Petit, 2m 22.921s; **18** Nakajyo, 2m 23.150s; **19** Casanova, 2m 23.165s; **20** Manako, 2m 24.073s; **21** Prein, 2m 24.314s; **22** Stief, 2m 24.570s; **23** McCoy, 2m 24.752s; **24** Giro, 2m 24.900s; **25** Spaan, 2m 25.848s; **26** Alzamora, 2m 26.090s; **27** Hodgson, 2m 26.489s; **28** Geissler, 2m 26.720s; **29** Dussauge, 2m 27.076s; **30** Debbia, 2m 27.254s; **31** Torrontegui, 2m 27.520s; **32** Lopez, 2m 27.639s; **33** Baumann, 2m 28.328s; **34** Cecchinello, 2m 29.337s; **35** van Etten, 2m 30.724s.

World Championship: 1 Sakata, 121; **2** Raudies, 80; **3** Öttl, 79; **4** Ueda, 77; **5** McCoy, 48; **6** Saito and Tsujimura, 46; **8** Martinez and Torrontegui, 41; **10** Gresini, 34; **11** Tokudome, 32; **12** Petrucciani, 30; **13** Nakajyo, 27; **14** Koch, 26; **15** Perugini, 25; **16** Bodelier, 19; **17** Manako, 16; **18** Casanova, 15; **19** Aoki, 8; **20** Cuppini, 7; **21** Amano, Katoh and Scalvini, 4; **24** Debbia, 32; **25** Cecchinello, Geissler and Igata, 2; **28** Prein, 1.

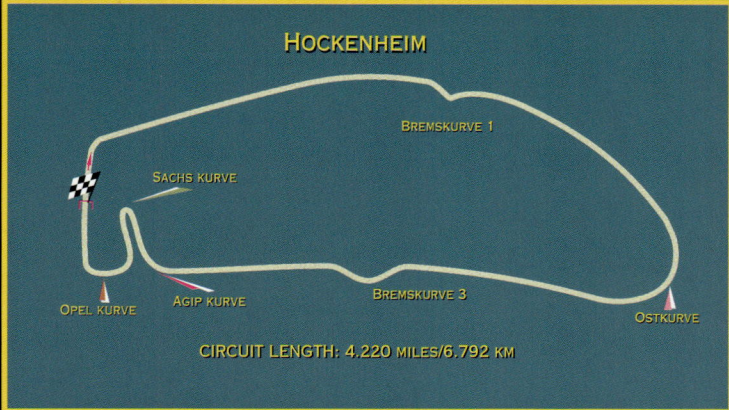

HOCKENHEIM

CIRCUIT LENGTH: 4.220 MILES/6.792 KM

Above: Second was enough to maintain Schwantz's smile – his good tracks were coming next ...

Noboru Ueda *(left)* was a potential winner until his gearlever snapped off.

Photos: Gold & Goose

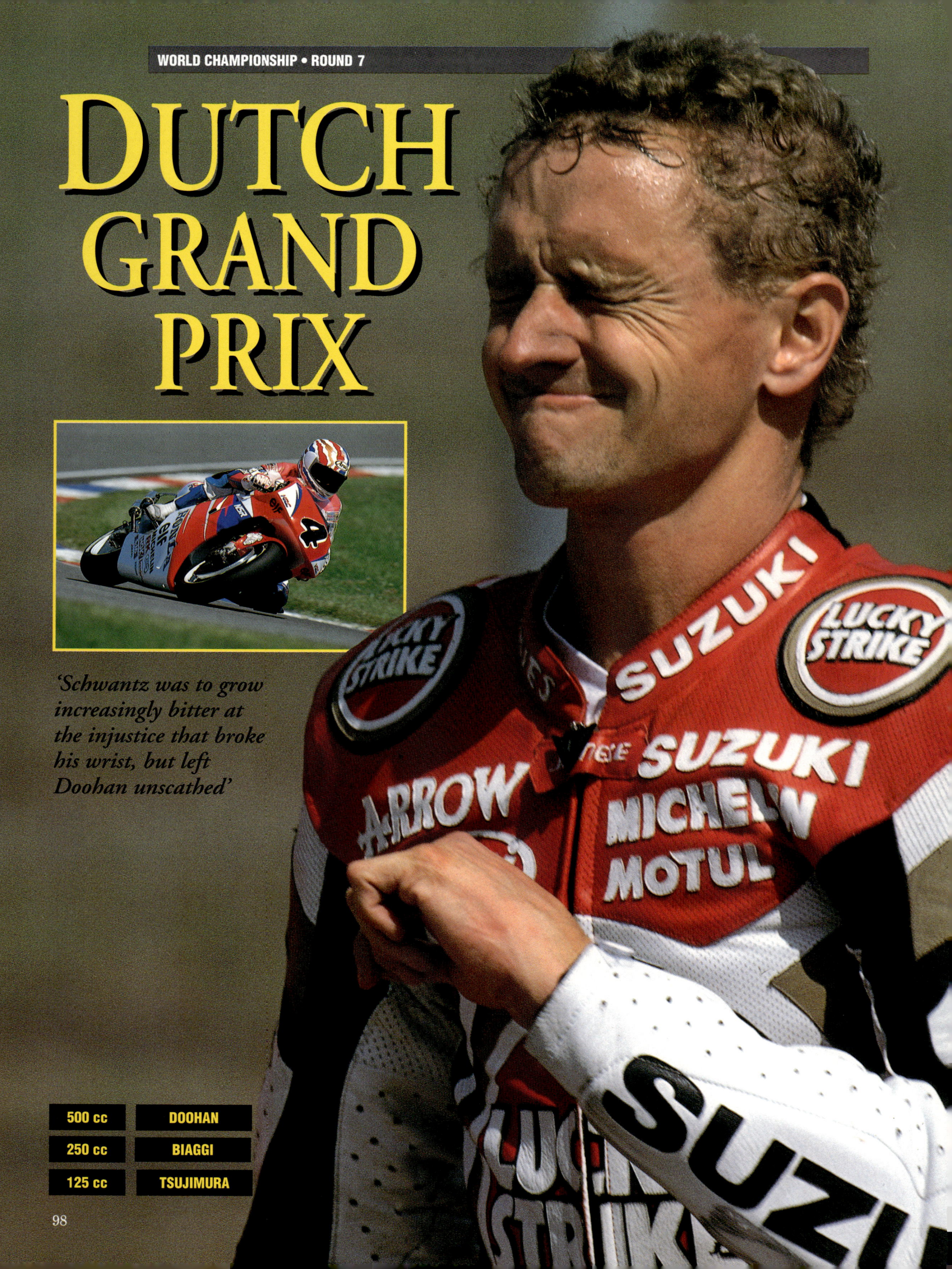

WORLD CHAMPIONSHIP • ROUND 7

DUTCH GRAND PRIX

'Schwantz was to grow increasingly bitter at the injustice that broke his wrist, but left Doohan unscathed'

500 cc	DOOHAN
250 cc	BIAGGI
125 cc	TSUJIMURA

DUTCH GRAND PRIX

Opposite page: Kevin Schwantz grimaces in two-fold agony – one the result of serious derangement of his wrist, the other the certain ruin of his title defence.

Amid important changes, traditions were upheld at Assen, and the Dutch GP was again a pivotal race in the World Championships.

As has become increasingly frequent, it was crashes that defined the significance, and the most significant was that of Kevin Schwantz, for it effectively ended his title defence.

Assen is a favourite track, where he has won thrice, and been beaten only by machine failure and as a hapless crash victim. Here, and at the following more technical circuits, he expected to start turning the tables on the Doohan-Honda steamroller. Instead he raced with his left wrist in a plaster cast, weak and in pain, to an heroic fifth. Back in the pits, Dr Claudio Costa dropped to his knees and said in his best (almost his only) English: 'I love you.' But the race had redamaged the injury, and with the next round just one week later, the omens were bad.

The 250 race was also significantly affected by an early collision between Capirossi and Harada. Later on the same lap early leader Romboni also went down. This left Biaggi to coast to an easy win and the clear title lead once again. The 125s also saw two front-runners in both race and title take a tumble: the ever-impetuous pole-qualifier Nobbie Ueda and (within mere yards of the line) erstwhile race leader Peter Öttl.

Practice crashers also numbered Doohan and Beattie, both lucky to get away with high-speed tumbles. Beattie's happened after he lost the front briefly at the fastest part of the track. He'd recovered but run onto the grass. Heading straight for the bank, he took the brave man's option and jumped off. Others were hurt in a small spate of get-offs: 125 riders Bruno Casanova and Oliver Koch broke a leg and the left arm and wrist respectively; 250 rider Alessandro Gramigni his shoulder and foot.

Tradition notwithstanding, there had been something of a sea-change at the senior race on the GP calendar. Assen has been a public roads circuit since long before it shrunk to its present length. In 1994, completion of a bypass meant it had become a closed circuit for the first time ever. Among other things, this means that Assen will not be a bikes-only track for much longer.

Many things remained as before – the massive crowds, the mid-season timing, the arrival of important new equipment. There was also the predictable blistering criticism from Doohan.

Since it was Assen that ruined his 1992 title bid and left him with a permanent limp, it is not surprising he harbours a grudge. But if this were all, it would surely have been settled by victory this year. Not so. 'I'm glad to have won here, but my opinion hasn't changed,' he said after the race. Earlier, he'd explained his continuing invective with more logic than in the past. 'I don't think we should be riding GP bikes on public roads. They have a crowned profile, which may be good for drainage but is lousy for racing. We're used to riding on corners with a flat profile, whether they're banked or not. You come out of corners with the wheel spinning and the bike sliding. With a crown on the road, as you really start drifting out the camber drops away and the bike spins and slides much more. It's unpredictable, and it causes a lot of crashes. I don't think we should race here, but maybe none of the other riders has the balls to agree with me.'

Challenging words, delivered unequivocally and as publicly as possible at the post-practice 'front-row' press conference. Alberto Puig, sitting alongside, agreed – if guardedly. 'On a 250 you don't have the wheelspin. On a 500, Assen is a very different track.' Schwantz, sitting injured at the far end, was in a tricky position. Apart from his past successes on the subtle sweeps, his sponsors Lucky Strike are also long-time Dutch TT backers. But his own crash was proof enough, and he did allow that 'It can catch you out.' Only Alex Barros, on the eve of his best race of the year so far, stood up for Assen: 'It's my favourite track.'

The complaint applies only to some sections of the track, which was recently fully resurfaced and widened. Now with no more public road obligations the way is open to bank the remaining kinks and corners, but it is unlikely to happen for a few years.

Schwantz was to grow increasingly bitter at the injustice that broke his wrist, but left Doohan unscathed. The Australian fell at high speed, but could not blame the circuit. He suspected a dragging front brake. 'The front started sliding at a place where it is already light, then when I corrected it, it just carried on sliding. I was in over-rev in a gear that tops at 230 km/h,' he said, well aware of the implications of his lucky escape.

Schwantz's crucial crash happened at the end of the first day of practice, in the closing minutes of a frustrating timed session, with one bike giving engine trouble and the other suffering a continuing reluctance to turn, especially under braking. He'd been down in seventh, and in the last laps set about improving matters. 'It was my own fault,' he said. 'I was trying to go faster than the bike's ability.'

Chasing Barros, engaged in a similar exercise and in fact slightly faster, he gassed it too early at Mandeveen, the first of a tricky pair of rights at the furthest point of the circuit. The Suzuki stepped out, flicked him out of the seat, then dropped him on the low side and followed him towards the barrier. 'I put out my left hand to fend it off and the gas tank landed on my wrist.' This dislocated three of the eight small bones in two rows at the bottom of the wrist, fractured a bone in his hand, and cracked the crucial scaphoid bone. He was not expected to race.

But Schwantz is special. He was out again for an exploratory three laps the next afternoon, which turned into a full-scale practice session, still searching for better handling. He even led the race briefly. It was marvellous. But it was a long way short of turning the tables on Doohan.

Others had brought their left hand injuries with them. John Kocinski had a broken finger and Luca Cadalora a bad gash, both from Hockenheim; Niall Mackenzie had a broken radius and ulna from a testing crash at Donington, after a hose-clip broke and spilled water onto his rear tyre. Then there was 125 ace Garry McCoy's right little finger. This had been scraped on the track in Germany, but treatment at the track had missed bone damage and dirt underneath a flap of skin. A day later McCoy's own doctor discovered the full extent of the injury. The Australian was riding with difficulty, and facing possible amputation.

Assen traditionally sees new equipment, but such is the pace of development that everybody already had their new ram-air fairings (Suzuki 500s and Honda 125s), while Suzuki actually dropped the still-secret shrouded straight-rate rear damper. But Yamaha followed tradition, with a new frame for Cadalora, at last replacing the die-hard 1992-based Roc-built frame of the past two seasons. It was a revival of the factory's own complex-section extruded tube unit, first used and rejected last year by Rainey, and rejected again at pre-season tests. Said team boss Roberts: 'We've had a problem with our bike not turning into the corners fast enough. It seems the new frame will be better, though with Luca's injury we can't tell too much yet. It only arrived Monday.' Luca said good things; but so did Beattie, still on a Roc, of the latest Dunlops. The biggest problem was horsepower, with the Australian well up in twisty section times – second in one session on the last third of the track, but only 12th on the part including the back straight.

One more aftermath of the German GP was a settlement of the potentially dangerous grudge match between Romboni and Biaggi after the latter's adventurous Hockenheim tactics. Race director Roberto Nosetto called a special class meeting on the first day of practice to defuse the situation. He replayed the video, then said something along the lines that it hadn't been dangerous riding, but that they shouldn't do it again. Biaggi was thus somewhat exonerated, and when asked if he would make the same move again said: 'Yes, but not so hard.' Romboni was also conciliatory. 'For a few hours after the race I was very angry, but when I watched the video in the week afterwards my view changed. I did not lodge any complaint about Max, and I did not ask Nosetto to call the meeting.'

500 cc PRACTICE

Schwantz is always a pole-position candidate here, but his effort ended while trying to ride through suspension problems. He'd just snuck onto the front row when he crashed, and who knows what he might have done the next day – though, to be fair, none of the top six actually improved in a windy session.

By then Doohan had also fallen, but retained pole anyway with a first day time more than half a second outside Schwantz's 1991 lap record, but an even greater distance out of reach of second-placed Puig. Like the track or not, nobody was able to go round it faster.

There are no more adjectives to describe the prowess of Alberto Puig. At the hardest track in his first 500 year he qualified second, the best-ever Spaniard in the class. He admitted he'd been close to crashing several times as he worked to adapt 500 cc speed and wheelspin to 250 rider's track knowledge, saying again: 'In racing you have to take risks.'

Next to the pair of Hondas, both Suzukis. Barros was third at his best

Photos: Gold & Goose

99

DUTCH GRAND PRIX

Right: Victorious, but glad to be leaving – Michael Doohan didn't soften his attitude to Assen.

Below: Alberto Puig shone in practice, but ran into familiar physical problems.

Bottom left: Alex Criville, a former Assen winner, was on the rostrum again.

Bottom right: This patchwork pink Roc, Jeandat at the helm, is a typical 500 privateer bike, for sale by the square foot, and trying hard just to get close to the top ten.

Luca Cadalora *(opposite page)* was back, but with his hand injury even wiping his eye was hard work.

Photos: Gold & Goose

DUTCH GRAND PRIX

track, and having crashed out of the lead last year was trying to stay calm and smooth. He had engine problems on the second day, wasting a lot of time walking back to the pits. 'At least I am happy with the settings we had yesterday,' he said. Then in race morning warm-up both bikes broke down again, triggering a massive team effort, including Schwantz's mechanics, to fit up a new engine that had to be ready to race in less than three hours.

Schwantz also had engine problems in his first session, which may have contributed to his unseemly and expensive haste at the end of the afternoon. He was still hunting balance and stability, especially on corner entry under braking. When he went out the next day, his left arm in a cast and holding a specially shaped handlebar grip, he planned just three laps to run in a new engine, but became involved not only in 'seeing if I could do it', but also continuing suspension work. He ran 18 laps, almost full race distance.

The first positions in row two were also set on the first afternoon, with former Assen winner (the year Doohan, Rainey, Schwantz and Lawson all crashed) Criville's Honda leading it, more than a second down on pole.

Then came Chandler's Cagiva, the American looking as though he was working hard, which is not a good style for Assen. He knew that too, but when he smoothed out on day two to his more usual relaxed style, the times relaxed too. 'It's a strange track,' he said. 'It seems to get harder to ride a 500 here every year.'

Itoh's Honda was alongside, with Kocinski next, well below par at a track where he had expected much. His second left-hand finger, broken a fortnight before, was stiff and sore. 'I usually use two fingers on the clutch but now I have to use my whole hand. I'm not even holding the bike the way I am used to,' he said.

Beattie led row three, amazingly unhurt after pushing the 'Eject' button on the fastest part of the course; but he was little closer to regaining competitive form, in spite of some improvement from new front Dunlops. Weaned on Hondas, with their plentiful power, his style leaves him short of corner exit speed and resultant top speed on a Yamaha. As Rainey's press-on style showed, the Yamaha needs to be ridden more aggressively, offering in exchange more sympathetic handling to accommodate such a technique. But when Beattie tried it, he was just chewing up his front tyre.

Reggiani's 400 V-twin Aprilia was next, tenth fastest, not as good as expected. It wasn't fast enough, and the time it lost on the flat-out back section, taking the bikes from first gear to sixth, was at least as much as it made up on the twists. New crankcases and cylinders were, said chief engineer Witteveen, simply rationalised versions of the Hockenheim equipment. 'We'd used up all the available development on the old set, now we start again with these,' he said.

Cadalora was alongside, using the new Yamaha chassis but really in trouble with his painful hand injury. 'It's not good to feel that I may not be able to control anything that might happen,' he said. 'I don't know if I will be able to finish.'

John Reynolds completed the row, ready as usual to step into the gap left for top privateer by Niall Mackenzie, who qualified 18th, riding with his own plaster cast.

Jeandat led row four from McWilliams, Naveau and Bernard Garcia. All 31 entrants qualified.

500 cc RACE – 20 LAPS

There wasn't much doubt about who was going to win before the race, nor in the last lap. It was only the bit in the middle that was unexpected, as clear favourite Doohan found himself unable to shake off the pursuit of Barros and a dogged Criville, and obliged to put his earlier hopes on hold. 'I thought I might clear off at the beginning, but I got a bad start. Then I thought I might do the same thing in the middle of the race, and that didn't work either. I decided to wait until the last two laps, and if that didn't work there was nothing left.'

He'd got away fourth, as Kocinski grabbed the early lead, Schwantz on his tail and Barros next, an order they held for two laps more, all in each other's pockets, until Schwantz – arm in a cast, teeth gritted – made his move at the end of the pit straight. He was as amazed as anybody to be leading in his condition. 'I thought there must have been a crash behind me.'

Barros followed past at the end of the back straight, then Kocinski was consigned to fourth by Doohan after the pit straight. Next it was Criville's turn and the American was fifth at the end of lap four, in a much closer race than anyone had expected.

Now Schwantz's injury started to tell and he slowed marginally, leaving Barros in front, with Doohan shadowing and preparing to pounce. He did so at the Strubben horseshoe, and was in the lead at last. But the anticipated escape simply didn't happen. Doohan went faster to break up the group, and Barros and Criville just went along with him.

At half-distance, Barros nosed in front again for two laps; then Doohan took his turn, seeing that he was faster in some parts. 'But when he followed me after that he must have picked up some tips,' grinned Doohan, for when the Brazilian passed him again on lap 15 he was noticeably quicker. Doohan elected to play it cool to the finish, tucking in behind as Criville dropped off the back of the group, complaining later about a spinning rear tyre.

Two laps from the end, the showdown began. Barros was tight into the bends, then on the kink after the pits he was too tight and the Honda too fast. Doohan swept past on the outside. Head down, he charged away. Head down, Barros followed him. Both riders made their fastest laps now, Barros on lap 19 and Doohan on 20, although both were still short of the record. And while the gap never really closed right down, nor did it open up.

The likelihood of a repeat of Barros's crash last year grew. He was in the lead then; now he saw Doohan just tantalisingly out of reach, and the temptation to try that bit harder must have been almost unbearable. To his credit, he resisted. 'The Honda was faster past the pits, but the Suzuki was faster on the back straight,' he said, rather surprisingly. 'I was hoping to attack, but I had a couple of wheelspins, and he was too far away. I decided second would be better than nothing.'

Thus Doohan flashed across the line 1.9 seconds ahead, a far smaller margin than he would have wanted after a most unexpectedly tense and difficult race.

Criville had meanwhile dropped into the clutches of Puig, but he fought back, hanging on his rear wheel. The issue was resolved on the last lap when Puig had a huge slide and was thrown out of the seat, smashing the screen with his helmet, but landing right side up and pointing the right way. He finished in fourth.

Some way back, Schwantz had been dogging Chandler's back wheel, conserving his strength for a last-lap attack on the back straight. It went perfectly to plan, and he led the Cagiva across the line by half a second. 'Doug was riding well, but the bike seemed to be leaking oil, with his feet coming off the pegs,' said Kevin. Chandler in turn complained that though he was fine on his own, anyone in front would slow him mid-corner, losing him valuable momentum and even dropping him out of the powerband.

What Schwantz didn't reveal was the full extent of the pain he had suffered. Reset two evenings before, the same bones were dislocated again after the race.

Arch-enemy Kocinski complained later that Schwantz had deliberately blocked him as he and Puig caught up with the fading champion. 'He let the other guy through then closed the door on me. I guess I should expect that of him.' Schwantz had his own version: 'I could see Alberto was fast so I let him by. But I'm racing John for the championship.' It almost ended in tears, with Kocinski attempting an over-ambitious outbraking move at the first corner, and being forced to lift and run straight onto the grass. By the time he got going again, he was lying in 15th.

This left Beattie to a lonely but at least untroubled seventh, his best so far. 'I feel at last we're going in the right direction,' he said, after noting

101

Main picture: Bayle, Waldmann and Okada practise psyche-out games under braking for the chicane. The Frenchman (22) had really arrived as a GP racer.

Above: Wilco Zeelenberg's only rostrum of the year left him thrilled enough to throw his helmet into the crowd.

Left and inset left: 'I just felt a bang from behind.' Collision imminent, Harada is about to be launched by Capirossi, who later (briefly) blamed his victim. Damage to the Yamaha's seat clearly shows the point of impact.

Photos: Gold & Goose

DUTCH GRAND PRIX

Right: And for Max Biaggi, it was just a cruise in the 250 cc race.

that for once his front tyre finished the race well used but still working. But he was still short of speed, a fact made obvious when he was dicing with Itoh before the Japanese rider crashed on lap six. 'I'd pass him into the chicane, and he'd be ahead of me again when we crossed the finish line, barely 100 yards away.'

Kocinski worked his way back to finish eighth and 14 seconds adrift. His last victim was the pained Cadalora, who had earlier been tussling for his honour with privateer Reynolds and Reggiani's V-twin before the former had crashed and the latter suffered a massive crankshaft/con rod failure, reportedly the bike's first ever.

Bernard Garcia was a solitary tenth, with Jeandat just beating Naveau to 11th. Then came Miralles, Bonhuil and Foray in a race with only 19 finishers. As well as those already mentioned, 12 retirements included Emmett after a crash, Migliorati and Pedercini after a private collision, and the luckless Mackenzie, whose bike dropped onto two cylinders on the second lap.

Thus Doohan left Assen with a slightly smaller points lead than in 1992, but in a very different position. This time his rival was hurt, while the well-rounded combination of Mick, the Honda, and the fettling of crew chief Jerry Burgess was looking unbeatable.

250 cc PRACTICE

Biaggi went from the 1994 Aprilia engine of Hockenheim back to the old faithful 1993 motor to claim pole position in the closing minutes of the final session. 'The older one is easier to ride in the mid-range. That's better here,' he explained.

Capirossi was second, only a quarter of a second down after also leaving his best efforts until the last.

The timing may not have been contrived to unsettle third Italian superstar Romboni, but it was perfect all the same. Rombo, a 125 Assen winner in 1990, who broke his leg here last year to spoil his championship chances, had been consistently fastest until then. He had some justification. 'We changed the gearing very slightly compared with yesterday, and it made a very big difference, even though it was only by a couple of km/h,' he said. 'We'll go back to what we had before and go faster again.'

Final front-row man was again Okada, in his second Assen visit and only starting to get things right on the second day. 'It's a hard track and the settings have been difficult, but now we have found the right direction,' he said. 'If we had more practice I would expect to get faster again.'

Aoki led row two from Ruggia, who was having engine trouble yet again with machinery that doesn't seem to be a problem for the other Aprilia riders, reinforcing his reputation for being rough on bikes.

Then came Harada, close to full strength now but hampered by a works Yamaha that is short of the class standard. He was visibly trying hard to make even the second row, and ending up only a tenth ahead of Waldmann's NSR, in the German's first Assen 250 outing. Ralf's combination of aggression and experience, gained in the 125 class, was backed by improving confidence and clear natural talent, and he was getting ready to join in at the top levels.

Some enthusiasts were starting to say similar things about Bayle, and indeed his steady progress continued. He led row three from disappointing top Dutchman Zeelenberg's NSR, and the similar bike of D'Antin, with Suter's Aprilia completing the row. Then came the van den Goorbergh brothers, Jurgen the faster to lead row four, with Assen novice Honma alongside on the Marlboro Rainey Yamaha.

There were 33 qualifiers.

250 cc RACE – 18 LAPS

Romboni burst into the lead, with Biaggi hot on his heels. Capirossi and Harada were emerging behind, not only to chase the leaders but also to scrap it out themselves. It didn't last the first lap.

The first clash saw Capirossi try too hard to get back underneath Harada at the looping Strubben: he found himself running out of road with nowhere to go. He pushed Harada off the track before going into a graceful high-side of his own that left him heavily concussed. At first he blamed Harada, but later went and apologised. The Japanese rider had a simple tale. 'I was in the corner when something hit me from behind.'

At the far end of the same lap came Romboni's tumble, at the Bult left-hander. 'I don't really know what happened. The front just slipped away,' he said. But Biaggi was happy to suggest that his rival was just pushing too hard in a vain attempt to escape.

Anyway, it left Biaggi already almost ten seconds in the clear, and free to charge away to a faultless third win of the year. 'I saw Romboni fall, then I got the signal Capirossi Out, but I continued to push hard. It was very important to win here.'

The real race was for second, where Aoki, Okada and Waldmann were caught by Zeelenberg and Bayle by the tenth lap, and a tooth-and-nail battle commenced that lasted to the flag. It was a little surprising that Okada didn't manage to break away, and impressive that both Waldmann and especially Bayle were able to hold their own. The French ex-dirt biker was up to second on one occasion. And all the while Zeelenberg was at or near the back, watching and waiting.

The last lap was a masterpiece of tension. Bayle was generally just out of touch as the other four went at it, arriving four abreast into the final chicane. Aoki easily won the out-braking battle, only to run straight across the grass as the others fought on underneath his elbow.

Okada, very properly, won out, while Zeelenberg's tactics turned out to be excellent for a popular and opportunistic third place, his first rostrum in almost three years. Waldmann was right up behind – then Aoki wobbled into fifth. Unfortunately he had rejoined all crossed up and forced Bayle into the dirt, and the Aprilia team lodged a protest, without much hope of success.

D'Antin had been left 25 seconds adrift for a solitary seventh; Suter defeated Jurgen van den Goorbergh for eighth, while brother Patrick survived a first-lap pushing match to come through to tenth, narrowly ahead of Checa, Fiorillo and the dogged Honma.

Others of the ten retirements included the Aprilias of Ruggia and Preining, both with engine trouble.

Thus luck and the points lead swung back Biaggi's way, not to mention Okada's: another swoop in a roller-coaster season.

125 cc RACE – 17 LAPS

Japanese Honda privateer and general hero Takeshi Tsujimura stalled on the startline, then achieved the almost impossible at the difficult Dutch circuit to ride right through the field to take victory. He had to fight for it all the way, with a five-strong group of bikes battling right up to the final corners.

The race had started rather differently, with pole-qualifier Ueda setting off furiously in an attempt to break away, hotly pursued by Raudies's similar airbox-equipped Honda and the Aprilias of Öttl and Sakata. Ueda's effort lasted only until the second lap, when he fell trying too hard through typically difficult Assen kinks; Raudies went one lap later with a crank bearing failure, the first such problem in three years.

Tsujimura, left to push-start after stalling his engine on the line, had immediately commenced a storming recovery, passing 17 riders on the first lap to cross the line 16th (Akira Saito had helped him by crashing). When Raudies went, he was up to seventh, and he was soon forging his way to the front of the leading group, now dominated by Sakata and Öttl. He took the lead for the first time on lap 12.

It was a superb race, with six riders disputing the lead until Hockenheim hero and still Team FCC substitute Manako's Honda broke down with five laps left. Then there were five, weaving and ducking and slipstreaming, then breaking formation to enter corners three or four abreast.

At the finish Tsujimura crossed the line barely two-tenths ahead of veteran Jorge Martinez's Yamaha. Öttl was with them but ran too fast into the chicane, cutting the second apex then rejoining off-line so that he crashed, almost taking down Sakata. This left the way open for Dutch private Honda rider Loek Bodelier, in the race of his life, to claim third, with Sakata fourth.

Öttl could still have had fifth if he'd picked up his bike and pushed across the line; instead he stalked off in a rage, leaving the position to Tokudome, 15 seconds down but mere hundredths ahead of Herri Torrontegui's Aprilia. Petrucciani took seventh.

Another five seconds down, Garry McCoy, hampered by his badly injured right hand, managed to fend off Nakajyo's Honda. Debbia and Alzamora were next, ahead of Aoki, Scalvini, Petit and Cecchinello. Yoshiaki Katoh crashed out on the second Yamaha; other fallers included Perugini, Prein and Geissler.

The puzzling Giro pulled out on the startline, complaining of engine trouble on the warm-up lap. His mechanics were unable to find anything wrong, and the strange Spanish saga continued.

Sakata's luck was holding, while the hoped-for mid-season difficulties for Japanese riders simply weren't happening this time round.

103

FIM WORLD CHAMPIONSHIP • ROUND 7
LUCKY STRIKE
GROTE PRIJS VAN NEDERLAND
25 JUNE 1994

500 cc

20 laps, 75.180 miles/120.980 km

Place	Rider	Nat.	Machine	Laps	Time & speed	Fastest lap	Lap
1	Michael Doohan	AUS	Honda	20	41m 35.272s 108.454 mph/ 174.541 km/h	2m 03.144s	20
2	Alexandre Barros	BR	Suzuki	20	41m 37.172s	2m 03.905s	19
3	Alex Criville	E	Honda	20	41m 42.718s	2m 04.013s	19
4	Alberto Puig	E	Honda	20	41m 53.228s	2m 03.824s	16
5	Kevin Schwantz	USA	Suzuki	20	41m 59.131s	2m 04.852s	20
6	Doug Chandler	USA	Cagiva	20	41m 59.736s	2m 04.857s	19
7	Daryl Beattie	AUS	Yamaha	20	42m 10.304s	2m 05.545s	4
8	John Kocinski	USA	Cagiva	20	42m 24.409s	2m 04.890s	6
9	Luca Cadalora	I	Yamaha	20	42m 31.978s	2m 06.335s	20
10	Bernard Garcia	F	Yamaha	20	42m 44.141s	2m 06.664s	8
11	Jean-Pierre Jeandat	F	Yamaha	20	43m 08.553s	2m 07.829s	5
12	Laurent Naveau	B	Yamaha	20	43m 09.455s	2m 08.542s	8
13	Julian Miralles	E	Yamaha	20	43m 31.748s	2m 09.480s	18
14	Bruno Bonhuil	F	Yamaha	20	43m 32.033s	2m 09.427s	20
15	Jean Foray	F	Yamaha	20	43m 32.825s	2m 09.580s	18
16	Bernard Hänggeli	CH	Yamaha	20	43m 32.904s	2m 09.511s	18
17	Kevin Mitchell	GB	Yamaha	19	41m 58.308s	2m 10.598s	3
18	Cees Doorakkers	NL	Yamaha	19	42m 58.668s	2m 10.289s	3
19	Vittorio Scatola	I	Paton	19	44m 02.594s	2m 12.688s	11
	John Reynolds	GB	Yamaha	14	DNF	2m 06.501s	13
	Loris Reggiani	I	Aprilia	11	DNF	2m 06.108s	10
	Sean Emmett	GB	Yamaha	11	DNF	2m 08.320s	11
	Jeremy McWilliams	GB	Yamaha	7	DNF	2m 09.828s	2
	Shinichi Itoh	J	Honda	5	DNF	2m 05.656s	3
	Cristiano Migliorati	I	Yamaha	4	DNF	2m 10.746s	2
	Lucio Pedercini	I	Yamaha	4	DNF	2m 11.445s	2
	Lothar Neukirchner	D	Yamaha	4	DNF	2m 12.756s	3
	Andreas Leuthe	D	Yamaha	2	DNF	2m 13.645s	2
	Niall Mackenzie	GB	Yamaha	2	DNF	2m 19.198s	1
	Marc Garcia	F	Yamaha	2	DNF	2m 20.960s	1
	Juan Lopez Mella	E	Yamaha	1	DNF	2m 38.255s	1

Fastest lap: Doohan, 2m 03.144s, 109.881 mph/176.837 km/h.
Lap record: Kevin Schwantz, USA (Suzuki), 2m 02.443s, 110.519 mph/177.849 km/h (1991).

Qualifying: 1 Doohan, 2m 03.035s; 2 Puig, 2m 03.655s; 3 Barros, 2m 03.721s; 4 Schwantz, 2m 04.123s; 5 Criville, 2m 04.156s; 6 Chandler, 2m 04.503s; 7 Itoh, 2m 04.754s; 8 Kocinski, 2m 04.996s; 9 Beattie, 2m 05.213s; 10 Reggiani, 2m 05.578s; 11 Cadalora, 2m 05.988s; 12 Reynolds, 2m 06.514s; 13 Jeandat, 2m 07.174s; 14 McWilliams, 2m 07.229s; 15 Naveau, 2m 07.814s; 16 B. Garcia, 2m 07.855s; 17 Lopez Mella, 2m 07.894s; 18 Mackenzie, 2m 07.997s; 19 Emmett, 2m 08.435s; 20 M. Garcia, 2m 08.801s; 21 Miralles, 2m 09.088s; 22 Hänggeli, 2m 09.130s; 23 Foray, 2m 09.320s; 24 Bonhuil, 2m 09.345s; 25 Doorakkers, 2m 09.940s; 26 Pedercini, 2m 10.288s; 27 Migliorati, 2m 11.053s; 28 Mitchell, 2m 11.108s; 29 Leuthe, 2m 12.185s; 30 Scatola, 2m 13.025s; 31 Neukirchner, 2m 13.517s.

World Championship: 1 M. Doohan, 161; 2 Schwantz, 119; 3 Kocinski, 87; 4 Criville, 83; 5 Barros, 81; 6 Puig, 77; 7 Itoh, 66; 8 Cadalora, 53; 9 Chandler, 48; 10 Reynolds, 32; 11 Mackenzie, 28; 12 Beattie and B. Garcia, 23; 14 Emmett, 14; 15 Lopez Mella, 11; 16 Honma, Jeandat and McWilliams, 10; 19 Naveau, 9; 20 Migliorati, Miralles and Reggiani, 7; 23 Moineau, 5; 24 S. Doohan, 4; 25 Bonhuil, 3; 26 Foray and Pedercini, 1.

250 cc

18 laps, 67.662 miles/108.882 km

Place	Rider	Nat.	Machine	Laps	Time & speed	Fastest lap	Lap
1	Massimiliano Biaggi	I	Aprilia	18	38m 19.086s 105.939 mph/ 170.492 km/h	2m 06.357s	18
2	Tadayuki Okada	J	Honda	18	38m 47.788s	2m 08.522s	10
3	Wilco Zeelenberg	NL	Honda	18	38m 48.052s	2m 08.001s	8
4	Ralf Waldmann	D	Honda	18	38m 48.307s	2m 08.419s	2
5	Nobuatsu Aoki	J	Honda	18	38m 48.818s	2m 08.275s	11
6	Jean-Michel Bayle	F	Aprilia	18	38m 49.025s	2m 08.153s	8
7	Luis D'Antin	E	Honda	18	39m 15.716s	2m 09.238s	2
8	Eskil Suter	CH	Aprilia	18	39m 17.806s	2m 09.892s	18
9	Jurgen van den Goorbergh	NL	Aprilia	18	39m 18.208s	2m 09.758s	5
10	Patrick van den Goorbergh	NL	Aprilia	18	39m 27.822s	2m 10.286s	3
11	Carlos Checa	E	Honda	18	39m 27.909s	2m 09.966s	5
12	Giuseppe Fiorillo	I	Honda	18	39m 27.967s	2m 10.485s	13
13	Toshihiko Honma	J	Yamaha	18	39m 28.494s	2m 10.385s	12
14	Bernd Kassner	D	Aprilia	18	39m 37.507s	2m 10.716s	10
15	Adi Stadler	D	Honda	18	39m 58.162s	2m 11.934s	7
16	Luis Maurel	E	Honda	18	39m 58.268s	2m 11.790s	5
17	Christian Boudinot	F	Aprilia	18	39m 58.454s	2m 11.916s	5
18	Noel Ferro	F	Honda	18	39m 58.485s	2m 11.902s	5
19	Kristian Kaas	SF	Yamaha	18	40m 28.042s	2m 13.156s	5
20	Manuel Hernandez	E	Aprilia	18	40m 32.226s	2m 12.849s	5
21	Rudi Markink	NL	Honda	17	38m 40.872s	2m 14.872s	4
22	Rodney Fee	CAN	Honda	17	38m 45.079s	2m 15.252s	4
23	Juanlino Kirindongo	NL	Honda	17	38m 45.644s	2m 15.082s	12
	Alan Patterson	GB	Honda	11	DNF	2m 14.692s	4
	José Luis Cardoso	E	Aprilia	10	DNF	2m 12.244s	8
	Enrique de Juan	E	Aprilia	9	DNF	2m 13.997s	9
	Frédéric Protat	F	Honda	7	DNF	2m 13.206s	4
	Adrian Bosshard	CH	Honda	6	DNF	2m 10.843s	2
	Doriano Romboni	I	Honda	2	DNF	2m 07.202s	2
	Loris Capirossi	I	Honda	2	DNF	2m 07.155s	2
	Tetsuya Harada	J	Yamaha	2	DNF	2m 07.676s	2
	Andy Preining	A	Aprilia	1	DNF	2m 28.957s	1
	Jean-Philippe Ruggia	F	Aprilia	1	DNF	5m 28.223s	1
	Alessandro Gramigni	I	Aprilia		DNS		

Fastest lap: Biaggi, 2m 06.357s, 107.087 mph/172.340 km/h (record).
Previous record: John Kocinski, USA (Suzuki), 2m 06.951s, 106.586 mph/171.534 km/h (1993).

Qualifying: 1 Biaggi, 2m 05.997s; 2 Capirossi, 2m 06.253s; 3 Romboni, 2m 06.389s; 4 Okada, 2m 07.150s; 5 Aoki, 2m 07.286s; 6 Ruggia, 2m 07.390s; 7 Harada, 2m 07.761s; 8 Waldmann, 2m 07.838s; 9 Bayle, 2m 07.931s; 10 Zeelenberg, 2m 08.716s; 11 D'Antin, 2m 09.372s; 12 Suter, 2m 09.794s; 13 J. van den Goorbergh, 2m 09.957s; 14 P. van den Goorbergh, 2m 10.000s; 15 Honma, 2m 10.128s; 16 Preining, 2m 10.141s; 17 Fiorillo, 2m 10.447s; 18 Bosshard, 2m 10.530s; 19 Checa, 2m 10.897s; 20 Kassner, 2m 11.225s; 21 Cardoso, 2m 11.523s; 22 Maurel, 2m 12.116s; 23 Boudinot, 2m 12.699s; 24 Ferro, 2m 13.087s; 25 Stadler, 2m 13.268s; 26 Kaas, 2m 13.546s; 27 Hernandez, 2m 13.746s; 28 Protat, 2m 13.802s; 29 de Juan, 2m 14.344s; 30 Markink, 2m 15.580s; 31 Patterson, 2m 15.699s; 32 Fee, 2m 16.165s; 33 Kirindongo, 2m 16.250s.

World Championship: 1 Biaggi, 128; 2 Okada, 116; 3 Capirossi, 102; 4 Romboni, 93; 5 Ruggia, 78; 6 Waldmann, 66; 7 D'Antin, 57; 8 N. Aoki, 53; 9 Bayle, 48; 10 Zeelenberg, 43; 11 Harada, 25; 12 Suter and J. van den Goorbergh, 22; 14 P. van den Goorbergh, 21; 15 Checa, 19; 16 Ukawa, 16; 17 Preining, 14; 18 T. Aoki, 11; 19 Kassner and Stadler, 8; 21 Bosshard and Gramigni, 7; 23 Connell, 5; 24 Fiorillo, 4; 25 Castilla and Honma, 3; 27 Cardoso, 1.

ASSEN RACING CIRCUIT

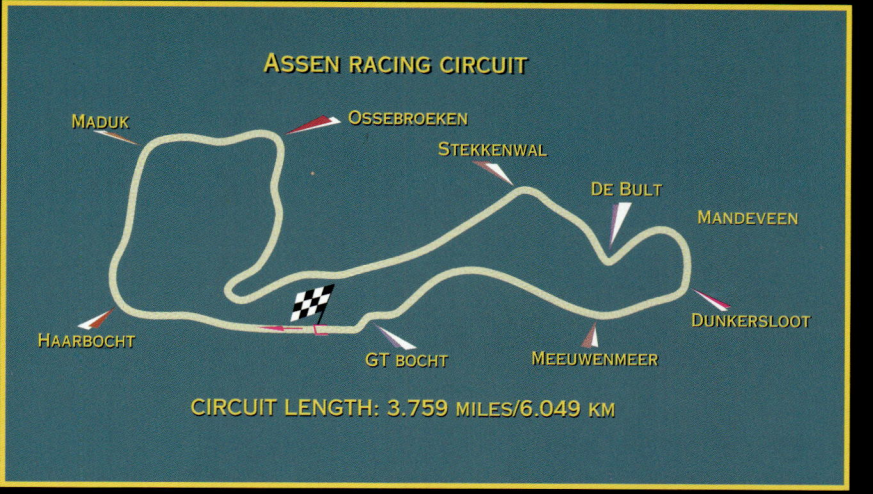

CIRCUIT LENGTH: 3.759 MILES/6.049 KM

Maduk, Ossebroeken, Stekkenwal, De Bult, Mandeveen, Dunkersloot, Meeuwenmeer, GT bocht, Haarbocht

125 cc

17 laps, 63.903 miles/102.833 km

Place	Rider	Nat.	Machine	Laps	Time & speed	Fastest lap	Lap
1	Takeshi Tsujimura	J	Honda	17	39m 07.728s 97.980 mph/ 157.684 km/h	2m 16.586s	8
2	Jorge Martinez	E	Yamaha	17	39m 07.958s	2m 17.026s	11
3	Loek Bodelier	NL	Honda	17	39m 08.670s	2m 16.703s	6
4	Kazuto Sakata	J	Aprilia	17	39m 09.082s	2m 16.638s	13
5	Masaki Tokudome	J	Honda	17	39m 24.977s	2m 17.689s	3
6	Herri Torrontegui	E	Aprilia	17	39m 24.982s	2m 17.852s	3
7	Oliver Petrucciani	CH	Aprilia	17	39m 39.890s	2m 17.884s	8
8	Garry McCoy	AUS	Aprilia	17	39m 44.615s	2m 19.211s	10
9	Hideyuki Nakajyo	J	Honda	17	39m 44.750s	2m 18.905s	3
10	Gabriele Debbia	I	Aprilia	17	39m 47.394s	2m 18.460s	3
11	Emili Alzamora	E	Honda	17	39m 52.866s	2m 19.582s	16
12	Haruchika Aoki	J	Honda	17	39m 53.017s	2m 19.168s	16
13	Gianluigi Scalvini	I	Aprilia	17	39m 53.134s	2m 19.087s	17
14	Frédéric Petit	F	Yamaha	17	39m 53.472s	2m 19.314s	3
15	Lucio Cecchinello	I	Honda	17	39m 53.733s	2m 19.489s	17
16	Fausto Gresini	I	Honda	17	40m 19.852s	2m 19.558s	2
17	Manfred Baumann	A	Honda	17	40m 23.368s	2m 20.709s	9
18	Neil Hodgson	GB	Honda	17	40m 32.108s	2m 21.031s	9
19	Vittorio Lopez	I	Honda	17	40m 36.491s	2m 21.993s	5
20	Hans Spaan	NL	Honda	17	40m 43.223s	2m 22.093s	5
21	Rick van Etten	NL	Honda	17	41m 11.270s	2m 23.976s	2
22	Marcel Nooren	NL	Honda	17	41m 12.582s	2m 23.998s	3
	Peter Öttl	D	Aprilia	16	DNF	2m 17.182s	13
	Tomoko Manako	J	Honda	12	DNF	2m 16.921s	6
	Manfred Geissler	D	Aprilia	12	DNF	2m 20.666s	9
	Stefano Perugini	I	Honda	9	DNF	2m 19.278s	8
	Stefan Prein	D	Yamaha	9	DNF	2m 20.411s	9
	Dirk Raudies	D	Honda	3	DNF	2m 17.594s	3
	Bert Smit	NL	Honda	3	DNF	2m 23.465s	2
	Noboru Ueda	J	Honda	2	DNF	2m 17.726s	2
	Yoshiaki Katoh	J	Yamaha	2	DNF	2m 27.888s	1
	Akira Saito	J	Honda	0	DNF		
	Carlos Giro	E	Aprilia		DNS		
	Bruno Casanova	I	Honda		DNS		
	Oliver Koch	D	Honda		DNS		

Fastest lap: Tsujimura, 2m 16.586s, 99.068 mph/159.434 km/h.
Lap record: Kazuto Sakata, J (Honda), 2m 16.539s, 99.101 mph/159.498 km/h (1993).

Qualifying: **1** Ueda, 2m 15.444s; **2** Sakata, 2m 16.320s; **3** Raudies, 2m 16.746s; **4** Tsujimura, 2m 16.858s; **5** Öttl, 2m 17.212s; **6** Petrucciani, 2m 17.385s; **7** Saito, 2m 17.513s; **8** Bodelier, 2m 17.755s; **9** Aoki, 2m 17.780s; **10** Perugini, 2m 17.904s; **11** Debbia, 2m 17.965s; **12** Manako, 2m 17.987s; **13** Alzamora, 2m 18.008s; **14** Gresini, 2m 18.073s; **15** Katoh, 2m 18.097s; **16** Tokudome, 2m 18.127s; **17** Martinez, 2m 18.226s; **18** McCoy, 2m 18.348s; **19** Torrontegui, 2m 18.367s; **20** Nakajyo, 2m 18.593s; **21** Cecchinello, 2m 18.677s; **22** Giro, 2m 18.734s; **23** Petit, 2m 18.827s; **24** Scalvini, 2m 19.242s; **25** Baumann, 2m 20.036s; **26** Geissler, 2m 20.195s; **27** Lopez, 2m 20.261s; **28** Hodgson, 2m 20.280s; **29** Spaan, 2m 20.665s; **30** Prein, 2m 21.252s; **31** Smit, 2m 22.560s; **32** van Etten, 2m 23.088s; **33** Nooren, 2m 24.326s.

World Championship: **1** Sakata, 134; **2** Raudies, 80; **3** Öttl, 79; **4** Ueda, 77; **5** Tsujimura, 71; **6** Martinez, 61; **7** McCoy, 56; **8** Torrontegui, 51; **9** Saito, 46; **10** Tokudome, 43; **11** Petrucciani, 39; **12** Bodelier, 35; **13** Gresini and Nakajyo, 34; **15** Koch, 26; **16** Perugini, 25; **17** Manako, 16; **18** Casanova, 15; **19** Aoki, 12; **20** Debbia, 9; **21** Cuppini and Scalvini, 7; **23** Alzamora, 5; **24** Amano and Katoh, 4; **26** Cecchinello, 3; **27** Geissler, Igata and Petit, 2; **30** Prein, 1.

Top right: Loek Bodelier, 125 rostrum first-timer.

Centre: Peter Öttl and Kazuto Sakata, going for inches.

Photos: Gold & Goose

WORLD CHAMPIONSHIP • ROUND 8

ITALIAN GRAND PRIX

Gold & Goose

500 cc	DOOHAN
250 cc	WALDMANN
125 cc	UEDA

'The resumption of battle by Yamaha was both welcome and overdue'

The Italian GP was very hot stuff. This applied in several areas. Most notably climatic – the race took place as June turned to July, and high summer arrived with a vengeance. Some reports were of Italy's hottest day for 50 years, while not far off in Rome several deaths by heatstroke were recorded. At Mugello, only one rider actually collapsed – Doriano Romboni, erstwhile 250 front-runner, who had the sense to pull into the pits after his vision went, rather than racing on into the danger of an on-track black-out. But the hottest ambient and track surface temperatures since Malaysia took their toll of men and equipment, especially tyres.

One problem was the differential between morning and afternoon. In all classes riders found that they could get their suspension and tyres matched up in the morning only to find them sliding and chattering in the afternoon. It was not only the reduced grip, explained Dunlop's Jeremy Ferguson, but the way the heat affects the flexibility of the carcase itself. Thus chassis fine-tuning included a strong element of educated guesswork, extrapolating known data to decide which tyre specifications and suspension/geometry settings would work best at whatever the temperature would be during the race.

Most of the top teams found their way through this maze successfully. One notable failure, though, was Loris Capirossi, whose Marlboro-Pileri team was without their regular tyre guru, injured in a road accident. Others thought they had it right, but turned out to be wrong – among them John Kocinski in the 500 class and likely 250 winner Max Biaggi, both of whom fell at the same corner without any real understanding of why it had happened. It was one of Mugello's many difficult downhill-entry loopers.

The track outside Florence is a superb facility, set in the achingly gorgeous Medici scenery of Tuscany, following an 'old-fashioned' long lap of 3.259 miles as it loops and S-bends up and down both sides of a broad valley. Lavishly updated and equipped with Fiat money in the name of Ferrari in 1991, it represented the only visit to Italy this year, with the on-and-off San Marino GP dropped from the calendar, along with alternate circuit Misano Adriatico. This was one reason for the fair crowd turnout, some 70,000 pitching up over the three days, 90 per cent on race day.

Opposite page: Pole at home broke the long drought for Luca Cadalora and the Yamaha.

Doug Chandler *(right)* was fast and comfortable on the Cagiva at his 'home' track, Daryl Beattie stiff and apprehensive in case of a front-wheel slide from his Yamaha.

Another reason was the likelihood of a very Italian day on the rostrums. Cadalora was on pole in the 500 class, Biaggi in the 250s, and stunning wild card Roberto Locatelli in the 125s. Furthermore a Cagiva (Chandler's) was second on the 500 grid, with Kocinski's not far behind. As it turned out, most were out of luck. Only two out of nine denizens of the rostrums were Italian, and the 125 top three was all Japanese.

Indeed, in the end, the premier 500 class was more of the same. Cadalora's (and Team Roberts's) revival had surely only been a matter of time; far more significant was the continuing steamroller superiority of Doohan and his HRC Honda. Yet again the win was achieved with assurance, at close to the slowest possible speed, underlined by a show of strength in the closing laps. It also lifted Doohan's points lead to more than 50 – a two-race cushion that was far more important to the matter-of-fact Australian than that his victory here put him in the record books: the first rider to win five GPs in a row since Giacomo Agostini in 1972. 'It's 1994 now,' he commented gruffly. 'I'm only interested in what the position will be in October.'

One factor in his favour was the state of Kevin Schwantz. The Lucky Strike Suzuki rider's left wrist injury was little better than the week before at Assen, and possibly worse, since he had incurred further damage during his brave ride to fifth in Holland. This was to the critical scaphoid bone near the base of the thumb, which was 'cracked' in Holland (Kevin wryly confirmed in private that a 'crack' was a fracture way of saying you didn't want to think about) and required resetting after it had been further displaced during the race. Schwantz showed many fine qualities in taking third – but the uncomfortable truth was that his injury would linger for several more races, and his title defence was effectively over.

The resumption of battle by Yamaha was both welcome and overdue. Over the past races, his potential blunted by handling and horsepower shortcomings, and then by injury to his left hand, Cadalora has privately insisted, 'I am not going to be a hero.' In Mugello he put the same argument more tactfully. 'When the bike is right, then I can ride at my full potential.'

The necessary improvements had come on all fronts. This was Luca's second race with the new Yamaha-built extruded-spar chassis, working well; and he had fresh development Dunlops that performed likewise. There were also whispers of a change of fuel – some said, to Elf from their usual Sunoco. Kenny Roberts played ignorant. 'I honestly don't know what we're using here. We've used Elf – we're always testing other fuels. Agip as well. Sunoco have a new formulation, but I don't know if it's arrived yet, because it has to come by sea.' In the pits, the cans were marked 'Sunoco', while Roberts insisted: 'The important change is new cylinders and pipes, developed within the Yamaha organisation' – which was a polite way of saying they'd been developed by team two-stroke guru, Bud Aksland.

Certainly something was different, and even Beattie went a bit better, though still short of his expected potential. His new frame hadn't arrived yet, but he was in any case more worried about tyres and engines, and sixth was his best yet this year.

The other big-time comeback was made by Chandler. Recently nicknamed 'Dud' because of his lacklustre season, Doug was back at the track where he had the crash and concussion that slowed his GP career. Now he was as fast as anyone, outqualifying Doohan without appearing stretched, his cautious riding style still reminiscent of Eddie Lawson's. Of course it helped that he was at Cagiva's test circuit, where he has done many miles this year alone. 'I've been faster here during testing,' he said after practice. 'I don't feel like I'm doing anything special.' Cynics also remarked that contract renewal time was drawing near, and Doug knows well how deep the Cagiva pockets can be in this respect, making a bit of extra effort very worthwhile.

The 500 result may have made the title even more of a routine affair; that in the 250 class did the opposite, opening it up again after Biaggi threw away a secure race lead. This very human error prevailed after a mechanical turnaround. Last year an Aprilia (ridden by Reggiani) lost the race here to a Honda (Capirossi's) by inches, due to the Japanese bike's better power surge out of the last bend and along almost the full length of the pit straight. This year the positions were clearly reversed: the NSR Hondas handled more sweetly than ever in their ten years of evolution, but were clearly outpowered. At least by Biaggi's bike. Chesterfield Aprilia team-mate Jean-Philippe Ruggia, well known for a bellicose attitude, was now complaining loudly that Max was getting better treatment and a faster bike. Here he was also beleaguered by factory tester Marcellino Lucchi, the 37-year-old veteran in as a wild card on a full 1994 works Aprilia, and proving a serious nuisance all race long.

Career developments elsewhere were also shaky. East German 500 rider Lothar Neukirchner, perennial back-marker and occasional non-qualifier, was finally sacked by his team after another crash and ensuing altercation.

Meanwhile the Giro saga continued. This race was make or break, after his mystery no-go at Assen. Ducados were insisting on a top ten finish, or dismissal. In fact he finished 15th, scoring one point; but given that his team would face a hefty fine from IRTA if they switched riders this was enough for him to keep the job.

There were two injuries in practice, the worst to luckless Yoshiaki Katoh, All-Japan 125 champion, whose high-pressure entry into GPs as a Yamaha development rider had seen him crash at every track. This time he suffered a broken knee-cap, and was out for the rest of the European season at least. The other victim was Nobuatsu Aoki, who dislocated and fractured his shoulder while trying to improve his second-row position.

500 cc PRACTICE

For the past four races, only Schwantz had been able to challenge Doohan, and with his injury it seemed this race would be straightforward. Thus it was unexpected, to say the least, when the Australian was pushed to third on the grid by hitherto rank outsiders Cadalora and Chandler.

To be fair, there were only hundredths in it, and as Doohan said: 'I

ITALIAN GRAND PRIX

feel as though the whole front row is on pole.' But Cadalora's sudden rise from the doldrums was more than surprising. He was last on pole in Japan, four races ago, and hadn't even been on the front row since then. Serenely calm as ever, he attributed his ascendancy to a package of improvements: the new frame working well, a fresh batch of Dunlops ditto, and the engine also having woken up from a long doze thanks to Aksland's new confection of old parts. As important, his injured hand was much better, with the stitches removed. However he'd collapsed on Friday evening, and been ill all night. 'I must have drunk something too cold,' he surmised, leading to the unspoken suggestion that he take less ice with it. 'Dr Costa put me on a drip before practice, and I was fit again.'

Chandler was an even greater surprise, suddenly back on the form that made him a frequent front-row man two years ago on the Suzuki. Doug has a lot of miles at Mugello, but even so nobody expected a leap from the back of the works bikes (always behind team-mate Kocinski) right up to the front. 'The main thing is there isn't much stop-go here. You keep the speed up so acceleration is not so important.'

With Luca at lap record speeds, Doug was some five-hundredths slower, and Doohan three-hundredths slower than him. In fact he'd been fastest throughout until Cadalora's fliers with seven minutes left. Doohan was already fitting up a new rear, and set out immediately to recapture the psychological advantage. But while he went faster than before, his third and final quick one was thwarted by a pair of slower riders at a track with a notable shortage of overtaking points. Last year he won largely because his tyres lasted while Schwantz's chunked. 'It's a long race,' he said. 'I've been able to pick good tyres that I think can last. The second half will decide the result.'

Barros was alongside for his second successive front-row start. He'd been working steadily all weekend improving set-up. 'It's different from Assen,' he explained. 'The long corners make it important to have the bike stable when it is leaned over. We made a lot of geometry changes.' But he'd certainly been helped when Doohan came by in the closing minutes. Barros couldn't stay with him, but he followed for his best time, more than half a second slower. 'I don't think the others can ride at that speed in the race,' he said. 'I hope not.'

The heat was a problem for everybody, and for the tyres. Kocinski also had his hand injury. 'It's not 100 per cent, but it's a lot better,' he said. He'd been on the front row on the first day of practice, but was knocked to fifth overall on the second day, when he only managed a marginal improvement. 'I've missed too much practice and testing because of illness and injury,' he said.

Criville ended up a tenth slower, much surprised at the speed of the unexpected front-row interlopers. Another tenth or so down came Schwantz, wrist still in a cast, and again overcoming pain and weakness to qualify 1.5 seconds off pole. 'This track's harder on me than Assen because of the longer turns and because it's not so grippy,' he said. 'I've changed my style so I don't go so deep and hard into the turns, but try and keep more corner speed. We've altered the bike's geometry too to make it more comfortable. But when I get settled I find I'm riding in my usual way again. If the guys in front can match their practice times,' he added dubiously, 'I can only watch.'

Last man on row two was Itoh, still aching after his Assen crash, and hunting for the right suspension to improve his corner exits.

Row two was led by Puig, a little short of his usual speed, with Beattie alongside, the Australian disappointed that improved tyres and engine power didn't yield the improvement he expected after running fifth in morning warm-up.

Only then came Reggiani's Aprilia – the V-twin 400's usual position, but disappointing after he'd been up to sixth fastest on day one. 'We've done such a lot of testing here that the bike almost knows its own way round,' he said. 'I'd hoped for more, but we have increased the gap on the private V4s and got closer to the works bikes. I just need more power now,' he said.

Bernard Garcia completed the row, while Mackenzie led the next, his painful left arm injury still in a cast. He was less than half a second ahead of Reynolds in the usual tight privateer battle, with Lopez Mella next and McWilliams – who survived a heavy fall on Friday – completing the fourth row.

With Neukirchner withdrawing from the race, all 31 remaining entrants qualified.

First-lap scramble: Schwantz leads Kocinski, Itoh (8), Criville, Beattie, Barros and Chandler. Puig (17) and Cadalora loom; Doohan is making ground fast, out of picture to the left.

500 cc RACE – 23 LAPS

The start was a real surprise, as Schwantz burst off the second row, ricocheting off Barros and Doohan to take an immediate lead – he'd decided to race hard for as long as his wrist could stand it. 'We chose tyres we knew would work from the start, and it went perfectly,' he said. He even pulled away, helped somewhat by the fact that Kocinski was in second while Doohan had to work his way through from sixth, finally moving past the Cagiva on the third lap.

At that point, Schwantz was 1.7 seconds ahead, but by the end of lap five Doohan had closed up and dived inside him on the way out of one of the circuit's many S-bends – and from then on the Australian was never headed. He was, however, severely pressured, with Schwantz hanging on, and more trouble to come.

Pole-starter Cadalora was slow away, finishing lap one in tenth, but he too had been relentlessly picking his way through, to the delight of the crowd, gaining four places in the second lap alone, and arriving in third on lap six after surging past Criville up the hill.

He quickly closed on Schwantz, passing him at the end of the pit straight as they started lap eight. At this time he was the only one lapping below the 1m 55s mark, with times well below the best in practice because of the searing heat. Luca's best lap was his sixth, and it was the fastest lap of the race, half a second off the record.

Cadalora immediately started to attack Doohan, nosing alongside on the straight once, and never more than inches from the Honda's back wheel. Doohan, for his part, withstood the pressure manfully, turning one consistent lap after another; Schwantz meanwhile was a close spectator.

The order didn't change, but the tension remained high. Then Schwantz dropped away slightly, and Cadalora tried to up the pace. Doohan was able to respond in kind, and to win the day. 'I'd tried to get away but the other two were always there,' he explained later. 'When I saw there were five laps to go, I gave it my best shot. I was really happy to see on my lap board that I got an advantage.' At the finish he had stretched it to 5.7 seconds. His best lap was his 21st, when he too dipped below 1m 55s.

For Cadalora, the last kick was too much. 'My bike was running really well and I could stay in his slipstream. When he speeded up, it was more than I could do.' But his first podium since the opening round at least gave hope of better results from now on.

Schwantz lost a little ground, then a lot, a gap of 2.4 seconds on lap 16 opening to 10.5 seconds on lap 17. 'I had a little misfire that slowed me for half a lap,' he said. 'I was having some trouble with my wrist going numb, though I was able to rest it on the straight. When I slowed, I thought I'd better just keep going and see who passed me, then see what I could do about that at the end.'

In fact, the 17th lap had dealt with two potential challengers. Chandler's Cagiva was closing fast, after he'd worked his way through from eighth on lap one. He was stuck a long while behind Kocinski. 'He was fast into the corners, but not so fast through them, which made him hard to pass,' said Doug. Now he could see Schwantz and was hopeful of catching him. Instead, the bike suddenly started vibrating badly and he thought the crankshaft had gone. His mechanics later found a loosened cylinder bolt. 'It's real frustrating – I thought I could finish on the podium, but we never have any luck here.'

The other would-be attacker was Schwantz's arch-enemy, Kocinski. Instead he crashed, losing the front, then the rear and sliding off unhurt at the last downhill right-hander. 'I don't really know why,' he said later. 'It was nothing to do with my hand.'

This left only Criville in a position to attack, and he did so, catching and passing Schwantz quite easily on the 19th lap as the American took his hand off the bars and shook it to try and restore circulation. Schwantz stuck to his back wheel, but said later: 'I looked for ways I might pass on the last lap, but I couldn't out-drag him or outbrake him. He was riding really fast. I don't think I could have got him.' Then Criville did it himself, sliding off on the same corner as Kocinski, half a mile from the flag. 'I was determined to beat Schwantz to help Doohan and Honda in the championship,' he said. 'But I made a mistake.'

There'd been a lot of action behind in one of the better 500 races of the year. While Itoh and Beattie were riding steadily in the group that had contained the Cagivas, Barros was up and down. A partial seizure into the first corner had knocked him down to 11th, but the engine picked up again, and he put his head down to catch the works bike group again within a couple of laps. This punished his tyres and, though he tried hard to pass Criville, he had to accept defeat and started dropping back. Meanwhile Puig was coming hard from behind in the closing laps, his tyres obviously better than those of his rivals. He came from tenth on lap 16 past Barros and Beattie, then made a superhuman effort to catch and pass Itoh on the last lap. Thus he claimed fourth, with Itoh less than a tenth behind in fifth, followed by Beattie and Barros.

Behind them came Bernard Garcia after a strong if lonely race as top privateer, with Mackenzie another 13 seconds down, nursing his arm and riding alone throughout. Lopez Mella was tenth, with Jeandat triumphing in a good battle with Migliorati, Hänggeli, Emmett and McWilliams, with the latter two dropping out of touch at the finish. McWilliams took the last point.

There were 21 finishers. Retirements included Briton Reynolds, who had crashed in morning warm-up, and – disappointingly – Reggiani's V-twin Aprilia 400, which nipped up yet again after less than two laps.

109

ITALIAN GRAND PRIX

Top left: Ruggia's Aprilia control centre; wild card Marcellino Lucchi *(top right)* pushed Ruggia all the way to the finish.

Main picture: Sakata obscures Ueda, Raudies shades Locatelli, then come Öttl, Perugini and Tsujimura: typical 125 action, with plenty of change to follow.

Bottom: Second-time winner Ueda and girlfriend Maki grinned as usual, with good reason.

250 cc PRACTICE

There were few upsets in the qualifying order of the 250 class, but a significant upset of the other sort when, in the final session, Andy Preining cut across the front wheel of Biaggi and sent him tumbling into the sand trap in such a flurry that even his mouth was full of grit. So was he, of the other kind, running back to the pits and improving his existing pole time still further, to end up first by almost three-quarters of a second. The Aprilia's speed really seemed to tell at this track where they do so much testing. It was only after practice that he realised he had pulled a muscle in his neck, and left the track for treatment.

The only front-row surprise came from Waldmann, with the former 125 rider fastest on day one, and ending up second after cutting almost a second off his time, proving it was no flash in the pan. He dutifully praised his mechanics; an important change was simply to his riding position. With footrests moved back and clip-ons forward, he was tipped further forward on the bike and not only fitted better behind the fairing, but also felt more comfortable. At this level, such marginal changes can make a crucial difference.

Romboni was alongside and might have been ahead but for running into chatter problems in the heat – he'd been fastest in the cooler morning session. 'We know the problem, and I hope we can make the right adjustments.' As it transpired, the bike was not the weak link in his package.

Then came Capirossi, working hard but also falling victim to the increased heat of the afternoon, which put his suspension settings out. 'We will make changes for the race. It won't exactly be a guess, but it would have been nice to have had a chance to test the changes,' he said. He was 1.2 seconds slower than Biaggi, a big gap.

Italy threw up some hot wild cards, mainly courtesy of Aprilia. The man in the 250 class was Lucchi, Aprilia's veteran factory tester and the only man on a full 1994 bike: his track knowledge had him threatening a front-row start. Ruggia was next, three-tenths slower, working hard on troublesome carburettor settings to try and get his bike as fast as team-mate Biaggi's.

Harada was seventh, disappointed as he regained strength for the second half of the season. In the final session, he heard 'a strange sound' from the engine. Unwilling to risk disaster, he parked his best bike and practised on his spare.

The top seven places went to Dunlop riders; the last place on the second row was taken by Nobuatsu Aoki's Honda, but he crashed heavily in the last session, breaking and dislocating his shoulder, and did not start. This left the place to countryman Okada, below his usual form as he ran into a familiar Michelin problem, a lack of steering bite, exacerbated by the many downhill corners here.

Bayle was next, with D'Antin alongside, and flying Aprilia privateer Eskil Suter slotting into 11th. Then came Honma, who moved gradually up throughout practice for his second race at a difficult circuit he had never seen before. 'There are a lot of blind corners here that make it hard to learn,' he said.

250 cc RACE – 21 LAPS

Romboni was first away, pursued by Capirossi, and the pair stretched away to head the first lap with Harada leading the pursuit. Until they got to the pit straight, that is, when Biaggi's Aprilia simply motored past the Yamaha and Max started work closing on the leaders.

The black Aprilia was in second on lap three, and ahead of Romboni to lead on lap four. Biaggi was making ground hand over fist as Waldmann joined a fierce three-way fight with Romboni and Capirossi; Harada seemed to lose ground behind, only to catch up again in a clear message that the World Champion was back.

By lap six, Max was almost two seconds clear and apparently in complete control. Likewise after lap seven, when Romboni pulled into the pits unexpectedly. 'I felt ill before the race and worse after it started,' he said later. Nauseous and with blurring vision, he thought it wiser to get medical attention than to press on. He collapsed in his pit and was stretchered away to recover in the Clinica Mobile.

With Biaggi charging, the pursuit was getting stretched. Then it all changed on the tenth lap as Max slid to earth on one of the track's many downhill corners, leaping straight to his feet, then kicking up a plume of stones from the gravel trap in his frustration. 'I hit a bump, the forks bottomed and bounced back, and suddenly the front slid away. I don't know why – the tyres were perfect,' he explained later.

Now all the pressure was on Waldmann, who had a gap of 2.5 seconds over Capirossi and Harada. He did well to preserve it as Harada slipped ahead on lap 12. The Yamaha rider gradually drew clear of Capirossi, but Waldmann was on top of the situation, and maintained a lead of two seconds to the finish. 'To win my first 250 race over the fast Italians in their own GP is great,' he said. 'As good as my first-ever GP win. We used a long first gear so I knew I would be slow from the start. But when I saw how much Capirossi was sliding early on while my tyres were still good, I felt I had a chance. My bike was perfect today. I must also thank Romboni. He has tested a lot here, and he gave me a lot of good advice about gear settings.'

Harada was delighted with second, his best finish all season, and also the first time he'd been able to ride like a champion. 'My bike needs more power, and my hand isn't perfect. But things are coming better,' he said.

And Capirossi was glad to finish well, admitting that he'd had tyre problems. 'When I saw Max crash, I knew I must be sure to get points,' he said. 'It was impossible to hope for better than third.'

Unusually for the class, there wasn't an excess of action down the field. Ruggia was fourth, chased all race long by Lucchi but having found the top-end power he needed to stay ahead.

The next group were disputing sixth in the dice of the race, D'Antin, Okada, Bayle and Zeelenberg finishing in that order. A fine result, after fierce fighting, for D'Antin, but disappointing for Okada, deep into the same understeer problems that so troubled Biaggi when he rode the Kanemoto Honda last year. Bayle complained of a lack of acceleration; Zeelenberg had used up his energy and his tyres catching up from a mediocre start, and had nothing left for the final sprint.

Checa finally escaped from Bosshard to claim tenth, some 18 seconds back; then came Preining, Gramigni and Patrick van den Goorbergh in a tight pack. Three seconds back another pair, with Kassner taking the last point less than a tenth ahead of Jurgen van den Goorbergh, who'd caught up from last after being batted across the gravel at the first turn.

There were 23 finishers. Other retirements included Honma, with engine trouble.

125 cc RACE – 20 LAPS

A race of great excitement and wildly changing fortunes closed the day. Dirk Raudies (HB Honda) led the first two laps from the usual brawl, chased for the first one by surprise pole-qualifier Roberto Locatelli.

Soon seniority established itself, with Raudies disputing the lead with Sakata's works Aprilia, Öttl's similar machine and Ueda's Honda. Locatelli, a bright hope in Italy, hung on impressively for several laps before dropping back to the larger group close behind, from whence came Tsujimura's Honda.

Sakata soon started to make a breakaway, and by lap 11 had stretched his lead to an impressive five seconds. Then he had a little slip, but recovered, only to find himself heading across the grass at very high speed on the inside of the second part of the S-bend. He rejoined in fifth, but was severely criticised afterwards by both Raudies and Öttl for careless riding. 'I was doing more than 160 km/h, and I missed him by ten centimetres,' said Öttl.

Now Ueda was in front and pulling away slightly; then Raudies took his turn at a gravel short-cut on lap 13, dropping from third to an out-of-touch fifth after rough-riding across the gravel.

Sakata was riding brilliantly, and picked his way through the group to reclaim second from Tsujimura on lap 15. One lap later he had caught and passed Ueda, and there ensued a brilliant battle, the pair inches apart and swapping back and forth.

Ueda was narrowly ahead with less than half a lap to the flag when Sakata had his second lucky escape. A slide flicked him half out of the seat, but he managed to stay wheels down. It was enough to give Ueda his second win of the season, though, by 3.4 seconds. Tsujimura was third, another five seconds down, pipping Öttl by less than a tenth.

Raudies was a lone fifth, with Tokudome's Honda narrowly leading the next big group from Martinez (Yamaha), Manako (Honda), Aoki (Honda), Locatelli and Petrucciani (both Aprilia). The group was covered by less than one second. Loek Bodelier had been in the thick of the group, but handling problems meant his Aprilia was two seconds adrift at the finish.

Torrontegui, Saito and Giro took the last points, crucially in the case of the last-named. Up front, the Japanese were firmly in control.

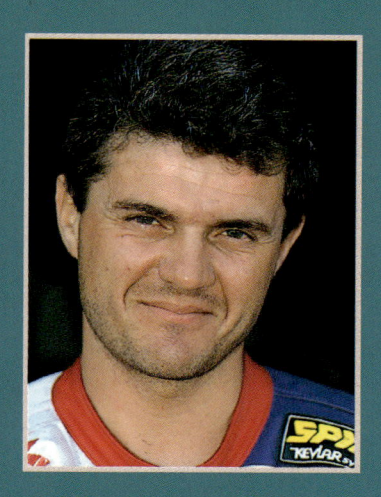

Photos: Gold & Goose

FIM WORLD CHAMPIONSHIP • ROUND 8
GRAN PREMIO D'ITALIA
3 JULY 1994

500 cc
23 laps, 74.957 miles/120.635 km

Place	Rider	Nat.	Machine	Laps	Time & speed	Fastest lap	Lap
1	Michael Doohan	AUS	Honda	23	44m 20.402s 101.433 mph/ 163.241 km/h	1m 54.765s	21
2	Luca Cadalora	I	Yamaha	23	44m 26.186s	1m 54.354s	6
3	Kevin Schwantz	USA	Suzuki	23	44m 37.738s	1m 55.219s	11
4	Alberto Puig	E	Honda	23	44m 44.506s	1m 55.322s	23
5	Shinichi Itoh	J	Honda	23	44m 44.584s	1m 55.707s	9
6	Daryl Beattie	AUS	Yamaha	23	44m 49.138s	1m 55.167s	10
7	Alexandre Barros	BR	Suzuki	23	44m 54.962s	1m 55.714s	7
8	Bernard Garcia	F	Yamaha	23	45m 08.972s	1m 56.153s	7
9	Niall Mackenzie	GB	Yamaha	23	45m 21.912s	1m 56.780s	13
10	Juan Lopez Mella	E	Yamaha	23	45m 44.398s	1m 58.011s	4
11	Jean-Pierre Jeandat	F	Yamaha	23	45m 46.518s	1m 58.011s	13
12	Cristiano Migliorati	I	Yamaha	23	45m 47.376s	1m 58.308s	6
13	Bernard Hänggeli	CH	Yamaha	23	45m 48.567s	1m 58.394s	6
14	Sean Emmett	GB	Yamaha	23	45m 54.240s	1m 58.426s	15
15	Jeremy McWilliams	GB	Yamaha	23	45m 54.974s	1m 58.592s	7
16	Laurent Naveau	B	Yamaha	23	46m 10.062s	1m 59.529s	20
17	Bruno Bonhuil	F	Yamaha	22	44m 24.720s	2m 00.320s	22
18	Ermanno Bastianini	I	Yamaha	22	44m 25.220s	1m 59.031s	16
19	Jean Foray	F	Yamaha	22	44m 26.456s	2m 00.179s	3
20	Lucio Pedercini	I	Yamaha	22	44m 36.804s	1m 59.716s	3
21	Cees Doorakkers	NL	Yamaha	22	46m 32.950s	2m 01.913s	2
	Alex Criville	E	Honda	22	DNF	1m 55.375s	21
	Marc Garcia	F	Yamaha	18	DNF	1m 59.181s	5
	Julian Miralles	E	Yamaha	17	DNF	1m 59.305s	8
	Doug Chandler	USA	Cagiva	16	DNF	1m 55.146s	10
	John Kocinski	USA	Cagiva	16	DNF	1m 55.348s	16
	Vittorio Scatola	I	Paton	9	DNF	2m 02.963s	4
	Andreas Leuthe	D	Yamaha	3	DNF	2m 01.880s	2
	Loris Reggiani	I	Aprilia	2	DNF	1m 57.366s	2
	John Reynolds	GB	Yamaha	2	DNF	1m 59.490s	2
	Kevin Mitchell	GB	Yamaha	0	DNF		

Fastest lap: Cadalora, 1m 54.354s, 102.600 mph/165.119 km/h.
Lap record: Michael Doohan, AUS (Honda), 1m 53.829s, 103.073 mph/165.880 km/h (1993).

Qualifying: 1 Cadalora, 1m 53.730s; 2 Chandler, 1m 53.787s; 3 Doohan, 1m 53.817s; 4 Barros, 1m 54.478s; 5 Kocinski, 1m 55.026s; 6 Criville, 1m 55.120s; 7 Schwantz, 1m 55.251s; 8 Itoh, 1m 55.375s; 9 Puig, 1m 55.398s; 10 Beattie, 1m 55.478s; 11 Reggiani, 1m 55.583s; 12 B. Garcia, 1m 56.400s; 13 Mackenzie, 1m 56.603s; 14 Reynolds, 1m 57.034s; 15 Lopez Mella, 1m 57.270s; 16 McWilliams, 1m 57.562s; 17 Jeandat, 1m 58.286s; 18 Emmett, 1m 58.295s; 19 Hänggeli, 1m 58.389s; 20 Migliorati, 1m 59.054s; 21 Foray, 1m 59.444s; 22 Miralles, 1m 59.710s; 23 Pedercini, 1m 59.922s; 24 Bastianini, 2m 00.028s; 25 Bonhuil, 2m 00.172s; 26 M. Garcia, 2m 00.246s; 27 Naveau, 2m 00.318s; 28 Doorakkers, 2m 00.554s; 29 Leuthe, 2m 00.632s; 30 Scatola, 2m 01.479s; 31 Mitchell, 2m 01.535s.

World Championship: 1 M. Doohan, 186; 2 Schwantz, 135; 3 Barros and Puig, 90; 5 Kocinski, 87; 6 Criville, 83; 7 Itoh, 77; 8 Cadalora, 73; 9 Chandler, 48; 10 Mackenzie, 35; 11 Beattie, 33; 12 Reynolds, 32; 13 B. Garcia, 31; 14 Lopez Mella, 17; 15 Emmett, 16; 16 Jeandat, 15; 17 McWilliams and Migliorati, 11; 19 Honma, 10; 20 Naveau, 9; 21 Miralles and Reggiani, 7; 23 Moineau, 5; 24 S. Doohan, 4; 25 Bonhuil and Hänggeli, 3; 27 Foray and Pedercini, 1.

250 cc
21 laps, 68.439 miles/110.145 km

Place	Rider	Nat.	Machine	Laps	Time & speed	Fastest lap	Lap
1	Ralf Waldmann	D	Honda	21	41m 05.128s 99.949 mph/ 160.852 km/h	1m 56.404s	5
2	Tetsuya Harada	J	Yamaha	21	41m 07.188s	1m 56.389s	9
3	Loris Capirossi	I	Honda	21	41m 10.332s	1m 56.466s	7
4	Jean-Philippe Ruggia	F	Aprilia	21	41m 13.585s	1m 56.510s	4
5	Marcellino Lucchi	I	Aprilia	21	41m 14.376s	1m 56.696s	3
6	Luis D'Antin	E	Honda	21	41m 46.234s	1m 57.640s	2
7	Tadayuki Okada	J	Honda	21	41m 46.494s	1m 58.051s	6
8	Jean-Michel Bayle	F	Aprilia	21	41m 46.579s	1m 57.688s	6
9	Wilco Zeelenberg	NL	Honda	21	41m 46.804s	1m 57.899s	7
10	Carlos Checa	E	Honda	21	42m 04.816s	1m 58.435s	4
11	Adrian Bosshard	CH	Honda	21	42m 07.872s	1m 58.560s	3
12	Andy Preining	A	Aprilia	21	42m 18.358s	1m 59.282s	9
13	Alessandro Gramigni	I	Aprilia	21	42m 18.490s	1m 59.759s	10
14	Patrick van den Goorbergh	NL	Aprilia	21	42m 18.528s	1m 59.671s	4
15	Bernd Kassner	D	Aprilia	21	42m 21.268s	1m 59.888s	16
16	Jurgen van den Goorbergh	NL	Aprilia	21	42m 21.324s	1m 59.313s	6
17	Noel Ferro	F	Honda	21	42m 30.101s	1m 59.790s	8
18	Adi Stadler	D	Honda	21	42m 30.274s	2m 00.196s	8
19	Luis Maurel	E	Honda	21	42m 42.520s	2m 00.327s	9
20	Frédéric Protat	F	Honda	21	43m 14.122s	2m 01.611s	4
21	Kristian Kaas	SF	Yamaha	20	41m 10.062s	2m 01.870s	4
22	Christian Boudinot	F	Aprilia	20	41m 22.716s	2m 02.437s	2
23	Rodney Fee	CAN	Honda	20	42m 03.351s	2m 04.493s	2
	Giuseppe Fiorillo	I	Honda	12	DNF	1m 59.928s	11
	Massimiliano Biaggi	I	Aprilia	10	DNF	1m 56.102s	5
	Toshihiko Honma	J	Yamaha	10	DNF	1m 58.871s	5
	Doriano Romboni	I	Honda	6	DNF	1m 56.671s	6
	Eskil Suter	CH	Aprilia	6	DNF	1m 58.578s	4
	Davide Bulega	I	Aprilia	6	DNF	2m 00.792s	4
	Alan Patterson	GB	Honda	4	DNF	2m 03.365s	3
	José Luis Cardoso	E	Aprilia	1	DNF	2m 12.946s	1
	Manuel Hernandez	E	Aprilia	1	DNF	2m 14.763s	1
	Enrique de Juan	E	Aprilia	1	DNF	2m 16.320s	1
	Nobuatsu Aoki	J	Honda		DNS		

Fastest lap: Biaggi, 1m 56.102s, 101.055 mph/162.633 km/h (record).
Previous record: Jean-Philippe Ruggia, F (Aprilia), 1m 56.224s, 100.950 mph/162.462 km/h (1993).

Qualifying: 1 Biaggi, 1m 55.856s; 2 Waldmann, 1m 56.591s; 3 Romboni, 1m 56.716s; 4 Capirossi, 1m 57.092s; 5 Lucchi, 1m 57.290s; 6 Ruggia, 1m 57.600s; 7 Harada, 1m 57.704s; 8 Okada, 1m 57.730s; 9 Bayle, 1m 57.934s; 10 D'Antin, 1m 58.255s; 11 Suter, 1m 58.423s; 12 Honma, 1m 58.489s; 13 Zeelenberg, 1m 58.620s; 14 Bulega, 1m 58.906s; 15 Preining, 1m 59.043s; 16 Bosshard, 1m 59.067s; 17 Kassner, 1m 59.345s; 18 Fiorillo, 1m 59.371s; 19 Checa, 1m 59.407s; 20 J. van den Goorbergh, 2m 00.267s; 21 Gramigni, 2m 00.402s; 22 Ferro, 2m 00.447s; 23 P. van den Goorbergh, 2m 00.846s; 24 Maurel, 2m 01.090s; 25 Protat, 2m 01.125s; 26 Stadler, 2m 01.132s; 27 de Juan, 2m 01.637s; 28 Boudinot, 2m 01.740s; 29 Cardoso, 2m 02.110s; 30 Kaas, 2m 02.140s; 31 Hernandez, 2m 02.214s; 32 Patterson, 2m 03.297s; 33 Fee, 2m 03.604s.

World Championship: 1 Biaggi, 128; 2 Okada, 125; 3 Capirossi, 118; 4 Romboni, 93; 5 Ruggia and Waldmann, 91; 7 D'Antin, 67; 8 Bayle, 56; 9 N. Aoki, 53; 10 Zeelenberg, 50; 11 Harada, 45; 12 Checa, 25; 13 P. van den Goorbergh, 23; 14 Suter and J. van den Goorbergh, 22; 16 Preining, 18; 17 Ukawa, 16; 18 Bosshard, 12; 19 T. Aoki and Lucchi, 11; 21 Gramigni, 10; 22 Kassner, 9; 23 Stadler, 8; 24 Connell, 5; 25 Fiorillo, 4; 26 Castilla and Honma, 3; 28 Cardoso, 1.

AUTODROMO INTERNAZIONALE DEL MUGELLO

CIRCUIT LENGTH: 3.259 MILES/5.245 KM

Left: Kenny Roberts in characteristic pose as his team gathers strength.

Below: Loris Reggiani's mint-condition Sixties Corvette was more dependable than his 400 cc V-twin.

Bottom: Ralf Waldmann did everything right, including not crashing, to claim his maiden 250 cc victory.

And Michael Doohan (*bottom left*) looked invincible.

125 cc

20 laps, 65.180 miles/104.900 km

Place	Rider	Nat.	Machine	Laps	Time & speed	Fastest lap	Lap
1	Noboru Ueda	J	Honda	20	41m 25.510s 94.409 mph/ 151.937 km/h	2m 03.107s	20
2	Kazuto Sakata	J	Aprilia	20	41m 28.980s	2m 02.541s	8
3	Takeshi Tsujimura	J	Honda	20	41m 34.248s	2m 03.406s	15
4	Peter Öttl	D	Aprilia	20	41m 34.310s	2m 03.330s	8
5	Dirk Raudies	D	Honda	20	41m 43.343s	2m 03.622s	7
6	Masaki Tokudome	J	Honda	20	41m 50.922s	2m 03.627s	3
7	Jorge Martinez	E	Yamaha	20	41m 50.980s	2m 03.650s	13
8	Tomoko Manako	J	Honda	20	41m 51.006s	2m 03.748s	14
9	Haruchika Aoki	J	Honda	20	41m 51.067s	2m 04.207s	19
10	Roberto Locatelli	I	Aprilia	20	41m 51.356s	2m 03.920s	4
11	Oliver Petrucciani	CH	Aprilia	20	41m 51.470s	2m 04.145s	16
12	Loek Bodelier	NL	Honda	20	41m 53.376s	2m 04.218s	6
13	Herri Torrontegui	E	Aprilia	20	42m 01.269s	2m 04.612s	12
14	Akira Saito	J	Aprilia	20	42m 08.486s	2m 05.121s	8
15	Carlos Giro	E	Aprilia	20	42m 08.508s	2m 04.306s	17
16	Stefan Prein	D	Yamaha	20	42m 09.212s	2m 04.870s	17
17	Fausto Gresini	I	Honda	20	42m 11.670s	2m 05.182s	14
18	Emili Alzamora	E	Honda	20	42m 11.726s	2m 05.188s	14
19	Gabriele Debbia	I	Aprilia	20	42m 25.486s	2m 05.147s	6
20	Manfred Geissler	D	Aprilia	20	42m 30.430s	2m 05.696s	10
21	Luigi Ancona	I	Honda	20	42m 30.520s	2m 05.146s	4
22	Hans Spaan	NL	Honda	20	42m 55.186s	2m 07.003s	9
23	Vittorio Lopez	I	Honda	20	42m 55.214s	2m 07.329s	2
24	Yasuaki Takahashi	J	Honda	20	43m 32.590s	2m 09.032s	14
25	Bertrand Stey	F	Honda	20	43m 34.065s	2m 08.191s	3
	Hideyuki Nakajyo	J	Honda	13	DNF	2m 05.630s	7
	Garry McCoy	AUS	Aprilia	13	DNF	2m 04.139s	7
	Neil Hodgson	GB	Honda	10	DNF	2m 06.382s	2
	Stefano Perugini	I	Aprilia	9	DNF	2m 03.828s	4
	Manfred Baumann	A	Yamaha	7	DNF	2m 05.365s	6
	Lucio Cecchinello	I	Honda	5	DNF	2m 04.016s	5
	Gianluigi Scalvini	I	Aprilia	3	DNF	2m 07.482s	2
	Frédéric Petit	F	Yamaha	1	DNF	2m 17.118s	1
	Frank Baldinger	D	Honda	0	DNF		
	Ivan Cremonini	I	Aprilia	0	DNF		
	Yoshiaki Katoh	J	Yamaha		DNS		

Fastest lap: Sakata, 2m 02.541s, 95.745 mph/154.087 km/h (record).
Previous record: Carlos Giro, E (Aprilia), 2m 03.309s, 95.150 mph/153.128 km/h (1993).

Qualifying: 1 Locatelli, 2m 02.401s; **2** Ueda, 2m 02.566s; **3** Sakata, 2m 02.640s; **4** Öttl, 2m 03.862s; **5** Raudies, 2m 03.924s; **6** Martinez, 2m 04.194s; **7** Nakajyo, 2m 04.225s; **8** Manako, 2m 04.231s; **9** Tokudome, 2m 04.232s; **10** Petrucciani, 2m 04.271s; **11** Giro, 2m 04.455s; **12** Ancona, 2m 04.503s; **13** Tsujimura, 2m 04.668s; **14** McCoy, 2m 04.804s; **15** Perugini, 2m 04.812s; **16** Cremonini, 2m 04.822s; **17** Saito, 2m 04.845s; **18** Cecchinello, 2m 04.944s; **19** Debbia, 2m 05.170s; **20** Aoki, 2m 05.223s; **21** Gresini, 2m 05.224s; **22** Petit, 2m 05.307s; **23** Scalvini, 2m 05.453s; **24** Hodgson, 2m 05.468s; **25** Prein, 2m 05.721s; **26** Torrontegui, 2m 05.944s; **27** Bodelier, 2m 06.203s; **28** Alzamora, 2m 06.404s; **29** Lopez, 2m 06.535s; **30** Geissler, 2m 06.566s; **31** Baumann, 2m 06.578s; **32** Stey, 2m 08.070s; **33** Spaan, 2m 08.089s; **34** Baldinger, 2m 08.136s; **35** Takahashi, 2m 08.174s.

World Championship: 1 Sakata, 154; **2** Ueda, 102; **3** Öttl, 92; **4** Raudies, 91; **5** Tsujimura, 87; **6** Martinez, 70; **7** McCoy, 56; **8** Torrontegui, 54; **9** Tokudome, 53; **10** Saito, 48; **11** Petrucciani, 44; **12** Bodelier, 39; **13** Gresini and Nakajyo, 34; **15** Koch, 26; **16** Perugini, 25; **17** Manako, 24; **18** Aoki, 19; **19** Casanova, 15; **20** Debbia, 9; **21** Cuppini and Scalvini, 7; **23** Locatelli, 6; **24** Alzamora, 5; **25** Amano and Katoh, 4; **27** Cecchinello, 3; **28** Geissler, Igata and Petit, 2; **31** Giro and Prein, 1.

113

WORLD CHAMPIONSHIP • ROUND 9

FRENCH GRAND PRIX

'Three years ago I felt ten feet tall and bullet-proof. Now I'm just bullet-proof'

Kevin Schwantz on shifting safety perceptions

500 cc	DOOHAN
250 cc	CAPIROSSI
125 cc	UEDA

Photos: Gold & Goose

FRENCH GRAND PRIX

Frozen, Doohan's launch looks okay. In fact, he's travelling 20 miles an hour slower than Schwantz, shooting through from the second row.

Bottom: *The luckiest man in France, Michael Doohan, is flanked by John Kocinski and Alex Criville, the second-luckiest.*

Luck has a lot to do with it – a sentiment acknowledged by every World Champion in recent memory.

In France, crashes savaged Daryl Beattie's foot, trumped Kevin Schwantz's last-lap joker, and dumped Michael Doohan in the dirt in his third practice spill of the year. This was at a low speed and, like the others, a front-wheel low-sider, and he was again luckily unhurt. But Doohan's real good fortune came in the race, with a trio of escapes that proved quite clearly that whatever cruel fates denied him the title in 1992 had taken the weekend off.

It began when he muffed the start. Trying way too hard to recover places, he charged into the first chicane too fast and, as Barros turned across him, he was obliged to release the brakes, lift the bike and run straight across the gravel inside the second apex, taking the hapless Criville dirt-tracking with him. As he rejoined, Schwantz had to swerve and he ran off the track himself. It was too close for comfort to a repeat of the infamous 'human bowling ball' exploit at Donington last year.

Two laps later, fast-starting Bernard Garcia crashed his Roc on the corner before the pits. His bike landed right under Doohan's front wheel, but slid out of his way in time.

The last reprieve came only 300 yards from home. Confident of victory after preserving his tyres for the last ten laps or more, Mick gave the bike an exuberant handful of throttle on the last left-hander, and slid wildly almost into the pit road – on full opposite lock, he later admitted. He saved it, because his luck seemed to have made him invulnerable.

This was the first race at the too tight Bugatti circuit since 1991, and a rebirth for the French GP, which was missing believed wounded from last year's calendar. The wounds were the result of the total national ban on tobacco advertising, and the cigarette-sponsored bikes all required special paintwork to disguise their trademarks even more than at the cover-up events in Germany and Britain. Marlboro machines appeared for the first time as 'Team Red and White', likely to become almost a trademark in itself.

Enthusiastic new promoters made a festival of the weekend, and they were rewarded with a fair crowd of some 40,000. A rock concert, a pit walkabout and sundry stunts including a rocket car (it fizzled out on the line) formed a backdrop, while one-price go-anywhere tickets were a popular innovation. A bungee-jumping crane near the first hairpin was in constant use. This earned criticism from Schwantz, who complained that it was distracting while braking hard to spy some terrified punter plummeting earthwards.

Schwantz was in general not too keen on the track, which is short of run-off in a few spots, notably at the end of the pit straight, where the chicane used last time has had little done to improve its safety. Kevin's comment was quotable: 'It seems less safe than three years ago. Since the track hasn't changed it must be my attitude. Back then I felt ten feet tall and bullet-proof. Now I'm just bullet-proof.'

Beattie's crash was no fault of the circuit. It happened before he'd even seen all of it. On his first lap, on cold tyres, he was caught out by the chicane at the end of the back straight and was unfortunate enough to get his foot tangled in the drive chain and sprocket as he fell. As well as fracturing his left wrist, this mangled his foot more than somewhat, removing the tips of all five toes in a far from surgical manner. The segments were carefully packed in ice, but surgeons in Paris found it impossible to reattach them. His foot was substantially saved, however, and the message was that while he would be out for several races, he would ride – and even walk – again. This gruesome episode raised the question of whether chain-guards should be fitted, but technical director Jack Findlay felt that since the bikes had so many differences it would probably be best left to the teams themselves to take precautions against this rare if not unknown type of injury. Team Roberts bikes immediately sprouted a rudimentary sprocket-guard.

Cagiva gave their fuel-injected bike a first public outing, following tests at Mugello earlier in the week. Now they felt ready to test it against other machinery. It ran well, reported Chandler, with a rather heavy throttle, but good performance. 'It feels so smooth you think it's slow, but you're coming out with the other guys and they're not getting away from you.' But testing a third bike diluted his efforts at a time when he was gathering strength, and he only used it in the 'untimed' morning sessions.

Yet more promise came from Serge Rosset, who showed his new Roc engine, run for the first time the weekend before. The V4 is fundamentally an improved (probably) Yamaha Big Bang, with revised reed valves, a narrower 76-degree vee and a flap-type exhaust powervalve, compared with Yamaha's rotary barrel valve. Rosset claimed about 175 horsepower at 12,000 rpm, with riders reporting good torque if a relative reluctance to rev. Designed with the privateer in mind, the motor's future depended to a large extent on the level of interest they might display. It had been hoped that endurance star Hervé Moineau, who won a magazine readers' poll for the 500 class wild card, would ride the bike at Le Mans, but he was concussed after a heavy crash at the Spa 24-hour race the weekend before.

Also absent, Reggiani's Aprilia. After the spate of seizures, the Italians had withdrawn to try and solve the problem in private. After its promising Jerez debut, the 400 cc V-twin had run well in practice for the next four races, but failed in the early laps. Now culprits were to be sought, with suspects ranging from poor-quality pistons or cylinder lining material to gassing up with a full tank of fuel. Each race missed, under IRTA's rules, incurred a fine of US$10,000 – the price of honesty. As team boss Carlo Pernat explained: 'If we had told a lie and said Loris had hurt his finger while testing, no problem. But we told the truth, and now we must pay.' And pay again, and again, for that was the last we saw of the Aprilia until the final race of the year.

Julian Miralles was also out after the collapse of a sponsorship deal, replaced on his Team Roc bike for the moment by German Superbike hero Udo Mark, while the collapse of the Krona sliding-door firm backing Sakata's Aprilia team left the factory to carry the burden alone, though they left his and Torrentegui's bikes in the same red livery for the sake of appearances.

The Honda/Aprilia battle for 250 honours was intensified with a factory power-up kit available to Capirossi and Romboni. The Honda had a speed deficit, and new carburettors with an electronic power-jet, new ignition electronics and exhausts were designed to address the problem. Le Mans comprises mainly drag strips linked by hairpins, so this was not the place to measure its effectiveness, yet the promise was clear. Romboni also raced a new 16-in. rear Dunlop, the first time in the class.

500 cc PRACTICE

The problems of Le Mans were two-fold and related – a slippery surface along with low overall gearing. The result for the 500s is a propensity to violent wheelspin, and there were a number of crashes and near-misses apart from the Queenslander cobbers Doohan and Beattie. Victims included Chandler, Barros and Emmett, without serious injury.

Doohan fell on Saturday morning, by when he had stamped his authority with a Friday time that remained unassailable. He was inside the race lap record, but almost a second slower than Kocinski's 1991 pole. He tried to explain the continuing decline in speed, suggesting the 500 class weight limit of 130 kg should be dropped to break the circle of stagnation. 'We keep getting more horsepower, which means we get more wheelspin. It makes it even harder to get the bike turned. We also arrive at the corners faster, so we have to brake harder. If the bikes were lighter, I believe times would drop as with the 250s.'

Schwantz was second almost throughout, also on a Friday time. Then, in the closing quarter of the final session, things came alive, and by the finish the World Champion wasn't even on the front row.

Hottest on the charge (another contract-time flier) was Cadalora, with a pair of fast laps that lifted him from seventh to an ultra-close second, just three-hundredths down. The success came, he said mysteriously, 'after a crucial change at the end of the session', but he knew they were flash laps, and was worried both about consistency and tyre wear.

Redoubtable, remarkable Alberto Puig was next, on the front row for the fifth time, and also worried about tyre wear. 'It seems okay, but because I have no 500 experience, I never know until the race. I can't set the bike up so it is smooth under wheelspin, which is hard on the tyre.'

And on the far end of row one, for the first time since the Spanish GP five races ago, came Kocinski, his hand still sore though less troublesome now. Half a second off Doohan and two seconds off his own previous pole, he said optimistically: 'I know what it takes to do the 1m 39s time here. The track seems more slippery, but it's just a case of getting the bike set up.'

Schwantz now led row two, saying: 'I've been getting better starts from the second row recently anyhow.' He

115

FRENCH GRAND PRIX

Right: Luca Cadalora chases Alex Barros chases Shinichi Itoh, early in the race.

Bottom: Heading for a first top-ten finish, Irish privateer Jeremy McWilliams compares times with team boss Joe Millar.

was working on tyre endurance, but his real problem was his wrist, though he was loath to admit it. The fractures in his hand were healing well, but the dislocated bones were still 'floating', he said; and he was still very definitely racing with the full plaster cast.

An on-form Chandler was alongside, less than two-tenths slower. 'After riding with the fast guys at Mugello, you kinda get carried along by them,' he said, the gentle smile now more frequently in evidence than earlier this year.

Criville was seventh and Itoh eighth, the pair of Honda riders pattering and wallowing respectively. Barros led row three, complaining of geometry problems that were losing him time mid-turn and on the exit. He crashed again in race day warm-up, and would come to the line with bruised ribs, stiff and sore.

Three-tenths behind came Mackenzie, with a flash time. 'The bike's a dog,' he said succinctly. 'There's no way I can keep that up for the race.'

Frenchmen Bernard Garcia and Jeandat were next, concluding the third row; McWilliams led the fourth from Reynolds, Migliorati and Lopez Mella. Udo Mark qualified 19th; Marco Papa's replacement, Ermanno Bastianini, was 22nd, ahead of crasher Emmett. Last out of 30 qualifiers was Evren Bischoff, replacing sacked slowcoach Lothar Neukirchner. He'd got up to speed, in spite of his dismay at the primitive state of the team's effort, then hurt his foot in a high-sider, and was out.

500 cc RACE – 27 LAPS

The starter held the lights a fraction longer than usual, and caught out both poleman Doohan and Cadalora alongside him. Both moved, but stopped just in time (before their rear-wheel spindles crossed the line), only to be left behind as the rest took off.

As Doohan embarked on his potentially disastrous first-corner adventure, Puig led away chased by the two Cagivas, Chandler taking control of second by the end of the lap.

Doohan was working his way through to the front, with Schwantz recovering from their encounter in his wake. He couldn't match the Honda's pace, though, and was still fourth as Doohan took the lead at the start of lap eight. Almost all Doohan's overtaking moves came under brakes at the end of the pit straight or for the next hairpin – there are few other places where passing is possible.

Once ahead, nobody could touch him, even though his best lap was four-tenths slower than his own three-year-old record and the race average down at 154.395 km/h as against 156.256. Only a mistake could ruin his day, and it came close with his unguarded fistful of throttle on the last left-hand bend. 'It slid straight onto opposite lock. I pulled in the clutch and it came back in line. I won't be trying that in a race again,' he said later.

Puig was hanging on to second, with Schwantz getting among the Cagivas, Kocinski now ahead and Chandler riding much harder and more riskily than for over a year. Then, on lap eight, his race was over – his engine suffered a broken con rod and subsequent major blow-up, and he pulled off the track forthwith.

Kocinski took second off Puig under brakes for the first hairpin on the next lap, and kept pulling ahead. 'I tried to stay with Doohan, and that meant I ran away from the others,' he said. But it was a hopeless quest, and second was the best he could hope for.

Now Puig came under renewed pressure from Criville and Schwantz, while behind them Itoh, Barros and Cadalora were also battling. That fight fizzled out, but the trio ahead had plenty of action to come.

As the race wore on, Criville moved ahead and gained some clear air. Schwantz was following Puig a little way back. Then, with five laps left, he was closing again. All race long he had been taking his left hand off the bars on every straight to shake his arm and restore circulation. But now he was hunkered down and going for it.

He outbraked Puig into the first right hairpin – la Chapelle – then started cutting away at a gap of more than a second on Criville. In the final bends, he seemed just a little too distant; but the Spaniard was running wide and the target was there. 'I could hear Schwantz coming, but there was nothing I could do about it,' he said.

The American was surprised at how quickly he caught up. But it suckered him into a crazy move that brought him cutting inside Criville in the final left just as he turned across him. The Suzuki left tyre marks on the Honda's seat, and though the surprised Criville survived his second close encounter, Schwantz did not. He quickly got to his feet, his wrist mercifully unhurt, but the bike had hit the barrier hard. He walked back to his pit to a standing ovation from the grandstand crowd.

Puig was thus fourth, while Itoh had gradually drawn clear of Barros, the pained Brazilian reporting a lack of mid-corner grip as the race wore on. Cadalora fell way short of practice form and also blamed fading tyres after losing touch with Barros, then slowing even more to cross the line more than 11 seconds adrift.

Three Britons were leading the privateer battle. Mackenzie was in charge until his bike started misfiring with nine laps remaining. He pitted, and left the circuit at once in high dudgeon, not for the first time in a year when all hopes have been dashed jointly and severally. That left McWilliams and Reynolds, the issue resolved on the penultimate lap when Reynolds seized and was thrown off. Eighth was a best-ever result for Ulsterman McWilliams.

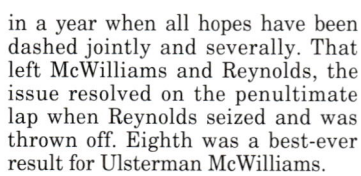

With Emmett also pitting in the closing stages with a serious misfire, Marc Garcia was ninth, also a career best, with Lopez Mella tenth, the Spaniard one lap down on the leaders. With just 18 finishers, only the last three didn't score points.

Bastianini crashed heavily, and though at first he seemed unhurt he later collapsed, and required emergency surgery to cure internal injuries including a ruptured spleen.

Schwantz's no-score helped Doohan reach another landmark as his points lead stretched to 76 – a three-race buffer. His train just kept on rolling, in spite of his own attempts to leap off the rails.

250 cc PRACTICE

Biaggi seemed dominant again, but was finally tipped off pole by a charging Romboni, who said the new power-up kit helped the engine to rev out better. He expressed some surprise at his speed. 'I wondered why the back was sliding so much, but when I saw the lap time I understood.'

He was almost four-tenths faster than Biaggi, whose hopes of improving his Friday time were thwarted by heavy traffic on the short circuit. But he was finding it difficult anyway, with the disc-valve Aprilia's abrupt throttle a handful on the slow, low-gear bends. 'I'll play the jackal tomorrow,' he said, 'waiting for others to make a mistake. If Romboni breaks away, he can go. But if Capirossi does, I'll have to go with him.'

Loris was next, but another six-tenths down, the spread of times being most unusual in the class. 'I'm not so worried,' he said. 'I have a good engine and a good chassis: they just weren't in the same bike this afternoon.'

Next up was Waldmann, whose plan was the opposite of his victorious Mugello tactics. This time he would fit an especially low first gear and try and seize control from the start, on a track where overtaking opportunities are very limited. With a 1.3-second deficit on fellow-HB Honda man Romboni, this seemed somewhat optimistic.

Ruggia led row two, also troubled with tricky Aprilia handling that meant he had to hunch over the front to keep it stable. He looked wild and close to crashing, and missed a front-row start at his home GP by just five-hundredths.

Harada was close behind the Frenchman, but feared his injured right hand wouldn't last the race because of the heavy braking. It was the reigning World Champion's first time at Le Mans, and he wasn't impressed. Then came Aoki, bravely defying the effects of his crash in Italy and riding with his injured shoulder strapped up, with Bayle completing row two after some spectacular motocrossing across the gravel at the final turns.

An off-form Okada was ninth, though he was too polite publicly to blame his Michelins for the usual lack of front grip. Next on row three was Honma's Rainey Yamaha – the Japanese rider had at least seen the circuit before, having raced here in 1989.

Zeelenberg was 11th, then D'Antin, but the Spaniard was in hospital with concussion after a heavy fall, and was not expected to race. In fact he did start, but didn't last long. There were 34 qualifiers, Carlos Checa, Eskil Suter, Adrian Bosshard and Luis Maurel filling the next row.

250 cc RACE – 25 LAPS

On the endless twists and slow turns, this was not for once a particularly exciting race. Biaggi led off the line, but by the end of lap one he was third, with Romboni up front and Capirossi a close second. And so it stayed, more or less, for the next 23 laps.

Ruggia was fourth, and did nose ahead of Biaggi from laps nine to 13, even closing on the leading pair. But Max moved back to continue lurking like a jackal as the race wore on.

Capirossi's plan was to wait for the last lap for a decisive assault on Romboni. 'I'd been watching to see where I could attack him. He was riding very well, but I was faster out of the corner before the back straight, so I could draft him, then take the lead at the end of the straight.' And so he did, to cross the line almost seven-tenths ahead.

117

FRENCH GRAND PRIX

Clockwise from right: Ruggia chased team-mate Biaggi for a while, but as usual his bike wasn't fast enough – or something; Marlboro girl in non-tobacco disguise; Ueda celebrates not crashing with a mineral water toast; Tsujimura leads Perugini and the 125 mob; Bayle uncaged looked casual for his fans, cool on the bike.

Biaggi had also closed up for the final battle, and may have been close enough to attack Romboni in the last bends, though it would have been a miracle if he'd prevailed. Instead Romboni had a big slide on the last left, and held both of them up. Later Romboni complained that his engine had been 200 or 300 revs down. 'If I'd had power I'd have stayed with Capirossi easily,' he said.

New-found speed notwithstanding, Biaggi said it was again their better braking and acceleration on the tight bends that beat him. 'The Aprilia lifts its back wheel and the power is very sharp, so the low-gear corners are difficult,' he explained.

Waldmann had been a little disadvantaged in the next battle, because his gearing choice left him with only five usable gears. His group comprised Ruggia, an ever-determined Aoki and a sparkling Bayle, who had lost touch after missing a gear, then caught right up again.

The last lap resolved matters, when group leader Ruggia was hit from behind by Aoki, and sent off into the dirt as both fought to regain control. This gave Waldmann the room he needed to nip through and claim fourth, with Bayle less than half a second behind. Aoki was three-tenths away; Ruggia three seconds behind and spitting mad. 'I was riding carefully to protect fourth, then Aoki came into the corner much too fast and ran into me. There's no way that sort of riding is acceptable. If so, we will have kicking fights out on the track.'

Harada had an up-and-down race, dropping right back to 15th after a mediocre start when his factory Yamaha's engine stalled on lap two. It restarted, but never did run right, with erratic power and no bottom end. He showed his class by storming through all the same, to claim a worthy eighth.

With Dunlop dominant again, Michelin man Okada spent most of the race trailing Zeelenberg. Then, in the final bends of the last lap, the Dutchman made a slip and ran off into the gravel. This gave ninth to the Japanese title contender, while Zeelenberg recovered to trail him across the line by seven seconds.

Honma was 11th. A long way back came Bosshard, Checa, then Suter, with Maurel narrowly defeating the Yokohama-shod Patrick van den Goorbergh for the last point.

D'Antin had made a surprise race appearance, but though his concussion was apparently cured, his left arm was painful, and when he dropped back out of the points he retired. There were 25 finishers, but few crashes, with only Rodney Fee falling.

The points situation was more tense than the race. Biaggi retained his lead by one point over Capirossi, with Okada only 12 adrift. Hold your breath, and keep watching.

125 cc RACE – 23 LAPS

The race was close, as usual, especially for the first few laps, but the front-running was all between Takeshi Tsujimura and Noboru Ueda, with the latter taking the lead on lap seven and holding it from there to the flag. 'Crashing is finished for me,' the ever-smiling Japanese rider joked later.

Tsujimura's pressure had been pitiless, and at the finish there was only just over a tenth of a second in it. The last-lap sprint had left Kazuto Sakata trailing, and he was so disheartened that he almost fell back into the clutches of Peter Öttl, who had earlier moved up to attack the leading group before dropping away again.

There had been six bikes battling behind them, but this group also stretched out towards the finish. Raudies had his hands full with Martinez, and only just prevailed over the Yamaha; then came Perugini. Two seconds behind was Torrontegui, who had worked through from a poor start: his arrival had helped break up the group.

Tokudome was ninth, with Gresini overpowered and losing touch at the end for tenth. Eleventh-placed Nakajyo had earlier set a new lap record, but he went grass-tracking on the last lap and was lucky to finish at all. Two seconds back came Aoki junior, all alone.

Young Spaniard Juan Maturana took over the injured Katoh's Yamaha, finishing a fighting 13th at the head of a five-strong group of much more experienced riders, Akira Saito and Stefan Prein collecting the final points on offer ahead of Geissler and McCoy.

Girl racer Tomoko Igata was back to reclaim her FCC Technical Sports Honda from Manako, but crashed out after 17 laps. Cecchinello and Takahashi also crashed. Likewise Giro, with an all-too-familiar first-lap first-corner tumble. Bodelier was another of the nine non-finishers, out of the leading group after his gear linkage broke early on.

Photos: Gold & Goose

FIM WORLD CHAMPIONSHIP • ROUND 9
GRAND PRIX DE FRANCE
17 JULY 1994

500 cc

27 laps, 74.331 miles/119.610 km

Place	Rider	Nat.	Machine	Laps	Time & speed	Fastest lap	Lap
1	Michael Doohan	AUS	Honda	27	46m 28.917s 95.937 mph/ 154.395 km/h	1m 41.686s	12
2	John Kocinski	USA	Cagiva	27	46m 35.018s	1m 41.809s	16
3	Alex Criville	E	Honda	27	46m 40.230s	1m 42.133s	5
4	Alberto Puig	E	Honda	27	46m 41.244s	1m 42.354s	9
5	Shinichi Itoh	J	Honda	27	46m 49.004s	1m 42.479s	5
6	Alexandre Barros	BR	Suzuki	27	46m 54.986s	1m 42.715s	4
7	Luca Cadalora	I	Yamaha	27	47m 05.790s	1m 42.476s	4
8	Jeremy McWilliams	GB	Yamaha	27	47m 41.676s	1m 44.555s	21
9	Marc Garcia	F	Yamaha	27	48m 12.425s	1m 45.004s	5
10	Juan Lopez Mella	E	Yamaha	26	46m 30.630s	1m 45.262s	20
11	Jean Foray	F	Yamaha	26	46m 31.062s	1m 45.599s	20
12	Bernard Hänggeli	CH	Yamaha	26	46m 31.288s	1m 45.418s	12
13	Bruno Bonhuil	F	Yamaha	26	46m 32.402s	1m 45.717s	7
14	Udo Mark	D	Yamaha	26	46m 36.013s	1m 45.425s	16
15	Cristiano Migliorati	I	Yamaha	26	47m 06.793s	1m 46.224s	7
16	Kevin Mitchell	GB	Yamaha	26	47m 33.342s	1m 47.581s	8
17	Andreas Leuthe	D	Yamaha	26	47m 41.197s	1m 48.231s	18
18	Philippe Monneret	F	Yamaha	26	47m 46.636s	1m 47.508s	6
	Kevin Schwantz	USA	Suzuki	26	DNF	1m 48.182s	26
	John Reynolds	GB	Yamaha	25	DNF	1m 44.066s	25
	Sean Emmett	GB	Yamaha	24	DNF	1m 45.723s	4
	Niall Mackenzie	GB	Yamaha	18	DNF	1m 43.648s	8
	Doug Chandler	USA	Cagiva	8	DNF	1m 42.879s	7
	Ermanno Bastianini	I	Yamaha	8	DNF	1m 45.712s	5
	Lucio Pedercini	I	Yamaha	6	DNF	1m 46.780s	4
	Cees Doorakkers	NL	Yamaha	6	DNF	1m 49.608s	5
	Laurent Naveau	B	Yamaha	2	DNF	1m 46.744s	2
	Bernard Garcia	F	Yamaha	1	DNF	2m 05.140s	1
	Jean-Pierre Jeandat	F	Yamaha	1	DNF	2m 27.541s	1
	Evren Bischoff	D	Yamaha		DNS		
	Paul Pellisier	I	Faton		DNQ		

Fastest lap: Doohan, 1m 41.686s, 97.453 mph/156.836 km/h.
Lap record: Michael Doohan, AUS (Honda), 1m 41.200s, 97.921 mph/157.589 km/h (1991).

Qualifying: 1 Doohan, 1m 40.759s; **2** Cadalora, 1m 40.944s; **3** Puig, 1m 41.143s; **4** Kocinski, 1m 41.493s; **5** Schwantz, 1m 41.497s; **6** Chandler, 1m 41.664s; **7** Criville, 1m 42.524s; **8** Itoh, 1m 42.703s; **9** Barros, 1m 42.737s; **10** Mackenzie, 1m 43.080s; **11** B. Garcia, 1m 43.092s; **12** Jeandat, 1m 43.326s; **13** McWilliams, 1m 44.024s; **14** Reynolds, 1m 44.106s; **15** Migliorati, 1m 44.708s; **16** Lopez Mella, 1m 44.786s; **17** Naveau, 1m 44.813s; **18** Bonhuil, 1m 45.225s; **19** Mark, 1m 45.314s; **20** M. Garcia, 1m 45.451s; **21** Hänggeli, 1m 45.493s; **22** Bastianini, 1m 45.563s; **23** Emmett, 1m 45.644s; **24** Foray, 1m 45.818s; **25** Mitchell, 1m 45.993s; **26** Pedercini, 1m 46.248s; **27** Doorakkers, 1m 47.193s; **28** Leuthe, 1m 47.646s; **29** Monneret, 1m 48.112s; **30** Bischoff, 1m 49.068s; **31** Pellisier, 1m 55.454s.

World Championship: 1 M. Doohan, 211; **2** Schwantz, 135; **3** Kocinski, 107; **4** Puig, 103; **5** Barros, 100; **6** Criville, 99; **7** Itoh, 88; **8** Cadalora, 82; **9** Chandler, 48; **10** Mackenzie, 35; **11** Beattie, 33; **12** Reynolds, 32; **13** B. Garcia, 31; **14** Lopez Mella, 23; **15** McWilliams, 19; **16** Emmett, 16; **17** Jeandat, 15; **18** Migliorati, 12; **19** Honma, 10; **20** Naveau, 9; **21** M. Garcia, Hänggeli, Miralles and Reggiani, 7; **25** Bonhuil and Foray, 6; **27** Moineau, 5; **28** S. Doohan, 4; **29** Mark, 2; **30** Pedercini, 1.

Udo Mark's Team Roc debut gave him two points.

250 cc

25 laps, 68.825 miles/110.750 km

Place	Rider	Nat.	Machine	Laps	Time & speed	Fastest lap	Lap
1	Loris Capirossi	I	Honda	25	43m 46.089s 94.338 mph/ 151.823 km/h	1m 44.030s	16
2	Doriano Romboni	I	Honda	25	43m 46.778s	1m 44.333s	14
3	Massimiliano Biaggi	I	Aprilia	25	43m 47.270s	1m 44.318s	24
4	Ralf Waldmann	D	Honda	25	43m 51.212s	1m 44.517s	24
5	Jean-Michel Bayle	F	Aprilia	25	43m 51.617s	1m 44.578s	20
6	Nobuatsu Aoki	J	Honda	25	43m 51.910s	1m 44.313s	7
7	Jean-Philippe Ruggia	F	Aprilia	25	43m 55.107s	1m 44.636s	6
8	Tetsuya Harada	J	Yamaha	25	44m 10.148s	1m 44.626s	17
9	Tadayuki Okada	J	Honda	25	44m 15.132s	1m 45.090s	6
10	Wilco Zeelenberg	NL	Honda	25	44m 22.362s	1m 45.351s	7
11	Toshihiko Honma	J	Yamaha	25	44m 27.876s	1m 45.450s	6
12	Adrian Bosshard	CH	Honda	25	44m 38.578s	1m 45.742s	7
13	Carlos Checa	E	Honda	25	44m 43.295s	1m 45.593s	14
14	Eskil Suter	CH	Aprilia	25	44m 47.592s	1m 46.016s	17
15	Luis Maurel	E	Honda	25	44m 49.442s	1m 46.450s	25
16	Patrick van den Goorbergh	NL	Aprilia	25	44m 50.366s	1m 46.556s	17
17	Adi Stadler	D	Honda	25	45m 02.516s	1m 46.867s	6
18	Juan Borja	E	Honda	25	45m 05.696s	1m 46.997s	17
19	Christian Boudinot	F	Aprilia	25	45m 06.252s	1m 46.878s	8
20	Bernd Kassner	D	Aprilia	25	45m 06.850s	1m 46.902s	16
21	Andy Preining	A	Aprilia	25	45m 12.953s	1m 47.446s	15
22	Noel Ferro	F	Honda	25	45m 13.098s	1m 47.226s	25
23	Sebastian Scarnato	F	Honda	25	45m 22.410s	1m 47.387s	15
24	Kristian Kaas	SF	Yamaha	24	44m 25.327s	1m 49.097s	4
25	Donnie Hough	USA	Honda	24	45m 25.524s	1m 51.992s	3
	Jurgen van den Goorbergh	NL	Aprilia	21	DNF	1m 47.200s	18
	Alessandro Gramigni	I	Aprilia	17	DNF	1m 46.822s	9
	Frédéric Protat	F	Honda	16	DNF	1m 47.972s	7
	Giuseppe Fiorillo	I	Honda	14	DNF	1m 47.105s	10
	Rodney Fee	CAN	Honda	13	DNF	1m 49.347s	9
	Enrique de Juan	E	Aprilia	10	DNF	1m 48.775s	7
	José Luis Cardoso	E	Aprilia	7	DNF	1m 49.064s	4
	Luis D'Antin	E	Honda	6	DNF	1m 47.576s	5
	Manuel Hernandez	E	Aprilia	3	DNF	1m 51.422s	2

Fastest lap: Capirossi, 1m 44.030s, 95.257 mph/153.302 km/h (record).
Previous record: Helmut Bradl, D (Honda), 1m 45.375s, 94.041 mph/151.345 km/h (1991).

Qualifying: 1 Romboni, 1m 42.967s; **2** Biaggi, 1m 43.322s; **3** Capirossi, 1m 43.701s; **4** Waldmann, 1m 44.265s; **5** Ruggia, 1m 44.312s; **6** Harada, 1m 44.354s; **7** Aoki, 1m 44.626s; **8** Bayle, 1m 44.716s; **9** Okada, 1m 44.760s; **10** Honma, 1m 44.771s; **11** Zeelenberg, 1m 44.984s; **12** D'Antin, 1m 45.009s; **13** Checa, 1m 45.272s; **14** Suter, 1m 45.417s; **15** Bosshard, 1m 45.949s; **16** Maurel, 1m 46.497s; **17** Boudinot, 1m 46.532s; **18** Preining, 1m 46.644s; **19** J. van den Goorbergh, 1m 46.759s; **20** P. van den Goorbergh, 1m 46.844s; **21** Fiorillo, 1m 47.213s; **22** Protat, 1m 47.267s; **23** Kassner, 1m 47.301s; **24** Ferro, 1m 47.512s; **25** Borja, 1m 47.632s; **26** Stadler, 1m 47.715s; **27** Scarnato, 1m 47.818s; **28** Gramigni, 1m 48.034s; **29** Fee, 1m 48.482s; **30** Hernandez, 1m 48.876s; **31** Kaas, 1m 49.180s; **32** Cardoso, 1m 49.387s; **33** de Juan, 1m 49.511s; **34** Hough, 1m 50.159s.

World Championship: 1 Biaggi, 144; **2** Capirossi, 143; **3** Okada, 132; **4** Romboni, 113; **5** Waldmann, 104; **6** Ruggia, 100; **7** Bayle and D'Antin, 67; **9** N. Aoki, 63; **10** Zeelenberg, 56; **11** Harada, 53; **12** Checa, 28; **13** Suter, 24; **14** P. van den Goorbergh, 23; **15** J. van den Goorbergh, 22; **16** Preining, 18; **17** Bosshard and Ukawa, 16; **19** T. Aoki and Lucchi, 11; **21** Gramigni, 10; **22** Kassner, 9; **23** Honma and Stadler, 8; **25** Connell, 5; **26** Fiorillo, 4; **27** Castilla, 3; **28** Cardoso and Maurel, 1.

Le Mans – Bugatti Circuit

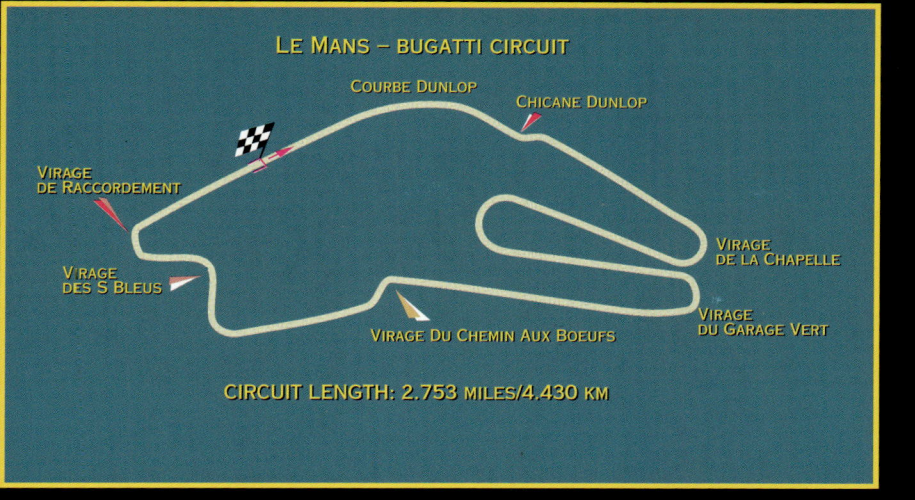

- Virage de Raccordement
- Virage des S Bleus
- Courbe Dunlop
- Chicane Dunlop
- Virage de la Chapelle
- Virage du Garage Vert
- Virage du Chemin aux Boeufs

CIRCUIT LENGTH: 2.753 MILES/4.430 KM

125 cc

23 laps, 63.319 miles/101.890 km

Place	Rider	Nat.	Machine	Laps	Time & speed	Fastest lap	Lap
1	Noboru Ueda	J	Honda	23	42m 59.000s 88.376 mph/ 142.227 km/h	1m 51.289s	7
2	Takeshi Tsujimura	J	Honda	23	42m 59.112s	1m 51.144s	9
3	Kazuto Sakata	J	Aprilia	23	43m 02.118s	1m 51.186s	13
4	Peter Öttl	D	Aprilia	23	43m 03.034s	1m 51.144s	8
5	Dirk Raudies	D	Honda	23	43m 08.738s	1m 51.571s	7
6	Jorge Martinez	E	Yamaha	23	43m 08.830s	1m 51.405s	4
7	Stefano Perugini	I	Aprilia	23	43m 11.029s	1m 51.352s	9
8	Herri Torrontegui	E	Aprilia	23	43m 13.428s	1m 51.737s	16
9	Masaki Tokudome	J	Honda	23	43m 13.721s	1m 51.508s	9
10	Fausto Gresini	I	Honda	23	43m 20.779s	1m 51.479s	4
11	Hideyuki Nakajyo	J	Honda	23	43m 26.086s	1m 50.818s	8
12	Haruchika Aoki	J	Honda	23	43m 28.174s	1m 51.990s	5
13	Juan Maturana	E	Yamaha	23	43m 41.752s	1m 52.855s	8
14	Akira Saito	J	Honda	23	43m 41.919s	1m 52.749s	2
15	Stefan Prein	D	Yamaha	23	43m 42.360s	1m 52.740s	22
16	Manfred Geissler	D	Aprilia	23	43m 42.500s	1m 52.692s	14
17	Garry McCoy	AUS	Aprilia	23	43m 43.162s	1m 52.571s	3
18	Oliver Petruccciani	CH	Aprilia	23	43m 46.123s	1m 53.004s	3
19	Gabriele Debbia	I	Aprilia	23	43m 58.934s	1m 52.890s	14
20	Neil Hodgson	GB	Honda	23	44m 11.794s	1m 52.792s	8
21	Gregory Fouet	F	Yamaha	23	44m 38.540s	1m 54.660s	11
22	Bertrand Stey	F	Honda	23	44m 42.111s	1m 55.427s	7
23	Hans Spaan	NL	Honda	23	44m 49.448s	1m 54.238s	5
24	Frank Baldinger	D	Honda	22	43m 10.352s	1m 54.076s	5
25	Luigi Ancona	I	Honda	22	43m 55.006s	1m 52.996s	8
26	Yasuaki Takahashi	J	Honda	22	44m 59.761s	1m 54.917s	5
27	Fabien Rousseau	F	Aprilia	22	44m 16.134s	1m 56.492s	6
	Vittorio Lopez	I	Honda	21	DNF	1m 53.558s	7
	Manfred Baumann	D	Yamaha	21	DNF	1m 55.337s	3
	Gianluigi Scalvini	I	Aprilia	20	DNF	1m 53.054s	7
	Tomoko Igata	J	Honda	17	DNF	1m 55.194s	11
	Lucio Cecchinello	I	Honda	16	DNF	1m 52.408s	4
	Emili Alzamora	E	Honda	10	DNF	1m 53.223s	3
	Loek Bodelier	NL	Honda	6	DNF	1m 51.196s	5
	Frédéric Petit	F	Yamaha	3	DNF	1m 56.919s	2
	Carlos Giro	E	Aprilia	0	DNF		

Fastest lap: Nakajyo, 1m 50.818s, 89.423 mph/143.912 km/h (record).
Previous record: Doriano Romboni, I (Honda), 1m 54.006s, 86.922 mph/139.887 km/h (1990).

Qualifying: 1 Sakata, 1m 50.552s; **2** Ueda, 1m 50.638s; **3** Tsujimura, 1m 50.925s; **4** Raudies, 1m 51.130s; **5** Martinez, 1m 51.323s; **6** Perugini, 1m 51.336s; **7** Aoki, 1m 51.508s; **8** Öttl, 1m 51.623s; **9** Nakajyo, 1m 51.627s; **10** Tokudome, 1m 51.798s; **11** Bodelier, 1m 51.812s; **12** Torrontegui, 1m 51.828s; **13** Petrucciani, 1m 51.903s; **14** Giro, 1m 51.932s; **15** Gresini, 1m 51.935s; **16** Saito, 1m 51.986s; **17** Scalvini, 1m 52.096s; **18** Alzamora, 1m 52.152s; **19** Debbia, 1m 52.348s; **20** Cecchinello, 1m 52.375s; **21** Prein, 1m 52.598s; **22** Igata, 1m 52.868s; **23** Maturana, 1m 52.902s; **24** Lopez, 1m 52.933s; **25** Geissler, 1m 53.006s; **26** McCoy, 1m 53.098s; **27** Petit, 1m 53.387s; **28** Hodgson, 1m 53.498s; **29** Takahashi, 1m 53.547s; **30** Ancona, 1m 54.210s; **31** Spaan, 1m 54.443s; **32** Baldinger, 1m 54.494s; **33** Rousseau, 1m 54.824s; **34** Stey, 1m 54.849s; **35** Fouet, 1m 55.383s; **36** Baumann, 1m 55.804s.

World Championship: 1 Sakata, 170; **2** Ueda, 127; **3** Tsujimura, 107; **4** Öttl, 105; **5** Raudies, 102; **6** Martinez, 80; **7** Torrontegui, 62; **8** Tokudome, 60; **9** McCoy, 56; **10** Saito, 50; **11** Petrucciani, 44; **12** Gresini, 40; **13** Bodelier and Nakajyo, 39; **15** Perugini, 34; **16** Koch, 26; **17** Manako, 24; **18** Aoki, 23; **19** Casanova, 15; **20** Debbia, 9; **21** Cuppini and Scalvini, 7; **23** Locatelli, 6; **24** Alzamora, 5; **25** Amano and Katoh, 4; **27** Cecchinello and Maturana, 3; **29** Geissler, Igata, Petit and Prein, 2; **33** Giro, 1.

From top: Niall Mackenzie stoops, but not to conquer; Doriano Romboni was so close; Max Biaggi in full bloom.

Photos: Gold & Goose

WORLD CHAMPIONSHIP • ROUND 10

BRITISH GRAND PRIX

Photos: Gold & Goose

'Schwantz not only needed to win. To be blunt, he needed for Doohan to get hurt'

500 cc	SCHWANTZ
250 cc	CAPIROSSI
125 cc	TSUJIMURA

BRITISH GRAND PRIX

You had to arrive early if you wanted to see Abe (left), *Fogarty* (below) *or Jamie Robinson* (bottom).

Opposite: Schwantz started the race without hope. Poised on Doohan's back wheel *(main picture)*, he gets an inkling he may have been wrong. The plaster-cast victory may have been his best race ever.

When it comes to heroic last-ditch title defences, Kevin Schwantz's British GP was an epic. He arrived with his dislocated wrist bones 'floating' again after Le Mans, and worried that the continual sweeps of Donington Park would be harder on him than France because there is no chance to rest. Then he had a huge crash on Saturday afternoon, escaping further fractures, but bruised and battered. His hopes of victory were not high.

Practice had been hot throughout, but race day was overcast and cooler, complicating tyre choice at a track that seems more slippery and sensitive every year. It was only after the race was well under way that the Texan had an inkling that victory might be possible. Intent on staying as close as possible to Doohan, he found instead that his gamble on a harder compound Michelin worked better than the Australian's softer choice. He could do more than stay with his rival. He could pass him, and then forge ahead to win his second race of the year.

In title terms he was only staving off the inevitable, but it did wonders for his self-respect and morale. 'When I was laying on the ground yesterday, I thought my season was over,' he said while still dripping with victory champagne. 'If you'd asked me last night if I thought I had a chance of winning I'd have told you no.'

Then again, in racing, for every one who succeeds there are at least two who fail. This time it was a pair in the 500 class who attracted much interest – but not for long.

The first was Abe, making his foreign GP debut on Beattie's Yamaha, and much hyped. Alas, the long-haired Tokyo rider crashed on only his third practice lap, exiting the final hairpin by the pit straight, breaking a bone in his hand and suffering concussion. This short-lived outing was blamed by team boss Kenny Roberts on the youngster being given tyres that were too hard even for his exploratory first outing. 'I've done the same thing myself,' he said.

The other was erstwhile World Superbike title leader Carl Fogarty, scheduled to ride a third Cagiva as a wild card. Not only that, he might also give the injected Cagiva its race debut, having a choice between the all-new squirter or a carburated bike. For thunder-faced Foggy, nothing went right. The injected machine proved a handful at a track where a 500 is on part throttle almost all the time. It even tossed him off on Friday, at the same spot as Abe. The other bike was just a dog, breaking down several times and never running right. Fogarty had been refused the extra start money he had demanded on the grounds that he would swell the crowd. He left on Saturday, after a meeting with Cagiva owner Claudio Castiglioni, blaming increasing pain in the hand he'd banged when he fell. In fact, the team had decided that staying fit for the World Superbike Championship was more important than risking all trying to impress Carl's home fans on an underdeveloped motor cycle.

Crashes were a major theme of the British GP. Twenty-three riders fell on Friday, and 16 on Saturday, some for a second time. The list included defending World Champions in all three classes and race numbers were reduced, although there were no serious injuries. Most blamed Donington's notorious surface, always a difficulty for tyre manufacturers and suspension engineers. And riders. Nobody knows why the track is so weather-sensitive and slippery, though many blame descending fuel droplets from aircraft taking off at the adjacent East Midlands airport. The sidecars were also blamed for leaving rubber on the racing line, as was a German Touring Car Championship meeting the weekend before.

Another difficulty is that many of the corners are only slightly cambered or even off-camber; one bend runs into the next, so a small mistake or slip off line can land riders in serious trouble a little further along.

Then there is the problem of the left side of the tyre cooling, particularly acute at the notorious left-hander at the bottom of Craner Curves, the first swing over that way for some distance and a favourite (but far from the only) place to crash.

In between Abe in the opening minutes and Schwantz at the end, 500 practice fallers included Criville, Jeandat, Reynolds (twice), Marc Garcia, McWilliams, Lopez Mella and Fogarty. Jeandat damaged his bike too badly to race. Barros didn't actually fall, but he ran over his foot and broke a toe in avoiding doing so.

In the 250 class, Harada led the listings, joined in the gravel at various times by Zeelenberg, Checa, Waldmann, Hernandez, Romboni and Bosshard (both twice), Kassner, Patrick van den Goorbergh and Ruggia. Another was wild card Jamie Robinson, riding a Roberts Yamaha TZ that he had also raced in the Spanish Ducados series. The young Briton broke his collarbone in the first untimed session. Roberts was less sympathetic in this case, shaking his head and muttering 'dickhead' in a stage whisper.

Raudies was one of the 125 men to go, likewise Ueda, Perugini, Geissler, McCoy and Petit.

Reduced ticket prices – down from £35 to £25 for advance bookings and £30 at the gate on race day – went some way towards bringing the crowds back. Another move was a full programme of racing, including a Triumph Triple one-make challenge and an international Superbike race attended by Honda men Doug Polen and Aaron Slight, who didn't race once the weather turned nasty. This began after the GP was over, so that racing continued until almost 9 pm. Race day crowds were officially put at 35,000, poor by the standards of a few years ago, but a big improvement on the 22,500 of last year. It was still not enough to put the beleaguered promoters into profit, though.

123

500 cc PRACTICE

Let nobody complain about a lack of variety, with four different makes of machine on the front row, likewise on the second.

Yet there were few surprises at this unpredictable race track. Doohan claimed his fifth pole of the year, only fractions slower this time than the 1991 lap record of Schwantz, who was a close second. But this order was established only in the closing minutes. Schwantz is superb at Donington, and he transcended his broken wrist and was fastest throughout until Mick pulled a fast one.

With well under ten minutes left, Schwantz put new tyres on and went out again. Intent on reclaiming pole, he crashed in a looping high-sider just after cutting inside Swiss privateer Bernard Hänggeli at the Old Hairpin. Hänggeli was also thrown out of the seat as he ran over the Suzuki, and very narrowly missed the rider while himself only just hanging on to the handlebars, legs streaming out straight behind him. Schwantz stood up, staggered off the track, then slumped to the ground, clearly in pain. His second crash in six days had been spectacular: by sheer luck he was 'beat up', but hadn't damaged his wrist.

Doohan stayed firmly wheels down throughout, making only minor suspension adjustments, but also finding unpredictable results. 'It seems we can use much softer tyres here. This morning I tried one made from a rain-tyre compound. It was like a cut slick, without the cuts. After four laps it was starting to move around a little. Anywhere else that tyre would have been destroyed in two laps.' To rivals, this suggested that Michelin were in trouble matching grip with endurance, and that continued heat might favour the Dunlop runners, as has happened here before. In the event the weather went the other way – but the result still hinged on tyres.

Mathematically, Mick Doohan was in a position to secure the title here. Winning the race would do it. But he was more reluctant than ever to discuss it, looking vague and uneasy when pressed, and saying: 'There's no point talking about it.' He'd just ride this, he insisted, like any other race.

Schwantz's chances of stopping this march to overall victory were slender. He not only needed to win, but (to be blunt) he needed for Doohan to get hurt either here or at the next race: not something either would relish, but always possible. His favourite track was physically punishing for his injury, which cost him development. 'I can't ride the bike the way I want so we're not really finding out things we should in practice. We find them in the race instead.' Then came his cold-tyre tumble, which puzzled him. 'Of all the corners I didn't expect it there. The left-handers are bad here; the right side felt fine down the hill. But when I put on the gas at the next right-hander it just spun up WHING and spat me off. Maybe I was on a little tighter line because of passing that other guy on the way in.'

He was exactly two-tenths slower than Doohan, having also improved slightly on day two; Cadalora didn't, but was still less than a tenth down. Winner here last year, his rhythmic style also suits the British circuit, and he blamed his lack of improvement on some misdirected chassis settings: in trying to make the bike better on the two hairpins that finish the lap, he'd spoiled it for the other dozen bends.

Kocinski completed the front row after carving a chunk off his previous best time. He is not a big fan of the track, but said he felt his bike was more settled than on previous visits, although not fast enough to challenge the three ahead. The Cagiva has been on pole here before (with Lawson riding), and is always a threat.

Leading row two and less than two-tenths down came the revived Chandler, again trying the anti-dive front end. 'It slows the rate of dive, which is good; but the bike feels kinda unsettled when you get off the brakes,' he said.

Puig was next, well in touch at just over two-tenths slower; then came Barros, more than half a second away. He'd suffered a freak injury, a broken toe, after running over his foot while fighting a big slide on Friday afternoon. After that he rode wearing a cast, and was having trouble changing gear, so it was not surprising he did not improve his time. 'Actually I am having more trouble with the ribs I hurt at Le Mans,' he insisted.

Alongside, top Briton Mackenzie was mere hundredths slower on the strength of a Friday time. 'The bike's handling and braking well, but the engine's not good. You don't use power so much here, but it would be nice to be as fast as the other privateers at least,' he joked grimly.

Criville led row three from Itoh,

BRITISH GRAND PRIX

Left: Chandler (10) had the jump, but Cadalora (5) the inside line for the first corner. Note Mackenzie (50) and McWilliams (14) in the thick of it.

Below: Doohan has just passed Schwantz as they chase Cadalora and Chandler.

both experiencing balance problems with their Hondas – their usual complaint. The next qualifier was early bather Fogarty. Then came Reynolds and McWilliams, who had posted identical times to the nearest thousandth of a second. Both had crashed in practice, both had injured fingers. McWilliams's tumble came because he was carved up by a cruising Marc Garcia, who claimed the racing line and took away the Ulsterman's front wheel. He was enraged, but imminent fisticuffs were narrowly averted by the marshals.

Bernard Garcia led row four from Briton James Haydon, riding as a substitute for the injured Marco Papa; then came Naveau and wild card Nick Hopkins, in his first GP. There were 29 qualifiers but only 27 starters, with Jeandat joining Fogarty in scratching, after damaging his bike on Friday.

500 cc RACE – 30 LAPS

Cadalora leapt into the lead, followed by Chandler, Schwantz and Doohan, with the Australian passing the Texan before half the lap was done. There was still some shuffling, not all of it exactly as expected, as Chandler moved into the lead under brakes at the end of the back straight on lap two. He stayed there until halfway round lap seven.

By this time Doohan was second and Cadalora third, and it looked as though the trio would outdistance Schwantz. Indeed, he was coming under pressure from the group behind, led by an inspired Puig from Criville and Kocinski. Mackenzie was losing ground behind, quite alone; Itoh was a similar distance behind him, after working his way through the privateers following a first-corner collision.

Doohan rode bravely round the outside of the leading Cagiva on the swooping Craner Curves, immediately pulling away to lead by almost a second by the end of lap 10. But now Schwantz was on the charge. He picked off Cadalora under braking for the Melbourne Hairpin at the end of the next lap, and likewise Chandler next time round.

Victory still seemed Doohan's for sure. It was only what everyone was used to. Schwantz had other ideas and was helped by the fact that his wrist was, surprisingly, somewhat better than at Le Mans, largely because a problem there of a too-tight cast had been avoided here. He set fastest lap of the race, half a second short of his own 1991 record, on lap 13 as he worked on closing up.

Bit by bit, at about two-tenths a lap, he closed on the Honda. By lap 17 he was on Doohan's tail and starting to show his front wheel. Next time round the Australian was obliged to close the door with a tight entry to the Melbourne Hairpin. Then, on lap 19, Schwantz pulled off a double bluff, just as he had on Rainey three years ago, attacking on the other side and riding right around the outside.

Mick was looking rattled and Kevin smooth, and the gap immediately began to stretch until it was 1.7 seconds on lap 21, at about the time they ran into heavy lapped traffic. This generally helped Schwantz more than Doohan, as is often the case, with the Australian complaining afterwards that riders were ignoring the blue flag. And by lap 28 Schwantz's lead was almost 3.5 seconds.

'I guess some of the other riders don't like this track, but I seem to adapt to it pretty well,' he smiled later. 'The Suzuki is also pretty good here.' It was one of his best-ever victories.

Then again, Doohan didn't have to beat him and, considering his title position, was probably wise in not attempting what he admitted would have been very difficult. His soft tyre choice didn't help. 'I was having a few problems, and when I saw how hard he was riding I felt it would be better to let him go and concentrate on staying ahead of whoever was behind. If not for the title, I think the result would have been the same but I'd have been closer.'

Cadalora faded towards the end. 'I was able to go well in some parts of the race, but not in others,' he said enigmatically.

Kocinski had moved through in the middle part of the race, but had lost too much time stuck behind Puig to make the most of his speed. 'I had no problems with the tyres. I feel sure I could have run in the top three,' he said. He was seven seconds down on Cadalora, and four ahead of Chandler, who had faded after his brilliant start. 'Pretty early on the rear started to slide. I tried to baby it, but it was moving around too much and I had to ease off. It was me who chose the wrong tyre, the bike was great. It was a pity. This was our kind of circuit, because acceleration is not so important.'

Criville was another three seconds down, after passing a disappointed Puig. His storming start was followed by problems after half-distance with the return of pain and pumping-up problems with his arms, a nagging counterpoint to his obvious talent.

Mackenzie was eighth, left behind by the top works bikes but well ahead of the rest. Itoh was seven seconds behind him, then came McWilliams, victor in a long battle with Bernard Garcia and Emmett. Naveau was less than a second behind, with the pained Reynolds narrowly ahead of Bonhuil for the last points, both one lap down on the leaders.

Crashers included Hänggeli, Haydon (spectacularly at the last hairpin, almost mowing down several photographers), and wild card Hopkins. And Barros, who had been in fourth place and going well when he lost the front wheel at the last hairpin in the opening laps.

250 cc PRACTICE

Business much as usual in this class, too, with the expected extra fillip of excitement and another change of pole at the end, when Capirossi grabbed the position by a relatively substantial margin of three-tenths from Biaggi in the closing minutes.

The Honda rider was again enjoying the new power-up kit, but said: 'Le Mans and this track are not really fast enough for us to be able to measure the improvement.' He said the bike felt unsettled down the hill, but that he'd been able to run consistently fast laps. 'What you need is a tyre that will be good on the last lap, because I think this will be another close race.'

Biaggi had tested the new Aprilia carbon-fibre swing arm, but preferred to stick with his old aluminium one for the race. 'I'm not worried about Capirossi's time,' he said. 'I think he used qualifying tyres.'

Waldmann was next, with fellow-HB Honda rider Romboni alongside. Both had crashed, the German at more than 200 km/h on Friday and counting himself lucky to have walked away; Romboni twice, neither time with serious consequences. He was almost a second down on Capirossi, giving a wider spread of front-row times than the 500s.

Okada was next in a close second row, still chasing the understeering front Michelins which had condemned him to play a secondary role to the Dunlop men over the past few races. Whisker-close came Harada, another to crash. Then came Ruggia, another Friday faller; and Bayle, who had earlier threatened to claim his first front-row position, placing fourth on day one.

Nobuatsu Aoki led row three, still stiff and sore, from Suter, Checa and Zeelenberg. Honma's works Yamaha was one row back, in 14th place, in his second ride for Team Rainey in place of regular absentee Kenny Roberts Junior.

There were 34 qualifiers.

250 cc RACE – 27 LAPS

The first race of the day saw Biaggi first into the first bend, but third by the end of the lap. Both Romboni and Okada had surged past him, and the Italian immediately set about opening up a gap as Capirossi joined the pursuit pack and they slowed each other up somewhat.

Of course in this company a slender gap doesn't last long, and by lap five the leading four were together again, Romboni first, then Capirossi, Biaggi and Okada. But again they seemed to be slowing each other, and the next group was now closing gradually, led by Waldmann, with Ruggia, Aoki and Bayle locked together. At the same time Harada was working his way up from a poor start to join in.

There was plenty of shuffling and then, on lap eight, Biaggi put in a charge to move to second at the Old Hairpin. Before the end of the lap, though, Okada had dived inside him at the Melbourne Loop, and next time round he outbraked Romboni at the chicane to take the lead.

There were now nine bikes in the leading group, though Aoki was dropping off the back of it.

Next to put in a big charge was Waldmann, who outbraked Capirossi and Biaggi in one move to hold third for four laps. Capirossi fought back, but Biaggi was having a little trouble, nearly outbraking himself at the Melbourne Hairpin and dropping to seventh behind Bayle as a result.

As he fought his way back, having real trouble trying to find a way past Waldmann, Capirossi made his move – inside Romboni down the hill and then inside Okada at the Macleans right-hander to lead for the first time on lap 18. He immediately embarked on his own attempt at running away, and it worked. He was 1.8 seconds ahead on lap 19, and 2.9 ahead one lap later, a gap he stretched a little further by the finish. 'Like Biaggi, I chose a slightly harder tyre, because I knew it would be better towards the end of the

BRITISH GRAND PRIX

Left: Like a scattering of shrapnel, the 250s jostle for position just behind the leaders: from left to right, Harada, Aoki, Ruggia, Bayle and (obscured) Waldmann.

Neil 'Too-Tall' Hodgson *(below right)* was again out of luck for the points.

Bottom: Working up to the final sprint, the 125 leaders play for inches – Tsujimura, Perugini, Sakata, Öttl and Torrontegui. By the finish, Öttl was up into third.

125 cc RACE – 26 LAPS

Tsujimura qualified third, behind Sakata and an inspired Torrontegui, and hit top form on race day, leading from the start and again at the finish. In the middle he'd been behind Sakata for three laps, but it was only temporary. It was all very close stuff, though, with the rising Perugini up with the leading pair all the time, and also nosing ahead now and then.

A little way back, Öttl, Ueda and Torrontegui were locked in combat, but Ueda was in pain after a practice crash, and when the others closed on the leaders in the last few laps he was unable to go with them.

Öttl was really on the charge, and on lap 24 he started to attack Sakata. This prevented the Japanese Aprilia rider from carrying through any plans he might have had for a last-lap attack of his own, and he finished fourth, right on Öttl's rear wheel.

Tsujimura had won in the meantime, less than three-tenths ahead of Perugini.

Torrontegui was a close fifth, Ueda a distant sixth, five seconds ahead of what remained of an earlier gigantic group. This was led by Aprilia man Oliver Petrucciani from Raudies, Charlie Giro, and Jorge Martinez on the best Yamaha; then a little way back came Nakajyo, Tokudome, Aoki, Debbia and Saito.

New Yamaha rider Maturana failed to repeat his points-scoring French ride, finishing 18th, while the unfortunate Neil 'Too-Tall' Hodgson was 21st at his home GP.

race,' he said. 'Everything else about the bike was perfect.'

Biaggi might have caught up, having passed Waldmann on lap 18, and still only a second behind Romboni. Instead his engine seized on the way into the Melbourne Hairpin, and he crashed. 'Two laps before I felt the engine tighten a little. Then it locked solid,' he said later. His team blamed break-up of the metallic coating inside the cylinder.

The battle for second went to the wire. The cooler conditions seemed to have solved Okada's front-tyre grip problems, and he was riding well. Romboni, meanwhile, had chosen soft tyres and was sliding badly. Even so he attacked on the last lap, taking second place at the Old Hairpin, only to come under attack himself at the penultimate hairpin. Okada had just enough left to win the day by less than a tenth.

Harada rode a masterful race to lead the next group, only half a second behind Romboni. The faithful Yamaha handling allowed him to come out of the corners better than the rest, and in this way he beat Bayle by 1.7 seconds. Ruggia was on his team-mate's back wheel, saying: 'I chose higher gearing than him, and it was a mistake.' Then came Waldmann, losing two places in the last lap after a back-marker baulked him and he lost his rhythm.

Less than seven seconds covered the first seven places.

Aoki was eighth, 20 seconds adrift at the finish, while Luis D'Antin narrowly won the next dice for ninth, leading a closely matched group of five riders across the line: Eskil Suter, Wilco Zeelenberg, Carlos Checa and the impressive Honma. Adrian Bosshard was 14th, with Luis Maurel stealing the last point from Jurgen van den Goorbergh at the last gasp.

Thus Capirossi took the title lead back, with Biaggi, having failed to add to his score, dropping to third behind Okada, the forgotten man in what most saw as a two-man title battle.

500 cc

30 laps, 75.000 miles/120.690 km

Place	Rider	Nat.	Machine	Laps	Time & speed	Fastest lap	Lap
1	Kevin Schwantz	USA	Suzuki	30	47m 31.632s 94.674 mph/ 152.363 km/h	1m 34.161s	13
2	Michael Doohan	AUS	Honda	30	47m 33.998s	1m 34.242s	6
3	Luca Cadalora	I	Yamaha	30	47m 37.442s	1m 34.387s	18
4	John Kocinski	USA	Cagiva	30	47m 43.892s	1m 34.405s	13
5	Doug Chandler	USA	Cagiva	30	47m 48.096s	1m 34.472s	6
6	Alex Criville	E	Honda	30	47m 51.406s	1m 34.692s	18
7	Alberto Puig	E	Honda	30	48m 11.288s	1m 34.490s	9
8	Niall Mackenzie	GB	Yamaha	30	48m 24.696s	1m 35.382s	4
9	Shinichi Itoh	J	Honda	30	48m 32.415s	1m 35.458s	4
10	Jeremy McWilliams	GB	Yamaha	30	48m 44.010s	1m 36.628s	25
11	Bernard Garcia	F	Yamaha	30	48m 47.041s	1m 36.474s	5
12	Sean Emmett	GB	Yamaha	30	48m 56.720s	1m 37.143s	6
13	Laurent Naveau	B	Yamaha	30	48m 56.988s	1m 37.046s	7
14	John Reynolds	GB	Yamaha	29	47m 41.562s	1m 37.086s	7
15	Bruno Bonhuil	F	Yamaha	29	47m 42.108s	1m 37.504s	11
16	Kevin Mitchell	GB	Yamaha	29	48m 06.090s	1m 38.228s	29
17	Udo Mark	D	Yamaha	29	48m 07.136s	1m 38.135s	4
18	Lucio Pedercini	I	Yamaha	29	48m 07.542s	1m 38.068s	5
19	Jean Foray	F	Yamaha	29	48m 07.875s	1m 38.516s	6
20	Andreas Leuthe	D	Yamaha	29	48m 51.362s	1m 40.084s	18
21	Cees Doorakkers	NL	Yamaha	29	49m 10.664s	1m 38.837s	4
	Bernard Hänggeli	CH	Yamaha	24	DNF	1m 37.617s	10
	Marc Garcia	F	Yamaha	20	DNF	1m 38.092s	4
	Cristiano Migliorati	I	Yamaha	9	DNF	1m 37.890s	7
	Alexandre Barros	BR	Suzuki	5	DNF	1m 34.747s	3
	James Haydon	GB	Yamaha	1	DNF	1m 46.392s	1
	Nick Hopkins	GB	Yamaha	1	DNF	1m 46.990s	1
	Carl Fogarty	GB	Cagiva		DNS		
	Jean-Pierre Jeandat	F	Yamaha		DNS		

Fastest lap: Schwantz, 1m 34.161s, 95.572 mph/153.809 km/h.
Lap record: Kevin Schwantz, USA (Suzuki), 1m 33.569s, 96.106 mph/154.667 km/h (1991).

Qualifying: 1 Doohan, 1m 33.611s; **2** Schwantz, 1m 33.811s; **3** Cadalora, 1m 33.893s; **4** Kocinski, 1m 34.075s; **5** Chandler, 1m 34.204s; **6** Puig, 1m 34.462s; **7** Barros, 1m 35.038s; **8** Mackenzie, 1m 35.061s; **9** Criville, 1m 35.404s; **10** Itoh, 1m 35.438s; **11** Fogarty, 1m 35.460s; **12** Reynolds, 1m 36.309s; **13** McWilliams, 1m 36.309s; **14** B. Garcia, 1m 36.604s; **15** Haydon, 1m 36.678s; **16** Naveau, 1m 36.748s; **17** Hopkins, 1m 37.405s; **18** Hänggeli, 1m 37.456s; **19** Emmett, 1m 37.714s; **20** Bonhuil, 1m 37.966s; **21** Pedercini, 1m 38.081s; **22** Mitchell, 1m 38.119s; **23** Migliorati, 1m 38.161s; **24** Foray, 1m 38.220s; **25** Jeandat, 1m 38.479s; **26** Mark, 1m 38.504s; **27** Doorakkers, 1m 40.002s; **28** M. Garcia, 1m 40.050s; **29** Leuthe, 1m 40.350s.

World Championship: 1 M. Doohan, 231; **2** Schwantz, 160; **3** Kocinski, 120; **4** Puig, 112; **5** Criville, 109; **6** Barros, 100; **7** Cadalora, 98; **8** Itoh, 95; **9** Chandler, 59; **10** Mackenzie, 43; **11** B. Garcia, 36; **12** Reynolds, 34; **13** Beattie, 33; **14** McWilliams, 25; **15** Lopez Mella, 23; **16** Emmett, 20; **17** Jeandat, 15; **18** Migliorati and Naveau, 12; **20** Honma, 10; **21** Bonhuil, M. Garcia, Hänggeli, Miralles and Reggiani, 7; **26** Foray, 6; **27** Moineau, 5; **28** S. Doohan, 4; **29** Mark, 2; **30** Pedercini, 1.

250 cc

27 laps, 67.500 miles/108.621 km

Place	Rider	Nat.	Machine	Laps	Time & speed	Fastest lap	Lap
1	Loris Capirossi	I	Honda	27	43m 18.624s 93.503 mph/ 150.478 km/h	1m 34.953s	18
2	Tadayuki Okada	J	Honda	27	43m 21.857s	1m 35.685s	22
3	Doriano Romboni	I	Honda	27	43m 21.980s	1m 35.603s	23
4	Tetsuya Harada	J	Yamaha	27	43m 22.500s	1m 35.282s	27
5	Jean-Michel Bayle	F	Aprilia	27	43m 24.140s	1m 35.508s	13
6	Jean-Philippe Ruggia	F	Aprilia	27	43m 24.731s	1m 35.496s	25
7	Ralf Waldmann	D	Honda	27	43m 25.110s	1m 35.629s	20
8	Nobuatsu Aoki	J	Honda	27	43m 45.957s	1m 36.088s	4
9	Luis D'Antin	E	Honda	27	43m 54.114s	1m 36.475s	26
10	Eskil Suter	CH	Aprilia	27	43m 54.934s	1m 36.766s	17
11	Wilco Zeelenberg	NL	Honda	27	43m 55.519s	1m 36.907s	12
12	Carlos Checa	E	Honda	27	43m 55.744s	1m 36.727s	17
13	Toshihiko Honma	J	Yamaha	27	43m 56.524s	1m 36.662s	13
14	Adrian Bosshard	CH	Honda	27	44m 22.616s	1m 37.244s	10
15	Luis Maurel	E	Honda	27	44m 28.290s	1m 37.154s	27
16	Jurgen van den Goorbergh	NL	Aprilia	27	44m 28.412s	1m 37.454s	26
17	Patrick van den Goorbergh	NL	Aprilia	27	44m 50.335s	1m 38.541s	4
18	Adi Stadler	D	Honda	27	44m 50.530s	1m 38.647s	7
19	José Luis Cardoso	E	Aprilia	26	43m 20.644s	1m 38.957s	13
20	Eugene McManus	GB	Yamaha	26	43m 21.742s	1m 39.050s	5
21	Christian Boudinot	F	Aprilia	26	43m 51.576s	1m 39.412s	11
22	Rodney Fee	CAN	Honda	26	43m 55.485s	1m 39.801s	26
23	Enrique de Juan	E	Aprilia	26	43m 56.103s	1m 40.086s	25
24	Donnie Hough	USA	Honda	25	43m 38.680s	1m 42.762s	3
	Massimiliano Biaggi	I	Aprilia	19	DNF	1m 35.538s	13
	Noel Ferro	F	Honda	18	DNF	1m 38.921s	17
	Giuseppe Fiorillo	I	Honda	13	DNF	1m 38.364s	4
	Kristian Kaas	SF	Yamaha	13	DNF	1m 40.745s	11
	Frédéric Protat	F	Honda	9	DNF	1m 39.373s	6
	Alessandro Gramigni	I	Aprilia	7	DNF	1m 39.608s	3
	Andy Preining	A	Aprilia	1	DNF	2m 21.788s	1
	Juan Borja	E	Honda	0	DNF		
	Bernd Kassner	D	Aprilia		DNS		
	Manuel Hernandez	E	Aprilia		DNS		

Fastest lap: Capirossi, 1m 34.953s, 94.775 mph/152.526 km/h.
Lap record: Jean-Philippe Ruggia, F (Aprilia), 1m 34.888s, 94.840 mph/152.630 km/h (1993).

Qualifying: 1 Capirossi, 1m 34.990s; **2** Biaggi, 1m 35.319s; **3** Waldmann, 1m 35.710s; **4** Romboni, 1m 35.810s; **5** Okada, 1m 35.924s; **6** Harada, 1m 35.977s; **7** Ruggia, 1m 36.031s; **8** Bayle, 1m 36.371s; **9** Aoki, 1m 36.577s; **10** Suter, 1m 36.726s; **11** Checa, 1m 36.772s; **12** Zeelenberg, 1m 36.877s; **13** Bosshard, 1m 36.915s; **14** Honma, 1m 36.970s; **15** D'Antin, 1m 37.138s; **16** Preining, 1m 37.204s; **17** J. van den Goorbergh, 1m 37.898s; **18** Maurel, 1m 38.096s; **19** Kassner, 1m 38.352s; **20** P. van den Goorbergh, 1m 38.476s; **21** Fiorillo, 1m 38.610s; **22** Stadler, 1m 38.880s; **23** Borja, 1m 39.030s; **24** Boudinot, 1m 39.438s; **25** McManus, 1m 39.785s; **26** Cardoso, 1m 40.010s; **27** Gramigni, 1m 40.073s; **28** Protat, 1m 40.078s; **29** Kaas, 1m 40.247s; **30** Ferro, 1m 40.265s; **31** Fee, 1m 40.280s; **32** de Juan, 1m 40.470s; **33** Hernandez, 1m 41.616s; **34** Hough, 1m 43.261s.

World Championship: 1 Capirossi, 168; **2** Okada, 152; **3** Biaggi, 144; **4** Romboni, 129; **5** Waldmann, 113; **6** Ruggia, 110; **7** Bayle, 78; **8** D'Antin, 74; **9** N. Aoki, 71; **10** Harada, 66; **11** Zeelenberg, 61; **12** Checa, 32; **13** Suter, 30; **14** P. van den Goorbergh, 23; **15** J. van den Goorbergh, 22; **16** Bosshard and Preining, 18; **18** Ukawa, 16; **19** T. Aoki, Honma and Lucchi, 11; **22** Gramigni, 10; **23** Kassner, 9; **24** Stadler, 8; **25** Connell, 5; **26** Fiorillo, 4; **27** Castilla, 3; **28** Maurel, 2; **29** Cardoso, 1.

Alex Criville complained of handling problems – here's proof.

DONINGTON PARK

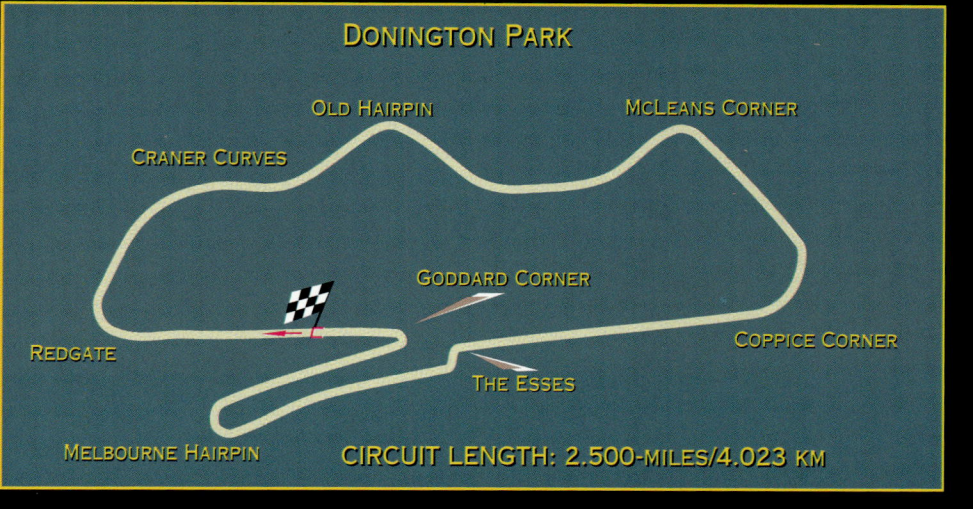

- Old Hairpin
- McLeans Corner
- Craner Curves
- Goddard Corner
- Redgate
- Coppice Corner
- The Esses
- Melbourne Hairpin

CIRCUIT LENGTH: 2.500-miles/4.023 km

Below: Flu victim Sakata's mask brought a touch of the east to the paddock village.

Okada *(bottom)* achieves an astonishing lean angle as he prepares to pounce on D'Antin.

125 cc

26 laps, 65.000 miles/104.598 km

Place	Rider	Nat.	Machine	Laps	Time & speed	Fastest lap	Lap
1	Takeshi Tsujimura	J	Honda	26	44m 22.659s 87.874 mph/ 141.420 km/h	1m 41.759s	13
2	Stefano Perugini	I	Aprilia	26	44m 22.926s	1m 41.788s	9
3	Peter Öttl	D	Aprilia	26	44m 24.118s	1m 41.643s	25
4	Kazuto Sakata	J	Aprilia	26	44m 24.290s	1m 41.669s	5
5	Herri Torrontegui	E	Aprilia	26	44m 24.512s	1m 41.703s	18
6	Noboru Ueda	J	Honda	26	44m 39.349s	1m 42.022s	4
7	Oliver Petrucciani	CH	Aprilia	26	44m 44.828s	1m 42.118s	7
8	Dirk Raudies	D	Honda	26	44m 46.480s	1m 42.408s	20
9	Carlos Giro	E	Aprilia	26	44m 46.969s	1m 42.536s	13
10	Jorge Martinez	E	Yamaha	26	44m 47.256s	1m 42.325s	4
11	Hideyuki Nakajyo	J	Honda	26	44m 54.412s	1m 42.652s	9
12	Masaki Tokudome	J	Honda	26	44m 56.305s	1m 42.715s	25
13	Haruchika Aoki	J	Honda	26	44m 58.976s	1m 42.664s	4
14	Gabriele Debbia	I	Aprilia	26	44m 59.096s	1m 42.719s	6
15	Akira Saito	J	Honda	26	44m 59.562s	1m 42.125s	4
16	Manfred Geissler	D	Aprilia	26	45m 06.808s	1m 42.177s	23
17	Stefan Prein	D	Yamaha	26	45m 07.932s	1m 42.947s	5
18	Juan Maturana	E	Yamaha	26	45m 12.595s	1m 42.740s	25
19	Tomoko Igata	J	Honda	26	45m 13.470s	1m 43.017s	25
20	Fausto Gresini	I	Honda	26	45m 13.730s	1m 43.160s	5
21	Neil Hodgson	GB	Honda	26	45m 29.472s	1m 43.491s	20
22	Emili Alzamora	E	Honda	26	45m 30.947s	1m 43.069s	4
23	Lucio Cecchinello	I	Honda	26	45m 31.420s	1m 43.832s	4
24	Frédéric Petit	F	Yamaha	26	45m 31.988s	1m 44.017s	6
25	Yasuaki Takahashi	J	Honda	26	46m 06.106s	1m 45.055s	26
26	Bertrand Stey	F	Honda	26	46m 06.674s	1m 45.290s	25
27	Vittorio Lopez	I	Honda	26	46m 44.619s	1m 45.204s	22
28	Darren Barton	GB	Honda	25	44m 46.166s	1m 46.028s	8
	Manfred Baumann	A	Yamaha	16	DNF	1m 44.676s	6
	Loek Bodelier	NL	Honda	14	DNF	1m 42.494s	13
	Luigi Ancona	I	Honda	12	DNF	1m 43.063s	5
	Garry McCoy	AUS	Aprilia	11	DNF	1m 43.910s	8
	Gianluigi Scalvini	I	Aprilia	10	DNF	1m 44.010s	7
	Kevin Mawdsley	GB	Honda	10	DNF	1m 46.160s	8
	Hans Spaan	NL	Honda	4	DNF	1m 47.650s	3
	Frank Baldinger	D	Honda		DNS		

Fastest lap: Öttl, 1m 41.643s, 88.537 mph/142.487 km/h.
Lap record: Kazuto Sakata, J (Honda), 1m 41.347s, 88.796 mph/142.903 km/h (1993).

Qualifying: 1 Sakata, 1m 41.027s; 2 Torrontegui, 1m 41.335s; 3 Tsujimura, 1m 41.386s; 4 Ueda, 1m 41.414s; 5 Öttl, 1m 41.427s; 6 Petrucciani, 1m 41.537s; 7 Gresini, 1m 41.880s; 8 Perugini, 1m 41.915s; 9 Martinez, 1m 41.982s; 10 Nakajyo, 1m 42.001s; 11 Hodgson, 1m 42.055s; 12 Scalvini, 1m 42.168s; 13 Giro, 1m 42.368s; 14 Tokudome, 1m 42.390s; 15 Prein, 1m 42.395s; 16 Raudies, 1m 42.428s; 17 Debbia, 1m 42.514s; 18 Alzamora, 1m 42.530s; 19 Aoki, 1m 42.631s; 20 Saito, 1m 42.647s; 21 Cecchinello, 1m 42.723s; 22 Ancona, 1m 42.733s; 23 Geissler, 1m 42.740s; 24 Bodelier, 1m 43.180s; 25 Maturana, 1m 43.381s; 26 Igata, 1m 43.562s; 27 McCoy, 1m 43.689s; 28 Petit, 1m 43.928s; 29 Baumann, 1m 44.240s; 30 Takahashi, 1m 44.247s; 31 Baldinger, 1m 44.301s; 32 Spaan, 1m 44.536s; 33 Mawdsley, 1m 44.776s; 34 Stey, 1m 44.922s; 35 Lopez, 1m 45.011s; 36 Barton, 1m 45.271s.

World Championship: 1 Sakata, 183; 2 Ueda, 137; 3 Tsujimura, 132; 4 Öttl, 121; 5 Raudies, 110; 6 Martinez, 86; 7 Torrontegui, 73; 8 Tokudome, 64; 9 McCoy, 56; 10 Perugini, 54; 11 Petrucciani, 53; 12 Saito, 51; 13 Nakajyo, 44; 14 Gresini, 40; 15 Bodelier, 39; 16 Aoki and Koch, 26; 18 Manako, 24; 19 Casanova, 15; 20 Debbia, 11; 21 Giro, 8; 22 Cuppini and Scalvini, 7; 24 Locatelli, 6; 25 Alzamora, 5; 26 Amano and Katoh, 4; 28 Cecchinello and Maturana, 3; 30 Geissler, Igata, Petit and Prein, 2.

Photos: Gold & Goose

WORLD CHAMPIONSHIP • ROUND 11

CZECH GRAND PRIX

'For the first time all season, Mick was happy to talk about the title'

500 cc	DOOHAN
250 cc	BIAGGI
125 cc	SAKATA

CZECH GRAND PRIX

Right: Biaggi would have won even if Capirossi hadn't crashed. The title lead was an unexpected bonus.

Opposite: Mick tried to stop everyone else thinking about the World Championship before the race – but he couldn't stop himself.

Bottom left: Doohan has escaped, while Cadalora steals inside Puig to give chase. Kocinski, Criville, Itoh, Abe and Chandler queue up behind.

One late and long-distant visit to Barcelona notwithstanding, the Czech GP marked the end of the European season. From here it was away offshore again, bikes crated, trucks and motor homes dismissed, leathers and helmets packed – 100 tonnes of freight on yet another Jumbo-ride between hell and high water. Or was it the other way round?

The consignment of containers was much the same as had arrived from Japan four months before, except for some important extra baggage: Capirossi's bright new set of bandages, Biaggi's regained title lead, Okada's renewed hopes, Kenny Junior's no-longer virginal leathers, Abe's first-ever finish, Sakata's now near-certainty...and while Schwantz took along his now-customary wrist injury, Doohan had something quite different to pack away in his personal crate. Nothing less, at last, than the World Championship.

The GP of the Czech Republic marked the first time all season he was happy to talk about the title. For the first time all season, there was no longer even the smallest possibility of doubt. Schwantz's last ditch turned out to be deep and muddy, and as he slumped to a disappointed seventh, Mick won the race as well. After losing the crown, and nearly losing his leg, in 1992, after enduring a gruelling 1993, after coming close more than once to quitting, the fight back had proved worthwhile, and there wasn't a soul at Brno who wasn't pleased for him. As Schwantz said, echoing his own chosen Queen song motif in his disappointment: 'Mick's done his time, and paid his dues.'

This was Brno's seventh GP, the first five in the name of the CSSR, the last two for the Czech Republic, and the venue has seen the 500 title decided four times now. It is a relatively long and rather different track, with a preponderance of downhill corner entries and indeed corners, putting a huge premium on secure turn-in and grip. Bad news for Schwantz. This is the current Suzuki's weakest area, and in an attempt to kill the bogey they had nominated Brno as their official test track. But injuries and other problems meant they'd used it only once, ten days before this race, and without Schwantz, home in Texas resting. He'd taken the cast off only the weekend before, and was now wearing a removable brace. 'It still bothers me some,' he admitted with customary understatement. Barros alone, with an injured foot, had run ball-park 2m 04s laps, and Schwantz was not without hope. Even after he fell, unhurt, on Saturday morning, then had engine problems in the afternoon that spoiled his chances of improving the handling.

Doohan, meanwhile, was on a bike that's been working ever since Jerez. Again, Brno is not the Honda's best track, but it has won here before. The only thing they'd changed was the paint job, rather unexpectedly (the bold NSR signwriting and zig-zag design to be echoed in the forthcoming production CBR600). And even when Cadalora flash-timed him off pole in the closing minutes, the Australian knew his fast laps were consistent and repeatable.

The title was open (if only a chink) until the green light, but it was settled by the second corner. Doohan was with the front men, Schwantz 11th after a bum start off the second row. More importantly, he discovered immediately that his front tyre choice was no good. It chattered in the first corner, and he knew at once the struggle was lost. It looked as though he was hardly trying from then on.

Doohan's luck has been with him this season, unhurt in four practice spills, surviving two big moments in the French GP. Now he pushed it still further. His opening laps as he strove to get to the front were as risky as any all year. But he soon got there, and that was, as usual, the end of that.

Other matters in the 500 class became a supporting act, especially at a time when all talk was of contracts and who-goes-where, with wild rumours sweeping the paddock. True, the battle for second occupied the minds of a bunch of riders, but hardly any more than the thought of next year's contracts. Indeed, the two are intertwined in some cases.

Abe had returned once more. His last essay, at Donington, had lasted only a matter of minutes, and he'd crashed again in private tests at Catalunya. Now, with Beattie still absent, the flowing-maned wonder of Suzuka had orders to take it easy and try to finish. In practice, his team were obliged to stop him from calling in every three or four laps for yet another adjustment, telling him to stay out and get some distance. In the race, however, the old Abe emerged again, a joy to see. This time he was with Puig, not Doohan, flouting convention, trying to force past him inside, outside, under and over, finally succeeding, only to find the fading Yamaha syndrome dropping him back again later. His first-ever GP finish left him touchingly overcome with emotion.

Beattie was present and walking, if not yet race fit. Reggiani was also to be seen, also not riding, his Aprilia V-twin still suffering persistent piston seizures in private tests, and a dubious prospect even for the final round in October. Each absence continued to cost the team US$10,000 per race; but compared with the cost of probably fruitless trips to the USA and Argentina, this represented fair value.

Aprilia in any case had their hands full with the 250 and 125 classes. A thorough engine reworking included new combustion chambers and exhausts and a reworked powervalve curve, aimed at broadening the 250's

Photos: Gold & Goose

131

range, in response to Honda's power-up parts of two races ago. Biaggi noted that his speed advantage had been restored at least somewhat.

Now Waldmann as well as Capirossi and Romboni had the HRC power-up parts. Brno is, furthermore, the rampant young German's test track, and he'd taken full advantage of his circuit knowledge to dominate most of practice. HB team-mate Romboni, meanwhile, had now heard he was to lose his sponsorship next season, while Waldmann retains his, a spur which might affect the temperamental Italian in any one of half a dozen ways. In the end he was a possible winner, right up until he highsided on the first lap.

Capirossi arrived in a controlling position in the championship, and left hanging his head and nursing a hand injury that was to cost him the title, all four metacarpals in his right hand painfully dislocated – the result of an impetuous last-lap error of a sort that he seemed to have put behind him. He was particularly unimpressive on the weekend that he had officially confirmed his move to the 500 class next year.

The battle was not over, however. Likewise in the 125 class, if only numerically, and all-Japanese to boot, with Sakata turning in an authoritative performance that stretched the arithmetic almost to breaking point; the rest brawled on behind him.

500 cc PRACTICE

Things went smoothly for World Champion-in-waiting Doohan until the closing minutes. He was comfortably faster than title rival Schwantz, and the Suzuki rider was all at sea, bike development going backwards. Then Cadalora went out, his Yamaha wearing soft 'qualifying' Dunlops, found a clear track, and set a flier to slot onto his third pole of the season by an impressive half a second.

The Yamaha's belated return to form left Cadalora calm and confident. This second quality is crucial for track as well as rider here, particularly confidence in the front wheel into the downhill corners. Luca included both aspects when he spoke about having found front-end geometry and suspension settings that worked. 'It means I can ride at 100 per cent,' he said.

Doohan, concentrating on endurance, had run a number of laps at close to his best time, inside the lap record, making sure his tyres would last, and reporting no difficulty. But while he too fitted new tyres and went out at the end to try and reclaim pole, he was thwarted by traffic.

If he was feeling the pressure of the championship, he was determined not to show it. Nor would he ride tactically, keeping an eye on his rival Schwantz. 'It's safer if I just ride in my usual way, fast as I can while trying to be sure of the finish,' he said. 'I haven't won the title yet, and until that happens it's just another race.'

Kocinski moved up to third in the closing session, after a somewhat fraught two days when he was making change after change to the bike, the ride height going up and down like a yo-yo. In the end he took it back to what he'd started with, and slotted in half a second down on Doohan. His team were becoming nonplussed with this repeated performance of pointless experiments, but that's the way John does it. 'I just want to get it competitive,' he insisted.

Puig also pushed onto the front row in the last session. It was no longer surprising that the ex-250 rider could go so fast, but he admitted it had been difficult. 'Each track is so different. You only know where it goes. The braking points must all be learned again. I was having trouble until the end when I tried to relax and follow other riders, and found some better lines,' he said.

Chandler led row two, after having been in the top four until the end. 'With the Cagiva you have to keep the bike leaned over such a long time to carry corner speed to make up for exit speed,' he said. 'You really lean on the front wheel. I had a real big slide that cost me a lot of confidence, though it actually happened on the uphill stretch rather than those hard downhillers,' he said.

Only then came Schwantz, whose second timed session was spoiled by niggling engine problems that meant he couldn't really get to work on the turn-in difficulties. But he had been faster in the morning. 'We have some good settings, so we can go back to them.' He shrugged off his crash, blaming a cold front tyre, and adding: 'Until the championship is mathematically impossible, I have to keep on pushing to win races. I have a chance tomorrow – we'll see how Doohan rides under the pressure of the title.' He practised with the straight-rate rear damper, still shrouded in mystery, saying it seemed easier on the tyre. But he discarded it for the race.

Itoh was next, recovering from the deleterious effects of a heavy spill on Friday that had hurt his hand, ribs and shoulder. Then came Criville, who also crashed, on Saturday, while trying to solve persistent patter problems.

Barros led row three, after failing to improve his time too, which left him baffled because he'd tested significantly faster ten days before in hotter weather and while still suffering from his Donington foot injury. Ironically enough, the team stayed on for more tests on Monday, and he was faster again.

Then came Mackenzie, going well after a long spell at Harald Bartol's workshop in Austria, including 75 dyno runs. The main change had been to ditch the airbox, but this was no magic solution. 'The bike's still not fast, but the chassis's really good,' he said. Thus his private Roc was ahead of Abe's works Yamaha.

Bernard Garcia completed the third row; McWilliams led the fourth from Reynolds, new Team Roc replacement Liedl and Emmett. There were 29 qualifiers, with Doorakkers last.

500 cc RACE – 22 LAPS

Puig swept into the lead, Doohan climbing all over him on the way out of the corners, only to be outbraked several times. Their contrasting

132

Too fast, too cold, too soon: Schwantz's practice slip-off was his third crash in three meetings.

Below left: 'I could have saved it' – not. Criville lost this battle and crashed in practice.

Bottom left: As Chandler tours to the pits, overheating, Barros and Mackenzie flash past, Schwantz watching behind. It was a dispirited end to his title defence.

Below: 'Good on yer, mate.' World Champion Doohan greets his crew chief Jerry Burgess.

lines and styles brought them close to collision at least once, then Doohan moved cleanly past halfway round the second lap, and the risk was over. Mick's only problem now was that his on-bike lap timer had failed and he was having trouble seeing his pit board, so it was hard to pace himself.

On lap three, a determined Cadalora also forced past Puig and closed up on the Honda's back wheel. That helped Doohan find the pace: he had to go a bit faster. This he did, fending off any potential challenge for the next four laps.

Itoh, meanwhile, full of painkillers after having had difficulty even riding his scooter in the morning, was charging through from seventh on the first lap. Riding better than for most of the year, he was in third on lap four, and in second on lap seven.

The leading trio remained close for three more laps. 'When nobody had come past me then I started to feel it would be alright,' said Doohan, who had so little time to look behind that he thought it was Kocinski on his tail. Two laps later, he'd opened up a second, with Cadalora about to run into trouble. 'I heard a noise from the engine, and it lost power. I knew then my chance was over,' he said later, and he started to drop back.

The leading trio finished in that order, with Doohan 3.3 seconds clear and Cadalora five seconds adrift of Itoh. After the interruption of Britain, it was yet another clear demonstration of just why Doohan deserves the title that he was now able – at last – to call his own.

Behind them, Puig delayed the pursuit: Criville, Kocinski, Abe and Chandler piled up behind. Criville was the first to escape, on lap six, with Kocinski following him through two corners later. This pair now started to draw away. Kocinski had several attempts at outbraking the faster Honda before he finally succeeded on lap ten, but then it was his turn to come under severe pressure, from a slower rider on a faster bike. Criville finally gave up and fell back five torrid laps later.

Kocinski had no chance of catching Cadalora, but seemed to have fourth sewn up. Then, on the second-last lap, he was missing as the bikes appeared on the start-finish straight, coasting into view soon afterwards to stop by the pit wall. His turn for a Cagiva breakdown, caused this time by catastrophic gearbox bearing failure.

Puig, Abe and Chandler stayed close as paint until the 12th lap, when Chandler also went missing. He too toured into the Cagiva pit with overheating problems again, this time a water leak at the cylinder base.

Now Abe started to push, repeating his dashing performance in Japan. Puig never knew where he would pop up next. Finally, on lap 13, he seemed to be ahead, even opening up a little gap over the next three laps. But his Yamaha was also to lose power, and the Spaniard came past decisively, to pull away and take fifth by nine seconds at the end, with Abe's sixth his first-ever GP finish.

Schwantz's last-ditch title defence had started badly, and got worse. He wasn't even in the top ten into the first corner, though he had just made it at the end of lap one. But he was in trouble. 'We tried two front tyres in the morning. One chattered, so I used the other one. But in the afternoon that one chattered too.'

It was a dispiriting sight as the 1993 World Champion tamely shadowed Barros, who had similar trouble, the pair losing ground at almost a second a lap. Then privateer Mackenzie caught up and passed Schwantz on lap ten. Three laps later the Scot was past Barros too. Now Kevin – shaking his injured wrist whenever he had the chance – dug a little deeper to lead both of them by lap 19.

Mackenzie might have challenged again. Instead his yellow bike slowed suddenly on the last lap, letting Barros through. Without the airbox, Mackenzie's team had also ditched the attendant fuel pump for the first time all year, and now with the tank low it momentarily starved. It picked up again, and he was a very disappointed ninth.

Twelve seconds back, McWilliams won a close battle from Bernard Garcia and Reynolds. Emmett was almost half a minute behind in 13th, leading another group consisting of Foray, Marc Garcia and Jeandat, the last-named just out of the points.

Itoh claimed the fastest lap, but short of Rainey's 1993 lap record.

Thus Doohan brought his total to 256 points, 87 ahead of Schwantz, and impossible to beat even if he didn't finish another race. Kocinski's non-finish cost him third overall and dropped him into the thick of the battle, with six riders within a spread of 15 points: Puig, Criville, Kocinski, Itoh, Cadalora and Barros.

133

250 cc PRACTICE

Pole was decided only in the closing minutes. Waldmann had held the advantage for most of practice, only to crash his kitted bike early in the last session. It was not damaged, but instead of remounting he ran back to the pits: an error, since he was not fast enough to maintain the lead.

Capirossi came through late in the session; then in the final moments Biaggi found the clear track he'd been waiting for, and scorched round to lead by better than half a second.

His new engine worked well, although the problem of instability under braking remained. Sporting a piratical bandanna, the latest move in the Italian rostrum fashion parade, he explained how in practice he'd put up with it, using settings that favoured corner stability and faster lap times. He planned to switch to more brake-friendly settings for the race on the grounds that, in a close battle, late braking might be more important than sheer speed. 'I'll try to break away tomorrow,' he said. 'But I'm afraid the others will follow me, and I will use up my tyres.'

Half a second on a long track is not a great advantage when the next man is a confident Capirossi. He'd made steady progress throughout, trying then rejecting the new 16-in. rear Dunlops to stay with the 17-inchers he knew well. The demands of the long fast track tipped the balance back towards the Aprilia, but not by much. 'A lot will depend on tyre choice,' Loris grinned.

Third was Romboni, three-tenths down and anxious for his first win of the year. He too was back on the larger tyre for the big corners here, and going well enough to feel that pole was only a risk or two away.

Waldmann was last on the front row, cursing the fact that he hadn't ridden his crashed bike back to the pits.

Harada led row two, the Yamaha improving steadily throughout practice as the team proved they have re-established direction somewhat, with their rider predicting a possible rostrum finish. Then came Ruggia, who might have been better if engine trouble hadn't restricted him to one bike in the last session; next was D'Antin, and finally Aoki, who was unhurt in a crash in the last minutes of the session which left the injured Kassner's replacement, Jurgen Fuchs, lying worryingly still for several minutes, though he was not badly hurt.

An off-form Okada was leading row three. Asked what his problems were, he just shrugged repeatedly. Then came Bayle who, like Ruggia, had trouble with one bike in the last session; Dutchmen Zeelenberg and Jurgen van den Goorbergh concluded the row.

Kenny Roberts Junior had arrived for his first GP of the year, but dropped from an impressive 11th on day one to 16th on day two, on the far end of row four. 'We improved everything on the bike except the lap times,' he said, unable to explain why.

All 33 entrants qualified at a track that really stretches the 250s.

250 cc RACE – 20 LAPS

Biaggi's tale is soon told. He started from pole, led from start to finish, broke the lap record on lap five and moved into a one-point championship lead. It sounds easy and it looked easy, but he was kind enough (or not) to pay a sort of compliment to Capirossi, whose pressure had kept him on the limit, although it had only lasted for the early part of the race.

In fact a gap of two seconds had stretched to five seconds by lap 12, and Capirossi was soon to slow with his tyres sliding badly.

Romboni had high-sided on the first lap just in front of Waldmann, which gave the German a bit of a scare; but soon afterwards he saw that he was not only able to hold off Ruggia, but was slowly closing the five-second gap on Capirossi. He began a remorseless pursuit, drawing steadily closer, and by lap 13 he was on the Italian's back wheel, and passed him quite easily next lap.

Waldmann didn't actually get away, though, and as they started the last lap Capirossi pulled out all the stops to close right up again – enough to tempt him into a costly indiscretion at the top of the hill. Braking too late, he fell, quickly remounted, but then parked the bike a few hundred yards later, in agony from his hand injury and also badly winded.

Thus Waldmann scored his second rostrum in his first 250 year after a strong and trouble-free race. He'd seen Capirossi slithering about, but his own bike and tyres were perfect.

Ruggia was third, some three seconds down, saying he didn't have quite enough power to catch the Hondas, but adding for once: 'I had a lot of fun.'

Aoki finished more than 20 seconds adrift after a mainly lonely race. He'd disposed of D'Antin quite easily in the early stages, as the Spaniard ran into intermittent misfiring problems, but he'd been unable to catch Harada up ahead. Instead, the Yamaha man had caught Ruggia and seemed set to make further progress, before dropping behind Aoki again as his tyres went away and his engine started to 'lose power' (a new Yamaha euphemism?) eventually causing his retirement on lap ten.

D'Antin dropped behind Bayle's Aprilia, then was soon in the thick of a fight with Zeelenberg and Okada, who had dropped from eighth to 11th with a near-crash on lap five. The works Honda man then outstripped the group and caught Bayle again.

CZECH GRAND PRIX

Left: Closely matched 250s skim the tarmac in the battle for second, but Capirossi *(left)* won't make the flag.

Kazuto Sakata *(below)* was simply in a class of his own at Brno.

125 cc RACE – 19 LAPS

Kazuto Sakata had qualified on pole by miles, and a runaway victory to the flag seemed highly likely. Instead it was young blood Perugini's Aprilia heading the first lap.

This was only delaying the inevitable, though. Sakata broke the lap record and the slipstream as he swept past on lap two. After that, he powered away as expected, and could throttle right back at the finish to win by 2.6 seconds.

Second was fiercely disputed, with Perugini riding wildly enough to earn criticism from Yamaha man Martinez. The Italian was in second at the start of the last lap, but Ueda was also part of the group, and seized the position into the first turn. From there to the finish he only had to stay in front and stay on board – a tall order, but accomplished successfully.

It was a good move, because Perugini had the red mist over his eyes. Trying to get back, he slid and ran wide over the kerbs on the downhill double left where most of the spectators gather, dropping to fourth and apparently out of touch. But he wasn't finished, and almost knocked Martinez off as he barged back past to reclaim third in the final chicane.

The next group was just as dramatic, though Tsujimura managed to take control at the finish for fifth. Then came Masaki Tokudome, closing right up in the last corners, and opening a two-second gap on last year's World Champion, Raudies. On his back wheel came Nakajyo, Petrucciani, Geissler and Prein: seventh to 11th positions were covered by less than half a second.

Japanese girl-racer Igata was 12th, her Honda heading the works Aprilia of Carlos Giro and Loek Bodelier's private Aprilia after a close scrap. The last point went to Gianluigi Scalvini, less than a tenth ahead of Garry McCoy (both Aprilia), with Cecchinello's Honda and Luigi Ancona hard up behind.

The race began badly with a start-line pile-up. Spaniard Torrontegui was on the front row, moved early, then stopped, only to be knocked off his bike by Perugini coming from behind. The fallen bike was promptly hit by the last qualifier, wild card Benjamin Weiss. Torrontegui's foot was caught up in the bike, and his leg and ankle badly broken. Officials only just managed to clear the start-line before the field came though again.

Öttl also failed to complete the first lap. He had qualified second, but fell after his engine seized.

Ueda pulled a little clear of Tsujimura in the championship table; Sakata was miles away from both of them, but he would have to wait one more race before final victory.

At the finish Okada took fifth by less than a tenth, with Bayle missing a gear to spoil his crucial last lap.

Eskil Suter joined Wilco and D'Antin on lap 13, and the trio went back and forth. At the finish, the Spaniard led Suter by less than half a second, but Zeelenberg was four seconds adrift. His throttle had jammed open briefly on the penultimate lap and he'd lost touch.

Andy Preining led the next group across the line, to claim tenth, closely followed by Maurel and Patrick van den Goorbergh.

Bosshard had lost touch in the closing stages and finished 13th; Fiorillo was a lone 14th, with Borja claiming the last point at the head of the next fierce group. Aggressive Briton James Haydon (Honda) was 16th, just missing a point in his first foreign GP.

Kenny Junior's crash was a highsider when trying to escape Zeelenberg while lying 11th on lap six. He was not hurt. Considering his position, it was not too bad a result in his first GP of the year.

Photos: Gold & Goose

135

FIM WORLD CHAMPIONSHIP • ROUND 11
CZECH GRAND PRIX
21 August 1994

500 cc
22 laps, 73.700 miles/118.668 km

Place	Rider	Nat.	Machine	Laps	Time & speed	Fastest lap	Lap
1	Michael Doohan	AUS	Honda	22	45m 39.974s 96.882 mph/ 155.916 km/h	2m 03.780s	11
2	Shinichi Itoh	J	Honda	22	45m 43.296s	2m 03.544s	4
3	Luca Cadalora	I	Yamaha	22	45m 48.796s	2m 03.852s	15
4	Alex Criville	E	Honda	22	46m 04.110s	2m 04.424s	6
5	Alberto Puig	E	Honda	22	46m 10.478s	2m 04.827s	19
6	Norifumi Abe	J	Yamaha	22	46m 19.970s	2m 05.010s	5
7	Kevin Schwantz	USA	Suzuki	22	46m 28.500s	2m 05.326s	15
8	Alexandre Barros	BR	Suzuki	22	46m 35.770s	2m 05.888s	15
9	Niall Mackenzie	GB	Yamaha	22	46m 36.478s	2m 05.519s	14
10	Jeremy McWilliams	GB	Yamaha	22	46m 48.194s	2m 06.589s	21
11	Bernard Garcia	F	Yamaha	22	46m 49.136s	2m 06.661s	4
12	John Reynolds	GB	Yamaha	22	46m 50.302s	2m 06.912s	7
13	Sean Emmett	GB	Yamaha	22	47m 18.513s	2m 07.904s	7
14	Jean Foray	F	Yamaha	22	47m 18.537s	2m 08.267s	5
15	Marc Garcia	F	Yamaha	22	47m 18.601s	2m 08.282s	15
16	Jean-Pierre Jeandat	F	Yamaha	22	47m 20.806s	2m 08.147s	18
17	Bernard Hänggeli	CH	Yamaha	22	47m 21.016s	2m 08.086s	16
18	Cristiano Migliorati	I	Yamaha	22	47m 36.662s	2m 07.971s	5
19	Marco Papa	I	Yamaha	21	45m 43.655s	2m 09.400s	18
20	Cees Doorakkers	NL	Yamaha	21	45m 44.988s	2m 08.948s	3
	John Kocinski	USA	Cagiva	21	DNF	2m 04.289s	8
	Juan Lopez Mella	E	Yamaha	17	DNF	2m 06.808s	11
	Laurent Naveau	B	Yamaha	15	DNF	2m 07.036s	6
	Doug Chandler	USA	Cagiva	12	DNF	2m 05.269s	5
	Kevin Mitchell	GB	Yamaha	9	DNF	2m 10.321s	4
	Lucio Pedercini	I	Yamaha	6	DNF	2m 10.285s	4
	Bruno Bonhuil	F	Yamaha	5	DNF	2m 09.205s	2
	Andreas Leuthe	D	Yamaha	3	DNF	2m 11.832s	3
	Michael Liedl	D	Yamaha	1	DNF	2m 45.531s	1

Fastest lap: Itoh, 2m 03.544s, 97.666 mph/157.178 km/h.
Lap record: Wayne Rainey, USA (Yamaha), 2m 03.266s, 97.886 mph/157.533 km/h (1993).

Qualifying: 1 Cadalora, 2m 02.380s; 2 Doohan, 2m 02.854s; 3 Kocinski, 2m 03.367s; 4 Puig, 2m 04.019s; 5 Chandler, 2m 04.115s; 6 Schwantz, 2m 04.607s; 7 Itoh, 2m 04.782s; 8 Criville, 2m 04.784s; 9 Barros, 2m 04.944s; 10 Mackenzie, 2m 05.586s; 11 Abe, 2m 05.644s; 12 B. Garcia, 2m 05.976s; 13 McWilliams, 2m 06.558s; 14 Reynolds, 2m 06.675s; 15 Liedl, 2m 06.859s; 16 Emmett, 2m 07.021s; 17 Lopez Mella, 2m 07.308s; 18 Naveau, 2m 07.424s; 19 Hänggeli, 2m 07.717s; 20 M. Garcia, 2m 08.050s; 21 Foray, 2m 08.500s; 22 Migliorati, 2m 08.789s; 23 Papa, 2m 08.838s; 24 Bonhuil, 2m 08.923s; 25 Leuthe, 2m 09.001s; 26 Pedercini, 2m 09.009s; 27 Jeandat, 2m 09.586s; 28 Mitchell, 2m 10.003s; 29 Doorakkers, 2m 10.340s.

World Championship: 1 M. Doohan, 256; 2 Schwantz, 169; 3 Puig, 123; 4 Criville, 122; 5 Kocinski, 120; 6 Itoh, 115; 7 Cadalora, 114; 8 Barros, 108; 9 Chandler, 59; 10 Mackenzie, 50; 11 B. Garcia, 41; 12 Reynolds, 38; 13 Beattie, 33; 14 McWilliams, 31; 15 Emmett and Lopez Mella, 23; 17 Jeandat, 15; 18 Migliorati and Naveau, 12; 20 Abe and Honma, 10; 22 Foray and M. Garcia, 8; 24 Bonhuil, Hänggeli, Miralles and Reggiani, 7; 28 Moineau, 5; 29 S. Doohan, 4; 30 Mark, 2; 31 Pedercini, 1.

250 cc
20 laps, 67.000 miles/107.880 km

Place	Rider	Nat.	Machine	Laps	Time & speed	Fastest lap	Lap
1	Massimiliano Biaggi	I	Aprilia	20	42m 09.445s 95.408 mph/ 153.539 km/h	2m 05.340s	5
2	Ralf Waldmann	D	Honda	20	42m 15.870s	2m 06.119s	3
3	Jean-Philippe Ruggia	F	Aprilia	20	42m 19.028s	2m 06.046s	2
4	Nobuatsu Aoki	J	Honda	20	42m 42.010s	2m 06.715s	4
5	Tadayuki Okada	J	Honda	20	42m 46.924s	2m 07.181s	17
6	Jean-Michel Bayle	F	Aprilia	20	42m 46.968s	2m 07.553s	8
7	Luis D'Antin	E	Honda	20	42m 52.079s	2m 07.249s	2
8	Eskil Suter	CH	Aprilia	20	42m 52.441s	2m 07.616s	9
9	Wilco Zeelenberg	NL	Honda	20	42m 56.993s	2m 08.058s	8
10	Andy Preining	A	Aprilia	20	43m 06.888s	2m 08.155s	3
11	Luis Maurel	E	Honda	20	43m 07.440s	2m 08.583s	13
12	Patrick van den Goorbergh	NL	Aprilia	20	43m 07.976s	2m 08.672s	13
13	Adrian Bosshard	CH	Honda	20	43m 12.760s	2m 08.478s	5
14	Giuseppe Fiorillo	I	Honda	20	43m 33.942s	2m 09.603s	4
15	Juan Borja	E	Honda	20	43m 41.668s	2m 09.901s	19
16	James Haydon	GB	Honda	20	43m 42.278s	2m 09.968s	3
17	Christian Boudinot	F	Aprilia	20	43m 42.692s	2m 09.951s	14
18	Jurgen Fuchs	D	Honda	20	43m 42.781s	2m 09.878s	17
19	Noel Ferro	F	Honda	20	43m 43.422s	2m 09.677s	20
20	Frédéric Protat	F	Honda	20	44m 11.716s	2m 10.424s	9
21	Kristian Kaas	SF	Yamaha	19	42m 09.560s	2m 11.960s	2
22	Enrique de Juan	E	Aprilia	19	42m 09.729s	2m 12.024s	3
23	Rodney Fee	CAN	Honda	19	42m 51.117s	2m 13.698s	2
	Loris Capirossi	I	Honda	19	DNF	2m 05.722s	2
	Adi Stadler	D	Honda	11	DNF	2m 09.783s	3
	Alessandro Gramigni	I	Aprilia	10	DNF	2m 10.591s	2
	Tetsuya Harada	J	Yamaha	9	DNF	2m 06.104s	2
	Kenny Roberts Jnr	USA	Yamaha	6	DNF	2m 07.645s	4
	Carlos Checa	E	Honda	5	DNF	2m 07.404s	2
	Jurgen van den Goorbergh	NL	Aprilia	5	DNF	2m 07.912s	2
	Bohumil Stasa	CS	Aprilia	1	DNF	2m 22.744s	1
	José Luis Cardoso	E	Aprilia	1	DNF	2m 53.716s	1
	Doriano Romboni	I	Honda	0	DNF		

Fastest lap: Biaggi, 2m 05.340s, 96.267 mph/154.926 km/h (record).
Previous record: Loris Capirossi, I (Honda), 2m 05.681s, 96.005 mph/154.505 km/h (1993).

Qualifying: 1 Biaggi, 2m 04.894s; 2 Capirossi, 2m 05.530s; 3 Romboni, 2m 05.893s; 4 Waldmann, 2m 05.933s; 5 Harada, 2m 06.024s; 6 Ruggia, 2m 06.440s; 7 D'Antin, 2m 06.816s; 8 Aoki, 2m 06.970s; 9 Okada, 2m 07.168s; 10 Bayle, 2m 07.228s; 11 Zeelenberg, 2m 07.344s; 12 J. van den Goorbergh, 2m 07.510s; 13 Suter, 2m 07.653s; 14 Preining, 2m 07.741s; 15 Bosshard, 2m 07.798s; 16 Roberts Jnr, 2m 07.846s; 17 Fuchs, 2m 08.532s; 18 Maurel, 2m 08.614s; 19 Fiorillo, 2m 09.012s; 20 Stadler, 2m 09.093s; 21 P. van den Goorbergh, 2m 09.469s; 22 Checa, 2m 09.492s; 23 Gramigni, 2m 09.774s; 24 Cardoso, 2m 10.018s; 25 Borja, 2m 10.126s; 26 Haydon, 2m 10.692s; 27 Protat, 2m 11.120s; 28 Boudinot, 2m 11.313s; 29 Stasa, 2m 11.759s; 30 Ferro, 2m 11.950s; 31 Kaas, 2m 12.422s; 32 de Juan, 2m 13.080s; 33 Fee, 2m 13.746s.

World Championship: 1 Biaggi, 169; 2 Capirossi, 168; 3 Okada, 163; 4 Waldmann, 133; 5 Romboni, 129; 6 Ruggia, 126; 7 Bayle, 88; 8 N. Aoki, 84; 9 D'Antin, 83; 10 Zeelenberg, 68; 11 Harada, 66; 12 Suter, 38; 13 Checa, 32; 14 P. van den Goorbergh, 27; 15 Preining, 24; 16 J. van den Goorbergh, 22; 17 Bosshard, 21; 18 Ukawa, 16; 19 T. Aoki, Honma and Lucchi, 11; 22 Gramigni, 10; 23 Kassner, 9; 24 Stadler, 8; 25 Maurel, 7; 26 Fiorillo, 6; 27 Connell, 5; 28 Castilla, 3; 29 Borja and Cardoso, 1.

Opposite page (top to bottom): Here at last: Kenny Roberts christened his pristine GP leathers with a touch of Brno gravel-rash. Low-price, open-borders, the Czech GP is these days a cosmopolitan affair. James Haydon was back again, now on a 250, and missed the points by less than a second.

AUTODROMO BRNO – CZECHOSLOVAKIA

CIRCUIT LENGTH: 3.350-MILES/5.394 KM

125 cc

19 laps, 63.650 miles/102.486 km

Place	Rider	Nat.	Machine	Laps	Time & speed	Fastest lap	Lap
1	Kazuto Sakata	J	Aprilia	19	42m 34.015s 89.763 mph/ 144.459 km/h	2m 12.500s	2
2	Noboru Ueda	J	Honda	19	42m 36.654s	2m 13.384s	4
3	Stefano Perugini	I	Aprilia	19	42m 37.310s	2m 13.643s	18
4	Jorge Martinez	E	Yamaha	19	42m 37.412s	2m 13.328s	4
5	Takeshi Tsujimura	J	Honda	19	42m 48.446s	2m 13.627s	12
6	Masaki Tokudome	J	Honda	19	42m 48.584s	2m 13.739s	2
7	Dirk Raudies	D	Honda	19	42m 50.603s	2m 14.192s	4
8	Hideyuki Nakajyo	J	Honda	19	42m 50.696s	2m 13.945s	16
9	Oliver Petrucciani	CH	Aprilia	19	42m 50.752s	2m 13.832s	2
10	Manfred Geissler	D	Aprilia	19	42m 50.908s	2m 13.898s	17
11	Stefan Prein	D	Yamaha	19	42m 51.002s	2m 13.864s	12
12	Tomoko Igata	J	Honda	19	43m 03.594s	2m 14.418s	12
13	Carlos Giro	E	Aprilia	19	43m 03.738s	2m 14.225s	7
14	Loek Bodelier	NL	Honda	19	43m 03.782s	2m 14.583s	12
15	Gianluigi Scalvini	I	Aprilia	19	43m 08.346s	2m 14.598s	8
16	Garry McCoy	AUS	Aprilia	19	43m 08.404s	2m 14.630s	19
17	Lucio Cecchinello	I	Honda	19	43m 08.626s	2m 14.832s	9
18	Luigi Ancona	I	Honda	19	43m 09.554s	2m 15.220s	13
19	Haruchika Aoki	J	Honda	19	43m 11.412s	2m 14.996s	7
20	Vittorio Lopez	I	Honda	19	43m 11.477s	2m 15.284s	6
21	Frédéric Petit	F	Yamaha	19	43m 24.315s	2m 15.470s	8
22	Juan Maturana	E	Yamaha	19	43m 26.360s	2m 15.744s	17
23	Manfred Baumann	A	Yamaha	19	43m 31.365s	2m 16.172s	16
24	Fausto Ricci	I	Aprilia	19	43m 41.932s	2m 16.362s	5
25	Nicolas Dussauge	F	Honda	19	44m 16.018s	2m 17.176s	2
	Oliver Koch	D	Honda	14	DNF	2m 15.337s	3
	Emili Alzamora	E	Honda	7	DNF	2m 16.060s	3
	Neil Hodgson	GB	Honda	7	DNF	2m 15.576s	2
	Massimiliano Gervasio	I	Honda	7	DNF	2m 17.970s	3
	Hans Spaan	NL	Honda	4	DNF	2m 18.135s	4
	Jaroslav Hules	CS	Honda	3	DNF	2m 16.788s	3
	Herri Torrontegui	E	Aprilia	0	DNF		
	Peter Öttl	D	Aprilia	0	DNF		
	Yasuaki Takahashi	J	Honda	0	DNF		
	Benjamin Weiss	D	Honda	0	DNF		
	Akira Saito	J	Honda		DNS		

Fastest lap: Sakata, 2m 12.500s, 91.064 mph/146.554 km/h (record).
Previous record: Kazuto Sakata, J (Honda), 2m 13.164s, 90.160 mph/145.823 km/h (1993).

Qualifying: 1 Sakata, 2m 11.689s; 2 Öttl, 2m 13.002s; 3 Torrontegui, 2m 13.298s; 4 Ueda, 2m 13.492s; 5 Perugini, 2m 13.567s; 6 Tsujimura, 2m 13.600s; 7 Martinez, 2m 13.603s; 8 Tokudome, 2m 13.626s; 9 Nakajyo, 2m 13.685s; 10 Saito, 2m 13.870s; 11 Raudies, 2m 14.035s; 12 Petrucciani, 2m 14.352s; 13 Hodgson, 2m 14.368s; 14 Prein, 2m 14.498s; 15 Cecchinello, 2m 14.532s; 16 Igata, 2m 14.549s; 17 Koch, 2m 14.562s; 18 Giro, 2m 14.572s; 19 Scalvini, 2m 14.620s; 20 Aoki, 2m 14.638s; 21 Geissler, 2m 14.724s; 22 McCoy, 2m 14.790s; 23 Petit, 2m 14.843s; 24 Ancona, 2m 14.919s; 25 Lopez, 2m 15.748s; 26 Bodelier, 2m 15.918s; 27 Spaan, 2m 16.506s; 28 Baumann, 2m 16.694s; 29 Alzamora, 2m 16.879s; 30 Ricci, 2m 16.978s; 31 Hules, 2m 17.195s; 32 Maturana, 2m 17.378s; 33 Gervasio, 2m 17.600s; 34 Takahashi, 2m 17.860s; 35 Dussauge, 2m 18.404s; 36 Weiss, 2m 19.448s.

World Championship: 1 Sakata, 208; 2 Ueda, 157; 3 Tsujimura, 143; 4 Öttl, 121; 5 Raudies, 119; 6 Martinez, 99; 7 Tokudome, 74; 8 Torrontegui, 73; 9 Perugini, 70; 10 Petrucciani, 60; 11 McCoy, 56; 12 Nakajyo, 52; 13 Saito, 51; 14 Bodelier, 41; 15 Gresini, 40; 16 Aoki and Koch, 26; 18 Manako, 24; 19 Casanova, 15; 20 Debbia and Giro, 11; 22 Geissler and Scalvini, 8; 24 Cuppini and Prein, 7; 26 Igata and Locatelli, 6; 28 Alzamora, 5; 29 Amano and Katoh, 4; 31 Cecchinello and Maturana, 3; 33 Petit, 2.

Photos: Gold & Goose

UNITED STATES GRAND PRIX

500 cc	CADALORA
250 cc	ROMBONI
125 cc	TSUJIMURA

WORLD CHAMPIONSHIP • ROUND 12

UNITED STATES GRAND PRIX

Luca Cadalora *(opposite)* finally felt able to give the last couple of per cent he'd been witholding.

Left: 'You have a nice day – or else.'

Below: Schwantz returned to hobble round the paddock.

For Kenny Roberts, novice race promoter, last year's US GP cost $2 million, the shortfall between the cost of staging the revived event and the disappointing ticket sales. One week after Wayne Rainey's accident, it was a dismal affair.

This year had to be considered a success. Losses were slashed to not much more than half a million dollars. What is more, this time round Kenny had someone to help pick up the tab. Dorna were now co-promoters, demonstrating a far greater commitment to the future of the US GP than the West Coast spectators.

Within weeks, it was already clear that the writing was on the wall for Laguna. If the moving finger had been able to find a wall, that is. One of the problems of the charity-run track within a nature reserve is the lack of permanent buildings.

Kenny's other consolation was his team's first race win of the year, at the tail end of a season that looked as though it might be the first without a victory since the 500 team's formation in 1986. It was not enough to prevent him seeking another circuit for next year's event, though, with Road America near Elkhart Lake in Wisconsin a prime candidate, if certain safety improvements can be made. This was, after all, the seventh GP at the Californian track, and it was now clear to all that the game wasn't worth the candle.

This was one of a number of undercurrents at the last waltz on the Monterey peninsula. Another was a sudden eddy in an increasingly troubled corner of the pool. The hitherto secretive Grand Prix Manufacturers' Association unexpectedly emerged from the shadows to host a press conference during practice, headed by a galaxy of industry heavy hitters surely never seen together in public before. They were there to throw their hats into the ring of the brewing battle about limiting the numbers of works bikes in the future, as a supposed cost-cutting measure, and while the sober-suited delegates from Honda, Yamaha, Suzuki and Cagiva didn't actually say much amid a lot of anodyne speechifying, there was plenty of menace to be read between the lines.

It was a relief to get back to the racing. The 500 title was decided, and now it was all down to sorting out the batch of riders currently disputing third, some way short of Kevin Schwantz. Then Schwantz suddenly offered them the chance of making it second instead.

This came about through a baffling crash while running in new engine parts during Saturday morning's free practice. High-sided on the exit from the infamous Corkscrew bend, he landed heavily, dislocating his left hip and breaking his left scaphoid (wrist) bone. And thereby ending his season. The hip was put back under anaesthetic in hospital, the wrist put in a cast and the apparently irrepressible, if finally not unstoppable rider was back in the paddock later that evening. 'I'd done three slow laps breaking in parts, and I had a new rear tyre on. Maybe it didn't get warm because I was on the dust off the racing line to stay out of the way. Stuart [Shenton] told me the tyre still looked brand new. I didn't gas it extra hard or anything, but the back stepped out, and it spat me off.' There was one crumb of comfort – now he could start early on a 14-week surgery and recuperation programme on his left wrist, injured at Assen, and again at every race since. It also resolved a conflict over whether he would attend the last two races. Schwantz had hoped to secure second overall in the USA, then quit to go under the knife; sponsors Lucky Strike and teams' association IRTA had wanted him to complete the season.

Last year, Doohan was also forcibly freed from remaining commitments to begin surgery early after crashing at Laguna.

Schwantz's accident further robbed the big class of interest, with the focus switched to the smaller classes, both still undecided. In the case of the 125s, Sakata had only to finish ahead of Ueda to secure the crown – as we shall see, circumstances prevented him from doing so. But there was still plenty to happen in the 250 class.

On paper, the struggle was still between Biaggi and Capirossi, with Okada an outsider. But Loris's personal fight was against pain and weakness. His right hand was clearly still very sore, and though he tried his best to ignore it, this was almost certainly the cause of his crash in the race that rendered infinitesimal his chances of slipping a 250 title alongside his two 125 crowns in the trophy cabinet before moving to 500s next year.

Unfortunately, perhaps, given the presence of the GPMA heavies, Laguna was the scene of some inspired rule-bending by an apparently slap-happy IRTA, barely two weeks after standing firm on rules as an excuse for kicking out the too-slow too-poor Sachsen team from the former East Germany as well.

Abe was allowed to start even though the rider he had been replacing, Daryl Beattie, was back. Of course this was good for the quality of the show, and a lot of fun besides – Norick rode a good race, climbing all over the back wheel of fifth-placed Doug Chandler before falling victim again to late-race fading. But it put out of joint the noses of the other works teams, all of whom had riders involved in the big group disputing the runner's-up position for the title. One of the guiding principles of the original closed-shop World Championship series, born in 1992, was to protect regular riders from losing vital points to fast one-race wonders, after all; and in the event the Japanese outsider did take points from Barros and Puig.

Team Roc were also allowed an unprecedented fourth rider change, the latest incumbent of the ex-Miralles/Mark/Liedl bike being American Chuck Graves. IRTA muttered sheepishly about 'special circumstances', thought to be a reference to the fact that the team (and Roc factory) owner Serge Rosset is their vice-president. The 500 class first-timer lived up to his name. He chucked the bike twice, the second time damaging it gravely, to the tune of almost $100,000.

There were some significant others in the paddock. One was former F1 GP winner Dan Gurney, the All-American Eagle driver the guest of Kenny Roberts. Another was Mick's brother Scott Doohan, who had originally been entered as a 500 class wild card on a spare Harris, though the deal foundered on a lack of finance. One week later he had a massive crash in the US Superbike round at Road Atlanta that resulted in a ban from future racing in the USA.

And there was Herri Torrontegui, a surprise arrival after sustaining bad leg and foot injuries on the startline in Brno. Now he tried to ride his

Photos: Gold & Goose

139

UNITED STATES GRAND PRIX

works 125 Aprilia, foot in a cast and a special boot – but the effort proved too much. It was too much also for Australian coming-man Garry McCoy, who had abruptly quit his usual AGV-Attac 125 team saying he lacked confidence in them, all the while trying to secure a go on Herri's presumably spare works Aprilia. Now McCoy had nothing but a pending lawsuit from his disgruntled former employers.

500 cc PRACTICE

Cadalora laid first claim to the hotly contested pole on Friday. He was deposed on Saturday by 1993 winner Kocinski, who was in turn moved down to second at the last gasp by Doohan, with his usual set of new tyres and the bike ready set up just right to trot out a hottie. But he beat the Cagiva by only eight-thousandths.

Doohan was determined to be determined. 'The championship may be over, but the season isn't,' he said. 'Maybe I'd like to quit now to start treatment, but I'm committed to the last three races, and as long as I'm here I'll try and win. Cruising round getting in other people's way would be dangerous for me and them.'

He didn't necessarily think the task would be easy after searching for grip, making more changes for this tight track than he is used to since getting the bike settled for the fourth race of the season. 'It feels different each time I go out,' he said. 'But I think we have it good enough now.'

Kocinski was frustrated by losing pole, and squarely blamed stagnant bike design. 'We just haven't improved. We should be doing 1m 24s, not 1m 26s. I don't know exactly what changes should be made, but something needs to be done to the design of the bikes to regain development.' John likes Laguna, and with Schwantz crashing his chances of achieving second overall improved considerably. One year before he'd achieved Cagiva's first-ever dry weather victory here.

Cadalora also improved, finishing less than a tenth adrift. 'The problem today was traffic,' he said. 'It's very hard to pass.' He praised new front tyres from Dunlop, adding: 'The front wheel is so important here.' A Laguna fan, he insisted: 'This track is real fun on a 500.'

Then came the first gap – Itoh was almost a full second down, at the head of his own tight pack. 'Like Mick we've been getting unpredictable handling results,' he said, 'though the Honda does have a speed advantage up the hill.'

Schwantz was fifth fastest on the strength of his Friday time, but no longer a factor. His place leading row two went instead to Chandler, happy to have improved after lowering the whole bike, though that brought problems of bump absorption. 'It's so much stop and go here and I felt like I was getting thrown over the front under brakes.' But he had another preoccupation: at home in nearby Salinas his second child was already overdue, and he left the track promptly after practice to be with his wife Sherry. (A daughter, named Rainee Layne, arrived the following week.)

Alongside was the returned Beattie, a strong and courageous showing considering his foot and hand injuries were not fully healed. 'I rode a dirt bike at Kenny's ranch. Now, though I can't feel my foot too well and I can't put a lot of weight on the left peg, I can ride,' he said.

Criville was eighth, but another non-starter after fracturing a bone in his right hand in the closing minutes. This left the second-row position to his great rival, Puig, making his 500 cc debut at Laguna. He also crashed unhurt on Friday, then failed to improve on his first-day time. Although the gap on the leader was now 1.7 seconds – a lot at such a short, tight track – the second-stringers were packed up close, with fourth to eleventh places within just over one second.

Next up, an off-form Barros scraped onto the second row thanks to the absences up front. The Brazilian was baffled by his failure to improve on the second day. 'We've got the bike good. Perhaps we need to change the rider,' he said prophetically.

Abe was close behind, last of the group. Seeing the track for the first time, he had clearly learned his lesson from his impetuous Donington debut, again running steadily, lap after lap, but with his excitingly aggressive style always evident.

McWilliams was 12th, leading the privateers and less than two-tenths down on Abe while better than four-tenths ahead of John Reynolds, who pushed Mackenzie down by a much smaller margin. Then came Jeandat, Bernard Garcia, Naveau and Emmett.

Niall Mackenzie had a lucky escape on Friday when a rear suspension link broke as he lined up for the left-hand bend following the Corkscrew. The bike dropped onto the bump-stop, but he was able to save it and ride back to the pits. According to Roc, this component had never broken before. They suspected a poor piece of metal.

Out of 30 entrants, only Roc-mounted Leuthe (pronounced 'loiter') failed to make the qualifying time. Criville and Schwantz were out hurt; Graves was a third non-starter, after placing a brave 21st in his first-ever 500 ride, then completely wrecking the bike. Lopez Mella was out after fracturing his right arm – an injury that he inadvertently exacerbated during the next week while driving a rentacar, simply by twirling the wheel too vigorously. Paul Pellisier's Paton also did not get past the first free practice.

In this way, an entry list of 31 was reduced to a bare 25 starters.

500 cc RACE – 33 LAPS

Doohan's plan was simple – to seize the advantage at a track where overtaking is notoriously hard. Accordingly he leapt away, chased by Kocinski, Cadalora, Barros and Itoh, the rest of the field streaming out behind as they looped down the hill again from the Corkscrew to complete the first of the 33 short laps.

Doohan led for the next seven, with Kocinski running wide the third time into the tight Turn Two, and letting Cadalora through under his elbow. By now the leading trio had already opened up a gap, with Itoh heading the distant pursuit.

Up front, Cadalora was on Doohan's back wheel, Kocinski within half a second. The first change came at the start of lap eight, when Doohan ran wide into Turn Two, already losing front-wheel bite, and Cadalora was more than ready to dive underneath him and immediately draw away, to lead by over a second just one lap later.

Then it was Kocinski's turn on the Turn Two dive. He ran in so close that Doohan had to lift to avoid getting hit, giving the impression that he'd missed his braking point and had overtaken by mistake. Doohan stayed with the Cagiva for a couple of laps, then by half-distance decided to play it safe. With Itoh more than ten seconds behind, and his own tyre problems getting worse, third would be good enough. 'The bike was consistent in the morning, but it was warmer in the afternoon and the front was sliding,' he explained. 'I had a couple of scares chasing John. He was sliding too, but I guess he was more determined than me. I decided there was nothing to gain by going down the road.'

At this point, Kocinski was some two seconds behind Cadalora. Riding with conspicuous determination he inched closer, so that by lap 18 he had halved the gap. But there was nothing left, and with Cadalora steadfast, Kocinski's effort was spent as they ran into traffic. When they came out the other side Cadalora was stretching away, to win by almost eight seconds, with Doohan in third, 17 seconds behind Kocinski. Not a thrilling finish for anyone apart from the ecstatic Team Roberts crew.

And their Dunlop tyre men, of course, finally vindicated at a track where Michelin were having trouble getting their bikes into the bends on a tight line. Kocinski blamed a poor tyre choice for his problems. 'I was scraping my boots on the road and my knee on the kerb in the bends. I figured that was the limit,' he said.

Itoh had been alone all race long. Chandler had had his hands full with Abe, who'd moved past Beattie and Puig to close right up on the eighth lap. He never did get ahead, in spite of several attempts. Only in the final third of the race did he fade slightly, blaming fatigue.

The pressure from Abe had brought Doug within sight of Itoh, and he forgot his own wheelspin problems and kicked again. A gap of just under one second on lap 29 was a tenth of that as they began the last lap, and when they crossed the line it took a photofinish to be sure that the Honda was still a few inches ahead of the Cagiva.

Puig was seventh, 14 seconds behind Abe after losing ground all race long. Behind him came Barros – dropping right back after a fourth-place start. At one point he was overtaken by privateer McWilliams, who was having the ride of his life, having deliberately turned his back on fashionable advice that he should learn to steer with the rear, and reverting to his own high-corner-speed style.

Barros did get back in front, if narrowly, until the Irish rider dropped away in the closing laps. 'My front suspension was too stiff and I had no confidence,' said Barros. 'The team already has one injured rider, and we don't need another one.'

McWilliams was five seconds away at the flag, but seven seconds ahead of Mackenzie's Roc: he'd had an unspectacular race. Emmett was

Above: Pressure from Abe helped lift Doug Chandler's game.

McWilliams *(left)* pushed his way up among the works bikes after changing his riding style.

Top: Schwantz fan watches John Kocinski enter the notorious Corkscrew.

Photos: Gold & Goose

another four seconds behind, after defeating Bernard Garcia and finishing as the last rider on the same lap as the leaders. Then came Naveau, Jeandat and Pedercini, claiming the last point less than a second ahead of Marc Garcia.

There were 21 finishers – Darryl Beattie not among them. He had started strongly in his comeback ride, only to lose power and retire after nine laps.

Kocinski claimed the fastest lap as he chased Cadalora, six-tenths slower than Schwantz's 1990 lap record.

250 cc PRACTICE

With Capirossi carrying seriously deleterious hand injuries, and Romboni adding gastro-enteritis to his own slight wrist injury, the medical profile favoured title leader Biaggi. But the results were not in line with predictions. Pole went to Romboni, Max was second and Capirossi led most of the final session to end up a close third.

And in fourth position, the forgotten man of the championship: Tadayuki Okada, poised for a strong finish after Erv Kanemoto had apparently stumbled on a cure for their persistent front-end handling problems.

Romboni had to come in and rest during the final session, due to his upset stomach, but he still hung on to the pole he had claimed on the first day. Again using the 16-in. rear Dunlop, he was for almost the first time not complaining about chatter problems. 'The bike is perfect after only minor suspension adjustments,' he said.

Biaggi was less than two-tenths down, but concerned. 'I'm still not happy with the suspension, especially at the back. The bike's moving around a lot. This track favours the Hondas: the Aprilia prefers faster tracks. I need some good luck.'

Capirossi's performance was remarkable. Nursing his hand off the bike, he showed no sign of any problems on it, looking particularly aggressive through the Corkscrew. That was where he expected to have trouble in the race, however. 'Braking and changing direction is not so easy,' he admitted.

Okada completed the front row, not really able to explain his paradoxical improvement at a track where front-wheel grip and quick turn-in – hitherto his weakest areas – are so important. 'I don't know why, except we have found a new combination of tyres and suspension settings that works better. They are tyres that were available before, not something new here,' he said.

Half a second covered the front row; one-tenth down, Ruggia led the second. He likes the track, and was confident of a good result, saying: 'Unlike the front men I did my time alone.' Aoki was alongside, the times still whisker close, with Harada next to him, after a crash at the Corkscrew on Friday. (Unhurt, he blamed gusting wind.)

Waldmann lost ground in the final session with engine trouble, ending up eighth.

Row three was led by D'Antin from Bayle and Checa, with Jurgen van den Goorbergh concluding the row, on his first visit to the track.

Kenny Roberts Junior led row four in his second race of the year, saying: 'The important thing is just to stay upright and try and finish.'

All 35 entrants qualified, with US wild cards Rich Oliver (Yamaha TZ) and Chris d'Alusio (Aprilia) 17th and 26th.

250 cc RACE – 31 LAPS

Biaggi led from the start, then on lap two Romboni pulled the usual Turn Two move and took to the front. He led for all but four of the remaining laps, with Okada ahead on laps 5 and 6, and 18 and 19, but it was only under the most severe and sustained pressure, with a pack of up to nine of the world's best 250 riders snapping at his heels.

Okada dropped from first to seventh with a slip on lap seven, but the pack was so close that he was able to pick his way back up to second again, from laps 14 to 28, before losing ground yet again.

In the interim, the action was hectic.

Capirossi had been right with the group, as high as second and threatening more. Then, after one-third distance, his hand started to cramp up. First he dropped from second to fourth under braking for the last corner; then, half a lap later, he wasn't able to brake hard enough for Turn Five, and fell. Happily he was not hurt, but it was a poor reward for a brave effort.

UNITED STATES GRAND PRIX

Öttl leads Tsujimura and Perugini in typical 125 action. The Japanese rider emerged in front.

Opposite: Romboni's first win of the year was hard-fought: he leads Okada, Biaggi, Ruggia and Aoki early on.

Below: Biaggi aims his Aprilia over the crest. The twisty, hilly track favoured the Hondas more.

Waldmann had also been at the back of the leading pack, moving up to sixth ahead of Harada on lap 12; then he too made an error at the same corner, running into the dirt without falling and rejoining in 14th.

Now there were seven.

And then six, with Jean-Michel Bayle crashing spectacularly on the uphill straight before the Corkscrew. The third Chesterfield Aprilia rider had been hanging on well at the back of the pack, but was unsighted by Harada before running into the dirt. It was his first-ever GP race crash.

Ruggia had been right there, up to third at half-distance, ahead of teammate Biaggi. Then, as the pace increased in the closing stages, he also fell, tumbling into the airfence at the end of lap 27. Now there were five.

Harada seemed to have lost touch with the group, after running into a carburation problem that meant he momentarily lost power. For the first time in 1994 he showed the sheer class that won him the title last year, closing up, then picking off his rivals one by one. He was third at the end of the penultimate lap, with Romboni finally having gained a small advantage over Biaggi.

Then came Biaggi's last adventure, on the final run down the hill. He tried way too hard to attack Romboni, and came within a whisker of getting flicked off. This slowed him enough to improve Harada's chances, and the Japanese rider made a superbly timed attack on the Italian, outbraking him into the last corner. It was only Biaggi's extra power that enabled him to get back in front over the line, to take second. Romboni was 1.4 seconds ahead, Harada just two-tenths behind.

Okada's up-and-down race was finally rewarded with fourth, less than a second behind Harada after another near-spill when he tried to run inside Aoki with less than three laps to go. He saved it and managed to pass his rival later the same lap. They were only two-tenths apart.

More than 20 seconds behind came Spaniards D'Antin and Checa, locked in combat for most of the race. D'Antin, on a works NSR, finished one-tenth ahead of the youngster's kitted RS production bike, an impressive result.

There had been a big group going for eighth, broken up somewhat when Waldmann rejoined in their midst. This gained Zeelenberg and Roberts Junior breathing space, and they spent the latter part of the race closely involved with one another. Roberts finally made the decisive overtaking move on the Corkscrew, on the last lap, to lead the more experienced Dutchman over the line by less than half a second.

Waldmann was tenth, with Preining four seconds behind, just two-tenths ahead of Suter. Close behind came Bosshard's works Honda, and Jurgen van den Goorbergh's Aprilia.

The last point went to Borja, fully 25 seconds adrift. And he was lucky. Wild card Oliver had been hanging on close to van den Goorbergh, only to seize on the last lap.

There were 22 finishers. Crashers included James Haydon, Adi Stadler and Kassner's replacement, Jurgen Fuchs.

125 cc RACE – 29 LAPS

This was a thrilling race, in spite of the crash that eliminated possible title winner Sakata.

The Aprilia rider had qualified on pole, but in the scramble through the Turn Two hairpin he collided with Raudies and fell, with Loek Bodelier running into his fallen bike. The Dutchman's bike was damaged, but Sakata climbed back on board his machine, eventually restarted after a push from a marshal, and set off in a hectic pursuit that was to end in the airfence after a spectacular high-side, one lap later.

At this stage, Öttl was already in the lead, pursued by Tsujimura and young Haruchika Aoki, after the Honda privateer had started from second overall alongside Sakata. Noboru Ueda was with them briefly, only to drop away after five laps with a mysterious power loss.

Stefano Perugini, meanwhile, had started in sixth, seemingly caught up in the next group. But the Aprilia rider was hot to trot, and quickly picked his way through to close the gap on the leaders after taking fourth place on the ninth lap. As he joined in and upped the pace, Aoki lost touch, and battle for victory was joined with less than ten laps left.

It was tooth and claw, with the trio close enough to touch, and Perugini apparently prepared to risk more than his more experienced rivals. He was second on lap 20, then hit the front in the usual Turn Two braking zone next time round, forcing Öttl wide, which let Tsujimura through to second.

The next moment came on lap 27 as they lapped Manfred Baumann. The Austrian let the first two past, then tried to hang on, slowing Öttl so that he lost almost a second – way too much to make up in this sort of company.

The last lap was a masterpiece for Tsujimura. He moved into the lead under braking for Turn Five and headed them up the hill towards the Corkscrew. He ran a little wide on the way in, tempting Perugini to try the inside line. But Tsuji was also going very fast, and not only did the Italian's bid fail, but it also sent him wide on the exit from the left-right bend, and slowed him so that he finished almost a second adrift, and only half a second ahead of Öttl.

Aoki was an excellent fourth, three seconds ahead of Yamaha rider Jorge Martinez, heading the next group of Nakajyo (Honda) and a strong Carlos Giro (Aprilia).

Raudies was eighth after a scary moment following his fateful first-lap bang. Ten seconds back came Ueda, with Gianluigi Scalvini bringing his Aprilia home in tenth.

There were 29 finishers. Perugini recorded a new lap record of 1m 32.432s, half a second inside Sakata's 1993 record. Fausto Gresini (Honda) did not start after crashing in practice.

Sakata's first non-finish of the year left him battered but not badly hurt, and still miles ahead in the championship. But it meant he would have to wait one more race before knowing it was his for sure. Meanwhile Tsujimura moved ahead of Ueda in their battle for second.

143

500 cc

33 laps, 72.468 miles/116.622 km

Place	Rider	Nat.	Machine	Laps	Time & speed	Fastest lap	Lap
1	Luca Cadalora	I	Yamaha	33	48m 00.370s 90.570 mph/ 145.759 km/h	1m 26.476s	19
2	John Kocinski	USA	Cagiva	33	48m 08.266s	1m 26.444s	15
3	Michael Doohan	AUS	Honda	33	48m 25.246s	1m 26.640s	13
4	Shinichi Itoh	J	Honda	33	48m 36.495s	1m 27.581s	7
5	Doug Chandler	USA	Cagiva	33	48m 36.500s	1m 27.490s	25
6	Norifumi Abe	J	Yamaha	33	48m 44.824s	1m 27.650s	19
7	Alberto Puig	E	Honda	33	48m 59.486s	1m 28.034s	12
8	Alexandre Barros	BR	Suzuki	33	49m 11.396s	1m 28.312s	5
9	Jeremy McWilliams	GB	Yamaha	33	49m 16.258s	1m 28.321s	11
10	Niall Mackenzie	GB	Yamaha	33	49m 23.286s	1m 28.522s	4
11	Sean Emmett	GB	Yamaha	33	49m 27.417s	1m 28.324s	11
12	Bernard Garcia	F	Yamaha	32	48m 01.750s	1m 28.516s	6
13	Laurent Naveau	B	Yamaha	32	48m 06.442s	1m 28.731s	12
14	Jean-Pierre Jeandat	F	Yamaha	32	48m 28.770s	1m 29.243s	7
15	Lucio Pedercini	I	Yamaha	32	48m 49.884s	1m 30.356s	32
16	Marc Garcia	F	Yamaha	32	48m 50.138s	1m 30.288s	26
17	Cristiano Migliorati	I	Yamaha	32	48m 58.608s	1m 30.387s	25
18	Bernard Hänggeli	CH	Yamaha	32	49m 01.213s	1m 30.571s	18
19	Bruno Bonhuil	F	Yamaha	32	49m 21.284s	1m 31.326s	13
20	Cees Doorakkers	NL	Yamaha	31	48m 05.102s	1m 31.424s	28
21	Jean Foray	F	Yamaha	31	48m 09.904s	1m 31.590s	4
	Marco Papa	I	Yamaha	13	DNF	1m 33.179s	7
	Daryl Beattie	AUS	Yamaha	9	DNF	1m 28.177s	5
	Kevin Mitchell	GB	Yamaha	7	DNF	1m 31.499s	4
	John Reynolds	GB	Yamaha	1	DNF	1m 45.247s	1
	Kevin Schwantz	USA	Suzuki		DNS		
	Alex Criville	E	Honda		DNS		
	Chuck Graves	USA	Yamaha		DNS		
	Juan Lopez Mella	E	Yamaha		DNS		
	Andreas Leuthe	D	Yamaha		DNQ		

Fastest lap: Kocinski, 1m 26.444s, 91.450 mph/147.175 km/h.
Lap record: Kevin Schwantz, USA (Suzuki), 1m 25.838s, 92.099 mph/148.219 km/h (1990).

Qualifying: **1** Doohan, 1m 26.068s; **2** Kocinski, 1m 26.076s; **3** Cadalora, 1m 26.128s; **4** Itoh, 1m 27.015s; **5** Schwantz, 1m 27.355s; **6** Chandler, 1m 27.401s; **7** Beattie, 1m 27.525s; **8** Criville, 1m 27.716s; **9** Puig, 1m 27.786s; **10** Barros, 1m 27.808s; **11** Abe, 1m 28.073s; **12** McWilliams, 1m 28.239s; **13** Reynolds, 1m 28.671s; **14** Mackenzie, 1m 28.696s; **15** Jeandat, 1m 28.959s; **16** B. Garcia, 1m 29.050s; **17** Naveau, 1m 29.124s; **18** Emmett, 1m 29.175s; **19** Pedercini, 1m 30.824s; **20** M. Garcia, 1m 31.063s; **21** Graves, 1m 31.084s; **22** Hänggeli, 1m 31.168s; **23** Bonhuil, 1m 31.178s; **24** Lopez Mella, 1m 31.188s; **25** Migliorati, 1m 31.765s; **26** Doorakkers, 1m 31.863s; **27** Mitchell, 1m 31.967s; **28** Foray, 1m 32.207s; **29** Papa, 1m 32.676s.

World Championship: 1 M. Doohan, 272; **2** Schwantz, 169; **3** Kockinski, 140; **4** Cadalora, 139; **5** Puig, 132; **6** Itoh, 128; **7** Criville, 122; **8** Barros, 116; **9** Chandler, 70; **10** Mackenzie, 56; **11** B. Garcia, 45; **12** McWilliams and Reynolds, 38; **14** Beattie, 33; **15** Emmett, 28; **16** Lopez Mella, 23; **17** Abe, 20; **18** Jeandat, 17; **19** Naveau, 15; **20** Migliorati, 12; **21** Honma, 10; **22** Foray and M. Garcia, 8; **24** Bonhuil, Hänggeli, Miralles and Reggiani, 7; **28** Moineau, 5; **29** S. Doohan, 4; **30** Mark and Pedercini, 2.

250 cc

31 laps, 68.076 miles/109.544 km

Place	Rider	Nat.	Machine	Laps	Time & speed	Fastest lap	Lap
1	Doriano Romboni	I	Honda	31	46m 01.397s 88.747 mph/ 142.824 km/h	1m 28.368s	30
2	Massimiliano Biaggi	I	Aprilia	31	46m 02.830s	1m 28.046s	30
3	Tetsuya Harada	J	Yamaha	31	46m 03.028s	1m 28.198s	23
4	Tadayuki Okada	J	Honda	31	46m 03.972s	1m 28.526s	21
5	Nobuatsu Aoki	J	Honda	31	46m 04.146s	1m 28.174s	29
6	Luis D'Antin	E	Honda	31	46m 25.938s	1m 29.230s	18
7	Carlos Checa	E	Honda	31	46m 26.094s	1m 28.948s	9
8	Kenny Roberts Jnr	USA	Yamaha	31	46m 38.830s	1m 29.571s	9
9	Wilco Zeelenberg	NL	Honda	31	46m 39.246s	1m 29.478s	20
10	Ralf Waldmann	D	Honda	31	46m 42.324s	1m 28.402s	13
11	Andy Preining	A	Aprilia	31	46m 46.312s	1m 29.407s	20
12	Eskil Suter	CH	Aprilia	31	46m 46.551s	1m 29.368s	14
13	Adrian Bosshard	CH	Honda	31	46m 47.896s	1m 29.472s	12
14	Jurgen van den Goorbergh	NL	Aprilia	31	46m 48.576s	1m 29.458s	14
15	Juan Borja	E	Honda	31	47m 13.282s	1m 30.292s	11
16	Patrick van den Goorbergh	NL	Aprilia	31	47m 26.130s	1m 30.267s	6
17	Luis Maurel	E	Honda	31	47m 29.399s	1m 30.564s	19
18	Noel Ferro	F	Honda	31	47m 30.240s	1m 30.677s	10
19	Chris d'Alusio	USA	Aprilia	30	46m 23.494s	1m 31.597s	22
20	José Luis Cardoso	E	Aprilia	30	46m 27.474s	1m 31.605s	13
21	Rodney Fee	CAN	Honda	30	46m 48.296s	1m 32.168s	19
22	Enrique de Juan	E	Aprilia	30	46m 48.960s	1m 32.176s	9
	Rich Oliver	USA	Yamaha	28	DNF	1m 29.682s	7
	Jean-Philippe Ruggia	F	Aprilia	26	DNF	1m 28.404s	23
	Jurgen Fuchs	D	Honda	25	DNF	1m 31.233s	7
	James Haydon	GB	Honda	24	DNF	1m 30.105s	19
	Adi Stadler	D	Honda	20	DNF	1m 30.250s	7
	Kristian Kaas	SF	Yamaha	19	DNF	1m 31.656s	13
	Jean-Michel Bayle	F	Aprilia	16	DNF	1m 28.721s	7
	Manuel Hernandez	E	Aprilia	14	DNF	1m 33.902s	9
	Frédéric Protat	F	Honda	13	DNF	1m 31.639s	13
	Alessandro Gramigni	I	Aprilia	13	DNF	1m 32.060s	7
	Loris Capirossi	I	Honda	11	DNF	1m 28.533s	3
	Giuseppe Fiorillo	I	Honda	8	DNF	1m 31.900s	6
	Christian Boudinot	F	Aprilia	5	DNF	1m 33.154s	4

Fastest lap: Biaggi, 1m 28.046s, 89.786 mph/144.497 km/h.
Lap record: Loris Capirossi, I (Honda), 1m 27.959s, 89.875 mph/144.640 km/h (1993).

Qualifying: 1 Romboni, 1m 27.499s; **2** Biaggi, 1m 27.622s; **3** Capirossi, 1m 27.960s; **4** Okada, 1m 28.050s; **5** Ruggia, 1m 28.151s; **6** Aoki, 1m 28.375s; **7** Harada, 1m 28.546s; **8** Waldmann, 1m 28.715s; **9** D'Antin, 1m 28.760s; **10** Bayle, 1m 28.808s; **11** Checa, 1m 28.992s; **12** J. van den Goorbergh, 1m 29.322s; **13** Roberts Jnr, 1m 29.392s; **14** Preining, 1m 29.488s; **15** Bosshard, 1m 29.771s; **16** Suter, 1m 29.978s; **17** Oliver, 1m 30.033s; **18** Zeelenberg, 1m 30.080s; **19** Borja, 1m 30.346s; **20** Maurel, 1m 30.356s; **21** Fuchs, 1m 30.621s; **22** Stadler, 1m 30.707s; **23** P. van den Goorbergh, 1m 30.762s; **24** Ferro, 1m 30.826s; **25** Haydon, 1m 31.106s; **26** d'Alusio, 1m 31.336s; **27** Cardoso, 1m 31.340s; **28** Protat, 1m 31.407s; **29** Fiorillo, 1m 31.450s; **30** Kaas, 1m 31.560s; **31** Boudinot, 1m 32.349s; **32** Gramigni, 1m 32.575s; **33** de Juan, 1m 32.608s; **34** Fee, 1m 33.145s; **35** Hernandez, 1m 34.361s.

World Championship: 1 Biaggi, 189; **2** Okada, 176; **3** Capirossi, 168; **4** Romboni, 154; **5** Waldmann, 139; **6** Ruggia, 126; **7** N. Aoki, 95; **8** D'Antin, 93; **9** Bayle, 88; **10** Harada, 82; **11** Zeelenberg, 75; **12** Suter, 42; **13** Checa, 41; **14** Preining, 29; **15** P. van den Goorbergh, 27; **16** Bosshard and J. van den Goorbergh, 24; **18** Ukawa, 16; **19** T. Aoki, Honma and Lucchi, 11; **22** Gramigni, 10; **23** Kassner, 9; **24** Roberts Jnr and Stadler, 8; **26** Maurel, 7; **27** Fiorillo, 6; **28** Connell, 5; **29** Castilla, 3; **30** Borja, 2; **31** Cardoso, 1.

Team Roberts celebrate their first win of what had threatened to be their first year ever without one.

Kocinski prepared a little all-American shrine in the press room. Schwantz was among throngs of worshippers.

Bottom: Perugini, Tsujimura and Öttl celebrate on the rostrum.

125 cc

29 laps, 63.684 miles/102.486 km

Place	Rider	Nat.	Machine	Laps	Time & speed	Fastest lap	Lap
1	Takeshi Tsujimura	J	Honda	29	45m 21.102s 84.250 mph/ 135.588 km/h	1m 32.778s	13
2	Stefano Perugini	I	Aprilia	29	45m 22.076s	1m 32.432s	13
3	Peter Öttl	D	Aprilia	29	45m 22.654s	1m 32.880s	14
4	Haruchika Aoki	J	Honda	29	45m 35.817s	1m 33.041s	13
5	Jorge Martinez	E	Yamaha	29	45m 38.954s	1m 33.221s	6
6	Hideyuki Nakajyo	J	Honda	29	45m 39.172s	1m 33.273s	6
7	Carlos Giro	E	Aprilia	29	45m 39.846s	1m 33.163s	9
8	Dirk Raudies	D	Honda	29	45m 44.518s	1m 33.722s	21
9	Noboru Ueda	J	Honda	29	45m 54.172s	1m 33.644s	6
10	Gianluigi Scalvini	I	Aprilia	29	46m 05.548s	1m 34.116s	9
11	Stefan Prein	D	Yamaha	29	46m 09.690s	1m 34.239s	12
12	Oliver Koch	D	Honda	29	46m 14.197s	1m 34.062s	17
13	Oliver Petrucciani	CH	Aprilia	29	46m 17.260s	1m 34.399s	21
14	Masaki Tokudome	J	Honda	29	46m 17.293s	1m 34.656s	9
15	Manfred Geissler	D	Aprilia	29	46m 17.504s	1m 34.400s	27
16	Juan Maturana	E	Yamaha	29	46m 24.490s	1m 34.557s	12
17	Lucio Cecchinello	I	Honda	29	46m 37.180s	1m 34.978s	13
18	Vittorio Lopez	I	Honda	29	46m 37.367s	1m 35.061s	28
19	Akira Saito	J	Honda	29	46m 37.656s	1m 34.316s	9
20	Gabriele Debbia	I	Honda	29	46m 38.044s	1m 35.253s	28
21	Emili Alzamora	E	Honda	29	46m 42.032s	1m 34.742s	5
22	Neil Hodgson	GB	Honda	29	46m 50.594s	1m 35.410s	4
23	Tomoko Igata	J	Honda	29	46m 54.970s	1m 35.574s	26
24	Yasuaki Takahashi	J	Honda	29	46m 55.063s	1m 35.801s	26
25	Max Gambino	I	Aprilia	28	45m 29.922s	1m 36.072s	13
26	Manfred Baumann	A	Yamaha	28	45m 31.741s	1m 36.357s	21
27	Takahito Mori	USA	Honda	28	45m 34.409s	1m 36.221s	5
28	Nicolas Dussauge	F	Honda	28	45m 53.028s	1m 36.570s	8
29	Kevin Murray	USA	Honda	27	46m 41.455s	1m 41.889s	26
	Frédéric Petit	F	Yamaha	16	DNF	1m 36.513s	11
	Maik Stief	D	Aprilia	14	DNF	1m 34.519s	11
	Hans Spaan	NL	Honda	4	DNF	1m 37.401s	3
	Kazuto Sakata	J	Aprilia	1	DNF	2m 36.873s	1
	Loek Bodelier	NL	Honda	0	DNF		
	Fausto Gresini	I	Honda		DNS		
	Herri Torrontegui	E	Aprilia		DNS		

Fastest lap: Perugini, 1m 32.432s, 85.526 mph/137.641 km/h (record).
Previous record: Kazuto Sakata, J (Honda), 1m 32.971s, 85.030 mph/136.843 km/h (1993).

Qualifying: 1 Sakata, 1m 33.170s; **2** Aoki, 1m 33.207s; **3** Martinez, 1m 33.512s; **4** Ueda, 1m 33.514s; **5** Öttl, 1m 33.526s; **6** Raudies, 1m 33.682s; **7** Tokudome, 1m 33.828s; **8** Giro, 1m 33.842s; **9** Tsujimura, 1m 34.028s; **10** Perugini, 1m 34.146s; **11** Debbia, 1m 34.160s; **12** Saito, 1m 34.239s; **13** Koch, 1m 34.356s; **14** Petrucciani, 1m 34.425s; **15** Stief, 1m 34.537s; **16** Prein, 1m 34.604s; **17** Cecchinello, 1m 34.614s; **18** Nakajyo, 1m 34.622s; **19** Bodelier, 1m 34.734s; **20** Scalvini, 1m 34.734s; **21** Hodgson, 1m 34.906s; **22** Alzamora, 1m 34.972s; **23** Geissler, 1m 35.199s; **24** Gresini, 1m 36.043s; **25** Igata, 1m 36.055s; **26** Maturana, 1m 36.068s; **27** Takahashi, 1m 36.116s; **28** Gambino, 1m 36.193s; **29** Petit, 1m 36.222s; **30** Lopez, 1m 36.598s; **31** Mori, 1m 36.788s; **32** Baumann, 1m 36.824s; **33** Dussauge, 1m 37.026s; **34** Spaan, 1m 37.144s; **35** Torrontegui, 1m 39.371s; **36** Murray, 1m 42.390s.

World Championship: 1 Sakata, 208; **2** Tsujimura, 168; **3** Ueda, 164; **4** Öttl, 137; **5** Raudies, 127; **6** Martinez, 110; **7** Perugini, 90; **8** Tokudome, 76; **9** Torrontegui, 73; **10** Petrucciani, 63; **11** Nakajyo, 62; **12** McCoy, 56; **13** Saito, 51; **14** Bodelier, 41; **15** Gresini, 40; **16** Aoki, 39; **17** Koch, 30; **18** Manako, 24; **19** Giro, 20; **20** Casanova, 15; **21** Scalvini, 14; **22** Prein, 12; **23** Debbia, 11; **24** Geissler, 9; **25** Cuppini, 7; **26** Igata and Locatelli, 6; **28**

LAGUNA SECA RACEWAY
CIRCUIT LENGTH: 2.196-MILES/3.534 KM

WORLD CHAMPIONSHIP • ROUND 13

ARGENTINIAN GRAND PRIX

500 cc	DOOHAN
250 cc	OKADA
125 cc	MARTINEZ

'All stories come to an end sometime. This one finished today'

Loris Capirossi, after kissing his title chances goodbye

The return to Buenos Aires was blissfully shambolic. Well, perhaps not blissful. Although the circus left in good order, the universal levity owed more to hysteria than bliss.

Any one of a number of things might have gone seriously wrong at this sticking-plaster last-minute bodged-up event. Instead, it came to conclusion without drama or disaster and, most important, without serious injuries, meaning that nobody discovered whether the medical treatment is as run-down and slap-happy (and amazingly expensive) as everything else in Argentina. But it was only by the skin of its teeth. And the relief at the averted trauma was enough to make anyone break into fatuous giggling.

Always controversial, the first Argentinian GP since 1987 defied all predictions of cancellation, but lived up to most people's fears, with several delays through the weekend at a track with dilapidated facilities and service, and a worrying new surface that started off slippery, then had more oil and diesel dumped on it by service vehicles, and was condemned as unridable in the wet by tyre technicians and riders.

The layout of the 4.350-km track, substantially reprofiled in parts and completely resurfaced since the last isolated visit in 1987, won general approval both on grounds of safety and in being interesting and enjoyable, although four first-gear corners make it rather tight for 500s. Selected from a number of possibilities at the old Municipal Autodrome of Buenos Aires, it followed the same route as in 1987 until the back straight, from where it U-turned back through a section with some Assen-style wiggles to another looping bend and short straight, itself then swerving interestingly left over a brow under braking for another fast right before a tightening final hairpin/chicane. Swathes of air-fence protected the pit wall and other potential trouble spots.

The surface problems were twofold. First, it was very 'green', with no wear, oils still rising and no rubber laid down. Second, there were the spillages. On Friday, an ambulance left a spoor of oil as it toured the track. The high-pressure cleaning machine that came to clear up only leaked more oil itself; then on Saturday 500 practice was delayed by almost an hour because of a big-time diesel spillage on turn one by the marshals' lunch truck.

Aprilia factory tester Marcellino Lucchi had come down less than a fortnight before in an attempt to give Max Biaggi an edge on gearbox and chassis settings, and found the slick-yet-bumpy surface so slippery that he was unable even to get his knee down. Riders' representative Franco Uncini then arranged for the track to be sandblasted, but this brought fresh problems. As Doohan said: 'The racing line is okay, but a few feet off it looks as though somebody's dumped a beach. If you get off line, the front just tries to fold. If this was Australia, we wouldn't ride, but I guess it's different being here. If it doesn't improve, we won't be able to race – just ride around. Whoever is first into the first bend will win.'

With strike threats on hold for the moment, the riders agreed to go out for the first untimed session to explore. This was what triggered Doohan's comments above, while some riders (notably Beattie) used intermediate tyres for grip even though it was quite dry. The organisers' response was to wash the racing line with high-pressure hoses. This helped, but only while the riders stayed on line, making overtaking manoeuvres difficult. 'We need more than three feet. We sometimes need the whole width of the race track,' commented Doohan. The track did gradually improve, though the spillages and consequent liberal sprinkling with cement dust hardly helped, and the riders still found it greasy and unpredictable on race day.

IRTA chief executive Paul Butler excused the surface, saying that the

Under southern skies – Chandler's Cagiva leads the 500s at the suburban Buenos Aires track.

Inset: Schwantz gives a master class to works-bike first-timer Sean Emmett.

tyre people should be able to come up with something to cope; and a Dunlop technician quietly agreed. However, they had all been caught out, expecting a more abrasive surface and bringing a generally too-hard selection of compounds to suit.

Their real fear concerned the possibility of rain, made more acute by a violent city-centre hailstorm on Saturday morning, which fortunately missed the track a few miles away. Dunlop and Michelin had an unprecedented meeting before practice began to discuss what might be done. The answer, by then, was: 'Nothing, but hope it stays dry.'

With the title won, little remained for Doohan except to demonstrate the mastery of a champion. His ninth win this year was his 19th career win, putting him one ahead of Gardner as the most successful Australian. The only obstacle was the Cagivas, with both Kocinski and, more especially, Chandler bang on form at a track where their faithful handling counted for a lot.

Schwantz was there – he was presented to the President Carlos Menem, while 1000 red roses were sent in his name to the president's daughter, Zulemita, who runs a motor cycle shop in the capital. Then the president's son, Carlos Junior, a rally driver of some note, took Kevin for several jaunts in his helicopter.

Schwantz thus dominated local TV coverage without even putting his leathers on – fresh from surgery, with both wrists plaster-casted, he had never intended to ride.

His bike went to British Shell Harris rider Sean Emmett, a controversial choice both with the sponsors, with paddock cynics, and with overlooked British riders Reynolds and McWilliams. Emmett jumped on a bike he pronounced faster at the top end than his Harris, but otherwise unsurprising, and proceeded to do everything right as he adapted to his first time on Michelin tyres. Instead of crashing, as many expected, each time he went out he was faster, culminating in a solid race spoiled only by his own reluctance to overtake temporary team-mate, the still lustrous Barros. Had he done so early in the race, when he was clearly faster, he might have finished even higher than tenth, and almost certainly ahead of the vengeful McWilliams, who produced a blinding ride to pip the works Suzuki in the closing laps.

This bike-switching had a knock-on effect most heartening in British racing circles, hungry for new talent. Emmett's unleaded-burning Harris was given to Neil Hodgson, a large lad who has for two years been labouring to overcome the disadvantage of his bulk in the 125 class. One of very few riders in the class not to have scored a single GP point, he redressed the balance with a solid ride to 15th first time on a 500.

In the 250 class, the final act of the championship was reaching a climax. By the end, Capirossi had been eliminated from the struggle for supremacy, his impetuous Brno hand injury proving as costly as had originally been feared. And as Biaggi produced a typically mercurial performance to claim a hard-won second, it was Okada who stepped out of the shadows to claim a masterful victory, and to close within eight points of Biaggi with just one race left. The forgotten man of the championship came back just at the right time.

It is hard to know exactly what role the other forgotten man, Tetsuya Harada, played in all this. Back to strength and at a track that suited the Yamaha (further evidence being sixth place for Kenny Roberts Jnr in an excellent ride), the Japanese man seemed on the surface to have judged his race perfectly, hanging with the leaders and saving strength and tyres, before mounting a challenge on Biaggi in the closing stages. He claimed the lap record, and did pass him on the last lap, but Max overtook him back under power. Harada did try to dive underneath him at the last left, but it may have been a half-hearted effort. Had Harada held back, so as to help Max in the title battle with his fellow-countryman and old rival Okada? Such is Harada's stature as a rider and tactician that it must be considered a possibility.

The 30,000 Argentinians who made it to the track did see one title settled – in the most undramatic manner. For once playing the calculating rider, Kazuto Sakata missed out on the hectic last-lap action of the most exciting finale of the season to cruise in ninth. It was enough to make him unassailable, and to release an unexpected torrent of emotional tears. The excitement came from Noboru Ueda and veteran Jorge Martinez, who changed places five times in a desperate last lap, with a final fairing-bashing victory worthy of a teenager going to the 34-year-old Spaniard. 'I was prepared to crash or win,' he said later. It was his 37th GP win, but Yamaha's first since 1974.

500 cc PRACTICE

There were a number of near-misses but no crashes worth mentioning, in spite of continuing complaints that the track was very treacherous off the racing line. As is often the case, the worst moans came from the fastest riders – which makes sense, because if they

Marlboro
Marlboro
Marlboro

Arai
elf
HRC
Racing
4
HONDA
elf
MICHELIN

ARGENTINIAN GRAND PRIX

Once again, 1994 World Champion Mick Doohan was in a class of his own.

Inset: **Not everything was tatty in Argentina: the Marlboro girls draw the attention of Beattie and Doohan from the peeling ceiling.**

were going slower they wouldn't be sliding around so much.

Winner of what became a fierce contest in the last session was Kocinski, his first pole since the first two races this year, but achieved by a substantial margin of seven-tenths over Doohan.

Kocinski was as unrevealing as usual, saying: 'We stayed conservative with the bike, and worked through the tyres for the race.' In spite of the improving times, he added: 'I don't think the surface continued to improve the way it did in the earlier sessions. I think it got worse, with oil on the track and cement dust on that. You had to avoid the oil and the guys cleaning it up.'

His pole reflected the nature of the track, where tight corners as well as the poor surface worked against the more powerful machines, while the Cagiva's faithful handling helped John to stay accurate on the narrow available line.

Doohan was a steadfast critic, though he liked the layout, finding several points of interest. One is a fast swerve at the end of the lap, braking from sixth to fourth and diving left over a brow and immediately into a fast right. The bike needed a lot of suspension travel there, but dialling this in left it unsettled elsewhere, and he was still looking for the right compromise.

The new World Champion was also caught out by carburation problems that prevented his planned bid for pole in the closing minutes, and he was still working on finding a tyre that would slide consistently. 'At least tyre wear won't be a problem,' he said drily. 'They're not wearing.'

With a lot of focus on the need for a good start on a one-line track with few passing places, Cadalora was also happy to have secured the front row, placing a close third after leading for much of the last session. He was on the ragged edge as he tried to get it back, and happy with the latest Dunlops after finding a good combination on Saturday. But he was having trouble braking for the track's four very slow corners, where some (though not all) riders were using first gear. 'There are a couple of places where I can't turn the bike until I'm off the brakes,' he said.

Chandler was on the far end of the front row, the first time Cagiva have had two out of four bikes there. In fact Doug had held pole for the first half of the last session, continuing to improve his form. He felt he might have been better but for engine trouble. 'The times came really easy early in the session, then my best bike quit running. I guess it was a bad plug or something. When I went out again I got stuck in the traffic.' He was also puzzled by the way the surface didn't work the tyres. 'This track is so strange there doesn't seem to be much difference between the tyres, and we have quite a selection.'

Row two was led by Itoh, clearly focused on aiming for a rocket start. 'We'll be queuing up for the slow corners, and the leaders will get away.' Puig pushed his way up alongside him in the closing minutes, displacing Barros as he claimed sixth. The Spaniard didn't look comfortable, and admitted, 'I prefer faster tracks.'

Barros's case was interesting, after his steady erosion over the last few races. Now he was not only using one of Schwantz's bikes, with slightly but significantly different chassis settings from his usual mount, but he had also switched to Schwantz's crew chief. He found the steering quicker and the chassis more communicative than with the direction he had been following with his own crew, and this seemed to be enough to boost his confidence, which is probably more important than nuances of geometry.

Beattie concluded the row, also gaining strength and looking more aggressive as his own recovery from injury proceeds. After intermediates on Friday he used a hand-cut slick on Saturday. 'We've been struggling with the front pushing,' he said. 'What works for Luca doesn't work for me, because our bikes are a lot different in settings.'

Row three was led by McWilliams, the Irish private Yamaha rider a revelation over the last two races as he moves clearly ahead of the privateer average. The improvement was the result, he said, of ceasing to take advice from others, and riding the bike his own way. Rather than trying to spin and slide, he is instead going for high corner speed and lots of revs, and along with much aggression this paid dividends. He was up to fourth more than once during the sessions, and still well placed in a close batch that included some works bikes.

Criville was alongside, the Spaniard wearing a dressing on his injured left hand and far from strong, having trouble changing direction, as well as under braking, when his familiar front-tyre chatter would rattle the injury painfully.

Then came Emmett, punting his ex-Schwantz Suzuki round with an impressive combination of safety and steady improvement. The temptation to try too hard must have been considerable, but while he was still far from familiar with the bewildering choice of Michelins after racing only Dunlops, he was moving steadily in the right direction, improving every session to cut better than three seconds off from day one to day two, and promising more on Sunday.

Reynolds completed row three, having been placed higher at a track that clearly suits British short-circuit scratchers. He ended up three-tenths ahead of the usual top privateer, Mackenzie, who led row four from Jeandat, Bernard Garcia, Naveau and local gaucho wild card Nestor Amoroso.

All 31 entrants qualified, among them 125 rider Neil Hodgson in 22nd on Emmett's bike, and Lopez Mella last after his US injuries. He did not start.

500 cc RACE – 27 LAPS

The front-row Cagivas leapt away in formation to lead into turn one, Kocinski ahead. At this stage Cadalora was third and Doohan fourth, but the Italian immediately began losing ground, blaming a lack of front-tyre grip.

Kocinski stayed in control for the first two laps, but was already troubled by a lack of grip, and when his team-mate attacked into the first corner at the start of lap three he was unable to resist. One lap later he succumbed to Doohan at the same place.

Chandler had a lead of almost a second, but Doohan quickly reduced it to nothing, and repeated his turn one move at the start of lap six. Having neatly proved himself wrong in the prediction that overtaking would be impossible, he was never headed, drawing steadily ahead, looking smooth and comfortable, to win by a commanding 8.7 seconds.

'It's different every time we go out, so I didn't know what to expect,' he said. 'I only knew it would be greasy. But I found a comfortable pace, and I could have run that speed all day. My only worry was that somebody might be able to run faster! I was worried about the Cagivas, but in the end, the Honda and the Showa suspension were kinder to the tyres. That made the difference.'

Chandler felt he could match the Honda's pace, but not consistently. 'He was smooth and I was making little mistakes. Perhaps I was too timid, but I decided to calm down and go at my own pace.' He too was never challenged again, and continued to his best result since he joined Cagiva two years ago.

Kocinski had a lot more drama. Lying third and hoping to improve, he outbraked himself going into the first corner and was forced to take to the escape road. By the time he rejoined he was almost 2.5 seconds behind the next pair of Hondas, Puig and Itoh, and it took him five laps to get back ahead, by which time Chandler was out of reach. 'I don't really know what happened,' he said. 'I guess it's the way the surface changes. We thought we had found some really good tyres, but after 20 laps they had no grip at all. At one point I thought about stopping to ask my mechanics what was wrong with them.'

Itoh and Puig continued scrapping, the Japanese rider finally getting ahead on lap 17. 'It was hard,' he said. 'He was so late on the brakes, then he would slow me up in the corners. Because of my hand injury [from Brno] I couldn't brake hard enough to attack him.' Once past, however, he drew slowly clear to claim fourth by some four seconds. Puig, meanwhile, was facing a return of his painful arm problem.

There was a good dice behind them for the first half of the race: four riders piled up high behind Barros as he lost ground.

First in the group was Emmett, riding one of Schwantz's bikes with the alternative rear suspension system, and challenging strongly. Later he cursed himself for not trying to overtake, while Lucky Strike Suzuki team chief Garry Taylor did the same in the pits for not having instructed Emmett to pass Barros if he could. 'I was a second a lap slower when I got stuck behind Barros, but I just didn't know how the team or the sponsors would feel if I did go by,' the Briton said. He stayed dutifully behind until the 12th lap, his concentration ruffled and his rhythm unsettled, so that when he did finally go by under braking he immediately ran wide, and slipped back behind not only Barros but also Cadalora and Criville.

Now the group started to break up, with Cadalora finding his way by Barros on the 15th lap, and moving slowly ahead in a lonely sixth. The below-par Criville took six more laps to get past the Suzuki, and was unable to get clear. In fact both closed up slightly on Cadalora, whose front tyre was getting worse towards the finish. On the last lap, Barros managed to get back ahead of Criville briefly, only to run onto the dirt, lucky to slot in behind the Spaniard to take eighth.

Emmett had now run into wheelspin problems, but was able to fend off the close attentions of Beattie. Then, three laps from the end, the Yamaha rider had one big slide too many on his fading tyres, and pulled into the pits rather than crash. With such a short distance remaining this was hardly impressive, but those who saw the carcase showing through his ruined front tyre were more understanding.

Emmett's problems weren't over. McWilliams was having another excellent race, and had escaped from Mackenzie's Roc – the Scotsman up and down as his slickshift mechanism kept cutting his ignition at awkward moments. Now McWilliams closed on Emmett and passed him with two laps left. Emmett fought back, but while wheelspin slowed his run onto the straight, McWilliams got a strong drive and blew by him again, taking ninth by just over a second.

Mackenzie was 11th, comfortably clear of Bernard Garcia, his brother Marc, Naveau, and Neil Hodgson, claiming the first point in a two-year GP career in his first-ever 500 outing.

There were two crashers among ten non-finishers. Briton Kevin Mitchell fell on the first lap, and was loaded onto a wooden stretcher, although not seriously hurt. Then the stretcher snapped in two as they lifted him into the ambulance. One lap later Reynolds crashed heavily but without injury after running off-line onto the slippery stuff.

Amoroso was a noble 20th and last, after one unscheduled stop, finishing a lap adrift but only half a second behind Hänggeli.

250 cc PRACTICE

As the best-planned things sometimes degenerate into farce, 250 practice did the opposite. After a tentative start from the first riders out on Friday, the last 15 minutes were thrill-a-minute, with a fierce contest for the front row illustrated by the fact that in that time Roberts Junior dropped from second to seventh, while Biaggi moved from 12th to second, but ended up third.

So hot was the pace at that stage that Capirossi, having already secured pole by an impressive seventenths, managed to run off the track – very lucky not to fall – after getting into a corner too fast and running wide onto the marbles. By that stage, Romboni had already crashed, unhurt, since like most of the relatively few get-offs it was at one of the many low-speed bends. He crashed again in race-day warm-up, and this time hurt his hand enough to be out of the race.

Capirossi was still far from fully fit. His hand didn't slow him down, but he was concerned. 'It's hard to predict how it will react. If I can break away and keep my rhythm it may be okay,' he said.

The focus remained on the battle between him and Biaggi, and the pair had one close encounter, luckily with no serious consequences. But just to remind everyone of the true title position, Okada moved smoothly and unobtrusively through in the closing stages to claim second place. 'Everything is really good,' he said. 'I only did a little fine tuning. I'm ready to race, and very relaxed.'

Not so Biaggi, showing the pressure mainly by his fraught reaction to the track, and by going fast only in the closing stages. 'If we're in a big group, it will be a risky race,' he said. 'The bike is good enough, but not the track.'

Romboni was fourth, his place on the front row taken by Ruggia for the race, with all times very close except for Capirossi's – second to 12th were all within a second. The Frenchman was having trouble getting the rear suspension settled. All three Chesterfield Aprilia riders were playing about with a selection of different swing arms, but Ruggia said: 'As soon as you open the throttle it slides.'

Harada was alongside, and complaining only a little. A 'handling' circuit suits both the Yamaha and the rider, and he was again looking like a serious threat, sixth overall but less than four-tenths slower than Okada.

And next to him, Roberts Junior, with a really strong showing in only his third race of the year. He'd even threatened a front-row start after tucking in behind Capirossi for a good tow. Some said it was because the circuit is similar to many in the USA – tight and slippery. 'Maybe so,' he said. 'I think it's more because we've done a few things to the bike that have worked, and I'm beginning to feel really confident on it.'

Checa was alongside, continuing to go well. Row three saw Bayle, who took time to get moving, ahead of D'Antin, Aoki and Waldmann, battling with terminal wheelspin.

All 35 entrants qualified, including wild cards Luis Lavado (32nd) and Sergio Granton (34th).

250 cc RACE – 25 LAPS

Okada led a tight pack through the first bends, with countryman Nobuatsu Aoki crashing his Jha Honda on the second corner in the middle of the rabble, luckily without getting hurt or bringing anybody else down. He rejoined, leaning over the front to rip away a section of broken mudguard. Andy Preining also collided with another rider and went off, his race over.

Biaggi had lost positions in the first corner, and was in the thick of the crowd, finishing lap one in tenth, his work cut out if he was to catch the leaders.

By the end of the second lap Capirossi was on Okada's back wheel and it looked as though they might break away. But Ruggia had other ideas, and gradually closed up, bringing Harada with him (through from seventh on lap one) to make a pack of four up front by lap four. Bayle was delaying the pursuit, and Biaggi working through fiercely, now sixth but suffering as the gap between the groups opened up. Then it looked even worse as Waldmann nipped in front of him, preparing his own attack on Bayle.

Capirossi took the lead on lap six and held it for five more laps. Then

ARGENTINIAN GRAND PRIX

Opposite: Impassive tower blocks oversee a towering struggle: Capirossi tries in vain to escape from eventual winner Okada and Ruggia.

Left: The best 125 race of all time? Perugini leads Martinez, Alzamora and Scalvini in the early stages.

Bottom: Bikes and bodies fly on lap one of the 125 race. Geissler (sliding on right), wild card Porco (obscured) and Dussauge (flying) were not hurt.

Okada, feeling threatened by Ruggia's increasingly close attention, decided it was time to make his move. He took to the front again on lap 12, and proceeded to pull away smoothly and certainly, to win by better than five seconds. It was only his second win of the year, but it came after a consistent finish record and at just the right time.

The battle was now for second, with Ruggia ahead of Capirossi, and Harada looming behind. The Japanese rider's tactics again looked exemplary as he kept the pressure on while saving his own strength and tyres. Meanwhile Biaggi had got by Waldmann on lap eight, and was slashing chunks off a gap of almost three seconds so that, by lap 14, he was also part of the group, and moving through steadily. Capirossi was back ahead of Ruggia on lap 15, and Biaggi promptly powered past the Frenchman one lap later.

The increased pace accorded badly with Capirossi's deteriorating condition. At the end of the back straight on the next lap he left his braking too late and didn't have the strength in his hand to recover the situation. He ran wide, and dropped straight to fifth, out of touch and out of hope. 'All stories come to an end sometime. This one finished today,' he said later.

The final act in the drama came as the chequered flag drew near. Harada really did look master of the situation, having waited until now to give everything. His first attack was actually on lap 20, trying to outbrake Max into turn one – and it was flawed. He lost the front and almost crashed, but recovered for his last-lap effort.

It came at the first left-hander, the second real corner, a place where nobody had overtaken anybody all weekend. The blue Yamaha slipped cleanly inside the black Aprilia, and that might have been that. But while the Japanese bike had a clear handling advantage, Max had power and heroism on his side. He used them to force his way past again, and to fend off another attack from Harada three corners from the end, winning second place by just over a quarter of a second.

Had Harada held back? Biaggi clearly didn't think so. 'In the last few laps I was sliding around like crazy. I even broke the screen with my head. That was a tough race, and the next one will be hard too. I won at Barcelona last year on a Honda with Michelins, and that is what Okada is riding.'

Ruggia was less than one second behind, a little down on power, he said, but happy after a strong and enjoyable race. Then came Capirossi, another seven seconds adrift by the finish.

By then, the next group was within six seconds – and Kenny Roberts was at the head of it. Bayle had been making the pace, and Waldmann was with them until the last couple of laps; but the young American was right on form, his bike handling well. When Bayle had a big slide on the last lap the issue was settled.

D'Antin prevailed in a race-long battle for ninth with Checa, works Honda only overtaking kitted RS with three laps left. A full 20 seconds back came Zeelenberg, who had been duelling the whole afternoon with Borja. At the end they both caught Bosshard but while Wilco got past, the Spaniard didn't, the trio crossing the line in just over one second.

Fiorillo was 14th, two seconds ahead of Cardoso, who took the last point. First-lap faller Aoki was 21st. There were nine non-finishers.

Capirossi's title hopes were over, but with Biaggi's lead shrunk to just eight points over Okada, the battle was going down to the wire.

125 cc RACE – 23 LAPS

The lead changed hands five times in a heart-stopping last lap in the fiercest race of the day, if not the year, with veteran former champion Martinez's Team Aspar Yamaha taking the flag by less than four-tenths of a second. It was a great day for the old man and the new Yamaha, and achieved with maximum risk.

Ueda's Honda weaved across the line on his tail, with the increasingly formidable Perugini another second away, awestruck after a grandstand view of his victors' antics.

Almost half a minute behind, Sakata's Aprilia cruised home a cautious ninth – enough to secure the world title for the Japanese rider, who had crashed twice in practice. He tearfully joined the top three on the rostrum, saying: 'I had no idea I would feel so emotional.'

Amazing young Spaniard Emili Alzamora's Marlboro Honda led the first lap, his first time ever up front; and he stayed in touch as a fierce four-bike battle developed, the lead changing back and forth between him, Martinez, Perugini and team-mate Scalvini. They were frequently two or three abreast in the corners, with Alzamora making up for a lack of power with ultra-daring braking.

Pole-qualifier Ueda, meanwhile, had started slowly, tenth at the end of lap one, but picking his way through to the front so that by half-distance it was a five-bike battle.

The Japanese rider took control seven laps from the end, but as he powered away Martinez took up station inches from his back wheel, waiting to pounce, leaving the other three to slow each other up.

Ueda had a power advantage, Martinez better brakes and handling, and he moved ahead on the first corner of the last lap. Ueda powered past on the back straight, Martinez dived inside again at the next bend, and now there seemed no more overtaking chances left. But Ueda found one, three corners from the end, only to be flabbergasted when Martinez promptly forced back underneath him at the last tight bend.

Perugini had escaped from his two rivals and almost caught up with the leaders on the last lap, only to run wide and lose touch again. He was still a comfortable third. Scalvini and Alzamora were fourth and fifth, scrapping to the end.

Raudies eventually prevailed over Tsujimura for sixth, with Tokudome leading a six-bike group over the line in pursuit – Sakata, Giro, Prein, Aoki and Öttl, the last named running off the track twice in the process.

Young Briton Darren Barton, making his foreign GP debut on Hodgson's Team Burnett Honda, lasted only five laps before being taken by surprise by another rider's early braking. 'He just stopped, and I hit him,' ran the blunt explanation. Geissler, Dussauge and wild card Porco were eliminated in a first-lap scrum.

With Sakata unassailable, Ueda's second was a boost in his battle with Tsujimura for second overall, putting him just seven points ahead. Öttl remained top European, but both Raudies and Martinez were poised to overtake him.

FIM WORLD CHAMPIONSHIP • ROUND 13
ARGENTINIAN GRAND PRIX
24 September 1994

500 cc

27 laps, 72.981 miles/117.450 km

Place	Rider	Nat.	Machine	Laps	Time & speed	Fastest lap	Lap
1	Michael Doohan	AUS	Honda	27	48m 12.812s 90.821 mph/ 146.162 km/h	1m 46.270s	8
2	Doug Chandler	USA	Cagiva	27	48m 21.554s	1m 46.681s	23
3	John Kocinski	USA	Cagiva	27	48m 29.781s	1m 46.424s	23
4	Shinichi Itoh	J	Honda	27	48m 41.093s	1m 47.160s	24
5	Alberto Puig	E	Honda	27	48m 45.202s	1m 47.290s	8
6	Luca Cadalora	I	Yamaha	27	48m 52.881s	1m 47.408s	16
7	Alex Criville	E	Honda	27	48m 54.054s	1m 47.858s	27
8	Alexandre Barros	BR	Suzuki	27	48m 55.862s	1m 47.881s	23
9	Jeremy McWilliams	GB	Yamaha	27	49m 09.561s	1m 48.088s	24
10	Sean Emmett	GB	Suzuki	27	49m 10.983s	1m 48.101s	7
11	Niall Mackenzie	GB	Yamaha	27	49m 25.766s	1m 48.311s	19
12	Bernard Garcia	F	Yamaha	27	49m 33.017s	1m 48.798s	6
13	Marc Garcia	F	Yamaha	27	49m 53.009s	1m 49.379s	6
14	Laurent Naveau	B	Yamaha	27	49m 54.446s	1m 50.038s	10
15	Neil Hodgson	GB	Yamaha	27	49m 54.782s	1m 49.912s	27
16	Cristiano Migliorati	I	Yamaha	27	49m 56.958s	1m 49.871s	13
17	Lucio Pedercini	I	Yamaha	26	48m 34.995s	1m 50.263s	8
18	Cees Doorakkers	NL	Yamaha	26	48m 35.637s	1m 50.735s	7
19	Bernard Hänggeli	CH	Yamaha	26	48m 36.178s	1m 50.938s	5
20	Nestor Amoroso	ARG	Yamaha	26	48m 36.606s	1m 50.772s	17
	Daryl Beattie	AUS	Yamaha	24	DNF	1m 47.976s	7
	Bruno Bonhuil	F	Yamaha	17	DNF	1m 51.064s	5
	Marco Papa	I	Yamaha	9	DNF	1m 54.403s	5
	Felipe Horta	RCH	Yamaha	8	DNF	1m 54.401s	5
	Vittorio Scatola	I	Paton	7	DNF	1m 56.374s	5
	Jean-Pierre Jeandat	F	Yamaha	5	DNF	1m 48.972s	5
	Jean Foray	F	Yamaha	5	DNF	1m 52.192s	4
	Andreas Leuthe	D	Yamaha	2	DNF	2m 03.612s	1
	John Reynolds	GB	Yamaha	1	DNF	1m 54.478s	1
	Kevin Mitchell	GB	Yamaha	0	DNF		
	Juan Lopez Mella	E	Yamaha		DNS		

Fastest lap: Doohan, 1m 46.270s, 91.566 mph/147.361 km/h (record).
Previous record: not available.

Qualifying: 1 Kocinski, 1m 45.346s; **2** Doohan, 1m 46.063s; **3** Cadalora, 1m 46.524s; **4** Chandler, 1m 46.598s; **5** Itoh, 1m 46.959s; **6** Puig, 1m 47.658s; **7** Barros, 1m 47.694s; **8** Beattie, 1m 48.062s; **9** McWilliams, 1m 48.116s; **10** Criville, 1m 48.217s; **11** Emmett, 1m 48.348s; **12** Reynolds, 1m 48.570s; **13** Mackenzie, 1m 48.899s; **14** Jeandat, 1m 49.536s; **15** B. Garcia, 1m 49.792s; **16** Naveau, 1m 50.196s; **17** Amoroso, 1m 50.220s; **18** M. Garcia, 1m 50.302s; **19** Bonhuil, 1m 50.969s; **20** Pedercini, 1m 51.008s; **21** Migliorati, 1m 51.480s; **22** Hodgson, 1m 51.554s; **23** Papa, 1m 51.631s; **24** Mitchell, 1m 51.632s; **25** Horta, 1m 51.658s; **26** Foray, 1m 51.938s; **27** Hänggeli, 1m 51.943s; **28** Scatola, 1m 52.007s; **29** Doorakkers, 1m 52.243s; **30** Leuthe, 1m 53.328s.

World Championship: 1 M. Doohan, 297; **2** Schwantz, 169; **3** Kocinski, 156; **4** Cadalora, 149; **5** Puig, 143; **6** Itoh, 141; **7** Criville, 131; **8** Barros, 124; **9** Chandler, 90; **10** Mackenzie, 61; **11** B. Garcia, 49; **12** McWilliams, 45; **13** Reynolds, 38; **14** Emmett, 34; **15** Beattie, 33; **16** Lopez Mella, 23; **17** Abe, 20; **18** Jeandat and Naveau, 17; **20** Migliorati, 12; **21** M. Garcia, 11; **22** Honma, 10; **23** Foray, 8; **24** Bonhuil, Hänggeli, Miralles and Reggiani, 7; **28** Moineau, 5; **29** S. Doohan, 4; **30** Mark and Pedercini, 2; **32** Hodgson, 1.

250 cc

25 laps, 67.575 miles/108.750 km

Place	Rider	Nat.	Machine	Laps	Time & speed	Fastest lap	Lap
1	Tadayuki Okada	J	Honda	25	45m 09.167s 89.794 mph/ 144.509 km/h	1m 47.584s	18
2	Massimiliano Biaggi	I	Aprilia	25	45m 14.450s	1m 47.464s	8
3	Tetsuya Harada	J	Yamaha	25	45m 14.770s	1m 47.336s	20
4	Jean-Philippe Ruggia	F	Aprilia	25	45m 15.680s	1m 47.866s	10
5	Loris Capirossi	I	Honda	25	45m 23.034s	1m 47.938s	15
6	Kenny Roberts Jnr	USA	Yamaha	25	45m 28.768s	1m 48.414s	23
7	Jean-Michel Bayle	F	Aprilia	25	45m 28.949s	1m 48.102s	23
8	Ralf Waldmann	D	Honda	25	45m 31.078s	1m 48.123s	6
9	Luis D'Antin	E	Honda	25	45m 37.925s	1m 48.489s	23
10	Carlos Checa	E	Honda	25	45m 38.902s	1m 48.699s	9
11	Wilco Zeelenberg	NL	Honda	25	45m 58.350s	1m 49.206s	24
12	Adrian Bosshard	CH	Honda	25	45m 59.352s	1m 49.130s	5
13	Juan Borja	E	Honda	25	45m 59.457s	1m 49.336s	21
14	Giuseppe Fiorillo	I	Honda	25	46m 11.092s	1m 49.906s	22
15	José Luis Cardoso	E	Aprilia	25	46m 13.760s	1m 49.962s	4
16	Luis Maurel	E	Honda	25	46m 22.366s	1m 50.373s	12
17	Frédéric Protat	F	Honda	25	46m 22.647s	1m 49.801s	10
18	Adi Stadler	D	Honda	25	46m 31.668s	1m 50.489s	6
19	Eskil Suter	CH	Aprilia	25	46m 34.006s	1m 50.014s	8
20	Jurgen Fuchs	D	Honda	25	46m 45.542s	1m 50.523s	6
21	Nobuatsu Aoki	J	Honda	25	46m 50.071s	1m 50.119s	8
22	James Haydon	GB	Honda	24	45m 21.103s	1m 50.998s	7
23	Kristian Kaas	SF	Yamaha	24	45m 46.550s	1m 52.471s	8
24	Sergio Granton	ARG	Yamaha	24	46m 07.305s	1m 53.656s	7
25	Manuel Hernandez	E	Aprilia	24	46m 34.772s	1m 54.562s	21
	Enrique de Juan	E	Aprilia	20	DNF	1m 52.062s	15
	Jurgen van den Goorbergh	NL	Aprilia	14	DNF	1m 50.216s	9
	Noel Ferro	F	Honda	10	DNF	1m 50.756s	8
	Alessandro Gramigni	I	Aprilia	9	DNF	1m 51.518s	5
	Christian Boudinot	F	Aprilia	9	DNF	1m 50.814s	6
	Patrick van den Goorbergh	NL	Aprilia	6	DNF	1m 52.210s	3
	Luis Lavado	YV	Yamaha	4	DNF	1m 55.026s	3
	Rodney Fee	CAN	Honda	2	DNF	1m 53.385s	2
	Andy Preining	A	Aprilia	2	DNF	2m 03.546s	1
	Doriano Romboni	I	Honda		DNS		

Fastest lap: Harada, 1m 47.336s, 90.656 mph/145.897 km/h (record).
Previous record: not available.

Qualifying: 1 Capirossi, 1m 47.576s; **2** Okada, 1m 48.242s; **3** Biaggi, 1m 48.302s; **4** Romboni, 1m 48.401s; **5** Ruggia, 1m 48.424s; **6** Harada, 1m 48.619s; **7** Roberts Jnr, 1m 48.642s; **8** Checa, 1m 48.702s; **9** Bayle, 1m 48.739s; **10** D'Antin, 1m 48.843s; **11** Aoki, 1m 48.947s; **12** Waldmann, 1m 49.045s; **13** Bosshard, 1m 49.298s; **14** J. van den Goorbergh, 1m 49.676s; **15** Suter, 1m 50.040s; **16** Borja, 1m 50.238s; **17** Maurel, 1m 50.457s; **18** Fiorillo, 1m 50.480s; **19** Cardoso, 1m 50.503s; **20** Zeelenberg, 1m 50.578s; **21** Protat, 1m 50.670s; **22** Preining, 1m 50.753s; **23** Stadler, 1m 50.920s; **24** Haydon, 1m 51.140s; **25** Ferro, 1m 51.144s; **26** Fuchs, 1m 51.150s; **27** Boudinot, 1m 51.435s; **28** P. van den Goorbergh, 1m 51.471s; **29** Gramigni, 1m 52.064s; **30** Fee, 1m 52.406s; **31** de Juan, 1m 52.488s; **32** Lavado, 1m 52.600s; **33** Kaas, 1m 52.926s; **34** Granton, 1m 54.576s; **35** Hernandez, 1m 54.933s.

World Championship: 1 Biaggi, 209; **2** Okada, 201; **3** Capirossi, 179; **4** Romboni, 154; **5** Waldmann, 147; **6** Ruggia, 139; **7** D'Antin, 100; **8** Harada, 98; **9** Bayle, 97; **10** N. Aoki, 95; **11** Zeelenberg, 80; **12** Checa, 47; **13** Suter, 42; **14** Preining, 29; **15** Bosshard, 28; **16** P. van den Goorbergh, 27; **17** J. van den Goorbergh, 24; **18** Roberts Jnr, 18; **19** Ukawa, 16; **20** T. Aoki, Honma and Lucchi, 11; **23** Gramigni, 10; **24** Kassner, 9; **25** Fiorillo and Stadler, 8; **27** Maurel, 7; **28** Borja and Connell, 5; **30** Castilla, 3; **31** Cardoso, 2.

CIRCUITO No 6 – DEL AUTODROMO DE LA CIUDAD DE BUENOS AIRES

CIRCUIT LENGTH: 2.668 MILES/4.350 KM

125 cc

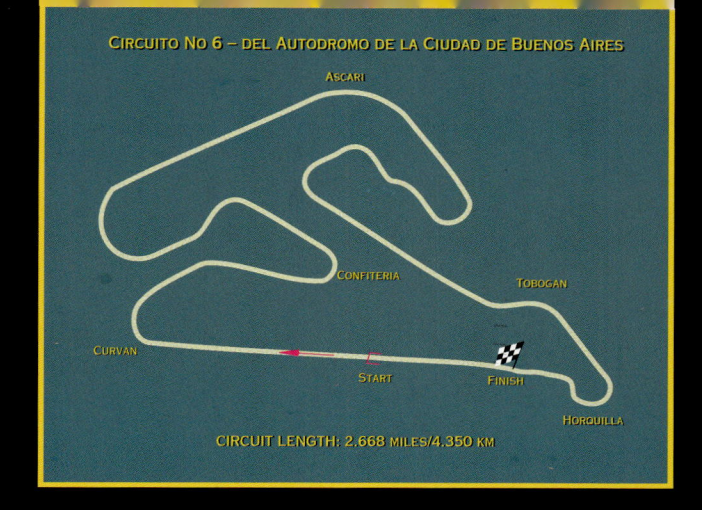

23 laps, 62.169 miles/100.050 km

Place	Rider	Nat.	Machine	Laps	Time & speed	Fastest lap	Lap
1	Jorge Martinez	E	Yamaha	23	43m 37.568s 85.501 mph/ 137.601 km/h	1m 52.828s	22
2	Noboru Ueda	J	Honda	23	43m 37.943s	1m 52.622s	14
3	Stefano Perugini	I	Aprilia	23	43m 38.902s	1m 52.268s	22
4	Gianluigi Scalvini	I	Aprilia	23	43m 40.682s	1m 52.864s	18
5	Emili Alzamora	E	Honda	23	43m 41.211s	1m 53.118s	19
6	Dirk Raudies	D	Honda	23	43m 51.575s	1m 53.210s	11
7	Takeshi Tsujimura	J	Honda	23	43m 53.647s	1m 53.501s	20
8	Masaki Tokudome	J	Honda	23	44m 04.011s	1m 53.705s	13
9	Kazuto Sakata	J	Aprilia	23	44m 04.278s	1m 53.727s	4
10	Carlos Giro	E	Aprilia	23	44m 04.426s	1m 53.832s	14
11	Stefan Prein	D	Yamaha	23	44m 05.210s	1m 53.660s	10
12	Haruchika Aoki	J	Honda	23	44m 05.301s	1m 53.574s	14
13	Peter Öttl	D	Aprilia	23	44m 06.238s	1m 53.188s	18
14	Akira Saito	J	Honda	23	44m 32.350s	1m 55.005s	23
15	Juan Maturana	E	Yamaha	23	44m 32.974s	1m 55.024s	20
16	Oliver Petrucciani	CH	Aprilia	23	44m 47.482s	1m 55.031s	18
17	Max Gambino	I	Aprilia	23	44m 54.459s	1m 55.640s	7
18	Manfred Baumann	A	Yamaha	23	45m 18.652s	1m 55.885s	9
19	Pablo Zeballos	ARG	Honda	22	44m 10.581s	1m 58.608s	5
	Loek Bodelier	NL	Honda	19	DNF	1m 53.928s	18
	Yasuaki Takahashi	J	Honda	19	DNF	1m 57.245s	7
	Hans Spaan	NL	Honda	16	DNF	1m 56.214s	9
	Fausto Gresini	I	Honda	14	DNF	1m 55.106s	7
	Gabriele Debbia	I	Honda	11	DNF	1m 55.914s	9
	Hideyuki Nakajyo	J	Honda	10	DNF	1m 53.659s	10
	Tomoko Igata	J	Honda	9	DNF	1m 55.418s	7
	Frédéric Petit	F	Yamaha	6	DNF	1m 56.857s	5
	Darren Barton	GB	Honda	5	DNF	1m 57.740s	5
	Lucio Cecchinello	I	Honda	4	DNF	1m 55.149s	3
	Vittorio Lopez	I	Honda	4	DNF	1m 59.370s	2
	Maik Stief	D	Aprilia	3	DNF	1m 55.754s	3
	Oliver Koch	D	Honda	1	DNF	2m 01.013s	1
	Manfred Geissler	D	Aprilia	0	DNF		
	Nicolas Dussauge	F	Honda	0	DNF		
	Sebastian Porco	ARG	Aprilia	0	DNF		

Fastest lap: Perugini, 1m 52.268s, 86.674 mph/139.488 km/h (record).
Previous record: not available.

Qualifying: 1 Ueda, 1m 52.688s; **2** Martinez, 1m 52.752s; **3** Perugini, 1m 52.791s; **4** Nakajyo, 1m 53.045s; **5** Giro, 1m 53.074s; **6** Alzamora, 1m 53.357s; **7** Scalvini, 1m 53.363s; **8** Koch, 1m 53.580s; **9** Tsujimura, 1m 53.582s; **10** Prein, 1m 53.607s; **11** Öttl, 1m 53.659s; **12** Sakata, 1m 53.668s; **13** Aoki, 1m 53.672s; **14** Raudies, 1m 53.741s; **15** Saito, 1m 53.848s; **16** Petrucciani, 1m 53.971s; **17** Porco, 1m 54.108s; **18** Petit, 1m 54.123s; **19** Tokudome, 1m 54.150s; **20** Stief, 1m 54.237s; **21** Bodelier, 1m 54.290s; **22** Geissler, 1m 54.522s; **23** Maturana, 1m 54.642s; **24** Gresini, 1m 54.796s; **25** Cecchinello, 1m 54.904s; **26** Debbia, 1m 54.912s; **27** Gambino, 1m 55.136s; **28** Dussauge, 1m 55.816s; **29** Baumann, 1m 56.018s; **30** Spaan, 1m 56.091s; **31** Igata, 1m 56.435s; **32** Barton, 1m 56.796s; **33** Lopez, 1m 56.856s; **34** Zeballos, 1m 58.470s; **35** Takahashi, 1m 58.715s.

World Championship: 1 Sakata, 215; **2** Ueda, 184; **3** Tsujimura, 177; **4** Öttl, 140; **5** Raudies, 137; **6** Martinez, 135; **7** Perugini, 106; **8** Tokudome, 84; **9** Torrontegui, 73; **10** Petrucciani, 63; **11** Nakajyo, 62; **12** McCoy, 56; **13** Saito, 53; **14** Aoki, 43; **15** Bodelier, 41; **16** Gresini, 40; **17** Koch, 30; **18** Scalvini, 27; **19** Giro, 26; **20** Manako, 24; **21** Prein, 17; **22** Alzamora, 16; **23** Casanova, 15; **24** Debbia, 11; **25** Geissler, 9; **26** Cuppini, 7; **27** Igata and Locatelli, 6; **29** Amano, Katoh and Maturana, 4; **32** Cecchinello, 3; **33** Petit, 2.

Neil Hodgson *(above)* scored his first-ever World Championship point in his first 500 outing on Emmett's vacant Shell-backed Harris Yamaha.

Teams rented 'luxury motorhomes' – the term was relative.

Photos: Gold & Goose

WORLD CHAMPIONSHIP • ROUND 14

EUROPEAN GRAND PRIX

500 cc	CADALORA
250 cc	BIAGGI
125 cc	RAUDIES

Biaggi *(below)* and Okada *(right)* were seldom close on the track, but ended up in a close final showdown.

'Usually I am at about four-and-a-half out of ten. Now six. Or maybe seven'

Max Biaggi on pre-race nerves

Floods in Barcelona. Placid streams turn to raging torrents, flotsam scours the banks. Lives are lost. Property is devastated. Roads are blocked. The racing circuit of Catalunya is rendered unridable. Knots of disconsolate people gather in the pits.

Thankfully, these events took place the day after the European GP, final showdown of the 1994 season. The only floods on race day were of Italian emotion – at Cadalora's victory, at Cagiva's imminent withdrawal. And, of course, for Massimiliano Biaggi's max-risk race win that gave him his first World Championship. Floods of champagne too, of course, with dapper Max – image carefully reworked for the occasion, with a new Vandyke goatee and moustache – drenched on the all-Italian 250 rostrum by bitter rivals but now (if temporarily) warm compatriots Capirossi and Romboni.

The last contest of the year had been resolved poetically, heroically and justly: Aprilia deserved their first 250 championship. Max was cockahoop; his last rival, Tadayuki Okada, dourly dignified in defeat. And it was all over bar the contracts.

Some of them didn't last much longer either, in a weekend of considerable turmoil. John Kocinski was released from his Cagiva contract shortly after the 500 race, during which he'd lost his chance of second overall, and after which he'd delivered stinging criticism of his too-slow bike. All a prelude to Cagiva's imminent withdrawal from GP racing. The day before his manager/girlfriend Toti Latorre had insisted that John had been offered a GP ride for 1995; now he looked stunned and started job-hunting, an activity that many of the Italian crew had already begun days or even weeks ago.

Job-hunting! Chandler was hovering round Team Marlboro Roberts, waiting to see if Luca Cadalora was going to stay on – the double race winner was hoping for a Honda ride instead next year. Romboni, in his last HB Honda 250 outing, had apparently already been met with enthusiasm at Aprilia, only to have the move blocked by Biaggi. Then there was Alex Barros, let go by Suzuki, also after the race. In his place slotted Daryl Beattie, rescued after an awful season (seven non-finishes with mechanical or tyre problems) to join Schwantz in next year's assault. And Ruggia, who already knew this was his last Aprilia race, and that Bayle would get the second team ride.

Goodbyes, also, from veterans Marco Papa and Hans Spaan, retiring at 37 and 36 respectively – Papa a racing journeyman who never quite made the big time and lost many years punting the Paton around, Spaan twice a 125 title contender.

The shrinking riders' pool was mirrored by a reduced number of bikes for next year. Word came at Catalunya that the GP Manufacturers' Association had agreed to IRTA's so-called cost-cutting plan of one bike per rider in the smaller classes. This was immediately challenged by a formal statement from Aprilia on Sunday, condemning the decision on grounds of safety, among other things, because they felt teams might rush repairs to a damaged bike to get the rider back out again. Their argument was cogent, but cynics also pointed across the paddock to where the 1995 privateer 125 and 250 Aprilias were on display and orders were being sought.

But the spirit of renewal was not entirely absent. For one thing, the V-twin Aprilia 400 was back; likewise Loris Reggiani, who confirmed his reputation as paddock jester by cruising around wearing a Chesterfield headscarf knotted under his chin washerwoman style – a jibe at Biaggi's piratical bandanna. But 'Reg Varney' had done something slightly farcical on his own account, which spoiled the last showing of the challenge to the V4s, fresh from testing while missing the last five races. The weekend before, racing saloon cars at Misano, he'd overturned and hurt his shoulder. As a result he couldn't give of his best in practice, and pulled in early during the race.

HRC evoked positive spirits with another of their unexpected moments of formal frankness, revealing that for two years they have been experimenting not only with electronic suspension, but also water injection. The suspension, developed by Showa, is less radical. Team Roberts flirted with an Ohlins version (named CES) three years ago, without much success, while Cagiva had such a bad time with an early version of Showa's black-box damping last year that it was a factor in their decision to switch to Ohlins. The

Photos: Gold & Goose

155

EUROPEAN GRAND PRIX

Sean Emmett, ahead of Niall Mackenzie, chases Daryl Beattie. Soon afterwards, he pushed too hard and fell.

news is that HRC seemed to have it working much better now – Criville rode it to fourth in the race – and plan an even more sophisticated version for the near future. Even the current version could be pre-programmed, with the rider having the option of various set responses via a handlebar switch.

The water-injection system is an additional method of fine-tuning exhaust responses to broaden the powerband. HRC men claimed that it filled in a slump in the power curve, at around 8000 rpm; but Doohan insisted the major difference was 'having to carry a four-litre water tank on the bike'.

Doohan, meanwhile, was also hoping to get fixed. He flew to San Francisco on Monday, for further surgery and Ilazaroff treatment to his right leg in the hope that it would restore more movement to the ankle than had previously been thought possible.

The other light on the horizon came, appropriately enough, from the furthest reaches of the paddock – the place to which the sidecars were banished. Rolf Biland, having already won the title, chose Catalunya for the GP debut of his own new Swissauto engine. This is a single-crank (Honda-style) V4 with a lot of promise for solo privateers as well as for the three-wheelers. Biland claimed 175 bhp from the 108-degree motor even without exhaust powervalves, let alone water injection. He qualified better than a second ahead of the rest, as usual, and was leading the race when forced to retire with ignition failure. The new motor weighs 36 kg, six less than the Yamaha motor currently available to 500 class privateers, and already both Harris and LCR (sidecar chassis makers who earlier built MBA and monocoque Krauser frames for solos) were looking at building chassis to house the new engine. Coming at the close of a year when confidence in the future of racing was shaky, at best, a lifeline from the sidecars was the richest of ironies.

IRTA's ability to bend their own rules to help their favourites reached new heights. The main beneficiary was again Serge Rosset, who just happens to be IRTA vice-president: he was permitted an unprecedented fifth rider change for his Team Roc entry. The bike was first ridden by Julian Miralles, then Udo Mark, followed by Michael Liedl, Chuck Graves – and now Andrew Stroud, the versatile Kiwi having a first GP of the year, partly as a shakedown run for a planned attack on the Macau GP for Rosset.

There had also been some convolutions on the way to getting Juan Lopez Mella out on a third Lucky Strike Suzuki. This happened at the behest of the Spanish branch of Lucky Strike; the team, meanwhile, were not inclined to dump Schwantz replacement Sean Emmett at the say-so of some local cigarette salesman. A compromise was worked out whereby Lopez Mella's usual Roc went to a wild card rider, who thus became a regular replacement rider – freeing Lopez Mella to take on the Suzuki, as a wild card. If you follow. Not many people did, especially when the wild card who formed a vital link in the equation turned out not to exist.

500 cc PRACTICE

Cadalora's flowing style suits this swooping track of almost continuous looping bends, and his fourth pole of the year came with assurance, after he had also led the first day of practice. His usual serenity was tested to the maximum in the last minutes, however, when he was obliged by a broken on-board rear suspension adjuster to sit in the pits and watch as Doohan moved to within hundredths, and Kocinski also nudged within spitting distance. The race would be close, opined the Italian; but he knew he had a good chance. His time hadn't come using soft-compound tyres. 'The front that worked best was harder,' he said. 'It will be perfect for the race.'

Doohan had spent the last session engaged in beautifully controlled power-slides out of the bends ('That's what we'll be doing in the race'), then put on a new rear tyre for a hot lap in the last three minutes. With the title already in his pocket, he'd departed from his usual conservatism to use new equipment – specifically Honda's exhaust water-injection system. He admitted he'd tried it from time to time over the past two seasons, but wouldn't be drawn on its merits, beyond saying: 'If you look at the top speed times, you'll see what effect it has.' (In the session he referred to, he was the slowest of the NSRs.) In mellower mood than usual, he added: 'We're treating these last races as test sessions for next year.'

He was within two-hundredths of Cadalora; Kocinski another three-tenths adrift, speeding up in the final session and insisting that Luca must have used soft tyres. 'This track is hard on tyres because you're leaned over such a long time. You need a lot of side grip; that's what qualifiers give you.'

Puig was the last man on the front row, under half a second down on the Cagiva, but it took the local man time to get there after a hatful of suspension changes. 'We've tested here twice already this year, but it is a difficult circuit, and we had problems on the first day. I think we've overcome them now.'

Row two saw his countryman and fellow-Honda-riding rival Criville in charge, with the gaps growing wider – Alex was more than half a second adrift. He was still troubled by his hand injury: 'Not because it is painful, but because we've adjusted the handlebar angle to relieve my hand, and that makes my arm very tired.' Criville was running Honda's latest programmable rear suspension. 'It's for sure better than the old suspension,' he said.

Beattie was in sixth, within hundredths of Criville, but still as worried in his last race on the Yamaha as he was in his first, at the start of the year. 'The rear is okay, but we've tried heaps of fronts, and it's still pushing.'

Itoh came next, three-tenths down, after a spill in the last session meant he was without his better bike in the crucial closing minutes. He was not hurt, but the crash was spectacular, with the bike somersaulting to destruction in the gravel trap, although the Japanese rider insisted: 'Only the parts that stick out were damaged.'

With many riders complaining of worsening ripple-bumps, brought up by the F1 cars, suspension was another key. Chandler, over half a second slower at the end of row two, was struggling. 'I've been trying to get a good balance, but it just doesn't feel right. Yesterday I was just trying to get the wheels to stay on the road; today it's a little better but if I get into the corners the speed I want to it runs wide.'

Barros led row three, far from happy as his form remained elusive right to the end of the season. He grinned, when asked about some lurid slides: 'I'm riding Kevin's bike, Kevin's style.' His only hope was that his tyre endurance testing would pay dividends.

John Reynolds was alongside and less than two-tenths slower, happy that his rhythmical riding was working well on the continual Catalun-yan swoops. Then came Emmett, on the second-best Suzuki, promising that he'd be faster in the race. 'I always am. It's something to do with the red mist,' he said.

Mackenzie was the last of the British trio, and three-tenths adrift after losing time in the final session with a broken sparking plug.

Bernard Garcia led row four from McWilliams, Roc first-timer Stroud, and Frenchman Jeandat.

There were no wild cards, and 30 qualifiers. Marco Papa was 28th, in the last GP of a 19-year career.

500 cc RACE – 25 LAPS

For the first eight laps, it was the closest race of the year, with six bikes packed together up front. The reason was Puig, who took a flier off the front row, and stayed in front by dint of his late braking. His corner speeds were relatively slow, hence the high-speed train behind him.

Kocinski was second for two laps, then Itoh came past, followed by Cadalora and Doohan. With few overtaking places, it took each of them another lap to do it.

Puig's glory was soon to fade. He succumbed to Cadalora at the start of lap nine, then tried to get back inside him a little further on, only to run wide. Doohan slipped through inside at once, followed by Kocinski and Criville. Now Puig was fifth, and then, with his right forearm again proving troublesome, he really started going backwards so that he ended up seventh. Itoh had already dropped to the rear of the group, after a slip on lap seven.

Up front, Doohan shadowed Cadalora, looking challenging, just half a second adrift. Then, on the 14th lap, rain started spotting his screen, and soon afterwards slippery spots began to appear on the track. 'I was wondering if they were waiting for some crashes before they stopped the race,' he said later. 'But Luca didn't slow down at all. Maybe he had such a dark face shield he didn't notice.'

Now unchallenged, Luca carried on pulling away, to win his second race of the season by four seconds. As he'd always promised, when he felt that the bike was right, he'd ride to 100 per cent. 'I took some risks when it started raining,' he said, 'but I just didn't care about it.'

Doohan raced the water-injection system, but was polite enough not to blame it for the fact that, for once, he didn't have a big speed advantage over the Yamaha. He did secure

EUROPEAN GRAND PRIX

Works rider for a day: Juan Lopez Mella rode the spare Suzuki to a steady 13th.

Far left: In between jokes, the injured Reggiani looked glum. The Aprilia 400's final failure of the year was all his fault.

Below: Mackenzie's last chance to get among the works bikes started well, but he ran into tyre problems.

Photos: Gold & Goose

157

EUROPEAN GRAND PRIX

After the Max: Romboni, Capirossi, Okada and Harada chase Biaggi as he starts to break away.

The 125 battle *(right)* was even closer: Martinez leads Ueda, Tsujimura, Raudies and Öttl.

fastest lap, but almost a second short of his own lap record.

From half-distance, Criville and Kocinski had been battling over third. John was clearly working hard, the Cagiva short of speed on the long straight so that he was obliged time and again to recoup lost ground by late braking, at least once so late that he promptly ran wide and let the Honda back through.

They went back and forth right to the finish, and almost once too often. Kocinski was in front as they started the last lap; Criville came close to outbraking him at the first chicane. He was still on his back wheel as they reached the end of the back straight, and he tried again. But this time he was too late on a patch that was still damp. The front slid, he ran into Kocinski's back wheel, and both came close to crashing.

Kocinski crossed the line a second ahead, and though he forgave Criville ('That's racing, and this is Spain'), he was far from happy. 'Cagiva didn't come up with a bike that was fast enough. I'd get a gap on Criville, but the problem was making it to the end of the straight without him coming by again.'

Criville, for his part, complained that his injured arm made braking difficult. 'On the last lap he shut the door on me. We were lucky not to crash. But he was luckier because he got to the next corner first.'

Beattie, Barros, Itoh and Puig had been disputing fifth in desultory style some way behind. The Australian led into the last lap and, at the end of it; Itoh went flying off the track behind Barros, falling heavily but escaping without serious injury.

Puig took seventh, four seconds adrift, with Mackenzie eighth. He'd been glued to Barros's back wheel for the first part of the race, but lost ground from half-distance with his front tyre ruined.

Bernard Garcia had dropped away to head a four-strong group for ninth. He'd been caught in the closing stages by Chandler, who had an awful last race on the Cagiva. 'No excuses. I didn't have the right set-up on the bike, and I had problems with the tyres sliding from the start.'

He just managed to fend off Reynolds, the British Harris rider less than a tenth away after another strong race. McWilliams also closed up in the last laps, and was another three-tenths behind.

Temporary Suzuki rider Lopez Mella was 13th, heading a group who had been battling all race long: with Naveau 14th, Stroud 15th and Neil Hodgson 16th, just out of the points. There were 20 finishers.

As well as Itoh, Scatola and Emmett crashed. The Briton had been up with Beattie and Barros in the early stages but lost the front wheel of the Suzuki after six laps.

Doohan could hardly improve his championship position, but second place did make him the first rider ever to score more than 300 points. Luca's win gave him second overall, two points ahead of Kocinski, and both ahead of race spectator Schwantz. Puig headed the next quartet from Criville, Itoh and Barros.

250 cc PRACTICE

The climax of the year approached amid full tension. There was hardly a rider among the top ten who didn't have an angle on the final showdown between Biaggi and Okada, whether through personal animosity or brand loyalty. Okada could count on the most support, from Honda colleagues Capirossi, Romboni and possibly even Waldmann, with the first two also bearing grudges against Max. Biaggi, apart from the questionable back-up of his French team-mates, Ruggia and Bayle, had only the possible support of Harada, who would prefer to remain as the only Japanese 250 World Champion.

Early on, it looked as though Max might need help; by the end it had all changed. Biaggi put on soft tyres in the last session, and moved from fifth on day one to pole by the end, three-tenths ahead of the rest.

Okada, meanwhile, was one of only four riders who failed to improve, and dropped from fourth overall to a lowly tenth, on the third row of the grid. Since his best chance required a race win, he would surely have his work cut out.

Biaggi admitted that his time was not repeatable for the whole race, and said he would drop his usual 'go-for-it' tactics in favour of a defensive approach, watching Okada. If the Honda came through, he would simply sit on his tail. And how nervous was he, on a scale of one to ten? 'Usually I am at about four-and-a-half. Now six. Or maybe seven.'

Hondas filled the front row: Romboni, Capirossi and Aoki, with a half-second spread of times. All had their own reasons for preferring not to get involved in the title battle. Romboni, sponsorless next year, was anxious for a victory to prove his worth; Capirossi wanted to win what he expected would be his last 250 race; Aoki's aim was to achieve his first podium of the year at his favourite European circuit.

Spaniard Luis D'Antin was fifth fastest, but was out after breaking his collarbone on Saturday morning. The injury had been plated previously, and the plate was bent. He had it replated on Saturday night so as to race on Sunday, but it proved impossible.

Thus the Chesterfield Aprilia pair of Ruggia and Bayle led the row, with Carlos Checa alongside, the Honda privateer running stronger and stronger as the season closes. Then came Harada, moving up from rows three to two courtesy of D'Antin, his qualifying effort spoiled when the temperatures dropped in the final session and he didn't have the tyres he needed.

Thus Okada led row three, a position from which only a lightning start might rescue him. He still insisted he was 'very relaxed' – but there was plenty of tension in the Team Kanemoto pit, where they couldn't get either of his bikes to work right on the second day. The problem persisted on Sunday – he ran warm-up with two different set-ups, then made a race bike out of a combination of the two.

Kenny Roberts Junior was alongside, then Waldmann and Bosshard.

All 35 entrants qualified: wild card Miguel Castilla (leading the Ducados Open Championship) was an impressive 16th on a TZ Yamaha; Luis Maurel, who had leased an NSR for the weekend in place of his usual RS Honda, still qualified in his usual place of 20th.

250 cc RACE – 23 LAPS

Okada's start was superb: he was fourth by the time they got to the first corner. Capirossi was leading from Biaggi and Aoki, with Romboni coming up, soon to pass fast starter Checa; Harada likewise from a bit further back.

Soon this sextet was in control, though the first ten remained in close company. Aoki was gradually losing ground, though, and was back to seventh behind Ruggia on the ninth lap. Trying too hard to get back up, he promptly crashed unhurt.

Now the leading five started to break away, Ruggia unable to hold the pace. The focus was on Biaggi and Okada.

Max had been shadowing Capirossi, and outbraked him at the end of the straight on lap six to take the lead. Romboni promptly followed him past, and the pair broke away for a while. Lap speeds were still relatively slow, but they were so close that it seemed highly likely that they might collide. Nervous watchers recalled Romboni's grudge after being nearly knocked off on the last lap at the Hockenheimring.

At this point, Okada was fourth. He slipped underneath Capirossi at the end of lap nine, and started to close. By lap 11 the first five were nose-to-tail again; and by lap 12 Okada was second.

Now came the attack. The Japanese rider found an unusual place to get past Biaggi after the last left, and led lap 13.

The next lap was hectic. Max passed him back on the straight, the Aprilia visibly faster. Okada stuck with him, and moved ahead again into the last left, to cross the line in the lead again. But Max had swerved right onto the other side of the track for the full run down the straight, and powered away from his surprised rivals as if he had one more gear, making perfectly sure nobody could catch his slipstream.

'At first I was calm and I wanted to wait for Okada. But he came past me so quickly and the others were so close that I realised I must think again. I knew that if another rider passed me I would lose the title,' he explained later. Thus he switched back to his usual Mad Max mode. 'I risked everything because that was the only way I was going to win.'

Riding on the limit, he immediately stretched away so that, at the end of lap 21, he had an advantage of better than four seconds – enough to indulge in wheel-popping antics on the last lap, and still win by almost two seconds – a well-deserved champion.

If the other Honda riders had been trying to help Okada, there was no point now, and they started scrapping harder. Romboni moved to second ahead of the Japanese rider on lap 17; two laps later Capirossi dived underneath both of them and, though Romboni was ahead again for the next two laps, Capirossi was not to be denied at least second in his last 250 race, breaking the lap record on the last lap. Remarkably, he said later that he had run much of the race without fifth gear.

Romboni held his position, his tyres sliding by the finish; and Okada was fourth, just four-tenths behind, the Honda trio crossing the line just over a second apart.

Okada's problem was side grip on the Michelins, which meant he couldn't get the power on as early as his rivals. He was dignified in defeat. 'I was at my maximum when I passed Biaggi, and when he started to pull away there was nothing I could do. I did my best today, so I'm not too disappointed. I'll use the experience positively for next season.'

Harada was just over a second down in fifth; Ruggia almost 15 seconds away in a lonely sixth. In the closing stages Waldmann had come closer, but not close enough. He finished three seconds down, with Bayle less than a tenth behind, as he had been for much of the race.

Checa had a strong ride after his good start, holding off Bosshard's NSR on his kitted RS. Then came Roberts Junior in 11th, after a storming ride from the back. He'd been delayed by Cardoso, who had high-sided in the first corner; then he'd run off into the gravel himself on lap two, trying to make up time, rejoining in last place. He moved steadily and impressively through to the points.

Zeelenberg was 12th, Maurel on his rented NSR just managing to beat Castilla's stock TZ Yamaha for 13th, with Andy Preining narrowly ahead of Fiorillo's Honda to take the last point.

As well as Cardoso and Aoki, Suter also crashed out, while lying 12th. There were 25 finishers.

Biaggi won the title by 20 points from Okada; Capirossi was third. Then came Romboni, Waldmann, Ruggia and Harada, with Bayle moving past D'Antin to claim ninth.

125 cc RACE – 22 LAPS

After the thrills of Argentina, the 125s had an even better race to close the season. The sheer size of the leading group was not surprising, with 17 riders qualifying within one second, and the spectacle was superb.

The lap chart showed five different leaders, but didn't tell the whole story. There were others who only led for part of a lap, in one of the biggest brawls many people could remember.

One such was Carlos Giro, who led much of the first lap, only to finish up seventh. Worse was to come when he was docked one minute for jumping the start.

Most of the leaders were predictable: Raudies; Aprilia stars Perugini and Öttl (who took the lap record on the third lap); and Martinez's Yamaha. Maik Stief (Aprilia) also had a lap and a bit of glory, before crashing while trying to regain the position.

Perugini had a wild time – a near high-sider on lap eight sent him running across the gravel. He then rejoined in 19th and set about a superlative recovery ride to fourth by lap 17, passing 15 riders in nine laps.

There were only 12 left in the front group by lap 15, and two laps later four riders made a slight break: Öttl leading Martinez, Raudies and the amazing Perugini, whose bike was plainly down on speed. So too was Martinez's, with both making up chunks under braking.

The last lap was decisive. Raudies led at the start, the rest all packed together. At the top of the hill Perugini moved outside Öttl and then tried to dive inside Martinez. He failed, and two bends later had a second high-sider. This one threw him off.

The final act was on the last two bends. Raudies was ahead, Martinez tried to swoop past outside of him. He succeeded, but was on the paint. The bike slewed gradually sideways, then threw him violently. Afterwards he said Raudies had hit him, but the German denied it – and it didn't look like it on the TV monitors either.

Thus Raudies won his third race of the year, with Öttl three seconds down at the end in second. Aoki Junior narrowly took third from Tsujimura (both Honda), with Petrucciani's Aprilia four seconds down. Then came Ueda, fighting for second in the championship, and only two-tenths ahead of Sakata, Nakajyo, Bodelier, Gresini and Scalvini, just over a second covering from sixth to 11th.

Ueda thus saved second from Tsujimura by four points, while Raudies's win took him past Öttl to be top European by two points. Martinez was sixth and Perugini seventh after a brilliant first season.

FIM WORLD CHAMPIONSHIP • ROUND 14
EUROPEAN GRAND PRIX
9 October 1994

500 cc

25 laps, 73.725 miles/118.675 km

Place	Rider	Nat.	Machine	Laps	Time & speed	Fastest lap	Lap
1	Luca Cadalora	I	Yamaha	25	46m 03.356s 96.067 mph/ 154.605 km/h	1m 49.498s	12
2	Michael Doohan	AUS	Honda	25	46m 06.844s	1m 49.452s	11
3	John Kocinski	USA	Cagiva	25	46m 09.922s	1m 49.944s	7
4	Alex Criville	E	Honda	25	46m 10.842s	1m 49.866s	12
5	Daryl Beattie	AUS	Yamaha	25	46m 22.093s	1m 50.065s	9
6	Alexandre Barros	BR	Suzuki	25	46m 23.350s	1m 50.653s	24
7	Alberto Puig	E	Honda	25	46m 27.884s	1m 50.192s	7
8	Niall Mackenzie	GB	Yamaha	25	46m 38.334s	1m 50.170s	7
9	Bernard Garcia	F	Yamaha	25	46m 58.256s	1m 51.706s	6
10	Doug Chandler	USA	Cagiva	25	46m 59.284s	1m 50.911s	4
11	John Reynolds	GB	Yamaha	25	46m 59.343s	1m 51.446s	3
12	Jeremy McWilliams	GB	Yamaha	25	46m 59.634s	1m 51.682s	12
13	Juan Lopez Mella	E	Suzuki	25	47m 14.196s	1m 51.889s	11
14	Laurent Naveau	B	Yamaha	25	47m 14.314s	1m 52.188s	12
15	Andrew Stroud	NZ	Yamaha	25	47m 14.415s	1m 52.012s	9
16	Neil Hodgson	GB	Yamaha	25	47m 14.637s	1m 52.185s	11
17	Jean-Pierre Jeandat	F	Yamaha	25	47m 14.730s	1m 52.035s	11
18	Cristiano Migliorati	I	Yamaha	25	47m 37.295s	1m 52.287s	9
19	Cees Doorakkers	NL	Yamaha	24	46m 36.752s	1m 53.982s	4
20	Bernard Hänggeli	CH	Yamaha	24	46m 39.248s	1m 53.998s	4
	Shinichi Itoh	J	Honda	24	DNF	1m 50.015s	3
	Bruno Bonhuil	F	Yamaha	19	DNF	1m 54.306s	5
	Marco Papa	I	Yamaha	15	DNF	1m 55.762s	3
	Marc Garcia	F	Yamaha	12	DNF	1m 52.657s	6
	Loris Reggiani	I	Aprilia	8	DNF	1m 51.816s	4
	Kevin Mitchell	GB	Yamaha	7	DNF	1m 56.199s	2
	Lucio Pedercini	I	Yamaha	7	DNF	1m 54.069s	6
	Sean Emmett	GB	Suzuki	6	DNF	1m 50.740s	6
	Vittorio Scatola	I	Paton	6	DNF	1m 55.737s	5
	Andreas Leuthe	D	Yamaha	5	DNF	1m 58.143s	4

Fastest lap: Doohan, 1m 49.452s, 97.017 mph/156.134 km/h.
Lap record: Michael Doohan, AUS (Honda), 1m 48.583s, 97.794 mph/157.384 km/h (1992).

Qualifying: 1 Cadalora, 1m 47.918s; 2 Doohan, 1m 47.934s; 3 Kocinski, 1m 48.264s; 4 Puig, 1m 48.641s; 5 Criville, 1m 49.226s; 6 Beattie, 1m 49.262s; 7 Itoh, 1m 49.591s; 8 Chandler, 1m 50.102s; 9 Barros, 1m 50.495s; 10 Reynolds, 1m 50.668s; 11 Emmett, 1m 50.951s; 12 Mackenzie, 1m 51.228s; 13 B. Garcia, 1m 51.408s; 14 McWilliams, 1m 51.446s; 15 Stroud, 1m 51.509s; 16 Jeandat, 1m 51.693s; 17 Naveau, 1m 51.796s; 18 Lopez Mella, 1m 51.830s; 19 Reggiani, 1m 51.840s; 20 Hodgson, 1m 51.991s; 21 M. Garcia, 1m 52.790s; 22 Hänggeli, 1m 52.939s; 23 Pedercini, 1m 53.352s; 24 Migliorati, 1m 53.424s; 25 Bonhuil, 1m 53.863s; 26 Doorakkers, 1m 54.117s; 27 Mitchell, 1m 55.947s; 28 Papa, 1m 56.641s; 29 Scatola, 1m 56.904s; 30 Leuthe, 1m 57.604s.

Final 500 cc World Championship points: see pages 162-3.

250 cc

23 laps, 67.827 miles/109.181 km

Place	Rider	Nat.	Machine	Laps	Time & speed	Fastest lap	Lap
1	Massimiliano Biaggi	I	Aprilia	23	42m 44.818s 95.223 mph/ 153.247 km/h	1m 50.494s	19
2	Loris Capirossi	I	Honda	23	42m 46.758s	1m 50.362s	23
3	Doriano Romboni	I	Honda	23	42m 47.426s	1m 50.756s	17
4	Tadayuki Okada	J	Honda	23	42m 47.874s	1m 50.746s	10
5	Tetsuya Harada	J	Yamaha	23	42m 49.047s	1m 50.447s	10
6	Jean-Philippe Ruggia	F	Aprilia	23	43m 03.311s	1m 50.992s	8
7	Ralf Waldmann	D	Honda	23	43m 06.886s	1m 51.708s	7
8	Jean-Michel Bayle	F	Aprilia	23	43m 06.968s	1m 51.570s	8
9	Carlos Checa	E	Honda	23	43m 15.975s	1m 51.794s	7
10	Adrian Bosshard	CH	Honda	23	43m 16.856s	1m 51.793s	7
11	Kenny Roberts Jnr	USA	Yamaha	23	43m 19.141s	1m 51.094s	19
12	Wilco Zeelenberg	NL	Honda	23	43m 24.723s	1m 52.352s	15
13	Luis Maurel	E	Honda	23	43m 41.416s	1m 52.700s	6
14	Miguel Castilla	E	Yamaha	23	43m 41.554s	1m 52.706s	7
15	Andy Preining	A	Aprilia	23	43m 44.328s	1m 52.746s	7
16	Giuseppe Fiorillo	I	Honda	23	43m 44.430s	1m 53.260s	22
17	Jurgen van den Goorbergh	NL	Aprilia	23	43m 50.381s	1m 52.576s	6
18	Juan Borja	E	Honda	23	43m 54.042s	1m 53.278s	12
19	Adi Stadler	D	Honda	23	43m 54.090s	1m 53.234s	3
20	Jurgen Fuchs	D	Honda	23	43m 54.123s	1m 53.236s	12
21	Mañuel Gibernau	E	Yamaha	23	43m 54.354s	1m 53.393s	5
22	Patrick van den Goorbergh	NL	Aprilia	23	44m 07.491s	1m 53.104s	9
23	Enrique de Juan	E	Aprilia	23	44m 25.350s	1m 54.711s	5
24	James Haydon	GB	Honda	23	44m 32.908s	1m 54.463s	6
25	Kristian Kaas	SF	Yamaha	22	42m 49.414s	1m 55.068s	5
	Eskil Suter	CH	Aprilia	16	DNF	1m 52.160s	5
	Frédéric Protat	F	Honda	13	DNF	1m 52.948s	4
	Noel Ferro	F	Honda	10	DNF	1m 53.913s	2
	Nobuatsu Aoki	J	Honda	9	DNF	1m 51.183s	9
	Rodney Fee	CAN	Honda	9	DNF	1m 56.422s	2
	Manuel Hernandez	E	Aprilia	5	DNF	1m 56.520s	3
	Alessandro Gramigni	I	Aprilia	4	DNF	1m 54.971s	2
	Christian Boudinot	F	Aprilia	1	DNF	2m 04.374s	1
	José Luis Cardoso	E	Aprilia	0	DNF		
	Luis D'Antin	E	Honda		DNS		

Fastest lap: Capirossi, 1m 50.362s, 96.217 mph/154.847 km/h (record).
Previous record: Loris Reggiani, I (Aprilia), 1m 51.304s, 95.403 mph/153.536 km/h (1992).

Qualifying: 1 Biaggi, 1m 49.942s; 2 Romboni, 1m 50.273s; 3 Capirossi, 1m 50.685s; 4 Aoki, 1m 50.730s; 5 D'Antin, 1m 51.148s; 6 Ruggia, 1m 51.239s; 7 Bayle, 1m 51.244s; 8 Checa, 1m 51.268s; 9 Harada, 1m 51.273s; 10 Okada, 1m 51.287s; 11 Roberts Jnr, 1m 51.429s; 12 Waldmann, 1m 51.560s; 13 Bosshard, 1m 51.808s; 14 Suter, 1m 51.811s; 15 Zeelenberg, 1m 52.291s; 16 Castilla, 1m 52.446s; 17 J. van den Goorbergh, 1m 52.521s; 18 Borja, 1m 52.773s; 19 Fiorillo, 1m 52.776s; 20 Maurel, 1m 52.899s; 21 Fuchs, 1m 52.984s; 22 Protat, 1m 53.033s; 23 Preining, 1m 53.082s; 24 Gibernau, 1m 53.649s; 25 Cardoso, 1m 53.691s; 26 Ferro, 1m 53.949s; 27 Haydon, 1m 53.980s; 28 Stadler, 1m 54.009s; 29 P. van den Goorbergh, 1m 54.371s; 30 Kaas, 1m 54.393s; 31 Gramigni, 1m 54.793s; 32 Boudinot, 1m 55.615s; 33 Fee, 1m 56.356s; 34 de Juan, 1m 56.380s; 35 Hernandez, 1m 56.665s.

Final 250 cc World Championship points: see pages 162-3.

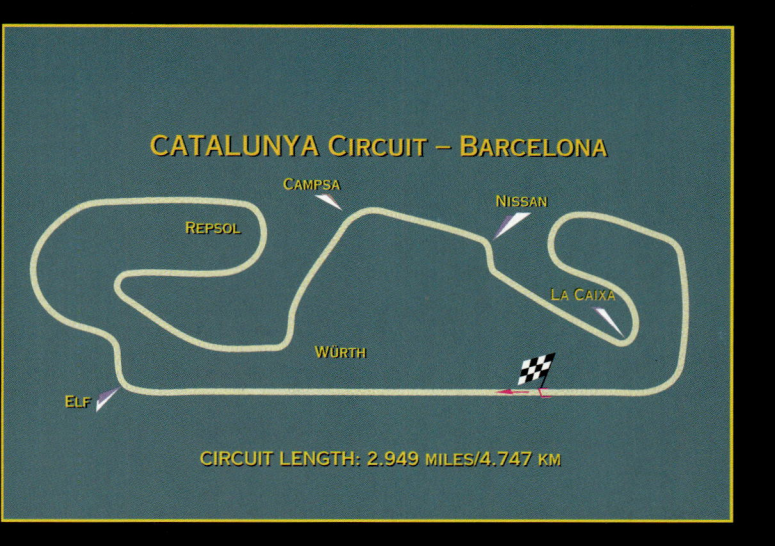

CATALUNYA CIRCUIT – BARCELONA

Campsa, Nissan, Repsol, La Caixa, Würth, Elf

CIRCUIT LENGTH: 2.949 MILES/4.747 KM

The exciting Perugini proved he'd come of age in his first GP season.

125 cc

22 laps, 64.878 miles/104.434 km

Place	Rider	Nat.	Machine	Laps	Time & speed	Fastest lap	Lap
1	Dirk Raudies	D	Honda	22	43m 26.974s 89.610 mph/ 144.214 km/h	1m 57.118s	18
2	Peter Öttl	D	Aprilia	22	43m 29.111s	1m 56.514s	3
3	Haruchika Aoki	J	Honda	22	43m 31.930s	1m 57.178s	11
4	Takeshi Tsujimura	J	Honda	22	43m 31.975s	1m 57.244s	3
5	Oliver Petrucciani	CH	Aprilia	22	43m 35.753s	1m 57.328s	11
6	Noboru Ueda	J	Honda	22	43m 39.465s	1m 56.832s	3
7	Kazuto Sakata	J	Aprilia	22	43m 39.617s	1m 57.359s	2
8	Hideyuki Nakajyo	J	Honda	22	43m 39.653s	1m 57.666s	8
9	Loek Bodelier	NL	Honda	22	43m 39.838s	1m 56.885s	11
10	Fausto Gresini	I	Honda	22	43m 39.938s	1m 57.329s	10
11	Gianluigi Scalvini	I	Aprilia	22	43m 40.088s	1m 57.386s	8
12	Yoshiaki Katoh	J	Yamaha	22	43m 45.777s	1m 56.840s	8
13	Masaki Tokudome	J	Honda	22	44m 07.615s	1m 58.068s	3
14	Lucio Cecchinello	I	Honda	22	44m 10.090s	1m 59.124s	19
15	Tomoko Igata	J	Honda	22	44m 10.100s	1m 59.096s	20
16	Vittorio Lopez	I	Honda	22	44m 22.902s	1m 58.874s	3
17	Luis Alvaro	E	Yamaha	22	44m 23.075s	1m 59.547s	5
18	Darren Barton	GB	Honda	22	44m 23.172s	1m 59.272s	14
19	Antonio Sanchez	E	Honda	22	44m 23.850s	1m 59.713s	14
20	Manfred Geissler	D	Aprilia	22	44m 31.330s	1m 58.455s	3
21	Stefan Prein	D	Yamaha	22	44m 39.720s	1m 57.446s	10
22	Frédéric Petit	F	Yamaha	22	44m 40.264s	1m 57.716s	8
23	Hans Spaan	NL	Honda	22	44m 45.241s	2m 00.656s	21
24	Max Gambino	I	Aprilia	22	44m 49.390s	2m 00.179s	2
25	Yasuaki Takahashi	J	Honda	22	45m 12.908s	2m 01.535s	11
	Jorge Martinez	E	Yamaha	21	DNF	1m 57.094s	18
	Stefano Perugini	I	Aprilia	21	DNF	1m 56.890s	19
	Herri Torrontegui	E	Aprilia	17	DNF	1m 57.086s	9
	Gabriele Debbia	I	Honda	14	DNF	1m 57.732s	7
	Maik Stief	D	Aprilia	13	DNF	1m 57.004s	8
	Nicolas Dussauge	F	Honda	11	DNF	1m 59.750s	10
	Carlos Giro	E	Aprilia	8	DNF	1m 56.970s	8
	Akira Saito	J	Honda	7	DNF	2m 00.632s	2
	Manfred Baumann	A	Yamaha	6	DNF	1m 59.358s	5
	Emili Alzamora	E	Honda	4	DNF	1m 57.762s	3
	Oliver Koch	D	Honda	0	DNF		

Fastest lap: Öttl, 1m 56.514s, 91.137 mph/146.671 km/h (record).
Previous record: Ralf Waldmann, D (Aprilia), 1m 57.230s, 90.580 mph/145.775 km/h (1993).

Qualifying: 1 Raudies, 1m 56.673s; 2 Perugini, 1m 56.684s; 3 Tokudome, 1m 56.821s; 4 Martinez, 1m 56.873s; 5 Tsujimura, 1m 56.952s; 6 Öttl, 1m 57.180s; 7 Sakata, 1m 57.225s; 8 Ueda, 1m 57.226s; 9 Katoh, 1m 57.261s; 10 Giro, 1m 57.320s; 11 Stief, 1m 57.330s; 12 Scalvini, 1m 57.341s; 13 Alzamora, 1m 57.348s; 14 Prein, 1m 57.360s; 15 Gresini, 1m 57.376s; 16 Petrucciani, 1m 57.528s; 17 Aoki, 1m 57.538s; 18 Nakajyo, 1m 57.745s; 19 Petit, 1m 57.926s; 20 Geissler, 1m 57.973s; 21 Cecchinello, 1m 58.174s; 22 Debbia, 1m 58.297s; 23 Bodelier, 1m 58.326s; 24 Baumann, 1m 58.502s; 25 Koch, 1m 58.549s; 26 Igata, 1m 58.606s; 27 Alvaro, 1m 58.734s; 28 Saito, 1m 58.801s; 29 Torrontegui, 1m 59.000s; 30 Sanchez, 1m 59.017s; 31 Barton, 1m 59.241s; 32 Dussauge, 1m 59.634s; 33 Lopez, 1m 59.635s; 34 Gambino, 1m 59.660s; 35 Spaan, 1m 59.929s; 36 Takahashi, 2m 00.763s.

Final 125 cc World Championship points: see pages 162-3.

aprilia max CAMPIONI del MONDO '94

500 cc

WORLD CHAMPIONSHIP RESULTS – 1994

Position	Rider	Nationality	Machine	Australia	Malaysia	Japan	Spain	Austria	Germany	Holland	Italy	France	Britain	Czech Republic	USA	Argentina	Europe	TOTAL
1	Michael Doohan	AUS	Honda	16	25	20	25	25	25	25	25	25	20	25	16	25	20	317
2	Luca Cadalora	I	Yamaha	20	13	13	–	–	–	7	20	9	16	16	25	10	25	174
3	John Kocinski	USA	Cagiva	25	20	7	16	11	–	8	–	20	13	–	20	16	16	172
4	Kevin Schwantz	USA	Suzuki	13	10	25	20	20	20	11	16	–	25	9	–	–	–	169
5	Alberto Puig	E	Honda	9	11	8	10	10	16	13	13	13	9	11	9	11	9	152
6	Alex Criville	E	Honda	10	8	9	11	16	13	16	–	16	10	13	–	9	13	144
7	Shinichi Itoh	J	Honda	11	16	16	–	13	10	–	11	11	7	20	13	13	–	141
8	Alexandre Barros	BR	Suzuki	8	9	11	13	9	11	20	9	10	–	8	8	8	10	134
9	Doug Chandler	USA	Cagiva	7	7	6	9	–	9	10	–	–	11	–	11	20	6	96
10	Niall Mackenzie	GB	Yamaha	–	5	–	8	7	8	–	7	–	8	7	6	5	8	69
11	Bernard Garcia	F	Yamaha	5	–	5	–	–	7	6	8	–	5	5	4	4	7	56
12	Jeremy McWilliams	GB	Yamaha	–	2	3	5	–	–	–	1	8	6	6	7	7	4	49
13	Daryl Beattie	AUS	Yamaha	–	6	–	–	8	–	9	10	–	–	–	–	–	11	44
14	John Reynolds	GB	Yamaha	6	4	4	6	6	6	–	–	–	2	4	–	–	5	43
15	Sean Emmett	GB	Yamaha/Suzuki	2	3	–	–	4	5	–	2	–	4	3	5	6	–	34
16	Juan Lopez Mella	E	Yamaha/Suzuki	3	–	1	3	–	4	–	6	6	–	–	–	–	3	26
17	Norifumi Abe	J	Yamaha	–	–	–	–	–	–	–	–	–	10	10	–	–	–	20
18	Laurent Naveau	B	Yamaha	–	–	2	–	1	2	4	–	–	3	–	3	2	2	19
19	Jean-Pierre Jeandat	F	Yamaha	–	–	–	2	3	–	5	5	–	–	–	2	–	–	17
20	Cristiano Migliorati	I	Yamaha	1	–	–	4	2	–	–	4	1	–	–	–	–	–	12
21	Marc Garcia	F	Yamaha	–	–	–	–	–	–	–	–	7	–	1	–	3	–	11
22	Toshihiko Honma	J	Yamaha	–	–	10	–	–	–	–	–	–	–	–	–	–	–	10
23	Jean Foray	F	Yamaha	–	–	–	–	–	1	–	5	–	2	–	–	–	–	8
24 =	Bruno Bonhuil	F	Yamaha	–	–	–	–	1	2	–	3	1	–	–	–	–	–	7
24 =	Bernard Hänggeli	CH	Yamaha	–	–	–	–	–	–	3	4	–	–	–	–	–	–	7
24 =	Julian Miralles	E	Yamaha	–	–	–	1	3	3	–	–	–	–	–	–	–	–	7
24 =	Loris Reggiani	I	Aprilia	–	–	–	7	–	–	–	–	–	–	–	–	–	–	7
28	Hervé Moineau	F	Yamaha	–	–	–	–	5	–	–	–	–	–	–	–	–	–	5
29	Scott Doohan	AUS	Yamaha	4	–	–	–	–	–	–	–	–	–	–	–	–	–	4
30 =	Udo Mark	D	Yamaha	–	–	–	–	–	–	–	–	–	2	–	–	–	–	2
30 =	Lucio Pedercini	I	Yamaha	–	–	1	–	–	–	–	–	–	–	–	1	–	–	2
32 =	Neil Hodgson	GB	Yamaha	–	–	–	–	–	–	–	–	–	–	–	–	1	–	1
32 =	Andrew Stroud	NZ	Yamaha	–	–	–	–	–	–	–	–	–	–	–	–	–	1	1

250 cc

Position	Rider	Nationality	Machine	Australia	Malaysia	Japan	Spain	Austria	Germany	Holland	Italy	France	Britain	Czech Republic	USA	Argentina	Europe	TOTAL
1	Massimiliano Biaggi	I	Aprilia	25	25	13	–	20	20	25	–	16	–	25	20	20	25	234
2	Tadayuki Okada	J	Honda	11	20	25	16	13	11	20	9	7	20	11	13	25	13	214
3	Loris Capirossi	I	Honda	16	16	20	–	25	25	–	16	25	25	–	–	11	20	199
4	Doriano Romboni	I	Honda	20	11	10	20	16	16	–	–	20	16	–	25	–	16	170
5	Ralf Waldmann	D	Honda	9	10	–	13	11	10	13	25	13	9	20	6	8	9	156
6	Jean-Philippe Ruggia	F	Aprilia	13	13	9	25	10	8	–	13	9	10	16	–	13	10	149
7	Tetsuya Harada	J	Yamaha	–	–	7	9	–	9	–	20	8	13	–	16	16	11	109
8	Jean-Michel Bayle	F	Aprilia	6	9	5	8	5	5	10	8	11	11	10	–	9	8	105
9	Luis D'Antin	E	Aprilia	8	8	6	10	9	7	9	10	–	7	9	10	7	–	100
10	Nobuatsu Aoki	J	Honda	10	–	8	11	–	13	11	–	10	8	13	11	–	–	95
11	Wilco Zeelenberg	NL	Honda	7	7	–	7	–	6	16	7	6	5	7	7	5	4	84
12	Carlos Checa	E	Honda	2	5	–	5	–	2	5	6	3	4	–	9	6	7	54
13	Eskil Suter	CH	Aprilia	1	–	1	6	6	–	8	–	2	6	8	4	–	–	42
14	Adrian Bosshard	CH	Honda	3	4	–	–	–	–	–	5	4	2	3	3	4	6	34
15	Andy Preining	A	Aprilia	4	3	–	–	4	3	–	4	–	–	6	5	–	1	30
16	Patrick van den Goorbergh	NL	Aprilia	–	–	3	–	8	4	6	2	–	–	4	–	–	–	27
17	Jurgen van den Goorbergh	NL	Aprilia	–	–	4	4	7	–	7	–	–	–	–	2	–	–	24
18	Kenny Roberts Junior	USA	Yamaha	–	–	–	–	–	–	–	–	–	–	8	10	5	–	23
19	Tohru Ukawa	J	Honda	–	–	16	–	–	–	–	–	–	–	–	–	–	–	16
20 =	Takuma Aoki	J	Honda	–	–	11	–	–	–	–	–	–	–	–	–	–	–	11
20 =	Toshihiko Honma	J	Yamaha	–	–	–	–	–	3	–	5	3	–	–	–	–	–	11
20 =	Marcellino Lucchi	I	Aprilia	–	–	–	–	–	–	–	11	–	–	–	–	–	–	11
23 =	Alessandro Gramigni	I	Aprilia	–	6	–	–	1	–	–	3	–	–	–	–	–	–	10
23 =	Luis Maurel	E	Aprilia	–	–	–	–	–	–	–	1	1	5	–	–	–	3	10
25	Bernd Kassner	D	Aprilia	–	2	–	2	2	–	2	1	–	–	–	–	–	–	9
26 =	Giuseppe Fiorillo	I	Honda	–	–	–	–	–	–	4	–	–	–	2	–	2	–	8
26 =	Adi Stadler	D	Aprilia	–	1	2	–	3	1	–	–	–	–	–	–	–	–	8
28 =	Juan Borja	E	Honda	–	–	–	–	–	–	–	–	–	–	1	1	3	–	5
28 =	Miguel Castilla	E	Yamaha	–	–	–	3	–	–	–	–	–	–	–	–	–	2	5
28 =	Craig Connell	AUS	Honda	5	–	–	–	–	–	–	–	–	–	–	–	–	–	5
31	José Luis Cardoso	E	Aprilia	–	–	–	1	–	–	–	–	–	–	–	–	1	–	2

125 cc

Position	Rider	Nationality	Machine	Australia	Malaysia	Japan	Spain	Austria	Germany	Holland	Italy	France	Britain	Czech Republic	USA	Argentina	Europe	TOTAL
1	Kazuto Sakata	J	Aprilia	25	20	20	25	11	20	13	20	16	13	25	–	7	9	224
2	Noboru Ueda	J	Honda	9	25	–	13	20	10	–	25	25	10	20	7	20	10	194
3	Takeshi Tsujimura	J	Honda	–	11	25	10	–	–	25	16	20	25	11	25	9	13	190
4	Dirk Raudies	D	Honda	6	13	–	11	25	25	–	11	11	8	9	8	10	25	162
5	Peter Öttl	D	Aprilia	20	–	13	20	13	13	–	13	13	16	–	16	3	20	160
6	Jorge Martinez	E	Yamaha	–	16	9	7	–	9	20	9	10	6	13	11	25	–	135
7	Stefano Perugini	I	Aprilia	–	–	–	4	10	11	–	–	9	20	16	20	16	–	106
8	Masaki Tokudome	J	Honda	7	2	10	6	–	7	11	10	7	4	10	2	8	3	87
9	Oliver Petrucciani	CH	Aprilia	11	9	–	3	1	6	9	5	–	9	7	3	–	11	74
10	Herri Torrontegui	E	Aprilia	8	7	8	16	2	–	10	3	8	11	–	–	–	–	73
11	Hideyuki Nakajyo	J	Honda	1	5	16	–	–	5	–	7	–	5	5	8	10	–	70
12	Haruchika Aoki	J	Honda	–	6	–	2	–	–	4	7	4	3	–	13	4	16	59
13	Garry McCoy	AUS	Aprilia	16	4	7	5	16	–	8	–	–	–	–	–	–	–	56
14	Akira Saito	J	Honda	10	8	11	–	9	8	–	2	2	1	–	–	2	–	53
15	Loek Bodelier	NL	Honda	5	–	5	8	–	1	16	4	–	–	2	–	–	7	48
16	Fausto Gresini	I	Honda	13	10	–	–	8	3	–	6	–	–	–	–	–	6	46
17	Gianluigi Scalvini	I	Aprilia	4	–	–	–	–	–	–	3	–	–	1	6	13	5	32
18	Oliver Koch	D	Honda	–	3	3	9	6	5	–	–	–	–	4	–	–	–	30
19	Carlos Giro	E	Aprilia	–	–	–	–	–	–	–	1	–	7	3	9	6	–	26
20	Tomoko Manako	J	Honda	–	–	–	–	–	–	16	8	–	–	–	–	–	–	24
21	Stefan Prein	D	Yamaha	–	–	–	1	–	–	–	–	1	–	5	5	5	–	17
22	Emili Alzamora	E	Honda	–	–	–	–	–	–	5	–	–	–	–	–	11	–	16
23	Bruno Casanova	I	Honda	–	1	6	1	3	4	–	–	–	–	–	–	–	–	15
24	Gabriele Debbia	I	Aprilia	3	–	–	–	–	–	6	–	–	2	–	–	–	–	11
25	Manfred Geissler	D	Aprilia	–	–	2	–	–	–	–	–	–	–	6	1	–	–	9
26	Yoshiaki Katoh	J	Yamaha	–	–	–	–	–	4	–	–	–	–	–	–	–	4	8
27 =	Emilio Cuppini	I	Aprilia	–	–	–	–	–	7	–	–	–	–	–	–	–	–	7
27 =	Tomoko Igata	I	Honda	2	–	–	–	–	–	–	–	–	–	4	–	–	1	7
29	Roberto Locatelli	I	Aprilia	–	–	–	–	–	–	–	–	–	6	–	–	–	–	6
30	Lucio Cecchinello	I	Honda	–	–	–	–	–	2	1	–	–	–	–	–	–	2	5
31 =	Kunihiro Amano	J	Honda	–	–	–	4	–	–	–	–	–	–	–	–	–	–	4
31 =	Juan Maturana	E	Yamaha	–	–	–	–	–	–	–	–	–	3	–	–	1	–	4
33	Frédéric Petit	F	Yamaha	–	–	–	–	–	–	–	2	–	–	–	–	–	–	2

SIDECAR WORLD CHAMPIONSHIP REVIEW

the GENERATION

The sidecar teams' 1994 season comprised eight races, split 5:3 between Grands Prix and Superbikes, a deal with Eurosport for their own TV show and an air of confidence that grew race by race. With all eight rounds of the series planned to be back with the Grands Prix for 1995, the sidecars finished the season in their strongest position for several years.

There were few major technical changes until the appearance of Rolf Biland's new Swissauto V4 at the last race. The engine was of great interest to the solo 500 privateers, who eagerly eyed the prospect of a competitive alternative to the YZR Yamaha at half the price. The thought that a sidecar engine could become the saviour of the 500s is supremely ironic.

Chassis-wise, several riders tried Louis Christen's 'new' multi-link steering system – actually his 1976 design as banned in 1978. It started the season still technically illegal, but after meetings at Assen in June ISRA decided to allow it. Bösiger, Derek Brindley, Klaffenböck and Reddington went on to race it but several top drivers, including Biland, Webster and Dixon, didn't feel it offered any advantage.

Once again Rolf Biland stood like a Colossus over the scene. This was the 43-year-old's 21st in the World Championships, and five wins and seven pole positions in eight races starkly demonstrated that his talent and racecraft just seem to get keener. It was the Swiss veteran's seventh world title.

Consistency from Steve Webster gave him second overall, despite a winless season for the first time since 1985. The young bloods closed the gap significantly, notably Derek Brindley and Darren Dixon, taking their first wins. The Güdel brothers, Markus Bösiger, Klaus Klaffenböck and Ralph Bohnhorst were all there or thereabouts. With the racing – behind Biland anyway – being closer than ever, potential future World Champions are not in short supply.

Round 1
Donington Park, England
2 May 1994
The opening race, held at a Superbike round, was notable for two significant events: the first Biland

GAP

by John McKenzie

A smear of glue and an ocean of skill and cunning took Rolf Biland *(below left)* to a dominant seventh title.

Main picture: Darren Dixon and passenger Andy Hetherington emerged as a new title threat, but only after they ditched their V4 motor.

Klaus Klaffenböck and Christian Parzer *(bottom left)* were almost a factor; likewise British GP runners-up Derek Brindley and Paul Hutchinson *(below)*.

crashing out; the second a richly deserved first win for 24-year-old Derek Brindley, passengered by Paul Hutchinson (26).

Second in practice, Brindley rocketed away at the start and was never headed throughout the 25 laps. By lap three, he had pulled out a 50-yard lead while Ralph Bohnhorst/Peter Brown, locals Steve Abbott/Julian Tailford, and the Swiss duo of Markus Bösiger and Jurg Egli battled for second.

Brindley's victory came after a winter devoted to preparation. With team organisation looked after by former racer Theo Van Kempen, they had improved aerodynamics. 'We've built a new fairing to get my shoulders in, and it seems better. And we put a dip in the back where the passenger goes on right-handers to get him out of the wind.'

Biland's crash came on lap five. Charging into the Goddard hairpin he lost all braking, cartwheeling the outfit into the gravel trap. Luckily, both he and Waltisperg walked away. Strangely, the brakes worked perfectly afterwards. 'They must have overheated. I suspect he does not have enough cooling going to the discs,' said chassis constructor Louis Christen.

Slow-starting Steve Webster moved up to sixth when Abbott pitted to replace a plug lead after he and Bösiger had a coming-together. Webster eventually found a way past Japanese Yoshi Kumagaya and Barry Brindley, but it took him six laps to reach fourth.

Up front, Brindley was under pressure from Bohnhorst until the German's engine quit on lap 18. This left Brindley alone with a ten-second advantage that he held to the flag.

Webster now inherited third behind Bösiger, but on the last lap ran low on fuel and lost almost seven seconds. He only just held off Barry Brindley by seven-tenths, and was grateful to finish at all, yet alone on the rostrum, after a weekend of vexing engine problems.

Round 2
Hockenheim, Germany
12 June 1994

The closest sidecar race for many years was violently curtailed by a horrifying crash. On lap 14, flat out in top gear on the fastest straight in GP racing, six outfits collided. Tragically, Simon Prior (40), passenger to Japanese driver Kumagaya, was thrown into the crash barrier, receiving serious head injuries from which he died two days later.

At the end of lap one Derek Brindley/Hutchinson led into the Motodrom, after passing 1991 winner Bohnhorst. But Brindley's hopes of a second win were dashed when, on lap six, his gearbox locked, snapping the chain.

Poleman Biland decided the racing was a bit too close and pulled clear of the pack behind – Webster, Abbott, Klaffenböck, Barry Brindley, Lauslehto, the Güdels, the Wyssen brothers and Kumagaya, all embroiled in a scrap for second. The very closeness of the action became its undoing.

Klaffenböck's data recorder showed the tragedy unfolded at 255 km/h – nearly 160 mph. Abbott moved out of Webster's slipstream to go for second under braking for the approaching chicane, but Klaffenböck was immediately on his left looking for the same gap. The two outfits touched and Klaffenböck lost control, running onto the grass before spinning back into the path of the following machines. Three outfits were destroyed as the accident spread.

Kumagaya, at the back of the pack, tried to go to the right-hand side, but there was nowhere to go. 'It was all so quick and there was nothing we could do. The accident was not our fault and we hit somebody, I don't know who,' he said later.

By a tragic miracle, only Prior was badly hurt. Klaffenböck's passenger, fellow-Austrian Christian Parzer, was also thought to be seriously injured but was later released from hospital.

The race was stopped immediately, with the results taken from the end of lap 13, giving Biland the win by five seconds from Webster and Abbott; second to ninth covered by a mere 1.671 seconds. Webster took an 11-point lead in the championship, but the sheer violence of the accident had shocked the competitors and there were sombre faces on the rostrum. Nobody felt like celebrating anything.

Round 3
Assen, Holland
25 June 1994

The sidecars regrouped in a subdued frame of mind at the Dutch GP. Kumagaya had a new passenger, Dutchman Rinie Bettgens; the Wyssen brothers were absent when they couldn't repair their machine in time.

Biland took pole, but his mechanic, ex-125 GP racer Thierry Feuz, found his six-year-old crankcases (yes,

Wet tyres and empty grandstands: Julian Tailford prepares to push driver Steve Abbott out for practice at Hockenheim.

Biland and long-time passenger Kurt Waltisperg *(right)* **were almost perfect all year long.**

Steve Webster and new passenger Adolf Hänni *(bottom right)* **were second again in spite of a season without a win.**

Round 4
Österreichring, Zeltweg, Austria
17 July 1994

Darren Dixon's sudden and unexpected good form as he joined the exalted ranks of GP winners with a contemptuously easy victory came after a crucial engine change. Until now he'd campaigned a V4 YZR500 Yamaha, supplied by sponsors Padgett's. Great things were expected from the '93-spec motor, but the solo engine's wide powerband was just too 'soft' for sidecars, and after a best of eighth and two DNFs they decided to switch to the more usual ADM/Honda.

The improvement was startling as they took pole four-tenths ahead of Biland. Webster was third, his first front row this year.

Bösiger, using an identical ADM engine, got away first but the versatile Brighton racer shot past on lap four, and disappeared over the horizon. He pulled out a second a lap until he was 16 clear, before easing off for a convincing and comfortable ten-second win.

Bösiger was second, three-tenths in front of Biland, who had tried everything to get past on the last lap after a troubled weekend. 'We were slower than last year, and we thought we had a problem with our ignition unit. It turned out to be a poor chassis earth, but we'd borrowed Webster's Swissauto ignition for the race, and the curve he uses didn't give as wide a powerband as we have. Then Klaffenböck crashed right in front of me and I had to slow right down. Then I couldn't get my rhythm going,' explained the new championship leader.

Webster finished fifth after a challenge from Derek Brindley ebbed away with a shredded rear tyre. Webster was using a standard clutch for the first time in three years. 'We broke our AP carbon clutch in practice, and borrowed a sintered clutch off Barry Brindley. I was too gentle and almost stalled, so we were absolutely last away. My fault, I messed up,' said a dejected Webster. He dropped to third overall, with Bösiger now second to Biland.

Locals Klaffenböck and Parzer flipped their outfit but righted it and continued, albeit out of the points. Klaffy was able to smile about it a week later: 'Home GP... trying too hard...'

The race was sidecar chassis constructor Louis Christen's (LCR) 100th consecutive GP win. The last time a non-LCR chassis won a GP

six...) had developed a slight crack. They glued it up and Biland continued – with his new V4 coming, he didn't want the expense of new cases for the old engine.

He led from the start, with Derek Brindley and Klaffenböck contesting second, Klaffy with the upper hand. Meanwhile, a furious Webster had rediscovered his old fire and was carving through the field. By lap three he was fourth, setting fastest lap; on lap four he took Brindley at the chicane and Klaffenböck on the brakes at the end of the back straight. For two laps he appeared to be catching Biland. Then on lap ten his gearbox locked in fifth, and he was out. After four retirements in six Dutch races, Webster is convinced he is jinxed.

Biland's victory margin was a perfectly programmed 4.5 seconds over Klaffenböck and Derek Brindley. Dixon had a non-finish due to ignition problems on what was to be his last outing with the YZR Yamaha engine.

Brindley had a strange explanation for being unable to catch Klaffenböck, who had found it hard to get motivated in practice after Hockenheim. 'I've put some shielding in the cockpit to stop brake dust blowing in. But Klaffy was going so quick that I had to stay tucked in – I couldn't breathe properly because it was so hot and I just didn't have the strength left to try to pass him. We'll have to put some ducts in for the next race!'

166

was way back in 1982, when Alain Michel won in Italy on a Seymaz.

Round 5
Donington Park, England
23 July 1994

The race was brought forward to the unusual time of 12.45 on Saturday to enable the BBC to film it for inclusion in the traditional Saturday afternoon sports programme, resulting in a hectic schedule of practice and race all within 24 hours. The last practice session didn't actually finish until eight pm on Friday, leaving a long – or rather, short – night ahead for those facing engine rebuilds.

After Zeltweg six days before, Dixon had high hopes of continuing his winning streak. He was fastest after the first session, just in front of Abbott. In the second session, he managed to knock another two seconds off his time, and looked set for pole. Then with just two laps left Biland came out of the pits and did a 1m 36.346s to knock Dixon off pole by the impossibly small margin of 0.099 seconds. It's tough out there...

Webster was fifth quickest, losing a large part of the second session after the 1.25-in. diameter rear axle sheared through as the wheel was changed. Louis Christen examined the part and was totally baffled. 'I've made over a hundred of these and I have never seen this happen before,' he said.

In the race Derek Brindley led the pack for the first half-lap but Dixon outbraked him into the esses and looked like repeating his Austrian runaway. He was ten seconds clear with ten of 26 laps to go when his hopes were dashed and he was sidelined by an electrical fault.

There was a tense three-way battle for third. Biland had squeezed past Klaffenböck into the esses on lap ten; going up to the Melbourne hairpin, Webster then tried inside-line outbraking on Klaffy but found the space suddenly occupied by Biland. The two outfits hit, damaging Webster's sidecar wheel arch. Biland ran wide, but held his place. Seconds later, at Goddards, Webster found the gap and finally ran inside Klaffenböck.

With a clear track, Biland went after Brindley, who was soon to inherit the lead. Stealthily Biland reeled him in, and with calculating efficiency he snatched the lead at the esses with five laps left.

He beat Brindley by 0.672 seconds after surviving a vicious slide on the last lap at Craner Curves, and expressed sympathy for Dixon. 'It should have been his race, but I'm happy with the points and the prize money!' he said. Brindley was content with second. 'We need carbon brakes, though. We thought we might be able to do without this season but proved today we can't.'

Webster took third, with Klaffenböck fourth.

Round 6
Brno, Czech Republic
21 August 1994

Dixon led for the third time in three consecutive GPs; for the second in a row he succumbed to machine problems. He had passed fast starter Bösiger at the first corner, and began to pull away. Then, on lap three, the fuel pump stopped and Derek Brindley was handed the lead.

A win the previous week, at the ISRA non-championship race at Schleiz in Germany, probably cost Dixon the victory. 'At first I thought the fuel pump had just packed up but we found out later the earth wire had broken. It was very bumpy at Schleiz so maybe it got shaken up a bit there.'

If Brindley hoped for a win, Biland had other ideas. After his customary poor start he began to pick off the field one by one. Within eight laps he was at the front and, as usual, pulled out just enough of a gap to ease off to save his tyres.

Bösiger was second for the third time after an unusual tyre choice – hard up front, soft at the rear – worked to his advantage.

Webster finally got the better of a race-long battle with Derek Brindley, and was less than seven-tenths behind Bösiger at the line. 'Another lap and I would have caught him. I could see his tyres were going off. But we're still second in the championship,' said Steve.

Race winner Biland was modest about the apparent ease with which he'd won. 'It was not an easy race at all. We were pushed very hard by Bösiger as well as by Webster and Brindley. I was afraid the tyres might not go the whole distance.' Biland now needed only a fourth place at the penultimate round at Assen to take the world title.

Round 7
Assen, Holland
12 September 1994

Maybe fourth would have been enough, but Biland confirmed his dominance by retaking the title with a flag-to-flag win. It was his 75th race win, yielding his third consecutive title and bringing his total to a record-breaking seven. 'Normally I don't have a very good start but today it went okay. Then I could take it at a steady pace and it worked out very well,' said Biland.

Once again, with Biland reading his pit-boards diligently to maintain his lead, interest centred on the tussle for second, and it kept the crowd of 60,000 on the edge of their seats. Dixon took it, a mere 0.43s in front of Webster; Klaffenböck half a second behind, with Brindley fifth. Only 1.28 seconds covered second to fifth.

Dixon explained later how a rare mistake by Webster benefited him: 'With Webster, Klaffenböck and Brindley pushing us hard, I'd cooked the brakes a bit by half-distance and they all caught up. Then, on the last but one lap, Webster came by me at the end of the straight – he thought it was the last lap – and I thought, "What's he doing taking tight lines and blocking us out?" Coming into the chicane he was hard on the brakes and a bit sideways. If it had been the last lap he would have done it but he'd lost all his drive and we passed him back going down the straight. By then, of course, he had showed his hand and I blocked him out for the last lap.'

Round 8
Catalunya, Spain
9 October 1994

Biland finally unveiled his 180 bhp Swissauto V4 and quickly demonstrated the whole point of the project by taking pole – for the 90th time in 166 GPs. Abbott was second: impressed by Dixon and Bösiger's new-found speed he had also switched to ADM power. For the first time in many years he had a truly competitive engine and, with his Windle chassis ruthlessly stripped down to bare bones, he was suddenly in contention.

Biland found the going harder after a damp start, spinning off on lap one and for once giving the others a chance. However, the race was stopped after only five laps of the scheduled 22 when the heavens opened. At that point Webster had just got to the front, but results were taken from the end of lap four, giving the advantage to Dixon.

After a 20-minute delay, including three laps of wet-tyre practice, a 16-lap second leg was restarted. Biland shot into the lead, keen to give his new engine a win and make up for the earlier indiscretion, but on lap 15 he was stopped by electrical problems.

Dixon inherited the lead and went on to his second win of the year with a ten-second aggregate-times advantage over Swiss brothers Paul and Charly Güdel, who had passed Dixon on the road with two laps to go for their best place of the season. 'It was unbelievably slippery out there,' said Dixon.

In third was Abbott, his best result of the year, in spite of a spin that brought them to a complete stop. 'Luckily we didn't go into the gravel,' he said.

Webster was now concentrating on second in the championship and watching his points rival Derek Brindley. He had a good lead on the clock over him, so drove to stay out of trouble.

Biland wasn't too depressed about his enforced retirement. 'I'm the 1994 World Champion and it was the first time with our new engine. The problem was only electrical – the motor went even better than we expected.'

Rolf has a contract for one more season with Schlossgold and Longines, his main sponsors, and says he will finally retire from racing at the end of 1995. 'I don't want another winter looking for sponsorship. If the engine sells well I will still come to GPs to give technical support – but I'll stay on this side of the Armco!'

SUPERBIKE WORLD CHAMPIONSHIP REVIEW

Carl Fogarty *(right and opposite)* would have made Scott Russell *(bottom left)* look over his shoulder more often, if only the defending champion on the Kawasaki had been able to get ahead of the Ducati.

Below: A Slight contretemps spoils the New Zealander's reputation for consistency on the disappointing new Honda RC45.

THREE MEN AND A

by Johan Vandekerckhove

DUKE

The 1994 edition of World Superbikes might have been devised by Alexandre Dumas. Everyone expected at least three musketeers to play a prominent part in the battle for the four-stroke crown. But the fourth musketeer scarcely featured. D'Artagnan Doug Polen was left behind in one of the early chapters by Scott Russell, Carl Fogarty and Aaron Slight.

The FIM took the role of the evil Cardinal Richelieu, meddling with the best-laid plans when the protagonists expected it least – in the intervals between their on-track battles.

But the thrills and spills persisted to the very end, with the threesome – duelling for the three works factories – crossing swords for the title at the final round in Australia. Chivalry was left in the pit lane, and the battle cry was One Against All and All Against One.

All three protagonists set about their missions with typical skill but, for one reason or another, they rarely spent an entire race in each other's company. Scott Russell would cruise to victory when Carl Fogarty was having trouble getting his new Ducati dialled in, while Fogarty rode from one win to another when Russell was desperately trying to make his war-horse Kawasaki behave. And Aaron Slight, riding steadily and consistently, watched their every move and waited for the chance to clinch his first win on the brand-new RC45, which lacked acceleration and ultimate handling, but proved incredibly reliable from the start.

Of course, it was never that simple. Four-stroke racing never is, and thanks to the likes of Giancarlo Falappa, James Whitham, Fabrizio Pirovano, Andreas Meklau, Paolo Casoli and Troy Corser, the outcome of the races always had an element of unpredictability.

The wicked Cardinal Richelieu, meanwhile, spoiled the fun right from the first race. At Donington, routine fuel samples from the bikes of Slight and Meklau were adjudged illegal, due to too high a content of diene, an additive that gained overnight fame in the Superbike paddock. Elf promptly admitted they'd made a mistake, absolving Castrol Honda and the Promotor teams from blame (and, in fact, most of the other Superbike teams, who had used the self-same fuel but had not been asked for samples). Unfortunately the FIM's rules, framed several years ago, did not take this into account. Instead, and even though samples had been taken before only one of the two races, Slight and Meklau lost the points they had won in both heats.

This triggered a judicial tug of war which would have given even experienced trial advocates a headache, and made this year's Superbike World Championship as exciting for statisticians as it was for the spectators. Both teams made a successful appeal, based on a number of technicalities; and both riders were reinstated just before the Asian tour. Then a counter-appeal from Ducati team boss Virginio Ferrari and the FIM's own Oriol Puig Bulto saw that decision partially rescinded. Just before Mugello both 'offenders' were informed they would be docked only the points gained in one of the Donington heats. At least a logical interpretation of the rules had prevailed.

All this had Slight roller-coasting up and down the points table – even leading at one point – but gave the statisticians a very different view of the balance of power than that gained by the crowds at the tracks.

At Donington, Russell and Fogarty

170

SUPERBIKE WORLD CHAMPIONSHIP REVIEW

Left: **Easy as one-two-three. Russell leads Fogarty and Slight at Donington as if they were alone in the world.**

James Whitham's style is unique, and remained so in his switch to Ducati.

sually at the read-outs before giving it all he had out on the track.

Russell's fourth consecutive win came at Misano, where he'd fended off likable Italian Piergiorgio Bontempi before the Kawasaki rider was forced to retire with engine trouble on the last lap. Falappa won the second heat. It was to be the last race of the year for Ducati's home-grown hard man, who only narrowly survived a heavy pre-race test crash at Albacete soon afterwards.

Spain was the first turning point. Russell crashed his best bike in the first heat, and his spare in the second. Now it was Fogarty's turn to start a run of four wins, at Albacete and the fast Österreichring, where Russell's Kawasaki proved way off the pace.

As the paddock packed up for Indonesia and Japan, with Slight temporarily stripped of all his Donington points, Fogarty was in charge with 128 points to Russell's 116, with Slight on 105. But even before the bikes had been taken out of their crates in the Sentul paddock, the FIM had done their first about-face. Slight had his points back...until the final decision a few days before Mugello, three races hence.

By now Russell was fighting again. He took two thirds in Indonesia, then a new engine at Sugo gave him victory in both legs there. Strangely, though, the Team Muzzy mechanics were asked to return the engine to the Kawasaki factory afterwards. Scott languished in sixth and ninth on his old bike at Assen, with Fogarty winning twice. After the Dutch round it was clear only three musketeers were battling it out, for fourth man Polen was already lagging more than 70 points behind the others.

Carl Fogarty did what was expected of him on Ducati's home track of Mugello...eventually. Only a retirement with electrical problems in the second heat stopped Russell from taking a masterful double victory. This unexpected bonus gave Fogarty the title lead, but it was substantially diminished when Russell again won twice at a soaking Donington in early October. (The British track stepped in to host the European round after Jerez backed out.) Fogarty was left struggling with tyre (and, he insisted, team-mate) problems, while Slight was short of traction.

Each of the three musketeers deserved the title, but only one could win it. Russell had again proved to be very stress-resistant, coming back several times from apparently dead-end difficulties. Fogarty lost fewer points at the crucial stages than last year, living up to his reputation of being able to ride hard on anything with two wheels and an engine – even the brand-new 916 in its debut season. And Slight did much better than had been expected, thanks to his consistency and a riding style apparently well suited to the understeering RC45.

The final showdown offered maximum tension as rain swept Phillip Island, stopping just in time for a shortened first leg. With only five points in it, both Fogarty and Russell needed to win, and the former scorched the first race. Russell led him for half a lap, but was outpaced, and only got second because new team-mate Anthony Gobert slowed to let him through. (The new Australian champion had switched from Honda to Kawasaki on the eve of the race after striking a deal for next season with Rob Muzzy.) Foggy could afford to dog his rival's wheel-tracks in the second leg as Gobert ran away up front. Then when the American's tyres started to break up and he pitted for a replacement, Fogarty could cruise to second to claim the title by 25 points. Slight also suffered from tyre problems to finish fourth in both legs and third overall, a good result considering the new Honda's teething troubles.

For Polen, on the other hand, fourth was something of a comedown. The former double World Champion was as professional and cool as ever, but never seemed able to get the best from the RC45. His fortunes made a telling contrast with those of Kiwi Simon Crafar, who took his only remotely factory-supported RC45 to a highly creditable fifth place in the final points table, and was one of the few Honda privateers not to suffer seemingly insurmountable handling problems.

Meklau almost pulled off the same stunt as last year on his home track at Zeltweg, taking two seconds there and notching up impressive results in almost every race.

Whitham missed the start of the season when he crashed at Donington,

looked to be the only ones able to go for gold consistently. Honda, while always a force to be reckoned with, would have to sort out their teething troubles first. But the musketeers left Britain with Slight only one point behind Fogarty and two ahead of Russell after a pair of seconds. Fogarty had won the first heat; Russell the second. It was the first in a series of four wins for the Georgian defending champion.

In Germany, Slight took second once more, and team-mate Polen his first rostrum of the year in heat two. It was a slow start for the Texan on the new RC45, but the team was relaxed: he'd been hired as much for his chassis development and telemetry skills as for his hard riding. Both Honda riders were doing what they did best, it was said. Doug spent hours at the computer, and undoubtedly understood the bike better, whereas Slight would glance only ca-

SUPERBIKE WORLD CHAMPIONSHIP REVIEW

and then found it hard to come to terms with the ill-handling 916, but two thirds in Spain and victory at Sentul made up for his slow start. Fellow-British hope Terry Rymer also had a hard time adapting to the Muzzy Kawasaki. Outranked by team-mate Russell, he finally lost motivation as the year wore on. He crashed heavily at Mugello and was forced to miss the European round at Donington.

Italian duo Fabrizio Pirovano and Piergiorgio Bontempi will both want to forget 1994. For the first time in his World Superbike career Pirovano was out of the top five, after a rash of mechanical gremlins with his Ducati, whereas Bontempi suffered from health and emotional problems.

Paolo Casoli and Australian youngster Troy Corser – a Superbike part-timer when not winning the US title – were among the big surprises of the year. The former 250 GP rider was very promising on the Belgarda YZF, towards the end of the season; and Corser proved he will certainly be a force to be reckoned with in 1995.

Ducati, winners of the constructors' title three times in a row, had expected to face stiff opposition in 1994. New limits narrowed the gap between the minimum weight for 750 cc fours (160 kg) and 1000 cc twins (145 kg). The Italians decided to meet the challenge by replacing the old faithful 888 with the 916.

Their showpiece was unveiled at the end of 1993. The aggressively styled new Duke was reserved at first for just four riders: Falappa and Fogarty in the Virginio Ferrari-run works team; Pirovano in the separate Davide Tardozzi team; and Whitham in a team based at Moto Cinelli, one of Britain's three Ducati importers. The plan was to make more machines available to privateers of substance as the year wore on and the 916 production line hit cruising speed. In fact, only two other riders saw them: Mauro Lucchiari, the factory tester who replaced the injured Falappa, and new bright hope Corser. Even fifth-placed Meklau waited in vain for a 916, and ran into problems common among such Ducati privateers as Stéphane Mertens and Valerio de Stefanis. All their campaigns took on the look of an economy run as spares became increasingly scarce. It says much for the tuning abilities of Charly Putz (Meklau) and Roland Simonetti (ex-Roche, now Mertens) that they gave the bikes enough power for several top five positions.

But the factory men were not overly blessed either. After getting their bikes only days before the first race, Fogarty and his colleagues found they were not easy to ride. The 955 cc engine delivered the goods as expected – it did not differ much from the smaller unit in the 888/926. The chassis proved a handful, though, due partly to a heavy front weight bias and a hard-to-set rear suspension linkage, and these problems were never quite solved, despite private test sessions later in the season.

The new Honda RC45 started the year with even more of a question mark hanging over it. The world's biggest manufacturer had decided, after a long absence, to take on the big four-stroke boys again with the long-awaited successor to the legendary RC30. The RC45 was outwardly similar, with a single-sided swing arm, a similar frame and a V4 engine. But it was an all-new bike, in an all-new campaign. The electronic fuel injection and the fact that Honda entrusted development to HRC rather than R&D saw to that.

The red and green Castrol Honda army soon found out that every dollar spent out of their enormous budget was not one too many. Unlike the RC30, the RC45 did not rule from the start, though its reliability and consistency served both Slight and Polen well over the year. And you certainly couldn't accuse the impressive team of not trying hard enough. Both racing bikes were taken apart after final practice, especially during the first race weekends of the year, with mechanics busy until very late every Saturday night performing crack tests on the frames and measuring every possible tolerance on every single moving engine part.

All this meticulous work resulted in a very reliable engine – but the bike wasn't yet ready to win races. A lack of acceleration was one problem, as shown when Slight came close to a win in Sentul, but had to let Whitham's Ducati go in the closing yards. They also had to overcome serious understeer problems and, as they discovered at the second Donington race, a lack of traction in the wet. Nevertheless, they achieved regular rostrum results.

Private Honda teams had even worse headaches with chassis and horsepower handicaps. Team Rumi, who started the season with an NL5 (factory-kitted) engine and Ohlins suspension, soon found it was a most effective package – some even whispered that Simon Crafar's bike steered better than the Showa-suspended works Castrol Hondas. When Crafar also got some engine parts and electronics, from Sugo onwards, it became clear that chips and software were responsible for much of the difference between the works and the private bikes.

Contrary to the time-honoured customs of HRC secrecy, the Castrol Honda team did not take long to fit in with the prevailing Superbike atmosphere, where outsiders are still able to have a look at the hi-tech machinery in the paddock. The candour of British team boss Neil Tuxworth did a lot to compensate for the entry of the megabuck trailers, campers and hospitality units which made their debut in the Superbike paddocks this year.

Strange as it may seem, curtains and 'prohibited area' stickers did appear – in the Team Kawasaki Muzzy pit boxes, despite the fact that they had the oldest bike in the Superbike fight. Their ZXR was as introduced at the start of 1993, but was still considered one of the bikes to beat in 1994, especially with Ducati and Honda facing inevitable teething troubles. Only minor engine changes had been made during the winter, and it turned out to be enough for the first couple of races. Then the team made trouble for themselves. A new stiffened chassis was tested and pronounced promising. At the Österreichring, however, the bikes did not handle at all, and Russell only gained six points from two disastrous heats. Desperate to regain an edge over the opposition, themselves gathering strength, Russell worked in vain to make the new chassis effective. Only when the factory race department gave them a different engine, for Sugo, did they return to winning form.

It is far from clear if such a rearguard action could succeed in 1995. Ducati and Honda both have intensive development programmes scheduled for the close season. Then there is Yamaha, planning a works entry for the first time next year. And the Japanese may face even stronger western opposition in the future, for whispers on the grapevine suggest that Harley-Davidson, Aprilia and Cagiva are also set to enter the fray.

That should certainly maintain the excitement and competition that has become such a hallmark of World Superbike racing.

Right: Whitham, Forgarty and Slight on the Albacete rostrum.

Kiwi Simon Crafar *(below)* was the only privateer to get good results from the new Honda.

Below right: Part-timer Troy Corser leads Pirovano, Fogarty and Russell in Britain.

Bottom: Fogarty steps off at Hockenheim.

Double Red Photographic

Gold & Goose

Kel Edge

QUIET START BIG FINISH

ENDURANCE WORLD CHAMPIONSHIP REVIEW

by Kel Edge

The light from the single headlight almost burned a hole in the back of Aaron Slight's leathers as he hurtled into the chicane for the last time. After nearly eight hours of racing, the gap between him and former team-mate Scott Russell was less than a bike length and the scene was set for the closest finish in Suzuka Eight Hour history. Could the new RC45 Honda record its first international race win or would reigning Superbike World Champion Russell give the ZXR Kawasaki victory for the second year in succession?

The New Zealander came out of the final turn first, with Russell almost alongside as they charged down the hill to the flag. They were side by side as they crossed the finishing line, and it was a few moments before the crowd realised that Slight was the winner. Honda had won a famous victory, Slight had won the world's biggest motor cycle road race for the second year running, and everybody present had witnessed one of the greatest races of all time.

And yet the season hadn't promised much when it started. The championship would consist of just four rounds – three 24-hour races (Le Mans, Spa and the Bol d'Or) and one eight-hour race (Suzuka). This was the first year that the Endurance World Championship was being run under Superbike rather than F1 regulations and it was obvious that the change wasn't being viewed with favour by many of the teams.

For the first round at Le Mans there were two 'factory' bikes each from Kawasaki, Suzuki and Ducati France, while Yamaha were making their endurance racing comeback and adding a little spice to the occasion by teaming Dominique Sarron with his older brother, Christian. Honda's flag was flown only by privateers, though there was some doubt that the RC45 was ready to race and some elected to use the venerable RC30 instead.

Christian Sarron is a superhero in France, and his presence drew a larger than normal crowd of 70,000 to the season's opener.

Briton Terry Rymer had set pole in practice, but stalled his Kawasaki on the line and was only 14th going into the first turn. To the unrestrained delight of the French *Ducatisti*, it was Mouchet away first, but it didn't take Rymer long to catch up: he was fourth at the end of the first lap and three laps later he was in the lead. He was still ahead when they all pitted for the first time, but behind him there was a terrific dogfight for second place between Dominique Sarron, Vieira, Mouchet and Moineau – all on different manufacturers' bikes.

For a while it seemed that Yamaha were on course for a glorious return to endurance racing, but then Christian Sarron threw it away spectacularly on his first lap at Museum Curve, destroying the bike in the

Night and day, the Bol d'Or pits are unforgettable. Pictured here is an Elf Honda rider change; opposite is the Kawasaki pit, title-winner Morillas's bike behind Rymer's.

From left: Slight, on an Eight-Hour mission; Holden at work in France; Yamaha hero Nagai pulls the trigger at Ricard's Mistral Straight; the Sarron brothers (Dominique here) take a long-awaited Bol d'Or win.
Below: Former GP rider Adrien Morillas took the championship.

process. He escaped with a bruised hand but admitted it had been his own fault – he had been adjusting his brake lever instead of looking where he was going!

With Yamaha out, the race developed into a classic Kawasaki versus Suzuki battle. Moineau, Lavieille and D'Orgeix on the number one Suzuki actually led Rymer, Morillas and Battistini at the nine-hour mark, but shortly afterwards retired with broken crankcases and the Kawasaki cruised to a comfortable victory ahead of Vieira, Khun and Nicotte's Honda. Third went to Bonhuil, Monneret and Gomez on the second factory Suzuki, but there was no luck for the British privateer Phase One team – they had retired with a broken gearbox after 15 hours.

It was three months before the next round, at the beautiful Spa-Francorchamps circuit in the Ardennes, and 20,000 spectators turned up, but the race was hardly a classic. Yamaha didn't enter and although Kawasaki France pitched up with two bikes, only one was raced, due to budgetary constraints. Suzuki France fielded their usual two-bike team and the rest of the grid was made up of privateers.

There were ominous grey clouds hanging over the circuit, but to everybody's relief the race started and continued in dry conditions. Mouchet got his Ducati away first again, chased by the factory bikes and Vieira's Honda, but the race was only five laps old when two of the leading bunch crashed in full view of the pits. Moineau and Nicotte's bikes had touched as they exited Eau Rouge and both riders lay motionless in the middle of the track. There were bits of bike everywhere – the scene resembled a disaster movie – but amazingly, apart from a few broken bones, both riders were OK. The pace car came out while the marshals cleared up the debris, and after 20 minutes racing recommenced at full blast.

Inevitably, now that two of the leading contenders were out, the race lost some of its gloss – a pity because Spa has been the scene of many memorable encounters. Mouchet, Mounier and Chambon's Ducati unbelievably led until the third hour, when Morillas, Battistini and Bonoris finally powered their Kawasaki to the front. In third were Manley, Holden and Graves, looking for their second Spa rostrum finish in two years, and that is how the pattern continued until the Ducati began having problems and lost ground.

The second half of the race passed almost uneventfully, with Morillas and Co. strolling to a problem-free victory ahead of Bonhuil, Monneret and Gomez, with the Phase One team taking a well-deserved third, cheered on by a huge contingent of Union Jack-waving British fans in the grandstand opposite the finish line.

The scene now moved away from Europe to the highly charged atmosphere of the Suzuka circuit. Undeniably the single most important race for the Japanese manufacturers, this year the Suzuka Eight Hour was without Schwantz, Mick Doohan (concentrating on the 500 title) and some of the other GP stars. But former champ Eddie Lawson was back on a Yamaha, with Nagai, and so were last year's winners, Russell and Slight – this time riding against each other. Honda fielded no less than five 'factory' RC45s, with Polen and Slight as their number one team.

Unlike the 24-hour marathons, Suzuka is just a very long sprint race. It began in its usual frenetic fashion, with Aoki leading Itoh, Nagai, Slight and Fujiwara, but after 30 minutes the red flag came out. Nagai had crashed and thought his race was over. Then a back-marker went down, spilling oil onto the track. His bike caught fire when it slid into the foam protectors in front of the Armco, and soon the foam was alight and dense clouds of black smoke filled the sky. Then another four riders slid off on the oil. It took four fire engines to put out the blaze, but when the race restarted, after half an hour, the fortunate Nagai was able to take part after all.

It was Aoki away first again, leading until lap 22 when he was overtaken by Nagai's team-mate, Lawson. In the last motor cycle race of his career, Eddie was determined to go out in style, but his lead lasted only ten laps before he was overtaken by Doug Polen.

Polen and Slight led until lap 47, but now Russell and Rymer were in second place. The race developed into a ferocious battle between the World Superbike regulars, the lead changing only because of pit stops. As dusk settled Rymer was clinically passed by Polen, while smart pit work by the Honda mechanics saw Slight go out for the final crucial session ahead of Russell. The American tried everything he knew, even overtaking a back-marker on the outside as the New Zealander passed him on the inside, but all to no avail. The final moments were desperate stuff, but Slight sneaked it, and the rest, as they say, is history. Honda were ecstatic, and the RC45 had broken its duck.

The thrilling nature of the Suzuka battle had lifted the whole endurance championship and now all attention was focused on the last round, at Paul Ricard. Seventy-five thousand fans braved the cool Mistral winds, many coming to see if Christian and Dominique Sarron could make history and win the Bol d'Or. The brothers were teamed with Japanese ace Nagai in the Yamaha France team – cynics said this was the only way that Yamaha Japan would provide a full factory bike.

There were two factory bikes from Kawasaki and Suzuki France, but the team on a mission were the French Ducati importers Sima, who had been given nine engines (for the two teams) including one 'Carl Fogarty special' and one 'qualifying' engine. And this was just for them to take pole and lead – of huge importance as the start of the race is shown live on French television. The plan worked and Mouchet took pole, ahead of Rymer, Moineau, Morillas, Sarron and Crafar. Morillas and Battistini were both in line for the title, so Kawasaki France had split them up: if one's bike broke, the other would have a chance of winning.

The race was given added glamour when film star Gérard Depardieu turned up to start the race, and on the stroke of three o'clock the air was shattered as 70 bikes thundered into life and charged down to turn one. Mouchet's Ducati led, its front wheel pawing the air in celebration as it came off the kerbstones at the last corner. Rymer was second, ahead of Dominique Sarron and Morillas, but the Briton soon took the lead and immediately began pulling away from his pursuers.

As the race progressed, Rymer, Battistini and Coutelle opened up a two-lap gap on the Sarrons and Nagai, who had a two-lap lead over Morillas, Haquin and Bonoris. Mouchet's team was soon out, after Ferracci crashed, but there was good news for the British fans as Manley, Holden and Edwards moved up to fifth place.

Problems began to beset all the fancied runners, including the leaders who had to come in for a new clutch, as day turned to night. This unscheduled stop allowed the Yamaha into the lead and from then on, despite pressure from Morillas, Moineau and then Manley and Co. in the closing stages, the Sarrons and Nagai were never headed on their way to the chequered flag.

On the rostrum, Christian Sarron was in tears as he embraced his brother. He had set pole and led the Bol d'Or five times before, but he had never won it. Manley, Holden and Edwards finished a superb second. Moineau, Lavieille and D'Orgeix were third, with fellow-countryman Adrien Morillas sixth – enough for him to be crowned 1994 World Endurance Champion.

The season started quietly at Le Mans and Spa, but Suzuka and the Bol d'Or were two of the most exciting and enjoyable endurance races of recent years. The new Superbike regulations produced no less drama or excitement than before. The gap between the factory and privateer teams has narrowed – and that can only be good for the health and future of the series.

175

UNITED STATES ROAD RACING REVIEW

THE YEAR THAT NOBODY BEAT THE BEST

by Paul Carruthers

The 1994 AMA Superbike racing season may go down in the annals as the year of the Australian invasion. Two Aussies joined the top-rung series in North American road racing in '94 – one with a resumé filled with credentials, the other virtually unknown outside his native country.

Former 500 cc Grand Prix winner Kevin Magee joined the newly named Smokin' Joe's Racing (formerly Camel Honda) for the 1994 AMA campaign, armed with the long-awaited, much-ballyhooed Honda RC45. Further bolstering Magee's reputation was a straight-fight win over Doug Polen in the Australian round of the World Superbike Championship at Phillip Island in 1992, as well as courageous efforts in the Suzuka Eight Hour in Japan. Magee, it seemed, was certain for AMA Superbike stardom, the man pencilled in to take the title from the Americans, the diamond in the rough who was going to make team owner Martin Adams the smartest man in the world.

Young Troy Corser, on the other hand, was a nobody. His Australian Superbike Championship meant little on this side of the Pacific, and he was given only token acknowledgment from those who mattered. Eraldo Ferracci, though, saw something in the freckle-faced wonderboy when the Aussie rode his Ducati during a Dunlop test session in December 1993, and the Italian V-twin guru fitted Corser into his two-man team as a replacement for non-defending champion Doug Polen. Big shoes to fill, indeed. But fit they did.

By season's end, nobody in the Smokin' Joe's Racing pit was smiling. Their Honda RC45 was the biggest bust since Dolly Parton and Magee fared no better. The combination of the newest, trickest superbike on the planet and the highest-paid rider in AMA Superbike racing ended the season a dismal 18th in the championship – 160 points behind the top-ranked racer in the ten-round series.

That rider was none other than Troy Corser, the man of the year in AMA Superbike racing. Talk about a turnaround. With a downtrodden Magee heading home at the end of the season, his racing future in doubt, Corser's was so bright he needed sunglasses. The 22-year-old had parlayed his AMA Championship into a Ducati factory ride for the 1995 World Superbike series, and the Woolongong Wonder II was suddenly the hottest thing to come out of Australia since, well...Mick Doohan.

The two other noteworthy men of the American Superbike wars were the Vance & Hines Yamaha teamsters, Jamie James and Colin Edwards II. James, the elder statesman and most popular rider in AMA racing, very nearly won a second AMA Superbike National Championship to go with his 1989 crown. Despite not winning a race James only missed out on the title by a single point, with the series not being decided until the late laps of the final race at Road Atlanta. It was then that James's Yamaha failed, with the EXUP exhaust valve sticking open and forcing Jamie to nurse the bike to a seventh-place finish – one point away from a championship. A gentleman to the end, James didn't throw what would have been an understandable tantrum in the back of the Vance & Hines truck – instead he went straight to the winners' circle to congratulate Corser.

While Corser made a name for himself with early-season dominance, the end of the year belonged to 20-year-old Colin Edwards II. The young Texan was simply masterful in the final rounds, winning three races in a row before ending the season with a third-place finish at Road Atlanta. His late-season heroics not only vaulted him to fifth in the series points standings after a dismal beginning to the season, but also jump-started his career. The one-time 250 cc phenomenon was suddenly back in demand, and will spend 1995 racing against the likes of Scott Russell and Carl Fogarty – and Troy Corser – in the World Superbike series aboard a factory Yamaha.

Corser's Most Excellent American Adventure began at Daytona in early March. After qualifying on the front row – ahead of four-times World Champion Eddie Lawson and two-times World Superbike Cham-

Troy Corser *(left and below left)* came from nowhere to beat the US riders at home.

Right: The USA proved ripe for invasion in 1994.

Pascal Picotte *(bottom left)*, team-mate to the stars, took two wins on his Ferracci Ducati.

Below: Colin Edwards leads Corser and Merkel – the end of the year belonged to the young Yamaha rider.

pion Doug Polen – Corser battled to the finish with the best Superbike racer in the world, Scott Russell. With what was a scintillating AMA debut, Corser immediately became a factor – but there was some talk of beginner's luck.

Russell's victory in the Daytona 200 was impressive. After hitting mechanical problems in the 50-mile qualifying race, Russell started the 200 from 64th starting position – but it didn't prevent him from winning his second race at the famed Speedway.

In what was probably his final Stateside appearance, Lawson finished third, riding an ultra-trick Yamaha that came directly from the factory in Japan. Lawson topped Polen in his first race aboard the Honda RC45. Magee was ninth in his AMA debut, and already complaining bitterly about the RC45. 'It doesn't do anything, anywhere. You just can't push it or you'll bust your ass. It's a big mix-up right now, but we'll get it sorted out and get it a lot closer.' Though disappointing, the Daytona outing would turn out to be one of Magee's best of the year.

Corser quickly dispelled the beginner's luck theory at the second round in Arizona. The Australian smashed the lap record during qualifying at a race track he'd never seen, then went out and blitzed the field to win his first AMA National. Second place at Phoenix International Raceway went to Muzzy Kawasaki's Fred Merkel, the two-times World Superbike Champion returning to AMA racing after a miserable few years riding inferior equipment at world level. Merkel, too, had never seen the race track on the outskirts of the city in the Valley of the Sun and he passed Edwards to finish second, some six seconds behind Corser. James was fourth.

There were some fireworks after the race when Rob Muzzy filed a protest through his number two rider, Takahiro Sohwa. His argument stemmed from the fact that Ferracci's Ducati 955s were homologated by the AMA as new motor cycles, despite being just Ducati 888s with stroked motors. It was the first of many protests regarding the V-twins in 1994.

The third round of the series very nearly blew up in the faces of the AMA. Constructed in a parking lot of the Pomona Fairplex on the outskirts of Los Angeles, the first-time event came under immediate fire from the riders for being unsafe. Chain-link fences, pedestrian bridges located dangerously close to the 2.1-mile track and a bumpy racing surface had the top riders up in arms. Talk of boycotts resulted in bridges being moved and extra hay bales being brought in – but when push came to shove most ended up racing. The most notable non-starter was Kevin Magee: 'If right now I could be picked up and dropped back in Japan racing superbikes – I'd do it,' the frustrated Australian said.

Despite the bumps, bridges and fences, the winner was again Corser. This time the Aussie led Japan's Sohwa and Canadian Steve Crevier (on the third Muzzy Kawasaki) across the line, marking the first time in AMA Superbike history that the winners' circle was made up entirely of non-Americans. Edwards was running third late in the race when he crashed on his own oil, the result of a mechanical failure and the beginning of a bad run for the young Texan.

For the second race in a row, Corser's Ducati was protested by Muzzy – this time his claims were based on the availability of the 955s which were being ridden by Corser and his team-mate, Pascal Picotte.

'The bottom line is that twin-cylinder motor cycles have to be made in quantities of 50 units and be available through regular channels for street use. That motor cycle isn't available,' Muzzy said.

Picotte was the forgotten man of AMA Superbike racing in early 1994. After being overshadowed in the Ducati team for the past few years by one Mr Doug Polen, the French Canadian was probably foaming at the mouth when the Texan departed to Honda. Finally, he was the number one rider in AMA racing's most successful road racing team – then came the Corser steamroller, and suddenly Picotte was dropped a notch once again.

Three years of futility finally ended for Picotte when the series reached its fourth round, at Laguna Seca. Picotte beat Corser in a straight fight, handing the Australian only his second defeat in four races. Third went to James after a gutsy, last-corner outbraking manoeuvre on Merkel. Edwards's unlucky streak continued as he crashed on oil dropped on the race track by Thomas Stevens's blown-up Yoshimura Suzuki.

The AMA handed down a decision the day after the Laguna Seca race – the Ducatis would be mandated to carry an additional 20 pounds. Not for next year, but for the very next race – making all the superbikes (twins and four-cylinders) equal in weight, at 355 pounds, and putting to an end the controversy of the Ducati's unfair advantage.

Weight gain or not, Picotte seemed to take well to this winning thing, following up his Laguna Seca victory with a win at Road America in Wisconsin. For the second race in a row, Picotte was the quickest in qualifying and the quickest in the race. Second place at the finish line went to James, but that was later taken away in a controversial decision by the AMA. With his team-mate Edwards lying on the outside of the final corner after a late-race crash, James ignored a waving yellow flag (which prohibits passing) and went by Picotte on the last lap. He missed a gearshift on the run to the flag and was repassed by Picotte – but then the AMA handed him a one-lap penalty, dropping him out of the points. Second place thus went to Merkel, with privateer Ducati rider David Sadowski finishing third. Corser, after making his first error of the season with an off-track excursion, finished fourth but maintained his tidy advantage in the points standings.

Just when it seemed that the pendulum was beginning to swing towards Picotte and away from Corser, the Aussie reached out and pulled it back with a crucial pole position and race win at New Hampshire International Speedway. The man who came closest to stopping Corser at Loudon was again Merkel, who scored his third runner-up finish of the season. It would really be the last hurrah for the Californian, though, as mechanical ills seemed to cause him to lose interest late in the season and basically he became a non-factor.

Third was James, starting to claw his way back into the hunt for the championship. Still, he trailed Corser by 43 points with only four rounds remaining – he needed a miracle just to make it close.

The near-miracle came at Mid-Ohio. With Corser's Ducati failing early in the race, James's second-place finish in the National moved him to within 16 points. Suddenly, there was a championship battle again.

But taking away from all that was the performance of Edwards. The Yamaha rider finally got the monkey off his back with his stunning first-time victory at the Mid-Ohio Sports Car Course. The ever-confident Edwards of old was back, giving credit to motivational tapes and a refined set-up on his YZF750. In the National, Edwards held off the advances of his veteran team-mate in record-setting fashion, after already breaking the lap record during qualifying. Third place went to the ever-consistent Sohwa.

Mid-Ohio will also long be remembered as the place where the Harley-Davidson VR1000 finally became a force to be reckoned with. Hard-riding Miguel DuHamel put the first-year bike on the front row and ran at the front of the pack – leading the first lap much to the delight of the record crowd of American iron fans – until the shift linkage came apart on the 14th lap. But the team had finally made a statement, after starting the season as the laughing stock of AMA racing. It was definitely a case of he who laughs last laughs loudest – and Harley appeared to be on the verge of a good chuckle.

A few weeks later, Edwards continued what was a late-season domination of the Superbike class. The Texan came out the best in what may have been the most exciting superbike race in AMA history – with eight riders fighting it out to the chequered flag at Brainerd International Raceway in Minnesota. As they crossed the stripe it was Edwards, Corser and James – one, two, three. And the Harley with DuHamel aboard was fourth – after leading early on – with only a last-lap slide keeping him from finishing second, or at the very least, third.

Corser was lucky even to be in the

UNITED STATES ROAD RACING REVIEW

Left: Phoenix rising – or just another hog roast? Harley-Davidson were a welcome arrival, on the pace by year's end, if not yet reliable.

Jamie James *(opposite)* missed the title for the sake of a stuck Yamaha exhaust valve.

Japan's Sohwa *(below)* rode a strong and consistent season on the Muzzy Kawasaki.

Below left: Colin Edwards, the coming man of US racing.

race, after suffering a difficult weekend. First, he'd rolled a rent-a-car while doing a hot lap around the race track during press day on Thursday. He followed that stunt with an horrific crash through the 150 mph first turn, destroying one of his Ducatis and gouging his right hand. He spent Friday night and Saturday in hospital, but shook off the pain to finish second in the race: a gutsy performance worthy of a champion-to-be.

Corser's comfort zone in the championship completely disappeared one round later, though, when he crashed at Sears Point while running with eventual winner Edwards. The crash wasn't Corser's fault. The frame fractured near the shock linkage, causing the bike to bottom-out and tossing the Aussie off the high-side. With Edwards riding unmolested to victory, Picotte came a narrow second over James and Sadowski. Just like that, James held the lead in the championship by three points – with only Road Atlanta remaining.

If things weren't interesting enough, World Superbike Champion Scott Russell returned for the final round at Road Atlanta – only 30 miles or so from his home on the outskirts of the city. Although he was out-duelled by Edwards in the battle for pole position, Russell waited around for nobody in the National as he streaked away to win by some ten seconds.

What went on behind him was much more interesting. Once he realised there was no matching Russell, Edwards slowed the pace, hoping to spur on his team-mate James who was at the rear of the pack contesting third. Suddenly, James caught fire and worked his way past Corser, Picotte and Sadowski to take over second. On the 20th lap, though, it all fell apart for the likeable Louisiana rider as he lost the edge, victim of a stuck exhaust valve. James dropped to eighth place, but that turned into seventh on the final lap when the Harley pulled out with a broken fuse.

There was still hope for James –

but on the last lap Corser was able to move past Sadowski (who was later accused by many of letting his fellow-Ducati rider by) to finish fourth – taking the extra championship point he needed for the title.

So Corser took the AMA Superbike title back to Australia after a very impressive season, in stark contrast to his countryman. Magee's pitiful year ended fittingly with him in hospital, the victim of – believe it or not – a spider bite that forced him to miss the final round of the series.

So much for pre-season predictions. The man who may have been even more impressive than Corser in AMA road racing was Rich Oliver. The veteran from northern California won eight of the ten 250 cc Grand Prix Nationals. He was beaten fair and square by Jimmy Filice at Daytona (in Filice's only AMA race of the year), but he was never headed again. His only other non-victory came at Brainerd International Raceway where a tyre failure caused him to crash.

179

ISLE OF MAN TT REVIEW

HEROES AND VICTIMS

Class act Hislop made a victorious return to the Formula One TT.

Above right: Joey Dunlop: when you've just made history, what better than a quiet fag?

The TT promised much for the radical Britten (opposite), but brought only heartbreak. This is Nick Jefferies in practice.

by Mac McDiarmid

The 1994 Isle of Man TT, like so many before it, was a saga of viciously mixed fortunes. The year may be remembered for Joey Dunlop's Junior and Lightweight double, taking his tally to 17 wins, way ahead of the all-time field. It may equally be remembered for the welcome return of Steve Hislop, by far the classiest act of the field. Consummate victories in the Formula One and Senior races gave the Scot 11 career TT wins, overhauling one G. Agostini and another Hawick flier, Jimmy Guthrie, to stand a clear third in the rankings.

Other memories are grimmer, not least Robert Dunlop's terrifying crash when his rear wheel collapsed, catapulting him into a Ballaugh garden wall. The four-times TT winner faces a long recuperation with serious arm and leg injuries.

But the blackest cloud to settle on Mona's Isle came on the Thursday of practice week, when Mark Farmer died after crashing the Britten V1000 at Black Dub. One of the most able riders never to win a TT, and one of the most cheerful and engaging characters in motor cycle sport, Farmer will be hugely missed. Practice week also claimed the life of former Scottish champion, Rob Mitchell.

Then there was the weather, which did much to dampen the increasingly important festival side of proceedings. The opening race, the Formula One TT, was allowed to start with a violent shower sweeping across the Island, and visibility on the Mountain manifestly too poor for racing. Just as mystifying was the decision to halt the race on lap two, when conditions were just as manifestly acceptable. Bad weather also caused Monday's races to be postponed to Tuesday.

Yet, despite its shortcomings, the Isle of Man continues to hold a special magic for competitors and spectators alike. While essentially now a British affair, this year riders from no less than 19 countries competed in an event which is like no other. For most of them the TT is a dream which surpasses danger and hardship, if not understanding. And the Manx authorities are at last putting into the festival the imagination it has always begged.

ISLE OF MAN TT REVIEW

MARK FARMER

One of two fatalities during TT fortnight, the death of Mark Farmer was a quite superfluous reminder that the Mountain Circuit has no favourites. The hazards are equal no matter how skilful, popular or well-respected you may be. Farmer was all those things, and when he died instantly after apparently being high-sided at notorious black-spot Black Dub the island was a very sombre place.

Farmer, who was making an increasing mark on British short circuits, had planned a full TT programme. The picture shows one of his last practice rides, on his Supersport 600 Yamaha, on which he set a fastest practice lap that was not equalled.

PRACTICE

If Hislop was rusty after a two-year absence, it didn't show. In his very first session he dragged his RC45, kicking and weaving, to a 120 mph lap, scaring spectators and rider alike: a kerb clipped with a wheel at Bray Hill, a wall clouted with a leg at Ginger Hall.

By Thursday Hislop had discarded Doug Polen's Superbike chassis in favour of his own. The result: 123.53 mph, just 0.8 seconds slower than Carl Fogarty's outright lap record – with a video pack strapped to his back! 'It didn't feel particularly quick. I just wanted to give Duke Video a good recording,' reported the laconic Scot.

Performance like this put Hislop in a class of his own. The only other 120 mph laps, both on Hondas, were by Phillip McCallen (121.15 mph, Wednesday evening) and Robert Dunlop (120.69 mph, Thursday afternoon). Handling problems or not, things were looking good for the brand-new RC45.

Meanwhile, the anticipated face-off with John Britten's radical V1000 was still-born, as the big V-twin suffered a succession of electrical and mechanical problems, as well as the trauma of Farmer's accident. The best Britten lap, eighth overall, was Farmer's, at 118.21 mph on Wednesday evening.

In the other classes, a lap at 116.07 mph allowed Phillip McCallen to edge out Robert Dunlop in a Junior event in which Hondas secured the top four times. Joey Dunlop was third, Ian Lougher fourth.

Mark Farmer's Tuesday morning lap at 116.89 mph on his Supersport 600 Yamaha survived the week, a tribute to a rider less fortunate. Ian Simpson, Steve Ward, Jim Moodie and Iain Duffus held the next four places, with honours shared between CBR Honda and FZR Yamaha 600s. Jason McEwen, one of ten Maudes Trophy competitors from New Zealand, impressed with a lap at 113.10 mph on his first IoM visit.

If most classes were tight, Jim Moodie was in one of his own among 400 Supersport qualifiers, almost 30 seconds ahead of the field. Yet the Scot was still outside his own lap record in a week in which no unofficial solo records were set (although Hislop's time in combined F1/Senior practice shaded his 1991 F1 record by 0.4 seconds). Fellow-Yamaha rider, Iain Duffus, was second, with Bob Jackson's Kawasaki third.

In 125 cc practice, it was the usual tight story. Just 21 seconds separated a top four comprising Robert Dunlop, Mick Lofthouse, David Brown and that man, Joey Dunlop.

In the very first practice session for the new single cylinder class, New Zealand's Robert Holden thundered to a lap at 109.79 mph, a speed no one was to approach all week. Second, also Ducati-mounted, was Bill Swallow – unknown as a TT rider, but a near-legend in the Classic Manx Grand Prix.

For new faces, and new speeds, you had to look to the sidecars. In only their second TT, Rob Fisher and Mike Wynn, using a stock FZR600 engine bought from a breaker's en route for the Island, blasted to the week's fastest three-wheeler time – an unofficial record at 104.53 mph.

FORMULA ONE TT

Steve Hislop actually sets his stall out to practise blistering laps on cold tyres from a standing start. If it works come race time – and usually it does – the opposition is demoralised and the race all but won.

So it was this year. By Glen Helen, on lap one, Hislop led McCallen by seven seconds, pulling away inexorably to win by 84.6 seconds after six laps. McCallen came home second, Joey Dunlop third – a Honda 1-2-3 and their 13th Formula One victory in succession.

'I couldn't find the rhythm at first...it wasn't flowing. I only got going at the end,' said McCallen, who set the fastest lap of the race, his last, at 122.08 mph. By then Hislop was long gone, for the crucial quick lap was his first, 121.79 mph from a standing start.

'Once the lead got to 30 seconds,' said Hislop afterwards, 'I knew I'd be safe even if a mistake was made at a pit stop.' In fact it was McCallen's pit work which was slower, his two stops costing 24 seconds more than the Scot's.

Joey Dunlop's third place came after a five-lap dice with Yorkshire's Steve Ward, including evasive action against a stray dog – and a van. Ward looked set for a comfortable rostrum place until his clutch broke. He eventually limped home in 16th.

Gary Radcliffe and Nigel Davies brought their RC30s into fourth and six places, separated by Iain Duffus on an elderly, intermediate-tyred OW01 Yamaha. For Davies this was some consolation after the disappointment of leading the aborted first running of the race.

The anticipated challenge from the younger generation evaporated when Jason Griffiths and Simon Beck both retired. TT debutant Michael Rutter placed 17th at an average of 109.83 mph.

With Robert Holden declining to ride the 'underdeveloped' Britten, it was left to last year's F1 winner, Nick Jefferies, to fly the Kiwi flag. Riding with a black armband in tribute to team-mate Mark Farmer, he retired at Ballacraine after a 20-minute pit stop failed to cure an ignition fault.

ISLE OF MAN TT REVIEW

Right: Iain Duffus, winner of the Supersport 600 TT.

Jim Moodie *(below)* flies at Ballaugh. While not the first single TT winner, he was the first winner of the new Single Cylinder TT.

Joey Dunlop *(main photo)* cleaves a path through typical Manx *chiaroscuro* scenery on his 125 Honda as he heads for the 16th of 17 TT wins.

Far right, top: TT veteran Brian Reid brushes past the wall on the way to second in the Junior.

There was a double sidecar win for Rob Fisher and Mick Wynn *(far right).*

SINGLE CYLINDER TT

No one knew quite what to expect of the TT's newest class, although the wags were laying bets that insufficient would finish to populate the rostrum. But the big banger boys had learned from the carnage of their North-West 200 outing: out of 29 starters, a creditable 18 finished.

More surprising still were the speeds, from a grid largely composed of tricked-out trail bikes. Jim Moodie flew round at 112.66 mph on his second lap, to overhaul early leader Robert Holden. The Scot maintained the advantage to the finish, catching Holden on the road on lap three, and thereafter spraying him with oil from the XTZ600 motor. A frustrated Holden claimed he could have eased his Ducati Supermono past at any time, if only he could see.

Jason Griffiths was a distant third, but fancied riders Bill Swallow (Ducati) and Simon Beck (701 Rumi) retired when in strong positions on the final lap with a split tank and electrical problems respectively.

125 cc TT

'This one was for Robert,' said Joey Dunlop after victory in the 125 cc TT, as his younger brother lay in hospital recovering from his freak Formula One crash. The win, which took Joey's personal tally to 16 (the first was in 1977), was one of his most emphatic. He was never headed, reaching the flag 71 seconds ahead of Irish up-and-comer Denis McCullough. Between them, the brothers Dunlop have won every 125 cc TT since the class was reintroduced in 1989.

'Yer Maun's' closest challenge came from Yamaha-mounted Mick Lofthouse, until the Lancastrian's silencer came loose at two-thirds distance. Manxman Chris Fargher placed third after a five-year lay-off (during which time he acted as a travelling marshal, 'but this is more fun'), with Noel Clegg fourth and Glen English fifth. Luckless Ian Lougher lay fourth until his Aprilia sprung a water leak, while fancied runners Bob Heath and Brian Reid also retired with mechanical problems.

SUPERSPORT 600 TT

In an exhilarating Yamaha and Scottish one-two, Iain Duffus got the better of compatriot Ian Simpson to clinch his first TT win in Tuesday's rescheduled Supersport 600 race. After many years of ill-luck and near-misses, the Pirelli tyre salesman's victory was one of the sweetest and most popular of the week. At the flag Duffus led by just 9.4 seconds, with Steve Ward a mere 2.4 seconds adrift in third.

At half-distance, it had looked like a Scottish triple, with Jim Moodie leading by three and five seconds from Duffus and Simpson respectively. Then, in the cruellest of ironies, Moodie crashed out at Black Dub, the same corner which had claimed the life of his Mitsui teammate just five days earlier. Fortunately his injuries were minor.

The seeds of Duffus's win came in a lightning mid-race pit stop, when he gained a further seven seconds on Simpson, putting them almost level on the road. As well as these precious seconds, Simpson lost his contact lenses, one of which he swallowed!

Steve Ward claimed third place, aided by the fastest bike through the speed trap at 149 mph. Phillip McCallen, detuned by a stomach bug, battled to within two seconds of Simpson on lap three but eventually slowed to fourth. Bob Jackson was fifth and Nick Jefferies sixth in a race in which Honda took six of the top eight places – but not the ones that mattered most.

A compelling aside to the race was an ultimately successful attempt on the Maudes Trophy, awarded for feats of exceptional machine endurance, by a squad of ten Kiwi riders on FZR600 Yamahas. All ten machines – completely standard but for race-compound Metzeler tyres – were sealed before the meeting, having to endure practice and racing with no more than routine service replacements.

With the exception of 'team mentor' Robert Holden, the entire squad were Isle of Man novices. All ten finished, with 26-year-old Jason McEwen the star of the show (FZRs notwithstanding). He finished 13th at an average speed of 110.79 mph, 'loved the course', and promised to be back. One to watch for the future.

JUNIOR TT

Phillip McCallen's Junior pit stops are improving, but there's still some way to go. Last year the Portadown man forgot to stop altogether and ran out of fuel while leading. This year he remembered, but took on too little fuel in an over-hasty pit stop, spluttering to a heart-breaking halt just three miles from the chequered flag.

This handed the lead to Joey Dunlop, trailing by 16 seconds at the time, for his 17th TT win. A delighted Dunlop, struggling with a loose footrest for most of the race, confessed he had no idea he was leading until he heard his reception at the grandstand.

Brian Reid, a 250 cc specialist, claimed second, after a stirring tussle with local man Chris Fargher which ended when the Manxman slid off at Governor's Bridge on the final lap.

Ian Lougher, still trying to recapture the form that brought victory and the current lap record in 1990, had led at Glen Helen on the opening lap. But first McCallen, hustled past and then he dropped from third to fifth when his exhaust pipe cracked on the final lap.

As with the Irish, one Welshman's misfortune was another's good luck. Young Jason Griffiths inherited the final rostrum position, to add to his third in the Singles event. Scotland's Ian Simpson was fourth in a rare 250 cc outing, his first Junior TT.

SUPERSPORT 400 TT

The last Supersport 400 TT (the event is deleted from the 1995 programme) turned out to be a triple whammy for Jim Moodie: his second win of the week, his second double in two years, including back-to-back SS400 wins. And, despite a broken thumb and lacerated hand from his SS600 crash, the tough Glaswegian made it look easy, setting the fastest lap of the race from a standing start, and never seeming remotely under pressure. At the flag he was 77 seconds ahead of Steve Linsdell, third in the same event last year.

Dave Morris completed a Yamaha monopoly of the rostrum after a race-long dice with Derek Young, who placed fourth. Iain Duffus's engine blew while he was lying second on lap three. And Bob Jackson, starting from the back of the field, battled through to third before crashing, miraculously without serious injury, at the frighteningly fast 11th Milestone.

SENIOR TT

Friday's Senior was a carbon copy of Sunday's Formula One race, with Steve Hislop leading home the same Honda clean sweep of Phillip McCallen and Joey Dunlop. Again, Hislop's success was founded on an audacious opening lap, this time at 122.5 mph, the fastest of the race. Victory hoisted him to third in the all-time list, behind Dunlop and Mike Hailwood.

Both leaders experienced minor difficulties. Hislop incurred a ten-second penalty after failing to halt in the stop box on lap two; later the edge went off his brakes. McCallen hit a bird, suffered an over-tight steering damper and nearly came to grief at Bishopscourt on oil from Nick Jefferies's Britten. Only Dunlop, using Hislop's spare forks, reported a trouble-free outing – although his RC45 had been so lively at the start of practice, the Ballymoney man had thought of going home.

Again, the battle between Castrol Honda Britain's RC45s and the ill-fated Britten squad failed to materialise. A lap at 118 mph put Jefferies seventh after lap one, before a holed clutch cover ended the V1000's race.

Welshmen Nigel Davies (Honda RC30) and Jason Griffiths (Kawasaki ZXR) were fourth and fifth, with Gary Radcliffe bringing another RC30 into sixth.

SIDECAR TT: RACE A

Rob Fisher and Mick Wynn proved their practice form was no fluke with a start-to-finish win in the first sidecar event, shattering race and lap records in the process. Last year's double winner, Dave Molyneux, was second, 25 seconds behind, with Mick Boddice Senior – still chasing that elusive tenth TT win – a further minute adrift in third.

It was a victory, too, for Yamaha, whose FZR600 engines collected five of the top six places. And with the first two-stroke ninth (and the second 35th) four-strokes were utterly dominant.

After practising with a stock road motor, Fisher bolted in his tuned race engine to spectacular effect. Only Molyneux could mount a serious challenge, playing lap record leapfrog with the Cumbrians before Fisher put the issue beyond reply on the final circuit. Despite damp patches and blustery winds, he lapped at 106.49 mph, over 2 mph up on the previous best, and within sight of Boddice's outright 750 cc record.

SIDECAR TT: RACE B

The 1-2-3 was the same, but conditions were vile. Yet even a downpour at the start of the second sidecar TT failed to dampen the pretensions of Fisher and Wynn as they slithered to their second win of the week.

Fisher didn't quite get it all his own way, however, for Roy and Tom Hanks, using intermediate tyres, held a 19-second lead by Glen Helen on lap one. But, as conditions improved, Fisher came into his own, easing ahead progressively, then holding off a last-lap charge to win by 46 seconds from Dave Molyneux. The Hanks brothers eventually dropped to fourth as Mick Boddice slipped by on the final circuit.

183

BRITISH NATIONAL RACING REVIEW

MUCH ADO ABOUT NORTON

by Gary Pinchin

Ian Simpson took the Norton rotary to a championship win; team-mate Phil Borley (inset) shared the wins and rostrums. Sadly it may have been the unorthodox machine's last season.

Change and change again. For 1994 the Motorcycle Race Promoters Committee (MRPC) decided to be rid of the confusion caused by 1993's two virtually identical national series (the BBC-televised six-round H.E.A.T. Supercup and the eight-round ACU British championship) and amalgamate them into one 11-round Supercup Championship. The rest of the calendar was padded out with numerous non-championship nationals – ironically with some paying considerably more prize money than the (socalled) prestigious Supercup.

The downside was that the BBC were only interested in televising four rounds (Anglia's 'Wheels' programme screened the Snetterton round) while 1993 Supercup sponsors H.E.A.T. (Heat Electric Advisory Team) declined to sponsor the full championship so put their name only to televised rounds plus the Pembrey meeting (Wales being a strong region for H.E.A.T.). It was not surprising, then, that the part-sponsored series was both difficult to promote and confusing to the public.

There was also a shift of power on the race track, namely in the TT Superbike class – which went some way towards maintaining the profile of the major class in the series – especially since it was a British-built bike in command. In 1992 John Reynolds and the ZXR750 Kawasaki dominated British TT Superbike racing; last year it was the turn of Yamaha's new YZF750 with James Whitham doing the lion's share of the winning from the saddle of the Fast Orange machine. But 1994 will be remembered for the all-conquering team effort by Duckhams Norton, which surpassed even the glories of the mega-buck JPS Norton team of 1989-92.

Even though the crowd-pleasing Norton was again winning, some of the Supercup rounds failed to draw big crowds. There were 12,500 people for the Cadwell Park round in late August but the rest of the late-season meetings – four in five weeks – simply failed to attract the paying public. Yet at the non-championship Mallory Race of the Year, the weekend between those four meetings, there was a huge crowd for a lacklustre national entry, with only a 'Past Masters' Triumph race to enliven the proceedings. Perhaps a little variety needs to be breathed into Supercup?

Norton's Ian Simpson and Phil Borley amassed 31 podium finishes, including 14 race wins, on the rotary-powered machines and the duo finished first and second on no less than 11 occasions in the 11-round, 22-race Supercup series.

Yet the success story could in fact be the swansong for the Colin Seeley-managed, Brian Crighton-engineered team – at least as far as using Norton machines is concerned. 'I'd like to keep the Norton team going,' admitted the patriotic Seeley towards the end of his team's victorious Supercup campaign. 'We even have the resources within our team to build replica race bikes, but we've had no positive vibes from the Norton company and unless they agree to support our efforts we'll wrap the Norton thing up and consider racing other machinery.'

Scot Simpson, from Dalbeattie, and Essex man Borley began the season under-rated as Superbike riders – especially on the hard-to-master Norton. Previously running a selection of Japanese superbikes, Simpson had only achieved the mediocre success one might expect from a hard-up privateer and was better known for his Supersport 600 performances. Borley, 1992 Supercup SS600 champion, earned a reputation in Europe (particularly in Spain) for his Supersport efforts and had only had limited outings on a Ducati before this season.

For the first three rounds the Norton team looked anything but championship material. The season only came alive for them in the fourth round, at Donington Park in mid-June. Until then neither Simpson nor Borley had particularly impressed. Both riders were acclimatising themselves to the unique power characteristics of the rotary engines and the taut, 500 GP-like handling of the Spondon chassis. Perfecting a new exhaust system took longer than expected, Borley had trouble adjusting to a newly built bike compared to his older number two machine, and a series of minor technical problems left everyone on the team at a low ebb.

The series began at a freezing cold Donington Park in April when Carl Fogarty took the factory development 916 Ducati to two wins amidst squally snowstorms. He beat James Whitham, who was racing a 1993 spec Moto Cinelli Ducati 926. But these two were only using the meeting as a shakedown for their respective World Superbike campaigns so their results were academic in terms of the championship.

The official Yamaha team, the force of '93, had a completely new look. Whitham was long gone to Ducati, team boss Rob McElnea was still recovering from his end-of-season Mallory crash, and the bikes now sported red and white Loctite livery rather than the previous year's exciting Fast Orange logos. There were two new riders in Jim Moodie (Norton's solitary team member in 1993) and Mark Farmer – but they also took time to get into their stride.

Farmer failed to score in the opening round but won both races at Mallory Park, beating his team-mate into second place. At third-round, rain-lashed Snetterton Farmer struggled while Moodie grabbed his first win of the year in the second leg – a dry race – after sliding off in the wet first leg.

Then the series took a recess for the annual Isle of Man TT races. Sadly Mark Farmer never returned. He was killed during practice aboard the Britten V-twin. The Loctite ride was 30-year-old Farmer's first real breakthrough after several years of being on the fringe of greatness.

Moodie dedicated his first race at Donington on 19 June to his lost friend and team-mate, but the Loctite team would have to wait until the last race of the year before recording their next win.

Borley won the second leg at Donington from Simpson, with Moodie pushed back to fourth. This was the start of the Norton steamroller – stage-managed to perfection by Seeley. Simpson racked up five straight wins and only once did Moodie manage to sneak ahead of Borley in a period of nine one-two victories for Norton in ten races.

When Borley broke down with an ignition failure in the second leg at ninth-round Brands Hatch it meant Simpson had a 25-point lead over his team-mate with Moodie a further seven points behind. Borley won both races at penultimate-round Oulton but Simpson went into the final round 17 points clear and clinched the title by winning the first leg at Brands, ahead of Borley, with Moodie third.

Borley only needed three points from the final race to make it a Norton 1-2 in the series but his clutch centre nut worked loose (for the second time in the season – it also happened in the Snetterton Race of Aces) and Moodie's second leg race win meant the Yamaha rider took runner-up spot in the championship.

After a lacklustre 1993 aboard a disappointingly slow Kawasaki, Matt Llewellyn was one of the revelations of the class on his Joe Meakin/Saber 926 Ducati. He was something of an enigma – fast enough to qualify on pole four times and capable of cutting hot laps in the races but somehow never quite capable or confident enough to put together a race win.

Llewellyn won several non-championship races in the year but at Supercup level his best result came right at the end of the year when he finished second in the final Brands race.

A couple of crashes and some mechanical problems kept him from scoring in six of the races and that hurt his final points tally, but fourth place in the championship was still a highly commendable effort from the 26-year-old privateer. He'll be even stronger in 1994 with a Meakin-supplied 916.

After a terrible season, despite a great start with the Medd team in 1993, 21-year-old Michael Rutter hit the headlines with some promising rides on his McCulloch-backed Ducati which alternated between 888 cc and 926 cc. Rutter's consistency was only hindered by a huge confidence-crunching crash (not his fault – oil on the track) at Pembrey when he damaged knee ligaments, but he'll be one of Britain's hot prospects in 1995 whether he gets a

Main photo: Double Red Photographic   Inset photo: Clive Challinor

185

Right: **The Medd team did everything right, but had a poor year with the troublesome Hondas. Former champion Roger Marshall wonders why.**

Ex-GP man Steve Patrickson *(below right)* **won a close 125 title battle.**

Opposite: **James Haydon's helmet design** *(top left)* **was well 'ard; David Jefferies and Mike Rutter showed promise on their Ducatis** *(top right)*; **newcomer Jason Vincent** *(below left)* **emerged triumphant over the luckless 250 class veterans; Steve Abbott and Julian Tailford** *(below right)* **took the sidecar title again over high-class opposition.**

manufacturer team ride or stays with McCulloch backing and opts for a 916 Ducati.

Loctite Yamaha chose to fill Mark Farmer's berth with a Kiwi. They claimed all the up-coming Brits were tied to contracts. Although Andrew Stroud finished every race in the points on the YZF, he never produced the sort of form many expected from the former 500 GP Shell Harris rider, although he did lack track knowledge. He finished sixth in the points.

The major disappointment of the year was the new Honda RC45. Castrol Honda's number one rider, Steve Hislop, got a lot of flack for his public slating of the bike early in the year, but he was ultimately proved right. The bike was slow and didn't handle and it was only after he got the Ohlins suspension he'd asked for – and tuner Tony Scott had worked his magic – that the Castrol Honda became anything like competitive.

Hislop's Honda looked like a crash waiting to happen at some tracks and the fans were denied the excitement of seeing him on the edge, at his aggressive best, until late in the season. Ironically when he did get the bike on the pace, at Pembrey, he high-sided, caught out by the track's vicious bumps.

Hislop's best result came at Snetterton, early in the year, when he was second to Moodie in the dry. The same meeting saw Honda's only win of the season when James Haydon ignored the slippery conditions to take a waterlogged first race win on the Medd Honda.

That, and Robert Dunlop's North West 200 win, were the only high spots of a trouble-torn year for the Medd team. They failed to finish the season, blaming HRC for not releasing the computer access codes to the fuel-injection system. Medd had worked closely with F1 car engineers Cosworth to tune up the V4 engines but it was wasted work without a re-programmed fuel system.

The team left a trail of disaster behind them. Ray Stringer, after realising the RC45 would not be competitive, quit the team early on to go his own, more successful, way with Ducati. Robert Dunlop crashed at the TT when his rear Marvic wheel collapsed: he was pitched into a wall and suffered terrible arm and leg injuries. Then Haydon and the team went their separate ways, when the Amersham-based 20-year-old was offered a 250 GP ride.

Kiwi Chris Haldane had some steady, if unspectacular rides on the bike and helped sort out some suspension problems, and 125 GP rider Neil Hodgson made a spectacular one-off showing at Pembrey, finishing sixth in the second leg on a bike that resembled a bucking bronco. The team eventually pulled out of the final Brands Supercup and miscellaneous end-of-season non-championship meetings.

Jason Vincent and Eugene McManus became the new order of 250 racing in the UK. Twenty-two-year-old Vincent, a former Shell Scholarship clubman, took the title when he won the penultimate round of the championship at Brands riding his A & P Windows-backed Yamaha, while a superb second half of the season saw Ulsterman McManus (also 22) come on strong with two wins and two seconds in the final five races to take the runner-up slot.

It had all looked so different after six rounds: Vincent held a two-point advantage over experienced Aprilia pilot Ian Newton; and defending national 250 champion Paul Brown was sitting in third, only eight points further adrift on his Keppel Yamaha.

Newton had sprung into contention by virtue of three straight wins but his title hopes disappeared with 14th place at Pembrey, and two missed races due to injury. He eventually finished fourth in the points behind Yamaha-mounted Steve Sawford.

Brown took the spare Medd Honda in the TT Superbike class at Cadwell in late August but shocked everyone when he parked his TZ250, even though he was still in with a shot at the title.

Also out of contention was Nigel Bosworth. He broke his scaphoid in a crash at Donington in June, but when he returned a 20-second penalty dropped him out of the points at Pembrey and his Hein Gericke RS250 Honda wouldn't fire up for him to take pole in the next round at Cadwell.

Most observers agreed that 19-year-old Darren Barton was the 'find' of the 125 class. 'The Flying Flea' won three races, placed second twice, then missed the final round to take over Neil Hodgson's vacated Burnett Honda at the Argentine GP.

Barton finished only fourth in the championship, which was won by vastly experienced Steve Patrickson. The former GP runner and nine-times British Champion didn't win a race but scored steadily in every round to claim title number ten. The quality of racing in the class was second to none, with packs of as many as ten riders fighting for the lead each weekend.

Kevin Mawdsley won three races on his way to runner-up spot in the championship with the McCready RS125. Robin Appleyard took one win and finished third overall, while Chris Palmer won two rounds after parking his Yamaha in favour of a Paul Bird Honda. Andy Hatton won one race and Neil Hodgson also took one.

Mark Norman, Fernando Mendes, Barry Stanley and Les Wood might not have won races but they figured in the action at the front of the field almost every weekend.

The new TZ125 was the other major let-down of the season. Only in the final four races of the year, after continuous work on Frank Wrathall's dyno, did Mick Lofthouse finally get the Denis Trollope-entered machine up into the leading pack. He finished second in the final Brands races – an indication of things to come next year

BRITISH NATIONAL RACING REVIEW

when Honda bring out their latest generation 125?

The blue and yellow Duckhams-inspired hues didn't just dominate the TT Superbike class. Colin Seeley's team fielded Ian Simpson in the Supersport 600 class on an Avon-shod Yamaha, and he clinched the title in the penultimate round after several race-long scraps with arch rival Mike Edwards.

'Simmo' won six races to Edwards's five, but the V & M-backed rider would have provided even sterner opposition had organisers at the Snetterton round in May not made a diabolical call, handing out a 20-second penalty to Edwards for jumping the start. Video evidence clearly showed he hadn't infringed the law but the ACU refused to back down from the decision.

Edwards, under pressure to deliver a win every race, then slipped off at Pembrey and the series was virtually handed to Simpson. But Edwards's efforts didn't go unnoticed, for his name was being linked with a Castrol Honda ride for 1995 by the end of the year.

Scot Iain Duffus, who achieved his first TT win after ten years of trying, was a constant threat on his Akito/Shirlaws Yamaha if either of the two leaders ever showed signs of hitting trouble.

The Single Cylinder class was promoted to Supercup level in 1994 for an eight-round championship. No one could argue against the wide variety of machinery the singles attracted, but early races were boring processions. However, the class took off at Oulton Park in June after a thrilling wheel-to-wheel scrap between Mike Edwards on the factory MZ and Nick Hopkins on Team GB's official works Over Yamaha which the latter won.

Edwards, after teething troubles with the Martin Sweet-tuned, Dave Pearce-built MZ early in the series, came good in the final four races, placing second to Alan Carter's Ducati Supermono at Pembrey after another frantic dice and then won the final three rounds going away.

Carter had also won the Mallory round but a series of problems ruled the Top Gun-entered former GP rider out of the championship reckoning. The title went instead to the official Shell Team Harris Yamaha 'works' rider, Dave Rawlins. The Triumph Motorcycles tester scored in every round, winning at Knockhill and even jetting back from Texas (where he was testing Triumphs, naturally!) for the Pembrey weekend, to bag a few more points.

Scott Smart, son of former international star Paul and nephew of Barry Sheene, took the ACU Superteen Challenge title. He finished equal on points with Neil Baker, but got the verdict after winning three races to Baker's two.

Smart's end of season was laced with crashes and pain, however. He broke his collarbone when he went down in qualifying at Pembrey, after his Yamaha engine blew up. With the Superteen title sewn up he raced Team Pelsall's Yamaha TZ250 at Oulton, but rebroke his collarbone after high-siding out of the race. Then he crashed Team GB's spare Yamaha in testing prior to the Donington World Superbike meeting, breaking bones in his hand and ankle.

Once again there were two sidecar championships. Veterans Mick Boddice Senior and Dave Wells retained their Formula Two title in a thrilling last race at Brands. They finished fourth to equal Geoff Bell and Nick Roche's 67-point tally, but took the title on more second places; each crew had won a race apiece. Manxman Dave Molyneux and Peter Hill won the final round, their second win of the series, to finish third overall while other winners were Rob Fisher/Mick Wynn and Gary Smith/Tony Balazs.

The Open Class was won by Steve Abbott and Julian Tailford. They led the five-race series after winning the second round at Mallory but would have been pushed much harder for the title had Derek Brindley and Paul Hutchinson not suffered a gearbox failure in the opening Donington round.

And so to 1995...and more change. Rumours suggest that Supercup will be back to eight rounds with television coverage by Sky Sports while the BBC will be offered a four-race, non-championship international programme. As usual, the format of the championship was still to be announced as we went to press. The only definite change will be reducing Superteens from Supersport 400 machines to Supersport 125s, with backing from Cagiva and Aprilia.

187

OTHER MAJOR 1994 RESULTS

Compiled by Kay Edge

Sidecar World Championship

DONINGTON PARK CIRCUIT, England, 2 May. 2.500-mile/4.023-km circuit.
Sidecar World Championship, round 1 (25 laps, 62.500 miles/100.575 km)
1 Derek Brindley/Paul Hutchinson, GB/GB (LCR Honda). 2 Markus Bösiger/Jurg Egli, CH/CH (LCR-ADM); 3 Steve Webster/Adolf Hänni, GB/CH (LCR-Krauser); 4 Barry Brindley/Scott Whiteside, GB/GB (LCR-Yamaha); 5 Paul Güdel/Charly Güdel, CH/CH (LCR-ADM); 6 Klaus Klaffenböck/Christian Parzer, A/A (LCR-Bartol); 7 Jukka Lauslehto/Juha Joutsen, SF/SF (LCR-ADM); 8 Darren Dixon/Andy Hetherington, GB/GB (LCR-Yamaha); 9 Tony Wyssen/Kilian Wyssen, CH/CH (LCR-Krauser); 10 Steve Abbott/Julian Tailford, GB/GB (Windle-Krauser); 11 Reiner Koster/Oscar Combi, CH/I (LCR-ADM); 12 Mark Reddington/Trevor Crone, GB/GB (LCR-ADM); 13 Kevin Webster/Phil Coombes, GB/GB (LCR-Krauser); 14 Benny Janssen/Frans van Kessel, NL/NL (LCR-Yamaha); 15 Billy Gälross/Shaun Smith, S/GB (LCR-Yamaha).
Fastest lap: Abbott, 1m 37.590s.
Championship points: 1 D. Brindley, 25; **2** Bösiger, 20; **3** S. Webster, 16; **4** B. Brindley, 13; **5** Güdel, 11; **6** Klaffenböck, 10.

HOCKENHEIMRING, Germany, 12 June. 4.220-mile/6.792-km circuit.
Sidecar World Championship, round 2 (13 laps, 54.860 miles/88.296 km)
1 Rolf Biland/Kurt Waltisperg, CH/CH (LCR-Swissauto), 28m 35.190s, 115.156 mph/185.324 km/h.
2 Steve Webster/Adolf Hänni, GB/CH (LCR-Krauser); 3 Steve Abbott/Julian Tailford, GB/GB (Windle-Krauser); 4 Klaus Klaffenböck/Christian Parzer, A/A (LCR-Bartol); 5 Barry Brindley/Scott Whiteside, GB/GB (LCR-Yamaha); 6 Jukka Lauslehto/Juha Joutsen, SF/SF (LCR-ADM); 7 Paul Güdel/Charly Güdel, CH/CH (LCR-ADM); 8 Tony Wyssen/Kilian Wyssen, CH/CH (LCR-Krauser); 9 Yoshisada Kumagaya/Simon Prior, J/GB (LCR-ADM); 10 Ralph Bohnhorst/Peter Brown, D/GB (LCR-Steinhausen); 11 Markus Bösiger/Jurg Egli, CH/CH (LCR-ADM); 12 Mark Reddington/Trevor Crone, GB/GB (LCR-ADM); 13 Gary Knight/Trevor Hopkinson, GB/GB (Windle-Krauser).
Fastest lap: Güdel, 2m 09.838s, 117.017 mph/188.321 km/h.
Championship points: 1 S. Webster, 36; **2** Biland, Bösiger and D. Brindley, 25; **5** B. Brindley, 24; **6** Klaffenböck, 23.

CIRCUIT VAN DRENTHE, Assen, Holland, 25 June. 3.759-mile/6.049-km circuit.
Sidecar World Championship, round 3 (17 laps, 63.903 miles/102.833 km)
1 Rolf Biland/Kurt Waltisperg, CH/CH (LCR-Swissauto), 37m 44.428s, 101.584 mph/163.484 km/h.
2 Klaus Klaffenböck/Christian Parzer, A/A (LCR-Bartol); 3 Derek Brindley/Paul Hutchinson, GB/GB (LCR-Honda); 4 Ralph Bohnhorst/Peter Brown, D/GB (LCR-Steinhausen); 5 Paul Güdel/Charly Güdel, CH/CH (LCR-ADM); 6 Steve Abbott/Julian Tailford, GB/GB (Windle-Krauser); 7 Markus Egloff/Urs Egloff, CH/CH (LCR-Yamaha); 8 Jukka Lauslehto/Juha Joutsen, SF/SF (LCR-ADM); 9 Markus Bösiger/Jurg Egli, CH/CH (LCR-ADM); 10 Yoshisada Kumagaya/Rinie Bettgens, J/NL (LCR-ADM); 11 Kevin Webster/Harry Hofsteenge, GB/NL (LCR-Krauser); 12 Gary Knight/Trevor Hopkinson, GB/GB (Windle-Krauser); 13 Markus Schlosser/Giancarlo Cavadini, CH/CH (LCR-ADM); 14 Bert Janssen/Frans van Kessel, NL/NL (LCR-Yamaha); 15 Reiner Koster/Oliver Combi, CH/I (LCR-ADM).
Fastest lap: Steve Webster/Adolf Hänni, GB/CH (LCR-Krauser), 2m 11.423s, 102.960 mph/165.697 km/h.
Championship points: 1 Biland, 50; **2** Klaffenböck, 43; **3** D. Brindley, 41; **4** S. Webster, 36; **5** Abbott and Bösiger, 32.

ÖSTERREICHRING, Zeltweg, Austria, 17 July. 3.636-mile/5.853-km circuit.
Sidecar World Championship, round 4 (16 laps, 58.176 miles/93.650 km)
1 Darren Dixon/Andy Hetherington, GB/GB (LCR-ADM), 34m 36.887s, 113.468 mph/182.609 km/h.
2 Markus Bösiger/Jurg Egli, CH/CH (LCR-ADM); 3 Rolf Biland/Kurt Waltisperg, CH/CH (LCR-Swissauto); 4 Paul Güdel/Charly Güdel, CH/CH (LCR-ADM); 5 Steve Webster/Adolf Hänni, GB/CH (LCR-Krauser); 6 Jukka Lauslehto/Juha Joutsen, SF/SF (LCR-ADM); 7 Ralph Bohnhorst/Peter Brown, D/GB (LCR-Steinhausen); 8 Steve Abbott/Julian Tailford, GB/GB (Windle-Krauser); 9 Yoshisada Kumagaya/Michael Finnegan, J/GB (LCR-ADM); 10 Barry Brindley/Scott Whiteside, GB/GB (LCR-Yamaha); 11 Markus Egloff/Urs Egloff, CH/CH (LCR-Yamaha); 12 Kevin Webster/Harry Hofsteenge, GB/NL (LCR-Krauser); 13 Billy Gälross/Peter Berglund, S/S (LCR-Yamaha); 14 Tony Wyssen/Kilian Wyssen, CH/CH (LCR-Krauser); 15 Reiner Koster/Oscar Combi, CH/I (LCR-ADM).
Fastest lap: Dixon, 1m 53.810s, 115.040 mph/185.139 km/h.
Championship points: 1 Biland, 66; **2** Bösiger, 52; **3** S. Webster, 47; **4** Güdel, 44; **5** Klaffenböck, 43; **6** D. Brindley, 41.

DONINGTON PARK CIRCUIT, England, 23 July. 2.500-mile/4.023-km circuit.
Sidecar World Championship, round 5 (26 laps, 65.000 miles/104.598 km)
1 Rolf Biland/Kurt Waltisperg, CH/CH (LCR-Swissauto), 42m 54.342s, 90.889 mph/146.271 km/h.
2 Derek Brindley/Paul Hutchinson, GB/GB (LCR-Honda); 3 Steve Webster/Adolf Hänni, GB/CH (LCR-Krauser); 4 Klaus Klaffenböck/Christian Parzer, A/A (LCR-Bartol); 5 Paul Güdel/Charly Güdel, CH/CH (LCR-ADM); 6 Yoshisada Kumagaya/Michael Finnegan, J/GB (LCR-ADM); 7 Steve Abbott/Julian Tailford, GB/GB (Windle-Krauser); 8 Barry Brindley/Scott Whiteside, GB/GB (LCR-Yamaha); 9 Mark Reddington/Trevor Crone, GB/GB (LCR-ADM); 10 Bert Janssen/Frans van Kessel, NL/NL (LCR-Yamaha); 11 Kevin Webster/Harry Hofsteenge, GB/NL (LCR-Krauser); 12 Ralph Bohnhorst/Peter Brown, D/GB (LCR-Steinhausen); 13 Ian Willford/Greig Hallam, GB/GB (LCR-ADM-Yamaha); 14 David Hoskin/David James, GB/GB (LCR-ADM-Yamaha); 15 Gary Knight/Trevor Hopkinson, GB/GB (Windle-Krauser).
Fastest lap: Biland, 1m 37.486s, 92.313 mph/148.563 km/h.
Championship points: 1 Biland, 91; **2** S. Webster, 63; **3** D. Brindley, 61; **4** Klaffenböck, 56; **5** Güdel, 55; **6** Bösiger, 52.

AUTODROMO BRNO, Czech Republic, 21 August. 3.352-mile/5.394-km circuit.
Sidecar World Championship, round 6 (19 laps, 63.688 miles/102.486 km)
1 Rolf Biland/Kurt Waltisperg, CH/CH (LCR-Swissauto), 40m 52.767s, 93.468 mph/150.422 km/h.
2 Markus Bösiger/Jurg Egli, CH/CH (LCR-ADM); 3 Steve Webster/Adolf Hänni, GB/CH (LCR-Krauser); 4 Derek Brindley/Paul Hutchinson, GB/GB (LCR-Honda); 5 Ralph Bohnhorst/Peter Brown, D/GB (LCR-Steinhausen); 6 Paul Güdel/Charly Güdel, CH/CH (LCR-ADM); 7 Yoshisada Kumagaya/Michael Finnegan, J/GB (LCR-ADM); 8 Markus Egloff/Urs Egloff, CH/CH (LCR-Yamaha); 9 Barry Brindley/Scott Whiteside, GB/GB (LCR-Yamaha); 10 Bert Janssen/Frans van Kessel, NL/NL (LCR-Yamaha); 11 Billy Gälross/Peter Berglund, S/S (LCR-Yamaha); 12 Kevin Webster/Harry Hofsteenge, GB/NL (LCR-Krauser); 13 André Vögli/Hansueli Wickli, CH/CH (LCR-Yamaha); 14 David Hoskin/David James, GB/GB (LCR-ADM-Krauser); 15 Kieron Kavanagh/David Horne, GB/GB (LCR-Krauser).
Fastest lap: Biland, 2m 07.963s, 94.293 mph/151.750 km/h.
Championship points: 1 Biland, 116; **2** S. Webster, 79; **3** D. Brindley, 74; **4** Bösiger, 72; **5** Güdel, 65; **6** Klaffenböck, 56.

CIRCUIT VAN DRENTHE, Assen, Holland, 11 September. 3.759-mile/6.049-km circuit.
Sidecar World Championship, round 7 (17 laps, 63.903 miles/102.833 km)
1 Rolf Biland/Kurt Waltisperg, CH/CH (LCR-Swissauto), 36m 56.510s, 103.780 mph/167.018 km/h.
2 Darren Dixon/Andy Hetherington, GB/GB (LCR-ADM); 3 Steve Webster/Adolf Hänni, GB/CH (LCR-Krauser); 4 Klaus Klaffenböck/Christian Parzer, A/A (LCR-Bartol); 5 Derek Brindley/Paul Hutchinson, GB/GB (LCR-Honda); 6 Markus Bösiger/Jurg Egli, CH/CH (LCR-ADM); 7 Steve Abbott/Julian Tailford, GB/GB (Windle-Krauser); 8 Yoshisada Kumagaya/Steve Pointer, J/GB (LCR-ADM); 9 Barry Brindley/Scott Whiteside, GB/GB (LCR-Yamaha); 10 Tony Wyssen/Kilian Wyssen, CH/CH (LCR-Krauser); 11 Ralph Bohnhorst/Peter Brown, D/GB (LCR-Steinhausen); 12 Markus Egloff/Urs Egloff, CH/CH (LCR-Yamaha); 13 Jukka Lauslehto/Juha Joutsen, SF/SF (LCR-ADM); 14 Mark Reddington/Trevor Crone, GB/GB (LCR-ADM); 15 Paul Güdel/Charly Güdel, CH/CH (LCR-ADM).
Fastest lap: D. Brindley, 2m 09.230s, 104.706 mph/168.508 km/h.
Championship points: 1 Biland, 141; **2** S. Webster, 95; **3** D. Brindley, 85; **4** Bösiger, 82; **5** Klaffenböck, 69; **6** Güdel, 66.

CIRCUIT DE CATALUNYA, Barcelona, Spain, 9 October. 2.949-mile/4.747-km circuit.
Sidecar World Championship, round 8 (22 laps, 64.878 miles/104.434 km)
1 Darren Dixon/Andy Hetherington, GB/GB (LCR-ADM), 50m 02.148s, 77.815 mph/125.231 km/h.
2 Paul Güdel/Charly Güdel, CH/CH (LCR-ADM); 3 Steve Abbott/Julian Tailford, GB/GB (Windle-Krauser); 4 Klaus Klaffenböck/Christian Parzer, A/A (LCR-Swissauto); 5 Derek Brindley/Paul Hutchinson, GB/GB (LCR-Honda); 6 Jukka Lauslehto/H. Metsaranta, SF/E (LCR-ADM); 7 Steve Webster/ Adolf Hänni, GB/CH (LCR-Krauser); 8 Billy Gälross/Peter Berglund, S/S (LCR-Yamaha); 9 Kieron Kavanagh/M. Puyvelde, GB/NL (LCR-Krauser); 10 Markus Bösiger/Jurg Egli, CH/CH (LCR-ADM); 11 Yoshisada Kumagaya/Steve Pointer, J/GB (LCR-ADM); 12 Mark Reddington/Trevor Crone, GB/GB (LCR-ADM); 13 Gary Knight/Trevor Hopkinson, GB/GB (Windle-Krauser); 14 Kevin Webster/Harry Hofsteenge, GB/NL (LCR-Krauser); 15 Reiner Koster/Peter Höss, CH/CH (LCR-ADM).
Fastest lap: Rolf Biland/Kurt Waltisperg, CH/CH (LCR-Swissauto), 1m 53.800s, 93.311 mph/150.169 km/h.

Final World Championship points:

1	Rolf Biland, CH	141
2	Steve Webster, GB	104
3	Derek Brindley, GB	96
4	Markus Bösiger, CH	88
5	Paul Güdel, CH	86
6	Klaus Klaffenböck, A	82

7 Darren Dixon, GB, 78; 8 Steve Abbott, GB, 74; 9= Barry Brindley, GB and Yoshisada Kumagaya, J, 52; 11 Jukka Lauslehto, SF, 50; 12 Ralph Bohnhorst, D, 48; 13 Markus Egloff, CH, 26; 14= Kevin Webster, GB and Tony Wyssen, CH, 23.

Superbike World Championship

DONINGTON PARK CIRCUIT, England, 2 May. 2.500-mile/4.023-km circuit.
Superbike World Championship, round 1 (2 x 25 laps, 62.500 miles/100.575 km)
Leg 1
1 Carl Fogarty, GB (Ducati), 40m 16.42s, 93.100 mph/149.830 km/h.
2 Aaron Slight, NZ (Honda); 3 Fabrizio Pirovano, I (Ducati); 4 Scott Russell, USA (Kawasaki); 5 Giancarlo Falappa, I (Ducati); 6 Simon Crafar, NZ (Honda); 7 Piergiorgio Bontempi, I (Kawasaki); 8 Brian Morrison, GB (Honda); 9 Doug Polen, USA (Honda); 10 Mauro Moroni, I (Kawasaki); 11 Valerio de Stefanis, I (Ducati); 12 Jean-Yves Mounier, F (Ducati); 13 Michael Rutter, GB (Ducati); 14 Jim Moodie, GB (Yamaha); 15 Andreas Meklau, A (Ducati).
Fastest lap: Troy Corser, AUS (Ducati), 1m 35.52s, 94.212 mph/151.620 km/h.

Leg 2
1 Scott Russell, USA (Kawasaki), 40m 05.37s, 93.529 mph/150.520 km/h.
2 Carl Fogarty, GB (Ducati); 3 Troy Corser, AUS (Ducati); 4 Giancarlo Falappa, I (Ducati); 5 Simon Crafar, NZ (Honda); 6 Brian Morrison, GB (Honda); 7 Doug Polen, USA (Honda); 8 Mauro Lucchiari, I (Yamaha); 9 Jean-Yves Mounier, F (Ducati); 10 Mauro Moroni, I (Kawasaki); 11 Nick Hopkins, GB (Yamaha); 12 Alex Vieira, F (Honda); 13 José Kuhn, F (Honda); 14 Denis Bonoris, F (Kawasaki); 15 Serafino Foti, I (Ducati).
Fastest lap: Russell, 1m 35.02s, 94.703 mph/152.410 km/h.
Championship points: 1 Fogarty, 37; **2** Russell, 33; **3** Falappa, 24; **4** Crafar, 21; **5** Morrison, 18; **6** Slight, 17.

HOCKENHEIMRING, Germany, 8 May. 4.220-mile/6.792-km circuit.
Superbike World Championship, round 2 (2 x 14 laps, 59.080 miles/95.088 km)
Leg 1
1 Scott Russell, USA (Kawasaki), 29m 08.36s, 121.660 mph/195.793 km/h.
2 Aaron Slight, NZ (Honda); 3 Terry Rymer, GB (Kawasaki); 4 Adrien Morillas, F (Kawasaki); 5 Doug Polen, USA (Honda); 6 Jean-Yves Mounier, F (Ducati); 7 Simon Crafar, NZ (Honda); 8 Edwin Weibel, D (Ducati); 9 Rob Phillis, AUS (Kawasaki); 10 Roger Kellenberger, D (Yamaha); 11 Alex Vieira, F (Honda); 12 Andrea Perselli, I (Ducati); 13 Michael Paquay, B (Honda); 14 Brian Morrison, GB (Honda); 15 Udo Mark, D (Ducati).
Fastest lap: Russell, 2m 03.74s, 122.783 mph/197.601 km/h.

Leg 2
1 Scott Russell, USA (Kawasaki), 29m 07.49s, 121.720 mph/195.890 km/h.
2 Fabrizio Pirovano, I (Ducati); 3 Doug Polen, USA (Honda); 4 Giancarlo Falappa, I (Ducati); 5 Keiichi Kitagawa, J (Kawasaki); 6 Terry Rymer, GB (Kawasaki); 7 Valerio de Stefanis, I (Ducati); 8 Edwin Weibel, D (Ducati); 9 Udo Mark, D (Ducati); 10 Andreas Meklau, A (Ducati); 11 Mauro Moroni, I (Kawasaki); 12 Christer Lindholm, S (Yamaha); 13 Jochen Schmid, D (Kawasaki); 14 Jean-Yves Mounier, F (Ducati); 15 Denis Bonoris, F (Kawasaki).
Fastest lap: Pirovano, 2m 03.52s, 123.002 mph/197.953 km/h.
Championship points: 1 Russell, 73; **2** Polen, 42; **3** Falappa and Fogarty, 37; **5** Slight, 34; **6** Pirovano, 32.

AUTODROMO SANTAMONICA, Misano, Italy, 29 May. 2.523-mile/4.060-km circuit.
Superbike World Championship, round 3 (2 x 25 laps, 63.075 miles/101.500 km)
Leg 1
1 Scott Russell, USA (Kawasaki), 40m 44.221s, 92.892 mph/149.495 km/h.
2 Giancarlo Falappa, I (Ducati); 3 Aaron Slight, NZ (Honda); 4 Stéphane Mertens, B (Ducati); 5 Mauro Lucchiari, I (Ducati); 6 Valerio de Stefanis, I (Ducati); 7 Simon Crafar, NZ (Honda); 8 Gianmaria Liverani, I (Honda); 9 Massimo Meregalli, I (Yamaha); 10 Andreas Meklau, A (Ducati); 11 James Whitham, GB (Ducati); 12 Doug Polen, USA (Honda); 13 Camillo Mariottini, I (Ducati); 14 Andrea Perselli, I (Ducati); 15 Mauro Moroni, I (Kawasaki).
Fastest lap: Piergiorgio Bontempi, I (Kawasaki), 1m 36.484s, 94.130 mph/151.486 km/h.

Leg 2
1 Giancarlo Falappa, I (Ducati), 40m 35.836s, 93.212 mph/150.010 km/h.
2 Scott Russell, USA (Kawasaki); 3 Mauro Lucchiari, I (Ducati); 4 Aaron Slight, NZ (Honda); 5 Carl Fogarty, GB (Ducati); 6 Fabrizio Pirovano, I (Ducati); 7 Piergiorgio Bontempi, I (Kawasaki); 8 Valerio de Stefanis, I (Ducati); 9 Terry Rymer, GB (Kawasaki); 10 Andreas Meklau, A (Ducati); 11 Simon Crafar, NZ (Honda); 12 Massimo Meregalli, I (Yamaha); 13 Serafino Foti, I (Ducati); 14 Mauro Moroni, I (Kawasaki); 15 Doug Polen, USA (Honda).
Fastest lap: Falappa, 1m 36.439s, 94.173 mph/151.556 km/h.
Championship points: 1 Russell, 110; **2** Falappa, 74; **3** Slight, 62; **4** Fogarty, 48; **5** Polen, 47; **6** Crafar, 44.

CIRCUITO DE ALBACETE, Spain, 19 June. 2.199-mile/3.539-km circuit.
Superbike World Championship, round 4 (2 x 28 laps, 61.572 miles/99.092 km)
Leg 1
1 Carl Fogarty, GB (Ducati), 44m 21.492s, 83.285 mph/134.034 km/h.
2 Aaron Slight, NZ (Honda); 3 James Whitham, GB (Ducati); 4 Piergiorgio Bontempi, I (Kawasaki); 5 Terry Rymer, GB (Kawasaki); 6 Doug Polen, USA (Honda); 7 Andreas Meklau, A (Ducati); 8 Simon Crafar, NZ (Honda); 9 Stéphane Mertens, B (Ducati); 10 Brian Morrison, GB (Honda); 11 Serafino Foti, I (Ducati); 12 Adrien Morillas, F (Kawasaki); 13 Carlos Cardus, E (Ducati); 14 Stefano Caracchi, RSM (Ducati); 15 Michael Paquay, B (Honda).
Fastest lap: Fogarty, 1m 33.081s, 85.049 mph/136.874 km/h.

Leg 2
1 Carl Fogarty, GB (Ducati), 44m 33.685s, 82.905 mph/133.685 km/h.
2 Aaron Slight, NZ (Honda); 3 James Whitham, GB (Ducati); 4 Andreas Meklau, A (Ducati); 5 Terry Rymer, GB (Kawasaki); 6 Piergiorgio Bontempi, I (Kawasaki); 7 Doug Polen, USA (Honda); 8 Carlos Cardus, E (Ducati); 9 Adrien Morillas, F (Kawasaki); 10 Stéphane Mertens, B (Ducati); 11 Fabrizio Pirovano, I (Ducati); 12 Serafino Foti, I (Ducati); 13 Brian Morrison, GB (Honda); 14 Simon Crafar, NZ (Honda); 15 Gianmaria Liverani, I (Honda).
Fastest lap: Fogarty, 1m 33.675s, 84.510 mph/136.006 km/h.
Championship points: 1 Russell, 110; **2** Slight, 96; **3** Fogarty, 88; **4** Falappa, 74; **5** Polen, 66; **6** Crafar and Rymer, 54.

ÖSTERREICHRING, Zeltweg, Austria, 17 July. 3.636-mile/5.853-km circuit.
Superbike World Championship, round 5 (2 x 18 laps, 65.448 miles/105.350 km)
Leg 1
1 Carl Fogarty, GB (Ducati), 33m 32.793s, 117.081 mph/188.424 km/h.
2 Andreas Meklau, A (Ducati); 3 Doug Polen, USA (Honda); 4 Aaron Slight, NZ (Honda); 5 Stéphane Mertens, B (Ducati); 6 Simon Crafar, NZ (Honda); 7 James Whitham, GB (Ducati); 8 Fabrizio Pirovano, I (Ducati); 9 Roberto Panichi, I (Ducati); 10 Rob Phillis, AUS (Kawasaki); 11 Piergiorgio Bontempi, I (Kawasaki); 12 Massimo Meregalli, I (Yamaha); 13 Serafino Foti, I (Ducati); 14 Scott Russell, USA (Kawasaki); 15 Christer Lindholm, S (Yamaha).
Fastest lap: Meklau, 1m 50.408s, 118.585 mph/190.844 km/h.

Leg 2
1 Carl Fogarty, GB (Ducati), 33m 31.787s, 117.148 mph/188.532 km/h.
2 Andreas Meklau, A (Ducati); 3 Doug Polen, USA (Honda); 4 Aaron Slight, NZ (Honda); 5 Stéphane Mertens, B (Ducati); 6 Simon Crafar, NZ (Honda); 7 Paolo Casoli, I (Yamaha); 8 Jochen Schmid, D (Kawasaki); 9 Piergiorgio Bontempi, I (Kawasaki); 10 Serafino Foti, I (Ducati); 11 Terry Rymer, GB

(Kawasaki); **12** Scott Russell, USA (Kawasaki); **13** Rob Phillis, AUS (Kawasaki); **14** Christer Lindholm, S (Yamaha); **15** Massimo Meregalli, I (Yamaha).
Fastest lap: Fogarty, 1m 50.769s, 118.199 mph/190.223 km/h.
Championship points: **1** Fogarty, 128; **2** Slight, 122; **3** Russell, 116; **4** Polen, 96; **5** Meklau, 75; **6** Crafar and Falappa, 74.

SENTUL INTERNATIONAL CIRCUIT, Indonesia, 21 August. 2.464-mile/3.965-km circuit.
Superbike World Championship, round 6 (2 x 25 laps, 61.600 miles/99.125 km)
Leg 1
1 James Whitham, GB (Ducati), 37m 13.266s, 99.288 mph/159.788 km/h.
2 Aaron Slight, NZ (Honda); **3** Scott Russell, USA (Kawasaki); **4** Doug Polen, USA (Honda); **5** Simon Crafar, NZ (Honda); **6** Andreas Meklau, A (Ducati); **7** Adrien Morillas, F (Kawasaki); **8** Terry Rymer, GB (Kawasaki); **9** Stéphane Mertens, B (Ducati); **10** Valerio de Stefanis, I (Ducati); **11** Piergiorgio Bontempi, I (Kawasaki); **12** Brian Morrison, GB (Honda); **13** Mauro Moroni, I (Kawasaki); **14** Gérald Muteau, F (Ducati); **15** Alex Vieira, F (Honda).
Fastest lap: Carl Fogarty, GB (Ducati), 1m 28.406s, 100.326 mph/161.459 km/h.

Leg 2
1 Carl Fogarty, GB (Ducati), 37m 01.075s, 99.834 mph/160.665 km/h.
2 Aaron Slight, NZ (Honda); **3** Scott Russell, USA (Kawasaki); **4** James Whitham, GB (Ducati); **5** Andreas Meklau, A (Ducati); **6** Doug Polen, USA (Honda); **7** Terry Rymer, GB (Kawasaki); **8** Adrien Morillas, F (Kawasaki); **9** Stéphane Mertens, B (Ducati); **10** Simon Crafar, NZ (Honda); **11** Piergiorgio Bontempi, I (Kawasaki); **12** Valerio de Stefanis, I (Ducati); **13** Brian Morrison, GB (Honda); **14** Alex Vieira, F (Honda); **15** Mauro Moroni, I (Kawasaki).
Fastest lap: Fogarty, 1m 28.064s, 100.717 mph/162.088 km/h.
Championship points: **1** Slight, 156; **2** Fogarty, 148; **3** Russell, 146; **4** Polen, 119; **5** Meklau, 96; **6** Crafar, 91.

SUGO CIRCUIT, Japan, 28 August. 2.335-mile/3.737-km circuit.
Superbike World Championship, round 7 (2 x 25 laps, 58.375 miles/93.425 km)
Leg 1
1 Scott Russell, USA (Kawasaki), 38m 49.703s, 89.717 mph/144.385 km/h.
2 Fabrizio Pirovano, I (Ducati); **3** Yasutomo Nagai, J (Yamaha); **4** Carl Fogarty, GB (Ducati); **5** Wataru Yoshikawa, J (Yamaha); **6** Aaron Slight, NZ (Honda); **7** Takuma Aoki, J (Honda); **8** Anthony Gobert, AUS (Honda); **9** Andreas Meklau, A (Ducati); **10** Doug Polen, USA (Honda); **11** Akira Yanagawa, J (Suzuki); **12** Piergiorgio Bontempi, I (Kawasaki); **13** Adrien Morillas, F (Kawasaki); **14** Alex Vieira, F (Honda); **15** Kenichiro Iwahashi, J (Honda).
Fastest lap: Pirovano, 1m 31.994s, 90.881 mph/146.260 km/h.

Leg 2
1 Scott Russell, USA (Kawasaki), 38m 38.123s, 90.204 mph/145.107 km/h.
2 Carl Fogarty, GB (Ducati); **3** Keiichi Kitagawa, J (Kawasaki); **4** Wataru Yoshikawa, J (Yamaha); **5** Yasutomo Nagai, J (Yamaha); **6** Anthony Gobert, AUS (Honda); **7** Aaron Slight, NZ (Honda); **8** Takuma Aoki, J (Honda); **9** Terry Rymer, GB (Kawasaki); **10** James Whitham, GB (Ducati); **11** Norihiko Fujiwara, J (Yamaha); **12** Noriyuki Haga, J (Ducati); **13** Shoichi Tsukamoto, J (Kawasaki); **14** Simon Crafar, NZ (Honda); **15** Shinya Takeishi, J (Honda).
Fastest lap: Fogarty, 1m 32.00s, 90.874 mph/146.248 km/h.
Championship points: **1** Russell, 186; **2** Fogarty, 178; **3** Slight, 175; **4** Polen, 125; **5** Meklau, 103; **6** Crafar, 93.

CIRCUIT VAN DRENTHE, Assen, Holland, 11 September. 3.759-mile/6.049-km circuit.
Superbike World Championship, round 8 (2 x 16 laps, 60.144 miles/96.784 km)
Leg 1
1 Carl Fogarty, GB (Ducati), 34m 11.400s, 105.537 mph/169.846 km/h.
2 Paolo Casoli, I (Yamaha); **3** Aaron Slight, NZ (Honda); **4** Terry Rymer, GB (Kawasaki); **5** James Whitham, GB (Ducati); **6** Scott Russell, USA (Kawasaki); **7** Simon Crafar, NZ (Honda); **8** Jochen Schmid, D (Kawasaki); **9** Andreas Meklau, A (Ducati); **10** Stéphane Mertens, B (Ducati); **11** Doug Polen, USA (Honda); **12** Jean-Yves Mounier, F (Ducati); **13** Michael Paquay, B (Honda); **14** Jeffry de Vries, NL (Yamaha); **15** Arpad Harmati, H (Yamaha).
Fastest lap: Fogarty, 2m 06.750s, 106.755 mph/171.805 km/h.

Leg 2
1 Carl Fogarty, GB (Ducati), 34m 06.650s, 105.782 mph/170.240 km/h.
2 Aaron Slight, NZ (Honda); **3** Mauro Lucchiari, I (Ducati); **4** Paolo Casoli, I (Yamaha); **5** James Whitham, GB (Ducati); **6** Terry Rymer, GB (Kawasaki); **7** Simon Crafar, NZ (Honda); **8** Jochen Schmid, D (Kawasaki); **9** Scott Russell, USA (Kawasaki); **10** Christer Lindholm, S (Yamaha); **11** Fabrizio Pirovano, I (Ducati); **12** Andreas Meklau, A (Ducati); **13** Serafino Foti, I (Ducati); **14** Jean-Yves Mounier, F (Ducati); **15** Jeffry de Vries, NL (Yamaha).
Fastest lap: Fogarty, 2m 06.400s, 107.050 mph/172.281 km/h.
Championship points: **1** Fogarty, 218; **2** Slight, 207; **3** Russell, 203; **4** Polen, 130; **5** Meklau, 114; **6** Crafar, 111.

AUTODROMO INTERNAZIONALE DEL MUGELLO, Italy, 25 September. 3.259-mile/5.245-km circuit.
Superbike World Championship, round 9 (2 x 20 laps, 65.180 miles/104.900 km)
Leg 1
1 Scott Russell, USA (Kawasaki), 39m 07.526s, 99.958 mph/160.867 km/h.
2 Carl Fogarty, GB (Ducati); **3** Troy Corser, AUS (Ducati); **4** Aaron Slight, NZ (Honda); **5** Fabrizio Pirovano, I (Ducati); **6** Andreas Meklau, A (Ducati); **7** Paolo Casoli, I (Yamaha); **8** James Whitham, GB (Ducati); **9** Simon Crafar, NZ (Honda); **10** Piergiorgio Bontempi, I (Kawasaki); **11** Doug Polen, USA (Honda); **12** Serafino Foti, I (Ducati); **13** Christer Lindholm, S (Yamaha); **14** Massimo Meregalli, I (Yamaha); **15** Stéphane Mertens, B (Ducati).
Fastest lap: Russell, 1m 56.499 km/h, 100.710 mph/162.078 km/h.

Leg 2
1 Carl Fogarty, GB (Ducati), 39m 12.621s, 99.741 mph/160.518 km/h.
2 Aaron Slight, NZ (Honda); **3** Mauro Lucchiari, I (Ducati); **4** James Whitham, GB (Ducati); **5** Fabrizio Pirovano, I (Ducati); **6** Piergiorgio Bontempi, I (Kawasaki); **7** Doug Polen, USA (Honda); **8** Jochen Schmid, D (Kawasaki); **9** Simon Crafar, NZ (Honda); **10** Massimo Meregalli, I (Yamaha); **11** Brian Morrison, GB (Honda); **12** Christer Lindholm, S (Yamaha); **13** Jeffry de Vries, NL (Yamaha); **14** Stéphane Mertens, B (Ducati); **15** Mauro Moroni, I (Kawasaki).
Fastest lap: Scott Russell, USA (Kawasaki), 1m 56.305s, 100.878 mph/162.348 km/h.
Championship points: **1** Fogarty, 255; **2** Slight, 237; **3** Russell, 223; **4** Polen, 144; **5** Whitham, 126; **6** Crafar, 125.

DONINGTON PARK CIRCUIT, England, 2 October. 2.500-mile/4.023-km circuit.
Superbike World Championship, round 10
Leg 1 (24 laps, 60.000 miles/96.552 km)
1 Scott Russell, USA (Kawasaki), 42m 45.140s, 84.196 mph/135.500 km/h.
2 Troy Corser, AUS (Ducati); **3** Paolo Casoli, I (Yamaha); **4** Alan Carter, GB (Ducati); **5** Simon Crafar, NZ (Honda); **6** Piergiorgio Bontempi, I (Kawasaki); **7** Andreas Meklau, A (Ducati); **8** Aaron Slight, NZ (Honda); **9** Brian Morrison, GB (Honda); **10** Michael Rutter, GB (Ducati); **11** Jochen Schmid, D (Kawasaki); **12** Doug Polen, USA (Honda); **13** Valerio de Stefanis, I (Ducati); **14** Carl Fogarty, GB (Ducati); **15** Massimo Meregalli, I (Yamaha).
Fastest lap: Corser and Russell, 1m 45.640s, 85.184 mph/137.090 km/h.

Leg 2 (25 laps, 62.500 miles/100.575 km)
1 Scott Russell, USA (Kawasaki), 44m 57.140s, 83.413 mph/134.240 km/h.
2 Troy Corser, AUS (Ducati); **3** Mauro Lucchiari, I (Ducati); **4** Paolo Casoli, I (Yamaha); **5** Carl Fogarty, GB (Ducati); **6** Alan Carter, GB (Ducati); **7** Piergiorgio Bontempi, I (Kawasaki); **8** Brian Morrison, GB (Honda); **9** Andreas Meklau, A (Ducati); **10** Aaron Slight, NZ (Honda); **11** Massimo Meregalli, I (Yamaha); **12** Fabrizio Pirovano, I (Ducati); **13** Jeffry de Vries, NL (Yamaha); **14** Matt Llewellyn, GB (Ducati); **15** Simon Crafar, NZ (Honda).
Fastest lap: Russell, 1m 45.490s, 85.308 mph/137.290 km/h.
Championship points: **1** Fogarty, 268; **2** Russell, 263; **3** Slight, 251; **4** Polen, 148; **5** Meklau, 140; **6** Crafar, 137.

PHILLIP ISLAND, Australia, 30 October. 2.764-mile/4.448-km circuit.
Superbike World Championship, round 11
Leg 1 (21 laps, 58.044 miles/93.408 km)
1 Carl Fogarty, GB (Ducati), 33m 50.946s.
2 Scott Russell, USA (Kawasaki); **3** Anthony Gobert, AUS (Kawasaki); **4** Aaron Slight, NZ (Honda); **5** Troy Corser, AUS (Ducati); **6** Kirk McCarthy, AUS (Honda); **7** Mat Mladin, AUS (Kawasaki); **8** Shawn Giles, AUS (Ducati); **9** Piergiorgio Bontempi, I (Kawasaki); **10** Simon Crafar, NZ (Honda); **11** Doug Polen, USA (Honda); **12** Peter Goddard, AUS (Suzuki); **13** Roy Leslie, AUS (Ducati); **14** Andreas Meklau, A (Ducati); **15** Steve Martin, AUS (Suzuki).
Fastest lap: Fogarty, 1m 35.575s.

Leg 2 (22 laps, 60.808 miles/97.856 km)
1 Anthony Gobert, AUS (Kawasaki), 35m 32.853s.
2 Carl Fogarty, GB (Ducati); **3** Troy Corser, AUS (Ducati); **4** Aaron Slight, NZ (Honda); **5** Kirk McCarthy, AUS (Honda); **6** Simon Crafar, NZ (Honda); **7** Shawn Giles, AUS (Ducati); **8** Fabrizio Pirovano, I (Ducati); **9** Piergiorgio Bontempi, I (Kawasaki); **10** Andreas Meklau, A (Ducati); **11** Doug Polen, USA (Honda); **12** Stéphane Mertens, B (Ducati); **13** Peter Goddard, AUS (Suzuki); **14** Martin Craggill, AUS (Kawasaki); **15** Steve Martin, AUS (Suzuki).
Fastest lap: Fogarty, 1m 36.026s.

Final Championship points

1	Carl Fogarty, GB	305
2	Scott Russell, USA	280
3	Aaron Slight, NZ	277
4	Doug Polen, USA	158
5	Simon Crafar, NZ	153
6	Andreas Meklau, A	148

7 James Whitham, GB, 126; **8** Piergiorgio Bontempi, I, 116; **9** Fabrizio Pirovano, I, 111; **10** Terry Rymer, GB, 106; **11** Troy Corser, AUS, 80; **12** Mauro Lucchiari, I, 79; **13** Paolo Casoli, I, 76; **14** Stéphane Mertens, B, 75; **15** Giancarlo Falappa, I, 74.

World Endurance Championship

24 HEURES DU MANS, Bugatti Circuit, Le Mans, France, 16-17 April.
World Endurance Championship, round 1. 757 laps of the 2.753-mile/4.430-km circuit, 2084.021 miles/3353.510 km
1 Terry Rymer/Adrien Morillas/Jean-Louis Battistini, GB/F/F (750 Kawasaki), 23h 58m 55s, 86.889 mph/139.835 km/h.
2 Alex Vieira/José Kuhn/Rachel Nicotte, F/F/F (750 Honda), 751 laps; **3** Bruno Bonhuil/Philippe Monneret/Juan Eric Gomez, F/F/F (750 Suzuki), 733; **4** Vincent Vivoli/Philippe Cambray/Olivier Ulmann, F/F/F (750 Suzuki), 732; **5** Herbert Graf/Stefan Ambord/Rolf Ammann, CH/CH/CH (750 Kawasaki), 729; **6** Christophe Guyot/Jean-François Damide/Pascal Guigou, F/F/F (750 Honda), 725; **7** Bruno Soulon/Michel Almaric/Wilfrid Veille, F/F/F (750 Honda), 722; **8** Serge David/Jean-Luc Romanens/Peter Krummenacher, CH/CH/CH (750 Honda), 719; **9** Eric L'Herbette/Jean-Paul Leblanc/Jean Marchand, F/F/F (750 Honda), 715; **10** Joel Petit/Patrick Lelan/Alain Agogue, F/F/F (750 Honda), 714; **11** Philippe Mouchet/Stéphane Chambon/Florian Ferracci, F/F/F (888 Ducati), 712; **12** Jacques Lenoxaic/Alain Cornil/Jean-Philippe Guinand, F/F/F (750 Honda), 709; **13** Gérard Jolivet/Georges Furling/Philippe Pinchedez, F/F/F (750 Suzuki), 707; **14** Patrick Beltzung/Alain Bousseau/Alexandre Jeannin, F/F/F (750 Suzuki), 705; **15** Gérard Bonnet/Serge Kuenemann/André Lacroix, F/F/F (750 Honda), 700.
Fastest lap: Rymer, 1m 46.09s, 93.408 mph/150.325 km/h.
Championship points: **1** Rymer, Morillas and Battistini, 40; **4** Vieira, Kuhn and Nicotte, 34; **7** Bonhuil, Monneret and Gomez, 30.

24 HEURES DE LIEGE, Spa-Francorchamps, Belgium, 9-10 July.
World Endurance Championship, round 2. 523 laps of the 4.340-mile/6.985-km circuit, 2269.820 miles/3653.155 km
1 Adrien Morillas/Jean-Louis Battistini/Denis Bonoris, F/F/F (750 Kawasaki), 24h 01m 47s, 94.465 mph/152.026 km/h.
2 Bruno Bonhuil/Philippe Monneret/Juan Eric Gomez, F/F/F (750 Suzuki), 520 laps; **3** Steve Manley/Robert Holden/Peter Graves, GB/NZ/GB (750 Kawasaki), 518; **4** Jean-Michel Mattioli/Thierry Autissier/Michel Simeon, F/F/B (750 Honda), 514; **5** Leo Planken/F. Millet/Michel Graziano, NL/F/F (750 Yamaha), 512; **6** Joel Petit/Patrick Lelan/Patrick Dubois, F/F/F (750 Honda), 498; **7** J. Bosch/H.V. den Broek/A. Colet, NL/NL/NL (750 Kawasaki), 496; **8** Gérard Bonnet/Serge Kuenemann/André Lacroix, F/F/F (750 Honda), 496; **9** Jean-Paul Leblanc/Eric L'Herbette/Jean Marchand, F/F/F (750 Honda), 494; **10** Dierk Kretschmer/Hans Günter Ziegenfuss/J. Berg, D/D/D (750 Yamaha), 493; **11** Philippe Mouchet/Jean-Yves Mounier/Stéphane Chambon, F/F/F (888 Ducati), 490; **12** Ch. Rosenfeld/D. Crassous/C. Jaggi, CH/F/CH (888 Ducati), 489; **13** Benoit Lacrosse/Michel Nickmans/Alexandre Legrand, B/B/B (750 Kawasaki), 488; **14** Breintenstein/Hans Keller/K. Askar, CH/CH/CH (750 Yamaha), 486; **15** Per Backstrom/Stefan Johansson/Ben Nyman, S/S/SF (750 Kawasaki), 485.
Fastest lap: Morillas/Battistini/Bonoris, 2m 31.29s, 103.279 mph/166.211 km/h.
Championship points: **1** Battistini and Morillas, 80; **3** Bonhuil, Gomez and Monneret, 64; **6** Rymer, 40; **7** Graves, Holden, Kuhn, Manley, Nicotte and Vieira, 34.

SUZUKA EIGHT HOURS, Suzuka International Racing Course, Japan, 31 July.
World Endurance Championship, round 3. 183 laps of the 3.662-mile/5.859-mile circuit, 670.146 miles/1072.197 km
1 Doug Polen/Aaron Slight, USA/NZ (750 Honda), 6h 52m 49s, 96.909 mph/155.960 km/h.
2 Scott Russell/Terry Rymer, USA/GB (750 Kawasaki), 183 laps; **3** Shinichi Itoh/Shinya Takeishi, J/J (750 Honda), 183; **4** Eddie Lawson/Yasutomo Nagai, USA/J (750 Yamaha), 182; **5** Keichi Kitagawa/Shoichi Tsukamoto, J/J (750 Kawasaki), 182; **6** Shunji Yatsushiro/Shuya Arai, J/J (750 Honda), 180; **7** Kenichiro Iwahashi/Haruchika Aoki, J/J (750 Honda), 180; **8** Akira Yanagawa/Thomas Stevens, J/USA (750 Suzuki), 179; **9** Toshiya Kobayashi/Alex Vieira, J/F (750 Honda), 179; **10** Michio Izumi/Hitoyasu Izutsu, J/J (750 Kawasaki), 178; **11** Niall Mackenzie/Shawn Giles, GB/AUS (750 Suzuki), 178; **12** Akira Ryo/Trevor Jordan, J/AUS (750 Kawasaki), 177; **13** Takeshi Tsujimura/Tomoko Manako, J/J (750 Honda), 177; **14** Kenji Osaka/Keiji Tamura, J/J (750 Honda), 176; **15** Hiroshi Maruyama/Jun Maeda, J/J (750 Honda), 176.
Fastest lap: Russell, 2m 11.026s, 112.537 mph/181.110 km/h.
Championship points: **1** Battistini and Morillas, 80; **3** Bonhuil, Gomez and Monneret, 64; **6** Rymer, 57; **7** Vieira, 41.

58e BOL D'OR, Circuit Paul Ricard, France, 17-18 September.
World Endurance Championship, round 4. 667 laps of the 3.610-mile/5.810-km circuit, 2409.204 miles/3875.270 km
1 Dominique Sarron/Christian Sarron/Yasutomo Nagai, F/F/J (750 Yamaha), 23h 57m 46s, 100.834 mph/162.276 km/h.
2 Steve Manley/Robert Holden/Mike Edwards, GB/NZ/GB (750 Kawasaki), 664 laps; **3** Hervé Moineau/Christian Lavieille/Jehan D'Orgeix , F/F/F (750 Suzuki), 662; **4** Bruno Bonhuil/Philippe Monneret/Juan Eric Gomez, F/F/F (750 Suzuki), 662; **5** Christophe Guyot/Jean-François Damide/Pascal Guigou, F/F/F (750 Honda), 659; **6** Adrien Morillas/Christian Haquin/Denis Bonoris, F/F/F (750 Kawasaki), 657; **7** Jean-Michel Mattioli/Thierry Autissier/Michel Simeon, F/F/B (750 Honda), 656; **8** André Lussiana/Doug Tolan/Peter Linden, F/USA/S (750 Honda), 651; **9** Stéphane Chambon/Thierry Rogier/Gérald Muteau, F/F/F (888 Ducati), 645; **10** Patrice Perin/Gilles Ferstler/Eric Kermarec, F/F/F (750 Suzuki), 643; **11** Gérard Jolivet/Philippe Pinchedez/Jean-Yves Besson, F/F/F (750 Suzuki), 640; **12** Jean-Louis Tranois/Arpad Harmati/Arnaud Vandenbossche, F/H/F (750 Yamaha), 637; **13** Joel Petit/Patrick Lelan/Patrick Dubois, F/F/F (750 Honda), 636; **14** Philippe Cambray/Georges Furling/Olivier Ulmann, F/F/F (750 Suzuki), 634; **15** Yves Besson/F. Montels/Eric Mizera, F/F/F (750 Honda), 633.
Fastest lap: Terry Rymer, GB (750 Kawasaki), 2m 00.24s, 108.461 mph/174.551 km/h.

Final World Championship points:

1	Adrien Morillas, F	100
2=	Bruno Bonhuil, F	90
2=	Juan Eric Gomez, F	90
2=	Philippe Monneret, F	90
5	Jean-Louis Battistini, F	80
6=	Steve Manley, GB	64
6=	Robert Holden, NZ	64

8 Denis Bonoris, F, 60; **9** Terry Rymer, GB, 57; **10** Yasutomo Nagai, J, 53; **11** Thierry Autissier, F, Jean-Michel Mattioli, F and Michel Simeon, B, 44; **14** Jean-François Damide, F, Pascal Guigou, F and Christophe Guyot, F, 42.

AMA National Championship Road Race Series (Superbike)

DAYTONA INTERNATIONAL SPEEDWAY, Daytona Beach, Florida, 13 March 1994. 200 miles/321.869 km
1 Scott Russell (Kawasaki); **2** Troy Corser (Ducati); **3** Eddie Lawson (Yamaha); **4** Doug Polen (Honda); **5** Jamie James (Yamaha); **6** Steve Crevier (Kawasaki); **7** Mike Smith (Honda); **8** Thomas Stevens (Suzuki); **9** Kevin Magee (Honda); **10** Dale Quarterley (Kawasaki).

PHOENIX INTERNATIONAL RACEWAY, Goodyear, Arizona, 27 March 1994. 63 miles/101.389 km
1 Troy Corser (Ducati); **2** Fred Merkel (Kawasaki); **3** Colin Edwards II (Yamaha); **4** Jamie James (Yamaha); **5** David Sadowski (Ducati); **6** Steve Crevier (Kawasaki); **7** Takahiro Sohwa (Kawasaki); **8** Thomas Stevens (Suzuki); **9** Mike Smith (Honda); **10** Dale Quarterley (Kawasaki).

POMONA FAIRPLEX, Pomona, California, 10 April 1994. 52.5 miles/84.491 km
1 Troy Corser (Ducati); **2** Takahiro Sohwa (Kawasaki); **3** Steve Crevier (Kawasaki); **4** Jamie James (Yamaha); **5** Pascal Picotte (Ducati); **6** Dale Quarterley (Kawasaki); **7** Thomas Stevens (Suzuki); **8** Mike Smith (Honda); **9** Tom Kipp (Suzuki); **10** Scott Gray (Ducati).

LAGUNA SECA RACEWAY, Monterey, California, 22 May 1994. 63 miles/101.389 km
1 Pascal Picotte (Ducati); **2** Troy Corser (Ducati); **3** Jamie James (Yamaha); **4** Fred Merkel (Kawasaki); **5** David Sadowski (Ducati); **6** Takahiro Sohwa (Kawasaki); **7** Steve Crevier (Kawasaki); **8** Dale Quarterley (Kawasaki); **9** Mike Smith (Honda); **10** Kevin Magee (Honda).

ROAD AMERICA, Elkhart Lake, Wisconsin, 12 June 1994. 64 miles/102.998 km
1 Pascal Picotte (Ducati); **2** Fred Merkel (Kawasaki); **3** David Sadowski (Ducati); **4** Troy Corser (Ducati); **5** Takahiro Sohwa (Kawasaki); **6** Steve Crevier (Kawasaki); **7** Kevin Magee (Honda); **8** Thomas Stevens (Suzuki); **9** Mike Smith (Honda); **10** Dale Quarterley (Kawasaki).

NEW HAMPSHIRE INTERNATIONAL SPEEDWAY, Loudon, New Hampshire, 19 June 1994. 64 miles/102.998 km
1 Troy Corser (Ducati); **2** Fred Merkel (Kawasaki); **3** Jamie James (Yamaha); **4** Mike Smith (Honda); **5** Colin Edwards II (Yamaha); **6** Thomas Stevens (Suzuki); **7** Takahiro Sohwa (Kawasaki); **8** Pascal Picotte (Ducati); **9** Mike Hale (Honda); **10** Steve Crevier (Kawasaki).

MID-OHIO SPORTS CAR COURSE, Lexington, Ohio, 17 July 1994. 64.8 miles/104.285 km
1 Colin Edwards II (Yamaha); **2** Jamie James (Yamaha); **3** Takahiro Sohwa (Kawasaki); **4** Steve Crevier (Kawasaki); **5** Dale Quarterley (Kawasaki); **6** Thomas Stevens (Suzuki); **7** Mike Hale (Honda); **8** Scott Doohan (Ducati); **9** Tom Kipp (Suzuki); **10** Brad Hazen (Ducati).

BRAINERD INTERNATIONAL RACEWAY, Brainerd, Minnesota, 31 July 1994. 63 miles/101.389 km
1 Colin Edwards II (Yamaha); **2** Troy Corser (Ducati); **3** Jamie James (Yamaha); **4** Miguel DuHamel (Harley-Davidson); **5** Takahiro Sohwa (Kawasaki); **6** Pascal Picotte (Ducati); **7** Steve Crevier (Kawasaki); **8** Brad Hazen (Ducati); **9** Tom Kipp (Suzuki); **10** Scott Gray (Ducati).

SEARS POINT RACEWAY, Sonoma, California, 21 August 1994. 62.5 miles/100.584 km
1 Colin Edwards II (Yamaha); **2** Pascal Picotte (Ducati); **3** Jamie James (Yamaha); **4** David Sadowski (Ducati); **5** Scott Gray (Ducati); **6** Takahiro Sohwa (Kawasaki); **7** Dale Quarterley (Kawasaki); **8** Thomas Stevens (Suzuki); **9** Donald Jacks (Suzuki); **10** Brad Hazen (Ducati).

ROAD ATLANTA, Braselton, Georgia, 18 September 1994. 63 miles/101.389 km
1 Scott Russell (Kawasaki); **2** Pascal Picotte (Ducati); **3** Colin Edwards II (Yamaha); **4** Troy Corser (Ducati); **5** David Sadowski (Ducati); **6** Mike Smith (Honda); **7** Jamie James (Yamaha); **8** Steve Crevier (Kawasaki); **9** Dale Quarterley (Kawasaki); **10** Takahiro Sohwa (Kawasaki).

Final Championship points

1	Troy Corser	273
2	Jamie James	272
3	Takahiro Sohwa	251
4	Pascal Picotte	245
5	Colin Edwards II	239

6 Steve Crevier, 235; **7** Dale Quarterley, 219; **8** Mike Smith, 181; **9** Thomas Stevens, 166; **10** Fred Merkel and Brad Hazen, 152.

Isle of Man Tourist Trophy Races

ISLE OF MAN TOURIST TROPHY COURSE, 4-10 June. 37.73-mile/60.72-km course.
Formula 1 TT (6 laps, 226.38 miles/364.32 km)
1 Steve Hislop (750 Honda), 1h 53m 37.2s, 119.54 mph/192.38 km/h.
2 Phillip McCallen (750 Honda), 1h 55m 01.8s; **3** Joey Dunlop (750 Honda), 1h 56m 23.6s; **4** Gary Radcliffe (750 Honda), 1h 59m 00.2s; **5** Iain Duffus (750 Yamaha), 1h 59m 36.0s; **6** Nigel Davies (750 Honda),

1h 59m 39.2s; **7** Derek Young (750 Honda), 2h 00m 09.6s; **8** Steve Linsdell (750 Yamaha), 2h 00m 22.4s; **9** Colin Gable (750 Honda), 2h 00m 35.8s; **10** Glenn Williams (750 Honda), 2h 01m 11.0s; **11** Bob Jackson (640 Honda), 2h 01m 11.4s; **12** Brian Gardiner (750 Honda), 2h 01m 38.8s.
Fastest lap: McCallen, 18m 32.6s, 122.08 mph/196.47 km/h.

125 cc TT (4 laps, 150.92 miles/242.88 km)
1 Joey Dunlop (Honda), 1h 25m 38.0s, 105.74 mph/170.17 km/h.
2 Denis McCullough (Honda), 1h 26m 49.2s; **3** Chris Fargher (Yamaha), 1h 27m 55.6s; **4** Noel Clegg (Honda), 1h 29m 20.4s; **5** Glen English (Honda), 1h 30m 25.8s; **6** Gary Dynes (Yamaha), 1h 30m 50.6s; **7** Mark Watts (Honda), 1h 31m 17.6s; **8** Alan 'Bud' Jackson (Honda), 1h 31m 30.4s.
Fastest lap: Dunlop, 21m 04.6s, 107.40 mph/172.84 km/h.

Single Cylinder TT (4 laps, 150.92 miles/242.88 km)
1 Jim Moodie (660 Yamaha), 1h 21m 21.6s, 111.29 mph/179.10 km/h.
2 Robert Holden (560 Ducati), 1h 21m 29.6s; **3** Jason Griffiths (680 Yamaha), 1h 27m 36.6s; **4** Gary Radcliffe (660 Yamaha), 1h 30m 22.0s; **5** Matthew Wood (580 Harris), 1h 30m 23.0s; **6** Derek Young (680 Honda), 1h 30m 40.0s.
Fastest lap: Moodie, 20m 05.6s, 112.66 mph/181.31 km/h.

Supersport 600 TT (4 laps, 150.92 miles/242.88 km)
1 Iain Duffus (Yamaha), 1h 18m 32.0s, 115.30 mph/185.56 km/h.
2 Ian Simpson (Yamaha), 1h 18m 41.4s; **3** Steve Ward (Honda), 1h 18m 43.8s; **4** Phillip McCallen (Honda), 1h 18m 52.6s; **5** Bob Jackson (Honda), 1h 19m 16.2s; **6** Nick Jefferies (Honda), 1h 19m 36.0s; **7** Joey Dunlop (Honda), 1h 19m 48.6s; **8** Derek Young (Honda), 1h 20m 29.8s; **9** Robert Holden (Yamaha), 1h 21m 02.6s; **10** Marc Flynn (Honda), 1h 21m 05.0s; **11** Chris Day (Honda), 1h 21m 14.2s; **12** Nigel Davies (Honda), 1h 21m 25.2s; **13** Jason McEwen (Yamaha), 1h 21m 43.6s; **14** Brian Gardiner (Honda), 1h 22m 04.4s; **15** Loren Poole (Honda), 1h 22m 07.2s; **16** Simon Beck (Honda), 1h 22m 26.6s.
Fastest lap: Jim Moodie (Yamaha), 19m 23.8s, 116.71 mph/187.83 km/h.

Junior TT (4 laps, 150.92 miles/242.88 km)
1 Joey Dunlop (250 Honda), 1h 18m 57.8s, 114.67 mph/184.54 km/h.
2 Brian Reid (250 Yamaha), 1h 19m 23.4s; **3** Jason Griffiths (250 Yamaha), 1h 19m 45.4s; **4** Ian Simpson (250 Honda), 1h 19m 48.4s; **5** Ian Lougher (250 Honda), 1h 19m 58.0s; **6** Gavin Lee (250 Yamaha), 1h 20m 43.4s; **7** James Courtney (250 Honda), 1h 20m 44.8s; **8** Richard Coates (250 Yamaha), 1h 21m 20.6s.
Fastest lap: Reid, 19m 31.2s, 115.97 mph/186.64 km/h.

Supersport 400 TT (4 laps, 150.92 miles/242.88 km)
1 Jim Moodie (Yamaha), 1h 23m 41.2s, 108.20 mph/174.13 km/h.
2 Steve Linsdell (Yamaha), 1h 24m 58.8s; **3** David Morris (Yamaha), 1h 25m 18.0s; **4** Derek Young (Honda), 1h 25m 27.6s; **5** Gary Long (Yamaha), 1h 26m 27.0s; **6** Nigel Piercy (Yamaha), 1h 27m 24.8s; **7** Simon Trezise (Kawasaki), 1h 27m 27.6s.
Fastest lap: Moodie, 20m 26.2s, 110.77 mph/178.27 km/h.

Senior TT (6 laps, 226.38 miles/364.32 km)
1 Steve Hislop (750 Honda), 1h 53m 53m 8s, 119.25 mph/191.91 km/h.
2 Phillip McCallen (750 Honda), 1h 55m 08.8s; **3** Joey Dunlop (750 Honda), 1h 56m 20.2s; **4** Nigel Davies (750 Honda), 1h 56m 37.8s; **5** Jason Griffiths (750 Kawasaki), 1h 56m 59.4s; **6** Gary Radcliffe (750 Honda), 1h 57m 34.0s; **7** Chris Day (750 Honda), 1h 57m 43.8s; **8** Paul Hunt (750 Yamaha), 1h 58m 05.8s; **9** David Goodley (750 Kawasaki), 1h 58m 46.4s; **10** Derek Young (750 Honda), 1h 58m 48.2s; **11** Colin Gable (750 Honda), 1h 59m 37.8s; **12** Alan Bennallick (750 Honda), 2h 00m 03.2s; **13** Brian Gardiner (750 Honda), 2h 00m 47.2s; **14** Glenn Williams (750 Honda), 2h 00m 59.2s.
Fastest lap: Hislop, 18m 28.8s, 122.50 mph/197.14 km/h.

Sidecar TT: Race A (3 laps, 113.19 miles/182.16 km)
1 Rob Fisher/Michael Wynn (600 Yamaha), 1h 04m 14.6s, 106.19 mph/170.90 km/h.
2 Dave Molyneux/Peter Hill (600 DMR), 1h 04m 39.2s; **3** Mick Boddice Snr/Dave Wells (600 Honda), 1h 05m 39.4s; **4** Kenny Howles/Rob Parker (600 Yamaha), 1h 06m 14.6s; **5** Geoff Bell/Nick Roche (600 Yamaha), 1h 06m 24.0s; **6** Roy Hanks/Tom Hanks (600 Ireson), 1h 06m 30.2s; **7** Dave Kimberley/Tony Darby (600 Kawasaki), 1h 07m 05.4s; **8** Eddy Wright/Richard Long (600 Yamaha), 1h 08m 40.8s; **9** Vince Biggs/Jamie Biggs (350 Shelbourne), 1h 09m 08.2s; **10** Lars Schwartz/Doug Jewell (600 Yamaha), 1h 09m 32.6s; **11** Martin Clark/Boyd Hutchinson (600 Yamaha), 1h 09m 38.0s; **12** Bill Davie/Neil Miller (600 Yamaha), 1h 09m 44.6s; **13** Gary Horspole/Kevin Leigh (600 Honda), 1h 09m 54.6s; **14** David Wallis/Tim Kirkham (600 Yamaha), 1h 10m 00.6s.
Fastest lap: Fisher/Wynn, 21m 15.4s, 106.49 mph/171.38 km/h.

Sidecar TT: Race B (3 laps, 113.19 miles/182.16 km)
1 Rob Fisher/Michael Wynn (600 Yamaha), 1h 05m 41.0s, 103.39 mph/166.39 km/h.
2 Dave Molyneux/Peter Hill (600 DMR), 1h 06m 27.8s; **3** Mick Boddice Snr/Dave Wells (600 Honda), 1m 06m 54.0s; **4** Roy Hanks/Tom Hanks (600 Ireson), 1h 06m 56.4s; **5** Geoff Bell/Nick Roche (600 Yamaha), 1h 07m 52.8s; **6** Dave Kimberley/Tony Darby (600 Kawasaki), 1h 07m 56.2s; **7** Kenny Howles/Rob Parker (600 Yamaha), 1h 08m 54.0s; **8** Peter Nuttall/Raymond Burns (600 Yamaha), 1h 10m 11.6s; **9** Rod Bellas/Geoff Knight (600 Yamaha), 1h 10m 41.6s; **10** Lars Schwartz/Doug Jewell (600 Yamaha), 1h 10m 45.8s; **11** Graham Hayne/Mark Beaumont (600 SAFF), 1h 10m 56.4s; **12** Eddy Wright/Richard Long (600 Yamaha), 1h 11m 09.4s; **13** Mick Boddice Jnr/Chris Hollis (600 Honda), 1h 11m 38.6s.
Fastest lap: Fisher/Wynn, 21m 28.0s, 105.45 mph/169.71 km/h.

H.E.A.T./British Supercup

DONINGTON PARK CIRCUIT, 4 April. 2.500-mile/4.023-km circuit.
H.E.A.T./British Supercup, round 1
125 cc (15 laps, 37.500 miles/60.345 km)
1 Andy Hatton (Honda), 27m 21.06s, 82.26 mph/132.39 km/h.
2 Kevin Mawdsley (Honda); **3** Steve Patrickson (Honda); **4** Robin Appleyard (Honda); **5** Patrick Corrigan (Yamaha); **6** Mark Norman (Honda); **7** Barry Stanley (Honda); **8** Ian Emberton (Honda); **9** Martin Johnson (Yamaha); **10** Les Wood (Honda); **11** Gavan Morris (Honda); **12** Stuart Nicholls (Honda); **13** Neil Durham (Honda); **14** Pete Jennings (Honda); **15** Chris Mintoff (Honda).
Fastest lap: Hatton, 1m 47.23s, 83.93 mph/135.07 km/h.
Championship points: **1** Hatton, 20; **2** Mawdsley, 17; **3** Patrickson, 15; **4** Appleyard, 13; **5** Corrigan, 11; **6** Norman, 10.

250 cc (8 laps, 20.000 miles/32.184 km)
1 Jason Vincent (Yamaha), 15m 21.37s, 87.91 mph/141.48 km/h.
2 Paul Brown (Yamaha); **3** Steve Sawford (Yamaha); **4** Adrian Clarke (Yamaha); **5** Ian Newton (Aprilia); **6** Greig Ramsay (Yamaha); **7** Eugene McManus (Yamaha); **8** Graeme Thompson (Yamaha); **9** Mark Snell (Yamaha); **10** Stephen Farmer (Yamaha); **11** Iain Challinor (Yamaha); **12** Woolsey Coulter (Aprilia); **13** Nigel Bosworth (Honda); **14** Gary Haslam (Yamaha); **15** Gary May (Yamaha).
Fastest lap: Vincent, 1m 40.61s, 89.45 mph/143.96 km/h.
Championship points: **1** Vincent, 20; **2** Brown, 17; **3** Sawford, 15; **4** Clarke, 13; **5** Newton, 11; **6** Ramsay, 10.

Supersport 600 (15 laps, 37.500 miles/60.345 km)
1 Ian Simpson (Yamaha), 26m 56.32s, 83.52 mph/134.41 km/h.
2 Mike Edwards (Yamaha); **3** Iain Duffus (Yamaha); **4** Tim Poole (Honda); **5** Steve Cunningham (Honda); **6** Gary Weston (Yamaha); **7** Alan Harland (Honda); **8** Iain Macpherson (Honda); **9** Mark Ditchfield (Honda); **10** Andrew Tinsley (Honda); **11** Gordon Whitaker (Honda); **12** Alan Batson (Honda); **13** Peter Jennings (Honda); **14** Mark Coleing (Honda); **15** Simon Smith (Honda).
Fastest lap: Duffus, 1m 44.55s, 86.08 mph/138.53 km/h.
Championship points: **1** Simpson, 20; **2** Edwards, 17; **3** Duffus, 15; **4** Poole, 13; **5** Cunningham, 11; **6** Weston, 10.

TT Superbike (2 x 15 laps, 37.500 miles/60.345 km)
Leg 1
1 Carl Fogarty (Ducati), 24m 57.14s, 90.17 mph/145.11 km/h.
2 James Whitham (Ducati); **3** Michael Rutter (Ducati); **4** Steve Hislop (Honda); **5** Jim Moodie (Yamaha); **6** Matt Llewellyn (Ducati); **7** James Haydon (Kawasaki); **8** Phil Borley (Norton); **9** Ray Stringer (Honda); **10** Nick Hopkins (Yamaha); **11** Ian Simpson (Norton); **12** Robert Dunlop (Honda); **13** David Jefferies (Ducati); **14** Phillip McCallen (Honda); **15** Peter Graves (Ducati).
Fastest lap: Whitham, 1m 38.07s, 91.77 mph/147.69 km/h.
Leg 2
1 Carl Fogarty (Ducati), 24m 45.68s, 90.86 mph/146.23 km/h.
2 James Whitham (Ducati); **3** Jim Moodie (Yamaha); **4** Matt Llewellyn (Ducati); **5** Steve Hislop (Honda); **6** Michael Rutter (Ducati); **7** Phil Borley (Norton); **8** James Haydon (Kawasaki); **9** Robert Dunlop (Honda); **10** David Jefferies (Ducati); **11** Lee Pullan (Yamaha); **12** Peter Graves (Ducati); **13** Nick Hopkins (Yamaha); **14** Phillip McCallen (Honda); **15** Shaun Muir (Yamaha).
Fastest lap: Fogarty, 1m 36.86s, 92.91 mph/149.53 km/h.
Championship points: **1** Fogarty, 40; **2** Whitham, 34; **3** Moodie, 26; **4** Rutter, 25; **5** Hislop, 24; **6** Llewellyn, 23.

Single Cylinder, round 1 (15 laps, 37.500 miles/60.345 km)
1 Royston Keen (Yamaha), 32m 04.41s, 70.15 mph/112.89 km/h.
2 David Rawlins (Yamaha); **3** Paul Harrison (Rotax); **4** Peter Branton (Tigcraft); **5** Scott Richardson (Tigcraft); **6** Steve Ruth (Yamaha); **7** Jonathan Sinclair (Over); **8** Paul Marris (Suzuki); **9** Stephen Marlow (Yamaha); **10** Bruce Stevenson (Yamaha); **11** Kevin Rance (Tigcraft); **12** Peter Rayfield (Suzuki); **13** Steve Allen (Harris); **14** Carl James (Harris); **15** Steve Tannock (Yamaha).
Fastest lap: Rawlins, 2m 05.29s, 71.83 mph/115.60 km/h.
Championship points: **1** Keen, 20; **2** Rawlins, 17; **3** Harrison, 15; **4** Branton, 13; **5** Richardson, 11; **6** Ruth, 10.

Open Sidecars, round 1 (11 laps, 27.500 miles/44.253 km)
1 Steve Webster/Adolf Hänni (LCR-Krauser), 18m 47.70s, 87.78 mph/141.28 km/h.
2 Steve Abbott/Julian Tailford (Windle-Krauser); **3** Barry Brindley/Scott Whiteside (LCR-Yamaha); **4** Mark Reddington/Trevor Crone (LCR-Honda); **5** Darren Dixon/Andy Hetherington (LCR-Yamaha); **6** Roger Lovelock/Jeff Haines (Asco); **7** Kieron Kavanagh/Michael Finnegan (Krauser); **8** Brian Gray/Steve Pointer (LCR); **9** Steve Dobson/Liz Dobson (Windle-Suzuki); **10** Simon Christie/Adrian Walduck (Christie); **11** Roger Body/Andy Peach (LCR-Krauser); **12** Ian Wilford/Dudley Tomlinson (LCR-Krauser); **13** Phil Croft/Nigel Stevens (Suzuki); **14** Ian English/Steve English (Krauser); **15** Barry Fleury/Jane Fleury (LCR-JPX).
Fastest lap: Webster/Hänni, 1m 40.80s, 89.28 mph/143.69 km/h.
Championship points: **1** Webster, 20; **2** Abbott, 17; **3** B. Brindley, 15; **4** Reddington, 13; **5** Dixon, 11; **6** Lovelock, 10.

MALLORY PARK CIRCUIT, 17 April. 1.37-mile/2.025-km circuit.
H.E.A.T./British Supercup, round 2
125 cc (18 laps, 24.66 miles/36.45 km)
1 Kevin Mawdsley (Honda), 15m 59.68s, 92.50 mph/148.87 km/h.
2 Darren Barton (Honda); **3** Barry Stanley (Honda); **4** Steve Patrickson (Honda); **5** Andy Hatton (Honda); **6** Robin Appleyard (Honda); **7** Les Wood (Honda); **8** Chris Palmer (Yamaha); **9** Fernando Mendes (Honda); **10** Darran Gawley (Honda); **11** Gavan Morris (Honda); **12** Stuart Nicholls (Honda); **13** Ian Emberton (Honda); **14** Lindsay Gordon (Yamaha); **15** Adrian Coates (Yamaha).
Fastest lap: Stanley, 52.12s, 94.62 nph/152.28 km/h.
Championship points: **1** Mawdsley, 37; **2** Hatton, 31; **3** Patrickson, 28; **4** Stanley, 24; **5** Appleyard, 23; **6** Barton, 17.

250 cc (18 laps, 24.66 miles/36.45 km)
1 Paul Brown (Yamaha), 15m 18.12s, 96.69 mph/155.61 km/h.
2 Jason Vincent (Yamaha); **3** Woolsey Coulter (Aprilia); **4** Steve Sawford (Yamaha); **5** Ian Newton (Aprilia); **6** Eugene McManus (Yamaha); **7** Jamie Robinson (Yamaha); **8** Greig Ramsay (Yamaha); **9** Max Vincent (Yamaha); **10** Adrian Butcher (Yamaha); **11** Adrian Clarke (Yamaha); **12** Mark Linton (Yamaha); **13** Kevin Wholey (Yamaha); **14** Gavin Lee (Yamaha); **15** Stephen Farmer (Yamaha).
Fastest lap: Newton, 50.06s, 98.52 mph/158.55 km/h.
Championship points: **1** Brown and J. Vincent, 37; **3** Sawford, 28; **4** Newton, 22; **5** Coulter and McManus, 19.

Supersport 600 (18 laps, 24.66 miles/36.45 km)
1 Ian Simpson (Yamaha), 15m 39.53s, 94.48 mph/152.06 km/h.
2 Mike Edwards (Yamaha); **3** Iain Duffus (Yamaha); **4** David Heal (Yamaha); **5** Iain Macpherson (Honda); **6** Steve Cunningham (Honda); **7** Mick Corrigan (Honda); **8** Tim Poole (Honda); **9** Peter Jennings (Honda); **10** Dave Martin (Honda); **11** Andrew Tinsley (Honda); **12** Jason Emmett (Honda); **13** Tony Goldstraw (Yamaha); **14** Howard Whitby (Honda); **15** Stuart Wickens (Yamaha).
Fastest lap: Edwards, 51.44s, 95.87 mph/154.30 km/h.
Championship points: **1** Simpson, 40; **2** Edwards, 34; **3** Duffus, 30; **4** Cunningham and Poole, 21; **6** Macpherson, 19.

TT Superbike (2 x 18 laps, 24.66 miles/36.45 km)
Leg 1
1 Mark Farmer (Yamaha), 15m 05.37s, 98.05 mph/157.80 km/h.
2 Jim Moodie (Yamaha); **3** Matt Llewellyn (Ducati); **4** Michael Rutter (Ducati); **5** Ian Simpson (Norton); **6** Peter Graves (Ducati); **7** Roger Bennett (Kawasaki); **8** Dean Ashton (Yamaha); **9** Phillip McCallen (Honda); **10** Ray Stringer (Honda); **11** Alex Buckingham (Yamaha); **12** Shaun Muir (Yamaha); **13** Philip Weston (Kawasaki); **14** Jason Griffiths (Kawasaki); **15** Graham Ward (Kawasaki).
Fastest lap: Phil Borley (Norton), 49.44s, 99.75 mph/160.54 km/h.
Leg 2
1 Mark Farmer (Yamaha), 15m 05.59s, 98.03 mph/157.76 km/h.
2 Jim Moodie (Yamaha); **3** Peter Graves (Ducati); **4** Dean Ashton (Yamaha); **5** Roger Bennett (Kawasaki); **6** Ian Simpson (Norton); **7** James Haydon (Honda); **8** David Jefferies (Ducati); **9** Phillip McCallen (Honda); **10** Nick Hopkins (Yamaha); **11** Alex Buckingham (Yamaha); **12** Jason Griffiths (Kawasaki); **13** Shaun Muir (Yamaha); **14** Colin Hipwell (Kawasaki); **15** Brett Sampson (Kawasaki).
Fastest lap: Michael Rutter (Ducati), 49.30s, 100.04 mph/160.99 km/h.
Championship points: **1** Moodie, 60; **2** Farmer and Fogarty, 40; **4** Llewellyn and Rutter, 38; **6** Whitham, 34.

Single Cylinder, round 2 (18 laps, 24.66 miles/36.45 km)
1 Alan Carter (Ducati), 15m 52.36s, 93.21 mph/150.01 km/h.
2 Nick Hopkins (Over); **3** Mike Edwards (MZ Scorpion); **4** Steve Ruth (Yamaha); **5** Roger Banks (Tigcraft); **6** David Rawlins (Yamaha); **7** Mike Hose (Yamaha); **8** David Morris (Chrysalis); **9** Royston Keen (Yamaha); **10** Colin Sturgeon (Yamaha); **11** Richard Cutts (Yamaha); **12** Scott Richardson (Tigcraft); **13** Paul Harrison (Spondon); **14** Richard Shepherd (Shepherd); **15** Paul Wilson (Tigcraft).
Fastest lap: Carter, 52.11s, 94.64 mph/152.31 km/h.
Championship points: **1** Keen and Rawlins, 27; **2** Ruth, 23; **3** Carter, 20; **4** Harrison, 18; **5** Hopkins, 17; **6** Edwards and Richardson, 15.

Open Sidecars, round 2 (18 laps, 24.66 miles/36.45 km)
1 Steve Abbott/Julian Tailford (Windle-Krauser), 15m 06.29s, 97.95 mph/157.64 km/h.
2 Steve Webster/Adolf Hänni (LCR-Krauser); **3** Derek Brindley/Paul Hutchinson (LCR-ADM); **4** Barry Brindley/Scott Whiteside (Yamaha); **5** Roger Lovelock/Jeff Haines (Asco); **6** Mick Cookson/Alan Hibberd (LCR-Suzuki); **7** Steve Dobson/Liz Dobson (Windle-Suzuki); **8** Brian Gray/Steve Pointer (LCR); **9** Phil Croft/Nigel Stevens (Suzuki); **10** Alan Budge/George Hamilton (Suzuki); **11** Bruce Moore/Dave Bilton (LCR-Krauser).
Fastest lap: Abbott/Tailford, 49.45s, 99.73 mph/160.51 km/h.
Championship points: **1** Abbott and Webster, 37; **3** B. Brindley, 28; **4** Lovelock, 21; **5** Dobson and Gray, 16.

SNETTERTON CIRCUIT, 22 May. 1.952-mile/3.141-km circuit.
H.E.A.T./British Supercup, round 3
125 cc (15 laps, 29.28 miles/47.115 km)
1 Chris Palmer (Yamaha), 23m 44.71s, 73.98 mph/119.06 km/h.
2 Robin Appleyard (Honda); **3** Steve Patrickson (Honda); **4** Alan Green (Honda); **5** Fernando Mendes (Honda); **6** Mark Norman (Honda); **7** Oliver Hutchinson (Yamaha); **8** Jim Falls (Honda); **9** Lindsay Gordon (Yamaha); **10** Nick Lang (Yamaha); **11** Damien Cahill (Bill Bunn); **12** Barry Stanley (Honda); **13** Lee Dickinson (Yamaha); **14** Scott Summerfield (Honda); **15** Sanjay Sharma (Honda).
Fastest lap: M. del Guidice (Yamaha), 1m 31.97s, 76.40 mph/122.96 km/h.
Championship points: **1** Patrickson, 43; **2** Appleyard, 40; **3** Mawdsley, 37; **4** Hatton, 31; **5** Palmer and Stanley, 28.

250 cc (15 laps, 29.28 miles/47.115 km)
1 Nigel Bosworth (Honda), 18m 42.38s, 93.91 mph/151.14 km/h.
2 Jason Vincent (Yamaha); **3** Eugene McManus (Yamaha); **4** Jamie Robinson (Yamaha); **5** Greig Ramsay (Yamaha); **6** Steve Sawford (Yamaha); **7** Iain Challinor (Yamaha); **8** Adrian Clarke (Yamaha); **9** Paul Brown (Yamaha); **10** Robin Milton (Yamaha); **11** Gary Haslam (Yamaha); **12** Stuart Rider (Yamaha); **13** Gary May (Yamaha); **14** Graeme Thompson (Yamaha); **15** Mark Linton (Yamaha).
Fastest lap: Bosworth, 1m 13.20s, 96.00 mph/154.49 km/h.
Championship points: **1** J. Vincent, 54; **2** Brown, 44; **3** Sawford, 38; **4** McManus, 34; **5** Ramsay, 29; **6** Clarke, 26.

Supersport 600 (13 laps, 25.376 miles/40.833 km)
1 Ian Simpson (Yamaha), 17m 46.57s, 85.65 mph/137.84 km/h.
2 Tim Poole (Honda); **3** Dave Martin (Honda); **4** Iain Duffus (Yamaha); **5** Mark Ditchfield (Honda); **6** John Crawford (Honda); **7** Jonathan Peacock (Yamaha); **8** Robert Simm (Honda); **9** Mike Edwards (Yamaha); **10** Jason Emmett (Honda); **11** Iain Macpherson (Honda); **12** Stuart Wickens (Yamaha); **13** Tim Howells (Honda); **14** Adam Lewis (Yamaha); **15** Nik Robards (Honda).
Fastest lap: Martin, 1m 18.19s, 89.87 mph/144.63 km/h.
Championship points: **1** Simpson, 60; **2** Duffus, 43; **3** Edwards, 41; **4** Poole, 38; **5** Macpherson, 24; **6** Cunningham and Martin, 21.

TT Superbike
Leg 1 (9 laps, 17.568 miles/28.269 km)
1 James Haydon (Honda), 13m 32.58s, 77.83 mph/125.25 km/h.
2 Michael Rutter (Ducati); **3** Andrew Stroud (Kawasaki); **4** Lee Pullan (Yamaha); **5** Matt Llewellyn (Ducati); **6** Robert Dunlop (Honda); **7** Mark Farmer (Yamaha); **8** Peter Graves (Ducati); **9** James Bunton (Yamaha); **10** Geoff Dixon (Yamaha); **11** Colin Breeze (Kawasaki); **12** Phil Read (Kawasaki); **13** Tom Knight (Ducati); **14** Johnny Bennett (Kawasaki); **15** Bob Crabtree (Kawasaki).
Fastest lap: Haydon, 1m 28.57s, 79.34 mph/127.68 km/h.
Leg 2 (15 laps, 29.28 miles/47.115 km)
1 Jim Moodie (Yamaha), 18m 02.08s, 97.41 mph/156.77 km/h.
2 Steve Hislop (Honda); **3** Phil Borley (Norton); **4** Matt Llewellyn (Ducati); **5** Mark Farmer (Yamaha); **6** Robert Dunlop (Honda); **7** Michael Rutter (Ducati); **8** Phillip McCallen (Honda); **9** Alex Buckingham (Yamaha); **10** Les Pullan (Yamaha); **11** Roger Bennett (Kawasaki); **12** Dave Redgate (Yamaha); **13** Philip Weston (Kawasaki); **14** Colin Breeze (Kawasaki); **15** Brett Sampson (Kawasaki).
Fastest lap: Borley, 1m 11.33s, 98.51 mph/158.54 km/h.
Championship points: **1** Moodie, 80; **2** Rutter, 64; **3** Llewellyn, 62; **4** Farmer, 60; **5** Haydon, 47; **6** Hislop, 41.

F2 Sidecars, round 1 (15 laps, 29.28 miles/47.115 km)
1 Mick Boddice Snr/Dave Wells (Honda), 20m 32.21s, 85.54 mph/137.66 km/h.
2 Steve Noble/Mark Bingham (Yamaha); **3** Kenny Howles/Steve Parker (Yamaha); **4** Richard Nelson/Mark Camp (Yamaha); **5** Geoff Bell/Nick Roche (Yamaha); **6** Martin Clark/Boyd Hutchinson (Honda); **7** Dave Kimberley/Tony Darby (Kawasaki); **8** Mick Boddice Jnr/Chris Hollis (Honda); **9** John Childs/Sadie Childs (Honda); **10** Gary Horsepole/Kevin Leigh (Honda); **11** Eddy Wright/Richard Long (EMC); **12** Roger Winterburn/Tony Howard (Honda); **13** Dave Atkinson/Phil Roberts (Windle); **14** Howard Baker/Philip Biggs (Shelbourne).
Fastest lap: Dave Molyneux/Peter Hill (DMR Yamaha), 1m 20.24s, 87.57 mph/140.94 km/h.
Championship points: **1** Boddice Snr, 20; **2** Noble, 17; **3** Howles, 15; **4** Nelson, 13; **5** Bell, 11; **6** Clark, 10.

DONINGTON PARK CIRCUIT, 19 June. 2.500-mile/4.023-km circuit.
H.E.A.T./British Supercup, round 4
125 cc (15 laps, 37.5 miles/60.345 km)
1 Neil Hodgson (Honda), 26m 33.34s, 84.72 mph/136.35 km/h.
2 Steve Patrickson (Honda); **3** Fernando Mendes (Honda); **4** Robin Appleyard (Honda); **5** Darren Barton (Honda); **6** Steve Reape (Honda); **7** Barry Stanley (Honda); **8** Jeffrey Claridge (Honda); **9** Chris Palmer (Yamaha); **10** Martin Johnson (Yamaha); **11** Lindsay Gordon (Yamaha); **12** Gavan Morris (Honda); **13** Rob Frost (Honda); **14** Pete Jennings (Honda); **15** Mick Lofthouse (Yamaha).

Fastest lap: Kevin Mawdsley (Honda), 1m 44.56s, 86.07 mph/138.52 km/h.
Championship points: **1** Patrickson, 60; **2** Appleyard, 53; **3** Mawdsley and Stanley, 37; **5** Palmer, 35; **6** Mendes, 33.

250 cc (15 laps, 37.5 miles/60.345 km)
1 Ian Newton (Aprilia), 25m 07.67s, 89.54 mph/144.10 km/h.
2 Jamie Robinson (Yamaha); **3** Ron Haslam (Yamaha); **4** Max Vincent (Yamaha); **5** Jason Vincent (Yamaha); **6** Paul Brown (Yamaha); **7** Greig Ramsay (Yamaha); **8** Robin Milton (Yamaha); **9** Mark Snell (Yamaha); **10** Fernando Mendes (Honda); **11** Graeme Thompson (Yamaha); **12** Gary May (Yamaha); **13** Steve Sawford (Yamaha); **14** Adrian Clarke (Yamaha); **15** Stuart Rider (Honda).
Fastest lap: Newton, 1m 38.68s, 91.20 mph/146.77 km/h.
Championship points: **1** J. Vincent, 65; **2** Brown, 54; **3** Newton, 42; **4** Sawford, 41; **5** Robinson, 39; **6** Ramsay, 38.

Supersport 600 (15 laps, 37.5 miles/60.345 km)
1 Mike Edwards (Yamaha), 25m 40.64s, 87.62 mph/141.02 km/h.
2 Ian Simpson (Yamaha); **3** Iain Duffus (Yamaha); **4** Andrew Pallot (Yamaha); **5** Howard Whitby (Honda); **6** Steve Cunningham (Honda); **7** Mick Corrigan (Yamaha); **8** Paul Breslin (Yamaha); **9** Tony Goldstraw (Yamaha); **10** Peter Jennings (Honda); **11** Gordon Blackley (Honda); **12** Iain Macpherson (Honda); **13** Mark Ditchfield (Honda); **14** John Crawford (Honda); **15** Ian Knights (Honda).
Fastest lap: Edwards, 1m 42.08s, 88.16 mph/141.88 km/h.
Championship points: **1** Simpson, 77; **2** Edwards, 61; **3** Duffus, 58; **4** Poole, 38; **5** Cunningham, 31; **6** Macpherson, 28.

TT Superbike (2 x 15 laps, 37.5 miles/60.345 km)
Leg I
1 Jim Moodie (Yamaha), 24m 33.90s, 91.59 mph/147.40 km/h.
2 Ian Simpson (Norton); **3** Phil Borley (Norton); **4** Matt Llewellyn (Ducati); **5** Michael Rutter (Ducati); **6** Nick Hopkins (Yamaha); **7** Ron Haslam (Yamaha); **8** Phillip McCallen (Honda); **9** Alex Buckingham (Yamaha); **10** Steve Manley (Kawasaki); **11** Andrew Corbett (Yamaha); **12** Nigel Nottingham (Yamaha); **13** Tom Cuddy (Yamaha); **14** Jason Griffiths (Kawasaki); **15** Nick Jefferies (Britten).
Fastest lap: Borley, 1m 37.27s, 92.52 mph/148.90 km/h.
Leg 2
1 Phil Borley (Norton), 24m 29.45s, 91.87 mph/147.85 km/h.
2 Ian Simpson (Norton); **3** Matt Llewellyn (Ducati); **4** Jim Moodie (Yamaha); **5** Nick Hopkins (Yamaha); **6** Ron Haslam (Yamaha); **7** David Jefferies (Ducati); **8** Peter Graves (Ducati); **9** Dave Redgate (Yamaha); **10** Alex Buckingham (Yamaha); **11** Roger Bennett (Kawasaki); **12** Steve Manley (Kawasaki); **13** Jason Griffiths (Kawasaki); **14** Phillip McCallen (Honda); **15** Shaun Muir (Yamaha).
Fastest lap: Llewellyn, 1m 36.76s, 93.01 mph/149.69 km/h.
Championship points: **1** Moodie, 113; **2** Llewellyn, 90; **3** Rutter, 75; **4** Borley, 67; **5** Simpson, 61; **6** Farmer, 60.

F2 Sidecars, round 2 (15 laps, 37.5 miles/60.345 km)
1 Gary Smith/Tony Balazs (Honda), 27m 17.10s, 82.46 mph/132.71 km/h.
2 Dave Molyneux/Peter Hill (DMR Yamaha); **3** Rob Fisher/Michael Wynn (Yamaha); **4** Eddy Wright/Richard Long (EMC); **5** Roy Hanks/Tom Hanks (Ireson); **6** David Wallis/Tim Kirkham (Yamaha); **7** Martin Whittington/Steve Birkett (Regiarni); **8** Steve Noble/Mark Bingham (Yamaha); **9** John Childs/Sadie Childs (Honda); **10** Vince Biggs/Jamie Biggs (Yamaha); **11** Geoff Bell/Nick Roche (Yamaha); **12** Stephen Ramsden/Paul Coward (Yamaha); **13** Mick Boddice Jnr/Chris Hollis (Honda); **14** John Coates/Neil Carpenter (Honda); **15** Peter Knight/Paul Attwood (Honda).
Fastest lap: Smith/Balzazs, 1m 47.75s, 83.52 mph/134.42 km/h (record).
Championship points: **1** Noble, 25; **2** Boddice Snr and Smith, 20; **4** Wright, 18; **5** Molyneux, 17; **6** Bell, 16.

OULTON PARK CIRCUIT, 26 June. 2.769-mile/4.458-km circuit.
H.E.A.T./British Supercup, round 5
125 cc (7 laps, 19.383 miles/31.206 km)
1 Kevin Mawdsley (Honda), 12m 24.40s, 93.73 mph/150.85 km/h.
2 Darren Barton (Honda); **3** Mark Norman (Honda); **4** Fernando Mendes (Honda); **5** Mick Lofthouse (Yamaha); **6** Steve Patrickson (Honda); **7** Andy Hatton (Honda); **8** Les Wood (Honda); **9** Lindsay Gordon (Yamaha); **10** Gavan Morris (Honda); **11** Pete Jennings (Honda); **12** Steve Reape (Honda); **13** Martin Johnson (Yamaha); **14** Rob Frost (Honda); **15** Nick Lang (Yamaha).
Fastest lap: Barton, 1m 44.58s, 95.31 mph/153.40 km/h.
Championship points: **1** Patrickson, 70; **2** Mawdsley, 57; **3** Appleyard, 53; **4** Mendes, 46; **5** Barton, 45; **6** Hatton, 40.

250 cc (10 laps, 27.69 miles/44.58 km)
1 Ian Newton (Aprilia), 16m 45.32s, 99.15 mph/159.57 km/h.
2 Jamie Robinson (Yamaha); **3** Eugene McManus (Yamaha); **4** Max Vincent (Yamaha); **5** Steve Sawford (Yamaha); **6** Iain Challinor (Yamaha); **7** Paul Brown (Yamaha); **8** Greig Ramsay (Yamaha); **9** Fernando Mendes (Honda); **10** Mark Snell (Yamaha); **11** Robin Milton (Yamaha); **12** Jason Vincent (Yamaha); **13** Adrian Clarke (Yamaha); **14** Lee Masters (Yamaha); **15** Mark Linton (Yamaha).

Fastest lap: Newton, 1m 38.82s, 100.87 mph/162.34 km/h.
Championship points: **1** J. Vincent, 69; **2** Brown, 63; **3** Newton, 62; **4** Robinson, 56; **5** Sawford, 52; **6** McManus, 49.

Supersport 600 (10 laps, 27.69 miles/44.58 km)
1 Mike Edwards (Yamaha), 16m 53.22s, 98.38 mph/158.33 km/h.
2 Ian Simpson (Yamaha); **3** Tim Poole (Honda); **4** David Heal (Yamaha); **5** Andrew Pallot (Yamaha); **6** Howard Whitby (Honda); **7** Iain Macpherson (Honda); **8** John Crawford (Honda); **9** Steve Cunningham (Honda); **10** Dave Martin (Honda); **11** Peter Jennings (Honda); **12** Mark Ditchfield (Honda); **13** Andrew Murphy (Yamaha); **14** Andrew Tinsley (Honda); **15** Colin Gable (Honda).
Fastest lap: Simpson, 1m 40.16s, 99.52 mph/160.16 km/h.
Championship points: **1** Simpson, 94; **2** Edwards, 81; **3** Duffus, 58; **4** Poole, 53; **5** Cunningham, 38; **6** Macpherson, 37.

TT Superbike
Leg 1 (8 laps, 22.152 miles/35.664 km)
1 Ian Simpson (Norton), 12m 55.37s, 103.07 mph/165.88 km/h.
2 Phil Borley (Norton); **3** Jim Moodie (Yamaha); **4** Matt Llewellyn (Ducati); **5** Michael Rutter (Ducati); **6** James Haydon (Honda); **7** Alex Buckingham (Yamaha); **8** Nick Hopkins (Yamaha); **9** Andrew Stroud (Yamaha); **10** Roger Bennett (Kawasaki); **11** Lee Pullan (Yamaha); **12** Phillip McCallen (Honda); **13** Graham Ward (Kawasaki); **14** Nigel Nottingham (Yamaha); **15** Dave Redgate (Yamaha).
Fastest lap: Ray Stringer (Ducati), 1m 35.27s, 104.85 mph/168.75 km/h.
Leg 2 (12 laps, 33.228 miles/53.496 km)
1 Ian Simpson (Norton), 19m 21.56s, 102.98 mph/165.73 km/h.
2 Phil Borley (Norton); **3** Ray Stringer (Ducati); **4** Matt Llewellyn (Ducati); **5** Jim Moodie (Yamaha); **6** Michael Rutter (Ducati); **7** Nick Hopkins (Yamaha); **8** Andrew Stroud (Yamaha); **9** Alex Buckingham (Yamaha); **10** Roger Bennett (Kawasaki); **11** Shaun Muir (Yamaha); **12** Phillip McCallen (Honda); **13** John Barton (Kawasaki); **14** Dave Redgate (Yamaha); **15** Nigel Nottingham (Yamaha).
Fastest lap: Stringer, 1m 35.54s, 104.33 mph/167.91 km/h.
Championship points: **1** Moodie, 139; **2** Llewellyn, 116; **3** Borley and Simpson, 101; **5** Rutter, 96; **6** Farmer, 60.

Single Cylinder, round 3 (10 laps, 27.69 miles/44.58 km)
1 Nick Hopkins (Over), 17m 25.63s, 95.54 mph/153.75 km/h.
2 Mike Edwards (MZ Scorpion); **3** Roger Banks (Rotax); **4** David Rawlins (Yamaha); **5** Barry Rudd (Yamaha); **6** Steve Ruth (Yamaha); **7** David Morris (BMW); **8** Stephen Marlow (Yamaha); **9** Jason Griffiths (Yamaha); **10** Geoff Baines (Ducati); **11** Steve Campbell (Hyde); **12** Gary Cotterell (Rotax); **13** John Neate (Spondon); **14** Sean Waller (Rotax); **15** Royston Keen (Yamaha).
Fastest lap: Edwards, 1m 43.36s, 96.65 mph/155.54 km/h (record).
Championship points: **1** Rawlins, 40; **2** Hopkins, 37; **3** Ruth, 33; **4** Edwards, 32; **5** Keen, 28; **6** Banks, 26.

F2 Sidecars, round 3 (10 laps, 27.69 miles/44.58 km)
1 Dave Molyneux/Peter Hill (DMR Yamaha), 18m 06.47s, 91.75 mph/147.65 km/h.
2 Mick Boddice Snr/Dave Wells (Honda); **3** Gary Horsepole/Kevin Leigh (Honda); **4** Roy Hanks/Tom Hanks (Ireson); **5** Steve Noble/Mark Bingham (Yamaha); **6** Mick Boddice Jnr/Chris Hollis (Yamaha); **7** Geoff Bell/Nick Roche (Yamaha); **8** Rob Fisher/Michael Wynn (Yamaha); **9** Eddy Wright/Richard Long (EMC); **10** David Wallis/Tim Kirkham (Yamaha); **11** Martin Whittington/Steve Birkett (Regiarni); **12** Martin Clark/Boyd Hutchinson (Shelbourne); **13** Mick Haith/Shaun Stenson (Yamaha); **14** Paul Glendenning/Graham Biggs (Honda); **15** Martin/Harrington (Ireson).
Fastest lap: Molyneux/Hill, 1m 47.25s, 92.94 mph/149.58 km/h.
Championship points: **1** Boddice Snr and Molyneux, 37; **3** Noble, 36; **4** Bell and Wright, 25; **6** Hanks, 24.

KNOCKHILL CIRCUIT, 17 July. 1.30-mile/2.092-km circuit.
H.E.A.T./British Supercup, round 6
125 cc (18 laps, 23.4 miles/37.656 km)
1 Kevin Mawdsley (Honda), 17m 17.79s, 80.48 mph/129.52 km/h.
2 Steve Patrickson (Honda); **3** Chris Palmer (Honda); **4** Robin Appleyard (Honda); **5** Andy Hatton (Honda); **6** Mick Lofthouse (Yamaha); **7** Jeffrey Claridge (Honda); **8** Ian Emberton (Honda); **9** Rob Frost (Honda); **10** Les Wood (Honda); **11** Mark Norman (Honda); **12** Alan Green (Honda); **13** Chris Mintoft (Honda); **14** Scott Summerfield (Honda); **15** Neil Durham (Honda).
Fastest lap: Mawdsley, 56.63s, 81.94 mph/131.87 km/h (record).
Championship points: **1** Patrickson, 87; **2** Mawdsley, 77; **3** Appleyard, 66; **4** Hatton, 51; **5** Palmer, 50; **6** Mendes, 46.

250 cc (18 laps, 23.4 miles/37.656 km)
1 Ian Newton (Aprilia), 16m 20.82s, 85.16 mph/137.05 km/h.
2 Woolsey Coulter (Aprilia); **3** Jason Vincent (Yamaha); **4** Paul Brown (Yamaha); **5** Ron Haslam (Yamaha); **6** Eugene McManus (Yamaha); **7** Max Vincent (Yamaha); **8** Greig Ramsay (Yamaha); **9** Iain Challinor (Yamaha); **10** Callum Ramsay (Yamaha); **11** Fernando Mendes (Honda); **12** Paul Booler (Yamaha); **13** Robin Milton (Yamaha); **14** Adrian Clarke (Yamaha); **15** Stephen Farmer (Yamaha).
Fastest lap: Newton, 53.52s, 86.70 mph/139.53 km/h (record).

Championship points: **1** J. Vincent, 84; **2** Newton, 82; **3** Brown, 76; **4** McManus, 59; **5** Robinson, 56; **6** Ramsay, 54.

Supersport 600 (18 laps, 23.4 miles/37.656 km)
1 Mike Edwards (Yamaha), 16m 32.94s, 84.12 mph/135.37 km/h.
2 Ian Simpson (Yamaha); **3** David Heal (Yamaha); **4** Iain Macpherson (Honda); **5** Tim Poole (Honda); **6** Mick Corrigan (Yamaha); **7** Howard Whitby (Honda); **8** Steve Cunningham (Honda); **9** Howard Selby (Yamaha); **10** Paul Breslin (Yamaha); **11** Andy Murphy (Honda); **12** Peter Jennings (Honda); **13** Jonathan Peacock (Yamaha); **14** Tim Smith (Yamaha); **15** Bob Grant (Honda).
Fastest lap: Edwards, 54.33s, 85.41 mph/137.45 km/h (record).
Championship points: **1** Simpson, 111; **2** Edwards, 101; **3** Poole, 64; **4** Duffus, 58; **5** Macpherson, 50; **6** Cunningham, 46.

TT Superbike (2 x 20 laps, 26.0 miles/41.84 km)
Leg 1
1 Ian Simpson (Norton), 17m 46.40s, 87.02 mph/140.06 km/h.
2 Phil Borley (Norton); **3** Matt Llewellyn (Ducati); **4** Steve Hislop (Honda); **5** Nick Hopkins (Yamaha); **6** Michael Rutter (Ducati); **7** Ray Stringer (Ducati); **8** Andrew Stroud (Yamaha); **9** David Jefferies (Ducati); **10** Roger Bennett (Kawasaki); **11** Phillip McCallen (Honda); **12** Shaun Muir (Yamaha); **13** Dean Ashton (Yamaha); **14** Colin Breeze (Kawasaki); **15** Nigel Nottingham (Yamaha).
Fastest lap: Borley, 52.04s, 89.16 mph/143.50 km/h.
Leg 2
1 Ian Simpson (Norton), 17m 41.06s, 87.46 mph/140.76 km/h.
2 Jim Moodie (Yamaha); **3** Phil Borley (Norton); **4** Steve Hislop (Honda); **5** Matt Llewellyn (Ducati); **6** Michael Rutter (Ducati); **7** Andrew Stroud (Yamaha); **8** Ray Stringer (Ducati); **9** Phillip McCallen (Honda); **10** Shaun Muir (Yamaha); **11** Dean Ashton (Yamaha); **12** Colin Breeze (Kawasaki); **13** Nigel Nottingham (Yamaha); **14** Graeme Ritchie (Ducati); **15** Lee Humphries (Kawasaki).
Fastest lap: Borley, 52.03s, 89.18 mph/143.63 km/h.
Championship points: **1** Moodie, 156; **2** Llewellyn, 142; **3** Simpson, 141; **4** Borley, 133; **5** Rutter, 116; **6** Hislop, 67.

Single Cylinder, round 4 (18 laps, 23.4 miles/37.656 km)
1 David Rawlins (Yamaha), 17m 12.91s, 80.86 mph/130.14 km/h.
2 Barry Rudd (Yamaha); **3** Steve Ruth (Yamaha); **4** Roger Banks (Tigcraft); **5** Geoff Baines (Ducati); **6** David Morris (Chrysalis); **7** Simon Beck (Rumi Honda); **8** Phil Giles (Spondon Yamaha); **9** Scott Richardson (Tigcraft); **10** Royston Keen (Yamaha); **11** Paul Harrison (Spondon Rotax); **12** Gary Cotterell (Tigcraft); **13** Richard Cutts (Spondon Yamaha); **14** Steve Dey (Honda).
Fastest lap: Mike Edwards (MZ Scorpion), 56.08s, 82.74 mph/133.16 km/h (record).
Championship points: **1** Rawlins, 60; **2** Ruth, 48; **3** Banks, 39; **4** Hopkins, 37; **5** Keen, 34; **6** Edwards, 32.

F2 Sidecars, round 4 (18 laps, 23.4 miles/37.656 km)
1 Geoff Bell/Nick Roche (Yamaha), 17m 33.48s, 79.28 mph/127.59 km/h.
2 Gary Smith/Tony Balazs (Honda); **3** Gary Horsepole/Kevin Leigh (Honda); **4** Steve Noble/Mark Bingham (Yamaha); **5** Rob Fisher/Ian Simons (Yamaha); **6** John Childs/Sadie Childs (Honda); **7** Dave Molyneux/Peter Hill (DMR); **8** Roy Hanks/Tom Hanks (Ireson); **9** David Wallis/Tim Kirkham (Yamaha); **10** Eddy Wright/Richard Long (EMC); **11** Martin Clark/Boyd Hutchinson (Honda); **12** Martin Whittington/Steve Birkett (Regiarni); **13** Kenny Howles/Rob Parker (Yamaha); **14** Alan Budge/Neil MacKenzie (Honda); **15** Dave Atkinson/Phil Roberts.
Fastest lap: Noble/Bingham, 57.39s, 80.85 mph/130.12 km/h (record).
Championship points: **1** Noble, 49; **2** Molyneux, 46; **3** Bell, 45; **4** Boddice Snr and Smith, 37; **6** Horsepole, 36.

PEMBREY CIRCUIT, 7 August. 1.456-mile/2.343-km circuit.
H.E.A.T./British Supercup, round 7.
125 cc (12 laps, 17.472 miles/28.116 km)
1 Darren Barton (Honda), 12m 46.73s, 82.03 mph/132.02 km/h.
2 Fernando Mendes (Honda); **3** Kevin Mawdsley (Honda); **4** Mark Norman (Honda); **5** Ian Lougher (Aprilia); **6** Mick Lofthouse (Yamaha); **7** Steve Patrickson (Honda); **8** Darran Gawley (Honda); **9** Barry Stanley (Honda); **10** Lindsay Gordon (Yamaha); **11** Pete Jennings (Honda); **12** Jeffrey Claridge (Honda); **13** Simon Williams (Honda); **14** Rob Frost (Honda); **15** Nick Lang (Yamaha).
Fastest lap: Mendes, 1m 02.42s, 83.97 mph/135.14 km/h (record).
Championship points: **1** Patrickson, 96; **2** Mawdsley, 92; **3** Appleyard, 66; **4** Barton, 65; **5** Mendes, 63; **6** Norman, 53.

250 cc (15 laps, 21.84 miles/35.145 km)
1 Jason Vincent (Yamaha), 15m 14.83s, 85.94 mph/138.31 km/h.
2 Eugene McManus (Yamaha); **3** Iain Challinor (Yamaha); **4** Paul Brown (Yamaha); **5** Max Vincent (Yamaha); **6** Graeme Thompson (Yamaha); **7** Steve Sawford (Yamaha); **8** Stuart Edwards (Yamaha); **9** Robin Milton (Yamaha); **10** Mark Snell (Yamaha); **11** Adrian Clarke (Yamaha); **12** Fernando Mendes (Honda); **13** Gary May (Yamaha); **14** Ian Newton (Aprilia); **15** Gary Haslam (Yamaha).
Fastest lap: J. Vincent, 59.52s, 88.06 mph/141.72 km/h (record).
Championship points: **1** J. Vincent, 104; **2** Brown, 89; **3** Newton, 84; **4** McManus, 76; **5** Sawford, 61; **6** Robinson, 56.

Supersport 600 (15 laps, 21.84 miles/35.145 km)
1 Ian Simpson (Yamaha), 15m 46.11s, 83.10 mph/133.74 km/h.
2 Iain Macpherson (Honda); **3** Iain Duffus (Yamaha); **4** Tim Poole (Honda); **5** Andrew Pallot (Yamaha); **6** Mick Corrigan (Yamaha); **7** Tony Goldstraw (Yamaha); **8** Andrew Tinsley (Honda); **9** Dave Martin (Honda); **10** Gary Weston (Yamaha); **11** Mark Ditchfield (Honda); **12** Andy Murphy (Yamaha); **13** Damion Bailey (Honda); **14** Steve Marks (Honda); **15** Simon Smith (Honda).
Fastest lap: Mike Edwards (Yamaha), 1m 01.89s, 84.69 mph/136.29 km/h (record).
Championship points: **1** Simpson, 131; **2** Edwards, 101; **3** Poole, 77; **4** Duffus, 73; **5** Macpherson, 67; **6** Cunningham, 46.

TT Superbike
Leg 1 (10 laps, 14.56 miles/23.43 km)
1 Ian Simpson (Norton), 10m 00.99s, 87.21 mph/140.36 km/h.
2 Phil Borley (Norton); **3** Jim Moodie (Yamaha); **4** Ray Stringer (Ducati); **5** David Jefferies (Ducati); **6** Peter Graves (Ducati); **7** Nick Hopkins (Yamaha); **8** Andrew Stroud (Yamaha); **9** Neil Hodgson (Honda); **10** Chris Haldane (Honda); **11** Phillip McCallen (Honda); **12** Lee Pullan (Yamaha); **13** Michael Rutter (Honda); **14** Dean Ashton (Yamaha); **15** Jason Griffiths (Kawasaki).
Fastest lap: Matt Llewellyn (Ducati), 58.88s, 89.02 mph/143.26 km/h (record).
Leg 2 (20 laps, 29.12 miles/46.86 km)
1 Phil Borley (Norton), 19m 57.84s, 87.51 mph/140.84 km/h.
2 Ian Simpson (Norton); **3** Ray Stringer (Ducati); **4** David Jefferies (Ducati); **5** Andrew Stroud (Yamaha); **6** Neil Hodgson (Honda); **7** Chris Haldane (Honda); **8** Peter Graves (Ducati); **9** Phillip McCallen (Honda); **10** Jim Moodie (Yamaha); **11** Nick Hopkins (Yamaha); **12** Shaun Muir (Yamaha); **13** Jason Griffiths (Kawasaki); **14** Michael Rutter (Honda); **15** Dean Ashton (Yamaha).
Fastest lap: Moodie, 59.28s, 88.42 mph/142.29 km/h.
Championship points: **1** Simpson, 178; **2** Moodie, 177; **3** Borley, 170; **4** Llewellyn, 142; **5** Rutter, 121; **6** Hopkins, 79.

Single Cylinder, round 5 (15 laps, 21.84 miles/35.145 km)
1 Alan Carter (Ducati), 15m 40.51s, 83.59 mph/134.53 km/h.
2 Mike Edwards (MZ Scorpion); **3** Steve Ruth (Yamaha); **4** David Rawlins (Yamaha); **5** Jason Griffiths (Yamaha); **6** Barry Rudd (Yamaha); **7** David Morris (BMW); **8** Roger Banks (Rotax); **9** Phil Giles (Yamaha); **10** Geoff Baines (Ducati); **11** Mark Wilson (Harris); **12** Mike Hose (Yamaha); **13** Carl James (BMW); **14** John Neate (Spondon); **15** T. Ross-Martin (Yamaha).
Fastest lap: Edwards, 1m 01.73s, 84.91 mph/136.65 km/h (record).
Championship points: **1** Rawlins, 73; **2** Ruth, 63; **3** Edwards, 49; **4** Banks, 47; **5** Carter, 40; **6** Rudd, 38.

Open Sidecars, round 3 (12 laps, 17.472 miles/28.116 km)
1 Derek Brindley/Paul Hutchinson (LCR-ADM), 12m 00.03s, 87.35 mph/140.58 km/h.
2 Steve Abbott/Julian Tailford (Krauser); **3** Chris Wright/Paul Woodhead (Suzuki); **4** Barry Brindley/Scott Whiteside (Yamaha); **5** Brian Gray/Steve Pointer (LCR); **6** Trevor Robinson/Richard Graham (Krauser); **7** Mick Cookson/Gary Leach (LCR); **8** Alan Budge/William Middleton (Suzuki); **9** Ian English/Steve English (Krauser); **10** Simon Christie/Adrian Walduck (Suzuki); **11** Steve Dobson/Liz Dobson (Suzuki); **12** Keith Brown/Alan Brown (Suzuki); **13** Phil Croft/Nigel Stevens (Suzuki); **14** Barry Fleury/Jane Fleury (LCR-JPX).
Fastest lap: D. Brindley/Hutchinson, 58.96s, 88.90 mph/143.07 km/h (record).
Championship points: **1** Abbott, 54; **2** B. Brindley, 41; **3** Webster, 37; **4** D. Brindley, 35; **5** Gray, 27; **6** Dobson and Lovelock, 21.

CADWELL PARK CIRCUIT, 29 August. 2.17-mile/3.472-km circuit.
H.E.A.T./British Supercup, round 8
125 cc (7 laps, 15.19 miles/24.304 km)
1 Robin Appleyard (Honda), 11m 12.89s, 81.26 mph/130.78 km/h.
2 Kevin Mawdsley (Honda); **3** Chris Palmer (Honda); **4** Phelim Owens (Honda); **5** Steve Patrickson (Honda); **6** Alan Green (Honda); **7** Mark Norman (Honda); **8** Les Wood (Honda); **9** Lindsay Gordon (Yamaha); **10** Barry Stanley (Honda); **11** Jeffrey Claridge (Honda); **12** Pete Jennings (Honda); **13** Gavan Morris (Honda); **14** Martin Johnson (Yamaha); **15** Nick Lang (Yamaha).
Fastest lap: Darren Barton (Honda), 1m 34.01s, 83.09 mph/133.73 km/h (record).
Championship points: **1** Mawdsley, 109; **2** Patrickson, 107; **3** Appleyard, 86; **4** Barton and Palmer, 65; **6** Mendes, 63.

250 cc (6 laps, 13.02 miles/20.832 km)
1 Eugene McManus (Yamaha), 9m 14.11s, 84.58 mph/136.13 km/h.
2 Iain Challinor (Yamaha); **3** Steve Sawford (Yamaha); **4** Jamie Robinson (Yamaha); **5** Jason Vincent (Yamaha); **6** Mark Snell (Yamaha); **7** Robin Milton (Yamaha); **8** Alan Patterson (Yamaha); **9** Robin Frear (Yamaha); **10** Adrian Clarke (Yamaha); **11** Greig Ramsay (Yamaha); **12** Gary Haslam (Yamaha); **13** Roki Read (Yamaha); **14** Gary May (Yamaha); **15** Paul Booler (Yamaha).
Fastest lap: Ian Newton (Aprilia), 1m 30.28s, 86.53 mph/139.25 km/h (record).
Championship points: **1** J. Vincent, 115; **2** McManus, 96; **3** Brown, 89; **4** Newton, 84; **5** Sawford, 76; **6** Robinson, 69.

Supersport 600 (8 laps, 17.36 miles/27.776 km)
1 Ian Simpson (Yamaha), 12m 39.69s, 82.26 mph/132.39 km/h.

2 Mike Edwards (Yamaha); 3 Iain Duffus (Yamaha); 4 Iain Macpherson (Yamaha); 5 Tim Poole (Honda); 6 Andrew Pallot (Yamaha); 7 Steve Cunningham (Honda); 8 Mark Ditchfield (Honda); 9 Colin Gable (Honda); 10 Stuart Wickens (Yamaha); 11 Jason Emmett (Yamaha); 12 Peter Jennings (Honda); 13 John Crawford (Honda); 14 Andrew Tinsley (Honda); 15 Simon Smith (Honda).
Fastest lap: Simpson, 1m 33.37s, 83.66 mph/134.64 km/h.
Championship points: 1 Simpson, 151; 2 Edwards, 118; 3 Duffus and Poole, 83; 5 Macpherson, 80; 6 Cunningham, 55.

TT Superbike (2 x 14 laps, 30.38 miles/48.608 km)
Leg 1
1 Ian Simpson (Norton), 21m 09.72s, 86.13 mph/138.62 km/h.
2 Phil Borley (Norton); 3 Ray Stringer (Ducati); 4 David Jefferies (Ducati); 5 Peter Graves (Ducati); 6 Chris Haldane (Honda); 7 Michael Rutter (Ducati); 8 Andrew Stroud (Yamaha); 9 Lee Pullan (Yamaha); 10 Dean Ashton (Yamaha); 11 Steve Hislop (Honda); 12 Roger Bennett (Kawasaki); 13 Dave Redgate (Yamaha); 14 Richard Defago (Kawasaki); 15 Colin Hipwell (Kawasaki).
Fastest lap: Matt Llewellyn (Ducati), 1m 29.24s, 87.53 mph/140.86 km/h.
Leg 2
1 Phil Borley (Norton), 21m 07.55s, 86.28 mph/138.85 km/h.
2 Ian Simpson (Norton); 3 Steve Hislop (Honda); 4 Matt Llewellyn (Ducati); 5 Jim Moodie (Yamaha); 6 David Jefferies (Ducati); 7 Michael Rutter (Ducati); 8 Andrew Stroud (Yamaha); 9 Chris Haldane (Honda); 10 Peter Graves (Ducati); 11 Dean Ashton (Yamaha); 12 Lee Pullan (Yamaha); 13 Roger Bennett (Yamaha); 14 Dave Redgate (Yamaha); 15 James Bunton (Yamaha).
Fastest lap: Borley, 1m 28.88s, 87.89 mph/141.45 km/h.
Championship points: 1 Simpson, 215; 2 Borley, 207; 3 Moodie, 188; 4 Llewellyn, 155; 5 Rutter, 139; 6 Stringer, 89.

Single Cylinder, round 6 (12 laps, 26.04 miles/41.664 km)
1 Mike Edwards (MZ Scorpion), 19m 22.53s, 80.63 mph/129.77 km/h.
2 David Rawlins (Yamaha); 3 Barry Rudd (Yamaha); 4 Phil Giles (Spondon Yamaha); 5 Mike Hose (Spondon Yamaha); 6 Steve Campbell (Hyde Hornet); 7 David Morris (Chrysalis); 8 Sean Waller (Rotax); 9 John Neate (Spondon); 10 Mark Wilson (Harris Rotax); 11 Gary Robinson (Yamaha); 12 Richard Cutts (Spondon Yamaha); 13 Mark Ebbage (BMW).
Fastest lap: Edwards, 1m 35.33s, 81.94 mph/131.88 km/h.
Championship points: 1 Rawlins 90; 2 Edwards, 69; 3 Ruth, 63; 4 Rudd, 53; 5 Banks, 47; 6 Morris, 45.

Open Sidecars, round 4 (12 laps, 26.04 miles/41.664 km)
1 Darren Dixon/Andy Hetherington (LCR), 18m 20.85s, 85.15 mph/137.04 km/h.
2 Derek Brindley/Paul Hutchinson (LCR-ADM); 3 Barry Brindley/Scott Whiteside (Yamaha); 4 Steve Abbott/Julian Tailford (Krauser); 5 Trevor Robinson/Richard Graham (Krauser); 6 Chris Wright/Paul Woodhead (Suzuki); 7 Simon Christie/Adrian Walduck (Christie); 8 Brian Gray/Steve Pointer (LCR); 9 Keith Brown/Alan Brown (Suzuki); 10 Alan Budge/William Middleton (Suzuki); 11 Steve Dobson/Liz Dobson (Suzuki); 12 Mick Boddice Jnr/Chris Hollis (Krauser); 13 Ian English/Steve English (Krauser); 14 Phil Croft/Nigel Stevens (Suzuki); 15 Barry Fleury/Jane Fleury (LCR-JPX).
Fastest lap: Dixon/Hetherington, 1m 29.66s, 87.12 mph/140.22 km/h (record).
Championship points: 1 Abbott, 67; 2 B. Brindley, 56; 3 D. Brindley, 52; 4 Webster, 37; 5 Gray, 35; 6 Dixon, 31.

BRANDS HATCH GRAND PRIX CIRCUIT, 4 September. 2.6002-mile/4.185-km circuit.
H.E.A.T./British Supercup, round 9
125 cc (10 laps, 26.02 miles/41.85 km)
1 Darren Barton (Honda), 16m 25.06s, 95.02 mph/152.93 km/h.
2 Kevin Mawdsley (Honda); 3 Robin Appleyard (Honda); 4 Mick Lofthouse (Honda); 5 Fernando Mendes (Honda); 6 Mark Norman (Honda); 7 Steve Patrickson (Honda); 8 Rob Frost (Honda); 9 Pete Jennings (Honda); 10 Barry Stanley (Honda); 11 Lindsay Gordon (Honda); 12 Nick Lang (Yamaha); 13 Jeffrey Claridge (Honda); 14 Les Wood (Honda); 15 Simon Williams (Honda).
Fastest lap: Mawdsley, 1m 36.77s, 96.73 mph/155.67 km/h.
Championship points: 1 Mawdsley, 126; 2 Patrickson, 116; 3 Appleyard, 101; 4 Barton, 85; 5 Mendes, 74; 6 Norman, 72.

250 cc
Postponed. See under Brands Hatch, round 11, 25 September.

Supersport 600 (8 laps, 20.802 miles/33.480 km)
1 Ian Simpson (Yamaha), 14m 06.24s, 88.49 mph/142.41 km/h.
2 Gary Weston (Yamaha); 3 Mike Edwards (Yamaha); 4 David Heal (Yamaha); 5 Iain Macpherson (Honda); 6 Jason Emmett (Yamaha); 7 Adam Lewis (Yamaha); 8 Iain Duffus (Honda); 9 Steve Cunningham (Honda); 10 Steve Marks (Honda); 11 Steve Ellis (Honda); 12 Mark Ditchfield (Honda); 13 Simon Smith (Honda); 14 Gordon Blackley (Honda); 15 Peter Jennings (Honda).
Fastest lap: Macpherson, 1m 41.23s, 92.46 mph/148.81 km/h.
Championship points: 1 Simpson, 171; 2 Edwards, 133; 3 Duffus, 96; 4 Macpherson, 91; 5 Poole, 88; 6 Cunningham, 62.

TT Superbike
Leg 1 (12 laps, 31.202 miles/50.22 miles)
1 Phil Borley (Norton), 18m 13.35s, 102.73 mph/165.34 km/h.
2 Ian Simpson (Norton); 3 Jim Moodie (Yamaha); 4 Michael Rutter (Ducati); 5 Matt Llewellyn (Ducati); 6 Andrew Stroud (Yamaha); 7 Chris Haldane (Honda); 8 Nick Hopkins (Yamaha); 9 Phillip McCallen (Honda); 10 Lee Pullan (Yamaha); 11 Dave Rawlins (Yamaha); 12 Dave Redgate (Yamaha); 13 David Jefferies (Ducati); 14 James Bunton (Yamaha); 15 Phil Nicholas (Kawasaki).
Fastest lap: Borley, 1m 30.15s, 103.83 mph/167.10 km/h.
Leg 2 (9 laps, 23.402 miles/37.665 km)
1 Ian Simpson (Norton), 13m 42.65s, 102.40 mph/164.81 km/h.
2 Jim Moodie (Yamaha); 3 Matt Llewellyn (Ducati); 4 David Jefferies (Ducati); 5 Chris Haldane (Honda); 6 Andrew Stroud (Yamaha); 7 Nick Hopkins (Yamaha); 8 Phillip McCallen (Honda); 9 Lee Pullan (Yamaha); 10 Dave Redgate (Yamaha); 11 Dave Rawlins (Yamaha); 12 Paul Brown (Honda); 13 Phil Nicholas (Kawasaki); 14 James Bunton (Yamaha); 15 Richard Defago (Kawasaki).
Fastest lap: Simpson, 1m 30.26s, 103.70 mph/166.90 km/h.
Championship points: 1 Simpson, 250; 2 Borley, 227; 3 Moodie, 220; 4 Llewellyn, 181; 5 Rutter, 152; 6 Stroud, 102.

Single Cylinder, round 7 (8 laps, 20.802 miles/33.480 km)
1 Mike Edwards (MZ Scorpion), 12m 57.79s, 96.28 mph/154.94 km/h.
2 Nick Hopkins (Over); 3 David Rawlins (Yamaha); 4 Barry Rudd (Yamaha); 5 Ian Cobby (Ducati); 6 Ray Stringer (Harris); 7 Colin Sturgeon (Yamaha); 8 Phil Giles (Yamaha); 9 Steve Ruth (Yamaha); 10 David Morris (BMW); 11 Steve Campbell (Rotax); 12 Mark Wilson (Rotax); 13 Carl James (BMW); 14 Peter Rayfield (Harris); 15 Sean Waller (Rotax).
Fastest lap: Hopkins, 1m 35.98s, 97.52 mph/156.95 km/h.
Championship points: 1 Rawlins, 105; 2 Edwards, 89; 3 Ruth, 70; 4 Rudd, 66; 5 Hopkins, 54; 6 Morris, 51.

Open Sidecars, round 5 (7 laps, 18.201 miles/29.295 km)
1 Derek Brindley/Paul Hutchinson (LCR-ADM), 10m 49.66s, 100.86 mph/162.31 km/h.
2 Steve Abbott/Julian Tailford (Krauser); 3 Darren Dixon/Andy Hetherington (LCR); 4 Barry Brindley/Scott Whiteside (Yamaha); 5 Keith Brown/Alan Brown (Suzuki); 6 Mick Boddice Jnr/Chris Hollis (Krauser); 7 Ian English/Chris Ault (Krauser); 8 Steve Dobson/Liz Dobson (Suzuki); 9 Ian Wilford/Gary Broadley (Krauser); 10 Mick Cookson/Gary Leach (Suzuki); 11 Paul Rider/Joy Rider (Windle); 12 Phil Croft/Nigel Stevens (Suzuki); 13 John Morrissey/Karl Firmin (Krauser); 14 Barry Fleury/Jane Fleury (LCR-JPX).
Fastest lap: D. Brindley/Hutchinson, 1m 30.82s, 103.06 mph/165.87 km/h (record).
Championship points: see Final Open Sidecar Championship points.

OULTON PARK CIRCUIT, 11 September. 2.769-mile/4.458-km circuit.
H.E.A.T./British Supercup, round 10
125 cc (10 laps, 27.69 miles/44.58 km)
1 Darren Barton (Honda), 17m 41.83s, 93.87 mph/151.08 km/h.
2 Robin Appleyard (Honda); 3 Steve Patrickson (Honda); 4 Mark Norman (Honda); 5 Chris Palmer (Honda); 6 Les Wood (Honda); 7 Rob Frost (Honda); 8 Barry Stanley (Honda); 9 Lindsay Gordon (Honda); 10 Martin Johnson (Yamaha); 11 Pete Jennings (Honda); 12 Nick Lang (Yamaha); 13 Gavan Morris (Yamaha); 14 Adrian Coates (Yamaha); 15 Simon Williams (Honda).
Fastest lap: Appleyard, 1m 44.49s, 95.40 mph/153.53 km/h.
Championship points: 1 Patrickson, 131; 2 Mawdsley, 126; 3 Appleyard, 118; 4 Barton, 105; 5 Norman, 85; 6 Palmer, 76.

250 cc (10 laps, 27.69 miles/44.58 km)
1 Nigel Bosworth (Honda), 16m 34.81s, 100.20 mph/161.26 km/h.
2 Eugene McManus (Yamaha); 3 Jason Vincent (Yamaha); 4 Steve Sawford (Yamaha); 5 Greig Ramsay (Yamaha); 6 Ian Newton (Aprilia); 7 Jamie Robinson (Yamaha); 8 Robin Milton (Yamaha); 9 Ron Haslam (Yamaha); 10 Adrian Clarke (Yamaha); 11 Alan Patterson (Yamaha); 12 Lee Masters (Yamaha); 13 Fernando Mendes (Yamaha); 14 Mark Snell (Honda); 15 Paul Booler (Yamaha).
Fastest lap: Bosworth, 1m 38.05s, 101.66 mph/163.61 km/h.
Championship points: 1 J. Vincent, 130; 2 McManus, 113; 3 Newton, 94; 4 Brown and Sawford, 89; 6 Robinson, 78.

Supersport 600 (10 laps, 27.69 miles/44.58 km)
1 Mike Edwards (Yamaha), 16m 57.74s, 97.94 mph/157.62 km/h.
2 Ian Simpson (Yamaha); 3 Iain Duffus (Honda); 4 Howard Whitby (Honda); 5 Andrew Pallot (Yamaha); 6 David Heal (Yamaha); 7 Jason Emmett (Yamaha); 8 Mark Ditchfield (Honda); 9 Dave Martin (Yamaha); 10 Jonathan Peacock (Yamaha); 11 Adam Lewis (Yamaha); 12 Tony Shaw (Honda); 13 Simon Smith (Honda); 14 Stuart Wickens (Honda); 15 Mark Wainwright (Honda).
Fastest lap: Edwards, 1m 40.42s, 99.26 mph/159.75 km/h.
Championship points: 1 Simpson, 188; 2 Edwards, 153; 3 Duffus, 111; 4 Macpherson, 91; 5 Poole, 88; 6 Heal, 64.

TT Superbike (2 x 12 laps, 33.228 miles/53.496 km)
Leg 1
1 Phil Borley (Norton), 19m 17.43s, 103.35 mph/166.32 km/h.

2 Jim Moodie (Yamaha); 3 Ian Simpson (Norton); 4 David Jefferies (Ducati); 5 Ray Stringer (Ducati); 6 Andrew Stroud (Yamaha); 7 Peter Graves (Ducati); 8 Michael Rutter (Ducati); 9 Paul Brown (Honda); 10 Lee Pullan (Yamaha); 11 Shaun Muir (Yamaha); 12 Roger Bennett (Yamaha); 13 Nigel Nottingham (Yamaha); 14 Graham Ward (Kawasaki); 15 Dean Ashton (Yamaha).
Fastest lap: Moodie, 1m 35.83s, 104.02 mph/167.40 km/h.
Leg 2
1 Phil Borley (Norton), 19m 20.00s, 103.12 mph/165.95 km/h.
2 Ian Simpson (Norton); 3 Jim Moodie (Yamaha); 4 David Jefferies (Ducati); 5 Steve Hislop (Honda); 6 Michael Rutter (Ducati); 7 Andrew Stroud (Yamaha); 8 Nick Hopkins (Yamaha); 9 Peter Graves (Ducati); 10 Dave Redgate (Yamaha); 11 Phillip McCallen (Honda); 12 Lee Pullan (Yamaha); 13 Shaun Muir (Yamaha); 14 Graham Ward (Kawasaki); 15 Nigel Nottingham (Yamaha).
Fastest lap: Moodie, 1m 35.70s, 104.16 mph/167.63 km/h.
Championship points: 1 Simpson, 284; 2 Borley, 267; 3 Moodie, 252; 4 Llewellyn, 181; 5 Rutter, 170; 6 Jefferies, 123.

F2 Sidecars, round 5 (9 laps, 24.921 miles/40.122 km)
1 Rob Fisher/Michael Wynn (Yamaha), 16m 11.14s, 92.38 mph/148.67 km/h.
2 Mick Boddice Snr/Dave Wells (Honda); 3 Geoff Bell/Nick Roche (Yamaha); 4 Gary Horsepole/Kevin Leigh (Honda); 5 Mick Boddice Jnr/Chris Hollis (Honda); 6 Dawson/Jones (Honda); 7 David Wallis/Tim Kirkham (Yamaha); 8 John Childs/Sadie Childs (Honda); 9 Eddy Wright/Richard Long (EMC); 10 Peter Nuttall/Shutt (Yamaha); 11 Martin Whittington/Steve Birkett (Regiarni); 12 Rod Bellas/Geoff Knight (Yamaha); 13 Stephen Norbury/Guy Scott (Yamaha); 14 André Witherington/John Jackson (Honda).
Fastest lap: Fisher/Wynn, 1m 45.16s, 94.79 mph/152.55 km/h.
Championship points: 1 Bell, 60; 2 Boddice Snr and Fisher, 54; 4 Horsepole and Noble, 49; 6 Molyneux, 46.

BRANDS HATCH INDY CIRCUIT, 24-25 September. 1.2036-mile/1.937-km circuit.
H.E.A.T./British Supercup, round 11
125 cc (14 laps, 16.850 miles/27.118 km)
1 Chris Palmer (Honda), 13m 46.29s, 73.41 mph/118.14 km/h.
2 Mick Lofthouse (Honda); 3 Robin Appleyard (Honda); 4 Steve Patrickson (Honda); 5 Mark Norman (Yamaha); 6 Jeffrey Claridge (Honda); 7 Nick Lang (Yamaha); 8 Kevin Mawdsley (Honda); 9 Martin Johnson (Yamaha); 10 Nick Sergent (Honda); 11 Ian Emberton (Honda); 12 David Dawson (Yamaha); 13 Simon Williams (Honda); 14 Tim Wilson (Honda); 15 Barry Stanley (Honda).
Fastest lap: Lofthouse, 57.59s, 75.23 mph/121.08 km/h.

250 cc, round 10 (18 laps, 21.665 miles/34.866 km)
1 Jason Vincent (Yamaha), 14m 35.77s, 89.05 mph/143.32 km/h.
2 Nigel Bosworth (Honda); 3 Steve Sawford (Yamaha); 4 Alan Patterson (Yamaha); 5 Jamie Robinson (Yamaha); 6 Eugene McManus (Yamaha); 7 Adrian Clarke (Yamaha); 8 Ron Haslam (Yamaha); 9 Fernando Mendes (Yamaha); 10 Stuart Edwards (Yamaha); 11 Gavin Lee (Yamaha); 12 Stephen Farmer (Yamaha); 13 Lee Masters (Yamaha); 14 Mark Snell (Yamaha); 15 Robin Milton (Yamaha).
Fastest lap: Mendes, 47.74s, 90.76 mph/146.06 km/h.

250 cc (12 laps, 14.443 miles/23.244 km)
1 Eugene McManus (Yamaha), 9m 42.10s, 89.32 mph/143.75 km/h.
2 Steve Sawford (Yamaha); 3 Jason Vincent (Yamaha); 4 Nigel Bosworth (Yamaha); 5 Woolsey Coulter (Aprilia); 6 Adrian Clarke (Yamaha); 7 Alan Patterson (Yamaha); 8 Ian Newton (Aprilia); 9 Stuart Edwards (Yamaha); 10 John McGuiness (Yamaha); 11 Robin Milton (Yamaha); 12 Lee Masters (Yamaha); 13 Gavin Lee (Yamaha); 14 Stephen Farmer (Yamaha); 15 Roki Read (Yamaha).
Fastest lap: Mendes, 47.44s, 91.33 mph/146.99 km/h (record).

Supersport 600 (14 laps, 16.850 miles/27.118 km)
1 Mike Edwards (Yamaha), 11m 40.98s, 86.53 mph/139.26 km/h.
2 Andrew Pallot (Yamaha); 3 Adam Lewis (Yamaha); 4 Howard Whitby (Honda); 5 Jason Emmett (Yamaha); 6 Iain Macpherson (Honda); 7 David Heal (Yamaha); 8 Gary Weston (Yamaha); 9 Steve Cunningham (Honda); 10 Dave Martin (Honda); 11 Mark Ditchfield (Honda); 12 Simon Smith (Honda); 13 Jonathan Peacock (Honda); 14 Mark Coleing (Honda); 15 Tim Poole (Honda).
Fastest lap: Edwards, 49.16s, 88.13 mph/141.84 km/h.

TT Superbike (2 x 18 laps, 21.665 miles/34.866 km)
Leg 1
1 Ian Simpson (Norton), 14m 20.94s, 90.59 mph/145.79 km/h.
2 Phil Borley (Norton); 3 Jim Moodie (Yamaha); 4 Matt Llewellyn (Ducati); 5 Andrew Stroud (Yamaha); 6 Steve Hislop (Honda); 7 Peter Graves (Ducati); 8 Michael Rutter (Ducati); 9 Robert Holden (Ducati); 10 Ray Stringer (Ducati); 11 David Jefferies (Ducati); 12 Phillip McCallen (Honda); 13 John Barton (Kawasaki); 14 Dean Ashton (Yamaha); 15 Lee Pullan (Yamaha).
Fastest lap: Borley, 47.11s, 91.97 mph/148.02 km/h.
Leg 2
1 Jim Moodie (Yamaha), 14m 20.49s, 90.63 mph/145.86 km/h.
2 Matt Llewellyn (Ducati); 3 Ian Simpson (Norton); 4 Phil Borley (Norton); 5 Peter Graves (Ducati); 6 Michael Rutter (Ducati); 7 Nick Hopkins (Yamaha); 8 David Jefferies (Ducati); 9 John Barton (Kawasaki); 10 Phillip McCallen (Honda); 11 Nigel Nottingham (Yamaha); 12 Dean Ashton (Yamaha); 13 Shaun Muir (Yamaha); 14 Ray Stringer (Yamaha); 15 Dave Redgate (Yamaha).
Fastest lap: Steve Hislop (Honda), 47.11s, 91.97 mph/148.02 km/h.

Single Cylinder, round 8 (14 laps, 16.850 miles/27.118 km)
1 Mike Edwards (MZ Scorpion), 12m 48.20s, 78.96 mph/127.08 km/h.
2 Nick Hopkins (Over); 3 Ian Cobby (Ducati); 4 Roger Banks (Rotax); 5 Steve Ruth (Yamaha); 6 Barry Rudd (Yamaha); 7 Mark Norman (Suzuki); 8 David Rawlins (Yamaha); 9 Phil Giles (Yamaha); 10 Mark Wilson (Rotax); 11 Steve Campbell (Rotax); 12 Royston Keen (KTM); 13 Ray Stringer (Harris); 14 Stephen Marlow (Yamaha); 15 Richard Shepherd (Suzuki).
Fastest lap: Banks, 52.43s, 82.64 mph/133.00 km/h.

F2 Sidecars, round 6 (14 laps, 16.850 miles/27.118 km)
1 Dave Molyneux/Peter Hill (DMR Yamaha), 12m 17.37s, 82.26 mph/132.39 km/h.
2 Gary Horsepole/Kevin Leigh (Yamaha); 3 David Wallis/Tim Kirkham (Yamaha); 4 Mick Boddice Snr/Dave Wells (Honda); 5 John Childs/Sadie Childs (Honda); 6 Eddy Wright/Richard Long (EMC); 7 Mick Boddice Jnr/Chris Hollis (Honda); 8 Steve Noble/Mark Bingham (Yamaha); 9 Geoff Bell/Nick Roche (Yamaha); 10 Rob Fisher/Michael Wynn (Yamaha); 11 Gary Kimberley/Doug Jewell (Kawasaki); 12 Martin Whittington/Steve Birkett (Regiarni); 13 Roger Dixon/Lee Farrington (Yamaha); 14 Stephen Ramsden/Paul Coward (Yamaha); 15 André Witherington/John Jackson (Honda).
Fastest lap: Hallam/Camp (Yamaha), 51.19s, 84.64 mph/136.22 km/h (record).

Final 125 cc Championship points
1	Steve Patrickson	144
2	Kevin Mawdsley	134
3	Robin Appleyard	133
4	Darren Barton	105
5=	Mark Norman	96
5=	Chris Palmer	96

7 Fernando Mendes, 74; 8 Barry Stanley, 65; 9 Mick Lofthouse, 62; 10 Andy Hatton, 55; 11 Les Wood, 49; 12 Lindsay Gordon, 45; 13 Jeffrey Claridge, 39; 14 Rob Frost and Martin Johnson, 31.

Final 250 cc Championship points
1	Jason Vincent	165
2	Eugene McManus	143
3	Steve Sawford	121
4=	Ian Newton	102
4=	Jamie Robinson	102
6	Paul Brown	89

7 Greig Ramsay, 70; 8 Adrian Clarke, 69; 9 Iain Challinor, 65; 10 Nigel Bosworth, 60; 11 Max Vincent, 53; 12 Robin Milton, 52; 13 Woolsey Coulter, 47; 14 Ron Haslam, 41; 15 Mark Snell, 40.

Final Supersport 600 Championship points
1	Ian Simpson	188
2	Mike Edwards	173
3	Iain Duffus	111
4	Iain Macpherson	101
5	Tim Poole	89
6=	David Heal	73
6=	Andrew Pallot	73

8 Steve Cunningham, 69; 9 Howard Whitby, 58; 10 Mark Ditchfield, 54; 11 Dave Martin, 48; 12 Jason Emmett, 45; 13 Gary Weston, 41; 14 Mick Corrigan, 38; 15 Adam Lewis, 31.

Final TT Superbike Championship points
1	Ian Simpson	319
2	Jim Moodie	287
3	Phil Borley	284
4	Matt Llewellyn	211
5	Michael Rutter	188
6	Andrew Stroud	145

7 David Jefferies, 136; 8 Peter Graves, 119; 9 Nick Hopkins, 113; 10 Steve Hislop, 108; 11 Ray Stringer, 106; 12 Phillip McCallen, 100; 13 Lee Pullan, 70; 14 Roger Bennett, 61; 15 Mark Farmer, 60.

Final Single Cylinder Championship points
1	David Rawlins	113
2	Mike Edwards	109
3	Steve Ruth	81
4	Barry Rudd	76
5	Nick Hopkins	71
6	Roger Banks	60

7 David Morris, 51; 8 Phil Giles, 43; 9 Alan Carter, 40; 10 Royston Keen, 38; 11 Ian Cobby, 26; 12 Steve Campbell, 25; 13 Mike Hose, 24; 14 Geoff Baines and Paul Harrison, 23.

Final Open Sidecar Championship points
1	Steve Abbott	84
2	Derek Brindley	72
3	Barry Brindley	69
4	Darren Dixon	46
5	Steve Webster	37
6	Brian Gray	35

7 Steve Dobson, 34; 8 Mick Cookson and Chris Wright, 25; 10 Keith Brown, 22; 11 Simon Christie, Ian English, Roger Lovelock and Trevor Robinson, 21; 15 Alan Budge, 20.

Final F2 Sidecar Championship points
1=	Geoff Bell	67
1=	Mick Boddice Snr	67
3=	Gary Horsepole	66
3=	Dave Molyneux	66
5	Rob Fisher	60
6	Steve Noble	57

7 Eddy Wright, 57; 8 David Wallis, 47; 9 John Childs, 43; 10 Mick Boddice Jnr, 41; 11 Gary Smith, 37; 12 Roy Hanks, 32; 13 Martin Whittington, 27; 14 Martin Clark, 19; 15 Kenny Howles, 18.